What Is Mental Retardation?

Ideas for an Evolving Disability in the 21st Century

Revised and Updated Edition

What Is Mental Retardation?

Ideas for an Evolving Disability in the 21st Century

REVISED AND UPDATED EDITION

Editors

Harvey N. Switzky and Stephen Greenspan

AMERICAN ASSOCIATION ON MENTAL RETARDATION

Library of Congress Cataloging-in-Publication Data

What is mental retardation? : ideas for an evolving disability in the 21st
century / editors, Harvey N. Switzky & Stephen Greenspan. — Rev. and updated ed.

    p. 384; cm.
  Includes bibliographical references and index.
  ISBN 0-940898-93-4 (cloth)
  ISBN 0-940898-94-2 (paperback)
  1. Mental retardation. I. Switzky, Harvey N. II. Greenspan, Stephen. III.
American Association on Mental Retardation.

  [DNLM: 1. American Association on Mental Retardation. 2. Mental Retardation—
classification. 3. Mental Retardation—diagnosis. 4. Mentally Disabled Persons—
classification. WM 15 W555 2006]

  RC570.W527 2006
  616.85′88075—dc22

                                       2006014396

Table of Contents

Contributors

George S. Baroff, Ph.D. (Emeritus)
Developmental Disabilities Training Institute
University of North Carolina
Chapel Hill, NC

Alfred A. Baumeister, Ph.D. (Emeritus)
Vanderbilt University
Nashville, TN

Eva Bjorck-Akesson, Ph.D.
Maastricht University
Vasteras, Sweden

Wil H. E. Buntinx, Ph.D.
University of Maastricht
The Netherlands

David L. Coulter, M.D.
Boston University Medical Center
Boston, MA

Douglas K. Detterman, Ph.D.
Case Western Reserve University
Cleveland, OH

David Felce, Ph.D.
University of Wales College of Medicine
Cardiff, Wales, UK

Lynne Gabriel, Ph.D.
Case Western Reserve University
Cleveland, OH

William C. Gaventa, M.Div.
The Elizabeth M. Boggs Center on
Developmental Disabilities
Robert Wood Johnson Medical School
New Brunswick, NJ

Laraine Masters Glidden, Ph.D.
St. Mary's College of Maryland
St. Mary City, MD

Stephen Greenspan, Ph.D. (Emeritus)
University of Connecticut
Storrs, CT

Mats Granlund, Ph.D.
Malardalen University
Vasteras, Sweden

H. Carl Haywood, Ph.D. (Emeritus)
Vanderbilt University
Nashville, TN

John W. Jacobson, Ph.D., BCBA (Deceased)
Sage College Center for Applied Behavior
Analysis
Troy, NY

James S. Leffert, Ed.D.
University of Massachusetts Boston
Boston, MA

Donald L. MacMillan, Ed.D. (Emeritus)
University of California
Riverside, CA

James A. Mulick, Ph.D.
Department of Pediatrics and Psychology
Ohio State University
Columbus, OH

Alya Reeve, M.D.
University of New Mexico Health Sciences
Center
Albuquerque, NM

Robert L. Schalock, Ph.D. (Emeritus)
Hastings College
Hastings, NE

Rune J. Simeonsson, Ph.D., MPH
University of North Carolina
Chapel Hill, NC

Gary N. Siperstein, Ph.D.
University of Massachusetts Boston
Boston, MA

J. David Smith, Ed.D.
The University of Virginia-College at Wise
Wise, VA

Martha E. Snell, Ph.D.
University of Virginia
Charlottesville, VA

Herman H. Spitz, Ph.D. (Retired)
E. R. Johnstone Training & Research Ctr.
Bordentown, NJ

Harvey N. Switzky, Ph.D., ABPP (Emeritus)
Northern Illinois University
DeKalb, IL

Mary D. Voorhees, Ph.D
University of Virginia
Charlottesville, VA

Dedication

We dedicate this book to all the philosophers, scientists, service providers, teachers, families, and individuals who have ever perplexed over the meaning of mental retardation, its causes, and treatments, and those who wanted to improve the welfare of persons with mental retardation and their families and friends, especially to John W. Jacobson who died in 2004.

FOREWORD

Mental Retardation Is a Functional Model

DAVID L. COULTER

What Is Mental Retardation? Generations of professionals have struggled to answer this question, and the answers they have provided have changed over the past century. The American Association on Mental Retardation (AAMR) published its first definition of mental retardation in 1921 and its tenth definition in 2002. The authoritative nature of the AAMR definition is reflected in its adoption (in one form or another) by many public agencies to guide determination of eligibility for services and supports. AAMR continues to study this question and is already working on the next edition of its definition. For this reason AAMR welcomes the publication of this book, which will provide stimulating insights to consider carefully as it prepares the next edition.

I was given the honor of writing this Foreword on behalf of AAMR because I was President of AAMR at the time this manuscript was submitted for publication in May 2005. In that role, I commend all of the authors for their careful and scholarly contributions and assure them that we will study this volume carefully. AAMR is committed to maintaining its leadership in definition and classification and welcomes the opportunity to publish the accumulated wisdom which this volume represents. Besides serving as AAMR President, I was also a co-author of the 9th (1992) and 10th (2002) editions of the AAMR definition and classification manual. Indeed, four of the eight authors of the 1992 edition went on to become Presidents of AAMR, which must surely indicate the high priority that AAMR places on this work.

AAMR continues to struggle to determine the most appropriate name for the condition represented by the term "mental retardation." The name should not reflect the shifting currents of political correctness, but it should describe accurately the true nature of the condition as it is currently understood by professionals in the field. What is the implication of AAMR's functional model for designating this condition? Do we still believe that the condition is solely determined by a slowing or "retardation" of mental development, a problem located within the brains of persons with this condition? The term "mental retardation" suggests a medical model of disability in which the problem is located solely within the person, rather than a functional model in which the problem is located within the interaction between the person and the social environment. The World Health Organization's International Classification of Functioning (ICF) describes disability as a problem in functioning related to physical impairments, activity limitations, and participation restrictions. How should we apply the ICF model of disability in designating the condition which is the subject of this volume? Whatever name is eventually chosen, it should reflect this international consensus about the nature of disability and its effect on functioning.

AAMR seeks to be the meeting place where professionals from many different backgrounds can discuss the critical issues in the field. We believe that open, collegial, and respectful debate, based on the best scientific and applied research, is the proper way to answer questions such as those represented by this volume. Science is an ongoing process of discovery, based on diverse approaches and sometimes on conflicting results that need to be resolved through further study and analysis. We welcome the publication of the research-based knowledge contained in this book, which advances our field and helps us to answer the most important questions of our time.

David L. Coulter, M.D., President
American Association on Mental Retardation
May 1, 2005

FOREWORD

What Is Mental Retardation?

DAVID FELCE

Clarity of definition is clearly necessary to science. So the question "What Is Mental Retardation?" is of fundamental importance. How we answer it will affect whose internal and external worlds we seek to understand, the models by which we seek to understand them, and the way we interpret applied research. This book updates an essential debate which scientists in our field must have and be informed about. It, therefore, does us a great service.

Our field has a penchant for changing its terminology, perhaps no more than in other scientific areas but in ways which are not necessarily internationally coordinated or related to scientific principles. The multiplicity and divergence of terms across and within countries was neatly brought home to me as I typed three separate terms in just writing the book title and my affiliations above—three terms, all with blurred definitional edges, used as synonyms. The reasons why such terms are adopted, retained, or changed are complex, involving considerations broader than their scientific merits. It is important that scientists take an international perspective and, therefore, learn the meanings and applications of various terms in countries other than their own. While the conditions which give rise to mental retardation or intellectual disability are universal, how the resulting condition is conceptualized, assessed, and categorized, and the response which is made, will and does vary between countries, cultures, and economies.

There can be considerable differences even in countries with fairly similar cultures and economies. When David Braddock, Roger Stancliffe, Eric Emerson, and I wrote a joint paper to summarize where children and adults with mental retardation or developmental disabilities lived in the United States, Canada, Australia, and England and Wales (Braddock et al., 2001), we found that the United States and Australia identified similar proportions of the general population as having mental retardation or developmental disabilities (about 1.2%–1.3%), while the proportion in England and Wales with learning disabilities (previously mental handicap) was about 40% of this level. Such differences have a variety of important implications for different stakeholders. One I was immediately struck by for us as scientists is how we interpret and compare research evaluating the effectiveness of interventions or programs across different countries. For example, when we in the United Kingdom look toward the apparently greater success in the United States at supporting people with mental retardation in employment or in living independently, should we be assuming that descriptions of effectiveness concern similar people with similar difficulties in working or living independently, and therefore attribute differences in outcome to differences in the design or effectiveness of intervention and support, or should we fail to conclude or generalize until science provides more rigorous demonstration of the epidemiological representativeness of the people being served?

It is also interesting that in none of the countries did the proportion of the population identified above come anywhere close to the proportion of people we assume to be covered by agreed international scientific definitions. Apparently, we have set criteria in defining the condition which are not used or useful in practice. The almost universal finding that the 'administrative' prevalence of mental retardation (or intellectual disabilities) is substantially lower than the assumed "true" prevalence means that in practice most people with mental retardation make their way in society with only the help of the normal mechanisms which a society has to support its citizens, and that societies recognize only people with more severe or profound disabilities as needing special intervention. In the UK, for example, the number of people identified as having learning disabilities tends to be only just above the estimated prevalence of severe learning disabilities (IQ > 50). Under identification of people with severe learning disabilities, particularly in childhood, means that some people with mild learning disabilities will be included, but those included must be only a minority of the full number. Perhaps this should be telling us that there are greater differences between people encompassed within the term "mental retardation" than between those who could potentially be encompassed and those "without mental retardation." If so, there may be a case for restricting the definition to fit what societies do in practice, as some have argued herein.

Of course such a proposition would be controversial . . . but then the value of this book is to keep a debate essential to our developing understanding in front of us.

David Felce
President
International Association for the Scientific Study of Intellectual Disabilities
Welsh Centre for Learning Disabilities
Cardiff University
Cardiff, UK

REFERENCES

Braddock, D., Emerson, E., Felce, D., & Stancliffe, R. J. (2001). The living circumstances of children and adults with mental retardation in the United States, Canada, England and Wales, and Australia. *Mental Retardation and Developmental Disabilities Research Reviews, 7,* 115–121.

FOREWORD

Broader Perspectives on Mental Retardation[1]

H. CARL HAYWOOD

One fine day, I was trying to get some community leaders in New York to consider adopting an educational program whose anticipated effect would be, in part, to prevent many cases of mild mental retardation and to improve learning effectiveness of young children. One gentleman in particular was skeptical. His first question was, "How do you know it works?" I then laid out, in some detail, eight evaluative studies, all of which had shown quite positive effects. Grandly unimpressed, the skeptical gentleman then asked, "Where were these studies done?" I replied that the first had been done in Tennessee, and the others in Canada, Belgium, France, and Israel; whereupon, my skeptic observed, "Aha! Just as I thought! But this is New York!" Which, in his mind, laid the matter to rest. As I thought about the mental retardation that we would not be allowed to prevent, I wondered whether we should think of some new diagnostic categories, such as "Mental retardation, mild, New York type," or "Mental retardation, moderate, French type," . . . or "Tennessee type!" In other words, how much truth might there be in the notion that intelligence—and therefore mental retardation—must be defined at least in part by its geography?

In 1968 we had an important international conference at Peabody College, called the Peabody/NIMH Conference on Social-Cultural Aspects of Mental Retardation (Haywood, 1970). One thing that I recall vividly from that conference is a debate between Carlos Albizu-Miranda and James Miller. Miller defended the "x-percent" theory of mental retardation, according to which a constant percentage of any large population would be diagnosable as mentally retarded. According to this notion, 3% of the U.S. population were thought to be retarded, because, following the Heber (1959) manual on terminology and classification, about 3% were expected to deviate sufficiently from the population average IQ and adaptive behavior norm to be diagnosed as retarded.

On the other hand, Albizu argued that the number of persons in a population who are diagnosable as mentally retarded depends on the location, customs, social mores, cultural expectations, relative "developed" status, and educational level of the population. Thus,

1. Keynote Address (Abridged), 121st Annual Meeting of the American Association on Mental Retardation, 1997, New York, NY.

he believed that in an agrarian society there would be fewer persons with mental retardation than in a highly industrialized society. He found very few persons in rural areas of
Puerto Rico whose neighbors believed them to be retarded. He talked about waiters in
urban restaurants who could neither read nor write and who, if given a standardized intelligence test, would surely make low scores, but who could recite to a table of guests an
entire unwritten menu, take orders from 8 or 10 guests, and then bring the correct food
to each guest without having to ask, "Now, who had the Italian dressing?" His point, of
course, was that these persons were well adapted to their culture, held jobs, earned their
living, went about freely in their society, and often married, had children, and supported
their families. If from time to time some neighbor needed to help them plan their finances
or pay their taxes or figure out a new bus schedule, that was hardly grounds for segregat-
ing them or labeling them as deviant. Albizu also believed that if these persons had been
plunked down in the middle of Manhattan Island and expected to survive, they would
not have done so. In fact, they would have been diagnosed as mentally retarded. I rather
suspect that part of the resistance to Albizu's analysis was the reluctance of mainland
Americans to believe that the prevalence of mental retardation was lower in the
Commonwealth of Puerto Rico than in mainland USA!

This incident set me to thinking about the cultural roots of individual differences in
intelligence. We have gone through quite an odyssey in our search for the nature of intelligence—and we have not yet reached Ithaca (Albany, perhaps, but not Ithaca)! In my
youth, we thought of intelligence as somehow independent of culture, and we tried to
construct "culture-free" and "culture-fair" tests. Most American psychologists did not
know that L. S. Vygotsky, who died in 1934, had insisted that the growth of intelligence
is attributable in part to transmission of the culture from one generation to the next, and
that intelligence itself inheres in the culture (see, e.g., Vygotsky, 1978)!

The difficult task is to function across both of these alternative points of view, because
both have some validity. It is undoubtedly true that intelligence, and therefore mental
retardation, is culturally relative in the sense that adaptive behavior differs as a function
of the environment that one has to adapt to. The relative normative nature of behavior
depends to a very great extent upon social expectations and the demands of the physical
environment. It is also obviously true that there are conditions that impair the nervous
system to varying degrees, and that impairment of the nervous system itself is a clear basis
for impairment in behavior, including social and environmental adaptive behavior. That
is to say, with sufficient impairment of the nervous system, the consequent impairment in
behavior should be recognizable across cultures and will constitute some deviation from
cultural expectations of "normal" behavior.

With those considerations in mind, I have two suggestions. The first is that we begin a
quest for new concepts and new definitions of mental retardation, recognizing the inadequacy of present concepts and definitions to incorporate what is known about the behavior and development of persons with mental retardation, and the inadequacy of present
concepts and definitions to incorporate both the cultural relativism and the physical
absolute—i.e., cultural constancy—perspectives. I suggest at the outset that we shall almost
certainly have to abandon the idea that mental retardation is a single entity and therefore
that it can be understood according to a single set of concepts, even multi-dimensional

ones. My second quite modest suggestion is that we mount a renewed effort to incorporate knowledge about mental retardation from sources around the world, that is, that we adopt a global perspective on this phenomenon.

Concepts and Definition of Mental Retardation

On the first suggestion I shall say very little, having recently written a chapter (Haywood, in press) on re-conceptualizing mental retardation by re-conceptualizing intelligence itself and incorporating logical thinking processes and intrinsic motivation into the concept. The re-conceptualization and re-definition of mental retardation is a large enough topic to occupy many conferences and many books. I offer only a few observations that I hope will make it into the deliberations about this topic that will surely take place over the next few years. The first is the suggestion that mental retardation is not a single entity and can only be further misunderstood if we insist upon regarding persons who are profoundly retarded and multiply handicapped under the same broad concepts that govern our conception of persons who are barely discriminable from those who actually escape the "retardation" label altogether. The suggestion has cropped up frequently over the last 50 years at least that persons with severe and profound mental retardation are in many ways qualitatively different from persons with mild and perhaps moderate mental retardation, while the latter group, those with mild and moderate retardation, are only quantitatively different from persons in the non-retarded category.

There are many reasons to believe in such a separation of concepts of retardation. The first is that there are few persons with severe and profound retardation who do not have demonstrable central nervous system pathology, and relatively few in the mild category who do have such demonstrable pathology. Thus, one suspects quite different etiologic conditions for these two groups. Second, there is a growing body of evidence to support the notion that the cognitive developmental path that characterizes persons with mild mental retardation is not different, in qualitative aspects or in sequence of development, from that of persons without mental retardation. Third, my own impression is that the effects of environmental and experiential variables are relatively greater on the development of persons with mild or moderate retardation than on the development of persons with severe or profound retardation—although it is clear that persons in both groups are subject to significant developmental effects of environmental circumstances. Fourth, individual differences in intelligence of persons with mild and even moderate retardation can be understood quite well within the framework of normal genetic variation—that is, as the low end of the distribution of intelligence—without the necessary interference of accidental disastrous variables. The occurrence of individual differences that lie four, five, or six standard deviations below the population average cannot be explained within the framework of the laws of genetics, especially in view of the fact that such persons occur in the population at almost 1000 times the rate that one would expect from normal genetic variation on the basis of an assumed Gaussian distribution of intelligence (see, e.g., Haywood, 1974). Their retardation has to have been a result of genetic abnormality, or of accidental, traumatic events in the process of development itself, in order for one to understand their occurrence in the population in such numbers. Fifth, to the extent that social/cultural variables influence the development of individual differences in intelligence, that influence is more pronounced in those who are currently regarded as mildly and moderately mentally retarded than in those whose retardation is more severe or profound. Finally, the behavioral development of persons in the two groups is substantially different. There are demonstrable differences not only in how rapidly they learn, but in what they learn, and to what extent their learning is generalized to new situations. For these and many other reasons, I suggest that our concept of who is mentally retarded be greatly reduced, to include only those persons who now are regarded as severely and profoundly mentally retarded, and perhaps some portion of the moderate category. Those whose social adaptive behavior and learning lie between that group and the non-retarded population have retarded development in the sense that their development occurs less rapidly than for persons in the average and superior ranges of intelligence, and ultimately reaches a lower level only because of its slower developmental pace. Because they are more like persons who are not now defined within the retarded category than they are like those who are presently defined as having severe and profound retardation, there should be no pressures to segregate them educationally or otherwise from the general population.

Indeed, such pressures have lessened greatly in the last 30 years, but I still encounter such phenomena as teacher union contracts that specify the teachers' presumed right not to have children with mental retardation placed in their classrooms. At the same time, we could recognize the qualitatively different set of needs of persons who are now categorized as severely or profoundly retarded, and we could make public policy affecting their care, treatment, training, residential arrangements, and habilitation with greater confidence and greater clarity if they were not grouped diagnostically with persons who are not much like them.

Nothing that I have suggested about this issue is new, and I hope that nothing about it is very radical. For various reasons, some of them political, the Soviet state banned the use of standardized, normative intelligence tests more than 60 years ago. One result was abandonment of the concept of mild mental retardation. That does not mean that persons whose intellectual and social functioning was at the lowest end of the "normal" range were denied special services. Special educational services and social services have indeed been provided for such persons, but this has been done without the assumption that they are qualitatively different from the general population, or the assumption that they are more like persons whose low intellectual and social functioning is associated with demonstrable brain pathology.

Many in our field will already have thought that defining a large number of persons out of the diagnostic category of mental retardation might lead to loss of essential services for those persons. To say that a person does not belong in the group of persons with mental retardation does not in any way deny that person's need for specialized services, including those in the areas of health, education, vocational support, residential support, and social integration. Indeed, a very large number of persons who, because either their measured intelligence or their adaptive behavior might fall just above the traditional cutting points for a diagnosis of mental retardation, are defined as not retarded are nevertheless in frequent and urgent need of specialized services. It is also true that many persons in that higher range of functioning, as well as some in what is now the range of mental retardation, do not need a full range of social services, and can get along rather well with minimal supports. This Association (Luckasson et al., 1992) has pointed the way to the solution of that problem in public policy. The answer, of course, is to be less concerned with what people *are* than with what they *need*. I can hardly count the times that I have received a clinical referral with the request that I tell the state or some agency "whether this person is mentally retarded or emotionally disturbed." More often than not, I have advised the referring agency that this is not a proper question, first of all because there is no reason why one cannot be subject to both conditions. Second, the question I was prepared to answer was "What are this person's significant needs, and how can they be met?" When we are able to address the question in that way, it will not matter whether a person's IQ is 60 or 85, or whether adaptive behavior is one, two, or three standard deviations below average—or above, for that matter.

Re-conceptualizing the nature of mental retardation requires searching systematically, in as many places as possible, for knowledge that may not be readily at hand. It is unlikely that a pan-cultural set of concepts can come entirely from within a particular culture. Philosophers of science now agree that knowledge that is developed through the scientific method is nevertheless subject to influence from the contexts in which it was developed.

As we look over the recent history of mental retardation, we can point to important contributions from virtually every part of the world. We recall, for example, the contributions of Binet, Wallon, and Zazzo in France with respect to concepts of mental retardation and assessment of individual differences in intelligence; Luria, Vygotsky, Lubovsky, Pevsner, Zaporozhets, and others in Russia on neuropsychological and cognitive analyses and educational treatment of persons with mental retardation; Nirje, first in Denmark, then in Canada and in Sweden, as well as Tizard, O'Connor, the Clarkes, and others in the United Kingdom on community integration of persons with retardation; Folling in Norway and Lejeune in France on inborn errors of metabolism and the genetic determination of Down syndrome, as well as Barr in Canada for discovery of sex chromatin bodies that made karyotyping and eventually amniocentesis possible; Feuerstein in Israel, as well as Guthke in Germany and again Vygotsky, for development of methods of assessment of learning potential and education of the intellect. The list can be very long, and is certainly very diverse—and it is certain that I have left out some very important contributions. The point is simply that our knowledge about mental retardation has come from all over the world, and must continue to do so. We will derive the greatest benefit from the world's knowledge to the extent that we eschew the provincialism that we sometimes hide behind, open our concepts and our policies to advancing knowledge whatever its sources, share our own knowledge as widely as possible, and recognize in that way the world-wide citizenship of persons with mental retardation.

I have tried to suggest to you that persons with mental retardation are indeed citizens of the world, with, as we say in the academic world, "all the rights, privileges, and responsibilities thereunto appertaining." In partial recognition of that global citizenship, I have suggested that we re-examine our basic concepts of the nature and the boundaries of mental retardation itself, considering especially the relation of individual differences in intelligence to variables that inhere in cultures. I have suggested further that we seriously consider re-defining mental retardation in such a way as to separate from that diagnostic category those persons who are not qualitatively different from those now considered to be in the "normal" range of intelligence, that is, those whose variation in terms of intelligence is within the normal range of genetic variation, and reserve the diagnosis of mental retardation for those persons who are, by virtue of extreme genetic variation or severe alteration of the nervous system, functioning in a qualitatively different manner.

H. Carl Haywood
Vanderbilt University

REFERENCES

Haywood, H. C. (Ed.). (1970). *Social-cultural aspects of mental retardation.* New York: Appleton-Century-Crofts.

Haywood, H. C. (Ed.). (1974). Intelligence, distribution of. *Encyclopaedia Britannica* (15th ed., pp. 672–677). Chicago: Encyclopaedia Britannica.

Luckasson, R., Coulter, D. L., Polloway, E. A., Reiss, S., Schalock, R. L., Snell, M. E., et al. (1992). *Mental retardation: Definition, classification, and systems of supports* (9th ed.). Washington, DC: American Association on Mental Retardation.

Vygotsky, L. S. (1978). *Mind in society: The development of higher psychological processes.* Cambridge, MA: Harvard University Press.

The 2003 Preface: Why This Book?

How This Book Was Born

This book grew out of a discussion between the editors a few years ago concerning exactly what the construct of mental retardation means in the 21st century, i.e., what is the constitutive definition of mental retardation and how is it to be measured and operationalized? Also our minds were on the need for more formal input from the field into efforts by the AAMR Terminology and Classification (T&C) Committee to revise the definition and classification system for the field of mental retardation (MR). While early drafts of the Luckasson et al. (1992) manual were sent out for commentary by various individuals and groups, there was no concerted effort, to our knowledge, to seek comments at the outset regarding how the predecessor (Grossman, 1983) manual should be modified. Lack of such input may have contributed to the considerable resistance to that 1992 document, as exemplified by the decision of the Division of Mental Retardation and Developmental Disabilities of the American Psychological Association to publish its own alternative classification manual (Jacobson & Mulick, 1996) and by the reluctance of most governmental and human service organizations to adopt key elements of the 1992 AAMR manual.

The 1992 manual was seen, even by many of its authors, as a transitional document, reflecting the fact that the field of mental retardation itself is in a state of flux. Part of the transitional nature of the document stemmed from the apparent decision by the 1992 T&C to get "half a loaf," namely to make only minor modifications in the diagnosis of MR while making radical changes in the classification and description of mental retardation, identifying needs for support and jettisoning the severity-level classification system.

The conservative aspect of the definition change consisted mainly in raising the IQ ceiling by five points and substituting "adaptive skills" for "adaptive behavior." The radical aspect of the classification system change consisted of eliminating the idea of categorical severity levels and substituting instead a severity continuum based on support needs rather than IQ standard deviation units, reconceptualizing the disabling process as resulting from the interaction of the person with his or her environment, and presenting a paradigm shift from viewing mental retardation as an absolute trait expressed solely by an individual to seeing it as an expression of the interaction between the person with intellectual functioning and the environment.

While it is typical for T&C revisions following a major "paradigm shift" to involve mainly minor fine-tuning, we hoped that the next AAMR manual (scheduled tentatively for 2002) would involve some major changes—for several reasons:

1. Because of the problems which many respected MR professionals, particularly researchers, had with the 1992 manual.
2. Because the 1992 manual was radical in the classification system but conservative with respect to the definition, making it necessary that they be brought into closer alignment.
3. Because there is a movement within AAMR to throw out the term "mental retardation" and replace it with another term (such as "intellectual disabilities") that is less pejorative and possibly more inclusive, so that all of us need to revisit the definition of MR, even if the first two considerations noted above were not operative.

The main purpose of this book is to provide some guidance to the AAMR T&C Committee, and to the field of MR in this country and the world, as we all must undertake the task of rethinking and revisiting the constitutive and operational definitions of mental retardation and the classification and description of mental retardation (as well as being cognizant of the philosophical underpinnings of the models proposed), so that we all can with great insight ponder exactly what mental retardation is in the 21st century.

An inspiration for this book is a similar one (Millon & Klerman, 1986) written by psychopathology scholars aimed at assisting the American Psychiatric Association in approaching the fourth edition (DSM-4) of their classification manual. The contributions in that book addressed some fundamental questions about classification of humans and about the meaning of disability and incompetence. Another book that motivated us in undertaking the challenge of this one was mentioned previously, The Manual of Diagnosis and Professional Practice in Mental Retardation (Jacobson & Mulick, 1996), whose purpose was to affirm the validity of the scientist-practitioner behavioral science perspective that espoused a biosocial–broadly ecological perspective in the practice of psychology in mental retardation. Jacobson and Mulick were writing in strong reaction to the 1992 AAMR manual, which was implied to have a social or sociopolitical perspective. Not that we necessarily espouse Jacobson and Mulick's position, but we were impressed with the challenge to the field of mental retardation that their book represented as well as by its intellectual integrity. We believe that our job as editors is to remain neutral amid all the controversies, except in our own personal chapters. In all the chapters we have jointly written we have tried to summarize and describe the various positions of all the stakeholders without taking sides.

How Contributors Were Chosen

The two editors were joined by two distinguished associate editors, Robert Schalock and J. David Smith, in putting together a wish list of contributors. An effort was made to constitute the list as broadly as possible, in terms of authors' disciplines as well as the position they were likely to take with respect to the 1992 manual and the nature of MR. The starting point for the contributor wish list was all surviving members of the 1983 and 1992 AAMR T&C Committees, as well as all members of the T&C Committee preparing the next manual, expected to be published in 2002. (Because a few members were added to the T&C Committee after this book was initiated, it is possible that some current members were not invited.) We then added an extensive list of experts considered to have something important to say on the question, "What Is Mental Retardation?"

Perhaps half of those contacted agreed to participate, and most of them came through with chapters. Some who declined suggested replacements, and in most cases, these people agreed to participate. We recount all of this to explain why the final set of contributors does not include some obvious names, or is not as broad-based as it might have been, though we tried to make our pool of authors as diverse as possible. Nevertheless, we consider our authors to be a rare collection of leading thinkers in the MR field, representing a highly varied cross section of perspectives, world views, and suggestions for the future of the MR construct.

We also wanted to include a more global orientation and perspective, and so we invited some authors to discuss the International Classification of Impairments. Disabilities and Handicaps (ICIDH-2), sponsored by the World Health Organization, in order to familiarize an American audience with this model, since we know that the AAMR's current T&C Committee is considering the extent to which its behavioral classification system can be made congruent with ICIDH-2. We are also aware that the American Psychological Association is exploring how the ICIDH model may create a more user friendly, more functionally oriented classification system useful to patients, practitioners, and researchers (DeAngelis, 2001).

COMMON TOPICS COVERED IN CHAPTERS

To make the book more coherent than most edited books, we gave each chapter author(s) a common set of topics, which we wanted covered, in the same order. The model for this approach (and the inspiration for our title) was a similar book, edited by Sternberg and Determan (1986), titled *What is Intelligence? Contemporary Viewpoints on Its Nature and Definition*. Another similarity between the two books is that virtually every author answered the question differently. The subtopics to be included in each chapter are the following:

1. Assessment of the 1992 AAMR definition.
2. Proposed revision of the 1992 definition.
3. Rationale for the proposed definition.
4. Comment on other aspects of the AAMR manual or process.
5. The future of the MR field or construct.
6. References.

Each chapter was to be kept to about 20 manuscript pages. The section on ICIDH-2 was provided to describe this model and its implications for the field of MR. There would also be two overview chapters by the editors, an introductory chapter providing a historic presentation of the various AAMR efforts at defining and classifying MR, and a concluding chapter attempting to integrate the ideas presented by all the stakeholders (a daunting task, given the diversity of perspectives).

Contributors were free to pick a particular emphasis for their chapter, as reflected in their chosen title. Given the eminence of our authors, and our inclination toward flexibility, we have made only minor efforts to impose the guidelines, including the page-limit requirement—partly because we ourselves, being overly verbose, had a little trouble with the limit. We recognize that the deviation from the common format may make some readers uncomfortable, but even with such deviations; the book still has more coherence in form and content than is typically found in edited volumes. There may be some overlap in many of the points made by our contributors, depending upon the world views and perspectives of the stakeholders that may be repetitious to the reader. This overlap in consensus will be discussed at length in the concluding chapter.

ORGANIZATION OF THE CHAPTERS

The chapters are presented in three rather arbitrary groupings. Part I, "The Concept of Mental Retardation: Critical Issues," deals with more global theoretical and historical concerns of our authors and our introductory Chapter 1 provides a historical presentation of the various AAMR efforts at defining and classifying MR. Part II, "The 1992 AAMR System and Its Critics and Supporters," deals with a broad spectrum of opinions and attitudes of our authors vis-à-vis the 1992 AAMR model. Part III, "Emerging Models and Definitions of Mental Retardation," deals with more detailed revisions by our authors of the construct of mental retardation and with the presentation of WHO's International Classification of Impairments, Disabilities and Handicaps (ICIDH-2); it also includes our summary chapter attempting to integrate all the ideas presented by the stakeholders.

CONCLUSIONS

The field of mental retardation is currently in a period of great flux and transition. The primary purpose of this book is to provide a forum in which competing paradigms and models of mental retardation may be discussed and presented, so that we all can revisit the constitutive and operational definitions of mental retardation as well as its systems of classification and description. Our goal is to determine exactly what mental retardation is in the 21st century. We hope that this book will inspire everyone throughout the world to undertake this quest, so that all the diverse stakeholders—service providers, educators, researchers, advocates, and families—can come to some kind of consensus. We believe that this book will contribute to that process and be viewed as a positive contribution to the whole field of mental retardation (intellectual disability).

PREFACE TO THE 2005 BOOK

As chapters were received from the authors, they were immediately sent to the T&C Committee constructing the 2002 AAMR manual to help them in their task. The tenth edition of the *AAMR Manual of Definition, Classification, and Systems of Support* was published in the summer of 2002 in printed-book format, while our book, *What Is Mental Retardation? Ideas for an Evolving Disability*, was, owing to AAMR's financial difficulties, published the following summer in e-book format, available online from AAMR's Web site (http://www.disabilitybooksonline.com), which greatly diminished its availability to the community of readers. However, an examination of the 2002 AAMR manual shows that our e-book did greatly influence the ideas in it.

This current book was constructed for the most part by the original authors of the e-book, who used the original e-book's style of organization to comment on the 2002 manual rather than the 1992 manual and even more broadly on a model (both constitutive and operational) of mental retardation/intellectual disability useful for the 21st century. The goals of the current book are the same as those of the 2003 book, and the problems that face our field are still the same (Switzky, 2003). We hope that the revision of our original e-book will further energize the field and help to build consensus in these confusing times.

REFERENCES

DeAngelis, T. (2001). APA has leading role in revising classification system. *Monitor on Psychology, 2*(2), 54–56.

Grossman, H. J. (Ed.). (1983). *Manual on terminology and classification in mental retardation* (1983 revision). Washington, DC: American Association on Mental Deficiency.

Jacobson, J. W., & Mulick, J. A. (Eds.). (1996). *Manual of diagnosis and professional practice in mental retardation.* Washington, DC: American Psychological Association.

Luckasson, R., Borthwick-Duffy, S., Buntinx, W. H. E., Coulter, D. L., Craig, E. M., Reeve, A., et al.(2002). *Mental retardation: Definition, classification, and systems of supports* (10th ed.). Washington, DC: American Association on Mental Retardation.

Luckasson, R., Coulter, D. L., Polloway, E. A., Reiss, S., Schalock, R. L., Snell, M. E., et al. (1992). *Mental retardation: Definition, classification, and systems of supports* (9th ed.). Washington, DC: American Association on Mental Retardation.

Millon, T., & Klerman, G. R. (Eds.). (1986). *Contemporary directions in psychopathology: Toward the DSM-IV.* New York: Guilford.

Sternberg, R. J., & Detterman, D. K. (1986). *What is intelligence? Contemporary viewpoints on its nature and definition.* Norwood, NJ: Ablex.

Switzky, H. N. (2003). The plight of adults with mild cognitive limitations: Still forgotten? In A. J. Tymchuk, K. C. Lakin, & R. Luckasson (Eds.), *The forgotten generation: The status and challenges of adults with mild cognitive limitations. Contemporary Psychology, APA Review of Books, 48*(3), 363–365.

Switzky, H. N., & Greenspan, S. (Eds.). (2003). *What Is Mental Retardation? Ideas for an evolving disability.* Washington, DC: American Association on Mental Retardation [E-Book]. Available at http://www.disabilitybooksonline.com

PART I

The Concept of Mental Retardation: Critical Issues 2005

This part of the book deals with more universal, speculative, and historical issues regarding the nature of mental retardation/intellectual disabilities. Except for the first, the chapters are presented alphabetically by author and display a luxurious banquet of electrifying ideas for the reader to devour.

Greenspan and Switzky, in Chapter 1, present an extremely thorough analysis of the evolution of the concept of mental retardation from 1959 to 2002 in the manuals published by AAMR, giving the reader a reference point for all the discussions to follow. They describe in great detail in an unbiased way the various AAMR systems.

Baroff, in Chapter 2, presents his idea of mental retardation as a "disorder of chronic intellectual and emotional immaturity . . . viewed as an *intellectual disability* that adversely affects the capacity to cope successfully with the challenges of daily existence. Its most general effect is to increase the degree of *dependence* in meeting these challenges." Baroff discusses the 2002 AAMR model in the light of his thinking.

Glidden, in Chapter 3, provides a semantic feature analysis of the 2002 AAMR definition of mental retardation compared to the 1992 AAMR model in an attempt to find "meaning" in the various labels and definitions provided by the AAMR manuals.

Smith, in Chapter 4, provides a history of MR definitions and the implications for the field of MR of the paradigm shift explicit in the 1992 and 2002 AAMR manuals.

Snell and Voorhees, in Chapter 5, focus on the effects of the label of mental retardation on the individuals so labeled, their parents and family members, and the professionals and social system agencies that use the label. An interesting part of this chapter is the ethnographic analysis and description of the effects of the mental retardation label on three adults in their 30s and 40s residing in semi-independent community settings, providing a more personal perspective into the world of persons labeled as mentally retarded.

Spitz, in Chapter 6, comments on the paradigmatic ideological position of the 1992 and 2002 AAMR systems that "exchanges an absolutist view for relativism" and abolishes familial (hereditary) forms of mental retardation. Spitz argues in his chapter that the evidence for familial (hereditary) forms of mental retardation is overwhelming and cannot be abolished by fiat by the authors of the 1992 and 2002 AAMR manuals for ideological reasons.

1

Chapter One

Forty-Four Years of AAMR Manuals

Stephen Greenspan and Harvey N. Switzky

Introduction

The way in which the mental retardation (MR) construct is defined has important consequences for millions of people. It affects their social and legal status and consequently the services and supports for which they may be eligible. It also affects a range of activities that shape these services and supports, including administration, communication, and statistical reporting and research.

This book explores the future of the MR construct in the 21st century and comments upon the newest revision of the AAMR classification manual (Luckasson et al., 2002). In order to avoid repeating past mistakes and to understand the arguments, many of them still relevant, that underlie previous and current choices and compromises, we require some familiarity with the 2002 manual and those that preceded it. Accordingly, this chapter provides a historical frame of reference to the literature on the classification of MR. We have restricted our focus to the various manuals published by AAMR, including those issued in its previous incarnation as AAMD (American Association on Mental Deficiency). We have not considered any of the broader classification schemes, such as that of the Diagnostic and Statistical Manual (DSM) of the American Psychiatric Association, in part because MR is only one of many disorders they address, and also because their definition of MR is typically derived from or modeled after the AAMR definition. In focusing on AAMR manuals, in a volume being published by the AAMR, one of our motives is to influence the dialogue about mental retardation in the 21st century.

Writing in the year 2005, we begin our discussion of AAMR manuals with the 1961 edition—hence the chapter title, "Forty-Four Years of AAMR Manuals." We begin with the 1961 manual, rather than discussing earlier diagnostic manuals published by predecessor professional organizations in the 1920s and 1930s, for four reasons:

1. It is generally acknowledged to be the first one providing objective (i.e., test score) criteria.
2. It established the term that is still used (at least in the United States), mental retardation, to replace more pejorative terms such as idiocy or feeblemindedness.
3. It was the first classificatory scheme to become almost universally adopted.

3

4. It provided the framework (the dual criteria of intelligence and adaptive behavior) and the competing goals (getting people needed services while avoiding the pitfalls of over identification) with which the field is still struggling.

Description of the AAMR Manuals

Each manual will be discussed in terms of four features:

1. Background information.
2. The conceptual definition, which is a brief general description of the category of mental retardation.
3. The operational definition, which is a more concrete elaboration on the key terms contained in the conceptual definition.
4. The behavioral classification system, especially the mechanism for sub-grouping people according to the severity of their impairments and needs.

Owing to space limitations, we have not addressed other aspects of the manuals, such as the (highly valuable) material on medical etiology or service approaches.

The 1961 Manual

Background to the 1961 manual.

The 1961 manual grew out of the "Project on Technical Planning in Mental Retardation" of the American Association on Mental Deficiency (AAMD, the precursor to AAMR). Its stated purpose was to "achieve increased uniformity in terminology and in the medical and behavioral classification of persons who are mentally retarded" (Heber, 1961, p. vii), as an aid to communication, classification, treatment, administration, programming, education, habilitation, statistical reporting and research.

The AAMR viewed this as the fifth in a series of such manuals. The first had been published in 1919 by a precursor organization, the American Association for the Study of the Feebleminded (AASF). Revisions were published in 1933 and 1941 by the AASF, in cooperation with the National Committee for Mental Hygiene. These three manuals, and related statistical reports, played an important role in establishing mental retardation as a specialty field and in encouraging the publication of nationwide statistical data on MR by the federal government.

In 1952, driven by dissatisfaction with terminology then in use (e.g., idiocy, imbecility and so on), the AAMD established a Committee on Nomenclature, chaired by Gale H. Walker. In 1957, this committee published an etiological classification scheme, which is now viewed as the fourth edition of the manual initially published in 1919. It was considered an interim product, to be replaced in a few years by a more comprehensive one (which would incorporate the etiological scheme).

That effort was initially chaired by Dr. Walker. Upon his death in 1958, the work was taken up by Rick Heber, a psychologist and research associate employed by the project. In 1959 the new manual was published in provisional form as a Monograph Supplement of the *American Journal of Mental Deficiency.* After a period of comment and review, a revised final version was published in 1961 as a Monograph Supplement of *AJMD*, and later published in book form.

The 1959 and 1961 manuals usually are viewed as essentially identical and often are cited interchangeably. In fact, however, they differed in one very major respect. The concept of "adaptive behavior," which has been the cause of so much controversy and confusion, did not appear as part of the conceptual definition of MR in 1959 but did appear in the revised manual two years later. This distinction is discussed in more detail in the next section.

Unlike the later process used by AAMR, where a manual was written collectively by a "Terminology and Classification" (T&C) committee, the 1961 manual appears to have been written largely by Heber and then reviewed by two committees of the Association, one (made up entirely of physicians) addressing issues of medical classification, the other (made up largely of psychologists) addressing issues of behavior classification. It has been reported, although not explicitly stated anywhere in the 1961 manual, that one of the major considerations was deep dissatisfaction with the section dealing with MR in DSM-2, the second edition of the American Psychiatric Association's *Diagnostic and Statistical Manual of Mental Disorders*. If that was, indeed, a motivator, it achieved its purpose, as the third and fourth editions of *DSM* have largely deferred to the AAMR in matters pertaining to the definition and classification of MR.

Conceptual definition of MR in the 1961 manual.

In the 1961 manual, the conceptual definition went as follows:

> Mental Retardation refers to subaverage general intellectual functioning which originates during the developmental period and is associated with impairment in adaptive behavior. (Heber, 1961, p. 3)

The earlier provisional (Heber, 1959) AAMD manual contained a conceptual definition which went as follows:

> Mental Retardation refers to subaverage general intellectual functioning which originates during the developmental period and is associated with impairment in one or more of the following: (1) maturation, (2) learning, and (3) social adjustment. (p. 3)

Thus, three relatively clearly defined terms were replaced by a single, largely undefined, newly invented term, *adaptive behavior*.

Furthermore, the term *mental retardation* itself was chosen by the T&C committee as "at present . . . the most preferred term among professional personnel of all disciplines concerned" (Heber, 1961, p. 3). It was intended to replace earlier terms such as idiocy, moronity, imbecility, amentia, and mental subnormality that were now viewed as less acceptable and lacking in specificity.

Operational definition of MR in the 1961 manual.

The 1961 manual defined the term *subaverage* as:

> Performance which is greater than one Standard Deviation below the population mean of the age group involved on measures of general intellectual functioning. (Heber, 1961, p. 3)

It went on to define general intellectual functioning as:

> Performance on one or more of the various objective tests that have been developed for that purpose. (p. 3; the circularity of this definition has been noted by various commentators)

Thus, subaverage intellectual functioning was operationally defined as a score of 84 or less on any test generally accepted as an adequate measure of intelligence. The developmental period was defined as all ages up to approximately sixteen.

Adaptive behavior was defined as:

> The effectiveness of the individual in adapting to the natural and social demands of his environment. (p. 3)

Impaired adaptive behavior was to be reflected in limitations in one or more of the following: (1) maturation, (2) learning, and (3) social adjustment for different age groups.

Thus, the three terms in the second part of the conceptual definition in the 1959 provisional manual (maturation, learning, and social adjustment) were folded into the final 1961 manual in the form of an elaboration on the newly invented rubric of adaptive behavior.

These terms were further operationally defined as follows:

1. Maturation was to be used to refer to "the rate of sequential development of self-help and sensori-motor skills of infancy and early childhood, the preschool years."
2. Learning ability was to be used to refer to "the facility with which knowledge is acquired as a function of experience, particularly in school settings during the school years" (p. 3).
3. Social adjustment referred to "the degree to which the individual is able to maintain himself independently in the community and in gainful employment as well as by his ability to meet and conform to other personal and social responsibilities and standards at the adult level as set by the community. During the preschool and school age years, social adjustment is reflected in large measure in the level and manner in which the child relates to parents, other adults, and age peers" (p. 4).

The manual indicates that the maturity criterion is most relevant to diagnosing MR in early childhood, the learning criterion is most relevant to diagnosing MR in school-age children, while social adjustment is most relevant to diagnosing MR in adults.

Behavioral classification system used in the 1961 manual.

In the AAMR manuals, beginning with the 1961 edition, severity classification is viewed as separate from diagnosis. In the 1961 manual (and in the 1959 draft version), the severity subcategory names are not prominently featured. In fact, only in a footnote to Table I, "Standard Deviation Ranges Corresponding to Measured Intelligence Levels" (Heber, 1961, p. 58), do we find the terms "borderline retardation of measured intelligence," "mild retardation of measured intelligence," "moderate retardation of measured intelligence," "severe retardation of measured intelligence," and "profound retardation of measured intelligence."

In the main body of that table, retardation severity levels are given numbers 1 through 5 corresponding to statistical codes ("1" corresponding to minus 1 standard deviation units on a standardized IQ measure, "2" to minus 2 standard deviation units, and so on). One has to look at the table footnotes to find the following amplification:

> Where use of descriptive terminology is advisable for purposes of interpretation to legal authorities, parents, etc., the following terms are suggested: Level-1—Borderline retardation of measured intelligence; Level-2—Mild retardation of measured intelligence, and so on to Level-5—Profound retardation of measured intelligence. (p. 58)

In the section on Adaptive Behavior, the same subcategory names reappear, but this time in the body of Table III, "Standard Deviation Ranges Corresponding to Level of Adaptive Behavior" (Heber, 1961, p. 62) rather than in a footnote. In this table there are four sub-categories:

- "Level-I (Mild but apparent and significant negative deviation from norms and standards of Adaptive Behavior);
- Level-II (Moderate but definite negative deviation from norms and standards of Adaptive Behavior);
- Level-III (Severe negative deviation from norms and standards of Adaptive Behavior); and
- Level-IV (Profound negative deviation from norms and standards of Adaptive Behavior)."

Like Table I, described above, Table III describes retardation severity levels in terms of standard deviation units, this time (for unspecified reasons) in 1.25-unit steps (Level I = -1.01 to -2.25 standard deviation units, Level II = -2.26 to -3.50 standard deviation units, Level III = -3.51 to -4.75 standard deviation units, Level IV = less than -4.75 standard deviation units).

This seems like a rather abstract and arbitrary exercise, given that no standardized scale of adaptive behavior even existed in 1961. The manual was relatively vague about the kinds of behavioral deficits believed to correspond to these subcategories, though a table from Sloan and Birch (1955) was offered to illustrate levels of Adaptive Behavior for three broad age groups, Pre-School Age (0–5) in maturation and development, School Age (6–21) in training and education, and Adult (21) in social and vocational adequacy.

Additionally, a supplementary classification section included in both the 1959 and 1961 manuals tried to measure impairments in personal-social and sensory-motor factors that are frequently concomitants of mental retardation and influence an individual's total behavioral adaptation to the environment. These were not diagnostic indicators for mental retardation but were viewed as important in planning for education and habilitation and in prognosis. The personal-social factors were: impairments in interpersonal relations, impairments in cultural conformity, and impairments in responsiveness. The sensory-motor factors were impairments in motor skills, impairments in auditory skills, impairments in visual skills, and impairments in speech skills. These supplementary factors were characterized as behavior either in accord with or superior to expectations in relation to age level, or significantly deficient.

The personal-social factor of impairment in interpersonal relations was

> intended to reflect deficiencies in interpersonal skills. The individual with an impairment in interpersonal relations does not relate adequately to peers and/or authority figures and may demonstrate an inability to recognize the needs of other persons in interpersonal interactions. (Heber, 1961, p. 65)

The personal-social factor of impairment in cultural conformity

> reflected one of the following: behavior which does not conform to social mores, behavior which does not meet standards of dependability, reliability, and trustworthiness; behavior which is persistently asocial, anti-social, and/or excessively hostile. (Heber, 1961, pp. 65–66)

The personal-social factor of impairment in responsiveness

> is characterized by an inability to delay gratification of needs and a lack of long-range goal-striving or persistence with response only to short-term goals. Those individuals who respond only to bio-physical stimuli of comfort or discomfort would be classified at one extreme of the dimension of behavioral responsivity. Individuals classified at the other extreme would be characterized by responsiveness to abstract or very symbolic rewards. (Heber, 1961, p. 67)

The 1973 Manual

Background to the 1973 manual.

The 1973 manual was intended to build on the 1961 manual and to remedy its perceived problems, especially its creation of a Borderline category with an IQ ceiling of 85. This problem had been exacerbated by diagnosticians' widespread ignoring of the Adaptive Behavior criterion.

The period between manuals, 1961–1973, saw a greatly increased awareness of problems of race and class discrimination in the United States. Excessively literal use of the 85 IQ cutoff, combined with a great expansion in self-contained Special Education programs for children with mild disabilities, resulted in over assignment of the MR label to minority individuals, many of whom would not have qualified for it if the Adaptive Behavior criterion had been taken seriously.

Conceptual definition in the 1973 manual.

As defined in the 1973 manual:

> Mental Retardation refers to significantly subaverage general intellectual functioning existing concurrently with deficits in adaptive behavior and manifested during the developmental period. (p. 5)

This differed in two ways from the 1961 conceptual definition:

1. The 1961 definition referred to "subaverage general intellectual functioning," which the 1973 definition changed to "significantly subaverage general intellectual functioning," thus specifying a greater severity of intellectual impairment.
2. The 1961 definition noted that the subaverage intellectual functioning "is associated with impairment in adaptive behavior," while the 1973 manual stated that it exists "concurrently with deficits in adaptive behavior."

This latter change, while seemingly minor, has been interpreted by some commentators as suggesting a shift away from viewing adaptive behavior as an necessary outgrowth of low intelligence, toward seeing it as something separate and orthogonal from intelligence, akin in some ways to a personality axis in a multiaxial classification system.

Operational definition in the 1973 manual.
The biggest change in the 1973 manual was in recalibrating the upper boundary of the MR category. The manual makes clear that the first change in the conceptual definition, from "subaverage" to "significantly subaverage" intellectual functioning, was intended "to reflect the deletion of the Borderline category" (Grossman, 1973, p. 11). The upper level of MR was changed from minus one standard deviation (IQ = 85 on the Wechsler scales) to minus two standard deviations (IQ = 70 on the Wechsler scales, or IQ = 68 on the metric then in use by the Stanford-Binet).

The upper age limit of the developmental period was now set at 18 years (in 1961, it had been set at 16), which, in the words of the manual, "serves to distinguish mental retardation from other disorders of human behavior" (p. 11).

"Intellectual functioning" was described, rather than defined, as something that "may be assessed by one or more of the standardized tests developed for that purpose" (p. 11; in other words, intelligence is that which is measured by intelligence tests). The manual specified that the intelligence test had to be individually administered and pointed out that "quick" or group tests were to be avoided (p. 15).

Adaptive behavior was defined as:

> The effectiveness or degree with which the individual meets the standards of personal independence and social responsibility expected of his age and cultural group. (p. 11)

Because of differing age-related expectations, deficits in adaptive behavior were believed to manifest themselves as follows:

1. During infancy and early childhood, in sensory-motor skills development, communication skills, self-help skills, and socialization.
2. During childhood and early adolescence, in "application of basic academic skills in daily life activities," "application of appropriate reasoning and judgment in mastery of the environment" and "social skills."
3. During late adolescence and adult life, in "vocational and social responsibilities and performances" (p. 11).

Behavioral classification system in the 1973 manual.

As noted, the major change in the classification system from the 1961 manual was the dropping of the category of Borderline Retardation. In the 1973 manual, there are thus four levels of mental retardation: Mild, Moderate, Severe and Profound. These sub-category levels were prominently emphasized in the text. As in 1961, they progressed in steps of 1.0 IQ standard deviation units, ranging from minus two standard deviation units for mild MR to minus five standard deviation units for profound MR.

One minor change (though not minor to the individuals affected) is that while in 1961, mild MR translated as an IQ of 70 or less (on the Wechsler scale, which at that time was the individual IQ test to arbitrarily equate a standard deviation unit with an IQ score of 15), in 1973 mild MR translated to an IQ in the range of 69–52, and so on for the other categories. Thus, the IQ criteria for subcategory levels were now set at being *less than* minus one, minus two, and so on, standard deviation units, while in 1961 they had been set *at* minus one, two, and so on standard deviation units. In the section on Adaptive Behavior, the 1973 manual backed off from the idea of subclassifying people according to standard deviation units.

While the same four severity levels of adaptive behavior impairment are used as for intellectual impairment, the 1973 manual eschews a statistical basis for such subcategorization, noting that

> if more precise instruments were available for the measurement of Adaptive Behavior, and general norms could be precisely stipulated, [then] the upper limit of Level-I could presumably be set at minus two standard deviations from the population mean. (Grossman, 1973, p. 19)

The manual goes on to note that, while several scales of adaptive behavior had been developed,

> most of the scales developed for use with the retarded have major limitations. They were developed primarily on institutional populations and do not adequately embrace the broad range of behaviors characteristic of mildly retarded children and adults living in the community. (Grossman, 1973, p. 20)

And, as has been frequently noted, the biggest problem facing diagnosticians comes in differentiating between those with mild and low-normal intelligence. The proposed solution, until more adequate measures are developed, is to rely on

> a combination of pertinent test data, clinical observation, and utilization of all available sources of information regarding the person's everyday behavior. (Grossman, 1973, p. 20)
>
> Therefore, the ultimate determination of the presence or absence of mental retardation rests on clinical judgment. (Grossman, 1973, p. 21)

The predominant supplementary classification section included in both the 1959 and 1961 manuals, and in the 1973 manual, was addressed as follows:

> Mental retardation may co-exist with other handicaps, and frequently does in individuals with more severe degrees of retardation. Classification of such individuals is difficult and requires a multiple axial system. The system presented in

this manual attempts to make provision for as many of these problems as possible by providing supplementary categories through which other traits of the individual can be classified (e.g., hearing handicap, motor dysfunction, speech defects, psychiatric disorders. (Grossman, 1973, p. 7)

Impairments in interpersonal relations and in cultural conformity disappeared into Section IX of the statistical reporting section (p. 101), and impairments in responsiveness vanished into the glossary (p. 152).

The 1983 Manual

Background to the 1983 manual.

There was a 1977 edition, but most commentators consider it to be a minor updating of the 1973 edition. The 1983 edition, while still bearing close resemblance to the 1973 manual, made some change in emphasis. The main change was an attempt to loosen the literalness with which the IQ cutoff score was being applied, by emphasizing the need to take into account an IQ test's standard error (the range, typically 5 points, within which an individual's actual score is likely to fluctuate), and by encouraging greater use of clinical judgment in the diagnostic process. These concerns were present, to some extent, in the 1973 manual, but were given greater voice in the 1983 manual. Also, previous manuals (1959, 1961, 1973) were organized into sections on medical and behavioral classification, statistical reporting, and glossary. The 1983 manual dropped its statistical reporting section and added new expanded sections on the application of the classification system to the delivery of services and research and a section on clinical applications. Also there was an emphasis throughout the manual on making explicit the implicit philosophical model undergirding the model of MR proposed. The purposes of the 1983 classification system were to contribute to an acceptable system to be used throughout the world, to facilitate communication for diagnostic, treatment, and research purposes, and to facilitate prevention of mental retardation (p. 2).

Conceptual definition in the 1983 manual.

The conceptual definition of mental retardation is somewhat confusing, since it is defined in two parts of the manual (page 1 and page 11) which do not totally agree. The impression is that the definitions provided on page 1 are abbreviated ones, expanded in greater detail on page 11 and throughout pages 11–26 (Chapter 3) and in the rest of the manual. On page 1:

> Mental retardation refers to significantly subaverage general intellectual functioning existing concurrently with deficits in adaptive behavior and manifested during the developmental period,

which was the conceptual definition provided in the 1973 manual. On page 11, we read:

> Mental retardation refers to significantly subaverage general intellectual functioning resulting in or associated with concurrent impairments in adaptive behavior and manifested during the developmental period.

This elaboration appears to emphasize a causal link between low intelligence (as cause) and impaired adaptive behavior (as effect), rather than viewing these as coexisting but not necessarily causally linked. Thus, the 1983 definition seems to give somewhat more primacy to the notion that MR is at its core a condition marked by low intelligence, with various behavioral deficits flowing from such low intelligence, rather than a condition marked by low intelligence and associated behavioral deficits. However, the manual states that

> the AAMD definition does not distinguish causality from association because members of the AAMD committee concluded that since one can not determine in most cases whether the lowered intellectual functioning does in fact cause the adaptive behavior deficits it was unnecessary to add a phrase implying causality. (pp. 124–125)

In conclusion, the 1983 manual favored the conceptual definition provided in the 1973 manual.

Operational definition in the 1983 manual.

Significantly subaverage general intellectual functioning was "defined as IQ of 70 or below on standardized measures of intelligence" (p. 11; note that the 1961 formula of "or below" was restored, replacing the 1973 formula that established the ceiling at 69). Impairments in adaptive behavior were defined as "significant limitations in an individual's effectiveness in meeting the standards of maturation, learning, personal independence, and/or social responsibility that are expected for his or her age level and cultural group, as determined by clinical assessment and, usually, standardized scales." The definition of the developmental period remained as the period of time between conception and the 18th birthday (p. 11). It was noted that

> developmental deficits may be manifested by slow, arrested or incomplete development resulting from brain damage, degenerative processes in the central nervous system, or regression from previously normal states due to psychosocial factors. (p. 11)

Behavioral classification system in the 1983 manual.

The 1973 behavioral classification was carried over largely intact into the 1983 manual. Mention was made, for the first time, of the need to keep the classification system congruent with other major classification systems (primarily the American Psychiatric Association's DSM and the World Health Organization's ICD), especially as the sections on MR in those schemes were largely derived from the 1961 and 1973 AAMD manuals. The major change in the subcategorization system, in line with the attempt to emphasize the standard error of IQ tests, was that the manual now operationally defined mild MR as falling in an IQ range of "50–55 to approximately 70" (p. 13), moderate MR as "35–40 to 50–55," severe MR as "20–25 to 35–40," and profound MR as "below 20 or 25."

> Levels of retardation were identified with the same terms as those used in previous AAMD manuals. The IQ ranges for levels were generally consistent with those suggested by the American Psychiatric Association in their Diagnostic and Statistical Manual III, but a narrow band at each end of each level was used to indicate that clinical judgment about all information, including the IQs, and more than one test, the information about intellectual functioning obtained from other sources, etc. is necessary in determining level." (p. 13)

The procedure for determining level of retardation is as follows:

1. Recognize that a problem exists (e.g., delay in developmental milestones).
2. Determine that an adaptive behavior deficit exists.
3. Determine measured general intellectual functioning.
4. Make decision about whether or not there is retardation of intellectual functioning.
5. Make decision about level of retardation as indicated by level of measured intellectual functioning (Grossman, 1973, p. 13).

The term *mental retardation,* as used in the manual,

> embraces a heterogeneous population, ranging from totally dependent to nearly independent people. Although all individuals so designated share the common attributes of low intelligence and inadequacies in adaptive behavior, there are marked variations in the degree of deficit manifested and the presence or absence of associated physical handicaps, stigmata, and psychologically disordered states. These variations greatly affect the needs of retarded individuals, the nature of the problems and services required by their families, and the burdens posed to community agencies and supportive systems. The differences are highly related to etiological factors, setting biologically damaged persons apart from psychosocially disadvantaged individuals on a number of significant dimensions: performance, problems, potentials, and prognosis. (p. 12)

Two overlapping groups of mentally retarded populations were identified: the "clinical types" who demonstrated central nervous dysfunction and had low IQs in the moderate range or below composing 25 percent of the MR population, and individuals who were neurologically intact and functioned in the mild range of intelligence and were found primarily in the lowest socioeconomic segments of society, composing 75 percent of the MR population in the United States.

One innovation of the 1983 manual was its strong concern with bio-psychosocial factors and social milieus that can impede or facilitate intelligence and its extension of its multiaxial classification system by inclusion within its classification model of a multiaxial coding of social-environmental factors known to affect cognitive and developmental processes, such as:

> "(a) parental absence, apathy, rejection, neglect, abuse, or lack of controls and limits; (b) lack of appropriate mental, sensory, and verbal stimulation; (c) family organization and conflict; (d) inadequate role models, socialization, and teaching approaches; (e) limited opportunities for positive interpersonal relationships with peers, teachers, and other socializing agents; (f) limited access to social and vocational opportunity structures, and (g) cultural conflicts within families. (p. 51)

These factors were not diagnostic for mental retardation but helped researchers, clinicians, and service providers to understand their contributory role for the manifestation of impaired intellectual and behavioral functioning and their importance in developing a plan for intervention, habilitation, and treatment.

The 1983 manual stressed reliance for classification on cutting-edge research and not on the "vagaries of litigation, political processes and the pressure of special-interest groups" (p. 19). The 1983 classification system was concerned with both research and delivery of service programs. The manual devoted Chapter 6 to a thorough discussion of the application of its classification system to the delivery of service and research, including service-system management, planning, and evaluation of services. In terms of research, the manual wanted to provide a common terminology, because without a uniform method of classifying different subtypes of dysfunction, research would be impossible.

> Planning services, specifying possible causes, and identifying opportunities for prevention require uniform specification of clinical patterns found to exist in individuals labeled retarded. There are five factors coded for research purposes, currently being proposed in this classification that should be considered in the clinical evaluation of the clients: (a) severity of intellectual impairment, (b) assessment of adaptive behavior functioning, (c) etiology of the condition, (d) associated medical and behavioral problems, and (e) evaluation of the social environment. (p. 89)

In terms of personal-social and motivational factors, the 1983 manual folded such concerns into its conceptions of adaptive behavior and its multiaxial coding of social-environmental factors. On pages 14–15, the manual characterizes mentally retarded persons as having impairments in self-direction, social responsiveness, and interactive skills, and on page 27 it includes motivation as one of the psychosocial factors that can influence intelligence.

The 1992 Manual

Background to the 1992 manual.

Although the 1973 and 1983 manuals contained some meaningful innovations (e.g., the 1973 elimination of the category of Borderline MR and the 1983 call for greater flexibility and use of clinical judgment), they both operated within the basic framework laid down in the 1961 manual—namely, a low IQ score paired with a global impairment in adaptive behavior. The T&C committee preparing the 1992 manual assumed that fundamental changes in service models and values (e.g., the use of "support" as opposed to facility-based service models, and a more optimistic and respectful way of viewing persons with disabilities perhaps due to the rise of the self-advocacy movement) made it necessary to fundamentally change the MR definition and classification system. The 1992 manual states even more explicitly than the 1983 manual the philosophical underpinnings of the model of mental retardation proposed.

Although the manual states that the changes were made with no concern for their impact on prevalence rates, there are reasons to believe that the committee was concerned that provisions in previous manuals (e.g., eliminating the Borderline category, strict enforcement of a 70 IQ ceiling, and requirement for global adaptive behavior impairment) had resulted in too many cases of deserving persons being turned down for services on the basis that they did not meet technical diagnostic criteria. Another apparent concern was the muddled state of the adaptive behavior construct, particularly the inclusion of a "maladaptive behavior" (i.e., psychopathology) component. which, while relevant for programming purposes, was inappropriate for use in diagnosing MR. The T&C commit-tee strongly argued for reconceptualization of the disabling process as resulting from the interaction of the person with their environment.

> Mental retardation is not something you have, like blue eyes or a bad heart. Nor is it something you are, like being short or thin. It is not a medical disorder . . . Nor is it a mental disorder. Mental retardation refers to a particular state of func-tioning that begins in childhood and in which limitations in intelligence coexist with related limitations in adaptive skill. (Luckasson et al., p. 9)

Obviously, another of the T&C committee's major concerns was the rigid reliance on IQ standard deviation units, especially in the behavioral subclassification system (i.e., mild, moderate, and so on). A related concern was the failure to exercise clinical judgment or to take into account the standard error of IQ test scores, when making the diagnosis.

The purposes of the 1992 classification system were to:

1. Attempt to express the changing understanding of what mental retardation is.
2. Formulate what ought to be classified as well as to how to describe the systems of supports people with mental retardation require.
3. Represent a paradigm shift, from a view of mental retardation as an absolute trait expressed solely by an individual to an expression of the interaction between the person with intellectual functioning and the environment. "Mental retardation describes the "fit" between the capabilities of the individual and the structure and expectations of the individual's personal and social environment" (p. 9).
4. Attempt to extend the concept of adaptive behavior from a global description to specification of particular adaptive skill area (pp. ix–x).

The major changes are as follows:

1. The global term adaptive behavior has been extended to 10 specific adaptive skill areas.
2. Four assumptions for the application of the definition are asserted at the same time as the definition.
3. Rather than requiring subclassification into four levels of a person's mental retar-dation (mild, moderate, severe, and profound), the system subclassifies the inten-sities and patterns of supports into four levels (intermittent, limited, extensive, and pervasive) (p. x).

In summary, the concept of supports and their use is integral to the definition of mental retardation that incorporates the possible nonpermanent nature of men-tal retardation and the demonstrated fact that with appropriate supports over a sustained period, the life functioning of individuals with mental retardation will generally improve. (p. 109)

Conceptual definition in the 1992 manual.
In 1992, the following definition governed professional practice:

Mental retardation refers to substantial limitations in present functioning. It is characterized by significantly subaverage intellectual functioning, existing concurrently with related limitations in two or more of the following applicable adaptive skill areas: communication, self-care, home living, social skills, community use, self-direction, health and safety, functional academics, leisure and work. Mental retardation manifests itself before age 18. (p. 1)

This definition was based on four assumptions, which were essential to the application of the definition:

1. Valid assessment considers cultural and linguistic diversity as well as differences in communication and behavioral factors.
2. The existence of limitations in adaptive skills occurs within the context of community environments typical of the individual's age peers and is indexed to the person's individualized needs for supports.
3. Specific adaptive limitations often coexist with strengths in other adaptive skills or other personal capabilities.
4. With appropriate supports over a sustained period, the life functioning of the person with mental retardation will generally improve (p. 1).

The major innovation here is the substitution of "adaptive skills" for "adaptive behavior" and the use of a polythetic (2 out of 10) formula rather than the monothetic, and more global, requirement of "impairments in adaptive behavior." The theoretical section of the 1992 manual indicated a desire to ground the definition of MR (and of adaptive behavior) more fully in a model of multiple intelligences, specifically, a tripartite model consisting of "conceptual intelligence (IQ)" ("cognition and learning," page 11), "practical intelligence" ("the ability to maintain and sustain oneself as an independent person in managing the ordinary activities of daily life," page 15) and "social intelligence" ("the ability to understand social expectations and the behavior of other persons and to judge appropriately how to conduct oneself in social situations," page 15). However, the 1992 conceptual definition still maintained a distinction between "intellectual functioning" and adaptive behavior (now termed "adaptive skills"), and the list of 10 adaptive skills was derived, not from the tripartite model, but from a largely atheoretical community skills curriculum, the Syracuse Community Referenced Curriculum Guide (Ford et al. 1989).

Chapter 2, the theoretical basis of the definition ends as follows:

This theoretical framework is not intended to be the "last word" on the subject. Rather, it should be considered a statement of current thinking at this point in time. As such, it is intended to guide the further development of concepts about mental retardation. Many of the ideas in this chapter warrant further elaboration, model building and empirical validation. We anticipate that further research and thinking will result in necessary changes in the framework as presented here. (p. 19)

Operational definition in the 1992 manual.

As in the previous manuals, an IQ score approximately two standard deviations or more below the population mean is a necessary condition for the diagnosis of MR. In the 1992 manual, however, the criterion is established more loosely, as "a score of 70 to 75 or below" (p. 14), to take into account the standard error of any given IQ test (i.e., the like-lihood that one's true score falls within a range that is 5 points above or below the score obtained). This adding of the standard error of IQ tests into the cutting score (rather than continuing to caution diagnosticians to act flexibly in interpreting IQ scores) reflected, undoubtedly, frustration over the continuing tendency of professionals and agencies to apply the 70 IQ ceiling inflexibly, without taking into account either standard error or adaptive functioning level. One noted consequence of raising the IQ ceiling from 70 to 75, however, is that the incidence of newly diagnosed cases of MR can, theoretically, more than double, from 2 percent to about 5 percent of the population, if the new operational definition is, in fact, adopted and implemented widely (which, for the most part, has not been the case).

The 1992 definition of mental retardation is based on a multidimensional approach involving four dimensions: Dimension I—Intellectual Functioning and Adaptive Skills, Dimension II—Psychological/Emotional Considerations (assessed by measures of psychopathology, e.g., DSM III-R), Dimension III—Physical/Health/Etiological Considerations (assessed by ICD-9 and etiological factors such as biomedical, social, behavioral, and education), and Dimension IV—Environmental Considerations (as assessed by ecological analysis including educational/habilitation program, living environments, and employment environments). A three-step process of diagnosis, classification, and system of supports was followed (p. 24).

Step 1. Diagnosis of Mental Retardation—using Dimension I—to determine eligibility for supports. Mental retardation is diagnosed if:

1. The individual's intellectual functioning is approximately 70 to 75 or below. ["This criterion serves only to assist in the determination of whether an individual is to be classified as having mental retardation but by itself is insufficient to such diagnosis" (p. 49)].
2. There are significant disabilities in two or more adaptive skill areas. ["This part of the diagnosis is more substantive and subjective and requires clinical judgment that takes into account environmental demands and potential supports systems . . . Identified limitations in many educational, vocational, and community living skills may be irrelevant if appropriate supports or prosthetics are made available or if appropriate environmental accommodations are made. The person's adaptive skill profile must be considered in making a diagnosis of mental retardation. The general rule is that if two or more adaptive skill limitations fall substantially below the average level of functioning (as determined either by formal comparison to a normative sample or through professional judgment), then the individual would meet this second criterion for a diagnosis of mental retardation. . . . By shifting to a greater reliance on adaptive skills in the diagnosis of mental retardation, embedded within an orientation toward observation and clinical judgment, all persons who have significant limitations associated with the defined concept of mental retardation could be assured of eligibility for services" (p. 49)].
3. The age of onset is below 18.

Step 2. Classification and Description—using Dimensions I, II, III, and IV—to identify strengths and weaknesses and the needs for supports.

1. Describe the individual's strengths and weaknesses in reference to psychological/emotional considerations.
2. Describe the individual's overall physical health and indicate the condition's etiology.
3. Describe the individual's current environment placement and the optimal environment that would facilitate his/her continued growth and development.

Step 3. Profile and intensities of needed supports. Identify the kind and intensities of supports needed (intermittent, limited, extensive, or pervasive) for each of the four dimensions (p. 24).

The intent of this three-step process is to broaden the conceptualization of mental retardation, to avoid reliance on IQ scores to assign a level of disability, and to relate the person's needs to the intensities of supports necessary to enhance the person's independence/interdependence, productivity, and community integration (p. 25).

In summary, the purpose of the three-step approach to Definition, Classification, and Systems of Supports is to provide a detailed description of the individual and his or her needed supports. This permits recognition of all separate areas of need that may require intervention while recognizing their interdependence. It also facilitates the design of treatment approaches or service delivery plans that take into account all aspects of the person's functioning. From the viewpoint of the individual, it permits a more accurate description of change over time, including individual responses to personal growth, environmental changes, educational activities, and therapeutic intervention. Finally, it focuses on the potential of one's environment to provide the services and supports that will enhance the person's opportunities for personal life satisfaction (p. 34).

Behavioral classification system in the 1992 manual.

The most controversial feature of the 1992 manual was the elimination of the behavioral classification system based on four distinct severity subcategories ("mild," "moderate," "severe," and "profound"), replacing it with a single descriptive profile approach, the Support Planning Matrix (p. 106), the intensity and range of an individual's support needs across the 10 adaptive skills areas, the habilitation goals, and the environmental characteristics. The motivation was undoubtedly:

1. To reduce heavy reliance on IQ scores (since the diagnostic subcategorizing tended to be based solely on IQ standard deviation units).
2. To bring the notion of support needs, so central to the changing service paradigm in the MR field, into the definition of MR as operationalized in the Support Planning Matrix.

Opposition to this step reflects the view that subcategories have a long history in the MR field (in fact, they predate the invention of a unifying rubric of MR), that there are broad qualitative differences between people with mild and more severe forms of MR, and that these qualitative distinctions should not be obscured.

The 1992 manual in its discussion of Dimension III, Physical/Health/Etiology considerations, modified the broad etiological model of mental retardation due to biological origins vs. mental retardation due to psychosocial disadvantage as overly simplistic. Mental retardation reflects the cumulative or interactive effects of more than one factor, and so one cannot separate the etiology of mental retardation into biological and psychological categories that may be often blurred. Instead a multifactorial model of etiology was extended to include type of factors and timing of factors. Four types of factors were proposed (p. 71):

1. Biomedical: factors that relate to biological processes, such as genetic disorders or nutrition.
2. Social: factors that relate to social and family interaction, such as stimulation and adult responsiveness.
3. Behavioral: factors that relate to potentially causal behaviors, such as dangerous (injurious) activities or maternal substance abuse.
4. Educational: factors that relate to the availability of educational supports that promote mental development and the development of adaptive skills (p. 71).

The second direction describes the timing of the occurrence of casual factors according to whether these factors affect the parents of the person with mental retardation, the person with mental retardation, or both. This aspect of causality is termed intergenerational to describe the influence of factors present during one generation on the outcome in the next generation. (p. 71)

Thus mental retardation has both multifactorial and intergenerational origins.

The 1992 manual is heavily focused on educational, adult services, social policy, and legal applications in practice. In terms of the relationship of the diagnostic and classification system to research it can be summarized as follows:

We anticipate that the 1992 Definition, Classification, and Systems of Supports will challenge the research community. For example, a major anticipated change is in the description of research subjects. The new system requires greater precision in the description of subjects beyond the mild, moderate, severe, and profound categorization. Now practice will demand complete information on the person's assessed level of intellectual functioning (IQ), a profile of adaptive skills, the condition's etiology, and the types and intensities of supports needed by—and provided to—the person.

A second anticipated change relates to focusing on the assets and liabilities of the person's environment and the types and intensities of supports being received by the person. As a result, there will be less emphasis on the person's condition and functioning level as the independent variable. Rather, more emphasis will be given to environmental conditions and support structures as independent or intervening variables and the person's functioning level, living/employment status, or level of satisfaction as the dependent variable.

> In addition to the ongoing research in typical areas, and lines of research currently underway, some researchers should turn their attention to large utilization studies and large-scale field testing of the definition so that its effects, if any, can be monitored. (p. 149)

In terms of personal-social and motivational factors, the 1992 manual excludes personality, temperament, and character as not essential to the definition of mental retardation (p. 12). However, Self-Direction is included as one of the 10 adaptive skill areas. It is defined as:

> skills related to making choices, learning and following a schedule; initiating activities appropriate to the setting, conditions, schedule, and personal interests; completing necessary or required tasks; seeking assistance when needed; resolving problems confronted in familiar and novel situations, and demonstrating appropriate assertiveness and self-advocacy skills. (p. 40)

Self-Direction appears to be similar to modern models of self-regulation and self-determination.

Personal-social and motivational factors as outcomes (e.g., a person's sense of well being) are addressed in Dimension IV, Environmental Considerations, as the result of wholesome environments (pp. 95–96). Personal satisfaction, strengthening self-esteem, and an individual sense of worth are seen as primary outcomes of having appropriate supports (pp. 101–102). Interestingly, another result of appropriate supports, spirituality—the role of spiritual beliefs and their expression in the lives of people with mental retardation—is also mentioned in the 1992 manual (p. 108).

The 2002 Manual

Background to the 2002 manual.

After several years of deliberation by the Terminology and Classification (T&C) Committee, the 10th AAMR manual was published in 2002. Our book *What Is Mental Retardation? Ideas for an Evolving Disability* (Switzky & Greenspan, 2003) was intended to influence the debate over the development and adoption of the 10th AAMR manual. To that end, we hoped that it would come out a year or two before the 10th edition, while the T&C committee was still deliberating. However, it was delayed and came out in e-book form in 2003, almost a year later than AAMR 2002. A preliminary draft of our book was, however, circulated among the T&C members, as described by Robert Schalock in his foreword to *What Is Mental Retardation? Ideas for an Evolving Disability*, and influenced to some extent the final form of the 2002 AAMR manual. (This influence can also be seen in several references made in the AAMR 2002 manual to *What Is Mental Retardation?*)

The challenge facing the authors of the AAMR 2002 manual (10th edition) stemmed from the fairly widespread unhappiness that had been expressed over the AAMR 1992 (9th edition). This unhappiness was reflected in such things as a general ignoring of the 1992 definition by state MR/DD agencies, and by the action of the MR Division 33 of the American Psychological Association in publishing its own diagnostic manual (Jacobson & Mulick, 1996), which proposed a rival definition closer to the pre-1992 AAMR one, the 1983 version edited by Grossman, which was considered more scientific, more positivistic, and more modern. (See Jacobson and Mulick, 2003, for their critique of AAMR 1992; see also Jacobson and Mulick in this book.)

The two major stated reasons for unhappiness with the 1992 definition as discussed in the 2002 manual, pages 27–32, were: (a) the switch from a requirement of global deficit in "adaptive behavior" to a requirement of deficits in two out of ten "adaptive skills" (with the additional problem that the listed ten skills were of questionable validity); and (b) the dropping of the diagnostic severity levels of mental retardation (based on IQ score SD units) and its replacement with a model where severity level was based on intensity of support needs across all ten adaptive skill areas.

The 2002 T&C committee also was responding to the criticism that the tripartite model of intelligence was cited in 1992 as providing justification for a new approach to adaptive behavior, but was not actually reflected in the operational definition of adaptive skills that was presented. For these reasons, it was expected that the definition of MR contained within the 2002 manual would depart in significant ways from the one proposed in 1992. Also there was major unhappiness in the psychological community with AAMR's shift from a Functionalist-Objectivistic, Positivistic, "Scientific," Modern paradigm of mental retardation typical of the pre-1992 AAMR manuals to an Interpretive Post-Modern paradigm of mental retardation based on a Social System perspective announced in the 1992 AAMR manual. However, no one expected that the 2002 AAMR manual would shift back to a Functionalist-Objective perspective. (See Switzky and Greenspan, 2003, this book, for a discussion of the scientific paradigms underlying the various AAMR manuals.)

Conceptual definition in the 2002 manual.

In the 2002 manual, "Mental retardation is a disability characterized by significant limitations both in intellectual functioning and in adaptive behavior as expressed in conceptual, social, and practical adaptive skills. This disability originates before age 18" (Luckasson et al., 2002, p. 8). Included are five assumptions:

Assumption 1: "Limitations in present functioning must be considered within the context of community environments typical of the individual's age peers and culture." This means that the standards against which the individual's functioning must be measured are typical community-based environments, not environments that are isolated or segregated by ability. Typical community environments include homes, neighborhoods, schools, businesses, and other environments in which people of similar age ordinarily live, play, work, and interact. The concept of age peers should also include people of the same cultural or linguistic background.

Assumption 2: "Valid assessment considers cultural and linguistic diversity as well as differences in communication, sensory, motor, and behavioral factors." This means that in order for assessment to be meaningful, it must take into account the individual's diversity and unique response factors. The individual's culture or ethnicity, including language spoken at home, nonverbal communication, and customs that might influence assessment results, must be considered in making a valid assessment.

Assumption 3: "Within an individual, limitations often coexist with strengths." This means that people with mental retardation are complex human beings who likely have certain gifts as well as limitations. Like all people, they often do some things better than other things. Individuals may have capabilities and strengths that are independent of their mental retardation. These may include strengths in social or physical capabilities, strengths in some adaptive skill areas, or strengths in one aspect of an adaptive skill in which they otherwise show an overall limitation. (We find the sentence "Individuals may have capabilities and strengths that are independent of their mental retardation" a little confusing. To what domains of functioning that are independent of mental retardation is this referring, since mental retardation is a disability characterized by significant limitations both in intellectual functioning and in adaptive behavior as expressed in conceptual, social, and practical adaptive skills? Beyond those, what components of functioning are left?)

Assumption 4: "An important purpose of describing limitations is to develop a profile of needed supports." This means that merely analyzing someone's limitations is not enough, and that specifying limitations should be a team's first step in developing a description of supports that the individual needs in order to improve functioning. Labeling someone as mentally retarded should lead to a benefit such as a profile of needed supports.

Assumption 5: "With appropriate personalized supports over a sustained period, the life functioning of the person with mental retardation will generally improve." This means that if appropriate personalized supports are provided to an individual with mental retardation, improved functioning should result. A lack of improvement in functioning can serve as a basis for reevaluating the profile of needed supports. In rare circumstances, however, even appropriate supports may merely maintain functioning or stop or limit regression. The important point is that the old stereotype that people with mental retardation never improve is incorrect. Improvement in functioning should be expected from appropriate supports, except in rare cases (pages 8–9).

The 2002 System's theoretical model (page 10, Figure 1.1) maintains the ecological focus on the key elements in five dimensions derived from the International Classification of Functioning, Disability, and Health (ICF) (World Health Organization [WHO], 2001) model of disability: Dimension I. Intellectual Abilities, Dimension II. Adaptive Behavior (conceptual, social, and practical skills), Dimension III. Participation, Interactions, and Social Roles, Dimension IV. Health (physical health, mental health, and etiology), and Dimension V. Context (environments and culture), which influence the person's unique functioning.

The major elements, and changes, in the 2002 definition are discussed below:

1. By including the term "disability," the T&C committee sent the message that MR is a serious disorder, involving impairments significant enough to warrant provision of various supports in order for the person to function normally. Thus, adding the term "disability" brought the notion of "support needs" into the definition of MR more directly. Also by including the term "disability," AAMR 2002 tries to blend its model even more into the ICF, WHO 2001, model of disability.

2. By indicating that people with MR have significant limitations in both intellectual functioning and adaptive behavior, the T&C committee put the two criteria on an equal footing. This is in contrast to 1961 and 1973 (where low intelligence is "associated with impairment in adaptive behavior"), to 1983 (where adaptive behavior "exists concurrently with deficits in adaptive behavior,") and to 1992 (where adaptive behavior is "existing concurrently with related limitations in two

. . . adaptive skill areas.") Thus, unlike the earlier AAMR manuals, which gave intelligence primary emphasis and adaptive behavior (or skills) secondary status (by indicating that it is associated or exists concurrently with low intelligence), in 2002 neither criterion was given primacy, as reflected in the assertion that MR is characterized by significant limitations in both criteria.

3. In 2002, the term "adaptive behavior" was retrieved from the dust bin. In 1992 it had been replaced, by the term "adaptive skills." This retrieval is indicated in the statement in 2002 that MR is characterized by "significant limitations both in intellectual functioning and adaptive behavior." However, the adaptive skills term was retained by the further statement that "adaptive behavior is expressed in conceptual, social, and practical adaptive skills." This formula allowed the T&C committee to do three things: (1) return the term adaptive behavior to a prominent place in the definition, (2) retain the adaptive skills term (as an elaboration on adaptive behavior), and (3) bring the tripartite model directly into the definition of MR, even if as a tripartite model of adaptive behavior rather than a tripartite model of intelligence (which would have required dropping the construct of adaptive behavior altogether, and replacing it with a definition of MR based on deficits in multiple areas of intelligence). (See also Schalock, Chapter 17, 2003.)

4. The "developmental criterion" was retained in the 2002 manual, as reflected in the statement: "this disability originates before age 18." As in previous manuals, there is no indication in the definition of any particular type of known or inferred etiology or cause for the disability. A development that influenced to some extent the writing of the 2002 AAMR manual was the publication, in 2001, of the World Health Organization's (WHO) International Classification of Functioning, Disability and Health (ICF). The ICF model was intended to be more transactional and less defectology-oriented than its ICIDH predecessor, and some attention was paid in the 2002 AAMR manual to pointing out areas of convergence between the AAMR 2002 system for diagnosing MR and the 2001 ICF model of functioning, disability, and health. In the ICF model, a health disorder or disability, such as MR, is seen as the outcome of the interaction between various personal and environmental factors, as reflected in three domains: "Body Functions and Structures" (impairments, such as limited intelligence); "Activities" (the execution of various tasks, including difficulties an individual may have in playing various roles); and "Participation" (the extent to which an individual's environment facilitates or impedes the playing of various social roles). Both the 2002 AAMR system and the ICF systems are described in the 2002 manual as "multiparadigmatic ... that is, they do not rely on a singular [sic] objective or subjective worldview and they attempt to integrate medical, psychological, and social models of disability" (p. 109). But are they both multiparadigmatic? We have argued that the ICIDH model (Switzky and Greenspan, Chapter 24, 2003) and its successor, the ICF model appear to be multiparadigmatic and combine elements of the modernist and postmodernist philosophy of science, a kind

of a mixed-model, but that the AAMR 2002 model retains an interpretive post-modern perspective.

In an attempt to demonstrate the equivalence of the two systems, it was argued (p. 109) that the AAMR intelligence criterion loads on ICF's body functions and structures domain, while the AAMR adaptive behavior criterion loads on the ICF activities and participation domains. Luckasson et al. (2002) go on to state that "it may be concluded that the core concepts and criteria of the AAMR 2002 System fit the frame of reference of functioning and disability of the ICF" (p. 109). Clearly, the T&C committee felt that it was important to show that 2002 diagnostic system fits nicely with the ICF's theoretical orientation. (See Buntinx, Chapter 22, 2003; Griffin & Parmenter, Chapter 21, 2003; Jacobson, Chapter 23, 2003; Simeonsson, Granlund, & Bjorck-Akesson, Chapter 20, 2003, for a more detailed analysis.)

Operational definition in the 2002 manual.

In line with the ICF (WHO, 2001) , the term "disability" is "conceptualized as a significant problem in functioning and is characterized by marked and severe problems in the capacity to perform ('impairment'), the ability to perform ('activity limitations'), and the opportunity to function ('participation restrictions')" (p. 16). An individual's possible need for formal disability status, as reflected in a perceived need for special services and supports, is the starting point for assessment and diagnosis, and the outcome of that process is the confirmation or disconfirmation of that status.

An innovation in the 2002 manual is the effort to provide a conceptual definition of intelligence. This definition is "a general mental ability [that] includes reasoning, planning, solving problems, thinking abstractly, comprehending complex ideas, learning quickly, and learning from experience" (p. 51). However, in line with previous AAMR manuals, "intellectual functioning" is operationally defined as performance on a standardized measure of intelligence, and impairment in intellectual functioning is an IQ score, which is a measure of where one falls on the normal distribution of test performance across the general population. It is acknowledged in the manual that "although reliance on a general functioning IQ score has been heatedly contested by some researchers . . . it remains, nonetheless, the measure of human intelligence that continues to garner the most support within the scientific community" (p. 51).

The 2002 manual makes note of the movement among intelligence scholars away from a reliance on a single measure of "g" (general intelligence) but then goes on to state that

> until more robust instruments based upon one of the many promising multifactor theories of intellectual abilities are developed and demonstrated to be psychometrically sound, we will continue to rely on a global (general factor) IQ [score]. (p. 66)

In the 2002 manual, as in the 1992 manual,

> the 'intellectual functioning' criterion for diagnosis of mental retardation is approximately two standard deviations below the mean, considering the SEM [standard error of measurement, usually expressed in SD units] for the specific assessment instruments used and the instruments' strengths and limitations. (p. 58)

A difference between the 2002 and 1992 manuals is that in 1992, the IQ cut-off score was established as "a score of 70 to 75 or below," while in 2002 there was a return to the 1983 AAMR manual's injunction to take the SD of a scale into account, thus implying that a score of 75 makes one eligible, without specifying any particular score value. In the discussion of standardized intelligence tests, it is pointed out that a score below 70 has slightly different meanings across tests (for example, taking in a slightly larger percentage of the population with the Stanford-Binet than with the WAIS, even if both use a SD of 15 points) and that clinical judgment should be used in selecting tests and interpreting test scores.

There is much discussion in the 2002 manual of the need to reduce excessive reliance on IQ scores, and to raise the adaptive functioning criteria to an equal footing. However, in the summary for Chapter 4 (pages 51–71), which addresses intellectual assessment, it was stated that

> *subaverage intellectual functioning*, defined as two or more standard deviations below the mean, is a necessary but insufficient criterion to establish a diagnosis of mental retardation. (p. 66)

This seems to imply a continuation of the existing one-way practice, where a high adaptive behavior score will invalidate a (false positive) diagnosis of MR in someone who meets the IQ score criterion, but the same cannot be done in reverse (that is, avoiding a false negative nondiagnosis if a person with significant adaptive behavior deficits has an IQ score that falls above the cut-off ceiling). Thus, one consequence of continuing to view adaptive behavior and intellectual functioning as separate domains (rather than integrating them by adopting a tripartite model of intelligence and dropping adaptive behavior as a separate construct) is that, rhetoric to the contrary, IQ scores continue to be more important than adaptive behavior scores as the basis for defining and diagnosing MR.

In spite of continuing this view of IQ as the "necessary but insufficient criterion," considerably more space was devoted in the 2002 manual than in predecessor manuals to a discussion of adaptive behavior and how to measure and use it. As mentioned, a major difference between the 1992 and 2002 manuals is in dropping the 10 adaptive skill areas and substituting instead a tripartite model of adaptive behavior, with the three areas being "Conceptual Skills," "Practical Skills," and "Social Skills." The justification given for switching over to the tripartite model of adaptive skills is that they have been supported by "many years of empirical research on the construct of adaptive behavior" (p. 76), research that "supports the three dimensions that are in the current definition" (p. 76).

Table 5.1 (p. 77) of the 2002 manual lists several standardized measures of adaptive behavior and indicates which subscales on these various measures shed light on each of the three areas of an individual's adaptive functioning (i.e., conceptual skills, social skills, and practical skills). It is puzzling that information from intelligence or achievement tests was not recommended to shed light on deficits in conceptual skills, but this is understandable when one considers that the T&C committee wished to create the impression that adaptive skills are somehow different from what the first author (Greenspan, 1979, 1981) had previously termed "adaptive intelligence." This results in some confusion, as "daily living skills" and "personal living skills" (from the Vineland Adaptive scales and the Scales of

Independent Behavior, respectively) are placed in the "Practical Skills" column, while "Community Self-Sufficiency" and "Independent Living" (from the AAMR Adaptive Behavior Scale and Comprehensive Test of Adaptive Behavior, respectively) are placed in the "Conceptual Skills" column.

In previous manuals, adaptive behavior measurement was intended to be used more descriptively (the original AAMD Adaptive Behavior Scale did not even have norms), or else, as in the 1992 AAMR manual (in the selection of deficits in two out of ten adaptive skill areas), in a manner that could be considered to be criterion- rather than norm-referenced. In the 2002 manual, as part of the effort to treat adaptive behavior and intelligence as equal and parallel criteria, a requirement was established that "for the diagnosis of mental retardation, significant limitations in adaptive behavior should be established through the use of standardized measures based on the general population, including people with disabilities and people without disabilities" (p. 76).

As with IQ, the cut-off score for establishing significant limitations in adaptive behavior is "operationally defined as performance that is at least two standard deviations below the mean" (p. 76; however, there is no mention of the need to take into account the standard error of adaptive behavior instruments, as reflected in use of the language "approximately two standard deviations below the mean"). Two choices are given, however, regarding the score to which this minus 2SD criterion is to be applied. One choice involves an individual's score on a measure of "one of the following three types of adaptive behavior: conceptual, social, or practical," while the second choice involves "an overall score on a standardized measure of conceptual, social, and practical skills."

If the T&C committee's intent was to establish a parallel between adaptive behavior and intelligence, then the second choice (overall score) makes some sense, as an overall IQ score (and not solely a Verbal or Performance IQ score) is required for meeting the intelligence criterion. However, the first choice given (a low score in one of the three types of adaptive skills) makes less sense theoretically, in part because a low score on conceptual skills (in spite of the manual's effort to establish it as different from conceptual intelligence) means that a person can be found to have MR solely on the basis of academic limitations. The first choice also is puzzling in that no empirical or theoretical basis was provided for establishing the criterion at one skill, as opposed to two or all three skills, and this makes the definition vulnerable to the same charge of arbitrariness directed against the 1992 AAMR manual's setting the adaptive skill criterion at two-out-of-ten adaptive skills.

It was acknowledged in the 2002 manual that the option of using a significant deficit in only one of the three skill areas "may appear to be an overly inclusive criterion and one that might identify people who have deficits in a single, narrow area rather than the generalized adaptive skill deficit that is assumed to be present in a person with mental retardation" (p. 78). Three explanations were provided for giving such an easy choice. The first explanation is that since the correlations between the various aspects of adaptive behavior differ widely across various measures, requiring a finding of deficits on more than one measure would create an unfair situation in which a diagnosis of MR would depend too heavily on which adaptive behavior measure was used. The second explanation is that a finding of significant deficit in one area "will have a sufficiently broad impact on individual functioning as to constitute a general deficit in adaptive behavior" (p. 78), especially if this general deficit is confirmed through the use of clinical judgment. The third, and probably most important, explanation is that simulation studies have shown that a more stringent standard would cause many current persons with mild MR to be found not to have MR, and the T&C committee was concerned about devising a standard that would result in too many false negatives.

Behavioral classification system in the 2002 AAMR manual.

Perhaps the most controversial provision in the 1992 AAMR manual was the dropping of the four distinct severity subtypes of MR (mild, moderate, severe and profound) and replacing this discontinuous classification scheme with a continuum based on breadth and intensity of an individual's support needs. In 2002, the T&C committee decided to side-step this source of controversy, by enumerating the various goals of subclassification and listing one or more classification mechanisms for pursuing each of the goals, but without indicating its own preferred subclassification scheme.

The statement on classification systems contained in the 2002 manual (p. 99) goes as follows:

> The purposes of classification include grouping for service reimbursement or funding, research, services, and communication about selected characteristics. Multiple classification systems may be used so that the multiple needs of researchers, clinicians, and practitioners can be met. Such classification systems can be based, for example, on the intensities of needed supports, etiology, levels of measured intelligence, or levels of assessed adaptive behavior.

One obvious advantage of this wording is that one can use any classification system one likes (ranging from the pre-1992 reliance on IQ SD-based discontinuous categories to the post-1992 reliance on a continuum based on profile of support needs) without being in opposition to the AAMR manual.

CONCLUSION

In this chapter, we have provided a basic picture of the various AAMR diagnostic manuals over the past four decades, using their own words as much as possible. Our aims have been (a) to give the reader a "feel" of the style of the manuals, (b) to enable the reader to understand the historical references in the various chapters, and (c) to provide a historical perspective on current efforts to improve the 2002 AAMR manual and develop a model of mental retardation for the 21st century. Because the various contributors will be making evaluative comments (especially on the 2002 manual), we have attempted to avoid commenting on the manuals, although we have not always succeeded in keeping our biases from showing.

The basic problem with which AAMR has struggled, beginning with the 1961 manual, is how to keep the definition of MR grounded in a notion of low "intelligence" without getting locked into a rigid IQ formula or relying solely on an individual's IQ score. This has proven to be a great challenge, as reflected in the various changes that have been assayed during the past four decades in the AAMR manuals. Some familiarity with the historical record can only be helpful to the reader as this challenge is addressed.

REFERENCES

Ford, A., Schnorr, R., Meyer, L., Davern, L., Black, J., & Dempsey, P. (1989). *The Syracuse community-referenced curriculum guide*. Baltimore: Brookes.

Grossman, H. J. (Ed.). (1973). *Manual on terminology and classification in mental retardation (1973 revision)*. Washington, DC: American Association on Mental Deficiency.

Grossman, H. J. (Ed.). (1983). *Manual on terminology and classification in mental retardation* (1983 revision). Washington, DC: American Association on Mental Deficiency.

Heber, R. (1959). *A manual on terminology and classification in mental retardation* [Monograph Supplement]. *American Journal of Mental Deficiency, 64*(2).

Heber, R. (1961). *A manual on terminology and classification in mental retardation* (2nd ed.) [Monograph Supplement]. *American Journal of Mental Deficiency*.

Jacobson, J. W., & Mulick, J. A. (Eds.). (1996). *Manual of diagnosis and professional practice in mental retardation*. Washington, DC: American Psychological Association.

Luckasson, R., Coulter, D. L., Polloway, E. A., Reiss, S., Schalock, R. L., Snell, M. E., et al. (1992). *Mental retardation: Definition, classification, and systems of supports (9th ed.)*. Washington, DC: American Association on Mental Retardation.

Luckasson, R., Borthwick-Duffy, S., Buntinx, W. H. E., Coulter, D. L., Craig, E. M., Reeve, A., et al. (2002). *Mental retardation: Definition, classification, and systems of supports (10th ed.)*. Washington, DC: American Association on Mental Retardation.

Sloan W., & Birch, J. W. (1955). A rationale for degrees of retardation. *American Journal of Mental Deficiency, 60*, 258–264.

Switzky, H. N., & Greenspan, S. (Eds.). (2003). *What Is Mental Retardation? Ideas for an evolving disability*. Washington, DC: American Association on Mental Retardation [E-Book]. Available at http://www.disabilitybooksonline.com

World Health Organization. (2001). *International classification of functioning, disability, and health (ICF)*. Geneva: Author.

Chapter Two

On the 2002 AAMR Definition of Mental Retardation

George S. Baroff

Introduction

This is the second of two papers focused on the recent AAMR definitions of mental retardation (Luckasson et al., 1992, 2002). The first (Baroff, 2003b) appeared in Switzky and Greenspan's *What Is Mental Retardation?* and addressed areas of concern in the 1992 model, principally intelligence, etiology, and the term *mental retardation* itself. The current paper revisits some of the same issues but broadens its critique to all three of the diagnostic criteria in the AAMR model—intelligence, adaptive behavior, and age of onset. The reviewer's extensive publications in the field include two textbooks (Baroff, 1991; Baroff & Olley, 1999). In recent years he has applied his knowledge of the disability to criminal cases, most often capital in nature, where he has functioned as a forensic psychologist and expert witness (Baroff & Freedman, 1988; Baroff, 1990, 1991, 1996, 1998, 2003a; Baroff, Gunn, & Hayes 2004).

Mental Retardation from the Author's Perspective

In order to understand the author's reaction to the AAMR definition in the tenth edition of *Mental Retardation* (Luckasson et al., 2002), it is necessary to appreciate his conception of the disorder. Within a scientific and clinical tradition of more than a century, mental retardation has been recognized as a condition of incomplete or immature intellectual development. This intellectual immaturity affects virtually every aspect of functioning; most generally what is now called "adaptive behavior." More specifically, in the language of the seminal definition of Heber (1961), it affects maturation, learning, and social adjustment. Recent conceptions of "adaptive behavior" have characterized it in terms of three broad skills: conceptual, social, and practical (Greenspan, Switzky, & Granfield, 1996). Of particular significance in light of future comments is the representation of "practical skills" as "skills of *independent* living."

The individual with mental retardation will be delayed in the acquisition of age-related developmental skills in all adaptive domains, and his or her behavior, in comparison to that of the normally developing person, will appear "childlike"—that is, more appropriate to a younger age. To behave in a fashion befitting an age younger than one's own is, by definition, to behave "immaturely," and in this sense the author views mental retardation as a disorder of *chronic intellectual and emotional immaturity*. This immaturity is most often apparent in the social and emotional realms, especially in persons with more severe degrees of intellectual impairment. In persons less severely affected, where the level of intellectual impairment is not more than "mild," the immaturity is more evident in the cognitive realm. There, for example, one observes a greater degree of suggestibility (Baroff & Olley, 1999) and gullibility and credulity (Greenspan, Loughlin, & Black, 2001).

The "chronic" nature of the disorder stems from the limitations set by biology on the period when the brain develops, during which there is corresponding growth of intellectual abilities. Formal measures of intelligence have represented this period as from infancy to about age 17 (e.g., Stanford-Binet IV: Thorndike, Hagen, & Sattler, 1986). Although new learning is, obviously, not confined to this *developmental period* and we can continue to acquire knowledge throughout our lives, the basic biological capacity that we bring to new learning is set by this developmental time frame. Its effect is to influence the *rate* of new learning and the *complexity* of that which we can eventually grasp. This time-constrained growth period, a developmental reality that presumably affects all organs and their functions, is what gives mental retardation its chronicity or, in the language of an earlier time, its "incurability." While recent definitions of the disorder stress its dynamic nature—that is, viewing it as a state of *current* functioning—it is understood that changes of a magnitude meriting removal of the diagnosis are more apt to reflect improvement in adaptive behavior than in intelligence itself. It must be acknowledged, however, that given the extraordinary developments in genetics, even growth periods themselves may be subject to modification.

Reference has been made to the effect of mental retardation on "adaptive behavior." Its most general consequence, at any age, is to limit the mastery of the developmental skills appropriate to that age and thereby to increase the degree of dependency on others for their performance. In childhood and adolescence this means a greater dependence on parents and caregivers than is typical for that age. For some, though, since mental retardation varies so widely in its severity, the prolongation of dependency may be largely limited to the pre-adult years. For the individual with so-called cultural-familial and "mild" mental retardation, Mercer's "six-hour retarded child" (Mercer, 1973), or the "mildly retarded" segment of Tymchuk's "forgotten generation" (Tymchuk, Lakin, & Luckasson, 2001) the dependency may not extend into adulthood, although major academic limitations are going to affect functional reading and money-management skills. Moreover, the changes in America from a "manufacturing" to a "service and information" economy severely threaten the employability of persons with poor reading and arithmetic skills and will increase their difficulty in achieving full independence. They are "currently not served by community-based mental retardation systems, which focus on those having greater degrees of intellectual impairment and meeting the diagnostic criteria for "developmental disabilities." Responding to the needs of individuals with "mild" retardation as well as those with even lesser but permanent learning problems will require major additions to community health and social service systems and a reconsideration of how America addresses the adult needs of a population increasingly at risk. But where the degree of retardation is more than "mild"—from moderate to profound—a fully independent adjustment may never be achieved, and assistance or "supports" in varying intensity may be a lifelong necessity. Parenthetically, the term "mild cognitive limitations" as applied to adults with mild mental retardation is a gross misnomer. Functioning at the lower extreme of the intelligence range, they have "mild" limitations only in comparison to those of individuals with "moderate" to "profound" retardation.

In summary, mental retardation is viewed as an *intellectual disability* that adversely affects the capacity to cope successfully with the challenges of daily existence. Its most general effect is to increase the degree of *dependence* in meeting those challenges. With this as a background, we now consider the most recent AAMR definition of the disability, the 10th edition of *Mental Retardation* (Luckasson et al., 2002). This review examines each of its three elements—intelligence, adaptive behavior, and age of onset—as these are described and amplified in the AAMR model.

Here is the 2002 definition: "Mental retardation is a disability characterized by significant limitations both in intellectual functioning and in adaptive behavior as expressed in conceptual, social, and practical adaptive skills. This disability originates before age 18."

MENTAL RETARDATION AS A "DISABILITY"

The current definition reveals a greater willingness than its predecessor to acknowledge the disabling nature of the disorder. It specifically refers to mental retardation as a "disability" in terms of both "intellectual functioning" and "age of onset." This characterization, absent from previous versions, is an apt inclusion, conveying immediately the reality of the disorder. Presumably in response to pressure by advocates for persons with mental retardation, as well as by those persons themselves, an effort has been made to represent the condition in the least prejudicial form. This is perfectly understandable, given both the high value that our culture places on "intelligence" and the scorn often visited on those with intellectual impairment. The epithet "retard" as a term of ridicule epitomizes this attitude. Efforts to present the condition in a more favorable light have included changing the name itself, e.g., from "mental deficiency" to "mental retardation," and the term "intellectual disability" is coming into wider use, both here and abroad. In Great Britain, for example, the author learned that his textbook *Mental Retardation: Nature, Cause and Management"* (Baroff with Olley, 1999) would not now be publishable under that title. In Great Britain the term "learning disability" is now applied to the same population defined here as "mentally retarded" (e.g., Lindsay, Taylor, & Sturmey, 2004). This designation, in fact, represents a different meaning for "learning disability," at least as it is used in the United States, where it is intended to refer to students with grossly normal intelligence but with specific deficits in such academic skills as reading, writing, and arithmetic. But this usage, too, in the United States has been much modified. It is now commonly employed by school systems as a substitute for the presumably more pejorative label "mental retardation," at least where the IQ is above 60 (MacMillan, Gresham, Siperstein, & Bocian, 1996). As a consequence, in the 20-year period between 1977 and 1997, a time of *increased* national attention to the needs of children and adults with mental retardation, there was a 38% *decline* in pupils classified as "mentally retarded" by the schools and an extraordinary *increase* of 202% in those designated as "learning disabled"

(Annual Report to Congress on the Implementation of the Individuals with Disabilities Education Act [IDEA], U.S. Department of Education, 1995).

The quest for a less prejudicial label has a long history (e.g., Heber, 1962), though the term "mental retardation" persists and remains in standard psychiatric nomenclature (DSM-IV, 1994) and in international health classification systems (WHO, 1993). In earlier papers, the author suggested the term "general learning disorder" (Baroff, 1999, 2003b). It has the merit of calling attention to the central problem created by mental retardation, that of "learning."

INTELLECTUAL FUNCTIONING

The model within which the definition is embedded (Luckasson et al., 2002) seeks to broaden our understanding of the nature of intelligence but never directly presents it as a "developmental" phenomenon—that is, tied to a particular growth period. Since such characterization would imply awareness of explicit biological constraints, the omission suggests continued resistance to acknowledging the influence of intelligence itself on the disability. The two most recent editions of the definition have sought to mute the traditionally dominant role of intelligence in the diagnosis of mental retardation in favor of a greater emphasis on the "supports" or services necessary to maximize adaptive potential. Most dramatically, beginning with the 1992 definition, this took the form of the removal of the IQ "severity" category from the definition and the creation of a seemingly related one, the *intensity* of needed supports. The excision was much criticized, a criticism freely acknowledged in the 2002 AAMR model. Indeed, one of its admirable qualities is its readiness to acknowledge criticisms of the 1992 model and to respond to them. In this regard, the current version recognizes that there are settings within which knowledge of the severity of the intellectual impairment would be relevant, including the diagnostic framework of the definition itself. Nevertheless, it still seeks to carefully circumscribe the role of severity of intellectual impairment in one's appreciation of the disorder.

Major diagnostic and classification systems, however, have continued to incorporate a "severity" dimension, because knowledge of the depth of the intellectual impairment communicates useful information about the individual's adaptive potential (e.g., DSM-IV and WHO, 1993). The level of intelligence is, itself, an important predictor of adaptive behavior (e.g., Harrison & Oakland, 2003). Indeed, the three areas of "adaptive behavior" defined in the current model—conceptual, social, and practical—were terms originally applied to forms of *intelligence* that underlie personal competence (Greenspan et al., 1996).

Although "supports" are important in maximizing adaptive potential—they are, after all, analogous to the "treatment" dimension in the management of health problems—the severity of intellectual impairment conveys significant implications for the individual's current and future needs for assistance, that is, for the supports themselves. In terms of "personal independence," the dimension most broadly affected by intellectual impairment, persons with deficits greater than "mild"—that is, from "moderate" to "profound," roughly IQs below 60—are unlikely to achieve a fully independent or self-sustaining adult existence. They will always require at least some degree of assistance in their lives. This can be asserted without qualification where the retardation is severe or profound. It is this prognostic reality that the two recent definitions tend to obscure in favor of its earlier-mentioned representation as a "dynamic" state, one subject to change—principally, improvement. But the *degree* of change *is* limited by developmental growth-period constraints. While adjustment can vary as a function of the supports and services received, *intellectual capacity* will remain generally constant, subject only to the vagaries of health and old age. This was the basis for the earlier characterization of the disability as "incurable."

IQ 70: An Artificial Boundary

A perennial problem for definers of mental retardation is to establish a rational basis for setting an intelligence range that will distinguish it from other types of intellectual functioning. The current edition continues the practice of including IQs as high as 75 as compatible with the disorder. Recognizing the arbitrariness of fixed boundaries for the upper limit of the retardation range, it argues for flexibility based on the error of measurement tied to any given IQ score. This refers to sources of variation in IQ attributable to both the examiner(s) and examinee. Of greater significance, the 2002 model gets closer to the essence of the problem when it refers to a "hypothetical true score." Like a golfer's or bowler's handicap, a given IQ can never be more than an estimate of the score that best approximates the individual's *typical* functioning on that particular intelligence test. Apart from errors of measurement, presumably not a problem for golfers or bowlers, the problem consists of trying to distinguish differences between adjacent IQs that have no objectively measurable distinction. The trait measured by our intelligence tests exists only in the eye of the beholder; it has no referent in the world of physics. It is not a quality that can be directly known through our senses. Moreover, this qualitative trait exists on a continuum where categorical distinctions are inherently arbitrary. The line that is drawn at IQ 70 to differentiate between "mental retardation" and "borderline" intelligence is based on a *statistical* (standard deviation) and not *behavioral* distinction. It persists in usage because it captures virtually all of the population of concern.

In an earlier paper (Baroff, 2003a), the author likened the IQ continuum to the color spectrum, where color changes are so gradual, e.g., from yellow to orange, that only at the extreme of one color is its difference from the other obvious. We have no parallel in IQ for the dramatic alteration that can occur, for example, with change in temperature, when water drops from 33 to 32 degrees Fahrenheit and changes from liquid to solid. On our IQ scale, we have only a seamless continuity from one end of the scale to the other, rendering distinctions between *adjacent* scores that represent different IQ categories necessarily arbitrary. The designers of our intelligence tests have created these categories and we follow suit.

All of this is to say that, given the artificiality of diagnostic distinctions at the border between contiguous intelligence categories, e.g., "mental retardation" and "borderline" intelligence, the "adaptive behavior" component will assume particular significance in distinguishing them (Baroff, 2003a).

Borderline Intelligence

While acknowledging the arbitrariness of differences between adjacent IQ scores, we can draw distinctions between individuals who, for example, differ by more than two standard errors on the IQ scale. It is the view here that there are meaningful behavioral differences between persons functioning, for example, at the midpoints of the "borderline" (IQ 70 to 79) and "mildly retarded" (IQ 55 to 69) intelligence ranges, e.g., at IQs 75 and 62. But the recent AAMR definitions, 1992 and 2002, treat this categorical distinction as nonexistent. In accepting IQs as high as 75 as compatible with mental retardation, there is no acknowledgment that this score falls at the midpoint of the range of a *different* intelligence level. Although the 1983 revision (Grossman, 1983) wisely eliminated "borderline retardation" as a diagnostic category, "borderline intelligence" is a valid intelligence range on both the Wechsler scale (Wechsler, 1997) and the Binet test (Thorndike et al., 1986). On the latter, it is called "slow learner." In any case, this range is treated as distinct from that of retardation. But in neither of the two recent definitions is there any reference to this intelligence level, although the potential overlap creates a diagnostic quandary. For judges who must follow state legal statutes that set IQ 70, or 69, as the boundary for mental retardation, the distinction, in capital cases, may truly be one of life or death. If a capital defendant in one of the 38 states that still have the death penalty is adjudicated "mentally retarded" *by that state's law*, he's no longer subject to execution. This results from the recent Supreme Court decision (*Atkins* v. *Virginia*, 2002) outlawing the death penalty for defendants with mental retardation. In effect, the retarded defendant is viewed as having a lesser level of culpability or blameworthiness than his nonretarded counterpart, a conclusion with which the writer wholly agrees (Baroff, 1998; Baroff, Gunn, & Hayes, 2004). But the Court left it to the states to define mental retardation, leaving open possible variation between them. The need for national agreement in state criminal codes is obvious if we're to avoid situations in which individuals with very similar IQs have very different fates (e.g., Coleman & Shellow, 2003)!

Regarding the special diagnostic problem of persons whose IQ scores are at the ceiling of the "mentally retarded" range and at the floor of the "borderline" one, we've noted that particular weight must be given to "adaptive behavior." This speaks to "personal independence," the behavior seen as most generally affected by the intellectual disorder. In the author's experience, admittedly heavily influenced by evaluating adults with *criminal* histories, apart from their antisocial behavior, in those with retardation, one finds a breadth and severity of adaptive difficulties that impedes their achievement of a fully independent or self-sustaining adjustment. They appear to have always needed assistance from others in managing their daily lives. Virtually all functioning in the range of "mild" mental retardation, they're typically sustained, even in adulthood, by family, spouse, and partners who provide their living quarters and pay their bills. Those with "borderline" intelligence, however, though certain to have some functional academic difficulties, may be capable of maintaining themselves in the community independently. Where such independence is observed, even when the IQ is 70 or below, the attainment of an independent existence could rule out, on "adaptive behavior" grounds, the diagnosis of mental retardation.

ADAPTIVE BEHAVIOR: CONCEPTUAL, SOCIAL, AND PRACTICAL SKILLS: "SIGNIFICANT LIMITATIONS . . . IN ADAPTIVE BEHAVIOR AS EXPRESSED IN CONCEPTUAL, SOCIAL, AND PRACTICAL ADAPTIVE SKILLS"

The diagnostic criterion calls for significant deficit in at least *one* of the three areas of adaptive behavior, implying that deficit in "conceptual" skills is not necessary. On the face of it, this is absurd. Deficits in "conceptual" or "educational" skills are the very essence of mental retardation. Subnormal general intelligence *always* affects academic progress. School psychologists, for example, use IQ as one of the indicators of expected school achievement. The very basis for the distinction between the child with a "specific learning disability" and the one with mental retardation lies in general intelligence (IQ). The child with "learning disability" has educational difficulties *in spite of grossly normal intelligence*, and this distinguishes him from the inevitable and broader learning problems of the child with retardation.

This seeming reluctance of recent revisions to acknowledge the relationship between subnormal intelligence or "conceptual" impairment and school achievement is especially obvious in the continued representation of "functional academic skills" as only *one* of the ten areas of possible adaptive behavior deficit. To the contrary, it is not an "optional" deficit; if it is not present, there can be no mental retardation! Indeed, it is the relationship between subnormal general intelligence and major educational problems that led, in the first place, to the creation of special education services for children with retardation.

Will the definers of mental retardation ever acknowledge that "intelligence" or "conceptual" skills have something to do with school achievement? On page 82 of the current definition, reading, writing, and money (arithmetic) concepts are identified as "conceptual" skills. Do the definers really believe that there are children with histories of developmental delay and subnormal general intelligence who do *not* have these academic problems?

AGE OF ONSET: "THIS DISABILITY ORIGINATES BEFORE AGE 18"

Perhaps the most puzzling feature of the current definition is the absence of a section on "age of onset." It is, after all, one of the three criteria that define mental retardation. The '92 definition noted that the bulk of brain growth has occurred by age 7 and that the further elaboration of synapses and refinement of connections is largely completed by adulthood. It also distinguished between normal and mentally retarded persons with regard to the rate of cognitive growth and the levels of cognitive functioning ultimately achieved. This, as discussed earlier in this chapter, represents the learning consequences of altered brain development. Noting Heber's (1959) observation that the upper age limit of the developmental period, presumably referring to the "biological" one, could not be precisely fixed, recent revisions chose 18 because it represents the time when many youth assume the responsibilities of adulthood. Acknowledging the arbitrariness of 18, the '92 edition proposed a "cultural" alternative to a "biological" criterion for adulthood, viewing it as a function of a given society's social, cultural, and ethnic milieu. Undoubtedly this is a sociological truth, yet the relevant dimension in mental retardation pertains to the growth period for intelligence, a *biological* and not a cultural phenomenon! Presumably, the same growth period obtains in all humans, irrespective of culture.

With respect to that period, the designers of intelligence tests offer the most useful marker. Earlier tests recorded performance in terms of "mental age" and set its upper limit at 17 years. In effect, by age 17, our intellectual *capacity* is largely in place. Indeed, the '92 definition notes that from childhood onward, intellectual functioning is fairly stable and "limitations in intellectual functioning (low IQs) in most cases are not likely to change much beyond that point." (p. 18). Recognizing the reality of such limitations, it then adds, correctly, that their *impact* on functioning may change as a function of services and supports. But no mention of any of this is found in the 2002 version. In fact, there is no reference to "age of onset" even in the Subject Index!

But age 18 also serves to distinguish, for diagnostic purposes, between intellectual deficit of developmental origin and that *originating* in the post developmental or "adult" years. The latter is considered to be "dementia." The distinction is necessarily artificial and may not affect the services and supports needed. With 18 chosen as the upper limit of the time period during which intellectual impairment diagnosable as "mental retardation" must exist, the sudden loss of intellectual functioning due to brain injury at 17, for example, would still allow for that diagnosis. But the same loss at 19 would yield a different diagnosis, although the service needs might be identical. These are diagnostic distinctions of "convenience," allowing us, for example, to establish prevalence rates for the two disorders.

This author has also personally benefited from the '92 treatment of "age of onset," finding in it justification for labeling as "mentally retarded" a capital defendant who appears to have experienced a major decline in intelligence at age 14, although his history is silent as to its cause. (Inhaling intoxicating fumes has been suggested, and he acknowledges engaging in this activity.) Given that he now clearly functions in the mentally retarded range, his IQ at 25 is 68, and he is much impaired in "adaptive behavior," in order to meet the State's legal criterion for mental retardation he had to have shown retardation prior to age 18. The language of the '92 definition permits us to recognize his change in functioning at 14—that is, prior to 18—as within the purview of "mental retardation" as defined in our state statute. In its discussion of the "age of onset," the '92 definition asserts that, "an individual who develops typically and then sustains a significant developmental regression for any reason prior to age 18 years may (be) considered to have mental retardation" (Luckasson et al., 1992, p. 16). In light of the exclusion of the death penalty for capital defendants with mental retardation, this language contributed to saving a life!

The complete omission of "age of onset" from the current definition is mystifying. Is it purely inadvertent, or does it reflect the admitted desire to mute the role of "intelligence" in conceptualizing the disorder? One cannot appreciate the chronicity of the disability without understanding the significance of the "age of onset." The subject certainly deserves restoration in the next revision; indeed, AAMR may want to include a paper on this topic in one of its journals.

Summary

In this critique of the 2002 AAMR model of mental retardation, the author has focused on its treatment of the three criteria that define the disability—intelligence, adaptive behavior, and age of onset.

With respect to "intelligence," greater attention is given to its nature than in the '92 model, although its representation as a "developmental" phenomenon is largely ignored. As in the '92 edition, the wish is to mute the role of intelligence from a prognostic perspective in favor of an emphasis on plasticity through supports and services. Not only is the prognostic implication of a time-limited growth period for general intelligence ignored, but the developmental period is itself represented as a "sociological" rather than "biological" phenomenon.

To its credit, the 2002 edition does speak to the "arbitrariness" of diagnostic cutoff points on the IQ scale, an issue that has been examined earlier by the author (Baroff, 2003a) and is treated in this review in somewhat greater depth.

As in its 1992 version, the current model continues to try to reduce the influence of IQ categories that denote the "severity" of intellectual impairment. Much criticized for rejecting what continues to be a standard part of other diagnostic systems, it does acknowledge that such information can be of value.

With regard to "adaptive behavior," the 2002 model persists in treating "functional academics" as an *optional* deficit. It is the strong view here that this is *not* an "optional" deficit; indeed, it is the very essence of the learning difficulties created by subaverage general intelligence. If significant reading, writing, and arithmetic limitations are *not* present, one is not dealing with "mental retardation," at least as this disability has been understood for nearly two centuries!

The third criterion of the definition pertains to "age of onset." Dealt with in some depth in the 1992 version, it is almost totally ignored in the current model. Indeed, there is no reference to it at all in the Subject Index! This was a valuable section of the 1992 model, and its absence is either simply an inadvertence or further evidence of the wish to avoid the prognostic implications of a disability onset in the "developmental" years.

References

American Psychiatric Association. (1994). *Diagnostic and statistical manual of mental disorders* (4th ed.). Washington, DC: Author.

Atkins v. Virginia. U. S. Case No. 8452. (2002).

Baroff, G. S. (1990). Establishing mental retardation in capital defendants. *American Journal of Forensic Psychology, 8*(2), 35–44.

Baroff, G. S. (1991). *Developmental disabilities psychosocial aspects.* Austin, TX: Pro-Ed.

Baroff, G. S. (1996). The mentally retarded offender. In J. W. Jacobson & J. A. Mulick (Eds.), *Manual of diagnosis and professional practice in mental retardation* (pp. 311–322). Washington, DC: American Psychological Association.

Baroff, G. S. (1998). Why mental retardation is "mitigating." *The Champion, 22*(7), 33–35.

Baroff, G. S. (1999). General learning disorder: A new designation for mental retardation. *Mental Retardation, 37*(1), 68–70.

Baroff, G. S. (2003a). Establishing mental retardation in capital cases: An update. *Mental Retardation, 41*, 198–202.

Baroff, G. S. (2003b). Mental retardation: Some issues of concern. In H. N. Switzky & S. Greenspan (Eds.), *What Is Mental Retardation? Ideas for an evolving disability* (pp. 67–74). Washington, DC: American Association on Mental Retardation [E-Book]. Available at http://www.disabilitybooksonline.com

Baroff, G. S., & Freedman, S. C. (1988, April). Mental retardation and Miranda. *The Champion,* 6–9.

Baroff, G. S., Gunn, M., & Hayes, S. (2004). Legal issues. In W. R. Lindsay, J. L. Taylor, & P. Sturmey (Eds.), *Offenders with developmental disabilities* (pp. 37–47). Chichester, England: John Wiley & Sons, Ltd.

Baroff, G. S. (with Olley, J. G.) (1999). *Mental retardation: Nature, cause, and management* (3rd ed.). Philadelphia: Brunner/Mazel.

Coleman, P., & Shellow, R. A. (2003). Toward a uniform standard for mental retardation in death penalty cases. *Mental Retardation, 41*, 203–204.

Goldstein, H. (1964). Social and occupational adjustment. In H. Stevens & R. Heber (Eds.), *Mental retardation: A review of research* (pp. 214–259). Chicago: University of Chicago Press.

Greenspan, S., Loughlin, G., & Black, R. S. (2001). Credulity and gullibility in people with developmental disorders: A framework for future research. In L. M. Glidden (Ed.), *International review of research in mental retardation* (Vol. 24, pp. 101–135). New York: Academic Press.

Greenspan, S., Switzky, H. N., & Granfield, J. M. (1996). Everyday intelligence and adaptive behavior: A theoretical framework. In J. W. Jacobson & J. A. Mulick (Eds.), *Manual of diagnosis and professional practice in mental retardation* (pp. 127–135). Washington, DC: American Psychological Association.

Grossman, H. J. (Ed.). (1983). *Manual on terminology and classification in mental retardation* (1983 revision). Washington, DC: American Association on Mental Deficiency.

Harrison, P. L., & Oakland, T. (2003). *Adaptive behavior assessment system (ABAS-II)* (2nd ed.). San Antonio: PsychCorp/Harcourt Assessment.

Heber, R. (1959). System of classification. In J. H. Rothstein (Ed.), *Mental retardation reading and resources* (pp. 84–98). New York: Holt, Rinehart, & Winston.

Heber, R. (1961). Definition of mental retardation. In J. H. Rothstein (Ed.), *Mental retardation readings and resources* (pp. 9–12). New York: Holt, Rinehart, & Winston.

Lindsay, W. R., Taylor, J. L., & Sturmey, P. (2004). *Offenders with developmental disabilities* (p. xvii). Chichester, England: John Wiley & Sons, Ltd.

Luckasson, R., Borthwick-Duffy, S., Buntinx, W. H. E., Coulter, D. L., Craig, E. M., Reeve, A., et al. (2002). *Mental retardation: Definition, classification, and systems of supports* (10th ed.). Washington, DC: American Association on Mental Retardation.

Luckasson, R., Coulter, D. L., Polloway, E. A., Reiss, S., Schalock, R. L., Snell, M. E., et al. (1992). *Mental Retardation: Definition, classification, and systems of supports* (9th ed.). Washington, DC: American Association on Mental Retardation.

MacMillan, D. L., Gresham, F. M., Siperstein, G. N., & Bocian, K. M. (1996). The labyrinth of IDEA: School decisions on referred students with subaverage general intelligence. *American Journal on Mental Retardation, 101*, 161–174.

Mercer, J. R. (1973). *Labeling the mentally retarded*. Berkeley: University of California Press.

Thorndike, R. L., Hagen, E. R., & Sattler, J. M. (1986). *Stanford-Binet Intelligence Scale: Fourth edition*. Chicago: Riverside.

Tymchuk, A. J., Lakin, K. C., & Luckasson, R. (Eds.). (2001). *The forgotten generation: The status and challenges of adults with mild cognitive limitations*. Baltimore: Paul H. Brookes.

Wechsler, D. (1997). *Wechsler Adult Intelligence Scale: Third edition*. San Antonio: The Psychological Corporation.

World Health Organization. (1993). *International statistical classification of diseases and related health problems* (10th ed.). Geneva: Author.

CHAPTER THREE

An Update on Label and Definitional Asynchrony: The Missing Mental *and* Retardation *in Mental Retardation*

LARAINE MASTERS GLIDDEN

INTRODUCTION

When I first considered the dilemma of competing definitions of mental retardation in my chapter, "Label and Definitional Asynchrony: Where Are the *Mental* and *Retardation* in Mental Retardation?" in Switzky and Greenspan (2003), I was impatient. I was impatient with scientists who seemed too concerned with politics, prose, and policy, and not concerned enough with evidence. I was also impatient with process and progress that seemed to move too slowly and sometimes in the wrong direction, attentive to arguments that obfuscated as often as they clarified. That was more than five years ago. Today, although (as I will make clear in this chapter) I do not think that much essential has changed, I am less impatient, in part because of Seymour Sarason and my rereading of his brilliant and personally poignant paper about the nature-nurture controversy (Sarason, 1973). In the more than three decades since this paper was published, no one has made a more cogent argument for patience.

In this classic, *Jewishness, Blackishness, and the Nature-Nurture Controversy*, Sarason compares Jews and African Americans, two groups that have historical reasons to view the world as hostile. He describes the strong intellectual tradition that characterizes Jewish culture. For Jews, knowledge is power, and education is the route to success. This belief is transmitted from parent to child, across millennia. For African Americans, the culture is quite different. Indeed, during slavery illiteracy was forced, and even after emancipation opportunity for education was limited. Thus, it is not surprising that among African Americans intellectual traditions were not widespread, and that other pathways to success were and continue to be traveled.

Sarason reminds us that manifestations of intelligence are culturally rooted and that culture does not change in a matter of months or years, but rather decades, centuries, and

The writing of this chapter was supported, in part, by Grant # HD21993 from NICHD and from Faculty Development grants from St. Mary's College of Maryland.

even millennia. This reminder helped to restore my patience. I realized again that we will have many iterations of the definition of mental retardation, each of them time- and culture-bound, each needing revision quite frequently. Perhaps a new definition every ten years is not regress, but progress. After all, definitions attempt to specify the essential nature of a thing, a person, a concept. And that nature is not isolated from the time and culture in which it exists. The progress of science requires alterations of definition, as does social change.

In the current updated chapter, I analyze the definition in the 10th edition of the American Association on Mental Retardation's manual, *Mental Retardation* (Luckasson et al., 2002). Prior to the definitional analysis, however, I must summarize and reiterate some prefatory material from Glidden (2003) to place definitions and changes in meaning in a broader cultural and historical context.

Typically, and especially with complex concepts, definitions include multiple meanings. After all, reality is highly nuanced and difficult to capture in a relatively simple and small set of words. Luckasson and Reeve (2001) refer to this challenge and the importance to society that it be successfully met. One criterion that science and scientists rely upon is that a definition indicates clearly those that are members of a class and those that are not. Science would be a futile enterprise if what was being studied changed from one laboratory to another, but nonetheless had the same name—or, in linguistic terminology, if the *definiendum* specified multiple *definiens*. With increasing scientific precision allowing us to specify the nature of a thing, e.g., DNA analysis, we solve many scientific mysteries. For example, the *New York Times* (Broad, 2004) reported that what some thought to be a sea creature of monster proportions was shown by DNA typing to be only whale blubber. In this case, the definition of whale via DNA specification allowed competing views to be evaluated.

The sea monster/whale blubber case illustrates another important element of definitions. They change over time, as do the usage patterns of words. Definitions are, of course, problematic when they fail to match the word's current usage pattern. Many words have shifted their meaning over time. For example, O'Neill (1918) traces the origin of *villain* as referring to a laborer or serf in the Middle Ages, and that of *nice* as originally meaning foolish (from the Latin *nescious* or ignorant). Clearly, problems would arise if we used these words today as they were originally used.

Just as clearly, problems can also arise if definitions are changed abruptly, and a new definition does not match the dominant current usage. Even though the advantages of avoiding ambiguity and increasing communication clarity might encourage us to legislate word meanings, either by introducing sudden changes or preventing them, mandating changes in natural languages is not likely to be successful. Despite the origins of the word *gymnasium* from the Greek *gymnos*—naked—it would not do to mandate that gymnasium means a gathering place for nudists (Garrison, 1965). Indeed, if such legislation were to take place, boards of education might find themselves deluged with calls from parents about the "gym" classes that their children were required to take!

Scientific terms, however, are not exactly like ordinary words in the natural language. Some scientific terms are not used commonly, and therefore, are less subject to changes in usage patterns. Their agreed-upon meaning can be kept relatively pure. For example, trichotillomania—the recurrent pulling out of one's hair—has four diagnostic criteria as described in DSM-IV (American Psychiatric Association, 1994, pp. 618-619). Because most people do not recognize or use this word, it is unlikely to undergo change over time.

Thus, any changes in the diagnostic criteria are more likely to result from changes in scientific knowledge than from sociolinguistic usage patterns.

Other scientific terms, however, also have a history of usage in common parlance, and, indeed, may have even been borrowed or adapted from the natural language. Examples abound in psychology, and terms such as anxiety, depression, and hyperactivity have both precise scientific meanings as well as looser natural language usages. Mental retardation is one such term. This current phrase replaces earlier ones that we now think of as somewhat barbaric and certainly politically incorrect. Once mental retardation became differentiated from mental illness, terms such as feeble-mindedness, imbecility, and idiocy were used scientifically as labels for mental retardation. Indeed, the first name of the organization that is now the American Association on Mental Retardation was "The Association of Medical Officers of American Institutions for Idiots and Feeble-Minded Persons" (Scheerenberger, 1983). The Association underwent a number of name revisions before it adopted its present name in 1987.

The label *mental retardation* may be even more complex than some other terms that serve both a scientific and a lay community, because it is not just binary—that is, used differently by just two different communities. It certainly is used by nonprofessionals in common parlance. However, it also has different meanings to different professional communities, with medical, psychological, educational, and adult service-oriented communities focusing on very different aspects of its primary, secondary, and tertiary meanings. Thus, the definitional polemic that began in 1992 with the publication of a new definition by AAMR and was revisited 10 years later in 2002 with a revision of that definition must be evaluated, recognizing that these varied communities view the topic through different lenses.

In Glidden (2003) I took that approach and analyzed two definitions—the 1992 AAMR definition and the 1996 American Psychological Association (APA) definition. These are embedded in manuals devoted entirely to mental retardation and its meaning, and as such they provide not only a definition and a classification system, but also lengthy explorations of the implications of each. In the current chapter, I take the same approach with an analysis of the 2002 AAMR definition. Initially, I review the components or semantic features of the definition (Bolinger, 1975, chap. 7). I consider the order in which features are mentioned and elaborated with the presumption that order implies importance. Moreover, I examine the definition with regard to four important criteria for any definition:

1. Does it conform to current usage patterns?
2. Is it unambiguous?
3. Is it functional?
4. Does it define what the label suggests that it defines?

The 2002 definition exists not because scientific advances have made the 1992 definition obsolete. Rather, as stated in the preface (Luckasson et al., 2002, p. xii), it "reflects 10 years of experience with—and critiques of—the 1992 System." The critiques were wide-ranging, and the interested reader is referred to Switzky and Greenspan (2003) for both challenges to, and defenses of, the 1992 System. In addition, Chapter 2 of the 10th edition of *Mental Retardation* (Luckasson et al., 2002) provides summaries of both positive and

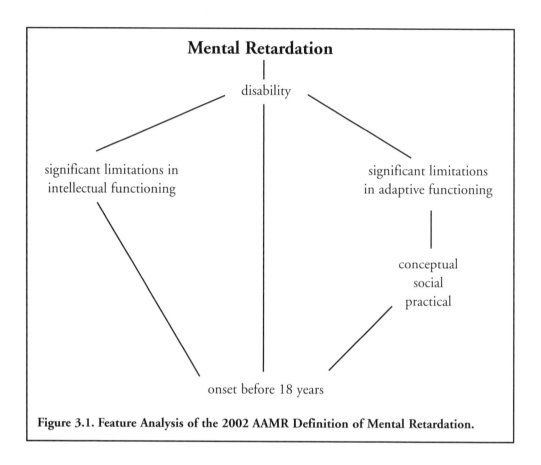

Figure 3.1. Feature Analysis of the 2002 AAMR Definition of Mental Retardation.

negative appraisals. We will consider these critiques after analyzing the features of the 2002 definition.

FEATURES AND ASSESSMENT OF THE 2002 AAMR DEFINITION OF MENTAL RETARDATION

Figure 3.1 presents a feature analysis of the definition of mental retardation. As presented in AAMR (2002),

> *mental retardation* is a disability characterized by significant limitations both in intellectual functioning and in adaptive behavior as expressed in conceptual, social, and practical adaptive skills. This disability originates before age 18.

The initial component of the definition is *disability*, which is "the expression of limitations in individual functioning within a social context and represents a substantial disadvantage to the individual" (p. 15). Because it is first, it is deemed to be the primary essential of the definition and represents the core concept which all other features embellish. The other components elaborate what constitutes this disability and when the disability must occur. In addition to its primacy, the term *disability* is important for another reason: It is new to the AAMR definition, and it replaces the first phrase that was new to the 1992 definition. The 1992 phrase defined mental retardation as *substantial limitations in present functioning*. What does this shift really mean and why was it taken? One rationale for the inclusion of *disability* was undoubtedly the anticipation that the label *mental retardation* would be replaced by the new label, *intellectual disability*. In March 2002 the Board of Directors of AAMR voted to change its name to the American Association on Intellectual Disabilities, but an organizationwide referendum later that year did not endorse the change.

As a result of this shift away from *present functioning* in the core of the definition, the emphasis has changed. An important focus of the 1992 AAMR definition was that mental retardation was not necessarily a permanent or a lifelong condition. Thus, the notion of "present functioning" was critical. The 2002 definition does not so obviously incorporate this focus. Indeed, by stating first that mental retardation is a disability, it implies permanency rather than a condition that can be cured. That this difference is not directly addressed seems remarkable. Indeed, in the summary in Chapter 1, pp. 16–17, in which the 1992 and 2002 definitions are compared and contrasted, no mention is made of this shift—quite an extraordinary omission, since the inclusion of one of the 'd' words (defect, deficiency, disability) as a first essential in the definition returns to the early definitions of Tredgold (1908, 1937) and Doll (1941) and their emphasis on incurability. Regardless of the intentions of the AAMR Ad Hoc Committee on Terminology and Classification, the effect of the shift is to emphasize the disability feature of mental retardation and de-emphasize the focus on current functioning.

The next two features of the AAMR 2002 definition are *significant limitations in intellectual functioning and in adaptive behavior*. Intellectual functioning is mentioned first, as it was in the 1992 definition, and the manual reinforces its importance to the diagnosis of mental retardation, stating explicitly that "The determination that an individual's intellectual functioning is significantly below the mean fulfills the first requirement for being diagnosed as having mental retardation" (p. 52).

Adaptive behavior is elaborated in the AAMR 2002 definition as it was in the 1992 definition, but the 10 adaptive behavior skills have been reduced to three—conceptual, social, and practical. Interestingly and consistently, these same three domains were used to explain the dimensions of present functioning in the 1992 definition (Luckasson et al., 1992, p. 5). In Glidden (2003) I wrote that the primacy of intellectual functioning was somewhat ameliorated by the weight given to the listing of 10 adaptive skill areas, because the definition made the measurement of adaptive skills seem more advanced and precise than the measurement of intellectual functioning, even though the latter almost always includes different dimensions such as memory, vocabulary, comprehension, and reasoning. Other critics responded similarly (Detterman, Gabriel, & Ruthsatz, 2000; Greenspan, 1999), and the imprecision in the use of adaptive behavior skills and their measurement was described as one of the rationales for the 2002 definition (Luckasson et al., 2002, p. 31).

The criterion of *before age 18* is not a conceptual shift from the 1992 definition. It is a change from the 1983 definition, which used the phrase "during the developmental period" and then interpreted that period as the time between conception and age 18. Mentioning a specific age in the definition adds precision, but not necessarily understanding. Use of the earlier term "developmental period" made the rational basis of the age criterion clear in the definition itself. With both the 1992 and 2002 definitions, one must read the explanation before understanding the rationale. (See Baroff, this book, for additional commentary.)

A highly controversial new element of the 1992 definition was the elimination of the precisely defined severity levels, and the introduction of the levels-of-support classification. The 2002 definition retains these changes. In addition, the definition of *supports* is much the same as it was in 1992: "resources and strategies that aim to promote the development, education, interests, and personal well-being of a person and that enhance individual functioning" (p. 151).

EVALUATION OF THE 2002 AAMR DEFINITION

Does It Conform to Current Usage Patterns?

As I wrote in Glidden (2003), it is important to specify usage in terms of *by whom?* With regard to professionals, my speculation is that the 2002 definition, like the 1992 definition, corresponds well to the way that professionals and other service staff working with adults with mental retardation think about them and about mental retardation more generally. They see it, foremost, as a disability, based on limited intellectual ability and on problems with daily skills of varying sorts. They are likely to be more concerned with social and practical adaptive behaviors than with conceptual skills, but they are intimately involved in providing the supports that these adults need in order to live as independent a life as is possible. Although these workers recognize that intellectual functioning is an essential portion of the definition, it is the manifestation of that functioning in everyday life, or adaptive behavior, that is most salient.

More than the 1992 definition, the 2002 definition also conforms more closely to the way educators and psychologists are likely to use the term mental retardation. For both of these groups the deficits in learning are paramount, loosely equating to limitations both in intelligence and in conceptual adaptive behavior skills. For educators, these deficits are critical, because they represent an adaptive behavior failure in the school environment. Psychologists tend to be cognizant of the long-term stability of intellectual functioning, particularly after age 5 or 6. Psychologists also are likely to recognize and assert that the intellectual limitation causes the adaptive behavior problems and not the reverse. Although measured intelligence and adaptive behavior have been found in many studies to correlate only modestly with each other (Jacobson & Mulick, 1996; Loveland & Tunali-Kotoski, 1998), it seems clear that early in life, especially for children with mental retardation, the relationship is quite strong (Kahn, 1983; Wachs & de Remer, 1978). Moreover, lower correlations later in life can usually be explained by a variety of other variables, such as physical or sensory disabilities resulting in lower adaptive behavior despite average or above-average intelligence, as well as the use of adaptive behavior scales that include maladaptive behaviors that may not bear any relation to intelligence.

Finally, because the levels-of-support classification is neither precisely defined, nor based on well-established data or psychometric evidence, it is likely to be a rather crude estimate that will have serious reliability problems. Some psychologists, particularly those with a research orientation, have been and will continue to be opposed to this part of the definition (MacMillan, Gresham, & Siperstein, 1995; Vig & Jedrysek, 1996). On the other hand, because this portion of the definition will require the most art and skill, including experienced clinical judgment, others will welcome its inclusion. Regardless, however, of whether psychologists or educators are happy with the definition, it is safe to say that it does not conform to their current usage patterns. Indeed, AAMR (2002) points out that only four states used the 1992 definition and none used the levels-of-support model.

Is It Unambiguous?

The 2002 definition is less ambiguous than the 1992 definition. Eliminating the phrase *limitations in present functioning* and stating that mental retardation is a *disability* implies stability. As in the 1992 definition, the IQ threshold of 70–75 has been retained. That threshold has been criticized by some as likely to increase the number of individuals classified with mental retardation (MacMillan, Gresham, & Siperstein, 1993), whereas others have argued that it will not do so (Reiss, 1994). And, as discussed earlier, the reference to levels of support that will be needed is a prognosis rather than a diagnosis. If this prognosis could be made with certainty, it would not be ambiguous. Although there has been substantial clarification of the construct and its assessment since 1992, there is also evidence that professionals from different disciplines who will need to work collaboratively will not readily achieve consensus (Siperstein, Wolraich, & Reed, 1994).

Is It Functional?

With regard to functionality, there appears to be little difference between the 1992 and 2002 definitions. Certainly, the revised definition is no more research-friendly. It does not restore the precisely defined IQ-based levels of functioning, nor does it substitute a system with easily described and relatively fixed boundaries—as in, for example, standard deviation units. On this point, also, the definition is at odds with competing classification systems, such as that of American Psychological Association (Jacobson & Mulick, 1996) and the International Classifications of Diseases (9th rev.), Clinical Modification (Medicode, 1998), both of which use an IQ basis for classification of levels.

The adaptive-behavior construct has been modified substantially from 1992 to 2002, based primarily on the criticism that the 10 dimensions in the 1992 definition did not have empirical validation (Luckasson et al., 2002, p. 31; Widaman & McGrew, 1996). The three dimensions of conceptual, social, and practical skills in the 2002 definition more closely correspond to some current models of competence, especially that of Greenspan (1999, 2003, 2004). Of course, these three dimensions are, by necessity, broader in range and therefore less likely to be easily anchored to specific behaviors, creating difficulties in measurement and therefore classification and diagnosis.

Specifically, in Table 5.1 of the 2002 manual, four different instruments for measuring adaptive behavior are outlined with respect to these three dimensions. The four instruments show some correspondence with each other, but also substantial variance. For example, the dimension of conceptual skills corresponds to community skills in two instruments, and to communication in two others, along with independent living in one of these two.

Arguably, deficits in conceptual adaptive skills are the most fundamental to the diagnosis of mental retardation. Indeed, if a person diagnosed with mental retardation had age-appropriate language in reading, writing, and speaking as well as unimpaired quantitative skills such as money concepts, we would certainly believe that he or she was misdiagnosed. An appropriate measure of conceptual skills should correlate positively with IQ scores, more so than either social or practical intelligence will correlate with IQ. Indeed, recent models of gullibility, for example, which is listed as a representative social skill vulnerability, assume that it is influenced by conceptual factors (Glinou, 2004; Greenspan, 2004; Greenspan, Loughlin, & Black, 2001; Hickson & Khemka, 1999, 2004; Khemka & Hickson, in press; Murphy, 2004; Switzky, 2004). It is critical that future research attend to the three adaptive-behavior dimensions to determine whether they should be weighted equally, as they are in the 2002 AAMR definition.

Does It Define What the Label Suggests It Defines?

As with the 1992 AAMR and the 1996 APA definitions, neither the word *mental* nor the word *retardation* appears in the definition of mental retardation. Although *mental* is frequently used as a synonym for intellectual, why use mental instead of intellectual? Indeed, there are significant reasons not to use mental, because of its similarity to, and frequent confusion with, mental illness. Retardation, of course, implies *slower* or *delay* rather than deficit or deficiency, and the definition does not state delay, but rather specifically states limitation. If the label were to conform to the definition, it should include the concepts [and words] of intelligence, of adaptive behavior, and of limitations.

In sum, the 2002 AAMR definition, like the 1992 definition that it replaces, is problematic with regard to all four criteria of assessment. It does not conform to the current usage patterns of all those who will be using it; it contains ambiguities; it is not likely to be functional for all groups who will be using it; and there is substantial label/definitional asynchrony because neither *mental* nor *retardation*, the two terms in the label, is specifically mentioned in the definition.

SUMMARY AND RECOMMENDATIONS

The features analysis of the 2002 AAMR definition of mental retardation results in a profile quite similar to my comparison of the 1992 AAMR definition with the 1996 APA definition (Glidden, 2003). I demonstrated that, although there were differences, the definitions shared many features. The core criteria in each were limitations in both intellectual functioning and adaptive behavior. The 2002 AAMR definition shares this similarity, thus continuing consensus on these components.

The evaluations of the three definitions also reach consensus on another issue. None of them includes either of the two component words, *mental* or *retardation*. There are good reasons for this exclusion, as I have noted below, and several international organizations such as the World Health Organization and the International Association for the Scientific Study of Intellectual Disability have chosen the alternative label of *intellectual disability*. One rationale for abandoning the label *mental retardation* is that the similarity between it and the quite different label *mental illness* is partially responsible for the lay confusion that surrounds the two concepts. Moreover, *mental*, although sometimes used as a synonym for *intellectual*, also encompasses a scope that is broader, including emotional as well as rational faculties. Furthermore, because retardation implies a delay or slowness rather than an ongoing limitation, it conveys an incorrect concept, because the definitions do not focus on slowness, but rather on limitations. Thus, there is label/definitional asynchrony. This asynchrony is not trivial, but neither is its elimination simple.

One obvious recommendation is to change the label or *definiendum* so that it is congruent with the *definiens* or definition. In this case, because the 2002 AAMR definition specifies limitations in intellectual functioning and adaptive behavior, changing the *definiendum* from *mental retardation* to *intellectual and adaptive behavior limitations* would seem to make sense. It is also consistent with the labels employed in some countries, such as China (Tao, 1988), and by some organizations, such as the International Association for the Scientific Study of Intellectual Disabilities. Of course, this change has also the disadvantage of sudden legislation attempting to alter decades of common and scientific usage. The various professional communities would need to decide whether this sudden shift in terminology conveys benefits that outweigh the disadvantages of the coexistence of multiple labels for the same condition and the need for reeducation.

A less scientific but nonetheless compelling argument for changing the term comes from advocates, both self-advocates and others, who view it as stigmatizing. There is little disagreement that persons with mental retardation are devalued and that the word or its derivatives, such as *retard*, are used frequently as epithets rather than as scientific nomenclature. In fact, many individuals know the term only as an insult. A few years ago, I was interviewed by a reporter who was writing an article on capital punishment and was focused on court cases in North Carolina and Virginia. As an aside he told me that he was shocked when he read a *New York Times* headline using the phrase *mental retardation*. He was reluctant to accept my explanation of the official diagnostic function of the phrase.

Nonetheless, empathy for individuals who are devalued is not a good reason for alteration of scientific terminology (Baumeister, 2003). There may be many supportable reasons to shift our diagnostic labels, but stigma is not one of them. History and good sense tell us that it is the condition that transfers the stigma to the label and not the reverse. Changing labels may reduce stigma in the short term, but attitudes will resurrect the devaluation, unless attitudes change to alter the fundamental view of the condition.

REFERENCES

American Psychiatric Association. (1994). *Diagnostic and statistical manual of mental disorders: DSM-IV* (4th ed.). Washington, DC: Author.

Baroff, G. S. (in press). On the 2002 AAMR definition of mental retardation. In H. N. Switzky (Ed.), *International review of research in mental retardation* (Vol. 31). New York: Academic Press.

Baumeister, A. A. (2003). The meaning of mental retardation: Sentiment versus science. In H. N. Switzky & S. Greenspan (Eds.), *What Is Mental Retardation? Ideas for an evolving disability* (pp. 127–146). Washington, DC: American Association on Mental Retardation [E-Book]. Available at http://www.disabilitybooksonline.com

Bolinger, D. (1975). *Aspects of language* (2nd ed.). New York: Harcourt Brace Jovanovich.

Broad, W. J. (2004, July 27). Ogre? Octopus? Blobologists solve an ancient mystery. *New York Times.* Retrieved July 27, 2004, from http://www.nytimes.com

Detterman, D. K., Gabriel, L. T., & Ruthsatz, J. M. (2000). Intelligence and mental retardation. In R. J. Sternberg (Ed.), *Handbook on intelligence* (pp. 141–158). New York: Cambridge University Press.

Doll, E. A. (1941). Notes on the concept of mental deficiency. *American Journal of Psychology, 54,* 116–124.

Garrison, W. (1965). *What's in a word?* Nashville: Abingdon.

Glidden, L. M. (2003). Where are the *mental* and *retardation* in mental retardation? In H. N. Switzky & S. Greenspan (Eds.), *What Is Mental Retardation? Ideas for an evolving disability* (pp. 75–86). Washington, DC: American Association on Mental Retardation [E-Book]. Available at http://www.disabilitybooksonline.com

Glinou, N. M. (2004). Impact of cognitive-motivational training on interpersonal negotiation strategies [Abstract]. *Journal of Intellectual Disability Research, 48,* 453.

Greenspan, S. (1999). What is meant by mental retardation? *International Review of Psychiatry, 11,* 6–18.

Greenspan, S. (2003). Perceived risk status as a key to defining mental retardation. In H. N. Switzky & S. Greenspan (Eds.), *What Is Mental Retardation? Ideas for an evolving disability.* Washington, DC: American Association on Mental Retardation [E-Book]. Available at http://www.disabilitybooksonline.com

Greenspan, S. (2004). Why Pinocchio was victimized: Factors contributing to social failure in people with mental retardation. In H. N. Switzky (Ed.), *International review of research in mental retardation* (Vol. 28, pp. 121–144). San Diego, CA: Elsevier/Academic Press.

Greenspan, S., Loughlin, G., & Black, R. S. (2001). Credulity and gullibility in people with developmental disorders: A framework for future research. In L. M. Glidden (Ed.), *International review of research in mental retardation* (Vol. 24, pp. 101–135). New York: Academic Press.

Hickson, L., & Khemka, I. (1999). Decision making and mental retardation. In L. M. Glidden (Ed.), *International review of research in mental retardation* (Vol. 22, pp. 227–265). San Diego, CA: Academic Press.

Hickson, L., & Khemka, I. (2004). Impact of ESCAPE on the cognitive and motivational aspects of self-protective decision making [Abstract]. *Journal of Intellectual Disability Research, 48,* 453.

Jacobson, J. W., & Mulick, J. A. (1996). Psychometrics. In J. W. Jacobson, & J. A. Mulick (Eds.), *Manual of diagnosis and professional practice in mental retardation* (pp. 75–84). Washington, DC: American Psychological Association.

Kahn, J. V. (1983). Sensorimotor period and adaptive behavior development of severely and profoundly mentally retarded children. *American Journal of Mental Deficiency, 88,* 69–75.

Khemka, I., & Hickson, L. (in press). The role of motivation in the decision making of adolescents with mental retardation. In H. N. Switzky (Ed.), *International review of research in mental retardation (Vol. 30).* San Diego, CA: Elsevier/Academic Press.

Loveland, K. A., & Tunali-Kotoski, B. (1998). Development of adaptive behavior in persons with mental retardation. In J. A. Burack, R. M. Hodapp, & E. Zigler (Eds.), *Handbook of mental retardation and development* (pp. 521–541). Cambridge, England: Cambridge University Press.

Luckasson, R., Borthwick-Duffy, S., Buntinx, W. H. E., Coulter, D. L., Craig, E. M., Reeve, A., et al. (2002). *Mental retardation: Definition, classification, and systems of supports* (10th ed.). Washington, DC: American Association on Mental Retardation.

Luckasson, R., Coulter, D. L., Polloway, E. A., Reiss, S., Schalock, R. L., Snell, M. E., et al. (1992). *Mental Retardation: Definition, classification, and systems of supports* (9th ed.). Washington, DC: American Association on Mental Retardation.

Luckasson, R., & Reeve, A. (2001). Naming, defining, and classifying in mental retardation. *Mental Retardation, 39,* 47–52.

MacMillan, D. L., Gresham, F. M., & Siperstein, G. N. (1993). Conceptual and psychometric concerns about the 1992 AAMR definition of mental retardation. *American Journal on Mental Retardation, 98,* 325–335.

MacMillan, D. L., Gresham, F. M., & Siperstein, G. N. (1995). Heightened concerns over the 1992 AAMR definition: Advocacy versus precision. *American Journal on Mental Retardation, 100,* 87–97.

Medicode. (1998). *International classification of diseases, ninth revision, clinical modification* (6th ed.). Salt Lake City: Medicode Publications.

Murphy, G. H. (2004). Making decisions [Abstract]. *Journal of Intellectual Disability Research, 48,* 285.

O'Neill, E. (1918). *Stories that words tell us.* London: T. C. & E. C. Jack.

Reiss, S. (1994). Issues in defining mental retardation. *American Journal on Mental Retardation, 99,* 1–7.

Sarason, S. B. (1973). Jewishness, blackishness, and the nature-nurture controversy. *American Psychologist, 28,* 962–971.

Scheerenberger, R. (1983). *A history of mental retardation.* Baltimore: Paul H. Brookes.

Siperstein, G. N., Wolraich, M. L., & Reed, D. (1994). Professionals' prognoses for individuals with mental retardation: Search for consensus with interdisciplinary settings. *American Journal on Mental Retardation, 98,* 519–526.

Switzky, H. N. (2004). The importance of motivational and personality variables for research in intellectual disabilities (ID) [Absract]. *Journal of Intellectual Disability Research, 48,* 453.

Switzky, H. N., & Greenspan, S. (Eds.). (2003). *What Is Mental Retardation? Ideas for an evolving disability.* Washington, DC: American Association on Mental Retardation [E-Book]. Available at http://www.disabilitybooksonline.com

Tao, K. T. (1988). Mentally retarded persons in the People's Republic of China: Review of epidemiological studies and services. *American Journal on Mental Retardation, 93,* 193–199.

Tredgold, A. F. (1908). *Mental deficiency: Amentia.* New York: W. Wood.

Tredgold, A. F. (1937). *The text-book of mental deficiency (amentia)* (6th ed.). Baltimore: W. Wood.

Vig, S., & Jerysek, E. (1996). Application of the 1992 AAMR definition: Issues for preschool children. *Mental Retardation, 34*, 244–246.

Wachs, T. D., & de Remer, P. (1978). Adaptive behavior and Uzgiris-Hunt scale performance of young, developmentally disabled children. *American Journal of Mental Deficiency, 83*, 171–176.

Widaman, K. F., & McGrew, K. S. (1996). The structure of adaptive behavior. In J. W. Jacobson & J. A. Mulick (Eds.), *Manual of diagnosis and professional practice in mental retardation* (pp. 97–110). Washington, DC: American Psychological Association.

Chapter Four

Quo Vadis Mental Retardation? Definition by Aggregation versus the Hope for Individual Futures

J. David Smith

Assessment of the 2002 AAMR Definition

In his book *Abandoned to Their Fate,* Phillip Ferguson speaks of people who have been judged "unfixable." Through his study of mental retardation in the 19th and 20th centuries, Ferguson found that the judgment of "chronicity" had the most profound impact on the lives of people. To be judged "chronic" meant that you were socially abandoned. The judgment of chronicity is reached when, in Ferguson's words, "badness becomes incorrigible, ugliness becomes inhuman, and uselessness becomes untrainable" (p. 16). The status of chronicity, he argued, not that of retardation or other comparable terms, has determined the fate of generations of people.

As more formal and elaborate definitions of mental retardation were developed during the first half of the 20th century, they tended to incorporate the judgment of chronicity. The most important of these, and the one that continues to influence the defining of mental retardation, was authored by psychologist Edgar Doll in 1941. His pioneering definition included six elements that he considered essential to the concept of mental retardation.

1. Social incompetence,
2. due to mental subnormality,
3. which has been developmentally arrested,
4. which obtains at maturity,
5. is of constitutional origin, and
6. is essentially incurable (p. 215).

The first four of these elements have continued to be overtly central to the prevailing conceptualization of mental retardation even as expressed in the 2002 American Association on Mental Retardation (AAMR) definition (Luckasson et al., 2002). Social incompetence associated with deficits in mental ability is a thread that runs from Doll's definition through subsequent ones to the most current. The same is true for his emphasis on mental retardation as a disability that originates during the developmental period.

51

The last two elements of Doll's definition, however, are not found as formal elements of contemporary definitions of mental retardation. Retardation is no longer viewed as always resulting from "constitutional" factors. It has long been recognized that environmental variables are important causes of mental retardation. Much retardation, for example, is associated with the depriving effects of poverty. This recognition, however, is not operative in many community and school contexts, where "true" retardation is still considered to be physiological in origin. Mental retardation is also no longer considered to be an "incurable" condition in official definitions. The goal of educational services for many students, in fact, is to help them achieve a level of competence at which it would no longer be appropriate describe them as having mental retardation. The belief in incurability of children and adults with mental retardation has continued to be held, however, in the minds of many people.

The legacy of Doll's conceptualization of mental retardation can be seen most clearly in definitions that were developed during the second half or the 20th century, and in 2002 by AAMR. Those definitions have always included the criteria of low measured intelligence and deficits in social competence. They have also consistently described mental retardation as a developmental disability.

In 1959 the AAMR, which at the time was called the American Association on Mental Deficiency (AAMD), published a definition of mental retardation that read: "Mental retardation refers to subaverage general intellectual functioning which originates during the development period and is associated with impairment in adaptive behavior" (Heber, p. 63).

The Heber definition was revised in 1961. That revision specified the meaning of "subaverage general intellectual functioning" in a manner that was to have considerable impact on the field of mental retardation. One standard deviation below the mean on an intelligence test was delineated as the point at which intellectual functioning should be considered subnormal. This specification meant that on an IQ test with a mean of 100 and a standard deviation of 15, any score below 85 would be diagnostic of mental retardation. If the total population were tested and classified on this basis, almost 16% would be diagnosed as having mental retardation. Even higher percentages would be expected in subpopulations where minority status, language factors, or socioeconomic background depresses intelligence test scores.

There were also criticisms of the concept of adaptive behavior as it appeared in the 1961 definition: it was not, critics said, actually functional for the diagnosis of mental retardation. In reality, it was argued, the determination of retardation continued to be based on intelligence test scores alone, and intelligence was not significantly "associated" with adaptive behavior in this process (Clausen, 1972).

In 1973, with the criticisms of the 1961 definition in mind, an AAMR committee chaired by Herbert Grossman developed another revision. It specified that "significantly subaverage general intellectual functioning" was to be determined by a score at least "two standard deviations" below the mean on an intelligence test. Essentially this moved the cutoff point for mental retardation downward from 85 to 70, thereby lowering the percentage of the population that might be identified as having mental retardation from 16% to approximately 2.25%. This revision meant that fewer people would be labeled "retarded" because of language differences, socioeconomic factors, or minority status. It also meant, however, that fewer students were eligible for special education services. This is a particularly important consideration, because the 1973 AAMR definition was adopted for defining mental retardation under Public Law 94-142, the Education of All Handicapped Children Act, in 1975. This definition also placed more emphasis on the importance of adaptive behavior and extended the developmental period upward from 16 to 18 years of age.

In 1977 the AAMR published another manual on mental retardation terminology and classification (Grossman, 1977). There was no substantive change to the definition, but the role of clinical judgment was given greater emphasis. Allowance was made as well for diagnosing people with IQs up to 10 points above the 70 cutoff as having mental retardation if they also showed marked deficits in adaptive behavior. A 1983 AAMR definition further expanded the developmental period from conception (instead of birth) to age 18. This change officially made people with mental retardation resulting from prenatal factors eligible to be classified (Grossman, 1983).

The 1992 AAMR definition (Luckasson et al., 1992) included dramatic changes and was presented by AAMR as a paradigm shift. Retardation was no longer to be viewed as characteristic of an individual. It was defined instead as the product of interactions between a person and the nature and demands of that person's environment. The phrase "limitations in present functioning" (p. 1) was used to indicate that mental retardation might be a transitory condition. The global term *adaptive behavior* was extended to 10 specific adaptive skill areas; each was discussed at some length in the manual. Levels of severity of mental retardation were replaced by a system that classified the intensities and patterns of support required by individuals.

The revision and its changes in the classification guidelines on mental retardation generated a great deal of professional and academic controversy. Even within the AAMR there were sharp differences of opinion. John Jacobson, former president of the AAMR Psychology Division, was quoted as saying, "The new AAMR manual is a political manifesto, not a clinical document" (as cited in Michaelson, 1993, p. 34). He described the AAMR's changes in diagnosing mental retardation as being politically motivated rather than research based. This position, and other criticisms of the revisions, appeared elsewhere in the professional literature (Jacobson & Mulick, 1993; MacMillan, Gresham, & Siperstein, 1993; MacMillan, Gresham, & Siperstein, 1995).

Greenspan (1995) observed that the AAMR 1992 revision presented a "less defectology-oriented approach to conceptualizing disorder, a view that is reflective of both new treatment approaches as well as new social trends" (pp. 684–685). On the other hand, he pointed out that the definition was not grounded on a research base of any kind. This, he argued, rendered the definition vulnerable to major criticism. According to Greenspan, relatively full acceptance of any radical new classificatory scheme (no matter how much philosophical or practical merit it might have) is likely to occur only if the promoters of the scheme are able to advance the illusion, if not the reality, that it is driven by scientific methods and findings (p. 685).

The 2002 AAMR manual clearly shows Greenspan's influence. It describes the domains of adaptive behavior as being "less differentiated than the 10 skill areas listed in the 1992 definition" and "more consistent with the conceptual models in the literature that describe major domains of personal competence" (Luckasson et al., 2002, p. 76). References that follow this statement clearly show that Greenspan and others have been heard concerning the complexities and intricacies of defining and measuring adaptive behavior and social intelligence. The 2002 definition describes adaptive behavior as being expressed in "conceptual social and practical adaptive skills" (p. 1). The definition itself reads:

> Mental retardation is a disability characterized by significant limitations both in intellectual functioning and in adaptive behavior expressed in conceptual social, and practical adaptive skills. This disability originates before age 18. (p. 1)

Ideas for a Revised Definition

The authors of the 1992 AAMR manual characterized their revisions as a paradigm shift consisting of two facets: first, a change in the conception of mental retardation from a trait existing in an individual to an expression of the interaction between a person with limited intellectual and adaptive skills and that individual's environment; and second, a focus on the pattern of the person's needs rather than on his or her deficits (Schalock et al., 1994). The authors of the 2002 AAMR manual reiterate that the challenge of the 1992 manual was to "reflect the paradigm shift" (p. xiii).

Paradigm shifts may be critical to advancement and improvement in any field of endeavor. Thomas Kuhn in his classic book *The Structure of Scientific Revolutions* (1962) defined paradigms as shared world views of scientists, shared ways of viewing certain realities. Kuhn argued that these shared views eventually become so strong and institutionalized that only a sudden and dramatic break from them can bring on a positive revolution of thought.

Unlike the situation in physics, however, where a paradigm shift from the world view of Newton to that of Einstein did nothing to change the reality of the physical universe, a paradigm shift in the field of mental retardation is likely to have profound implications for the education, care, and treatment of millions of human beings.

What is the purpose of defining mental retardation? If it is to create greater understanding of the people whose lives are touched by retardation, Robert Edgerton's words from the newest edition of *The Cloak of Competence* (1993) are important to consider:

> There are many cognitively limited people in the United States and the rest of the world who live in dramatically different social and cultural worlds. Until we enter those worlds and learn from the people who live in them, we will not know what mental retardation is or what people with it can accomplish, and that what they can accomplish can enlighten and enlarge us all. (p. 234)

The effort to define mental retardation with the greatest possible scientific accuracy continues. The effort to define it in a way that promotes greater sensitivity to the needs of people with mental retardation also continues. Successful resolution of the tension between meeting these two goals will determine the future of a social construct that promotes care rather than control for the people whose lives are central to its construction. Perhaps an even more dramatic paradigm shift than is attributed to the AAMR definition is needed. What shift might best serve the interests of the people who are and could be defined in the future as having mental retardation? The most positive paradigm shift might be, in fact, the deconstruction of the concept and terminology of mental retardation. The best definition may be no definition at all.

RATIONALE FOR THE SUGGESTED REVISION

The eminent American psychologist Seymour Sarason observed in 1985, "Mental retardation is never a thing or characteristic of an individual, but rather a social invention stemming from time-bound societal values and ideology that makes diagnosis and management seem both necessary and socially desirable" (p. 233).

The "time-bound" nature of social values was powerfully expressed by Supreme Court Justice Oliver Wendell Holmes in his book *The Common Law* (1881): "The life of the law has not been logic; it has been experience. The felt necessities of the time are the sources of law" (p. 1). When Holmes spoke for the majority of the Supreme Court in 1927 and supported the right of the Commonwealth of Virginia to sterilize people who had been diagnosed as "feebleminded," he was upholding a "felt necessity" of his time and culture. He was also acting in accordance with a "felt necessity" that had a long history in American society.

There is evidence to suggest that mental retardation carries the most debilitating socially constructed stigma. Gibbons (1985) contends that people with mental retardation themselves are acutely aware of this stigma and tend to react with derogation to their own peers' lack of social competence and physical attractiveness. The threat of a devalued identity provides a powerful incentive for maintaining both physical and social distance from people more seriously stigmatized. As Goffman (1963) suggests: "In general, the tendency for a stigma to spread from the stigmatized individual . . . provides a reason why such relations tend either to be avoided or terminated, where existing" (p. 30). Mental retardation is a powerfully stigmatizing and isolating construction.

In *Coming of Age in Samoa* (1928), Margaret Mead included a discussion of people with disabilities in the Samoan culture. She not only provided profiles of those Samoans with disabilities, but, perhaps more important, she described a Samoan society that possessed "more charity towards weakness than towards misdirected strength" (p. 182).

Mead returned to this theme many years later. In 1959 she spoke at a conference sponsored by the AAMD. She referred to a statement by a group of Catholic sisters who worked with children with mental retardation and said they were attempting to make it possible for these children to make a "contribution in time as well as in eternity" (p. 253).

Later in her speech, she again referred to the work of the Catholic Church with individuals having mental retardation. She gave the example of a child with Down syndrome who had been tested, diagnosed, and given every opportunity for the best skill training. In her early teens, however, the child was given religious instruction, and Mead described the change that took place in the girl's life in terms of "wholeness." She said that when the girl became Catholic, she became a human being in a way that she had not been before. "I think that what happened on the secular side with this little girl was that for the first time she met a situation where people were willing to teach her the *whole* instead of saying 'you are defective and you can only learn a part.'" (p. 260). Mead concluded her address to the AAMD by elaborating on the concept of education for "wholeness." She distinguished between societies where everyone participates in all aspects of the culture (e.g., Samoa) and a segmented, socially stratified society that no longer attempts to teach the "whole" to all people (e.g., the United States). She emphasized that what makes for a culture of full participants is genuine opportunity for most people to learn how to wholly participate. She warned of the "risks of complicating sections of our culture so much that we define them as things most people can't learn" (pp. 258–259).

Margaret Mead's insights, unfamiliar to most people, can enrich our understanding that in order to genuinely include those with "mental retardation" in their own culture we must strive to make accessible to them the essential "wholeness" of citizenship (Smith & Johnson, 1997). That piece of people referred to by "mental retardation," "feeble mind-edness," or some other diagnostic term must no longer be allowed to overshadow the "wholeness" of those individuals.

The Future of Mental Retardation as a Field

Steven Gelb (1997) has examined the persistence in the field of mental retardation of *typological thinking*—the belief that individual differences converge into underlying types or essences. Gelb finds that definitions of mental retardation, regardless of their differences or particulars, have been founded on the assumptions of typological thought. The axis or core of the field of mental retardation is the assumption that somehow there is an "essence of mental retardation" that eclipses all of the individual differences that characterize the people who are described by the term.

A glance at the panoply of causes associated with mental retardation illustrates the allure and power of typological thinking. The 1992 manual listed more than 350 conditions in which mental retardation occurs. This list did not, of course, take into account the varying degrees or specific types of disabilities associated with these etiologies. If these variables were taken into account, the number of contexts and expressions of what is called "mental retardation" would be staggering. The only "glue" that holds mental retardation together as a category is the typological notion that there is some underlying essence to the characteristics and needs of the people identified by this term. Clearly mental retardation is a term used for an aggregate of life conditions. The only rationale for this aggregation has been the typological assumptions that Gelb described.

In his book *Wayward Puritans*, Erikson (1965) observed that the amount of punishable deviancy that was recorded in Quaker 17th-century New England corresponded neatly with the supply of available stocks and whipping posts. If a community had an ample supply of stocks, it convicted and punished a corresponding number of individuals for their deviations from the norm. If stocks were in short supply, the rate of deviations detected and punished in that community dropped. It is a simple logistic fact, Erikson argued, that the degree of deviance a community perceives and acts on is largely determined by the kinds of equipment it uses to detect and manage different forms of deviancy. The magnitude of deviation found in a community is at least in part a function of the size and complexity of its social control mechanisms.

Mechanisms of social control will, as has been discussed previously, be influenced by the "felt necessities" of the time and place. They will also be influenced, however, by the tolerance or intolerance for certain traits or for degrees of certain attributes. In *The Rules of Sociological Method*, Emile Durkheim (1895/1958) invited his readers to

> imagine a society of saints, a perfect cloister of exemplary individuals. Crimes properly so called, will there be unknown, but faults which appear venial to the layman will create there the same scandal that the ordinary offense does in ordinary consciousness. If, then, this society has the power to judge and punish, it will *define* these acts as criminal and treat them as such. (p. 63)

During the 20th century in the United States, the number of individuals defined as being mentally retarded has shifted dramatically. As the emphasis on intelligence-test performance has changed, there have been major fluctuations in the demographics of mental retardation. The same is true of the other changes in the accepted definitions of mental retardation. In a sense we have established changing patterns of "intellectual and adaptive saintliness" and have thereby created the less-than-"exemplary individuals" whom society has the power to define as "retarded." In this way, and usually with the best of intentions, we have created the social equivalent of the Puritans' stocks. We have created mechanisms of social control waiting to be used.

In *Miles to Go: A Personal History of Social Policy*, former Senator Daniel Patrick Moynihan (1996) included a chapter entitled "Defining Deviancy Down," in which he described three ways that various forms of social deviance have been redefined. Moynihan finds that "altruistic redefinitions" may be the attempts of "good" people to do the "right" thing. These attempts, however, sometimes lead to losses that have a dramatic impact on those who are redefined. (Moynihan's example is deinstitutionalization.) "Opportunistic redefinitions," according to Moynihan, may result in the growth of the numbers of people defined as deviant and an increase in the resources and power available to those who "control" the deviant population affected. Moynihan describes a "normalizing redefinition" as a form of denial, which may result in neglect of the real needs of the people who have been redefined. Moynihan's analysis of redefinitions makes evident the caution that must be used in redefining mental retardation (pp. 136–167).

Perhaps it is time, therefore, to abandon the term *mental retardation* and the quest for a better, more humane, more scientific definition. The term and its various definitions may, in fact, be manifestations of typological thinking that inevitably creates a false and unhelpful categorization of people with very diverse needs and characteristics. The 1992 and 2002 AAMR definitions of mental retardation do not go far enough to diminish the tendency of society to place people in social stocks.

Alternatives must be considered for conceptualizing the needs of people currently referred to as having mental retardation. It may be helpful to use Moynihan's redefinition model as a way of asking ourselves what the abandonment of the term *mental retardation* and the definitions associated with it can mean in the lives of individuals and families (the altruistic implications)—and what it might mean for the allocation of resources and provision of services to people who need them (i.e., what are the opportunistic consequences?). Finally, we must consider the impact of the deconstruction of retardation in terms of the dichotomies of need versus norm. How much segregation is necessary to meet needs? How much service is justified, given the risk of stigma associated with these services? How can we achieve a balance between the need for assistance and the value of independence? These are only some of the questions associated with dismantling of the category of mental retardation.

The authors of the 2002 AAMR manual acknowledge that many people are urging the elimination of the term *mental retardation*. They also acknowledge that the term is "stigmatizing and is frequently mistakenly used as a global summary about complex human beings" (p. xii). They concluded, however, that there was "no acceptable alternative term, despite its acknowledged shortcomings" (p. xii).

With the arrival of the new millennium, however, the time is overdue for a more vigorous and fundamental questioning of the concepts, terms, and practices associated with mental retardation. While it will be very difficult, the millions of people with the myriad of developmental disabilities that have been subsumed under that term deserve this questioning of the manner in which they are being regarded and treated. A disassembling of the aggregation that mental retardation is may enhance our vision of what it should be.

References

Clausen, J. A. (1972). The continuing problem of defining mental deficiency. *Journal of Special Education, 6,* 97–106.

Doll, E. A. (1941). The essentials of an inclusive concept of mental deficiency. *American Journal of Mental Deficiency, 46,* 214–219.

Durkheim, E. (1958). *The rules of sociological method* (S. A. Solovay & J. H. Miller, Trans.). Glencoe, IL: Free Press.

Edgerton, R. B. (1993). *The cloak of competence: Revised and updated.* Berkeley: University of California Press.

Education for All Handicapped Children Act of 1975, 20 U.S.C.--1400 *et seq.*

Erikson, K. T. (1965). *Wayward Puritans.* New York: John Wiley.

Ferguson, P. M. (1994). *Abandoned to their fate: Social policy and practice toward severely retarded people in America, 1820–1920.* Philadelphia: Temple University Press.

Gelb, S. A. (1997). The problem of typological thinking in mental retardation. *Mental Retardation, 35,* 448–457.

Gibbons, F. X. (1985). Stigma perception: Social comparison among mentally retarded persons. *American Journal of Mental Deficiency, 90,* 98–106.

Goffman, E. (1963). *Stigma: Notes on the management of spoiled identity.* Englewood Cliffs, NJ: Prentice-Hall.

Greenspan, S. (1995). Selling DSM: The rhetoric of science in psychiatry. *American Journal on Mental Retardation, 99,* 683–685.

Grossman, H. J. (Ed.). (1973). *Manual on terminology and classification in mental retardation (1973 revision).* Washington, DC: American Association on Mental Deficiency.

Grossman, H. J. (Ed.). (1977). *Manual on terminology and classification in mental retardation* (1977 revision). Washington, DC: American Association on Mental Deficiency.

Grossman, H. J. (Ed.). (1983). *Manual on terminology and classification in mental retardation* (1983 revision). Washington, DC: American Association on Mental Deficiency.

Heber, R. (1959). A manual on terminology and classification in mental retardation [Monograph Supplement]. *American Journal of Mental Deficiency, 64*(2).

Heber, R. (1961). Modifications in the manual on terminology and classification in mental retardation. *American Journal of Mental Deficiency, 65(4),* 499–500.

Holmes, O. W. (1881). *The common law.* Boston: Little, Brown.

Jacobson, J., & Mulick, J. (1993). APA takes a step forward in professional practice. *Psychology in Mental Retardation and Developmental Disabilities, 19,* 4–8.

Kuhn, T. S. (1962). *The structure of scientific revolutions.* Chicago: University of Chicago Press.

Luckasson, R., Borthwick-Duffy, S., Buntinx, W. H. E., Coulter, D. L., Craig, E. M., Reeve, A., et al. (2002). *Mental retardation: Definition, classification, and systems of supports* (10th ed.). Washington, DC: American Association on Mental Retardation.

Luckasson, R., Coulter, D. L., Polloway, E. A., Reiss, S., Schalock, R. L., Snell, M. E., et al. (1992). *Mental retardation: Definition, classification, and systems of supports* (9th ed.). Washington, DC: American Association on Mental Retardation.

MacMillian, D. L., Gresham, F. M., & Siperstein, G. N. (1993). Conceptual and psychometric concerns about the 1992 AAMR definition of mental retardation. *American Journal on Mental Retardation, 98,* 325–335.

MacMillian, D. L., Gresham, F. M., & Siperstein, G. N. (1995). Heightened concerns over the 1992 AAMR definition: Advocacy versus precision. *American Journal on Mental Retardation, 100,* 87–97.

Mead, M. (1928). *Coming of age in Samoa: A psychological study of primitive youth for Western civilization.* New York: Willam Morrow.

Mead, M. (1959). Research cult: Or cure? *American Journal of Mental Deficiency, 64,* 253–264.

Michaelson, R. (1993). Tug-of-war is developing over defining retardation. *APA Monitor, 24*(5), 34.

Moynihan, D. P. (1996). *Miles to go: A personal history of social policy.* Cambridge, MA: Harvard University Press.

Sarason, S. (1985). *Psychology and mental retardation: Perspectives in change.* Austin, TX: Pro-Ed.

Schalock, R. L., Stark, J. A., Snell, M. E., Coulter, D. L., Polloway, E. A., Luckasson, R., et al. (1994). The changing conception of mental retardation: Implications for the field. *Mental Retardation, 32,* 181–193.

Smith, J. D., & Johnson, G. (1997). Margaret Mead and mental retardation: Words of understanding, concepts of inclusiveness. *Mental Retardation, 35,* 306–309.

CHAPTER FIVE

On Being Labeled with Mental Retardation

MARTHA E. SNELL AND MARY D. VOORHEES

MENTAL RETARDATION: DOES THE LABEL BRING SUPPORT OR STIGMA?

The tasks of naming and defining mental retardation have been undertaken repeatedly across history. Naming involves "assigning a specific term to something or someone" (Luckasson & Reeve, 1999, p. 2), while defining relates to "precisely explaining a name or term" (p. 3). Both activities seem basic to humans and their tendency to seek order and organization in life. While the name or label "mental retardation" has been in use for approximately 50 years, many other names were applied in earlier times to people identified as having this disability: fool, dolt, simpleton, idiot, imbecile, feebleminded, mental defective, mentally deficient (Schalock, 2002; Trent, 1994). Each of these old terms has become pejorative and demeaning, and new terms have been coined. The task of defining mental retardation may be more recent, coinciding with the use of dictionaries in the past century (Luckasson & Reeve, 1999). The American Association on Mental Retardation (AAMR), for example, has produced 10 definitions of the term since 1921. Because disability definitions operationalize the term they identify, they can create major consequences in the lives of those to whom they are applied.

In this chapter, we focus on the effects that the mental retardation label appears to have on those so labeled. This perspective has been studied and written about, but less often considered seriously in discussions regarding terminology and classification procedures. First, we review the purpose of the mental retardation definition and label as perceived by audiences who have a stake in the definition. Then we examine reactions to the label by those individuals whom educational and adult services systems have identified as having mental retardation. Finally, we set forth several recommendations to guide our thinking as the term and its definition are reexamined.

WHAT IS THE PURPOSE OF THE MENTAL RETARDATION DEFINITION AND LABEL?

The general *purposes* of disability definitions and labels are to clarify etiology, to suggest treatment, and to make individuals eligible for services. Many factors influence whether these purposes are achieved (e.g., state and country of residence, labeling process used, advocacy efforts of family members and professionals, and the individual's age, health, insurance, and family income and status). The intended purpose of disability definitions and labels also may differ depending upon whose perspective is examined:

1. Individuals labeled as having mental retardation.
2. Parents and family members.
3. Professionals.

Individuals Labeled as Having Mental Retardation

In order to write about the perspective of individuals who have the mental retardation label, we reviewed the works of Edgerton, Bogdan and Taylor, and others. We also interviewed three verbal adults with this label. The purpose of the mental retardation label was unclear to these adults we interviewed, while its meaning designated individuals who "can't do much of anything." One man explained mental retardation in this way: "Your brain is not functioning and you cannot speak clear, reading is not clear, writing is not clear . . . some of them will never walk, talk, pick up a soda by themselves, plus feed themselves or take a shower" (Snell & Voorhees, 1998). No one mentioned the purpose typically cited by families and professionals: to get services and supports. The views of the three adults we talked with were similar to the views of individuals with the same label reported over a 40 year period (Bogdan & Taylor, 1994; Edgerton, 1967, 1993; Ward, 1990). In most of these reports, including our own limited interviews, the adults did not view themselves as having the label.

Parents and Family Members

Parents are motivated to seek disability labels to explain the developmental and behavioral differences their child exhibits, to identify remedies, and to obtain services that match the label. The mental retardation label and definition may not meet the first purpose (to explain the child's differences), since it applies to a highly varied group. The etiology of mental retardation, and thus its prognosis, is nonspecific more than half the time (Luckasson et al., 1992). Determination of an etiologic label such as for a chromosome abnormality (like Down syndrome) or a neuromuscular condition (like cerebral palsy) may help the family realize the primary purposes they ascribe to disability labels: to clarify the developmental delay and to qualify for services needed by the family member with the disability (Seligman & Darling, 1989). Most parents of children who are not diagnosed early with a condition unmistakably associated with mental retardation (such as Tay-Sachs or certain chromosomal abnormalities) still come to suspect that a problem exists before they receive a diagnosis; receiving a diagnosis usually reduces stress and brings relief rather than shock (Bristol & Schopler, 1984).

The postdiagnosis period is characterized first by a search for more information about the prognosis, followed by an exploration for treatment (motivated not so much by hope of a cure as by a desire to be a "good" parent), and finally succeeded by the pursuit of emotional support (Seligman & Darling, 1989). The label of mental retardation is a broad term that often is ambiguous in the information it provides parents on an individual's prognosis, but rarely is neutral or positive in its effect on parents. Unless mental retardation is clearly associated with a diagnosed congenital condition, professionals infrequently use the label. When a child's delayed development is accompanied by no clear etiology or reflects more subtle developmental delays and minimal support needs, physicians may suggest to parents that the child "will outgrow it," and they will avoid using a label of mental retardation or developmental delay. For only about half the children who exhibit significant delay can physicians assign a specific diagnosis; for the rest, labels of "developmental delay," "developmental disabilities," or even "pervasive developmental delay" are used rather than specific labels like mental retardation, emotional disorders, learning disabilities, and autism (Luckasson, Schalock, Snell, & Spitalnik, 1996). However, having any of these labels as a diagnosis appears to make it easier for families to seek information on appropriate programs. But without a diagnosis, or with one that does not identify an etiology or assign a disability label, it is difficult for parents to understand what can be expected of their child. Without a disability label, parents may not seek additional assessment, postponing diagnosis and services even longer; they are less likely to seek any intervention, less able to gain emotional support from parent groups (which typically are associated with disability labels), and more likely to experience stress over their child's differences.

These two purposes which families ascribe to the mental retardation label—to explain their child's developmental delay and to obtain appropriate services—may be overshadowed by the label's negative connotations: The label of mental retardation may be rebuffed by family members, may lower their expectations for the child, and may lead to stigmatizing social reactions from others, which parents find stressful (Baxter & Cummins, 1992).

Professionals

Generally, professionals hold that the purposes of disability definitions and labels are to explain the condition and to make services available; these same purposes are applied to the mental retardation label and definition. However, a survey by Denning, Chamberlain, and Polloway (2000) on definition and classification practices in the United States reveals wide variation not only in the specific term used to denote mental retardation, but also in the definition and the IQ criteria. Only about half the states (26 of 51, counting the District of Columbia) reported using the label of mental retardation, while other states used related terms: mental disability (7 states), mental impairment (4), mental handicap (3), intellectual disability (3), cognitive disability (2), and other variations such as educational disability, significantly limited intellectual capacity, and the like (7). Most states (35) reported using the 1983 AAMR definition or an adaptation of it (9), while fewer states used the 1992 AAMR definition (1) or an adaptation (3) or their own definition (3). Similar variation occurred with IQ cutoff for the criterion of intellectual functioning: 12 states reported using no IQ score cutoff, 18 used a cutoff of two standard deviations below the mean on standardized, norm-referenced tests, and 1 state used 1.5 standard deviations below the mean. In 19 other states specific IQ scores or ranges were identified as the criteria of inclusion and exclusion from the label: IQ 70 (13 states), IQ 74 (1), IQ range of 70–75 (2), IQ greater than or equal to 75 (1), and IQ 80 or below (2). These findings emphasize both how dynamic the concept of mental retardation is, as defined by professionals in the field (Denning et al., 2000), and how relative it is to one's residence location and time of life. This variability may influence how well the purposes of the definition are achieved.

To confuse the labeling process even more, it also has been shown that when classifying students by disability, schools do not consistently apply the criteria specified in their state's guidelines (MacMillan, Gresham, Siperstein, & Bocian, 1996). No research has been reported on the use of the 2002 AAMR definition (Luckasson et al., 2002), in which criteria for assessing IQ and adaptive behavior are specified more fully and in alignment with current psychometric practices.

Educators and direct care workers.

For most professionals in this group, the label's chief purpose is to provide appropriate, individualized educational services across functional life skill areas (Dever, 1990). Professionals serving adults who have mental retardation expand that purpose to include getting the supports and instruction that promote independence and self-determination (having meaningful day activities, holding a job, and living in the community with as much independence as possible). The curricular overlap with other disability areas is large, particularly between those having mental retardation and intermittent or limited support needs and those with learning disabilities (LD) who do not go on to higher education (Polloway, Patton, Smith, & Buck, 1997). For special education teachers and administrators and adult service professionals, the mental retardation label has served other related purposes:

1. To guide instructional practices, though it has been reported to limit the service-provider's expectations for learning.
2. To guide placement, though it often has led to education in separate classrooms or segregated service settings like sheltered workshops, day programs, residences, and leisure programs that are organized by IQ levels.
3. To authorize public and private services, funding, insurance, etc. needed by students and clients, though many who qualify for the diagnosis of mental retardation and need only intermittent support do not seek or accept the label and therefore do not qualify for support (Edgerton, 1990; MacMillan, Gresham, Siperstein, & Bocian, 1996; Polloway et al., 1997).

Over the past decade, our school practices for diagnosing mental retardation and placing individuals in special education contrast with these assumed purposes of labeling. We have seen several trends by schools. First, in many states there has been an increasing tendency to avoid the mental retardation label (i.e., a reduction by 38% in 1993–94) as a means for obtaining school services, and to assign the LD label (an increase by 207% in 1993–94) (MacMillan et al., 1996; Smith, 1997). Thus, in many states and schools, the "service-getting" purpose of the mental retardation label appears to have been abandoned because of the bleak prognosis it has had for educators, the stigma it carries, and the separate placement it typically leads to. The LD label, which offers more optimism to educators, has been substituted, although, many feel, inappropriately (Gottlieb, Alter, Gottlieb, & Wishner, 1994; MacMillan et al, 1996; MacMillan, Gresham, Bocian, & Lambros, 1998). This trend indicates that while IQ is assessed, it has not been used to make classification decisions; achievement scores have been substituted to classify many such individuals for special education (MacMillan et al., 1996).

A second trend is "overrepresentation" or the tendency to overidentify school-aged African-American and Native American individuals as being mentally retarded and to place them in special education self-contained classrooms intended to serve students so labeled. While ethnic disproportionality has been reported to have declined since the 1980s, it is still a national concern (Coutinho & Oswald, 2000). The reasons stated in the literature for overplacing African American students into special education classrooms are many, including: prejudice, inappropriate assessment and diagnostic practices, lack of understanding by staff of cultural differences, and problems at all stages of the special education process (less frequent use of prereferral strategies, overreferral, errors in eligibility testing, etc.). Overrepresentation has been reported as occurring far more often in primarily white districts than in primarily African American districts (Oswald, Coutinho, Best, & Nguyen, 2001).

Psychologists and other clinicians.

The purpose of the mental retardation definition most often referred to by clinicians is to differentiate individuals with this condition from those without and to classify the former group as having mental retardation. Clinicians hold that the label serves to provide family members and professionals with information about an individual's thinking ability, adaptive behavior, and social competence, to make predictions about prognosis, and to classify individuals for services and supports. These purposes are realized when the definition is decisive and valid, although there is disagreement among clinicians as to what characterizes a "decisive and valid" definition (e.g., Greenspan, 1997; MacMillan, Gresham, & Siperstein, 1993, 1995). The following definition characteristics have been identified as important:

1. The mental retardation label rests upon a definition which has professional consensus.
2. Valid measures, suited to the definition and the population, are used.
3. The diagnostic process to classify individuals into this category is reliably followed.
4. Consensual, clinical judgment with the appropriate safeguards is drawn upon to supplement test scores or is used when scores are deemed questionable or invalid.

Following the publication of the 1992 AAMR definition (Luckasson et al., 1992), there was extensive discussion regarding these purposes and whether or not the 1992 definition could fulfill them (e.g., Greenspan, 1997; Gresham, MacMillan, & Siperstein, 1995; MacMillan et al., 1996; Reiss, 1994; Smith, 1997). Critics of the definition cited continuing problems with the following:

1. Eligibility procedures (IQ cutoff, application of adaptive areas, etc.).
2. Valid measures (adaptive behavior skill areas, support).
3. Categorization within mental retardation by levels or degrees of disability or, alternately, by etiology or support needs.
4. The decision process for determining supports.
5. Overrepresentation in diagnosis and classification of minority groups.
6. Using the construct of adaptive behavior or adaptive skills rather than a tripartite model of adaptive behavior or intelligence.
7. Segregated placement of students with mental retardation for educational services (Greenspan, 1997; MacMillan et al., 1996; Polloway et al., 1997).

The 2002 definition (Luckasson et al., 2002) responded to some of these concerns by incorporating recent measurement research and making the diagnosis of mental retardation more precise.

Researchers.

For researchers, the purpose of the mental retardation definition and label is to classify people with as little error as possible into two groups: those who have mental retardation and those who do not. These groups should have distinguishable and meaningful differences from each other in both intellectual functioning and adaptive behavior. Furthermore, many researchers in the field of mental retardation have relied upon a second sorting process—sorting by an individual's "level of functioning," which is traditionally based on assessed IQ but assumes further differentiation by learning potential, capacity for independence and social competence, etiology, etc. Researchers tend to agree that the definition and process used to assign the label must be widely accepted, rest on valid measures, and be applied with good reliability. When any of these characteristics are missing, it is believed by some that research on the population labeled as being mentally retarded will be flawed. Hodapp (1995) reasons in this vein: Because "[a]ny definition of mental retardation affects research," the changes present in the 1992 AAMR definition are capable of seriously incapacitating research progress in the field of mental retardation (p. 24). At the same time, other researchers have pointed out that there is no true definition of mental retardation. "Scientists already had produced eight different AAMR definitions" before the 1992 definition (Reiss, 1994, p. 5).

In the 2002 AAMR definition (Luckasson et al., 2002), a framework for the role of assessment in mental retardation was described that set forth three functions: diagnosis, classification, and the planning of needed supports. Each function not only serves identified purposes (for example, diagnosis establishes eligibility for services) but is addressed through the use of specific measurement tools and considerations for accurate assessment. This approach enables researchers, for example, to group participants by their IQ scores, adaptive behavior ranges, or support needs.

Courts and law enforcement agencies.

A diagnosis of mental retardation can affect the outcomes of a legal case by alerting judicial personnel to accommodations or protections needed by the accused or by the victim. Thus the criminal justice system has a history of looking to the mental retardation label and definition for precision in differentiating those who have mental retardation from those who do not. Still, not all states have treated those found guilty of serious crimes differently if they have the label of mental retardation. For example, prior to the *Atkins* Supreme Court decision, only 13 of the 38 states with death penalty laws prohibited executions of convicts with mental retardation; 44 persons with mental retardation in U.S. prisons have been executed since 1976 (Keyes, Edwards, & Perske, 2002). In *Atkins* v. *Virginia*, 122 S.Ct. 2242 (June 20, 2002), the Supreme Court concluded that "the execution of any individual with mental retardation violated the Eighth Amendment's prohibition on cruel and unusual punishment" and therefore prohibited all such executions (Ellis, 2002, p. 2). In time, as states reform their practices to match this decision and incorporate the more precise 2002 AAMR standards for diagnosing mental retardation, the *Atkins* decision will have an impact.

Similarly, people with the mental retardation label who experience our legal systems as victims or defendants do so more frequently than is expected and often go unrecognized and without needed accommodations (Conley, Luckasson, & Bouthilet, 1992; Denno, 1997; Ellis & Luckasson, 1985).

Past use of the mental retardation label has been criticized, sometimes unfairly, by lawyers and judges on many counts:

1. Imprecision in the definition and measurement of adaptive behavior.
2. Imprecision in the measurement of IQ (e.g., scores that change with each retesting; standard error which makes an individual's resultant IQ score ambiguous).
3. Disagreement over an IQ "cutoff."
4. Disagreement between experts about the competence of an individual and its assessment and an individual's ability to give consent.

Prior to reaching the courtroom, and once there, people who have had a label of mental retardation during their school years typically deny that label, do not volunteer information on their disability, and may attempt to cover the disability to avoid the stigma associated with mental retardation (Ellis & Luckasson, 1985). Other characteristics that have been documented in persons with mental retardation include a low tolerance for frustration, deficient self-esteem, social ineptness, a motivation to please those in authority and to be liked, credulity or gullibility, and a tendency to acquiesce to the expectations and desires of others, particularly to those in authority (Conley et al., 1992; Greenspan, 1999). These characteristics may cause individuals to confess to crimes they did not commit, to be inconsistent, or to agree to a level of guilt they are not responsible for. Often, even if identified as being mentally retarded, no accommodations are made for such individuals as they enter the legal system. Numerous aspects of the legal process may be confusing to people with mental retardation and require significant accommodations and protection, such as understanding one's legal rights and advocating for them, avoiding confusion over basic legal terms and the legal process, and being easily "led" by police and lawyers during questioning.

To address these well-documented facts about individuals with mental retardation inappropriately served by our legal system and to realize the purpose the legal system ascribes to the mental retardation label, several goals need to be realized:

1. Consensus on the definition among professionals in the field.
2. Improvement in the diagnostic process and the validity of using the label.
3. Improved understanding of mental retardation and an awareness of simple, informal screening methods to check victims or suspects early in the legal process.
4. Accommodations and support available for people suspected of having or diagnosed as having mental retardation.

Policymakers.

Policymakers, like most individuals in our criminal justice system, rely upon a categorization process that determines who has and who does not have mental retardation. From policymakers' viewpoints, the purposes of the definition and label are twofold: to identify those who qualify for public (and private) services, funding, insurance, etc., so that tax-supported services go to the right people, and to provide such individuals with any needed accommodations and adaptations so that their basic rights under the constitution and state law are not violated. Typically, bureaucratic systems for matching people with tax-funded services lead to rigidity in applying the qualifying criteria despite the relative nature of these criteria. Greenspan (1999, p. 10) noted that "as the experience of nearly a century has shown, no amount of tinkering with the IQ ceiling will completely solve the problem of determining who actually has or does not have mental retardation." Thus, systems that determine if someone qualifies for the label are both rigid at any point in time and changing across time in ways that surpass the sophistication of our psychological measures and diagnostic practices.

Conclusion

Even when accepted procedures are followed, the diagnosis of mental retardation, as with other broad disability labels (emotional disturbance, learning disabilities), is not made without error. Though many would like it not to be, the concept of mental retardation is imprecise. Still, most professionals in the field of mental retardation hold that the condition is of lifelong duration for the majority who have the label; but they also tend to agree that a diagnosis made at one time may be inaccurate at a later time. Professionals outside the field of mental retardation are less clear about these exceptions. The reasons for these inaccuracies involve the following:

1. Changes in the diagnostic criteria.
2. Errors in the initial diagnosis (e.g., unqualified diagnostician, inappropriate test) or in diagnoses made at a later point.
3. Changes in the individual such that an early diagnosis no longer applies (e.g., a curing treatment for a person with a severe seizure disorder; an effective communication system for a person with extensive cerebral palsy; someone who leaves school, fits into a community, and functions adequately in new environments without additional supports) (Luckasson et al., 1992).

Thus while some of the categorization problems we have discussed relate to measurement imprecision, error, and diagnostic criteria, other categorization "problems" relate to individuals' unique nature, their supports, and their life circumstances.

Among the groups we have discussed (consumers, families, and the array of professionals), there is some agreement that the purpose of the mental retardation label is to explain the condition and to obtain appropriate services and supports. However, these groups differ in how valuable they regard the "explanation." While the label may predict difficulties in learning basic skills, when it is used in making routine judgments about one's daily life, and about what is socially appropriate, it is applied to an immensely heterogeneous group of people. Furthermore, the label tends to be rejected by society because of its connotations of extensive incompetence, its gloomy outlook, and its tendency to lower others' expectations for the individual. Currently, the label of mental retardation fails one of the questions that names or labeling terms are meant to address: "Does this term contribute positively to the portrayal of people with the disability?" (Luckasson & Reeve, 1999, p. 3). Finally, there are differences of opinion among these groups (consumers, parents, and professionals) as to whether the label yields services and supports and, when provided, how appropriate those services and supports actually are. In the next section, we review some of the effects of being labeled "mentally retarded."

What Are the Effects of Having a Label of Mental Retardation?

Research Findings About the Label's Impact

Research findings about the impact of the mental retardation label have been mixed, leading some to conclude that "the demonstrated negative effects of labels have not been sufficient to outweigh the useful political [applications] (e.g., marshaling point for families and supporters), economic [applications] (e.g., the identification of a group of people who need special services), and clinical applications" (Hastings, 1994, p. 363). A different conclusion may be reached, however, if one only examines research that has investigated the effect of the label from the consumer's perspective. Landmark studies from the 1960s and 1970s (Brigansky & Brigansky, 1971; Castles, 1979, 1996; Edgerton, 1967; Mercer, 1978), as well as more current investigations (Bogdan & Taylor, 1994; Edgerton, 1993) and writings (Dudley, 1997; Lefkowitz, 1997), reveal the powerful stigmatizing effect this label has had for many consumers.

Castles (1996) concludes that while researchers may debate the severity of this stigma, people who have this label do not. Their perceptions of the term mentally retarded are "strong and clear; overwhelmingly, persons with mild and moderate retardation believe that others view their disability in starkly negative terms" (Castles, 1996, pp. 99–100). The label of mental retardation creates a "cloak of incompetence" (Bogdan & Taylor, 1994), as the stigma derived from the stereotypes and myths surrounding this label overwhelms all other characteristics of the individual (Dudley, 1997).

Consumer's Perspectives About the Label's Impact

In order to heighten our awareness of the consumer's perspective, we met individually with three adults in their 30s and 40s who had this label and lived in semi-independent community settings. Their descriptions of its impact on them coincide with the first-person accounts provided in other studies (Bogdan & Taylor, 1994; Castles, 1979, 1996; Edgerton, 1967, 1993). We believe that these effects can best be described in the consumers' own words (their actual names are not used).

Emotional reactions: "It really hurts."

All of the individuals we interviewed expressed strong emotional reactions to the label of "mental retardation" and indicated that they would never use the word to describe anyone due to the "hurt" it causes.

> Some people use the word mental retardation wrong. . . . They are talking about you, just like if they use "the 'N' word" with a black man. It really hurts . . . because they don't want to hear something like that, they would rather hear something like "disability." . . . You got to watch how you use different words. . . . It can bring a person down so low that you wouldn't believe it. That is just the

way it is. It hurts a lot of people. I've been around a lot of people who have had it and it's just not right. (Ralph, a formerly institutionalized man in his 40s who lives by himself in an apartment and has the label of mental retardation, in Snell & Voorhees, 1998)

I never use it [the word mental retardation] around them . . . because inside of me, it told me that if I said it, it would hurt their feelings . . . it would make them very angry . . . so I am very careful about what I am saying around people. There are people who are blind . . . I don't call them any names . . . I appreciate the way they are. (Joseph, a man in his 30s who lives in a group home and has the label of mental retardation, in Snell & Voorhees, 1998)

[It makes me] mad. . . . I don't know why they use it . . . you should ask Sam [my boyfriend] . . . they say, "You must be slow because you are with her." [That makes me feel] sort of let down. . . . [When someone called me that] I just told Sam to just get me away from them and he did. (Mildred, a women in her 30s who lives in a group home and has the label of mental retardation, in Snell & Voorhees, 1998)

Stigmatizing effect: "Sort of an outcast."

Each person we talked with voiced the defiling effects of this term. They gave concrete descriptions of its stigmatizing effect on people—that it made them feel blemished and displaced. Similar reactions, indicating the pain of coping with the stigma created by this label, have been reported in other studies investigating this topic. For example,

the word "retarded" is a word. What it does is put people in a class. . . . We're on one side of the wall and the stone throwers on the other. (Ed, a formerly institutionalized young adult living in the community who has the label of mental retardation, in Bogdan & Taylor, 1994, p. 77)

A lot of people on the outside world would run and make fun at retarded people, . . . but when you get in the position of being the person they are making fun of, it's different. That's why I won't poke fun at anybody. I have lived with that. I understand that if I had somebody poke fun at me I wouldn't like it. (Pattie, a formerly institutionalized young adult living in the community who has the label of mental retardation, in Bogdan & Taylor, 1994, p. 199)

I think I was sort of an outcast, because when I was growing up everyone was calling me retarded. It was hard for me to deal with. (Ward, 1990, p. 9)

I don't believe anyone from the hospital has it easy outside. There's problems from being in that place. I mean with the people you meet. They take me as if I'm not a smart person. That's what makes me so provoked. And I mean they act like I don't understand things, which I do understand things. That's a terrible thing: I'd never do that to anybody. I don't know why I have to suffer like this. Sometimes I'd rather be dead than have people act like I'm not a smart person. (An adult woman, Edgerton, 1967, p. 206)

Dudley (1997) provides the analogy that "stigma is to people with a mental retardation label what racism is to African Americans and other ethnic minority groups. . . . Stigma is pervasive, thwarts the opportunity for a normalized lifestyle, and separates persons with this label from the mainstream and into a 'mentally retarded' world" (Dudley, 1997, p. 9).

Limited expectations: "I fooled them."

The label not only affects a person emotionally, but it influences other's expectations of them and their resulting interactions. When asked to define the label, the individuals who we spoke with emphasized its "can't do" characteristics, which carried limited expectations. For example:

> I didn't go [to high school] because they thought I would never learn nothing. But don't get me wrong, I fooled them. I am a fast learner and get along with people. . . . I fooled them, I can do it. I can drive a car, a tractor, a skidloader. I get my hands on anything and I can do it. (Joseph in Snell & Voorhees, 1998)

> I don't know, maybe I used to be retarded. That's what they say anyway. I wish they could see me now. I wonder what they'd say if they could see me holding down a regular job and doing all kinds of things. I bet they wouldn't believe it. (Ed in Bogdan & Taylor, 1994, p. 92)

> The worst word that I hate is to be called retarded. That's because I am not retarded. Anyone that says that doesn't understand the way I can carry myself, and understand myself, and take care of myself. I don't call anybody retarded that can do that. I might call that needing professional help, but I wouldn't say she was retarded. (Pattie in Bogdan & Taylor, 1994, p. 200)

Disassociation: "I never thought of myself as a retarded individual."

The stigma associated with the label of mental retardation is so injurious, that people with this label disassociate themselves from it (Bogdan & Taylor, 1994; Dudley, 1997; Edgerton, 1967, 1993). It is their "ultimate horror" to be referred to in this manner (Edgerton, 1967, 1993).

> I never thought of myself as a retarded individual, but who would want to? I never really had that ugly feeling down deep. (Ed in Bogdan & Taylor, 1994, p. 86)

They define mental retardation as someone who "can't do much of anything" and is dependent on others for assistance.

> Handicapped means more like mental retardation. It's more like when you can't move . . . or do much of anything. . . . I would use mental retardation if I couldn't do nothing. I can do something, so that means I have a disability. That means I can work. If I can work then I got a disability—I don't have mental retardation. (Ralph in Snell & Voorhees, 1998)

> Mental retardation means the nerve in your body is not functioning. Your brain is not functioning and you cannot speak clear, reading is not clear, writing is not clear. Some of them will never walk, talk, pick up a soda by themselves . . . plus feed themselves or take a shower. (Joseph in Snell & Voorhees, 1998)

Some people with mental retardation can work; some people can speak, some people can cook. You would have to teach them how to do that. They could learn; it would be a lot harder than it would for me because they came into life having mental retardation. (Ralph in Snell & Voorhees, 1998)

Real retarded people . . . unfortunately can't do much of nothing really . . . they have to be taken care of. They have to depend on other people all the time, like to help them get up, or help them cook something, you know, or something like that. (Interview with a person in a sheltered workshop, Lorber, 1974, p. 86 in Castles, p. 102)

[Mental retardation] what does it mean? I don't know. . . . [I've heard the word] many times, at the [sheltered] workshop, the supper club, around the parties, and when I go out on dates. I hate [the word] handicap. It means you can't do anything by yourself. (Mildred in Snell & Voorhees, 1998)

These personal insights point to the demeaning and devastating effect of the label on those who carry it. The viewpoints of these individuals have consensus with those set forth by self-advocacy organizations (e.g., People First): The negative effects of the label outweigh any positive results. For these reasons, some have called for an abandonment of labeling (Bogdan & Taylor, 1994). Others have proposed that the negative effects may be mediated by changing the label to a term with more positive connotations (Edgerton, 1967, 1993; Hastings, 1994). We think that change needs to be more systemic. To quote Goldfarb (1990, p. v): "linguistic reform without systemic change conceals unhappy truths." The recommendations we will set forth next for the field of mental retardation in the 21st century emerge both from the varying purposes that groups have for the definition and label and from the effects consumers have described.

WHAT RECOMMENDATIONS CAN BE MADE FOR THE 21ST CENTURY?

Gelb (1997) offers some helpful ways to understand the contrasting purposes that stakeholders have for definitions and labels like mental retardation. For some, the primary way of understanding human characteristics involves *typological thinking,* which is the tendency to classify people into "fixed, immutable types" or distinct, measurable categories in order to identify and assign global traits, to allocate services and educational programs, and to organize research investigations (Gelb, p. 448, 1997) (Table 5.1). For others, the primary way of thinking about people is as unique organisms requiring individualization. This perspective reflects *population thinking* or the tendency to focus on the singular qualities of individuals, not the means within groups, in order to clarify these differences and provide individualized services and supports (Table 5.1).

Over this past century, our definitions of mental retardation have gradually replaced some of their typological features (e.g., the IQ test as infallible; mental retardation as an incurable, global trait) with features reflecting population thinking (e.g., the need to assess *current* levels of functioning; adaptive-behavior functioning as a critical characteristic which compares to normative standards in a given community). Both of the most recent AAMR definitions (Luckasson et al., 1992, 2002) take on more features of "population thinking" with an emphasis on individualization of limitations and support needs (Luckasson et al., 1992, p. 10).

> Mental retardation is not a *trait*, although it is influenced by certain characteristics of capabilities of the individual. . . . Rather, mental retardation is a *state* in which functioning is impaired in certain specific ways. This distinction between *trait* and *state* is central to understanding how the present definition broadens the concept of mental retardation and how it shifts the emphasis from measurement of traits to understanding the individual's actual functioning in daily living.

The compelling accounts of consumers quoted earlier reinforce the lasting typological influences on the mental retardation label which communicate a global trait of incompetence, leading to the following:

1. Minimal expectations of a person who "can't do much of anything."
2. Stigmatizing effects on consumers (and family members).
3. Pernicious and emotional reactions from those so-labeled and their disassociation from the label.

Table 5.1
Changing emphases during and following the diagnosis of mental retardation.

The Diagnosis Process: Eligibility and Labeling	The Postdiagnosis Process: Support and Intervention
<ul><li>Involves *typological thinking* or a focus on sorting people into groups that differ from other groups of people. Emphasis is on measurement of psychological characteristics (IQ and adaptive behavior)</li><li>Attention given to test performance and scores, identified limitations, and observations by team members (family and various professionals) in comparison to category standards and "cutoffs"</li><li>Discrimination of an individual's shortcomings and their match with population characteristics</li><li>Identification of etiology and associated psychological and medical characteristics</li><li>Emphasis on diagnosis: finding a label that fits measured characteristics</li><li>Less tolerance for ambiguity in the process</li></ul>	<ul><li>Involves *population thinking* or a focus on individual characteristics and current functioning</li><li>Emphasis is on discussion of strengths and weaknesses in the individual's functional skills and abilities across home, school, work, and community environments by team members (consumer, family, friends, and various professionals)</li><li>Team determination of support needs and intensity across life dimensions: intelligence and adaptive behavior, psychological, etiological, health, and environmental dimensions</li><li>Current functioning and needed supports drive the process, not diagnostic labels</li><li>Tolerance for ambiguity exists in the team process</li></ul>

In short, the label devalues and "marginalizes" those who are so identified. These realities lead us to make several recommendations regarding the 1992 definition of mental retardation, the process used to define mental retardation, and the future of mental retardation as a field or construct.

Seek Labels with a Positive Connotation

First, a new label is needed that has a more positive connotation. We cannot ignore the consumer's aversion to the label of mental retardation. The right of minority groups to select the name by which they wish to be called is respected in our society (Castle, 1996). The same regard has not been provided to those currently labeled with mental retardation.

Even as we make this recommendation we recognize some problems. The tendency for labels with neutral denotations or explicit meanings to take on negative connotations or implied meanings over time is well documented (Goldfarb, 1990; Hastings, 1994). We agree with Goldfarb (1990) "linguistic reform alone can't really change the world" (p. v). Prejudices and stigma stand no chance of change unless societal attitudes and values are considered the primary focus for change. We also concur with Baroff (1991): "labels cannot erase biologically determined differences, [but] the connotations that they evoke can affect the means through which those differences can be diminished" (Baroff, 1991, p. 100). In today's world the label "retarded" may not produce the types of services that are in the person's best interests (Bogdan & Taylor, 1994). As Ed, a person with this label, explains:

> It's very hard to go through life with a label. You have to fight constantly. Retarded is just a word. We have to separate individuals from the word. We use words like "retarded" because of habit—just like going shopping every week and getting up in the morning. The word "retarded" has to be there if you are going to give people help, but what the hell is the sense of calling someone retarded and not giving them anything? (Ed in Bogdan & Taylor, 1994, p. 77)

Every new term employed to label a stigmatic group of people is fated for eventual disposal as it accrues the negative connotations of the old labels (Dudley, 1997; Hastings, 1994). Still, we hold, this tendency does not justify maintaining the status quo. One future step that may be taken to select and prolong the utility of new terminology is to establish an empirical basis for selecting a label with more positive connotations. Research that compares the connotations of different labels and their effects on persons so labeled should provide a better means for selecting terminology (Hastings, 1994). Another critical step is to involve the people who have this label and their families in determining the preferred nomenclature (Dudley, 1997; Hastings, 1994). Additionally, these new names/labels should be simpler, easier to say, respectful but perhaps self-evident, and adopted with a goal of being widely accepted and understood (Goldfarb, 1990; Hastings, 1994).

Use Labels Only During the Diagnostic Process

Second, the label should be used solely during the diagnosis and classification process (the evaluation and eligibility phase) and be dropped after diagnosis (during the support phase) when planning for individualized supports and intervention programs. This recommendation is consistent with the logic that *typological thinking*—groups of humans differ fundamentally from other groups—is part of the diagnostic process; but it is only

population thinking—focusing on individual characteristics and current functioning—
that is essential to the planning of individualized supports. Accurate labeling (categorization) still seems necessary for diagnostic purposes such as determination of eligibility,
appropriation of services and funding, and implementation of the *Atkins* decision. But we
question the value of labels at times when teams are planning support provision. The heterogeneity within the group labeled as mentally retarded (and in subgroups labeled by
level of functioning) is so great that these labels serve little purpose during the postdiagnostic phase when supports are being planned. Information on the specific individual's
educational, environmental, medical, and psychological characteristics is drawn into the
postdiagnostic phase to plan supports. Disability labels and functioning level labels shift
the team's focus in several ways that work against planning supports:

1. From an individual's strengths or what he or she actually "can do" to a focus on
   distinguishing group deficits, averaged traits, and typically negative characteristics (what they "can't do").
2. From an individual's particular needs at a given time under individualized conditions of existing support (or lack of it) to a focus on generic needs associated with
   the label (e.g., someone functioning at a "mild" level needs a mild or "educable"
   curriculum and a classroom and teacher to match).

While the reliance on neat categories to plan supports may seem easier and more efficient,
it is the direct opposite of our cultural values (Goldfarb, 1990) and of our goals for providing services to people with disabilities. Ralph, a person with the label of mental retardation, states that

> you got to look at the person that has mental retardation and that you are working with and you have got to tell him: "Don't say no [that] you can't do this" . . .
> because you don't want them to say that . . . you want to build his strength up
> instead of coming down. (Ralph in Snell & Voorhees, 1998)

This recommendation to use labels only during the diagnostic phase is compatible with
the stance of the largest professional group in special education, the Council for
Exceptional Children (CEC). CEC's current professional standards call for the redesign of
teacher education programs so teachers learn that instruction and grouping for instruction should be driven by students' strengths and needs, not by their categorical identification (*CEC Today*, 1998, p. 9). For years, teacher education programs and direct services
for children with disabilities aged birth to 5 have emphasized individualized programs for
a mix of students with special needs, without division into categorical groups (Luckasson
et al., 1996). The 1997 reauthorization on IDEA extended schools' authority to provide
noncategorical services to children with developmental delays through age 8. In many
public schools practicing inclusion today, the student's team individualizes its planning for
inclusion, and avoids a "one size fits all" approach. Thus individualized special education
services and supports follow a student into the general education classroom, and being
included does not preclude the use of individually planned "pull out services" (in a
resource classroom or through school-based or community-based instruction).

We contend that this recommendation for using labels only during the diagnostic phase takes a step in the right direction and that other public and private agencies and organizations should follow this lead. When an individual's strengths and needs drive the postdiagnostic or support process:

> [W]e shift attention from the deficiencies of the person to those of the society and service systems. Thus, we cease to ask what is wrong with the person and begin to ask what kinds of environments and services we can create to be able to accommodate all persons in the society, to treat them with respect, and permit them dignity. Most important, when we abandon labels, we are forced to listen to those whose perspective we have ignored and to take what they have to say seriously. (Bogdon & Taylor, 1994, pp. 224–25)

Definitions Need Diagnostic and Support Processes

Third, the definition and classification procedures in our field should continue to employ a diagnostic process for eligibility and categorization and a postdiagnosis or support process to define an individualized support profile. The 1992 manual modified our procedures from simply providing a definition of mental retardation for diagnostic purposes to providing a comprehensive process that focuses on diagnosis, classification, and intervention (Polloway, 1997). While this shift has generated much controversy, we contend that it leads to an interdisciplinary or multidimensional understanding of mental retardation and a definition that is relevant to consumers, because skills and supports are the focus. As noted by Reiss (1994, p. 6) "Consumers have indicated in one forum after another that they desire inclusion, access, and independence."

Earlier, we reviewed the criticisms of some psychologists and researchers that the 1992 AAMR definition suffered from having no research base, being advocacy motivated, being imprecise, and lacking valid measures—limitations, these individuals claim, that greatly diminish the definition's value to them. The 2002 AAMR definition intended to respond to those criticisms and incorporates improved psychometric precision.

> There will never be a flawless definition of mental retardation, nor will there be universal agreement on any given definition. Definers of this construct, however sophisticated, cannot be free from some arbitrariness; but every definition of mental retardation has significant impact on the lives of many individuals. Thus it is critical that those who revise definitions of constructs like mental retardation seriously contemplate the comments of users and consumers as well as strive for improvement in accuracy and correspondence with current understanding of human functioning. (Luckasson et al., 2002, p. 36)

Judgments from the field on the 10th edition have not yet been published. Each time the field reexamines and rewrites the definition, we stand on the shoulders of an existing definition and feel the historical effects of several others. There is always an agenda for discussion and for research that might improve our efforts. For example, the diagnostic phase in mental retardation could be improved by developing better measures, lending more clarity to the construct of intelligence (e.g., perhaps as a tripartite model that omits adaptive behavior, Greenspan, 1997), and reaching consensus on clinical judgment. Improving the diagnostic phase will help meet the primary purpose most groups identify for the definition: *accuracy in diagnosis*. To the extent that the postdiagnosis process of identifying types of supports and their needed intensities is better defined and is shown to yield improved consumer outcomes, the second purpose of definitions is more likely to be met: *that the label yield meaningful supports and improved outcomes*.

Changing Language Is Not Enough

Fourth, a change in the label must be accompanied by systemic changes in society in order to have a true effect on stigma and improve the quality of life for persons who are so labeled. As Edgerton (1993) notes: "the label is only one consideration in shaping the life of a person; the socialization that goes along with it is much more formative" (p. 223). Hughes and Carter (2000), Snell and Janney (2000), and Dudley (1997) are several of many authors who provide specific suggestions for promoting this change, based on their work with persons who have the label of mental retardation:

1. Support the acceptance of these individuals at school through ability/disability awareness activities, peer support programs, and individually meaningful inclusion in general education classrooms and school activities.
2. Teach using cooperative group methods and peer and cross-age tutoring.
3. Increase social interaction, social support, and relationships among people with and without disabilities.
4. Teach individuals how to promote their own social acceptance.
5. Hold group discussions about stigma issues with persons who are labeled and seek their recommendations for change.
6. Increase choices and decision making.
7. Promote self-determination and self-advocacy.
8. Eliminate stigma in our schools and service systems (e.g., separate classrooms and wings for disability programs, in appropriate agency names and their public display; the practice of segregated social events for people with disabilities).
9. Help those who can leave the system.

While the far-reaching effects of expanded social networks and positive relationships between people with mental retardation and those without have been extensively documented, we are only beginning to understand the benefits of self-advocacy. These two changes alone would go far to replace prejudice with positive attitudes emanating from experience.

A Dynamic Process

Fifth, defining the concept of mental retardation must not be viewed as a static process. Our concept of mental retardation has been and should continue to be influenced both by changes in our society and by the advances in the field (e.g., the development of psychometric techniques relevant to individuals now labeled with mental retardation and effective intervention strategies to support these individuals) (Denning et al., 2000). As Reiss (1994) points out, there is not one "true" definition of mental retardation; definitions have changed over time, often as an exercise in public policy. Definitions will continue to change in the 21st century. While the 9th and the 10th AAMR definitions were heavily influenced by consumers' desire for inclusion, access, and independence (Reiss, 1994), future definitions will be shaped by additional societal influences.

Smith's (1997) observations on definition and labeling provide an appropriate conclusion for this paper:

> The effort to define mental retardation in a way that is as scientifically accurate as possible continues. The effort to define it in a way that promotes greater sensitivity to the needs of people with mental retardation also continues. The successful resolution of the tension between meeting these two goals will determine the future of a social construct that promotes care rather than control for the people whose lives are central to this construction. (p. 172)

REFERENCES

Baroff, G. S. (1992). What's in a name: A comment on Goldfarb's guest editorial. *American Journal on Mental Retardation, 96*, 99–100.

Baxter, C., & Cummins, R. A. (1992). Community integration and parental coping. *International Journal of Rehabilitation Research, 15,* 289–300.

Bogdan, R., & Taylor, S. J. (1994). *The social meaning of mental retardation: Two life stories.* New York: Columbia University Teachers College Press.

Brigansky, D., & Brigansky, B. (1971). *Hansels and Gretels.* New York: Holt, Rinehart, & Winston.

Bristol, M. M., & Schopler, E. (1984). A developmental perspective on stress and coping in families of autistic children. In J. Blacker (Ed.), *Severe handicapped young children and their families* (pp. 91–141). New York: Academic Press.

Castles, E. E. (1996). *"We're people first": The social and emotional lives of individuals with mental retardation.* Westport, CT: Praeger.

Conley, R., Luckasson, R., & Bouthilet, G. (1992). *The criminal justice system and mental retardation: Defenders and victims.* Baltimore: Paul H. Brookes.

Council for Exceptional Children Today. (1998). Multicategorical framework approved. *CEC Today, 5*(1), 1, 9.

Coutinho, M. J., & Oswald, D. P. (2000). Disproportionate representation in special education: A synthesis and recommendations. *Journal of Child and Family Studies, 9,* 135–156.

Denning, C. B., Chamberlain, J. A., & Polloway, E. A. (2000). An evaluation of state guidelines for mental retardation: Focus on definition and classification practices. *Education and Training in Mental Retardation and Developmental Disabilities, 35,* 226–232.

Denno, D. W. (1997). Sexuality, rape, and mental retardation. *University of Illinois Law Review, 1997*(2), 315–434.

Dever, R. B. (1990). Defining mental retardation from an instructional perspective. *Mental Retardation, 28,* 147–153.

Dudley, J. (1997). *Confronting the stigma in their lives: Helping people with a mental retardation label.* Springfield, IL: Charles C. Thomas.

Edgerton, R. B. (1967). *The cloak of competence* (Rev. ed.). Berkeley: University of California Press.

Edgerton, R. B. (1990). Quality of life from a longitudinal research perspective. In R. L. Schalock (Ed.), *Quality of life: Perspectives and issues* (pp. 149–160). Washington, DC: American Association on Mental Retardation.

Edgerton, R. B. (1993). *The cloak of competence: Revised and updated.* Berkley: University of California Press.

Ellis, J. W. (2002). *Mental retardation and the death penalty: A guide to state legislative issues.* Albuquerque: University of New Mexico School of Law.

Ellis, J. W., & Luckasson, R. A. (1985). Mentally retarded criminal defendants. *The George Washington Law Review, 53,* 414–493.

Gelb, S.A. (1997). The problem of typological thinking in mental retardation. *Mental Retardation, 35*, 448–457.

Goldfarb, M. (1990). Guest editorial. *American Journal on Mental Retardation, 95*, v–vi.

Gottlieb, J., Alter, M., Gottlieb, B. W., & Wishner, J. (1994). Special education in urban America: It's not justifiable for many. *Journal of Special Education, 27*, 453–465.

Greenspan, S. (1997). Dead manual walking? Why the 1992 AAMR definition needs redoing. *Education and Training in Mental Retardation and Developmental Disabilities, 32*, 179–190.

Greenspan, S. (1999). What is meant by mental retardation? *International Review of Psychiatry, 11*, 6–18.

Gresham, F. M., MacMillan, D. L., & Siperstein, G. N. (1995). Critical analysis of the 1992 AAMR definition: Implications for school psychology. *School Psychology Quarterly, 10*, 1–19.

Hastings, R. P. (1994). On "good" terms: Labeling people with mental retardation. *Mental Retardation, 32,* 363–365.

Hodapp, R. M. (1995). Definitions in mental retardation: Effects on research, practice, and perceptions. *School Psychology Quarterly, 10*, 24–28.

Hughes, C., & Carter, E. W. (2000). *The transition handbook: Strategies high school teachers use that work!* Baltimore: Paul H. Brookes.

Keyes, E., Edwards, W., & Perske, R. (2002). People with mental retardation are dying, legally: At least 44 have been executed. *Mental Retardation, 40*, 243–244.

Lefkovwitz, B. (1997). *Our guys.* New York: Vintage Books.

Luckasson, R., Borthwick-Duffy, S., Buntinx, W. H. E., Coulter, D. L., Craig, E. M., Reeve, A., et al. (2002). *Mental retardation: Definition, classification, and systems of supports* (10th ed.). Washington, DC: American Association on Mental Retardation.

Luckasson, R., Coulter, D. L., Polloway, E. A., Reiss, S., Schalock, R. L., Snell, M. E., et al. (1992). *Mental retardation: Definition, classification, and systems of supports* (9th ed.). Washington, DC: American Association on Mental Retardation.

Luckasson, R., & Reeve, A. (1999, July). *Naming, defining, and classifying in mental retardation.* Paper presented at the Task Force on Language, Washington, DC.

Luckasson, R., Schalock, R. L., Snell, M. E., & Spitalnik, D. M. (1996). The 1992 AAMR definition and preschool children: Response from the committee on terminology and classification. *Mental Retardation, 34*, 247–253.

MacMillan, D. L., Gresham, F. M., & Siperstein, G. N. (1993). Conceptual and psychometric concerns about the 1992 AAMR definition of mental retardation. *American Journal on Mental Retardation, 98*, 325–335.

MacMillan, D. L., Gresham, F. M., & Siperstein, G. N. (1995). Heightened concerns over the 1992 AAMR definition: Advocacy versus precision. *American Journal on Mental Retardation, 100*, 87–97.

MacMillan, D. L., Gresham, F. M., Siperstein, G. N., & Bocian, K. M. (1996). The labyrinth of IDEA: School decisions on referred students with subaverage general intelligence. *American Journal on Mental Retardation, 101*, 161–174.

MacMillan, D. L., Siperstein, G. N., & Gresham, F. M. (1996). A challenge to the viability of mild mental retardation as a diagnostic category. *Exceptional Children, 62*, 356–371.

Oswald, D. P., Coutinho, M. J., Best, A. M., & Nguyen, N. (2001). Impact of sociodemographic characteristics on the identification rates of minority students as having mental retardation. *Mental Retardation, 39*, 351–367.

Polloway, E. A. (1997). Developmental principles of the Luckasson et al. (1992) AAMR definition of mental retardation: A retrospective. *Education and Training in Mental Retardation and Developmental Disabilities, 32*, 174–178.

Polloway, E. A., Patton, J. R., Smith, T. E. C., & Buck, G. (1997). Mental retardation and learning disabilities: Conceptual and applied issues. *Journal of Learning Disabilities, 30*, 297–308.

Reiss, S. (1994). Issues in defining mental retardation. *American Journal on Mental Retardation, 99,* 1–7.

Schalock, R. L. (2002). Definitional issues. In R. L. Schalock, P. C. Baker, and M. D. Croser (Eds.), *Embarking on a new century: Mental retardation at the end of the 20th century* (pp. 45–66). Washington, DC: American Association on Mental Retardation.

Seligman, M., & Darling, R. B. (1989). *Ordinary families, special children.* New York: Guilford Press.

Smith, J. D. (1997). Mental retardation as an educational construct: Time for a new shared view? *Education and Training in Mental Retardation and Developmental Disabilities, 32,* 167–173.

Snell, M. E., & Janney, R. (2000). *Teachers' guides to inclusive practices: Social relationships and peer support.* Baltimore: Paul H. Brookes.

Snell, M. E., & Voorhees, M. D. (1998). *Transcribed interviews with three adults labeled as having mental retardation.* Unpublished manuscript.

Trent, J. W. (1994). *Inventing the feeble mind: A history of mental retardation in the United States.* Berkeley: University of California Press.

Ward, N. (1990). Reflections on my quality of life: Then and now. In R. L. Schalock (Ed), *Quality of life: Perspectives and issues* (pp. 9–16). Washington, DC: American Association on Mental Retardation.

CHAPTER SIX

How We Eradicated Familial (Hereditary) Mental Retardation—Updated

HERMAN H. SPITZ

INTRODUCTION

In 2003 Switzky and Greenspan edited an e-book titled *What Is Mental Retardation? Ideas for an Evolving Disability.* A year later, the contributors to that book were invited to submit their chapters to an updated version, now titled *What Is Mental Retardation? Ideas for an Evolving Disability in the 21st Century*, published in hard print rather than electronic format. This updated version would give the contributors an opportunity to comment on the new definition and classification system published in 2002 (Luckasson et al., 2002), mentioned by some authors of the Switzky and Greenspan (2003) e-book but not discussed in any great detail. This, and the opportunity to publish the book in hard print, accounts for the short interval between the e-book and this revised book. We were informed that we could, if we desired, make additions or changes to our chapters, or write a new chapter. My chapter was not originally a description of "what mental retardation is," as suggested by the e-book's title, nor is it now a "model of mental retardation." It was, and is, an examination of just one diagnostic classification of mental retardation, familial mental retardation, which I feel is being ignored for ideological reasons. Consequently the title of my original chapter is unchanged (except for the addition of "updated") and the contents of the chapter are updated by the addition of the very important paper by Spinath, Harlaar, Ronald, and Plomin (2004) on genetic influence on mild mental retardation in early childhood. That paper adds confirmatory evidence for my thesis and therefore is covered here in some depth near the end of the section on "The Evidence for Familial (Hereditary) Mental Retardation."

THE IDEOLOGICAL POSITION OF THE 1992 AND 2002 CLASSIFICATION SYSTEMS

In describing mental retardation the authors of the 1992 AAMR manual declared that it "is not something you have, like blue eyes or a bad heart" (Luckasson et al., 1992, p. 9). Then, inexplicably, they added: "Nor is it something you are, like being short or thin." Surely what we call mental retardation refers to something a person is; it refers to a person who, from an early age, has been of low intelligence.[1] We can understand their statement—that mental retardation is not something you are—only by understanding the belief system that shaped it. That belief system is initially expressed in the Preface, where the authors remark that this edition "represents a paradigm shift, from a view of mental retardation as an absolute trait expressed solely by an individual to an expression of the interaction between persons with limited intellectual functioning and the environment" (Luckasson et al., 1992, p. x). This so-called "new paradigm" (a term whose use was rather grandiose when we consider its original meaning) is at the heart of the controversy over this redefinition. It exchanges an absolutist view for relativism.

If the intellectual limitations have no real effect on functioning, then the person does not have mental retardation. This implies a certain relativity of the significance of the intellectual limitations, making it relative to the demands of the environment (see their p. 13). This kind of extreme diagnostic relativism minimizes the importance of absolutes and universals. A similar approach, manifested as extreme cultural relativism, led anthropology down a thorny garden path from which it is only now recovering (e.g., Brown, 1991).

According to the 1992 classification system, mental retardation is neither a medical nor a psychopathological disorder, because it is not a trait. Rather, it is a state, "a particular state of functioning that begins in childhood" (p. 9). To understand a person in this state requires not only knowledge of the individual's capabilities but also "an understanding of the structure and expectations of the individual's personal and social environment" (p. 9). "Mental retardation is a disability *only* as a result of this interaction [between individual capabilities and environments]" (p. 11, original italics, as are all italics in quotes unless otherwise noted).

Being a state, mental retardation is not a pervasive condition, as it would be were it a trait. People can be in a state of anger, for example, from which they recover. By the same token, the 1992 manual maintains that people who are mentally retarded when interacting with others under certain conditions are not necessarily mentally retarded in other conditions. I presume that means they are not mentally retarded when alone.

The ideological position of the 1992 manual was essentially unchanged in the 2002 revision (Luckasson, et al., 2002), although there were changes in the theoretical model in order to make it more inclusive.[2] In the 2002 classification manual mental retardation is described as "a particular state of functioning in a particular context of time and place that results from . . . ecological interactions" (Luckasson et al., 2002, p. 139). The 2002 model continued to stress and even upgraded the importance of a supports-based approach, making it a fundamental basis of classification and service delivery in the new system. Note that the levels-of-retardation schema (mild, moderate, severe, profound)—determined primarily by IQ—was no longer the only source of diagnosis in the 1992 and 2002 manuals, which used *intensities of needed support* (intermittent, limited, extensive,

1. The inclusion of impaired adaptive behavior and the problems its measurement entails, as well as the use of 18 as a delimiting age, will undoubtedly be discussed in detail by some of the other contributors. I will focus instead on how loyalty to a particular ideological frame of reference has resulted in a major omission.

2. However, the incomprehensible suggestion on page 123 of the 1992 classification manual—that facilitated communication be investigated for use with their sample case—was dropped in the 2002 edition. The flaws in this technique and its potential dangers are now indisputable (Shane, 1994; Spitz, 1997).

pervasive) in specified areas as a new schema. Readers quite naturally assumed that this new schema was a substitute for the levels of retardation. Surprisingly, however, "such substitution was never intended" (Luckasson et al., 2002, p. 30).

Clinicians' acceptance of the elimination of the old schema meant that the classification "mild mental retardation" was no longer an option and therefore—as noted by a number of critics—many such individuals have been purposely misdiagnosed as learning disabled in order to provide them with some help. This decreases the number of children diagnosed as mildly retarded—a range in which familial retardation is most frequently found—and obscures a real issue: the hereditary basis of intelligence based on the normal curve of intelligence. Note that, for the sake of precision, researchers invariably choose to stick with the venerable levels-of-retardation schema in defiance of its demotion in the 1992 and 2002 manuals.

The 2002 manual, as did the 1992 manual, avoids the topic of polygenic heredity (an inherited effect determined by more than one gene).[3] Instead, effects passed from parents to children are called "intergenerational effects," and furthermore: "Current ideas about intergenerational effects stress their origin in preventable and reversible influences of adverse environments" (Luckasson et al., 2002, p. 128). In other words, the origin of low intelligence that is passed from one generation to the next is declared in advance to be preventable and reversible—i.e., environmental. This rules out consideration of any contribution of genetic transmission. It is rather like the inebriated gentleman who despite having lost his keys elsewhere is searching for them under a street lamp because that's where the light is. He will never find his keys and we will never find a major source of low intelligence if we look only where it's more convenient or socially palatable to look.

Familial retardation, then, continued to be ignored or proscribed as a risk factor in the 2002 manual. Below, we will briefly examine the history of that benighted phrase (cultural-familial) as part of our consideration of the heredity of low intelligence.

History of a Concept

Although the relativist authors of the 1992 and 2002 manuals recognized specific, monogenic (single-gene) disorders, many of which are due to mutations and chromosomal causes and result in severe disability, they did not acknowledge the normal hereditary, polygenic contributions to the roughly bell-shaped curve of intelligence. To whatever extent this curve represents normal genetic distribution it has important consequences for the claim that familial (hereditary) processes are the largest single cause of mental retardation (followed by Fragile-X syndrome and Down syndrome).[4]

---

3. Because polygenic has come to mean many genes of so small a size that they are unidentifiable, the term is now usually replaced by quantitative trait loci (QTL), a term that "denotes multiple genes of varying effect size" (Plomin, 1997, p. 95). With that caveat in mind, I will nevertheless continue to use the term "polygenic," which more easily translates into the general point being made.

4. Fragile X syndrome, an X-linked cause of mental retardation, is a specific chromosomal disorder and therefore differs from the polygenic, hereditary mental retardation I am discussing. Down syndrome is not hereditary except for certain rare types that account for about 5% of the cases.

In ignoring the contribution of familial, hereditary processes to low intelligence, the 1992 and 2002 manuals followed the path progressively laid down by their predecessors. It is instructive to observe how the concept of familial retardation was extinguished—indeed, was made abhorrent—over the course of successive classification manuals. In finally banishing familial retardation the manuals' authors followed the early lead of an association- ist- and behaviorist-dominated psychology that for so long had denigrated genetic contributions to the variance in intelligence and embraced the idea that early environmental deprivation was the major source of low intelligence, which, consequently, could be rectified by compensatory stimulation (Bloom, 1964; Hunt, 1961). But whereas psychologists generally have come to appreciate and study the role of genes in intelligence, the mental retardation classification manuals have gone in the opposite direction.

According to Heber (1961), the first manual on terminology and classification in the United States was published in 1921, followed by editions in 1933, 1941, 1957, and 1959. A second edition of the 1959 manual was prepared, as was its predecessor, by Heber and published, with very minor changes, in 1961. I will start with the 1961 manual and follow the changing positions on heredity, which are very revealing (Baroff, 1995). In the 1961 manual, "Cultural-familial mental retardation" was included under the heading "Mental Retardation Due to Uncertain (or Presumed Psychologic) Cause with the Functional Reaction Alone Manifest" (Heber, 1961, p. 52). To be classified in the Cultural-familial category (Code 81) required not only "absence of reasonable indication of cerebral pathology" (p. 40), but also "evidence of retardation in intellectual functioning in at least one of the parents and in one or more siblings where there are such" (p. 40). This appeared to implicate hereditary processes, and indeed the manual then pointed out that "because of the parental inadequacy . . . there is usually some degree of cultural deprivation present." This deprivation is generally not severe enough "to warrant classification under *psychogenic mental retardation associated with deprivation of stimulation*" (p. 40). If not, then obviously the mental retardation must be due to unrecognized cerebral pathology or to polygenic hereditary processes. "In those cases," Heber continued, "where the cultural deprivation is of severe degree, classification under cultural-familial mental retardation takes precedence where there is a family history of intellectual subnormality" (p. 40). These assertions seemed to be a circumspect way of saying that when there is a family history of subnormality, heredity must be considered, although it is usually accompanied by environmental factors

> There is no intent in this category to specify either the independent action of, or relation between, genetic and cultural factors in the etiology of cultural-familial mental retardation. The exact role of genetic factors cannot be specified since the nature and mode of transmission of genetic aspects of intelligence is not yet understood. Similarly there is no clear understanding of the specific manner in which environmental factors operate to modify intellectual performance. (p. 40)

However, this did not prevent Heber from giving environmental deprivation its own classification and code number: "Psychogenic mental retardation associated with environmental deprivation (Code No. 82)" (p. 40). In sum, "familial," as a hereditary rather than a social term, was not permitted to stand alone but was accompanied by "cultural"—like a truculent child with a sheltering governess.

Even that did not last long. In the next revision cultural familial retardation (unhyphenated) was defined as an "obsolete term; condition of unknown etiology, presumably associated with family history of borderline intelligence or mild retardation and home environment which was either depriving or was inconsistent with the general culture" (Grossman, 1973, p. 130). The previous mention of genetic factors was dropped. Familial mental deficiency was a curiosity, "an obsolete term for a type of retardation, presumed to be polygenic, in which there is a history of borderline intelligence or mild retardation and poor accomplishments in society" (p. 137), and so on. What took the place of this obsolete term? The closest reference was a noncoded category called "Additional Medical Information Categories" under which we find "Undetermined genetic mechanism present, probably polygenetic" (p. 47), which was repeated in the 1977 revision (Grossman, 1977, p. 47). Nothing further was said about it.

The subsequent classification manual (Grossman, 1983) explained that although earlier manuals "included the term cultural-familial retardation," that term has now "been supplanted by retardation associated with sociocultural or psychosocial disadvantage. Each of these designations assigns increasing emphasis to the role of life experience in the nature-nurture equation" (p. 48). And further along in the manual:

> the polygenic model of inheritance, put forth to explain the concentration of retarded persons in the lower classes and among minority groups, enjoys less currency today. Largely, this stems from our growing awareness of the effects of early stimulation and strategies of environmental enrichment. Nevertheless, individuals vary genetically on intellectual as well physical traits, and it is highly probable that some disadvantaged people owe their retardation in large measure to genetic factors. (p. 70)

This was followed by an explanation that mental retardation is not randomly distributed among impoverished people, "but is most often encountered in families in which there is low maternal intelligence" (p. 70) and, the manual continued, although this may support the causal role of polygenic inheritance, an alternative is that the mothers cannot supply a suitable learning environment. In spite of this discussion there was no code for "polygenic inheritance," although there was one for "Psychosocial disadvantage" (p. 134).

The 1992 and 2002 manuals (Luckasson et al., 1992, 2002) excluded, as no longer acceptable to professionals in the field of mental retardation, what is arguably the largest single category of mental retardation: familial, hereditary retardation, found most frequently in the mildly retarded and borderline range. The 1992 manual did not even consider the evidence that genes contribute substantially to intellectual variance, despite the availability even then of convincing data (e.g., McGue & Bouchard, 1989; Plomin, 1986; Segal, 1985). Cultural-familial retardation (which I regard as familial retardation) was mentioned on page 126 of the 2002 manual: "biomedical risk factors may be present in people with mild retardation of cultural-familial origin" (Luckasson et al., 2002). But what did they mean by "cultural-familial"? Instead of defining it, they wanted no part of it. They simply absorbed the term into "intergenerational effects" and stressed the origin of these effects "in preventable and reversible influences of adverse environments" (p. 128). No room for genes here.

Based on this history one can readily understand (but not forgive) why recent decisions about the exclusion of familial mental retardation have nothing to do with scientific evidence. There appears to be little hope that the genetics of the normal curve will be incorporated in AAMR classification manuals as a primary source of low intelligence until knowledgeable and forthright scientists are included in future classification committees. We must have a committee that insists that decisions be based on data instead of wishful thinking. Have we not at last erected a barrier against eugenic solutions that is so indestructible that we can now freely examine, as true scientists, all the evidence, rather than selectively ignoring what we do not like?

THE EVIDENCE FOR FAMILIAL (HEREDITARY) MENTAL RETARDATION

What is the evidence that polygenic inheritance is a major cause of mental retardation, or, as Anderson (1974) put it, that "the majority of the retarded . . . represent the lower end of the multifactorial distribution of intelligence" (p. 31)? The normal curve of intelligence is interrupted when it goes below about 50 or 55 IQ, where there is a bulge in frequency produced by a larger-than-expected number of individuals suffering central nervous system damage or dysfunction caused by some specific trauma, disease, or chromosomal abnormality. Roberts (1952) judged the bulge to start below IQ 45. In response to criticism that Roberts (1952) classified subjects based on their siblings' IQs rather than their own, Nichols (1984) extracted data on severe and mild mental retardation from the sizable database of the Collaborative Perinatal Project. "Most (72%) of the severely retarded [Caucasian] children [IQs < 50] were found, when examined at age 7 years, to have severe central nervous system pathology. . . . In contrast, only 14% of the mildly retarded children [IQs 50–69]" (p. 162) had any of the same disorders. The situation was similar with African-American children. Dingman and Tarjan (1960), among many others, calculated and illustrated an intelligence curve that included this bulge.

There is, on the other hand, no evidence for a pronounced bulge in the upper range of mental retardation (IQ from about 50 to 70). In line with the Anderson quote above, and the writings of innumerable others, this suggests that the origin of most cases of mental retardation of unknown etiology—a classification that occurs much more frequently in the upper than the lower range of mental retardation (McLaren & Bryson, 1987)—is the normal distribution of whatever genes contribute to the behavior we call intelligence. Those who subscribe to this concept do not hesitate to use the term familial mental retardation (e.g., Nichols, 1984; Zigler, 1967, 1995).[5]

The chance environmental factors and single-gene and chromosomal afflictions that produce the pronounced bulge in the lower range of mental retardation have a low probability

---

5. The fact that people with familial mental retardation have deficient genetic endowment does not necessarily mean they are simply developmentally regressed to the level of their mental age (MA) and will perform at their MA level on all tasks, nor does it necessarily follow that when they function below their MA level it is because of environmental and motivational processes. The challenge to these assumptions is at the heart of the so-called developmental-difference controversy.

of also striking siblings or other family members, because the mental retardation is usually not hereditary. On the other hand, in the upper range of mental retardation, where the largest percentage of familial mental retardation is found, there is, because of its hereditary nature, an increased probability that retardation will be found in one or more siblings as well as in one or both parents and (to a lesser extent) in more distantly related relatives. Based on Reed and Reed's (1965) large database, Anderson (1974) calculated that the risk of having a child with mental retardation increases when the father is retarded, is even greater when only the mother is retarded, is greatest when both parents are retarded, and interacts with number of siblings who are retarded.

In Halperin's (1945) survey the higher the mental status of the mentally retarded participants the more likely it was that the parents were mentally retarded or of below-average intelligence, and the same held true for siblings. Johnson, Ahern, and Johnson (1976)—reacting as did Nichols (1984) to criticism of the Roberts (1952) study, and drawing as Anderson (1974) did from the Reed and Reed (1965) survey—found that people in the upper range of mental retardation were more likely to have mentally retarded siblings than were people in the lower range. They were also more likely to have parents who were more frequently in lower occupational levels than were the parents of severely retarded children, similar to Halperin's (1945) finding that 68% of the parents of children in the lowest level of retardation were of average and above average socioeconomic status, compared to 22% of the parents of children in the highest level of mental retardation. Johnson et al. (1976) were properly cautious, pointing out that the distinction between the family patterns is not absolute (cf. Costeff, Cohen, & Weller, 1983). There is much overlap.

In the Nichols (1984) study, many relatives of the children with mental retardation also participated in the project; consequently the intelligence test results of some siblings were available. None of the 20 participating siblings of the severely retarded Caucasian children had mental retardation, and their mean IQ was 103. On the other hand, "The 58 siblings of the mildly retarded children showed a different pattern: 12 . . . were retarded" (p. 163), and the mean IQ of the 58 siblings was 85. Interestingly, a similar sibling pattern was not found for the siblings of African-American children unless the cutoff points for mild and severe mental retardation were shifted downward. The severely retarded Caucasian children had 23 cousins in the study, none of whom was retarded (mean IQ of 102), whereas 4 of 58 cousins of mildly retarded Caucasian children were retarded (mean IQ of the 58 cousins was 92). Once again the pattern for the African-American participants differed, and the authors suggested that for the African-Americans, "most retardation appeared to be of the cultural-familial type" (p. 161).

The weight of the evidence from many studies points to a significant difference both in diagnostic categories and family resemblance patterns when people who are mildly retarded are compared with people who are severely retarded, although the differences are probabilistic, not absolute, and ethnic differences may play an as yet undetermined role.

Studies of twins with mental retardation also support the need for a classification of familial (hereditary) mental retardation. Twins are said to be concordant if both are alike on some continuously distributed trait such as intelligence (IQ), or on some discrete trait such as mental retardation. If a trait is heritable, concordance (percentage of co-twins with the same diagnosis or level of cognition) will be higher in the pairs of monozygotic (identical) twins than in the pairs of dizygotic (fraternal) twins. In one study of twins, 65% of the pairs of monozygotic twins with uncomplicated mental deficiency were concordant for IQ (no more than 5 IQ points apart), compared with 21% concordance in the dizygotic same-sex twins. "Uncomplicated" indicated exclusion of those with certain organic pathologies, psychoses, behavioral difficulties, delinquency and criminality (Rosanoff, Handy, & Plesset, 1937). In a 1939 German study (Juda, as cited in Baroff, 1955 and in Shields & Slater, 1961), when participants with known organic pathology were excluded, the concordance for some degree of mental retardation—a much less fine-grained, concordance classification than an IQ difference of 5 IQ points or less—was reported as 100% for pairs of monozygotic twins and half as much for pairs of dizygotic twins (45% according to Baroff, 58% according to Shields and Slater). However, as Baroff (1955) pointed out, this study was completed "during the Nazi regime which was most anxious for clear-cut genetic results so that they could implement sterilization programs" (p. 30). Still, a 1930 Danish study reported even more disparity for concordance of mental retardation: 85% for monozygotic twins and 8% for dizygotic twins (Smith, as cited in Baroff, 1955).

Baroff (1955) tested "high grade" undifferentiated mentally retarded twins and reported an IQ correlation of .88 for monozygotic twins and .06 for dizygotic twins, a difference that is startling considering the fact that he did not include any dizygotic pair if the co-twin was not in the institution. "There was," he wrote, "no case of discordance for high-grade mental defect among monozygotic twins but many dizygotic twin individuals had normal cotwins" (p. 83). A larger range of IQs for the 20 monozygotic (36–75) than for the 20 dizygotic (51–70) twins probably contributed to this exceptionally large difference. Also, 5 of the dizygotic pairs were not same-sex.

In a recent extensive and important study of the polygenic source of mild mental impairment,[6] Spinath et al. (2004) drew from a representative sample of 3,886 twins the 5% of children who scored lowest on a composite measure of verbal and nonverbal tests given to them when they were 2, 3, and 4 years of age by their parents. In the lowest 5% group there were 73 monozygotic, 53 same-sex dizygotic, and 55 opposite-sex dizygotic twins. Principal component factor analyses at each age indicated that 50% to 55% of the total variance was accounted for by a single factor, which they identified as g, or general intelligence.[7]

With ages 2, 3, and 4 combined, results for the impaired group indicated that for monozygotic twins there was 74% concordance, whereas for same-sex dizygotic twins the concordance was 45%, and for opposite-sex dizygotic twins it was 36% (see their Fig. 2). This substantial difference in concordance between the monozygotic and dizygotic twins in the lowest (5%) intelligence group indicates a high level of genetic influence on cognitive processes. At a 10% intelligence level cutoff point (N = 366) the results are quite similar,

---

6. Mild mental impairment in place of mild mental retardation because no adaptive behavior levels were obtained.

7. The authors of the 2002 manual (p. 55) accept, at least for now, the impressive evidence for the concept of g, also known as Spearmen's g, as the best measure of intellectual functioning. For the role of g in mental retardation, see Spitz (2003).

but from there on, as we include 2-, 3-, and 4-year-old twins with even higher intelligence levels, the genetic influence (as indicated by differences between the concordances of monozygotic and dizygotic twins) declines.

For the entire sample of 3,886 young twins there was a .96 correlation for the monozygotic twins, which is appreciably higher than is the .74 concordance for the lowest 5% monozygotic twins.[8] One might think that this higher correlation of the monozygotic twins in the entire sample is evidence of higher heritability, but this is deceptive, because it is the difference in concordance or correlation between monozygotic and dizygotic twins that determines heritability. The difference between the monozygotic twins and dizygotic twins in the entire sample (.96 minus .81 to .84) is much less than that between the monozygotic twins and dizygotic twins in the lowest 5% group (.74 minus .36 to .45) (see their Fig. 2), indicating higher heritability in the 5% (lowest intelligence) group.

Note that the monozygotic minus dizygotic difference (and therefore the heritability) found in the entire sample will increase, because in unselected groups the heritability of general cognitive ability increases over the lifespan. McClearn et al. (1997) wrote that "for general cognitive ability, heritability increases from infancy (about 20%) to childhood (40%) to adolescence (50%) to adulthood (60%)" (p. 1561). For twins 80 years and older they reported a heritability of 62%. These individual percentages are not meant to be etched in stone (the infancy percentage appears high, for example, and different studies have reported different percentages), but the general trend has been found in many publications and is unlikely to change (see, e.g., McGue, Bouchard, Iacono, & Lykken, 1993).

The data provide information about environmental sources of variance as well as heritability. The dizygotic correlations in the entire group indicated stronger environmental influences compared with the environmental influences on the low-intelligence group. A more discriminating behavioral genetic analysis confirmed these findings and revealed that the factor most responsible for the environmental influence was shared environment (the environment available within the same family). The low-intelligence group is less affected by shared environment than is the rest of the sample. This fact very likely reflects the difficulty experienced by massive all-day interventions over a period of years (essentially a shared environment) in attempts to permanently raise low intelligence.

Spinath et al. (2004) speculate that the results might be attributed to different genes in the two intelligence groups, but that it is also possible the two groups have the same genes and simply do not express them equally. That is, these genes are not expressed as much in the unimpaired group because it is more affected by shared environment. An answer to this question will have to await the identification of specific genes "associated with mild mental impairment or [associated] with individual differences in the normal range" (Spinath

---

8. Concordance was used for the subgroups and correlations for the entire sample because—even assuming that the range for the subgroups was less restricted—correlations for a subgroup would have provided irrelevant information about individual differences within the subgroup. The information desired was why some children were in a subgroup (were within a certain range of intelligence) and others were not, and the concordances provided twin resemblances for the affected (monozygotic) vs. nonaffected (dizygotic) dichotomy. In the entire sample, concordance could not be measured because there are no separated groups. Note that although concordance measurements are not the same as correlations, the two are reasonably comparable.

et al., 2004, p. 41). They also suggest that people with mild mental impairment can be "a target for brain research that goes beyond modularity to consider global brain function and dysfunction" (p. 41).[9] An interesting example of these types of "neurogenetic" studies (combining neurobiology and genetics) is Thompson et al.'s (2001) study with normal (nonretarded) twins. They found a possible brain site and brain functions for the action of genes related to differences in intelligence. Although that impressive study had a rather small sample, Gray and Thompson (2004) provide an extensive review of neurogenetic studies that should be an eye opener for many professionals who have not been able to keep up with the exciting and cascading developments in this field.

In summing up the results of studies with twins of low intelligence: when organic pathology is excluded there is overwhelming evidence (even if we omit the Juda study) that the probability of a mentally limited monozygotic twin having a co-twin who is also mentally limited is very much higher than in the same situation for dizygotic twins. When combined with the results of family studies (as well as with studies using unselected groups) a strong case can be made for a significant contribution of genetic heritability to intelligence and consequently to many instances of mild mental retardation—so strong a case, in fact, that it is inconceivable that it is ignored in the recent AAMR diagnostic manuals. It makes one realize that there continue to be instances where political and social pressures override scientific evidence. Galileo would understand.

CONCLUSION

Hopes raised during the dominance of behaviorism and environmentalism in the 1950s, 60s and 70s—that intervention and environmental enrichment would permanently raise intelligence and prevent mental retardation—have not been realized (Spitz, 1986, 1999; Zigler, 1995), although there are many who claim that intellectual decline can be slowed (Guralnick, 1998).

How then was familial mental retardation eradicated? Very easily: It was simply excluded as a diagnostic category despite overwhelming evidence that it deserves a place in any classification manual of mental retardation.

REFERENCES

Anderson, V. E. (1974). Genetics and intelligence. In J. Wortis (Ed.), *Mental retardation and developmental disabilities* (Vol. 6, pp. 20–43). New York: Brunner/Mazel.

Baroff, G. S. (1955). A psychomotor, psychometric, and projective study of mentally defective twins. *Dissertation Abstracts, 16*(3), 373–374.

Baroff, G. S. (1995). Letter to the editor. *Psychology in Mental Retardation and Developmental Disabilities, 20*(2), 25.

Bloom, B. S. (1964). *Stability and change in human characteristics.* New York: Wiley.

Brown, D. E. (1991). *Human universals.* New York: McGraw-Hill.

Costeff, H., Cohen, B. E., & Weller, L. E. (1983). Biological factors in mild mental retardation. *Developmental Medicine & Child Neurology, 25,* 580–587.

---

9. In a previous paper Plomin (1999) described how the findings in behavioral genetics can be applied to the study of mild mental retardation and provided a model for future research strategies. He and his colleagues are now searching for the genes responsible for the high inheritability of mild mental retardation.

Dingman, H. F., & Tarjan, G. (1960). Mental retardation and the normal distribution curve. *American Journal of Mental Deficiency, 64,* 991–994.

Gray, J. R., & Thompson, P. M. (2004). Neurobiology of intelligence: Science and ethics. *Nature Neuroscience Review, 5,* 471–482.

Grossman, H. J. (Ed.). (1973). *Manual on terminology and classification in mental retardation (1973 revision).* Washington, DC: American Association on Mental Deficiency.

Grossman, H. J. (Ed.). (1977). *Manual on terminology and classification in mental retardation* (1977 revision). Washington, DC: American Association on Mental Deficiency.

Grossman, H. J. (Ed.). (1983). *Manual on terminology and classification in mental retardation* (1983 revision). Washington, DC: American Association on Mental Deficiency.

Guralnick, M. J. (1998). Effectiveness of early intervention for vulnerable children: A developmental perspective. *American Journal on Mental Retardation, 102,* 319–345.

Halperin, S. L. (1945). A clinico-genetical study of mental defect. *American Journal of Mental Deficiency, 50,* 8–26.

Heber, R. (1961). A manual on terminology and classification in mental retardation [Monograph Supplement, 2nd ed.]. *American Journal of Mental Deficiency, 64*(2).

Hunt, J. M. (1961). *Intelligence and Experience.* New York: Ronald Press.

Johnson, C. A., Ahern, F. M., & Johnson, R. C. (1976). Level of functioning of siblings and parents of probands of varying degrees of retardation. *Behavior Genetics, 6,* 473–477.

Luckasson, R., Borthwick-Duffy, S., Buntinx, W. H. E., Coulter, D. L., Craig, E. M., Reeve, A., et al. (2002). *Mental retardation: Definition, classification, and systems of supports* (10th ed.). Washington, DC: American Association on Mental Retardation.

Luckasson, R., Coulter, D. L., Polloway, E. A., Reiss, S., Schalock, R. L., Snell, M. E., et al. (1992). *Mental retardation: Definition, classification, and systems of supports* (9th ed.). Washington, DC: American Association on Mental Retardation.

MacMillan, D. L., Siperstein, G. N., & Leffert, J. S. (2006). Children with mild mental retardation: A challenge for classification practices—revised. In H. N. Switzky & S. Greenspan (Eds.), *What Is Mental Retardation?* Washington, DC: American Association on Mental Retardation.

McClearn, G. E., Johansson, B., Berg, S., Pedersen, N. L., Ahern, F., Petrill, S. A., & Plomin, R. (1997). Substantial genetic influence on cognitive abilities in twins 80 or more years old. *Science, 276,* 1560–1563.

McGue, M., & Bouchard, T. J., Jr. (1989). Genetic and environmental determinants of information processing and special mental abilities: A twin analysis. In R. J. Sternberg (Ed.), *Advances in the psychology of human intelligence* (Vol. 5, pp. 7–45). Hillsdale, NJ: Erlbaum.

McGue, M., Bouchard, T. J., Jr., Iacono, W. G., & Lykken, D. T. (1993). Behavioral genetics of cognitive ability: A life-span perspective. In R. Plomin and G. E. McClearn (Eds.), *Nature, nurture, & psychology* (pp. 59–76). Washington, DC: American Psychological Association.

McLaren, J., & Bryson, S. E. (1987). Review of recent epidemiological studies of mental retardation: Prevalence, associated disorders, and etiology. *American Journal on Mental Retardation, 92,* 243–254.

Nichols, P. L. (1984). Familial mental retardation. *Behavior Genetics, 14,* 161–170.

Plomin, R. (1986). *Development, genetics, and psychology.* Hillsdale, NJ: Erlbaum.

Plomin, R. (1997). Identifying genes for cognitive abilities and disabilities. In R. J. Sternberg and E. Grigorenko (Eds.), *Intelligence, heredity, and environment* (pp. 89–104). Cambridge, England: Cambridge University Press.

Plomin, R. (1999). Genetic research on general cognitive ability as a model for mild mental retardation. *International Review of Psychiatry, 11,* 34–46.

Reed, E. W., & Reed, S. C. (1965). *Mental retardation: A family study.* Philadelphia: Saunders.

Roberts, J. A. F. (1952). The genetics of mental deficiency. *The Eugenics Review, 44,* 71–83.

Rosanoff, A. J., Handy, L. M., & Plesset, I. R. (1937). The etiology of mental deficiency. *Psychological Monographs, 48*(4, Whole No. 216).

Segal, N. L. (1985). Monozygotic and dizygotic twins: A comparative analysis of mental ability profiles. *Child Development, 56*, 1051–1058.

Shane, H. C. (Ed.). (1994). *Facilitated communication: The clinical and social phenomenon.* San Diego, CA: Singular.

Shields, J., & Slater, E. (1961). Heredity and psychological abnormality. In H. J. Eysenck (Ed.), *Handbook of abnormal psychology: An experimental approach* (pp. 298–342). New York: Basic Books.

Spinath, F. M., Harlaar, N., Ronald, A., & Plomin, R. (2004). Substantial genetic influence on mild mental impairment in early childhood. *American Journal on Mental Retardation, 109,* 34–43.

Spitz, H. H. (1986). *The raising of intelligence: A selected history of attempts to raise retarded intelligence.* Hillsdale, NJ: Erlbaum.

Spitz, H. H. (1997). *Nonconscious movements: From mystical messages to facilitated communication.* Mahwah, NJ: Erlbaum.

Spitz, H. H. (1999). Attempts to raise intelligence. In M. Anderson (Ed.), *The development of intelligence* (pp. 275–293). Hove, England: Psychology Press.

Spitz, H. H. (2003). Mental retardation and *g*. In H. Nyborg (Ed.), *The scientific study of general intelligence: Tribute to Arthur R. Jensen* (pp. 247–259). Oxford, England: Elsevier Science.

Switzky, H. N., & Greenspan, S. (Eds.). (2003). *What Is Mental Retardation? Ideas for an evolving disability.* Washington, DC: American Association on Mental Retardation [E-Book]. Available at http://www.disabilitybooksonline.com

Thompson, P. M., Cannon, T. D., Narr, K. L., Erp, T. van, Poutanen, V.-P., Huttunen, M., et al. (2001). Genetic influences on brain structure. *Nature Neuroscience, 4*(12), 1253–1258.

Zigler, E. (1967). Familial mental retardation: A continuing dilemma. *Science, 155,* 292–298.

Zigler, E. (1995). Can we "cure" mild mental retardation among individuals in the lower socioeconomic stratum? *American Journal of Public Health, 85,* 302–304.

PART II

The 2002 AAMR System and Its Critics and Supporters

This part of the book provides the reader with a broad spectrum of commentary, both positive and negative, more focused on the 1992/2002 AAMR systems themselves. The chapters are presented alphabetically by author.

Baumeister, in Chapter 7, provides a very detailed analysis of the historical, ideological, philosophical, theoretical, and scientific ideas underpinning the 1992 and 2002 AAMR systems and his reactions to them. He states, "Basically, my contention is that the authors of the 1992 and 2002 manuals failed to consider a number of consequential, elemental, and deep-seated epistemological concerns. As a consequence, they did not advance a compelling philosophical rationale for the 'new' paradigm. With their focus on 'supports,' services, and consumerism they ignored and greatly depreciated the vast biological and social complexities. 'Newness,' like beauty, is in the eye of the beholder." He concludes, "Science and the technology it generates contribute to both purposes: definition and treatment. But by confusing these issues, the AAMR T&C committee, intentionally or not, elevated ritual over reason while projecting a decidedly postmodernism, antiscientific, relativism mien [resulting in scientific substance being sacrificed for warm and fuzzy other ways of 'knowing' disguised as social virtue]. Committee paladins, guided by the blinking beacons of consumerism and political correctness, apparently relegated empirical rationality and analytic reasoning to steerage class in their Titanic voyage to uncover the 'true' meaning of mental retardation." For Baumeister, it is the paradigmatic distinctions between postmodernism and modernism that lie at the very center of the dispute over the 1992 and 2002 AAMR manuals and systems.

Coulter, in Chapter 8, provides his favorable rationale for the 1992 and 2002 AAMR systems based on his many years of experience as a pediatric neurologist dealing with the very practical experiences of children and families trying to get along with others in social contexts—the very essence of social intelligence. He clarifies why AAMR 2002 embraced the language and ideas of WHO's ICF model, and the need for "supports" in the AAMR 2002 model, and why supports are so important. He argues for a revised definition as follows: "Intellectual disabilities describes individuals who require meaningful supports in order to achieve optimal functioning within the community because of the presence of substantial limitations in social adaptation and intellectual abilities manifested initially during the developmental period prior to adulthood." He proclaims the importance of

93

"spirituality" in the life of persons with mental retardation and laments the removal of "spirituality" from the 2002 AAMR manual, though it was a part of the 1992 AAMR manual and system.

Detterman and Gabriel, in Chapter 9, point out that the 1992 and 2002 AAMR systems have some inherent problems that limit their usefulness for both researchers and service providers. They believe that the ambiguity of the 1992 and 2002 definitions makes it "difficult, if not impossible, for researchers to do their job." They also argue that deficient adaptive behavior has no place as a criterion of diagnosis, because for the most part psychometric intelligence is highly correlated with measures of adaptive behavior. "The addition of an adaptive-behavior criterion simply muddies the waters." They present a very interesting Monte Carlo simulation involving the correlations among the ten adaptive-skill tests of the 1992 AAMR system and how they affect the diagnosis of mental retardation in ways the writers of the 1992 AAMR manual did not foresee, which has implications for the 2002 AAMR manual. Detterman and Gabriel are extremely worried that the 1992 and 2002 AAMR manuals have caused increasing alienation between researchers and service providers, and they discuss ways to elevate the situation.

CHAPTER SEVEN

Mental Retardation: Confusing Sentiment with Science[1]

ALFRED A. BAUMEISTER

THE MEANING OF MENTAL RETARDATION

With great fanfare the American Association on Mental Retardation (AAMR) announced the arrival of the ninth edition of the AAMR terminology and classification system (Luckasson et al., 1992). The advertisement proclaimed: "Don't miss the most important book of the decade!" An "innovative" theoretical framework was proposed, guided by "an evolving understanding of the concept of mental retardation and how it can be best defined and classified in our times" (p. ix).

A decade later the tenth edition was published to elaborate, expand, and clarify features of the earlier version (Luckasson et al., 2002). Many of the same people contributed to both volumes, although membership on the Ad Hoc Committee on Terminology and Classification (T&C Committee) had changed some over the ten-year interval, as was to be expected.

The two manuals are based on the same assumptions, conceptions, and reasoning. The tenth is "a logical continuation" of the major paradigm shift proclaimed in the ninth (Luckasson et al., 2002, p. 5). To wit: Mental retardation is regarded no longer as an absolute individual trait but rather as an expression of interaction between a person with limited intellectual functioning and the environment. "Supports" are a major feature of the paradigm shift. Purportedly, "what is new is the belief that the judicious application of supports can improve the functional capabilities of individuals with mental retardation" (p. 145; italics theirs).

In pursuit of this lofty endeavor the Terminology and Classification (T&C) Committee has continued the long AAMR tradition of formulating, organizing, and disseminating information on terminology and classification of mental retardation. Of course, another tradition was certainly bound to carry on—commentary, criticism, and condemnation.

---

1. I wish to express my deepest gratitude to Dr. Herman Spitz, not only for his careful review of this paper, but also for our numerous stimulating discussions over the years of so many related topics.

As noted, the 1992 manual was proclaimed by the T&C Committee (Schalock et al., 1994) to reflect a "significant paradigm shift" (p. 181). At the same time there was recognition that "Change never comes easy" (p. 190). Perhaps the qualification arises from the detailed and sometimes frankly blistering assaults that rapidly surfaced (Borthwick-Duffy, 1994; Greenspan, 1994; Jacobson, 1994; Jacobson & Mulick, 1992; MacMillan, Gresham, & Siperstein, 1993, 1995; MacMillan & Reschly, 1997; among others, including some contributors to the e-book, *What Is Mental Retardation? Ideas for an evolving disability* edited by Switzky and Greenspan, 2003). If previous AAMR "systems" were considered morbid by some critics, the 1992 edition and its successor were pronounced moribund if not DOA.

Vigorous disapprovals have been directed at various conceptual and technical aspects of both the 1992 and 2002 manuals. Some of these criticisms are acknowledged in the more recent version, a few accepted, and most either disputed, qualified, or simply dismissed.

Relatively few references have been made in the professional literature to underlying historical, ideological, philosophical, theoretical, and scientific considerations, and how the 1992 and 2002 manuals derive from and measure up in these respects. Most of these substantive discussions are found in the recent volume edited by Switzky and Greenspan (2003). It is with regard to these broader, but fundamental, considerations that I primarily focus the commentary that follows.

I contend that the authors of the 1992 and 2002 manuals failed to consider adequately and in sufficient depth a number of consequential, elemental, and deep-seated epistemological concerns that have enormous bearing on scientific and social complexities involved in defining and classifying mental retardation. As a consequence, they did not advance a compelling philosophical rationale for the alleged "new" paradigm. Focusing on "supports," services, and consumerism, they ignored and greatly deprecated the vast biological and social complexities associated with mental retardation.

In fairness, in both editions but particularly in the 2002 version Luckasson et al. do properly draw attention to the multifactorial nature of etiology and expression. On the other hand, that point was made long ago (e.g., Brison, 1967) and has been elaborated far more completely and precisely in a number of conceptual schemes, particularly concerning prevention (e.g., Institute of Medicine, 1991; Baumeister, Kupstas, & Woodley-Zanthos, 1993). To call this a significant paradigm shift is a stretch that disregards many historical precedents and contemporary formulations.

The AAMR manuals do not present original and innovative formulations, based on contemporary empirical evidence, in which the many predisposing and mediating factors affecting the occurrence and expression of mental retardation are integrated into a coherent, comprehensive, and utilitarian explanatory paradigm. Instead much of their rationale is couched in affective and emotionally laden conceptions that are more compatible with spiritual discernment than with systematic empirically driven precepts.

The "new" design described in the manuals allegedly is responsive expressly to a "fundamental paradigm shift" (Luckasson et al., 1992, p. 135). This new formulation requires "significant changes in thinking" in ways that will "guide and shape future research and practice" (p. 11), that will force reconceptualization of decision making (p. 139), that "demands a redefinition of services" (p. 135), and that suggests "cures" might be in the offing "if a fully integrated society were to accept persons with intellectual limitations as equal members" (p. 18). In sum, the underlying premises seem to be: a) a functional orientation, b) an ecological perspective, and c) an emphasis on a supports model for both classification and service. These themes are again expressed and underscored in the 2002 edition of the manual.

Much of what they offer is rapturous and heady rhetoric, if perhaps a tad tinny, shallow, and redundant, wanting for definitive philosophical and empirical rationales. Just how revolutionary is the underlying premise and everything that supposedly follows from it? Is the "inclusion" doctrine derived from nascent scientific discoveries, or does it originate from transient political activism fueled by ephemeral moralist ideals? How far does this "System" advance empirical and scientific understanding of mental retardation? Does it illuminate, obfuscate, or suffocate? Is it proactive or reactive? Is it objective or subjective?

Let me frame this predicament in stark and somewhat discomfiting questions. Does the larger society continuously and deeply care about providing anything more than the basic survival resources, if that? What is the payoff for the common good? How does the appeal to egalitarianism expounded in the manuals comport with biological and social realities? How does our society benefit from, say, community inclusion of retarded people? Do retarded people benefit? Should finite resources not be allocated or redirected more *toward prevention* so that we can avert some of the dreadful costs, in both monetary and human terms? Has anyone ever absolutely "*cured*" mental retardation? Just how are public health interests served by enormous investment for supports in marginal and minority groups when there are so many other pressing and competing demands (such as universal health care and homeland security)? Who pays, who really benefits, and at what cost? When does treatment become coercion? Should a woman routinely be offered screening for deleterious genes in her and her partner's family line or directly in the embryo? Is that her right and should she be allowed to act on the information without religious or political coercion or interference? Should prenatal exposure to serious teratogens that on imaging reveal aberrant intrauterine development give cause for elective abortion? Should we be allowed to tamper with the human gene line, despite knee-jerk religious opposition? How seriously disruptive is the permanently impaired child to the family—psychologically, socially, and financially? Are there rational or economic limits to how far we should go in providing supports? Are there biological limitations to seeking remedies in nurture? Who defines quality of life and, in fact, what really is "quality of life"? Is there a "right" to refuse treatment, such as chronic tube feeding? Is there absolute entitlement? If so, to what and how much? Do human policies (e.g., No Child Left Behind) conflict with natural laws? Given the likelihood that intellectually superior children benefit relatively more than impaired children from an enriched environment, would society not be better served by redirecting resources from the intellectually frail to the superior? What should activists do when their principles clash with realities of political and economic forces—hold out or compromise?

These questions and many others that have been framed before are neither new nor idle speculation, beastly as they may sound to some. At the same time, as our understanding of biological/genetic mechanisms continues to grow, along with our ability to intervene, we cannot afford to commit the "naturalist fallacy," assuming that the way nature intended is best (Watson, 2003). A balance must be achieved. The definitions in the AAMR manuals do not further understanding of the serious social implications posed by these questions. History, as we shall see, is very instructive and we should be able to do better than repeat it.

If individuals or organizations, such as AAMR, are to advocate in behalf of those who are handicapped and who live in the shadowy margins, then egalitarian proponents are obliged to support their basic premises on logical, philosophical, and empirical grounds that are persuasive and enduring. The argument must be based on abiding principles, not on what is currently politically fashionable or on private interests. Either provide compelling empirically driven rationale, or give up the pretense.

Probably it is not good form (or adaptive) in our secluded academic environments, in polite company, in the press, or in professional forums to pose such severe and draconian questions. As Healy (2004) so aptly put it in his book describing the scandalous and calumnious power of the pharmaceutical industry and its drive for immense profits, along with its subversion of university researchers: "Protesting academics are likely to fall foul of their institutions (p. xiii) . . . we need to recognize the hazards (p. 288)."

Is there a soul among us, especially those of us who have attempted to provide services, who has not asked some of these questions of ourselves, or who has not been asked by others, lay people and professionals alike? To be convincing, the answers have to be forthcoming in more persuasive, honest, and compelling terms than as justified by vague belief in the doctrine of egalitarianism—which does not, in any case, exist in the real world. Where is the basic rationale?

HISTORICAL PERSPECTIVES

In contemplating answers to these questions, we should briefly ponder where more than two centuries of experience have brought us. The historical experience with mental retardation is highly relevant, because all the fundamental issues as to defining and classifying mental retardation, on the one hand, and societal responsibility, on the other, have been addressed in conceptual terms not unlike those expressed in the 1992/2002 manuals. This is no idle digression into trifling historical incidents; rather it is an essential part of the story and sets the foundation for much of the argument that follows in later sections.[2]

History also raises questions as to the originality of the "new paradigm." Assuming that scientific knowledge and technology have accumulated on a linear, even exponential, scale, one should be able to observe virtues of this so-called "new paradigm" in stark relief against the unsophisticated ideas and crude practices of earlier periods.

A chapter in the 2002 AAMR manual purports to describe the "evolution of the definition of mental retardation." The authors begin with the definition set forth by Tredgold in 1908. However, most of their account of the so-called "evolution" is devoted to activities of the AAMR. I suppose it is understandable that the Terminology and Classification Committee should desire to emphasize the role and importance of their Association. But

---

2. Throughout the literatures on mental retardation and mental illness one can find numerous accounts of the history of definition, classification, and treatment. For a particularly fascinating and authoritative historical treatment of care and study of the mentally retarded see Kanner (1964). Others such as Best (1965) provide detailed descriptions of historical attitudes, provisions, and political forces affecting care and provision in the United States.

failure to address other influential historical precedents leads to a one-sided, incomplete, distorted, and misleading picture. For it is the case that many of the ideas and remedies set forth, some of which are described as innovative or new, actually were voiced centuries earlier. If they did not work then, why should they now? In contemplating this history, one can only look askance at the veracity and validity of some of the claims made as to originality and effectiveness. How have they advanced our understanding of mental retardation, despite repeated assurances of that intent?

Deviancy, of course, has existed from the beginning of human history. Even in the Garden of Eden individual differences were apparent, the fig leaf notwithstanding. More to the point, individual differences in ability or competence and the adequacy with which we meet and adjust to our environments have been apparent at least since the dawn of recorded history.

Early explicit references to mental retardation are most frequent in religious and philosophical literatures. The term "idiot," for instance, comes from the Greek meaning "private person"—those limited in intelligence. Perhaps the first official acknowledgment of behavioral incompetence is to be found in the Twelve Tablets of Rome which appeared about 450 B.C. Under this Roman law a "fool" was regarded as incapable of managing his affairs, the "fool" to be placed under the protection of his family. This concept has many modern adherents.

Occasionally throughout the Middle Ages references were made to the condition of "idiocy," invoking most frequently the concept of understanding as the basis for defining retardation. The ability to comprehend and react in appropriate ways to ordinary events and demands of life became the basis for deciding whether an individual could manage for himself or whether someone must assume responsibility for his affairs—that is, provide supports. By the 14th century laws were enacted to deal equitably with the property of incompetent individuals.

At about the time Columbus was finding America Sir Anthony Fitzherbert was defining the idiot as "a person who cannot count or number, nor can tell who was his father or mother, not how old he is . . . so as it may appear he had not understanding of reason what shall be his profit or his loss." Here we see operational referents, such as abstract reasoning, memory, and academic skills, used to tie observed behavior (i.e., impaired intelligence) to the condition of mental retardation.[3]

By the 19th century a strong and rather sudden awakening of humane interest in the treatment of those afflicted with mental disorders began to emerge—first in philosophical terms, then in scientific, and finally in social expression. The convergence of 19th-century

---

3. Many of the early references to mental deviancy were couched in religious terms. The period of Protestant Reformation in Europe for a time lent a peculiar religious significance to deviant behavior. Those who behaved strangely were, according to the teachings of Luther and Calvin, possessed by the Devil "...in a mass of flesh...with no soul." An individual who lacked a soul was likely to be treated harshly, to the point of having the Devil beaten out of him. Deviants were beaten, whirled, bled, purged, drugged, drenched, and manacled – very emphatic if not empathetic therapy. Some of these treatments are still in use today, without the consent of the patient.

humanitarianism, the scientific method, and Locke's sensationalist philosophy resulted in profound changes in conceptions, definitions, and management of behavior disorders.

Of particular influence was the sensationalist doctrine of Rousseau that natural man is innately good, conceived in perfection, but corrupted by an imperfect society. Herein lies something of a philosophical quandary. If man is innately good, should not the society he creates be good? Those who do not conform to the general will are deviants who must be forced into conformity. Deviants are still not welcome to the communal table. In any case, nurture was in vogue—at least among those who had the time, leisure, and wherewithal to think about it. As the AAMR manuals abundantly reveal, nurture is considered ascendant. The very notion of biological determinism still rings alarm bells within the egalitarian village. Of course there were pesky characters such as Darwin, Mendel, Watson, Crick and others who suggested that maybe the tabula rasa was not so blank after all.

As concern for proper and humane treatment grew, it became apparent that uniform criteria for definition and classification were necessary for administrative, scientific, and educational purposes. With the establishment of special schools, institutions, and hospitals for the mentally ill and retarded, efforts were made to develop objective definitions and systems of classification.

One of the initial and important distinctions to be made was that between insanity and mental deficiency. The first significant development in this respect was the two-volume publication of *Des Maladies Montales* by the French physician Esquirol in 1838. He observed that retarded behavior varies along a continuum from very mild to severe. Thus he classified mental retardation, in five categories, according to degree of severity and etiology. He proposed a functional behavioral classification system in which ability to understand and express language was taken as the principal criterion for intellectual functioning.

Of course the primary problem was that Esquirol had no standardized instrument to measure linguistic and communication skills. That had to await the development of successful intelligence tests. But what is new? The behavioral referents in definition have not really changed—diminished intelligence and deficits in adaptation.

There was, however, a parallel set of developments during the late 18th century and continuing throughout the 19th that have had profound influences on the ways in which many scientists and practitioners conceptualize, define, classify, and treat mental retardation. This was a period of remarkable growth in the medical and biological sciences. As early as 1870 scientific neurology was well established as a discipline, having produced an elaborate account of brain pathology along with objective methods of assessment. By 1900 major types of central nervous system pathology had been described. Thus, the concepts and terminology were becoming available by which mental retardation could be defined as primarily a *biological*, not a behavioral, concept.

Not only was there progress in pathology, anatomy, and neurology, but also considerable evidence was beginning to accumulate that would link mental retardation to heredity. As early as 1857 genetic theories had been specifically proposed to account for hereditary defects associated with feeblemindedness. Of course, now we understand that single gene mutations account for many different diseases associated with mental retardation. We also know that polygenic factors contribute enormously to the individual differences reflected in the distribution of IQs.

The first attempt at complete medical classification based on etiological factors was published by Ireland in 1877. His book, *On Idiocy and Imbecility* (1877), has been cited as the first well-organized and medically oriented textbook of mental deficiency (Kanner, 1964). Ireland's classification system included the following types of mental deficiency:

1. Genetic.
2. Microcephalic.
3. Eclampsic.
4. Epileptic.
5. Hydrocephalic.
6. Paralytic.
7. Cretinism.
8. Traumatic.
9. Inflammatory.
10. Idiocy by deprivation.

While the medical classes identified by Ireland are now much broader and more complete, every one of them is contained in current medical classifications of mental retardation. Thus the two major types of classification approaches—etiological and functional—are well rooted in medical and behavioral science. Now the question is: Which is ultimately more useful and heuristic? Which approach has demonstrated significant effectual growth in diagnosis, treatment, and theory? These two conceptions have lived side by side for many years, not always peacefully. As biological science and the technology it generates continue to resolve uncertainties about mental retardation, bit by bit, we can anticipate the diehard proponents, both nurturists and nativists, will dig in even more solidly.

I maintain it is the biological orientation that has shown the greater advances and promise. Lest there be any apparent contradiction, general intelligence as revealed in behavioral measures is governed by biological laws. When Watson and Crick unraveled the mysteries of the DNA molecule, a world-historical event, our conceptions of the human condition and our ability to affect destiny were forever and profoundly altered.

T&C Committee members apparently agree, but only superficially, with the frequently expressed notion that the definition of mental retardation promulgated by AAMR is deceptively clear and simple (Luckasson et al., 2002). Then why not propose a comprehensive data-based descriptive and explanatory system encompassing and integrating critical variables with a degree of specificity commensurate with the complexity of the problem? Additional definitional ambiguity and generality only add noise to a complex human problem desperately wanting for signal.

Now what does the history of AAMR and its more immediate precursors have to say? On June 6, 1876, in Media, Pennsylvania, six physicians who represented institutions ("schools") founded "The Association of Medical Officers of American Institutions for Idiotic and Feebleminded Persons." Led by Edouard Seguin, arguably one of the most influential and charismatic individuals in the history of mental retardation, these institutional pioneers set forth as their mission treatment of "mental deficiency" with the avowed purpose of returning afflicted people to their communities where they would be assimilated into normal social and work cultures (Woodley-Zanthos & Baumeister, 1994).

Although there were skeptics, much of the literature of that period reveals an ardent faith in the educational efficacy of "physiological education" first suggested by Itard and then greatly elaborated by Itard's student Seguin in his highly touted books (e.g., Seguin, 1866/1907). These works were the culmination of sensory philosophy, humanitarianism, empiricism, and, as Spitz (1986) has underscored, the religious-socialistic-moralistic doctrine of the followers of Claude Henri de Rouvroy Saint-Simon.

Seguin, intensely optimistic, attempted to transform his philosophy of *moral treatment* into a practical and functional concept—meaning that the mental defective, regardless of the reasons for his/her backwardness, was entitled to treatment with dignity, warmth, and kindness utilizing the best skills and resources available. Nowadays these concepts may be known as "empowerment," "inclusion," "quality of life," "best practice," "valuing," and "supports."

The Paris Academy of Science was so greatly enamored by the principles and methods of the "physiological method" that in 1844 they were moved to declare officially that Seguin had definitely solved the problem of idiot education. (Later Pope Pius IX weighed-in with his appreciation in a letter to Seguin.)

In the United States, report after report announced great success in the application of Seguin's methods, declaring that the "popular air that idiocy is an incurable malady has been disproved" (Baumeister, 1970, p. 7). That judgment may have been a little premature.

This was a historical period of enormous professional enthusiasm and not a little self-aggrandizement, championed by blatantly excessive claims. The literature of that time reveals an abundance of hyperbole proclaiming that disabilities and disadvantages visited on some people by unfortunate circumstances of pedigree and accident could be substantially if not entirely corrected through all-purpose environmental, educational, and social means.

As Best observed: "Probably the world has never known, before or since, such a pouring out of sympathy for the afflicted of society, a more zealous resolve to speed to their relief, nor a more ornate faith in the possibilities of education" (Best, 1965, p. 185). Lest one condemn these workers for their enthusiasms and even euphoria, it should be understood they had to convince a skeptical citizenry and often recalcitrant legislators that their work was worthy of public support. Some things have not changed, especially when it comes to promoting special interests.

Of course, there was recognition even then that hope for completely remedying mental deficiency, in all its extreme forms, has rational limits. As noted by Hervey Wilbur: "We do not propose to create or supply faculties absolutely wanting" (cited in Baumeister, 1970, p. 7).

Undaunted professional optimism of those earlier days not withstanding, something went wrong. Despite reported success (no doubt exaggerated then as now) in returning people to the community from the "schools," the physiological method was no panacea for feeblemindedness. The afflicted were not restored to a normal state. Accomplishment could match neither hope nor hype. Benevolence became the mother of excess, for the claims were indeed extravagant. By the 1880s evidence was beginning to accumulate to show that many, if not all, of the earlier assertions of success were ill-founded.

For this reason and others, pendulums, as they are wont to do, began an extreme swing as overlyreactive disillusionment set in and long-term custodial care and segregation became a more prevailing philosophy and instrument of management (Baumeister, 1970;

Spitz, 1986). Whereas formerly the concern was with helping the defective, the goal soon became one of protecting society, including secluding the feebleminded in "villages of the simple." It is really quite remarkable how dramatically public and professional opinion had changed within a period of less than 50 years.

Despite professional entreaties for financial support, the general public was not convinced that much, if anything, could be done to alter the mental status of minds enfeebled by disease or descent. In his veto of a bill to increase appropriations to Howe's school, the governor of Massachusetts expressed a sentiment that has its contemporary supporters: "When the state shall have sufficiently educated every bright child within its borders, it will be time enough to undertake the education of idiots and feebleminded children" (Best, 1965). Apparently there were then, as now, different constituencies competing for finite resources, perhaps explaining some of the extreme and peculiar assertions made by the votaries of that time. This seems to be another of those enduring but quixotic traditions. Those old-time advocates probably never thought of class-action lawsuits.

The intervention philosophy and the technology derived from it, most notably the physiological method, were flawed in that sensory and motor training failed to appreciably increase intelligence. To be sure, most people, save for the most profoundly affected, can acquire skill and knowledge. But that is not the same as raising intelligence. The "new doctrine and new methods of education" prescribed by Seguin could not, through unconditional reliance on environmental means, return an individual's impaired intellect to the normal state (Baumeister, 1970; Spitz, 1986).

Then, of course, evidence was accumulating that intellectual deviancy is frequently hereditary, especially concerning familial resemblance at higher grades of retardation. Finally, there was increasing alarm, much of it fed by Association leaders, about the connection between intellectual limitation and social degeneracy. These beliefs contributed to the eugenics movement based not only on fatally flawed genetic reasoning, but also on social-political–nationalistic impulses and prejudices. It should be noted, in the interests of historical accuracy, that the early eugenics movement found its greatest expression and substantial foundation support (e.g., Carnegie Institution and Rockefeller Foundation) in the United States. The U.S. eugenics movement started in 1904 and continued through World War II advocated and sustained by a self-styled social, political, and academic elite with horrendous effects nationally and internationally (Black, 2003). Extremism, whether then or now, by any other name is extremism. Eugenics is still with us today, but in a much different and scientifically valid form. Genetic medicine, developments in biomedicine, advances in reproductive biology, prenatal screening, and molecular genetics are inspiring the "new eugenics." Of course, there are sharply differing opinions on that score, too.

Fast-forward a century or so and see where we now stand. Although there have been modifications in terminology, the physiological educational methods introduced by Seguin remain essentially unchanged—behavior modification, sensory education and integration, motor training, language acquisition, vocational preparation, and socialization. In short, *educational technology has not undergone any revolutionary transformation.*

On the other hand, scientific knowledge *concerning* causes and prevention of mental retardation has increased by dramatic proportions that could hardly be imagined even in 1962, when the National Institute of Child Health and Human Development was established to address health issues affecting mothers and children. That virtually all these startling discoveries have occurred in *biomedical fields* is a consideration worth keeping in mind, both when considering definition and classification of mental retardation and with respect to research and intervention strategies.

I have reviewed some of the history in light of the proclamation by members of the AAMR T&C Committee (Schalock et al., 1994) that they advanced a "new conception of mental retardation" (p.182) . . . in which "intervention planning is a primary purpose of diagnosis" (p. 183) leading to the provision of services "that result in the person's increased independence, productivity, and community integration" (p. 183). "The concept of supports is integral" (Luckasson, 2002, p. 145). Here is their definition of supports: "resources and strategies that aim to promote the development, education, interests, and personal well-being of a person and that enhance individual functioning" (p. 151).

One might wonder if Seguin, Samuel Howe, and other ardent advocates a century dead experience a tapping, an ever so gentle rapping, of deja vu on their coffin doors. If they were around today, they might be pleased by newspaper accounts, misleading as they are, that with intensive early education intervention IQ can be raised by 7 to 10 points, and that mental retardation can therefore be prevented. Certainly they would be delighted to see that their ideas are alive and well in the AAMR manuals. But those who experienced the vagaries of opinion and policy might also warn of backlash.

The American Association on Mental Retardation

"The tradition of [AAMR] has been to lead the profession and society in promoting increased understanding of mental retardation and to support people with this disability to attain their goals through services they may need, protection of their rights as citizens . . . to establish personal life satisfaction" (Luckasson et al, 1992, p. xi). Which "profession"? Is there now a "profession of mental retardation"? If the intent is really to influence and guide professional practice, then why is it that the committee is so many steps behind current knowledge foundations of the professions they propose to support? They seem to be much more adept at reliving history or short-changing it than they are in furthering science and clinical practice.

All these sentiments raise questions as to whether the AAMR has really provided proactive and informed leadership to the various professions that deal with mental retardation or whether the Association has been reactive to social and political fashion. Greatly swayed by shifting social, political, economic, and cultural currents (including upheavals such as economic depressions and wars), the nature, purposes, and positions of the Association have mutated over the decades. The name of the organization has been changed a number of times to keep up with political currency.

Descriptive terminology advocated by the AAMR as applied to people with diminished intellectual capability has similarly changed, typically not because of scientific discoveries, but in frenzied pendulumic response to political correctness and the latest social philosophy. Where once there were, for instance, "idiots," "the feebleminded," "mental defectives," and "mental retardates," there are now "people with mental retardation," and, inevitably, "consumers."

THE MEANING OF MENTAL RETARDATION—DIFFERING VIEWS

So What Is Mental Retardation? The orthodox wisdom always has been that people with mental retardation have diminished intelligence. (The standardized intelligence test was not necessary for recognition of the certainty that people vary greatly in ability to cipher, use words, and think.) Although on several occasions the AAMD manual was revised and expanded, low intelligence remained the primary delineating feature. (See Greenspan & Switzky, 2003; this book.)

The latest renditions also identify IQ as a major defining attribute, but with qualifications and reservations. In other respects, the 1992 and 2002 systems of terminology and classification are a departure not only from previous AAMR schemes but from those of other organizations as well, such as the American Psychiatric Association (Diagnostic and Statistical Manual of Mental Disorders, 4th edition, 1994) and the World Health Organization's 1993 International Classification of Diseases (ICD).

In the 2002 edition of the manual there is a comparison of the International Classification of Diseases (ICD) through the World Health Organization (WHO) and AAMR models and systems. In general, the authors express the view that the WHO and AAMR see the problems of mental retardation in complementary ways and, despite some criticisms (p. 103) of ICD, they conclude "the AAMR theoretical model is compatible with the ICF process model of disability" (p. 111). (The ICF = International Classification of Functioning, Disability, and Health. This is an international classification complementary to and following from ICD.) This seems to be a world overtaken by acronyms.

On the other hand, Luckasson and collaborators do note interesting differences. One is that "The ICF reflects a professional, objective view of functioning and disability, whereas the AAMR 2002 System includes subjective aspects of functioning (e.g., personal appraisal, personal satisfaction issues, and a strong orientation toward supports" (p. 113). Objectivity should give way to subjectivity? The term "subjectivity" means that the nature of something exists only in the experiencer's mind, incapable of external verification. I find that statement not only indefensible, but patently objectionable, for science is based on that which is objectively observable and verifiable, not on subjective mysticism.

The 2002 T&C Committee also says the ICF model was constructed "as a result of consensus procedures" with input from professionals and consumers. And just how was the AAMR constructed in a more sophisticated manner? With something called "field consultation," whatever that is? The claim is also made the AAMR 2002 system is more oriented toward empirically validated views. Is this science by poll? Where in the manuals is the warrant for this assertion?[4]

In response to the 1992 AAMR System, the American Psychological Association (APA) published its own version (*Manual of Diagnosis and Professional Practice in Mental Retardation*, Jacobson & Mulick, 1996). Much more complete discussion is

---

4. See also Buntinx, 2003, this book; Griffin & Parmenter, 2003, this book: Jacobson, 2003, this book; Simeonssson, Garland, & Bjorck-Akesson, 2003, this book; for further discussion of the relationship of the 1992 and 2002 AAMR Model and the ICF Model.

devoted to many relevant matters, such as intelligence, adaptive behavior, biological substrates, epidemiology, scientific methodology, and the like. Another difference is that the APA model considers assessment of mental retardation in concert with other clinical manifestations. Among other contrasts is the APA focus on degree of severity by IQ and extent of adaptive limitations, as opposed to the AAMR emphasis on systems of support.

The 1992 AAMR "System" has been heralded by proponents and advocates as a most profound transformation because the conception is now cast as responsive to that major paradigm shift, eliciting reactions "not unlike" those to the scientific paradigm shifts described by Kuhn (Schalock et al., 1994). That is, paradigm shifts are conditioned not only by "official" science, but by social factors and personal whim. Of course, this viewpoint is consistent with the obvious and sanctimonious appeal to popular social sensitivities for greater investment in supports and services while, at the same time, down-playing the grim and harsh realities of biological variance and the impossibility of making whole brains and bodies enfeebled by disease, accident, and genetic onslaught. There will be some comfort and succor, however ill-founded, in denying natural science in favor of social construction and its primary tenet of relativism. This is virtuous one-upmanship.

Yes, perhaps the greatest recent influence on social constructivism is Kuhn (1970) in his book *The Structure of Scientific Revolutions*. Here he seems to claim that social consensus determines nature, rather than the other way around. But Kuhn vigorously denied the strong form of relativism that some have read into his work and, indeed, is a firm believer in scientific progress. His writing has been distorted by cultural constructivists.

Although Kuhn does express doubt about the permanent value of regnant scientific paradigms, he also concludes that the governing elements in theory affirmation are those traditionally accepted by natural scientists. One may inquire: If science is so dependent on culture, how could it produce so many solid, enduring results? Of course, there is no doubt that personal factors, swayed by social events and political sensitivies, do influence choice of issues to be investigated.

"Paradigm shift" is a catchy phrase and sounds pretty formidable; but it is no Rorschach test either. Kuhn's is a book that deserves to be more than superficially read before being used to bolster claims beyond what are justified. He does argue, in his writing, that theory choice is more than a matter of politics and fashion. What the T&C Committee has done here, in relying on the Kuhn paradigm-shift conception, is distant from what Kuhn substantively offered. Not only that, but Kuhn's conceptualization has met with considerable skepticism by other philosophers of science.

The foremost feature of this paradigmatic revolution is that mental retardation is no longer considered an absolute individual characteristic, but rather is a relativist expression of the functional impact of a person × environment interaction. This is purported to be an advance, because unlike previous definitions it recognizes "the importance of the environment and its impact on functioning" (p. 9).

This is an advance? Even a cursory examination of the history of efforts to define, classify, and treat mental retardation invites the question: What is really so revolutionary or novel about recognition of organism × environment interactions and transactions? They are just now discovering that nature works its effects via nurture? That proposition has been around a long time, was certainly not unearthed by the Committee, and is generally accepted by both nurturists and hereditarians. (The term "transaction" is as important as "interaction" for describing development of certain attributes. People are not only exposed to environments, but we select and gravitate to environments that suit our natural inclinations.)

Perhaps it might be more revealing to consider what mental retardation supposedly *is not* in this "System." According to Luckasson and her collaborators, mental retardation is not something one has (like blue eyes or a bad heart or, presumably, a bad brain) or what one is (like being short in height or, presumably, IQ points); is not a medical or a mental disorder; is not synonymous with specific etiologies (e.g., Down syndrome), because "etiology is not destiny." (But look at various genetic disorders such as Tay-Sachs disease.) Mental retardation is not a *trait*; rather it is a *state* in which functioning in daily life is impaired as revealed by limitations in adaptive skills. The conceptual representation is neither medical nor psychopathological; it is a *functional* model in which the interaction between capabilities and environments is supposedly central.

Mental retardation is considered a *disability* because of and *only* because of the person × environment interaction. In this light, a major purpose of the new definition "is to hold the *environment responsible* for providing needed supports for greater *inclusion* of individuals with disabilities" (Reiss, 1994, p. 2; italics added). Clearly both sides of the interactive equation are not equally contributory in this model. The environment is at once the problem and the promise.

Given such heavy investment in the social-role construction of mental retardation, a central operative concept is the environment or, more broadly, the culture. The extreme egalitarian proposition is championed that "cure" lies in structuring a fully integrated society where people with intellectual limitations are accepted as equal members and who can function in a "typical way" without need for additional supports (Luckasson et al., 1992, p. 18).

Is utopian eruption of advocacy proclamations—cast within an ideological happiness-based egalitarian stance, unsubstantiated by hard scientific evidence, together with a congenital reluctance to face up to the realities of biological havoc and genetic diversity—to be taken seriously as a revolutionary paradigm swing? The critical underlying inadequacy reflected in these manuals, as well as in other elements of the normalization movement, has been the grievous dereliction in examining the weaknesses and contradictions of fundamental philosophical principles and suppositions. Here we witness failure to move beyond slogans to serious scrutiny of premises, to say nothing of the conspicuous decision to set aside reasoned and convincing principles in the competition for funds and public sympathy. (Sympathy is easier to win than funds.)

Detailed and serious examination of their premises is not an especially easy task, because advocates, including the T&C Committee, have never dealt systematically and critically with such fundamental issues as to whether their positions are choice-based, class-based, respect-based, or happiness-based. These are not the same philosophical positions, and they present important and conflicting policy distinctions, as Rose-Ackerman (1982) pointed out in clear detail in her penetrating discussion of the ethics and politics of normalization. What we observe in the manuals is some kind of hodgepodge of these political philosophies, loosely tied together, accompanied by many unsupported claims, empirically and conceptually.

The T&C committees do not seem to be particularly concerned with current scientific knowledge, as evidenced by their eschewing of certain well-established biological principles concerning developmental variability. About 35 years ago Zigler (1970) aptly summed up the conflict between biology and environment influences in a way that could easily be applied to the 1992/2002 AAMR system as well as much of the prevailing prejudice in the psycho-educational establishment: "Not only do I insist that we take the biological integrity of the organism seriously, but it is also my considered opinion that our nation has more to fear from unbridled environmentalists than those who point to such integrity as one factor in the determination of development" (p. 83). For a more explicit account of the glaring disregard (and implications therefrom) of behavioral genetics to understanding of intelligence differences, see Baumeister and Bacharach (2000) and Spitz (this book).

Consumerism, or the Customer Is Always Right

In the 1992 and 2002 manuals reference is made frequently to "consumers" and their contribution to the new definition. One is not entirely clear as to the identity of this group, although it is certainly reasonable to assume from a literal interpretation that the T&C committees actually requested and incorporated views of people who "have the disability" (1992, p. x). In any case, according to Reiss (1994) the committee determined that consumers should have a "substantial degree of influence." Consumer organizations (special-interest groups? parent groups? advocacy groups? legal representatives?) not only participated but have allegedly enthusiastically supported the new definition because "they desire inclusion, access, and independence" (p. 6). This begs the question as to who are the "consumers." In any case, as reported by Luckasson et al. (2002), consumer organizations praised the 1992 definition for its emphasis on community-based supports.

Clearly definitional concepts were designed with the intention of expanding and elaborating inclusionary services, such as mainstream education, competitive employment, and supported living. The critical strategy is to develop all needed supports that are "consumer directed" (p. 184), through an interdisciplinary team, consisting mostly of laypeople who do not risk professional liability.[5] Supports go beyond services to include social security, health care, accessible housing, employment, and so forth. In other words, an essential focus of the diagnostic process is provision of greater benefits from public sources—justified on ideological, not scientific grounds.

In order for the system to become person-oriented, an aspiration repeatedly emphasized in the manuals as a core feature of the "new paradigm," it will be necessary to move to a supports-based approach that will "require both evolution and transformations of public services systems" (Luckasson et al., 2002, p. 188). "The goal of a supports-based approach is to facilitate the inclusion of individuals in the full life of the community" (pp. 183–184).

That begs the question as to how these individuals as a very heterogeneous group, aside from anecdotal accounts, contribute to society with an empirically established positive benefit-to-cost ratio? Here is an example of another awkward compromise between

---

5. This brings up a special professional, legal, and ethical problem. If decisions are made by an interdisciplinary team, including non-professionals, do those licenced professionals incur special liability risks in having to defend decisions made on the basis of committee consensus?

ideological purity and aspiration for resources. These manuals appear to be driven more by monetary than by scientific concerns.

The authors of the manuals repeatedly talk about the public interest and the person-centered supports and service programs, as if they share a common cause. This is another area in which they engage in naive confusion. Do they not understand that the sickness of the person and the sickness of the population represent very different problems and approaches? Public health responses that may benefit an individual may help or hurt the community. Public health measures that benefit the community may do harm to the individual. Do you have a right to be sick? That depends. Suppose it is an infectious disease that endangers others? This is why we require immunization, for instance, even though a few actually die from the immunization. Public health is based on epidemiological strategies in which the intent is to protect groups of exposed individuals. Odds ratios and relative risks are important measures in public health. This is entirely distinct from individual health care, where the person is the object of attention. Odds ratios and relative risk measures are irrelevant in the case of the individual. For the individual, it is the absolute risk that is most relevant.

ANTISCIENCE DOGMA AND POSTMODERN PERVERSION

Underlying every system or structure of classification and terminology, whether concerning mental retardation or any other natural condition, there must be some fundamental premises, suppositions, and epistemological foundations. Nosology does not mysteriously appear to the observer "like an angel writing in a book of gold."

Although the T&C Committee do offer some surface rationale (such as their stated commitment to egalitarianism, contextualism, and an ecological perspective in the 2002 edition), a deeper ideological structure inevitably guides their formulations, whether or not explicitly stated. It is important to scrutinize critically that core structure and its historical source—or, to put the matter bluntly, determine "where they are coming from."

If the inclusionary/normalization credo is born of socialization manifestations, then they should explain clearly the basic premises of cultural-anthropological determinations that underlie their deductive premises, offering testable hypotheses. There seems to some sort of moral doctrine at work here; but the implications of this belief system are not explicated. Numerous conflicts result from a leap from a vaguely articulated belief system to public solutions without examination of the intervening tensions, interests, and theory. If resources are limited and we wish to take into account the interests of all people, then there will inevitably be conflict with positions advanced by advocates. In short, we cannot do it all, and choices must be made—unfortunately, including normative decisions as to individual worth. Nowhere in the manuals are such fundamental epistemological questions addressed.

We are solemnly alerted by the Committee (Schalock et al., 1994) that the paradigm shift "necessitates . . . significant changes in one's thinking" (p. 181) and that service delivery now focuses on "strengths and capabilities of the person, normalized and typical environments, integrated services with supports, and the empowerment of individuals served" (p. 182). Quite aside from the obvious imprecision of this grandiose terminology (or utter inanity, such as "empowerment"), blatant and outright advocacy has no standing in construction of a clinical nosology, no matter how philosophically honorable and well intentioned in principle.

The Preface to the 2002 manual says: "we needed to attend to ensuring adequate and appropriate services"(p. xiii). Why and when did definition transmute into service planning? This is more than a nuanced change in definition and classification of a health problem. It is a calculated partisan bid to reconstruct biological reality and to advocate rather than inform.

Such constructions are not only scientifically regressive, they slight the common trust. This is nothing more than affected obscurity in search of a cause. The AAMR definition amounts to reflection of the contemporary proclivity to empower the afflicted, even to the point of promoting the curious fiction that there is no biological affliction, as such, but that people are simply "differently abled."

For reasons that others have noted, the doctrinaire fervor so abundantly evident in the socially constructed system could actually harm the very individuals who are intended to be the beneficiaries. For example, several recent epidemiological studies have shown that the pell-mell rush to relocate people from institutions to community placement significantly increases their relative risk of avoidable mortality (Strauss & Shavelle, 1998). I suppose one might argue that this is a form of enlightened empowerment, in that they should share more equitably the jeopardy of premature death. If the reward, why not the risk? One wonders why these consumers were not "empowered" to make the choice.

In any case, there are those who do not find mortality risk to be such a critical issue, insisting instead that the real question concerns meaningful life, not death. In arguing this point, Blacher (1998) makes the curious and rather nonsensical observation "that there is dignity in risk" (p, 412). Although the point can be argued that people with mental retardation have the same right to fail as others, they seem to exercise this right with greater frequency.

How we as a society should treat people who are hurt, sick, or otherwise disabled is undeniably a public policy issue of enormous significance. But that is a far different proposition from objectively, empirically, and scientifically developing a reliable, valid, and useful system for terminology and classification. Defining a health problem is one thing; dealing with it quite another. Certainly it cannot make sense to define a health problem in terms of "supports" required. Is the construction tailored to justify the purveyors? For instance, if we have special educators, do we need to define some subgroup as requiring their professional services, with methods that have not changed from the very beginning of the trade?

Science and the technology it generates contribute to both purposes: definition and treatment. But by confusing these issues, the AAMR T&C committee, intentionally or not, elevated ritual over reason while projecting a decidedly postmodern, antiscientific, relativist mien. The concept of mental retardation was laid in a procrustean bed, shrouded by philosophical contradictions and tautologies. One result is that scientific substance was sacrificed for warm and cozy other ways of "knowing" disguised as social virtue. Committee paladins, guided by the blinking beacons of consumerism and political correctness, apparently relegated empirical rationality and analytical reasoning to steerage class in their Titanic voyage to uncover the "true" meaning of mental retardation.

Presumably it is more important to inculcate suitably acceptable attitudes toward the great issues than it is to impart genuine knowledge of their substance.

The postmodern antagonism, implicit throughout the AAMR manuals, is a reflection of a much broader, more widespread, and growing quarrel with and resentment of modern science—sometimes called the "new humanities." Of course, I do appreciate that a broad-brush characterization will capture thoughtful people who do not accept cultism, irrationality, spirituality, sloganism, romantic fantasies, and apocalyptic rhetoric as legitimate alternatives to science and reason. Nonetheless, the antiscience movement has found root in practically all facets of Western life, including our universities, religious organizations, the press, and governmental agencies.

This assault comes from many diverse and influential individuals and groups. (See Gross & Levitt, 1994; Gross, Levitt, & Lewis, 1997, for more detail and identities of these individuals and groups.) These assemblies include, among others, radical feminists who decry male domination, literal creationists, intelligent design proponents, multiculturalists, radical ecologists, romanticist individualists in literature and poetry celebrating the importance of "intuition," animal rights extremists, religious leaders with their righteous insistence on literal interpretations of biblical traditions, and many in liberal arts academia who resent the growing dominance of science. (After all, it is the scientists who bring into the university hoards of external funding from NIH and NSF and are rewarded accordingly.)

These groups are not always in concert on other matters, but they do set aside their differences to share a unifying demotic perspective that science is a nihilistic construction that ensconces power in a self-perpetuating elitist establishment that, in denying the objective ground of moral truth, seeks to devalue and stifle other discourse or knowledge not grounded in the language and precepts of modern science.

It is in romantic individualism literature and poetry that the strongest and most impassioned distrust of science first set in as reaction against Enlightenment values (Gross & Levitt, 1994). We now see deep-seated and growing reluctance to accept the premise that the human condition can be reformed through science.

According to these nihilists science is supposedly crippled by its artificiality and reductionism, by insistence on contrived measurable objectivity, replicability, and methodological exactness; by rejection of mind-body dualism, spirituality, and mysticism; and by allegiance to the interests of elitism, dominion, caste structure, and economic prerogative. Postmodern critics of science have effectively spread an antirealist doctrine that is not only so fundamentally flawed conceptually that it cannot hold up to honest scrutiny or verification, but also is demonstrably harmful in both systemic and personal ways. Because of their appeal to political puissant agendas, aided and abetted by misguided partisan sensibilities and professional vanities, postmodern advocates have become a powerful, but subversive, faction in the soft side of academia. At the same time, the point should be stressed that many of these partisans are influential and highly respected scholars who have greatly enriched literature and philosophy.

These are not idle loons by any stretch, and they must be regarded seriously. Take, for example, the constructive philosophy of Stanley Aronowitz, a sociological theorist, who is a leading oppositional figure aiming to demystify science. He proceeds from the theory that science is culturally situated and is reflective of historical circumstances embedded in ideological design of dominance and influence within contemporary society. Notwithstanding that his views and writings have been described as turgid, opaque, and incoherent, he has created a dedicated following with such conclusions as: "The point is that neither logic nor mathematics escapes the contamination of the social" (Aronowitz, 1988).

It is as if an infectious process has invaded the legitimate scientific body of knowledge and methods, the health of which will depend on the vitality of the collective immune reaction to join in and rid our culture of this destructively injurious viral nonsense. Those who advocate the science-as-social dogma equate their maddening meandering with "progress."

Of course, some scientists also equate their work with "progress." That is an unnecessary and gratuitous extrapolation, for it depends on what is meant by progress, especially that of the social variety. Progress is problematic and does inevitably give cause for concern about the uses to which science and technology are put (e.g., recombinant DNA, cloning, screening, drugs). In fact, most scientists themselves demonstrate as much apprehension as anyone among the contemporary critics about some of the uses to which science is put. I doubt that many scientists are devoted to meliorism, although the tendency to social improvement may be furthered through conscious human effort. In any case, science is a means; the ends are a separate issue that must inevitably be resolved in terms of ethical and moral discourse and principle. In fact, science creates conditions which require an ethic.

In arguing the case for postmodern thinking in understanding and defining mental retardation, Danforth (1997) refers to science as a "progressive myth" and encourages a postscientific dialogue that would "seek democracy over science, community over 'objective truth'" (p. 105). He adds: "Postmodern philosophers propose that the sources of hope in the field of mental retardation services erupt from precisely those mouths and writing (or typing) hands [meaning facilitated communication] that do not speak the language of science" (p. 104). In short, science is just another form of concocted discourse, no more objective than other sources of knowledge, and less humane at that. According to this view, science offers neither a superior epistemology nor, as concerns matters of health, the optimal approach. Indeed history is replete with "alternatives."

Mountebank healers are not an anachronism (Spitz, 1997). By donning the mantle of "scientific studies" now, more than ever, these pseudoscientists aggressively and effectively ply their potions, services, and wares to an unwary public and many gullible service providers, as well as to policymakers. Alternative forms of healing such as homeopathy, spirituality, extra-sensory communication, energy-field manipulation, acupuncture, magic cures, fringe medicine, and relaxation training are just some of the "unconventional" healing therapies. For example, the framers of the 1992 manual endorsed facilitated communication (p. 123), apparently absent knowledge of the facts. In his extensive scholarly historical examination of this and other mystical folly, Spitz (1997) has demonstrated just how insidious and threatening these cabalistic "movements" have become to rationality and human welfare "like a virus run rampant" (p. 175).

To be sure, the abuses and arrogance that are too often characteristic of practitioners of conventional healing methods certainly fuel resentment and distrust (e.g., the epidemic of psychotropic prescriptions). Some practitioners—including physicians, psychologists, special educators—who clothe themselves in the patois and rhetoric of science actually rely on faith in authority (including drug sales representatives), whose information is often wrong or self-serving. Many are not trained as scientists and, in fact, often misinterpret research. Researchers also misinterpret research, often inflating the value of our own. All this contributes to the illusion that disability and, ultimately, death are avoidable.

Our journals, court records, and popular press are full of testimony to this unfortunate and embarrassing circumstance. In addition there are occasional unethical abuses of science and some that are so common and perilous as to be outrageous (Healy, 2004). (See Alan Baumeister, 2000, for a well-documented description of egregious abuse involving human brain stimulation.)

Then there are mistakes. Consider recent reports that about 100,000 people die in hospitals annually due to medical errors. For various reasons this is certainly an underestimate. If so many people die in hospitals because of medical errors, just think of the many more who suffer debilitating illness and morbidity.

Science is a messy, uncertain, and often contentious endeavor (and regrettably, but infrequently, sometimes fraudulent) that can easily be misunderstood by policymakers and providers. But those are not grounds to take flight from rationality and reason.

So what is wrong with alternative constructions and ways of healing? The difference is that if an unconventional therapy (e.g., facilitated communication or sensory integration therapy) actually has an effect, then it must be unequivocally demonstrated to work by rigorous and replicable test. That requires the scientific method. A belief system may be held without evidence, or contrary to the evidence, or because of the evidence. Scientific knowledge advances, often fitfully, because of the evidence.

I am convinced that vociferous critics of science such as postmodernists and cultural constructivists—through misleading and misreading—are at the very heart of the dispute regarding the 1992 and 2002 AAMR manuals and a multitude of other issues in the field of mental retardation and beyond. It is a distinction that harkens back to the ascendancy of Enlightenment values in conflict with religious doctrine and the utopian prescience of spiritual-socialism promulgated by other groups such as the Saint-Simonians and other radical rightists and radical leftists. Rejection of the scientific world view, no matter how recondite that view, should not be taken lightly.

I also think that many postmodern critics (and their cultural constructivist brethren) of science have not bothered to acquaint themselves with serious science and the way it works, what it can and cannot do. Theirs is a conviction born more of a stance than of understanding. They hold that there is really little need to appreciate the details of science, because the postmodern skeptics, or the poststructuralist, impotence-of-human-reason camp (as best represented by the prolific French social-historical theorist Michel Foucault; e.g., 1973), insist there is no possibility of enduring universal truth in a scientific area. In this view reality is merely a chimerical abstraction, a socially constructed fiction, consisting only of texts or stories that are socially and politically "situated."

According to this doctrine the philosophy cultivated during the Enlightenment of the 18th century is destructively flawed because we are locked within an arbitrary structure of language and have no basis for knowing anything that exists outside this system. From this it follows that all we have access to is "texts" and there is no such thing as fixed meaning. Therefore, science does not have universal application, but is merely a product of the ideology of a particular era, and all classifications, whether derived by physical or social scientists, are arbitrary manifestations of language and, therefore, bear no direct relationship to the outside world. One may wonder whether there is even an "outside world" at all according to these formulations.

The culturist interpretation of science has a long history in philosophical discourse. Many of these ideas stem from the German philosopher Nietzsche, who rejected not only the idea that knowledge accumulates, but that conclusions drawn from science can ever be grounded in any type of certainty (Windschuttle, 1996). There are only interpretations, not fact or objective truth. Truth is simply an effect of power.

What most certainly ought to be a major embarrassment for the postmodern radicals, especially the influential French (notably Foucault, for whom language creates power and authority), is their affinity with famous German existentialist philosopher, Martin Heidegger. He followed the lead of Nietzsche (especially in adopting the critical role of language in interpreting natural events). Heidegger rejected modern social existence and rational domination of nature. His philosophy was a major cornerstone of Nazism. Heidegger deplored the destruction of the Nazi regime until his death in 1976. Despite his fall from political grace and from his exalted academic status, Heidegger greatly influenced all the major poststructuralist theorists, especially concerning such concepts as deviance (Windschuttle, 1996).

Notwithstanding all the claims of postmodern relativists, the scientific method has proven to be overwhelmingly powerful technologically, economically, and militarily. The Western scientific tradition has captured the only genuinely valid form of empirical and verifiable knowledge. Despite contentious assertions and lack of total agreement among contemporary philosophers of science, who for the most part endorse scientific traditions, the efficacy, precision, and sustained growth of the methodology is beyond doubt. The enormous success of science in explanation of natural phenomena and in promoting technological innovation stems from the focus on explanations inferred from comfirmable information. When it comes to pragmatic criteria, Western science trumps all other cognitive styles. This does not mean that science is the only way in which we acquire knowledge. There are other avenues to understanding, including literature, the arts, philosophical contemplation, and religion. Science may even enrich moral perceptions, but that is beyond the realm of science. The role of science is to understand the natural world. The uses to which scientific information is put compels a moral test. Science does not contend that all swans are or should be white. Science looks for the black swan.

In other words, science works. But not the way the postmodern critics say it does. There is, in science, much that transcends the particular—that is, basic knowledge that is accepted by the scientific community as accurate and consequential. Postmodern nihilism is not only corrosive in its effects on reason, but, as the T&C Committee's 1992 and 2002 manuals abundantly illustrate, places public health policy in a conceptual straight-jacket. What we have here is procrustean absurdity.

So what have the T & C Committees put in place of science?: "Valuing." One might, generously, I suppose, regard the vague philosophy driving the AAMR manual as a reflection of the "new humanities." But in my view this trend is nothing less than intellectual catastrophe. Allan Bloom, in his *The Closing of the American Mind*, argued that radical egalitarian theory has captured the agenda as to how we understand human beings as individuals. The result is that the humanities or social sciences abandoned objectivity and truth and became hopelessly and unabashedly mired in political correctness. The politicizing of academia is really an assault on the intellectual and moral substance of American society.

Here we have a world view permeated with internal inconsistencies that are logically vacuous and irresponsible from a broad public policy perspective. This phenomenon extends beyond the humanities to health and medicine, where such concepts as illness, disease, patient, and biological intervention are regarded as social fictions. These beliefs, although cloaked in virtuous tongue, are pervasive throughout the recent AAMR manuals. The T&C Committees have gotten lost in a tautological mess of epistemological meanderings that lead nowhere, except in a circle. This sort of epistemological wandering leads us nowhere in particular and can, as history has shown, be indulged indefinitely without having any real impact on advancing scientific knowledge. If left unchecked, sooner or later deconstructionists will undermine the traditional order and mess up convenient and effective ways of engaging harsh realities.

We are informed by Reiss (1994), writing on behalf of the Committee in response to MacMillan et al. (1993), that "There is no single God-given definition [of mental retardation] that scientists can discover" (p. 5). One wonders what that revelation has to do with anything. While some of us who undertake pursuit of science in the quest to comprehend and interpret natural events may occasionally, in desperation or exasperation, importune divine guidance, providence seems to be prudently impartial. In any case, there appears to be scant benefaction from ecclesiastical sources on any nosology. The essence and inner logic of the scientific enterprise, for all its well-publicized flaws and foibles, provide the principal basis for categorizing and ordering knowledge of natural events pertaining to matters of health, of which mental retardation is part.

RESEARCH

What effect will this 1992 definition and its 2002 successor have on research? The answer depends on whom you ask. The manual writers say one thing; researchers by their actions say another.

According to the Committee, the system will be a "challenge" (1992, p. 149) in that researchers will find it necessary to provide more precise description of their subjects including IQ, profile of adaptive skills, etiology, and types and intensities of support necessary or provided. There will be "less emphasis on the person's condition and functioning level as the independent variable . . . and more given to environmental conditions and support structures as independent variables and the person's functioning level, living/employment status or level of satisfaction as the dependent variable" (p. 149).

Of course, they also predict that there will be large-scale utilization and field testing of the definition and its effects. There is a certain credibility gap here when one examines the research credentials of Luckasson and her collaborators. Perhaps they should be a bit more cautious in their pronouncement about the future of research until they have established themselves as serious empirical investigators rather than as polemicists. In short, it would help if they knew what they are talking about.

I doubt the 1992 and 2002 manuals will have much, if any, effect on scientific research, as distinguished from pseudoscientific. The percentage of published researchers who have adopted the 1992 version is virtually nonexistent. Science requires a stable, reliable, and precise system for hypothesis formulation and testing, selection of variables for study, and measurable specification of the thing being studied.

Intelligence, as assessed by standardized procedures, will continue to be of major interest to behavioral researchers, increasingly concerning neurological substrates and behavioral genetics. Despite reservations expressed in the manuals about the IQ score and the emphasis on adaptive skills, the well-established fact is that the IQ is the most robust predictor of performance that psychology has ever produced, whether indexed by academic achievement, job success, income, social status, mental health, and more (Gottfredson, 1997; Lubinski & Humphreys, 1997).

Biomedical researchers, who conduct the vast amount of research on conditions related to mental retardation, did not pay much heed to earlier AAMR definitions, and there is no reason to believe that will change (Baumeister, Bacharach, & Baumeister, 1997). Biomedical research reports rarely find their way into mainstream mental retardation journals, such as the American Journal on Mental Retardation, but rather are published in high-impact biological journals. The primary reason is that biomedical research is usually etiologically or pathogenically oriented. In terms of research funding priorities, as reflected in NIH grants, it is clear that pathogenic mechanisms, genetic history, heredity, neuroscience, and etiology dominate clinical and scientific thrust (Baumeister, Bacharach, & Baumeister, 1997).

Focus is on the disease (e.g., fragile X), problem (e.g., low birth weight), or pathogenesis (i.e., cellular or other perturbations that occur during the course of the disease). Mental retardation may be phenotypically expressed; but so are other outcomes as well. As an example, premature low birth weight is associated with cerebral palsy, systemic disorders, residual lung disease, retinopathy, neurological illness, affective disorders, learning disabilities, and so on. Furthermore, most "heavier" premature LBW children develop quite normally. The very light premature babies, below 1500 g, whose brains are seriously damaged, present far greater relative risk of all manner of serious disabilities, not just mental retardation. Variable expressivity is the rule, not the exception.

There is still another complicating side to this multifactorial perplexity. We define and diagnose disorders according to signs and symptoms. But it is the case certainly that different causes, including different genes, produce similar symptoms—such as low IQ and deficits in some of the same realms of adaptive behavior. Prevention and treatment approaches will necessarily vary by cause.

One looks in vain for any extended discussion of these matters in the manuals. They do point out, correctly, that people with mental retardation are at far greater risk, as compared with the general population, for many health and mental problems. For most, especially those in the more severe range, low IQ is not their most pressing health concern. Again, far more is known about this concordance than they indicate. But it has tremendous implications for research, treatment, funding, and policy.

Mental retardation is a biological condition (obviously sometimes triggered and influenced by environmental circumstances). Nature reveals its influence via nurture. If we wish to prevent or minimize those conditions that produce mental retardation, we must understand the sequence of pathogenic disease processes and how these unfold. Interventions can occur any where along this sequence, but they differ in sensitivity, specificity, and cost-benefit.

Consider again the problem of premature low birth weight in light of our research understanding of this condition. Does mental retardation begin with an undernourished grandmother, an autosomal genetic anomaly, low maternal intelligence, a teen pregnancy, unhealthy maternal behavior, lack of appropriate prenatal care, intrauterine infection, maternal structural abnormalities or disease, preeclampsia, intracranial bleeds, impoverished home environment, abuse and neglect, poor school performance, or measured low IQ scores? The answer is: any, some, or all of the above. The more appropriate question is: Where should intervention (supports, if they wish) begin? In any case, we can recognize the pathogenic sequence only through scientific research. There is little in the system proposed by AAMR that informs this complex process. In fact, it stultifies.

ETIOLOGY

The optimal system for classification of mental retardation is by specific cause or etiology. As Durkin and Stein (1996) have indicated, classification by etiology serves three purposes: primary prevention, understanding pathogenesis, and informing families and providers. To this I would add that epidemiological ends, vital to public health policy, are served as well.

Both manuals include chapters dealing with etiological issues. Acknowledgment is made of the complex multivariate and intergenerational nature of causes and effects. The importance of prevention is recognized. Furthermore, the point is properly made that rigid distinction between biological and psychosocial causes is invalid and misleading. Unfortunately, these important issues were dealt with by the T&C Committee perfunctorily and often in an illusive, contradictory manner. They either did not understand or take the time to examine current scientific knowledge that bears on these issues.

The familiar organic-nonorganic (psychosocial) distinction is too crude, at both ends, to inform either research, clinical practice, or theory. There are by now hundreds of known organic causes, each of which has its distinctive characteristics, pathogenesis, prognosis, and intervention implications. Furthermore, research continues to whittle away at the uncertainties. Where once, for instance, some children previously characterized as "psychosocial" are now known to have been subjected to lead intoxication. Others presenting with clear neurological symptomatology, classified as "organic—cause unknown," have been prenatally exposed to teratogens or infections. Unfortunately, these important issues were dealt with by the Committee perfunctorily and often in a misleading manner, as reflected in their assumptions about the wonders of "inclusion."

The 1992 manual states that "One cannot prevent what one does not understand" (p. 69). This sentiment is echoed in the more recent edition. While that sounds respectable on the surface, I am not certain what is meant by such an assertion in the context in which it was offered. Just what level or kind of understanding is required? Definitive knowledge about an immediate cause is not always necessary to prevent mental retardation or other health disorders.

Perhaps the classic illustration is the "shoe-leather" epidemiology pursued by John Snow in his analysis of a cholera outbreak in London in 1854. He did not know about the pathogen that causes cholera. But he was able to prevent the disease by systematically demonstrating that it is transmitted by water and that the outbreak of the disease occurred among those who obtained their water from a particular pump. Removal of the handle of the water pump at Broad Street dramatically reduced the weekly death toll. Family planning in regard to genetic and congenital risks accomplishes similar goals today.

Similarly, premature low birth weight is a complex, multivariate, and only vaguely understood constellation of causes. But through research we do know that spontaneous premature labor and premature rupture of membranes together account for most premature births. Furthermore, research has shown that women diagnosed with bacterial vaginosis are 40% more likely to deliver a premature LBW baby. Following up on that finding, it has been reported that treatment with antibiotic may reduce by 50% preterm birth and premature rupture of membranes associated with bacterial vaginosis. Understanding of the pathogenic process thus allows for prevention of mental retardation associated with LBW.

The same sorts of intervention strategies can be applied to mental retardation associated with genetic causes. Yet despite some potential merit in their chapter on etiology, the Committee stubbornly refused to accept the scientifically established facts of polygenic or multigene influences on family resemblances in intelligence. (As we shall see, they do accept that some hitherto "cultural" retarded persons may owe their misfortune to genetic influences.) Again, appeal is made to inclusionary doctrine, such as comprehensive early educational intervention, to reverse the influence of adverse environments. Although this may be socially or politically laudable in intent, independent analyses of outcome data from large-scale, global, and undifferentiated early intervention programs disclose that effects on intelligence are meager and transient (e.g., Farran, 2000).

Although many of the early eugenics measures were misguided and politically motivated, as the manuals indicate, this does not mean that the hereditary principles were wrong. Political and racial biases so badly twisted these genetic principles, especially as concerns "negative" eugenics, that they became demonstrably untenable. History has shown how much grievous and widespread harm can arise from deliberate distortion of biological principles when used to further political and nationalistic goals. That generalization, though, cuts two ways.

In any case, the best predictor of child IQ is maternal IQ. There has been considerable progress in mapping gene loci and different mutations associated with general intelligence (Baumeister & Bacharach, 2000). For instance, mutations in the GDI1 gene have been found in families with X-linked nonspecific mental retardation (D'Adamo et al., 1998). A recent brain-mapping study by Thompson et al. (2001) shows that specific areas of the brain, related to variability in measured general intelligence, are under genetic control.

Recently Plomin and his associates have shown a high degree of group heritability (.49) for mild mental retardation in early childhood, in fact greater than heritability of individual differences in intelligence in the "normal" range (Spinath, Harlaar, Ronald, & Plomin, 2004). Although there have been many other studies of the familial genetic aspects of intelligence, there have been few studies of genetic influences on mild mental retardation. Certainly none approach the Spinath et al. study in terms of sophistication and definitiveness. These and other studies persuasively showing that "mild" mental retardation is strongly tied to genetic variability are carefully reviewed by Spitz in another chapter in this book.

Such empirical examples of genetic influences on mild mental retardation underlie a sea-wave of scientific change that is occurring at a dizzy pace as the messages buried in the genome are being rapidly deciphered. Every human trait is associated with genetic variation. Variability—genetic, environmental, and in combination—is the hallmark of the natural condition.

The implications are enormous for neuroscience understanding of mild mental retardation. Those in the mild category are by far the largest group. This fact must be reason for concern in that, as society becomes increasingly technologically dependent, these individuals will become even more marginalized with respect to employment, self-reliance, and socialization.

As implied by the reaction-range concept, with increasing environmental complexity requiring ever greater demands on cognitive skills, the contribution of genetic influences to phenotypic differences in adaptation enlarges. Heredity governs the capacity to utilize the environment. If the framers of the recent AAMR manuals are thoroughly committed to the idealized egalitarian society, then they logically must accept the certainty that innate abilities would account for more and more individual differences. The intellectually rich would become richer, because heritability assessed at the level of biology (genotype) transacts with the environment to as to increase heritability as the level of the observed (phenotype). But in the quest to serve special interests, fairness is not defined as equitable; it is construed as leveling. That is, let us differentially intensify services and opportunities for impaired people so as increase uniformity of outcome. But we can't have it both ways. The repercussion is continual ideological quarreling among advocates as adversaries talk past one another, as if sound volume were the measure of winning. I envision Mother Nature laughing aloud. As Wilson so adroitly captured the message: "Chose the society you wish to promote, then prepare to live with its heritabilities" (Wilson, 1998, p. 142)—that is, the innate individual differences that separate us. I add to Wilson's statement: Be prepared to live with the consequences.

In what I believe is the soundest chapter in the 2002 edition of the manual, "Etiology and Prevention," the authors briefly review some of the evidence concerning the classical two-group approach to mental retardation. (This is before they had access to the Spinath et al., 2004, report. Who knows whether it would have made a difference?) They are led to conclude that the "historical distinction between biological and psychosocial types may be blurred in many cases" (p. 125) and "that biomedical risk factors may be present in people with mild mental retardation of cultural-familial origin" (p. 126). Here they deal most directly with the multiple-risk model of mental retardation, revealing that definition, classification, management, and prevention of mental retardation is an exceedingly complex matter. Unfortunately, these considerations are not reflected in the standard definition of mental retardation given on page 1 of the manual. I do not understand why not, especially when there they twice mention "supports" as "essential" to the application of the definition.

Individual differences in intelligence are a fact of nature, arising from endogenous and exogenous sources and their interactions. Because we can predict that individual differences in cognitive ability will become an increasingly important determinant of adjustments to complex environments, the question is: How should we deal with this variability? As Detterman and Thompson (1997) have observed, there continues to be general confusion as to whether the goal of special education is to raise the mean or reduce the standard deviation of a distribution. They call this a "dangerous confusion" (p. 1087), because the implications are far different. In any case, they conclude that there is scant empirical evidence that educational intervention has any effect at all on the distribution of ability scores and that "fixes that are motivated more by emotion than rationality will be insufficient" (p. 1089).

I should add that special education practices typically do not take into account the many different predisposing, initiating, maintaining, and mediating factors that contribute to individual differences, despite all the evidence. At the very least we should structure our educational programs along multiple tracks, using intelligence as a base. But that is another story.

My inclination to describe mental retardation in terms of etiology, pathology, diseases, symptoms, and all the rest no doubt might be taken by some advocates as "typological thinking," which apparently is not good because it stands as a "potent obstacle to the appreciation of human uniqueness and dignity" (Gelb, 1997). In a bizarre and silly effort to rectify the wrongs committed by typologists (e.g., Down, Galton, Darwin) Gelb praises the AAMR definition for standing "genetic reductionism on its head" (p. 453), whatever that means. Gelb has created an obvious tautology and made it sound like a timeless profundity.

CURE VERSUS PREVENTION

Consider this humbling circumstance: There are fifteen to twenty thousand recognized human diseases, but only a thousand can be cured or completely reversed (WHO, 1977). "Cure" of mental retardation has proven to be an elusive goal. In fact, how does one define "cure"? Are "supports" curative? At best, treatment or amelioration of mental retardation (and myriad cofeatures) is marginal, expensive, and long-term. There never has been nor will there ever be a single all-purpose cure for mental retardation, whether in medical, psychological, educational, or sociological applications (Baumeister, 1997; Baumeister & Bacharach, 2000). Nevertheless, the Committee maintains that the functional approach to definition has actually resulted in a decrease of prevalence of developmental disabilities in the schools (Schalock et al., 1994).

In fact, it is true that prevalence of mental retardation and speech and hearing disorders did decrease from 1987 to 1993, with a leveling off after that. We seem to be curing mild mental retardation. The difficulty with this interpretation is that at the same time we have experienced an epidemic of learning disabilities (Baumeister & Baumeister, 2002). In view of incredible variations in definitional criteria, diagnostic unreliability, stigmatization, and legal hypersensitivities involved, these disability groupings become distinctions of ludicrous futility (MacMillan & Reschly, 1998). Definitions based on cultural and legal sensitivities are about as sturdy as a sand castle.

So what are the prospects for prevention of mental retardation? This is a much more promising approach than cure, provided that the tempting allure of the all-purpose fix is dodged (Baumeister, Kupstas, & Woodley, 1993). The causes, progression, manifestations, and prognosis of the many mental retardations (note the plural) are products of a complex and daunting myriad constellation of events. Prevention and treatment interventions can be no less. As I have previously indicated, to prevent a disease or disability we must have some reliable and valid information about its causative or pathogenic nature. Consider some of the following examples (from Baumeister, Kupstas, & Woodley-Zanthos, 1993) from a great many (leaving out the old standby PKU, which has its own serious public health problems that are not widely understood):

1. Until recently the most significant cause of acquired mental retardation was the invasive bacterium hemophilus influenza type b (Hib) that causes meningitis. About 18,000 children were infected annually, leading to a 10% mortality rate and 33% risk of mental retardation among survivors. After a great deal of painstaking research, scientists at the National Institute of Child Health and Human Development discovered a conjugate vaccine that was so effective that the number of reported cases has dropped to fewer than 100 per year.

2. Routine newborn screening revealed that congenital hypothyroidism occurred at the rate of about 1 per 3600 births. Deficient levels of thyroid hormone after birth affect brain development and cause mental retardation. A mass screening program, conducted from 1979 to 1986, identified 97% of infants with congenital hypothyroidism in time to prevent mental retardation.

3. Tay-Sachs disease is an autosomal recessive metabolic disorder that results in mental retardation and death, usually prior to age 3. Because of the population-specific nature of Tay-Sachs, genetic screening can identify carrier status for couples at risk for having a baby with this disease. The discovery of a relatively simple heterozygote screen led to an impressive decline in the number of new cases in regions where populations are at high risk.

4. Each year about 4000 babies are born with neural tube defects. Recent studies have shown that preconceptual vitamin supplementation with folic acid can reduce incidence of neural tube defects by more than 50%.

5. A major cause of pediatric mortality and acquired mental retardation is HIV transmission from mother to child. Contemporary studies have shown that transmission risk can be reduced by up to two-thirds by antenatal and intrapartum administration of zidovudine to the mother and the newborn.

6. Lead has long been known to be a serious toxin affecting many organ systems including the brain. Only fairly recently did convincing scientific evidence became available demonstrating adverse effects of low levels of exposure. With the ban of lead in gasoline, in 1978, the number of children in the United States with blood levels above 10 μg/dl declined from over 10,000,000 to 900,000. Intellectual impairment due to lead exposure has almost certainly been greatly reduced.

7. A multisite research project supported by the NICHD has found that fetal cells circulating in maternal blood can be isolated and examined for chromosomal and genetic defects. It will not be long before this noninvasive procedure is available to be incorporated into standard obstetrics practice, producing some very profound positive effects concerning incidence of numerous disorders. For example, now amniocentesis or chorionic villus sampling is offered to some pregnant women who, because they are older, may be at increased risk for a child with Down syndrome. But in the future all pregnant women can be screened—without jeopardy

to either fetus or mother. This will potentially produce an enormous reduction in incidence of Down syndrome (for those opting for abortion), because, despite the highly increased risk of delivering a child with Down syndrome among women over 35 years, the fact is that by far the greater number of Down syndrome children are born to younger women. The fetal cells can also be examined for numerous single-gene defects, such as the in-born errors of metabolism.

The list of scientific accomplishments that prevent mental retardation(s) could be greatly expanded, and is growing at an ever-increasing pace. The point is made, however, that understanding of etiology, pathogenesis, and targeted interventions makes the difference. The definition of mental retardation and classification promulgated by AAMR had nothing to do with these discoveries of such great social, economic, and health benefits.

Concluding Thoughts

To the extent that the 1992/2002 system proposed by AAMR furthers the goals of advocacy, service provision, empowerment (of consumers, providers, and AAMR), resource procurement, inclusion, humanistic or spiritual impulse, and social reform, then so be it, as credulous and scientifically corrupt as their view is. They concoct evidence with the appearance of science, but without the substance. In their confused farrago, they indefensibly dismiss serious science and fix emphasis on populist political goals. Here is a situation where political and social considerations are more influential than scientific ones. Such is the way of votaries, those devoted to a cause. Means have become ends in a predetermined direction. Nature is now denatured. How lamentable—because, whether we like it or not, *Homo sapiens* is a biological entity, governed by the rules of nature that apply to all species.

I am not persuaded that any measure of rational argument and counter evidence is likely to move many of these vaporific framers. At the very least, the authors are tenacious in their beliefs. From the standpoints of scientific inquiry, meaningful treatment, primary prevention, and effective epidemiology the 1992/2002 AAMR system is best ignored as vexatious and righteous folly. They convey the impression of warm and feeling do-gooders. But here they are not scientists.

Now the Committee claim to be theory driven in their deliberations and in their recommendations. Accordingly, they are obliged to design explanatory theory that holds in the face of evidence. This leaves questions of warrant: How good is the evidence and what is the standing of the theory in the scientific world? They neither articulated evidence in support, nor did they demonstrate sound procedures of inquiry as to test of their theory, whatever that is. One can only conclude that, in these respects, they squandered the challenge, acquiescing to vacuity and wishful thinking. By any sensible meaning, an agglomeration of impressions, diagrams, instincts, assertions, suppositions, and social conventions is not theory, at least in a scientific professional sense. Their view may be, and probably is in some respects, consistent with modish doctrine. But that is not tenable theory, either. Perhaps by championing a position to which one is nostalgically committed, advocacy will advance a cause. Incantation has taken the place of analytical reasoning.

As Luckasson et al. (2002) report, by 1999 only four states had adopted the 1992 AAMR definition, and then without the levels-of-support model, so central to their system. Fewer than 1% of authentic researchers had applied the 1992 system of classification. Clearly their promise of a revolutionary new paradigm has not been widely embraced. All this despite their claim in 1992 that "The next few years will be the transition period into the new definition and classification system. This will be a dynamic process" (p. xi). One must suspect, in their enthusiasm, they fell prey to pernicious premature speculation.

Who are the actual beneficiaries of the alleged "fundamental paradigm shift"? Perhaps the Association itself will be a primary beneficiary by appealing to reformers, advocates, consumers, and soft-headed academics who not only rail against the scientific tradition, but see little point in even learning about it. But maybe it will help boost the AAMR membership, which had fallen off rather markedly.

Uncertainty about the meaning of mental retardation continues, even in matters concerning life and death. A recent U.S. Supreme Court decision (*Atkins* v. *Virginia*), banning executions of mentally retarded offenders, relies heavily on the AAMR and DSM definitions (United States Supreme Court, 2002). But the majority opinion reveals that the Court did not find the matter of diagnosis straightforward and simple: "To the extent there is serious disagreement about the execution of mentally retarded offenders it is in determining which offenders are in fact retarded." In fact, the complexity was expressly recognized in the statement, taken from DSM-IV: "Mental retardation has many different etiologies and may be seen as a final common pathway of various pathological processes that affect the functioning of the central nervous system." They didn't say anything about supports. Apparently the AAMR manuals and the Association's participation in the trial did little to assuage the Court's uncertainty about diagnosing mental retardation.

Earlier, in *Daubert* v. *Merrill Dow Pharmaceuticals,* the Court held that Rule 702 of Federal Rules of Evidence requires that testimony must be grounded in the methods of science to avoid "cosmic understanding" (United States Supreme Court, 509 U.S., 1993). Fortunately for lawyers on both sides, as in the epidemic of class-action suits in the field of mental retardation, there is no shortage of know-it-all-have-visa-will-travel "experts-for-hire." There is curious irony here in that so little is known about so much. It is also a blight. The courts need to attend more seriously to the intent in *Daubert.*

Aside from my fervent wish they would learn more about research methodology and theory construction, I have one final suggestion for the next T&C Committee to consider. Before they start their deliberations they might wish to read the poem "The Calf Path" by Sam Walter Foss (1858–1911). Here is a stanza:

For men are prone to go it blind
Along the calf paths of the mind,
And work away from sun to sun
To do what other men have done.
They follow in the beaten track.
And out, and in, and forth, and back,
And still their devious course pursue
To keep the paths that others do.

REFERENCES

American Psychiatric Association. (1994). *Diagnostic and statistical manual of mental disorders* (4th ed.). Washington, DC: Author.

Aronowitz, A. J. (1988). *Science as power: Discourse and ideology in modern society.* Minneapolis: University of Minnesota Press.

Atkins v. Virginia. U.S. Case No. 8452. (2002).

Baumeister, A. A. (1970). The American residential institution: Its history and character. In A. A. Baumeister & E. Butterfield (Eds.), *Residential facilities for the mentally retarded* (pp. 1–28). Chicago: Aldine Publishing.

Baumeister, A. A. (1997). Behavioral research: Boom or bust? In W. E. MacLean, Jr. (Ed.), *Ellis' handbook of mental deficiency, psychological theory and research* (3rd ed., pp. 3–45). Mahwah, NJ: Erlbaum.

Baumeister, A. A., & Bacharach, V. R. (2000). Early generic educational intervention has no enduring effect on intelligence and does not cure mental retardation. *Intelligence, 28*(3), 161–192.

Baumeister, A. A., Bacharach, V. R., & Baumeister, Alan A. (1997). "Big" versus "little" science: Comparative analysis of program projects and individual research grants. *American Journal on Mental Retardation, 102*, 211–227.

Baumeister, A. A., Kupstas, F. D., & Woodley-Zanthos, P. (1993). *The new morbidity.* Washington, DC: U.S. Department of Health and Human Services, President's Committee on Mental Retardation.

Baumeister, Alan A. (2000). The Tulane electrical brain stimulation program: A historical case study in medical ethics. *Journal of the History of the Neuroscience, 9*, 263–278.

Baumeister, Alan A., & Baumeister, A.A. (2000). Mental retardation: Causes and effects. In M. Hersen & R. T. Ammerman (Eds.), *Advanced abnormal child psychology* (2nd ed., pp. 327–355). Mahwah, NJ: Erlbaum.

Best, H. (1965). *Public provision for the mentally retarded in the United States.* Worcester, MA: Hefferman Press.

Blacher, J. (1998). Much ado about mortality: Debating the wrong question. *Mental Retardation, 36*, 412–415.

Black, E. (2003). *War against the weak: Eugenics and America's campaign to create a master race.* New York: Four Walls Eight Windows.

Bloom, A. (1988). *The closing of the American mind: How higher education has failed democracy and impoverished the souls of today's students.* Harmonsworth, England: Penguin Books.

Borthwick-Duffy, S. (1994). [Review of *Mental retardation: Definition, classification, and systems of supports*]. *American Journal on Mental Retardation, 98*, 541–544.

Brison, D. W. (1967). Definition, diagnosis, and classification. In A. A. Baumeister (Ed.), *Mental retardation* (pp. 1–19). Chicago: Aldine.

D'Adamo, P., Menegon, A., Lo Nigro, C., Grasso, M., Gulisano, M., Tamanini, F.,et al. (1998). Mutations in GDI1 are responsible for X-linked non-specific mental retardation. *Nature Genetics, 19*, 134–139.

Danforth, S. (1997). On what basis hope? Modern progress and postmodern possibilities. *Mental Retardation, 35*, 93–106.

Daubert v. Merrill Dow Pharaceuticals, Inc., U. S. Case No. 509. (1993).

Detterman, D. K., & Thompson, L. A. (1997). IQ, schooling, and developmental disabilities: What's so special about special education? *American Psychologist, 52*, 1082–1091.

Durkin, M. S., & Stein, Z. A. (1996). Classification of mental retardation. In J. W. Jacobson & J. A. Mulick (Eds.), *Manual of diagnosis and professional practice in mental retardation* (pp. 67–73). Washington, DC: American Psychological Association.

Farran, D. C. (2000). Another decade of intervention for children who are low income or disabled: What do we know now? In J. P. Shonkoff & S. J. Meisels (Eds.), *Handbook of early childhood intervention* (2nd ed., pp. 51–548). Cambridge, England: Cambridge University Press.

Foucault, M. (1973). *The birth of the clinic: An archaeology of medical perception* (A. M. Sheridan Smith, Trans.). New York: Random House.

Gelb, S. A. (1997). The problem of typological thinking in mental retardation. *Mental Retardation, 35*, 448–457.

Gottfredson, L. S. (1997). Why *g* matters: The complexity of everyday life. *Intelligence, 24*, 79–132.

Greenspan, S. (1994). Review of 1992 AAMR manual. *American Journal on Mental Retardation, 98*, 544–549.

Gross, P. R., & Levitt, N. (1994). *Higher superstition: The academic left and its quarrels with science.* Baltimore and London: The Johns Hopkins Press.

Gross, P. R., Levitt, N., & Lewis, M. W. (Eds.). (1996). *The flight from science and reason.* New York: New York Academy of Sciences.

Healy, D. (2004). *Let them eat Prozac: The unhealthy relationship between the pharmaceutical industry and depression.* New York: New York University Press.

Institute of Medicine. (1991). *Disability in America: Toward a national agenda for prevention.* Washington, DC: National Academy Press.

Ireland, W. W. (1877). *On idiocy and imbecility.* London: Churchill.

Jacobson, J. W. (1994). Review of *Mental retardation: Definition, classification, and systems of supports. American Journal on Mental Retardation, 98*, 539–541.

Jacobson, J. W., & Mulick, J. A. (1992). A new definition of mental retardation or a new definition of practice? *Psychology in Mental Retardation and Developmental Disabilities, 18*(2), 9–14.

Jacobson, J. W., & Mulick, J. A. (Eds.). (1996). *Manual of diagnosis and professional practice in mental retardation.* Washington, DC: American Psychological Association.

Kanner, L. (1964). *History of the care and study of the mentally retarded.* Springfield, IL: Charles Thomas.

Kuhn, T. S. (1970). *The structure of scientific revolutions* (2nd ed.). Chicago: University of Chicago Press.

Lubinski, D., & Humphreys, L. G. (1997). Incorporating general intelligence into epidemiology and the social sciences. *Intelligence, 24*, 159–201.

Luckasson, R., Borthwick-Duffy, S., Buntinx, W. H. E., Coulter, D. L., Craig, E. M., Reeve, A., et al. (2002). *Mental retardation: Definition, classification, and systems of supports* (10th ed.). Washington, DC: American Association on Mental Retardation.

Luckasson, R., Coulter, D. L., Polloway, E. A., Reiss, S., Schalock, R. L., Snell, M. E., et al. (1992). *Mental retardation: Definition, classification, and systems of supports* (9th ed.). Washington, DC: American Association on Mental Retardation.

MacMillan, D. L., Gresham, F. M., & Siperstein, G. N. (1993). Conceptual and psychometric concerns about the 1992 AAMR definition of mental retardation. *American Journal on Mental Retardation, 98*, 325–335.

MacMillan, D. L., Gresham, F. M., & Siperstein, G. N. (1995). Heightened concerns over the 1992 AAMR definition: Advocacy versus precision. *American Journal on Mental Retardation, 100*, 87–97.

MacMillan, D. L., & Reschly, D. J. (1997). Issues of definition and classification. In W. E. MacLean, Jr. (Ed.), *Ellis' handbook of mental deficiency, psychological theory and research* (3rd ed., pp. 47–74). Mahwah, NJ: Erlbaum.

MacMillan, D. L., & Reschly, D. J. (1998). Overrepresentation of minority students: The case for greater specificity or reconsideration of the variables examined. *Journal of Special Education, 32*, 15–24.

Reiss, S. (1994). Issues in defining mental retardation. *American Journal on Mental Retardation, 99*, 1–7.

Rose-Ackerman, S. (1982). Mental retardation and society: The ethics and politics of normalization. *Ethics, 93*, 81–101.

Schalock, R. L., Stark, J. A., Snell, M. E., Coulter, D. L., Polloway, E. A., Luckasson, R., et al. (1994). The changing conception of mental retardation: Implications for the field. *Mental Retardation, 32*, 181–193.

Seguin, E. (1907). *Idiocy: And its treatment by the physiological method* (Rev. ed.). New York: Teachers College of Columbia University.

Spinath, F. M., Harlaar, N., Ronald, A., & Plomin, R. (2004). Substantial genetic influence on mild mental impairment in early childhood. *American Journal on Mental Retardation, 109*, 34–43.

Spitz, H. H. (1986). *The raising of intelligence: A selected history of attempts to raise retarded intelligence.* Hillsdale, NJ: Erlbaum.

Spitz, H. H. (1997). *Nonconscious movements: From mystical messages to facilitated communication.* Mahwah, NJ: Erlbaum.

Strauss, D., & Shavelle, R. (1998). What can we learn from the California mortality studies? *Mental Retardation, 36*, 406–408.

Switzky, H. N., & Greenspan, S. (Eds.). (2003). *What Is Mental Retardation? Ideas for an evolving disability.* Washington, DC: American Association on Mental Retardation [E-Book]. Available at http://www.disabilitybooksonline.com

Thompson, P. M., Cannon, T. D., Narr, K. L., Erp, T. van, Poutanen, V.-P., Huttunen, M., et al. (2001). Genetic influences on brain structure. *Nature Neuroscience, 4*(12), 1253–1258.

Watson, J. D. (2003). *DNA: The secret of life.* New York: Random House.

Wilson, E. O. (1998). *Consilience: The unity of knowledge.* New York: Alfred A. Knopf.

Windschuttle, K. (1996). *The killing of history: How literary critics and social theorists are murdering our past.* New York: Free Press.

Woodley-Zanthos, P., & Baumeister, A. A. (1994). American Association on Mental Retardation. In *Encyclopedia of Intelligence* (Vol. 1, pp 78–82). New York: MacMillan.

World Health Organization. (1980). *International classification of diseases* (9th ed.). Geneva: Author.

Zigler, E. (1970). The nature-nurture issue reconsidered. In H. C. Haywood (Ed.), *Social-cultural aspects of mental retardation* (pp 81–106). New York: Appleton-Century-Crofts.

CHAPTER EIGHT

Neighbors and Friends: Social Implications of Intellectual Disability

DAVID L. COULTER

ASSESSMENT OF THE CURRENT AAMR SYSTEM

Why change? Can we not define mental retardation once and for all? If mental retardation were just a thing—a biomedical disease state, a specific alteration in neuronal structure or function—then perhaps such a permanent definition would be possible. But "mental retardation is not something you have, like blue eyes or a bad heart. Nor is it something you are, like being short or thin" (Luckasson, Coulter, Polloway et al., 1992). Mental retardation is to an extent based on the statistical concept of the population distribution of intelligence and describes those at the low end of this bell-shaped distribution. If the distribution changed, then presumably the boundaries of the definition of mental retardation would follow. For example, if we could give everyone a "smart pill" that raised everyone's IQ by 30 points, the bell-shaped distribution would just be shifted to the right. People at the low end of this new distribution, who would be identified as having mental retardation, would now have an IQ below 100. Thus as long as intelligence is distributed in the population along some sort of bell-shaped curve, mental retardation will exist and cannot be "cured" or even prevented completely.

Clearly this is the description not of a fixed, immutable entity (like a disease state), but rather of a fluid concept that draws meaning from specific population and social norms. Mental retardation describes how people with low intelligence function in society. Thus as society changes, the meaning of mental retardation should change as well. Ultimately, the test of any definition is how well it matches current reality.

The 1992 AAMR system was written at a time when concepts of mental retardation were changing. Bridging the past and what was foreseen as the future, it acknowledged then-current concepts while striving to move the field forward. The definition contained the same three essential components as previous definitions, low intelligence, impaired adaptation, and developmental onset, but stressed that the purpose of the definition was to relate these limitations to the person's individualized needs for supports. The 1992 AAMR system did represent a radical break with the past, however, because it adopted a functional model in place of what was essentially a medical model of disability. Mental retardation was no longer just a "mental deficiency" or problem within the brain, but rather was a description of the interaction between intellectual limitations and the demands of the social environment. In other words, it is a state of functioning, not a fixed, immutable trait (Luckasson, Coulter, Polloway et al., 1992).

The 2002 AAMR system updated the 1992 system while retaining the core elements described above. It based the definition of mental retardation on explicit statistical concepts of intelligence and adaptive behavior. Acknowledging the extensive research on functioning that culminated in the World Health Organization's release of the International Classification of Functioning, or ICF (WHO, 2001), the 2002 system clarified the functional model that forms the basis of the definition. According to the ICF, disability is a problem in functioning. The 2002 system stated, "Disability is the expression of limitations in individual functioning within a social context and represents a substantial disadvantage to the individual" (Luckasson, Borthwick-Duffy, Buntinx et al., 2002). This problem in functioning is what generates the need for supports.

Is the current AAMR system still accurate? Or does the international recognition of the functional basis of disability require a new formulation? Does the current multidimensional approach include all aspects of functioning, or has something been left out? I think the answer to the first two questions is a qualified "yes" and will suggest some changes that could improve the accuracy and comprehensiveness of the AAMR system.

IDEAS FOR A REVISED DEFINITION

The United States is one of the few countries that still use the term *mental retardation*. *Intellectual disability* is the term most widely used and better expresses the concept of social dysfunction related to low intelligence. This term will be used in the rest of this article. Which types of intelligence are low in persons with this disability?

Theories of multiple intelligences propose many different types (Gardner, 1983), including analytical, practical, and creative (Sternberg, 1985, 1997), social (Greenspan, Switzky, & Granfield, 1996), and emotional (Goleman, 1995). In some cases, intellectual disability is more closely related to impaired social and practical intelligence than to low analytical intelligence (IQ). A revised definition should allow for identification of individuals with intellectual disability who have limitations in different types of intelligence.

This would require a new nosology of intellectual disability that specifies just which type of intelligence, or combination of types of intelligence, is in fact limited and is responsible for the individual's problem in functioning. One category might describe individuals who are limited only in social intelligence, such as some persons with Asperger's disorder, while another category might describe individuals who are limited only in practical intelligence, such as some persons with nonverbal learning disabilities. What we now think of as mental retardation might represent the category of persons who have significant limitations in social, analytical, and practical intelligence. Another important category would include persons with significantly limited analytical intelligence but satisfactory social and practical intelligence. Many of these persons live on the margins of society because they are often excluded from eligibility for supports based on the current definition. This new nosology of intellectual disability would provide a mechanism for identifying them and including them in the systems of supports.

Greenspan (1994) rightly criticized the 1992 system for talking about supports but not including it in the definition. The new way of thinking about functioning embodied in the ICF clarified that people have a disability because they need supports in order to improve their capacity to function, their performance of desired functions, and their access to opportunities to function in the community (WHO, 2001). A revised definition should incorporate this idea that people with intellectual disability need supports in order to achieve the "communal norm" (Turnbull, 1998) of full community inclusion and participation.

These considerations lead to the following proposal for a revised definition: "Intellectual disability describes individuals who require meaningful supports in order to achieve optimal functioning within the community because of the presence of substantial limitations in social adaptation and intellectual abilities manifested initially during the developmental period prior to adulthood." The specific types of intellectual abilities that are limited would then be explained in an accompanying description of the nosology of intellectual disabilities and an analysis of how they result in problems with social functioning.

RATIONALE

I am not a psychologist and will leave to others the scholarly analysis of the literature on the nature of intelligence (see, for example, many of the chapters in Jacobson and Mulick, 1996). I am a pediatric neurologist who treats children and some adults with developmental disabilities, many of whom have intellectual disability. I believe a rationale for the proposed changes can be found in the practical experiences of these children and their families. Parents of adolescents and young adults with mental retardation give consistent answers when I ask them about the most troublesome aspects of managing family life and planning for the future. They are not concerned primarily with cognitive or analytical limitations like difficulty in reading or solving mathematical problems. The major problems are social and involve understanding how to get along with others and how to behave in social settings.

For example, a teenage boy is very trusting and makes friends easily, but he uses poor judgment in selecting friends and interacting with them. His mother was understandably upset when he invited some of his undesirable friends over to the house while she was away and the friends stole her television set and some money. Another adolescent girl still wants to hug everyone she meets, and her mother is concerned that someone will take advantage of her. These individuals have limitations in social intelligence, understood as "the ability to understand social expectations and the behavior of other persons and to judge appropriately how to conduct oneself in social situations" (Luckasson et al., 1992, p. 15). Current difficulties in measuring social intelligence should not detract from appreciating the central role of limitations in social comprehension, insight, judgment and communication as they affect the everyday lives of people with mental retardation (Greenspan, Switzky, & Granfield, 1996).

Another example comes from an analysis of running, a common behavioral problem faced by some families of young people with intellectual disability. This phenomenon may be understood better by reconceptualizing it as a manifestation of limited social intelligence. These children and adolescents enjoy leaving the house or the company of their parents to wander freely for hours at a time without realizing that others may be worried about them. When found, they are perfectly happy and in no distress and cannot understand why anyone was concerned. The experiences of one teenage boy may provide some insight into this phenomenon. His mother readily describes him as a runner. Indeed, he will leave the doctor's office to go to the bathroom and then wander the hospital for an hour until he is found. He also shows poor social judgment in other areas. One time he stayed out late and then slept in the basement so that he would not awaken his mother. He was hungry when he woke up and still did not want to awaken his mother, so he left the house and broke into an ice cream store. He was sorry he got caught by the police but did not appreciate that he had done anything wrong. The psychiatrist thought that he might have difficulties forming a social conscience, which is one aspect of social intelligence.

What is the difference between those who run and those who do not? Why is running a problem primarily for individuals with intellectual disability? Analysis of this case suggests that perhaps those who run simply do not have the social insight and judgment to realize that others are concerned for them and that running may be unsafe or may lead to socially unacceptable activities. If so, then perhaps a social teaching approach to intervention would be more effective than a purely behavioral or pharmacological approach. But first we need to see it as a problem with intelligence, not a mental illness or abnormal behavior. This means it is an educational problem, not a medical problem. If we can teach students how to read books, then we should be able to teach students how to read people.

One of the great accomplishments of mental health research in the past decade has been the recognition of the importance of identifying children and adolescents with impaired social intelligence. The great interest in children with Asperger's disorder reflects this research, as does the research on the problem of bullying among schoolchildren. Recently, a curriculum was published that provides clear and explicit instruction on how to teach social skills to children with special needs (Siperstein & Rickards, 2004). One hopes that early adoption of such educational approaches will help young people with intellectual disabilities to achieve more successful social functioning.

I was once told by a state mental health official in Texas, "The largest institution for people with mental retardation in this state is the Texas Department of Corrections." Why do so many individuals with intellectual disability get into trouble with the law? Some (like Johnnie Lee Wilson and Richard LaPointe) confess to crimes they did not commit (Connery, 1996). Many, however, really do commit the crimes they are charged with but do so because of poor social judgment. Perhaps more attention to identifying limitations in social intelligence during childhood and adolescence and to teaching acceptable social behavior would also help prevent these young people from getting into legal trouble.

These experiences highlight two aspects of the rationale for changing the definition of intellectual disability. One is the need to broaden the concept of intelligence to give at least equal emphasis to limitations in analytical, social, and practical intelligence, and to develop a new nosology of intellectual disabilities based on this multifactorial concept of intelligence. The other is the need to emphasize the role of the educational and social community in shaping the experiences of people with intellectual disability and in determining the types and intensities of needed supports. Families are looking for help so that their child can become a valued, productive, and responsible member of the community.

The proposed changes in the definition will focus attention on the goal of achieving the communal norm for individuals with intellectual disability.

OTHER IDEAS FOR THE AAMR MANUAL

People-first language requires us to consider first the person who happens to have an intellectual disability. Yet the AAMR manual remains focused primarily on the definition and classification of the disability. Perhaps it would be appropriate to consider first what it means to be a human person, since an appreciation of personhood will likely influence our responses to the disability. This is partly a philosophical question, but philosophers have provided markedly different answers about the meaning of personhood, and there is probably no universally accepted answer (Mahowald, 1995). From an anthropological perspective, identification of what it means to be a human person is also unclear (Fernandez-Armesto, 2004). Different concepts of personhood lead to different ethical and social attitudes toward individuals with disabilities, which may influence what supports they receive (Byrne, 2000; Lusthaus, 1985). Perhaps AAMR should explain exactly what vision of personhood informs and guides the concept of intellectual disability and how this vision shapes the development of needed supports.

One approach to understanding what it means to be a person would include consideration of the roles of personal identity, value, meaning and relationships. These are essentially spiritual issues, when spirituality is understood as a belief system focusing on intangible elements that impart vitality and meaning to life's events. The 1992 AAMR system discussed spirituality as one of the implications of using supports (Luckasson et al., 1992, p. 108), but this was removed from the 2002 AAMR system for reasons that are not clear. It may be time now to give more attention to the central role of spirituality in determining what we mean when we encourage the use of people-first language.

As a pediatric neurologist, I would like to describe a clinical method that I have used for many years to help me understand the spirituality of my patients and their families. I call it "the three ways of looking," or a way to "look three times to see the person" who may or may not have a disability (Coulter, 2001).

The first look is to see the person as an individual human being, not just as a patient or a clinical case but rather as a being with the "breath of life" of human consciousness. This can be harder than it sounds. We are so used to seeing people objectively through a variety of discernible characteristics (short, tall, thin, fat, young, old, pretty, ugly, graceful, awkward, smart, and stupid) that it is much more difficult to see them subjectively as individuals with the experience of being alive. This first look is an attempt to grasp the spiritual ground of the individual's existence.

The *second* look is to see the person as a human being like us. From an awareness of our own spirituality, we can seek to recognize in the other person what we know to be central to our own existence. We can say, "This is not just a person, this is a person just like myself." If the first look was difficult, this second look is even more difficult. The theologian John Dunne referred to it as the process of "passing over and returning to oneself." By this he meant that one first tries to leave one's own point of view and enter into the other person's point of view, to "pass over from myself to the other" to try to experience the other person's subjectivity. By returning to oneself, we now can appreciate what it means to the other person to be alive (Dunne, 1987). Passing over is like what I have referred to as the first look, while returning to oneself is like what I have referred to as the second look. The real purpose of returning to ourselves in this second look is to understand in a fundamental way what we have in common at the core of our being. This second look also allows us to value in the other person what we most value in ourselves, and protect for others what we would protect for ourselves.

If the first look is to see the person, and the second look is to see ourselves, the *third* look is even more difficult: it is to see the face of God. By God I mean the ground of all being and all existence, the transcendence or divinity that informs our spirituality. Spirituality has been described as one's relationship with God, but it is equally God's relationship with us. When we share our spirituality with another and experience that person's spirituality as our own, we participate in the source of our spiritual nature. If one does not want to call it God, one can see in this third look a universality of human existence that links all persons together. This third look is rare and comes when we least expect it, but its impact can be profound (Kleinert, 2001).

These three ways of looking provide a way to experience and understand the personhood of persons with intellectual disability. Some years ago I was visiting a public institution for people with severe mental retardation (their term), as part of an investigation of the quality of care provided by the medical staff. As I visited one cottage where the residents were laid out on mats on the floor, I knelt to touch and talk to one particular young man who was nonverbal and unable to move. We could not have spent more than five minutes together, yet in those few minutes I experienced an intensely spiritual presence through my interactions with him. I still remember the look in his eyes as we touched. This was indeed an experience of the three ways of looking. It was clear to me that my report would have to convey the need to treat him and the other residents of the institution as fully human and valued persons whose dignity and spirituality deserved respect by the medical staff.

The point here is that perhaps the concept of intellectual disability in the AAMR manual should be grounded explicitly in a spiritual awareness of what it means to be a person who happens to have an intellectual disability. This awareness will likely shape and guide the provision of needed supports to assist the person to achieve the communal norm.

The Future

Turnbull provided a vision of what the future might look like when all people with intellectual disability have achieved the communal norm (Turnbull, 1998). What would this look like? I can imagine coming home from work, having just attended a team meeting at the local public school to develop a comprehensive supports plan for including one of my patients with intellectual disability in regular classroom activities. As I pass the school athletic field, I see another of my patients with intellectual disability working out with his teammates on the varsity track team. I drive past the old state institution for people with mental retardation, a marvelous Victorian brick structure long since closed by the state and sold to private developers who renovated it and turned it into luxury condominiums. I smile at the irony as I realize that several of the former residents of the state institution are now owners of condominiums in this complex and participate on the owners' board.

When I stop for dinner, a young woman with Down syndrome takes my order and delivers the meal flawlessly. I then attend a meeting at my fully accessible church, where the priest is seeking our advice about how she can include people with disabilities in the liturgy as readers and altar servers. At home, my neighbor explains how she was late getting home because she noticed that a young man with intellectual disability had taken the wrong bus home from his job at the newspaper and she had helped him get on the right bus. A political advertisement on television describes the success of a state representative with intellectual disability who was just reelected. Finally I go to sleep and dream of a day when everyone is fully valued, welcomed and assisted by the community to pursue their goals for life, liberty and happiness.

References

Byrne, P. (2000). *Philosophical and ethical problems in mental handicap*. New York: Palgrave.

Connery, D. S. (Ed.). (1996). *Convicting the innocent*. Cambridge, MA: Brookline Books.

Coulter, D. L. (2001). Recognition of spirituality in health care: Personal and universal implications. *Journal of Religion, Disability and Health, 5*(2/3), 1–11.

Dunne, J. S. (1987). *The homing spirit: A pilgrimage of the mind, of the heart, of the soul*. New York: Crossroad.

Fernandez-Almesto, F. (2004). *Humankind: A brief history*. New York: Oxford Press.

Gardner, H. (1983). *Frames of mind: The theory of multiple intelligences*. New York: Basic Books.

Goleman, D. (1995). *Emotional intelligence*. New York: Bantam Books.

Greenspan, S. (1994). Review of 1992 AAMR manual. *American Journal on Mental Retardation, 98*, 544–549.

Greenspan, S., Switzky, H. N., & Granfield, J. M. (1996). Everyday intelligence and adaptive behavior: A theoretical framework. In J. W. Jacobson & J. A. Mulick (Eds.), *Manual of diagnosis and professional practice in mental retardation* (pp. 127–135). Washington, DC: American Psychological Association.

Jacobson, J. W., & Mulick, J. A. (Eds.). (1996). *Manual of diagnosis and professional practice in mental retardation*. Washington, DC: American Psychological Association.

Kleinert, H. L. (2001). The three looks: The persons we profess to teach. *Journal of Religion, Disability and Health, 4*(4), 77–90.

Luckasson, R., Borthwick-Duffy, S., Buntinx, W. H. E., Coulter, D. L., Craig, E. M., Reeve, A., et al. (2002). *Mental retardation: Definition, classification, and systems of supports* (10th ed.). Washington, DC: American Association on Mental Retardation.

Luckasson, R., Coulter, D. L., Polloway, E. A., Reiss, S., Schalock, R. L., Snell, M. E., et al. (1992). *Mental retardation: Definition, classification, and systems of supports* (9th ed.). Washington, DC: American Association on Mental Retardation.

Lusthaus, E. W. (1985). Involuntary euthanasia and current attempts to define persons with mental retardation as less than human. *Mental Retardation, 23*, 148–154.

Mahowald, M. (1995). The person. In W. Reich (Ed.), *Encyclopedia of bioethics* (pp. 1934–1941). New York: Simon and Schuster Macmillan.

Siperstein, G. N., & Rickards, E. P. (2004). *Promoting social success: A curriculum for children with special needs*. Baltimore: Paul H. Brookes.

Sternberg, R. J. (1985). *Beyond I.Q.* New York: Cambridge University Press.

Turnbull, H. R. (1998, May). *Come the millennium: Rights and strategies for the future*. Paper presented at the annual meeting of the American Association on Mental Retardation, San Diego, CA.

World Health Organization. (2001). *International classification of functioning, disability, and health*. Geneva: Author.

CHAPTER NINE

Look Before You Leap: Implications of the 1992 and 2002 Definitions of Mental Retardation

DOUGLAS K. DETTERMAN AND LYNNE GABRIEL

ASSESSMENT OF THE 1992 AND 2002 AAMR DEFINITIONS

All definitions are political, at least to some extent. Whether the definition is of country boundaries, a word's meaning, or a psychological condition, political considerations are a factor. Understanding this as a starting point is essential for understanding any definition. From the beginning, the definition of mental retardation has been subjected to political forces that have caused it to be modified. Whether these modifications are desirable or not will, in part, depend on the observer's political orientation.

When Binet devised his first IQ test, it was because of a political mandate. At the time, if a child was judged by his or her teacher to be unfit for academic instruction, the child could be expelled from the school. In an attempt to remove arbitrariness from the system, Binet devised an objective test that predicted school achievement. He hoped that children identified as mentally retarded would receive the extra help that they needed.

The current definition of mental retardation is no less affected by political interests. Receiving appropriate schooling is still a concern for parents with children affected by mental retardation. But those concerns have expanded beyond education to the many aspects of adjustment to daily life and just getting along in the world. Such concerns reflect the many kinds of support that are now available or should be available for persons with mental retardation. The committee who authored the ninth edition of the definition of mental retardation (Luckasson et al., 1992) should be commended for their attempt to provide a comprehensive volume on the current state of knowledge in the field today. Clearly, this was no simple task.

The 1992 edition consists of three parts. Part 1 includes the latest interpretation of the definition of mental retardation, as well as the theoretical background behind the definition. This edition stresses the importance of functioning in every day life, and as a result, there are two major changes to the current edition.

The first change from the previous definition to the current version is a shift away from the criterion of an overall adaptive skill deficit to a more precise explanation of adaptive skill areas. Specifically, a person must have limitations in at least two out of ten adaptive skill areas, which are listed within the definition. The committee proposes that looking at adaptive skills in a global way does not provide a full picture of a person. While there may be limitations in some adaptive areas, they can coexist with strengths in other areas. Therefore, breaking down "overall adaptive behavior" into specific skill areas is intended to provide a more complete understanding of a person and the supports he or she needs to succeed.

The second major change from previous editions is the elimination of the four levels of mental retardation (mild, moderate, severe, and profound). Instead, the committee advocates replacing levels of mental retardation with intensities of supports needed (intermittent, limited, extensive, and pervasive).

Part 2 of the 1992 edition is devoted to explaining how to arrive at a diagnosis and decide on supports an individual might need. This whole process is based on what the committee terms a "multidimensional approach." Using this approach, they describe four dimensions that need to be considered in order to provide a complete description of a person with mental retardation. This section is extremely thorough, covering practically every aspect of mental retardation.

Finally, Part 3 provides readers with some practical applications of the definition. These applications include educational and work-related settings. Another practical issue discussed is current social policy and legal usage of the definition. This section provides readers with a sense of how this definition can be and is being used in real-world situations.

The political orientation of the 1992 definition was obviously in favor of those who provide treatment. The current edition probably meets the prima facie needs of several subdisciplines within the broad field of mental retardation. Advocacy groups and service providers have been given a tool with which to support people with mental retardation. However, the extent to which this definition will actually be of benefit to service providers is an unanswered question. One subdiscipline that the definition does not serve well is that of research. Once the ramifications of the definition are fully understood, providers and advocacy groups may not be so happy with it, either.

The most recent definition of mental retardation (Luckasson et al., 2002) is very similar to the 1992 definition. A few refinements were made, but for practical purposes the 2002 definition is essentially the same as the 1992 definition. Therefore, we will consider both 1992 and 2002 definitions as being roughly equivalent.

The purpose of this chapter is to show that both definitions: 1) have inherent problems that may make them less useful than originally intended for service providers, and 2) do not meet the needs of the research community. We will discuss the shortcomings of the current definition as they relate to service providers and researchers.. Specifically, we question the use of approximate IQ cutoffs and the inclusion of specific adaptive skill domains as a criterion for diagnosis. We also offer suggestions on how to modify the current definition to better meet the needs of both service providers and researchers interested in investigating mental retardation. Finally, we offer suggestions on where the research in this field is headed in the future and how a new definition could help this effort.

IDEAS FOR A REVISED DEFINITION

Mental retardation is defined as any person with an IQ two standard deviations below the mean of the population plus or minus two standard errors of the measuring instrument employed. Clinical judgment can and should be used within two standard errors of the 70 cutoff. The 10 adaptive skills used in the 1992 definition would have no part in the initial diagnosis of mental retardation but would be recommended for use as part of a comprehensive assessment of each person diagnosed with mental retardation and would be particularly important for persons with scores that fell within two standard errors of the cutoff in forming a clinical judgment. In the 2002 definition, adaptive behavior has been added as a dimension separate from the intellectual dimension but is still included in much the same way.

RATIONALE FOR A REVISED DEFINITION

To begin, we will discuss the impact of the 1992 definition on researchers. These problems are the most obvious and easiest to present. The ambiguity of the 1992 definition makes it difficult, if not impossible, for researchers to do their job. When formulating a research proposal, one of the most important things to consider is the population to be studied. Clearly, the 1992 definition presents researchers with quite a dilemma because of vague IQ cutoff recommendations and the inclusion of the specific adaptive skills. It is clear that the 1992 definition has serious problems. In the 2002 definition, the authors begin by considering the impact of the 1992 definition. They indicate that only four states used the 1992 definition and that "less than 1% applied the 1992 AAMR system of classification" (p. 30).

We have three suggestions for a revised definition that would better meet the needs of the research community and still allow flexibility for service providers. The 1992 definition recommends a cutoff of 70 or 75. Adaptive behavior aside, if an upper IQ limit of 70 is used, 2% of the population could be diagnosed with mental retardation. However, if an upper IQ limit of 75 is used, 5% of the population could be diagnosed with mental retardation (MacMillan & Reschly, 1997). On its face, this lack of precision would seem helpful for service providers because they anticipate being able to offer services to a larger number of individuals. However, this ambiguity is a problem when attempting to distinctly classify individuals for research purposes. How do we know who we are supposed to be studying? Indeed, the definition has already been criticized elsewhere for its imprecision regarding classification for scientific interests (Belmont & Borkowski, 1994; MacMillan, Gresham, & Siperstein, 1995; MacMillan, Gresham, & Siperstein, 1993).

Our suggestion is to impose an upper IQ limit of 70, with a range of plus or minus two standard errors. This addresses the committee's concern of statistical variance found in intelligence tests and the possibility of measurement error. Anyone who works in mental retardation can tell stories about state laws that require an IQ of exactly 50 or less to work in a sheltered workshop. Such arbitrary cutoffs deny the variability in human performance and the substantial portion of variance due to factors other than IQ. Laws like this put the professional in the position of either denying service to people who could profit from it or doctoring their IQ test results. Most find the second alternative best, but they are placed in the position of committing an ethical violation to accomplish a greater good. The problem in these situations is obviously the law's imposing an arbitrary cutoff. However, if the AAMR uses arbitrary cutoffs in its definitions, why should we expect less well-informed legislators to do differently?

One problem with our suggestion of using a two-standard-errors window is that interpretation would require some knowledge of psychometrics. Professionals would have to explain the complexities of psychological testing to laypersons. While this change might cause difficulty for service providers initially, it should ultimately help the field overall. That is, professionals would be providing an educational service to the community at large that would make them better consumers of psychological test information.

Our second suggestion is to do away with the notion of deficient adaptive behavior as a criterion for diagnosis. In fact, IQ was the dominant criterion for diagnosing mental retardation during the early part of the twentieth century when researchers first became interested in studying mental retardation (Reschly, 1992). The first official classification scheme published by the AAMD in 1921 recommended using a Binet IQ for diagnosis. However, as the years went by, there was a shift away from the stringent use of IQ alone to diagnose mental retardation, and the notion of adaptive skills became a more important component. Thus, since the early 1960s, the AAMR has required both subaverage intellectual functioning and deficits in adaptive behavior in order to diagnose a person with mental retardation. However, we feel that an "adaptive skills deficit" is an unnecessary criterion—for two reasons.

First, the instruments designed to measure adaptive skills are simply not adequate. When the concept of adaptive behavior was first introduced to the definition in the 1960s (Heber, 1961), it was criticized because measures of adaptive behavior were not well-standardized. Often, clinical judgment was substituted for a formal assessment of adaptive behavior. There tended to be low agreement between examiners when diagnosing impairment in adaptive behavior. Clinical judgment led to low agreement between examiners, and low agreement resulted in unreliable diagnosis (Zigler & Hodapp, 1984).

Even if one accepts the ten (1992) or three (2002) adaptive skill areas as being a pertinent part of a diagnosis of mental retardation, the same problem researchers and clinicians faced almost 40 years ago still plagues us today. That is, there is a lack of reliable instruments to assess adaptive behavior (Jacobson & Mulick, 1992). When considering the psychometric characteristics of adaptive behavior measures, Kamphaus (1987) stated that most measures lack adequate national norms, and MacMillan, Gresham, and Siperstein (1993) noted that domain scores have poor reliability. Overall, the psychometric properties of adaptive behavior measures fall far below the quality of standardized intelligence tests. In fact, Luckasson et al. (1992) admit that "many of the adaptive behavior scales fall short of appropriate standards for norming" (1992, p. 44).

Another problem with the inclusion of adaptive behavior is how the ten or three areas specified in the definition were derived. There are no agreed-upon factor-analytic studies to show that these ten domains actually exist and are independent of one another (MacMillan, Gresham, & Siperstein, 1993), and there are also no data to show the internal consistency of these areas. Overall, MacMillan, Gresham, and Siperstein (1993) state that "there does not seem to be an empirical basis for the designation of the ten adaptive skill areas" (p. 329). Evidence may be better for three skills than ten, but still not strong.

As if using inadequate measures of adaptive behavior weren't enough, the current versions of the definition allow for "professional judgment" when assessing adaptive behavior (Luckasson et al., 1992). The AAMR should learn from the mistakes of the past and realize that allowing such wide-ranging professional judgment can result in an (even more) unreliable classification system. If psychology has learned one thing, it is that actuarial decisions are almost always better than clinical decisions.

Another reason that an adaptive skill deficit is an unnecessary criterion is the relationship between IQ and adaptive behavior. That is, as IQ decreases, adaptive behavior decreases as well (Clausen, 1967, 1968, 1972). Because of the high correlation between IQ and adaptive behavior, it could be argued that a diagnosis of mental retardation could be made based on an IQ score alone. The addition of an adaptive-behavior criterion simply muddies the waters.

As we have shown, IQ and adaptive behavior are strongly positively correlated. Therefore, if we know what a person's IQ is, we have a pretty good idea about the tasks he might be able to do every day. That is not to say that in knowing a person's IQ score, we know exactly what his strengths and weaknesses are. In fact, knowing a person's strengths and weaknesses in measures of everyday functioning can be helpful when devising a service plan. However, standardized IQ tests are valid and reliable measures that can be employed for diagnosis. The same cannot be said for measures of adaptive behavior. Perhaps one compromise is to use IQ scores for diagnosis and use adaptive-behavior measures to determine what supports a person needs.

A section of the definition might suggest methods for evaluation for the provision of services, and this section could contain the adaptive skills now required as part of the definition. There seems to be a tendency in this direction in the 2002 definition.

Finally, an IQ of 70 or below is certainly predictive of academic difficulties. Persons with an IQ of 70 or less are going to need support to obtain sufficient education to exist independently in today's society. While a 70 IQ may not describe many other spheres of a person's functioning, it does provide one indication of almost certain problems with education. Though effective interventions may require a broader description of a person's strengths and weaknesses, diagnosis of potential problems can and should be done with an IQ test.

So far we have only discussed problems researchers have with the current definition. However, we believe there are unrecognized problems for clinicians treating people with mental retardation that result from the 1992 and 2002 definitions. These problems have to do with the additional requirement that a diagnosis of mental retardation requires a deficit in adaptive skills. Though the authors of the 1992 definition say they wished to make the definition multidimensional, they may not have been clear about implications of multidimensional criteria for a definition. The reduction to three areas in the 2002 definition suggests that they are at least partially aware of the problems a multivariate definition poses.

In order to see how the ten adaptive-skill categories of the 1992 definition would affect the diagnosis of mental retardation, we did a simulation or Monte Carlo study of expected outcomes. As indicated above, an important variable in the outcome of such a simulation would be the correlation between the adaptive-skill tests. Instead of trying to identify the correlations among these scales, we simulated the full range of potential correlations.

To carry out the simulation, we made the following extremely optimistic assumptions. We assumed that there was an identified, objective test for each adaptive-skill category and that these tests were every bit as reliable and valid as IQ tests across the full range of ability. Next, we assumed that all 10 adaptive-skill tests had the same correlation with IQ and with each other. This correlation was allowed to take the following values: 0, .2, .4, .6, .8, and 1.0. One simulation was done for each of the six chosen correlation values.

Datasim (Bradley, 1988), a simulation computer program, was used to generate the equivalent of 20,000 cases for 11 variables consisting of IQ and the 10 adaptive skill scales. (Actually, we only generated 10,000 cases but used both "tails" of the distribution to effectively double the n.) All variables were multivariate normal and were given a mean of 100 and a standard deviation of 15 for convenience. Once the data were generated, we then analyzed them in the following way.

First, we selected all cases on the IQ variable that had a score of 75 or less. This corresponds to the first step in classification according to the 1992 definition.

Next, for those with a 75 IQ or less, we counted the number of cases where two or more of the adaptive skill scores were 75 or below. This corresponds to the definition's requirement that two or more adaptive skills be deficient.

Now, the question is: What proportion of cases will be diagnosed as mentally retarded if tests of adaptive skill have a given correlation with each other and IQ? These results are shown in Figure 9.1. We obtained Figure 9.1 by plotting the proportion of cases that would be diagnosed as mentally retarded for each of the six correlation values and then fitting an exponential function to the data.

The results are quite counterintuitive in some respects. We begin by considering the case where all correlations among tests are zero. Most people, and certainly all psychometricians, would consider this the most informative situation. When tests have a zero correlation with each other, they are orthogonal and independent. That means each test is providing completely novel information unavailable from any other test. If this condition occurred, only about 30% of persons with IQs of 75 or less would be diagnosed as mentally retarded because they had two or more of the adaptive criteria below 75. In fact, this is exactly the same proportion of people with IQs above 75 who would score below 75 on two or more of the 10 adaptive-skill scales. In other words, people with IQs above 75 would show the same rate of occurrence of deficits in adaptive skill as persons with IQs of 75 or less. Put another way, if all tests were correlated zero, adaptive-skill tests would be no more informative for persons with mental retardation than for persons in the general population. Further, nearly 70% of persons with IQs of 75 or less would not qualify for the definition of mental retardation.

Now consider the other extreme. Suppose the correlation between IQ and each of the adaptive skill scales was 1.0. If the correlation among tests was perfect, each person would receive the identical score on all 11 tests. If a person scored 73 on the IQ test, she would score exactly the same on all other tests. If you knew a person's score on one test, you would know her score on all tests. Once an IQ test was given, all of the ten other adaptive-skill tests would be redundant, and so would provide no useful information.

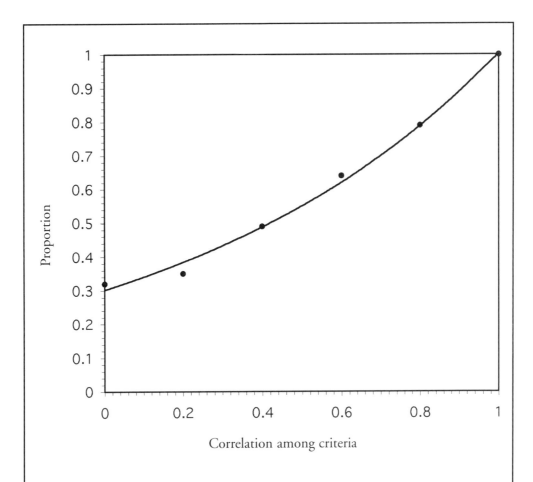

Figure 9.1. Results of a simulation of 20,000 cases for each data point. An exponential function was fit to the data points. The x-axis shows the correlation between IQ and 10 tests of adaptive skill. The y-axis is the proportion of persons with IQs of 75 or below who show two or more adaptive-skill deficits out of a possible 10.

It should also be obvious that, when test correlations are 1.0, no one with an IQ above 75 will have any deficits in adaptive skill. Thus, moving from a correlation of 0 to a correlation of 1.0 , the situation goes from one where deficits in adaptive skill occur at exactly the same proportion as they occur in the population to one in which they occur only in persons with IQs of 75 or less.

Now consider the middle cases, where the correlation among all tests ranges from .2 to .8. When the correlation is .2, about 35% of the cases would have two or more deficient adaptive-skill tests if their IQ was 75 or less. Corresponding figures are .4, 49% identified,

.6, 64% identified, and .8, 79% identified. As a rough rule of thumb, the proportion classified as mentally retarded will be about the same as the correlation among tests. We believe that the ten adaptive skills in the 1992 definition would probably have correlations of between .4 and .6 with IQ and with each other, if such tests could be devised. That means that between 36% and 50% of those previously classified as mentally retarded would not be so classified under the 1992 definition. We doubt that those who devised this definition were aware of the large number of persons they would be disenfranchising. This same argument applies to the 2002 definition.

In summary, our simulation of the 1992 definition provides empirical evidence that the addition of a required deficit in two of ten adaptive-skill areas to the definition of mental retardation poses real practical problems for service providers. On the one hand, if the tests of adaptive skills have high correlations with IQ, the tests will exclude a small number of persons from the definition but will provide little additional information beyond the IQ test that is useful for treatment purposes. On the other hand, if the adaptive-skills tests have low correlations with IQ, they will provide very useful information about the characteristics of the people in question and, indeed, all people in the population. But requiring these tests for a diagnosis of mental retardation will exclude up to 70% of those with IQs under 75 from being diagnosed as mentally retarded and getting appropriate services. Including these 10 adaptive skills places clinicians between a rock and a hard place.

We only have space for a cursory examination of the kinds of results that can be obtained from simulations. Certainly much more complete and comprehensive simulations are possible that take into account actual correlations of tests, their reliabilities, and so on. We have also not examined the characteristics of the resulting distributions that would arise from the 1992 definition. However, we do know that multivariate distributions of the kind that would result from this definition are often complex. What we are sure of from this simulation is that whoever writes the next definition would do well to simulate the outcome if the definition contains more than IQ. A simulation can prevent what could be disastrous mistakes. This obviously wasn't done for the 2002 definition, since it has the same general form as the 1992 definition.

Our third and final suggestion for modifying the 1992 definition is to do away with the new scheme of intensities of supports and revert back to the old scheme of levels of mental retardation. Others have pointed out elsewhere that there is a remarkable similarity between the two schemes and have implied that the change might not be truly necessary (MacMillan, Gresham, & Siperstein, 1995; MacMillan & Reschly, 1997).

Using the old terminology, researchers could write in the methods section of a paper that they "tested (for example) 20 people with mild mental retardation," and those reading the paper could gain some general sense as to the nature of the participants in the study. However, under this new scheme, brevity would be out of fashion in a methods section. The authors would have to state, in order to use the appropriate terminology, that they "tested one person with mental retardation who needed intermittent supports in communication and limited supports in home living, one person with mental retardation who needed limited supports in self-care and social skills, with intermittent supports in functional academics," and so on. This type of explanation would be a journal editor's worst nightmare! As can be seen by the small number of researchers who have adopted the 1992 definition (less than 1%), this type of definition will probably never be accepted by researchers.

Another consideration when discussing intensity of supports is the same problem as with the ten adaptive skills. Are there any instruments available that can objectively determine the difference between a person needing extensive or pervasive supports in a given domain? The committee does acknowledge that more accurate instruments of adaptive skills do need to be devised, and they hope that inclusion of particular criteria in the definition will lead to design of better measures. In essence, technology will "catch up" with the definition. However, doesn't it make more sense to do it the other way around? Have the instrument (or instruments) needed to measure these constructs before making them criteria for diagnosis. There seems to be something contradictory in having a definition that includes terms that are not, themselves, defined.

A compromise in this situation might be to rectify the old subclassification scheme to be used for reporting purposes. The new scheme of intensities of supports needed could certainly be used to devise unique service plans for people that would truly assist them in achieving as much independence as possible. Again, this scheme could be included in a recommended assessment section. However, before recommending any interventions, we should have evidence that these interventions will be effective. At least for educational interventions, there is very little evidence of any differential effectiveness of interventions (Detterman & Thompson, 1997).

OTHER IDEAS FOR THE AAMR MANUAL

In this edition of the manual, the committee acknowledges that "etiology of mental retardation is an important aspect of classification" (1992, p. 69). We wholeheartedly agree with that statement. The committee does an excellent job of convincing the reader that understanding the etiology of mental retardation will be important for the advancement of knowledge in the field. One final suggestion we have for the next revision of the manual is to somehow include etiology in the definition itself, rather than simply mentioning it. As we explain in the next section, we feel that understanding etiology will become critical for future research endeavors.

THE FUTURE OF MENTAL RETARDATION AS A FIELD

Mental retardation research holds an exciting future. In particular, research into behavioral phenotypes and phenotypic mapping should help us to better understand the concept of mental retardation.

A phenotype is the "observable or measurable expression of a gene or genes" (Berini & Kahn, 1987). A behavioral phenotype is seen in individuals with a specific genetic disorder, such as Down syndrome (O'Brien, 1992). In general, individuals with a specific genetic syndrome may tend to exhibit similar traits, such as physical or behavioral characteristics, as compared to individuals with other causes of mental retardation, because they share a common genetic anomaly (Dykens, 1995; Epstein, 1993). That is not to say that every individual with a particular disorder will exhibit every trait associated with the disorder. Rather, individuals with the same syndrome have an increased probability of exhibiting particular traits, even though there might be a great deal of variability within the syndrome (Dykens, 1995).

It is also important to note that the particular behaviors or physical features used to characterize a syndrome might not be specific only to that syndrome (Dykens, 1995). Some behaviors or physical features can be "shared" by a number of syndromes. For example, sociability and friendliness are qualities associated with both Down syndrome and Williams syndrome. However, there are qualitative differences in shared behaviors that make them "the same but different" across syndromes (Dykens, 1995). For example, the aggressiveness and temper tantrums associated with fragile X and Prader-Willi syndromes can be due to different causes. Some of the aggression found in individuals with fragile X might be associated with sensory sensitivity, while temper tantrums in individuals with Prader-Willi might be due to food limits (Dykens, Hodapp, Walsh, & Nash, 1992). Despite variability of expression of traits within syndromes and nonspecificity of traits between syndromes, attempts at defining several behavioral phenotypes have met with some success. Three examples are Lesch-Nyhan syndrome, Prader-Willi syndrome, and Rett's syndrome (Flynt & Yule, 1994).

Once behavioral phenotypes are identified, phenotypic mapping can be used. Phenotypic mapping is a molecular genetic technique. It involves defining the physical region of a chromosome that is likely to contain the gene(s) whose over- or underexpression is at least partly responsible for a phenotypic feature (Korenberg, 1993).

We believe that phenotypic mapping is one approach that will help researchers to find the underlying genetic basis for Down syndrome and other chromosomal abnormalities. It should be apparent why stressing etiology within the definition of mental retardation is so important. It is only when etiologies are well defined that these remarkable advances in technology can be utilized to facilitate a better understanding of the underlying causes of mental retardation. It is anticipated that molecular mapping will meet with continued success, provided that we can accurately classify individuals and continue to identify phenotypic features associated with particular disorders.

Though a large portion of mental retardation arises from genetic causes, there are other causes of environmental origin that could profit from more precise diagnoses. We are generally appalled at the lack of clinical information available about persons with mental retardation. An AAMR definition that includes diagnostic category as a required part would go a long way to solving this problem. Though many have resisted defining mental retardation as a medical problem, the biological nature of the disorder must be acknowledged if progress is to be made.

In summary, we realize that any definition is shaped by political forces. The 1992 and 2002 definitions of mental retardation are no exception. The committee who wrote the definition obviously had the commendable goal of providing better services to persons with mental retardation. Unfortunately, the definition they devised may have some extremely undesirable effects on both researchers and service providers. We think that a new revision of the definition could rectify many of its problems while still preserving the orientation it attempted to foster.

That AAMR should consider a new definition seems clear to us. From the 1960s through the 1980s, there was a close alliance between researchers and service providers.

Since the 1992 definition was introduced, it is our impression that researchers and service providers are more alienated than at any time in the history of the study of intellectual disability. We predict that if there is not a substantial modification in the definition of mental retardation to render it more sympathetic to the needs of researchers, researchers will become increasingly alienated. If this happens, we predict that an organization that meets researchers' needs will be established. This organization might be one that studies intellectual deficit, in general, and is not confined to just mental retardation. To avoid such an irreparable split, the AAMR should exercise its leadership to reunite service providers and researchers. Otherwise, they may find that they have defined mental retardation out of existence. This is not the way anyone should want to eliminate mental retardation. Such an outcome can only delay the day when mental retardation is really eliminated.

REFERENCES

Belmont, J. M, & Borkowski, J. G. (1994). Prudence, indeed, will dictate. Review of Mental retardation: Definition, classification, and systems of support (9th ed.). *Contemporary Psychology, 39,* 495–496.

Berini, R. Y., & Kahn, E. (1987). *Clinical genetics handbook.* Oradell, NJ: Medical Economics Books.

Bradley, D. R. (1988). *Datasim.* Lewiston, ME: Desktop Press.

Clausen, J. A. (1967). Mental deficiency: Development of a concept. *American Journal of Mental Deficiency, 71,* 727–745.

Clausen, J. A. (1968). A comment on Halpern's note. *American Journal of Mental Deficiency, 72,* 950.

Clausen, J. A. (1972). Quo vadis, AAMD? *The Journal of Special Education, 6,* 51–60.

Detterman, D. K., & Thompson, L. A. (1997). IQ, schooling, and developmental disabilities: What's so special about special education? *American Psychologist, 52,* 1082–1091.

Dykens, E. M. (1995). Measuring behavioral phenotypes: Provocations from the "new genetics." *American Journal on Mental Retardation, 99,* 522–532.

Dykens, E. M., Hodapp, R. M., Walsh, K., & Nash, L. J. (1992). Adaptive and maladaptive behavior in Prader-Willi syndrome. *Journal of the American Academy of Child and Adolescent Psychiatry, 31,* 1131–1136.

Epstein, C. J. (1993). The conceptual bases for the phenotypic mapping of conditions resulting from aneuploidy. In C. J. Epstein (Ed.), *The phenotypic mapping of Down syndrome and other aneuploid conditions* (pp. 1–18). New York: Wiley-Liss.

Flint, J., & Yule, W. (1994). Behavioral phenotypes. In M. Rutter, E. Taylor, & L. Hersov (Eds.), *Child and adolescent psychiatry: Modern approaches* (3rd ed., pp. 666–687). Oxford: Blackwell Scientific.

Heber, R. (1959). A manual on terminology and classification in mental retardation [Monograph Supplement]. *American Journal of Mental Deficiency, 64*(2).

Heber, R. (1961). Modifications in the manual on terminology and classification in mental retardation. *American Journal of Mental Deficiency, 65*(4), 499–500.

Jacobson, J. W., & Mulick, J. A. (1992). A new definition of mental retardation or a new definition of practice? *Psychology in Mental Retardation and Developmental Disabilities, 18*(2), 9–14.

Kamphaus, R. W. (1987). Conceptual and psychometric issues in the assessment of adaptive behavior. *The Journal of Special Education, 21,* 27–35.

Korenberg, J. R. (1993). Toward a molecular understanding of Down syndrome. In C. J. Epstein (Ed.), *The phenotypic mapping of Down syndrome and other aneuploid conditions* (pp. 87–115). New York: Wiley-Liss.

Luckasson, R., Borthwick-Duffy, S., Buntinx, W. H. E., Coulter, D. L., Craig, E. M., Reeve, A., et al. (2002). *Mental retardation: Definition, classification, and systems of supports* (10th ed.). Washington, DC: American Association on Mental Retardation.

Luckasson, R., Coulter, D. L., Polloway, E. A., Reiss, S., Schalock, R. L., Snell, M. E., et al. (1992). *Mental retardation: Definition, classification, and systems of supports* (9th ed.). Washington, DC: American Association on Mental Retardation.

MacMillan, D. L., Gresham, F. M., & Siperstein, G. N. (1993). Conceptual and psychometric concerns about the 1992 AAMR definition of mental retardation. *American Journal on Mental Retardation, 98*, 325–335.

MacMillan, D. L., Gresham, F. M., & Siperstein, G. N. (1995). Heightened concerns over the 1992 AAMR definition: Advocacy versus precision. *American Journal on Mental Retardation, 100*, 87–97.

Macmillan, D. L., & Reschly, D. J. (1997). Issues of definition and classification. In W. E. MacLean, Jr. (Ed.), *Ellis' handbook of mental deficiency, psychological theory and research* (3rd ed., pp. 47–74). Mahwah, NJ: Erlbaum.

O'Brien, J. (1992). Behavioral phenotypes and their measurement. *Developmental Medicine and Child Neurology, 34*, 365–367.

Reschly, D. J. (1992). Mental retardation: Conceptual foundation, definitional criteria, and diagnostic operations. In S. R. Hynd & R. E. Mattison (Eds.), *Assessment and diagnosis of child and adolescent psychiatric disorders: Volume II. Developmental disorders* (pp. 23–67). Hillsdale, NJ: Erlbaum.

Zigler, E., Balla, D., & Hodapp, R. (1984). On the definition and classification of mental retardation. *American Journal of Mental Deficiency, 89*, 215–230.

PART III

Emerging Models and Definitions of Mental Retardation

This part of the book provides the reader with more detailed revisions of the construct of mental retardation using the 1992/2002 AAMR systems as a springboard. It also provides a thorough introduction to the World Health Organization's International Classification of Impairments, Disability and Handicaps (WHO-ICIDH-2) and its revision, The International Classification of Functioning, Disability and Health (WHO-ICF), and their possible relationship to the AAMR 1992/2002 definitions, and comments on mental retardation and the law. The editor's summary chapter offers an integrative framework for the ideas provided by all the contributors to this book.

Chapters 10–17 are presented alphabetically by author and are primarily concerned with revisions of the 1992/2002 AAMR systems. Chapter 18 is concerned with the *Atkins* decision and its relationship to the AAMR 1992/2002 systems. Chapters 19–20 are concerned with the WHO models and are organized in such a way as to help the reader understand these complex systems and their theoretical and practical implications for the field of mental retardation. Chapter 21 is the editor's summary chapter.

Gaventa, who is a minister, in Chapter 10 discusses "spiritual considerations" in the life of persons with mental retardation and applauds the 1992 AAMR for recognizing the holistic, multidimensional nature of humans. He laments the lost opportunity of the 2002 AAMR to integrate spirituality into the understanding of persons with mental retardation, though he notices that "spiritual life" is included as a social role in Dimension III. His chapter is a detailed analysis of "spirituality" in both the 1992/2002 AAMR systems.

Greenspan, in Chapter 11, discusses how his ideas, as mentioned in both the 1992/ 2002 AAMR systems, do not reflect the essence of his propositions regarding mental retardation in the real world and the natural prototype or taxon of mental retardation, reflecting one or more essential qualities that a person with mental retardation has or does not have as based in practical and social intelligences, and berates the 2002 AAMR for relying on a mechanical formulistic approach ("an artificial cookbook formula"), in defining mental retardation rather than on "intuitive judgments from one's own gut" to avoid the past misuses of clinical judgment. "A major reason why mental retardation is defined in terms of an artificial numeric formula rather than an intuitively based natural taxon is that mental retardation, especially mild mental retardation, is a socially constructed disability category rather that a naturally constructed quasi-medical category." Greenspan

147

discusses the logical conclusions of his position. He applauds the 2002 AAMR for recognizing that low social intelligence, and gullibility, rather than low IQ scores and academic incompetence, are the universal and most important aspect of mental retardation's natural prototype, but believes that 2002 AAMR has not gone far enough.

Jacobson and Mulick, in Chapter 12, compare and contrast the 1992/2002 AAMR systems. They berate both manuals for not being sensitive to the practical problems of service providers living in a climate of dire fiscal emergencies, or being useful to pragmatic clinicians especially in the area of mild mental retardation, because there is not enough discussion of issues of diagnosis and classification and increased complexity of translating the numerous recommendations and guidelines into clinical practice, and too much space devoted to ideology. They conclude that the 2002 AAMR system, though it is better than the 1992 AAMR system, does not help practicing psychologists very much in doing their job. They conclude: "The manual continues to address system issues in a manner that is either hostile or indifferent to the conflicting and competing public policy priorities that are inherent in developmental and other human service settings today because of its idealistic base. The manual fails also to provide pragmatic guidance for clinicians that reflect the subtleties and complexities of issues and questions with which they grapple daily. Perhaps these characteristics are inherent in a manual that appears still to seek to appeal to all possible readers, but certainly the intent of the manual is to engender adoption as opposed to constituting a grand gesture. As a guide to clinicians, or to students of assessment and developmental disability, it is woefully inadequate, a primer at best. In short, AAMR, as the manuals demonstrate, has a stated objective of encouraging the adoption of a new definition of mental retardation by government and clinicians, then a new or additional vehicle is needed for this purpose, in the form of a clinician's manual that addresses the concerns of potential adopters, developed by scientist-practitioners, perhaps to augment rather than replace the 2002 AAMR manual."

MacMillan, Siperstein, and Leffert, in Chapter 13, argue that the 1992/2002 AAMR systems failed to address adequately the needs of individuals with milder forms of mental retardation (MMR) who make up 75–80% of individuals with mental retardation. MMR persons, they believe, may be better served if their needs and characteristics are conceptualized as a distinct form of mental retardation with separate classification criteria. MacMillan, Siperstein, and Leffert also argue that the 1992/2002 AAMR system is severely flawed for the dual purposes of service delivery and research, especially for MMR persons. Their chapter provides a revised definition and set of classification guidelines for MMR persons.

Reeve, in Chapter 14, provides a model of mental retardation that is considered medically useful. Rather than defining mental retardation in terms of limitations in social, practical, and social intelligence, these cognitive limitations need to be more closely aligned with medical/neurological limitations as expressed in behavioral outcomes. To Reeve, mental retardation is a medical condition of the brain, but not necessarily a disease, though it is a *chronic condition*. No complete phase of remission is possible, so ongoing supportive services and, should existing sources of support fail, a realistic safety net of support services are required. Reeve's chapter provides for a medical perspective on mental retardation to complement the other perspectives in the book. Reeve does recognize the need for a multidisciplinary approach.

Schalock, in Chapter 15, explores with the reader the impact of merging the constructs of intelligence and adaptive behavior on the conceptualization and measurement of mental retardation. Essentially, Schalock argues that mental retardation is a condition characterized by significant limitations in practical, conceptual, and social skills. In order to fully answer the question, "What Is Mental Retardation?" he tries to answer four questions:

1. What is a disability?
2. What are the essential characteristics of mental retardation?
3. What is the relationship of intelligence and adaptive behavior? and
4. How can we define the "class" of mental retardation?

He concludes, "Once the conceptual model of disablement and the focus of intervention are clear, then by combining the best of scientific and judgmental processes, we can collaboratively and successfully address key scientific and judgmental issues related to the essential characteristics of the condition, the relationship between intelligence and adaptive behavior, and how to define the class."

Simeonsson, Granlund, and Bjorck-Akesson, in Chapter 16, state a variety of concerns with the 1992 /2002 AAMR systems, including:

(a) Inadequate taxonomic structure; (b) Dichotomy between limitations of intelligence and adaptive skills; (c) Reliance on a single IQ score; (d) Lack of conception of multiple intelligences; (e) Lack of indicators of learning; (f) Inadequate description of the three adaptive-behavior skill areas; (g) Overlap of content across adaptive-behavior skill areas; (h) Overlap of content across adaptive-behavior skill areas and participation; and (i) Inadequate sensitivity to characteristics of children.

Their chapter provides numerous ideas for revision of the 2002 AAMR system, including its relationship to the WHO and DSM models.

Switzky, in Chapter 17, defines mental retardation as referring to substantial limitations in present functioning due to very inefficient problem-solving behaviors in various domains of life experiences as a result of significantly subaverage intellectual cognitive functioning (e.g., social, practical, and academic intelligences), interacting with *personality and motivational variables* (e.g., intrinsic motivation, mastery motivation, self-determination, and self-efficacy), as compared to behaviors of others of the same age and cultural group. Switzky argues that motivation along with cognition belongs in the "taxon" of mental retardation: "In the 2002 definition of MR, which stresses substantial limitations in present functioning as manifested in fundamental difficulties in learning and performance due to lesser amounts of conceptual, practical, and social intelligences, the distinction between learning and performance, characteristic of modern cognitive-motivational learning theories, is forgotten. Since cognitive-motivational mediators intervene between the stimuli (setting events) and the response (performance outcomes), and since motivational limitations are commonly present in persons with MR, [Switzky] finds it difficult to justify a definition of MR which makes no mention of intervening motivational processes (which was characteristic of all the [44 years of] AAMR manuals [since 1959]." Switzky's chapter provides a detailed rationale for his proposed definition, which stresses that the outcome performances of persons with mental retardation are a mediated function of the interaction of motivational and cognitive operators that directly relate to the fundamental "taxon" of mental retardation. Switzky also laments the veritable silence of AAMR 2002 regarding the construct of "mild mental retardation." He also worries whether "mental retardation is a functional state in the sense that one's status as being a person with or not being a person with mental retardation can *change* depending on the person satisfying the operational definition of mental retardation over time, since the AAMR 2002 definition now defines mental retardation as a 'disability' . . . and the operational definition of disability is unclear?" "Can a person have a diagnosis of mental retardation at age 6, or age 16, and not at age 25 even though the *'disability' of mental retardation* originated before the age of 18?"—and what are the forensic consequences, especially for *Atkins* cases? He worries about the model of adaptive behavior proposed in AAMR 2002, since no valid measures of conceptual, social, and practical skills presently exist.

Greenspan and Switzky, in Chapter 18, comment on the relationship between AAMR 1992/2002 and the *Atkins* decision and try to answer the question, "Does the 2002 AAMR diagnostic manual provide an adequate basis for resolving disputes regarding the diagnosis of mild mental retardation in capital cases in a just manner?" This question is very important, because the 2002 AAMR manual has become the gold standard typically used by clinicians on both sides, the State and the Defense, in deciding for the Court whether the defendant has or does not have mental retardation. Given that the Court is unlikely to even take on an *Atkins* case unless the defendant's IQ scores are at least fluctuating around the 70–75 ceiling, the crux of most *Atkins* decisions will often hinge on the individual's adaptive behavior. The chapter goes into a detailed practical analysis of all the concerns that a forensic psychologist will encounter in trying to measure adaptive behavior in the defendant.

Buntinx, in Chapter 19, focuses more specifically on two questions:

1. Are the 2002 AAMR system and WHO's International Classification of Functioning, Disability and Health (ICF) compatible?
2. What can be learned from the ICF for the further development of the AAMR system?

Buntinx gives detailed answers to his questions and his insights from his experiences in the Netherlands provides a very in-depth analysis of the complex ICF WHO system, and compellingly argues that the core concepts and criteria of the 2002 AAMR definition fit the frame of reference of the ICF, and indeed the theoretical models of the AAMR 2002 system and the ICF are comparable.

Jacobson, in Chapter 20, provides a case formulation of dual diagnosis treatment priorities using the ICF (ICIDH-2) system to provide a practical illustration of how the ICIDH-2 can be used in functional assessment.

Switzky and Greenspan, in Chapter 21, try to determine whether some consensus can be reached concerning the myriad perspectives of our authors and the implications for the future of the construct of mental retardation.

CHAPTER TEN

Defining and Assessing Spirituality and Spiritual Supports: Moving from Benediction to Invocation

WILLIAM C. GAVENTA

INTRODUCTION: A BEGINNING WITH PROMISE

In the 1992 American Association on Mental Retardation definition (Luckasson et al, 1992), the role of spirituality is mentioned in Chapter 9, "Appropriate Supports," as the fourth of a series of "implications of using supports" (pp. 107–109):

> A fourth implication of supports is associated with recognition of the significant role of spiritual beliefs and their expression in the lives of people with mental retardation, as its importance is increasingly acknowledged for all individuals (Naisbit and Aburdene, 1990). Acceptance and inclusion in the spiritual life of the community is an important source of support that is frequently overlooked for individuals with mental retardation. (p. 108)

The manual's section on spirituality stresses the "significant role of spiritual beliefs and their expression in the lives of people with mental retardation," the relationship of spiritual awareness to intelligence, and the importance of spirituality as a way of acceptance and inclusion in the community (p. 108).

From the perspective of those involved in ministries and spiritual supports with people with mental retardation and their families, the 1992 definition was a major step forward in the recognition of the holistic, multidimensional nature of human life. For many, it was a more accurate and truthful expression of the wondrous complexity of individuals, relationships, and environments, for at least four reasons:

1. It affirms a more holistic view of people with mental retardation, confirming the experience of many that strengths in some areas may exist side by side with limitations in others. Hence, many who have witnessed, affirmed, and experienced people (with significant limitations in some areas) primarily in terms of their gifts and strengths can see in that definition an affirmation of the value of each person.

2. It recognizes the importance of opportunity and experience for learning and development. Hence, those who have seen people with developmental disabilities change, learn, and grow through participation in faith communities have a way of defining the importance of opportunity and practice. Conversely, what might it mean to talk about being "at risk" in a spiritual sense, e.g., never having opportunities to experience love, to be part of a community of faith, or connected with sources of hope?

3. It correctly states that limitations and function must be explored in the context of culture, because different cultures and settings place different values and interpretations on what might appear to be the "same" human ability, disability, or behavior.

4. By including the importance of spiritual awareness and supports in a discussion of the implications of using supports, and delineating a distinction between spiritual awareness and intelligence, the definition took a major step toward creating a context for dialogue and collaboration among people, organizations, and communities who provide supports from different theoretical foundations or starting points, especially that of spirituality.

While a major step, this inclusion of spirituality as one of the appropriate supports and an "implication" to be considered is in some ways a beneficial afterthought, or, in other words, a "benediction." In the subsequent revision, the 2002 definition took out the discussion about the importance of spirituality as a social support and its relationship to intelligence. It did include "spiritual life" as a social role under Dimension III of its definition, and it included a place for that to be considered on the suggested diagnosis form in the accompanying Workbook (Luckasson et al., 2002), but it missed an opportunity to integrate the role of spirituality in more sophisticated ways that would reflect the advance in understanding of its role in personal well-being, supports, and outcomes.

From a Different Direction

To restart this discussion from a different direction, a "spiritual" or "theological" definition might begin with the fundamental affirmation that all human beings have within them a spark of divinity, or, as in the Judeo-Christian perspective, are created in the image of God. An attempt to assess, understand, or define a person with intellectual disabilities and functional limitations from a spiritual or theological dimension immediately puts one in touch with fundamental questions of meaning and purpose (Gaventa, 1997). What does it mean to be human? What and who is "God," that which is sacred or divine, in this person's life (and my own)? Why is there difference? Why is there pain or suffering? What is the purpose of that person's life and of my own in relation to him or her? And how are we connected to each other in our understanding of humankind?

The 1992 definition answers those fundamental questions in a decidedly Western context through the affirmed values of independence (Who am I?), productivity (Why am I?) and integration (Whose am I?) Thus, one of the questions for the definition is recognition of the paradox of its purpose. It is both means and end. It is meant to describe the nature of human experience while at the same time being a functional tool for identifying and organizing the kinds of support needed to assist growth and development toward desired ends.

From that perspective, the recognition of spiritual awareness as a dimension of human life and the importance of spiritual supports was an important first step, but just that—a first step. In the years since 1992, a growing body of literature and research has articulated the importance of spirituality, and the nature of spiritual supports in a wide variety of human services. Rather than being one of four "implications" of the concept of supports, the definition could be broadened to reflect spirituality as a basic dimension of human life. That's what this chapter will now turn its attention toward doing, and it will advocate moving the role of spirituality from an important "benediction" onto the 1992 definition to the more active role of being regularly "invoked" as a part of assessments, care, and supports.

REVISING THE DEFINITION: THE FIFTH/SIXTH DIMENSION AND/OR A TENTH SUPPORT AREA

Put simply, the basic revision needed is not to change the definition per se, but to add "spirituality" as the fifth dimension in the 1992 multidimensional approach to diagnosis, classification, and supports:

> Dimension I: Intellectual Functioning and Adaptive Skills.
> Dimension II: Psychological/Emotional Considerations.
> Dimension III: Physical Health and Etiology Considerations.
> Dimension IV: Environmental Considerations.
> Dimension V: Spiritual Considerations.

In the 2002 edition, it would become the sixth dimension:

> Dimension I: Intellectual Abilities.
> Dimension II: Adaptive Behavior (Conceptual, Social, and Practical Skills).
> Dimension III: Participation, Interactions, and Social Roles.
> Dimension IV: Health (Physical, Mental Health, and Etiological Factors).
> Dimension V: Context (Environments and Culture).
> Dimension VI: Spirituality.

Researchers, theorists, and practitioners define spirituality in a huge variety of ways. The most helpful definition for our discussion, I believe, comes from another interdisciplinary, multidimensional approach to diagnosis and supports, which views spirituality as one of seven dimensions of assessment and care (Fitchett, 1993a). Fitchett defines the "spiritual" as "the dimension of life that reflects the need to find meaning in existence and in which we respond to the sacred." In his work with nurses and other health care professionals in the late 1980s in Chicago, they developed what was envisioned as a "functional approach" to spiritual assessment, an approach that "focuses more on how a person makes meaning in his or her life than on what that specific meaning is" (Fitchett, 1993a, p. 16).

As defined by multiple researchers (Carder, 1984; Fitchett, 1993; Larson and Larson, 1994), spirituality is also seen as a broader category than religion. There is a spiritual dimension to life which may or may not be experienced or lived out in the context of a specific faith community, or what one might call a "substantive" approach to spirituality, i.e., specific beliefs with a defined community of practice. The implication for assessment is primarily that it needs to be more sophisticated than simply whether or not one goes to church, synagogue, or temple, wants to go or not, and has the appropriate supports to do so.

In Fitchett's 7 × 7 Model for Spiritual Assessment (Fitchett, 1993a, p. 42), spirituality is one of seven dimensions that need to be explored in a holistic process:

Holistic Assessment	Spiritual Assessment
Biological (Medical) Dimension	Belief and Meaning
Psychological Dimension	Vocation and Obligations
Family Systems Dimension	Experience and Emotion
Psycho-Social Dimension	Courage and Growth
Ethnic/Racial/Cultural Dimension	Ritual and Practice
Social Issues Dimension	Community
Spiritual Dimension	Authority and Guidance

In the Spiritual Dimension, Fitchett outlines seven areas of a person's spiritual life:

1. Belief and meaning, i.e., major beliefs, sense of purpose, symbols, affiliation.
2. Vocation and obligations, e.g., a sense of calling, duty.
3. Experience and emotion, i.e., experiences of the sacred, divine, or demonic, and feelings or interpretations associated with those experiences.
4. Courage and growth, or how is a person open to change in beliefs based on experience?
5. Ritual and practice, i.e., what are the rituals and practices associated with the beliefs and meaning systems of this person?
6. Community, e.g., Is the person a part of a formal or informal community of shared belief, meaning, ritual, or practice? What is the style of participation?
7. Authority and guidance, or, where does the person find authority for the beliefs and practices? Where does a person look for guidance when needed? To what extent does that guidance come from within or without? (Fitchett, 1993a)

The reason for outlining the comprehensiveness of this particular model is to articulate a base for including the spiritual as one of the major dimensions in the AAMR system rather than subsuming it under one of the others. Spirituality is, for many, related to intellectual functioning and adaptive skills, but one of the basic issues is that spirituality is too often equated with doctrine or intellectual understanding. Spirituality can be expressed in all of the adaptive skills in the current definition. For others, spirituality would seem to be emotional or psychological, yet in the current definition, this dimension is more closely related to identification of mental health issues. Other researchers (Larson & Larson, 1994) have comprehensively explored the historical way that spirituality or religiousness was too often dismissed as a "symptom" of mental illness without recognizing the ways it is also a powerful contributor to mental and emotional health. Increasingly, research has illuminated the impact of spirituality on physical health in terms of prevention, wellness, and recovery as well as support for coping with chronic conditions (Wallis, 1996, Matthews, Larson, and Barry, 1993). It certainly can relate to the 2002 dimension of "Participation, Interactions, and Social Roles," as participation in spiritual life and congregations can serve as a major pathway to community interaction and quality of life (Gleason, 2002, Gaventa, 2005). And, as part of the dimension of "Environmental Considerations" or "Context" (Environment and Culture) spirituality is clearly related to culture, community, and inclusion.

I would argue that the Fitchett model is much more sophisticated than the AAMR Assessment process in exploring the multiple dimensions of family, environment, and social contexts. Spirituality does not "fit" into one of the current dimensions, but rather is a "pervasive" dimension that needs to be assessed in dynamic relationships with the other four or five. Or, if it is not a separate dimension, the 2002 definition provided a framework that could have included spirituality as the tenth of a listing of major support areas: human development, teaching and education, home living, community living, employment, health and safety, behavioral, social, and protection and advocacy. As the Fitchett definition illustrates, the problem is that spirituality relates to all of the dimensions, or to each of these other nine support areas. That interactive complexity, and the recognition of spirituality's potential power, is a major reason for giving it its own place, so to speak, so that those who are assessing and planning supports can explore more fully the ways that spirituality can support many dimensions of growth.

To frame the argument more positively, there are at least four reasons for including and expanding the role of spirituality as a dimension of the assessment and diagnostic system.

First, it recognizes that the spiritual is a dimension of human experience in which people grow and develop as in others (Westerhoff, 1976; Fowler, 1981; Webb-Mitchell, 1993). Where does one find love, meaning, and hope, or experience mystery, trust, awe, the sacred or divine . . . or their opposites? We also need to be professionally honest about the impact that the "spirits" of others have on us and ours on them.

Second, as Fitchett and others have outlined, spirituality is a major way of finding meaning, coping, understanding, changing, and motivating. Whether or not one believes that spirituality is "substantive" part of human experience, we cannot ignore its functional role.

Third, spirituality is a major component of cultures and communities. If we are to be "culturally competent" as professionals, we have to recognize and utilize the spiritual beliefs of individuals, communities, and cultures as part of the context in which people live their own lives. If we want to mobilize inclusive, natural supports and empower both "consumers" and communities, understanding and collaboration with sources of spiritual supports is crucial (Heifitz, 1987; Gaventa, 1997; Dudley and Helfgott, 1990; Landau-Stanton, 1993).

Fourth, spirituality is a dimension of life and experience that begs for the honoring of "consumer" choice and empowerment. (Hoeksema, 1995). Indeed, in the theoretical base of self-determination, "spirituality" is articulated in the framework of freedom, authority, support, and responsibility as a "responsibility," an assumption that spirituality is a primary way of utilizing one's gifts in service to the wider community (Nerney & Shumway, 1996).

Before returning to some of the ways that the spiritual dimension might raise these and related issues for the 1992 and 2002 definition and classification systems, let's summarize some of the research and theoretical foundations for these four reasons for the expansion of "spirituality" in the AAMR system.

EXPANDING THE RATIONALE FOR A DIMENSION OF SPIRITUALITY

"Expanding a rationale for spirituality" may sound to some like a contradiction in terms, but the four areas are only a brief summation of the theoretical research and practice that are taking place in a number of disciplines and areas of human service in relation to the importance of spirituality as a dimension of holistic assessment and comprehensive supports.

Spirituality as a Dimension of Life and Growth

The seminal work on spiritual and faith development was begun by Westerhoff (1976) and Fowler (1981), whose work was based on developmental theories of Erickson. Wolfensberger pointed to fundamental theological, spiritual, and prophetic themes in services and supports with people with mental retardation. Providers and researchers began to hear about the work of Jean Vanier and the L'Arche communities, intentional communities of care and support that are based on a spiritual understanding of human growth in community. People from many faith, spiritual, and theoretical backgrounds knew the capacity of persons with mental retardation to appreciate and exhibit a spiritual life, but the systems of definition and classification made that very difficult to affirm in research and theory. One only has to remember the graphic passage in *The Man Who Mistook His Wife for A Hat* (Sacks, 1987, pp. 178–186), in which Oliver Sacks defines the difference between the Rebecca he saw in the examination room and the same person he saw outside in a garden, communing with the world of nature in a way in which the assessment instruments could not explain. Coles (1990) explored the spiritual lives of children, followed by Webb-Mitchell in an explicit examination of children with disabilities (1993). More recently, the Foundation of Learning Disabilities in the United Kingdom coordinated a national research project entitled *A Space To Listen*, which utilized participatory research to explore the understanding of adults with learning disabilities about their own spirituality (Swinton, 2004).

In The Right to Grow Up (Summers, J., Ed., 1986), I worked on an interdisciplinary model that utilized Westerhoff's understanding of faith development to explore the dimensions of spiritual and religious growth. In his model, spirituality (or faith) spiritual development is expressed as "styles":

1. "Experienced faith," in which individuals experience communities and times of love, trust, joy, and celebration.
2. "Affiliative faith," characterized often by emotional attachment to a set of beliefs and a particular community of faith, where the authority resides in the community.
3. "Searching," a style or period characterized by questioning, searching, and experimentation in beliefs, communities of faith, and social action.
4. "Owned faith," a coming to one's own faith style, often characterized by a renewed sense of the importance of spiritual practice and of shared community.

Others have taken the more explicit and elaborate stages of faith as defined by Fowler and applied them to their work and experience with persons with different levels of mental retardation (Schurter, 1994). In a more recent work, Schurter utilizes levels of support needs to delineate ways to provide support functions to individuals with mental retardation dealing with grief, death, and dying (Schurter, 1998). Glenda Prins, a chaplain serving people with developmental disabilities in Rochester, New York, utilized a theoretical model for spiritual diagnosis developed by Lex Tartaglia and other chaplains at the Strong Memorial Medical Center at the University of Rochester (Landau-Stanton, Clements, Tartaglia, Nudd, & Espillat-Pina, 1993) in development of a spiritual life plan for each person served by her agency. The Tartaglia framework is particularly thought provoking for the ways it combines both experience of fundamental spiritual questions and interpretation of that experience:

Spiritual Diagnosis	Image of God	Experience	Existential Question	Experience	Image of God	Spiritual Diagnosis
Fear	Unpredictable Capricious Chaotic	Mistrust Victimization Helplessness Passivity	"Am I safe?" "Is my world a threat or opportunity?"	Hope Courage Active agency Opportunity	Trustworthy Reliable	Faith
Alienation	Vengeful Divisive	Social stigma External judgment Rejection Estrangement	"Do I belong?"	Social acceptance, communion, embracement	Loving Inclusive	Community
Guilt	Punishing Judgmental	Internalized stigma Personal responsibility for illness	"Am I worthy?"	Grace Repentance	Merciful Compass-ionate	Reconciliation
Despair	Withholding Silent Absent	Meaning-lessness Death anxiety Nonbeing	"Am I valued?" "Do I leave a legacy?" "Did my life make a difference?" "Am I content?" "Regretful?"	Vocation Purpose Creativity Meaning Blessing	Affirming Revealing	Providence

Prins (1994) utilized this framework to assess spiritual strengths and needs and to plan ways to increase experiences of safety, hope. and trustfulness, enhance a sense of belonging, acceptance, and community, encourage experiences of self-worth, and strengthen a sense of personal value, purpose, or meaning. The plan utilized religious activities as ways to express and experience those spiritual needs, as appropriate to each individual, but the plans did not necessarily include religious participation, ritual, or belief.

Spirituality as Meaning, Purpose, and Coping

Besides the model and research of Fitchett cited earlier, literally hundreds of spiritual assessment instruments and research models have been developed to take into account the ways in which people utilize spirituality and religious faith to describe purpose and meaning in their lives, encourage spiritual growth as a means of motivation and coping, and articulate the impact of spirituality and religion on illness prevention and recovery, i.e., healing, or understandings of healing that do not involve cure or recovery (Matthews, Larson, Barry, 1993, Larson & Larson, 1994; Farrar, 1995; Smith, 1998). There has been extensive research on the importance of spirituality in the areas of aging, hospice care, HIV-AIDS, children, addictions, and mental illness. Those studies have led to standards of care in many service systems (e.g., Joint Commission for the Accreditation of Hospitals and Organizations) that address how spiritual needs of patients are met in hospitals and hospices, to headline-making national conferences on the relationships between spirituality and healing in medicine, and multiple forms of alternative therapies with spiritual components in addition to more attention to more traditional spiritual practices.

There has been more recent theoretical and research attention in developmental disabilities. Most of it has focused on spirituality and religion as a framework for coping and meaning in developmental disabilities have focused on families (e.g., Haworth, Hill, Glidden, 1996; Poston & Turnbull, 2004; Gaventa, 2005). The careful delineations of experience and interpretation in both Fitchett and Tartaglia point to a variety of ways in which research and practice could address spiritual gifts and needs of persons with mental retardation and other developmental disabilities.

Spirituality and Culture

With the growing imperative of public policy to be "culturally competent" in the design and delivery of services and supports, the role of spirituality, particularly as defined in the 7×7 model by Fitchett, becomes abundantly clear. What are the belief systems of this individual, family, and community? What meaning is placed on "disability" or even "diagnosis"? Can the community see and develop a place for this individual to live out his or her own sense of vocation, or, as we say, to make a contribution? What are the rituals and practice, the holidays and traditions, that give meaning to people's lives, particularly in periods of transition or change (Hornstein, 1997)? How do people grow and change, especially in terms of attitudes or practices that may be traditional but neglectful or harmful? Where are the experiences of community, belonging, and affirmation? Who does one turn to for guidance?

For many service providers and researchers, the question is even more fundamental: What authorities might we "invoke" to gain trust in a community in order to develop accurate assessments and effective supports? Whether one frames the research and planning in terms of eco-cultural issues (Gallimore, Weisner et al., 1989), community associations (Kretzmann & McKnight, 1993), family issues in particular cultures (Rogers-Dulan,

1998), religious identity (Moran & Weiner, 1991), or concerns for the "optimum environment that provides opportunities, fosters well being, and promotes stability" (Luckasson et al., 1992), the issue of effective and ethical practice begs for respect of the spiritual traditions and centers of cultural life and for enhanced research that can lead to more effective collaboration and practice. That importance is amplified when practitioners suspect or hear experiences of the ways in which spirituality can be used to hurt and harm as well as to help. One can dismiss spirituality as "bad" or "hurtful," but a deeper understanding may provide advocates, providers, and friends with alternative interpretations and/or practices within that same spiritual tradition.

Spirituality as Choice and Self-Determination

A number of researchers and practitioners have pointed to the importance of congregations and spiritual communities as pathways and supports into community life and relationships (Amado, 1993). A common dilemma faced by consumers, advocates, and supporters is that spiritual and religious rights may be affirmed in policy, but not supported in practice. The fear of "proselytizing" and of violating the "wall between church and state" points to real issues that need careful exploration, but they are not the same as recognizing, affirming, and supporting the importance of spirituality as a dimension of life for people with (or without) mental retardation (Gaventa, 1993a).

In an article that originated in work to resolve a lawsuit about proselytizing and agency policy, Hoeksema (1995) outlined the importance of respecting and supporting religious freedom in the group home context. He pointed the way toward responsible guidelines for policies and practices in those settings, and in doing so, helped focus the question of spirituality away from professional belief and practice to respecting citizenship and choice.

In the years since then, the importance of assisting individuals to make choices, and the relationship between choice, control, self-determination, and well-being, have received increasing attention in professional literature and practice. The theoretical basis for the growing self-determination movement (Nerney & Shumway, 1996), i.e., the values of freedom, authority, support, and responsibility, demonstrate the importance of values at the heart of practice and the ways in which these crucial expressions of spirituality (as defined by the meaning and purpose that is interpreted from experience) can impact practice. When it comes to spiritual expression, it does not take much imagination to recognize the ways in which spirituality becomes a field of potential choices waiting to be harvested, i.e., supported. Freedom to choose one's needed supports (Do I want to go to church today?), authority and power to make choice real (It's your job to help me get there, as we have defined it in your job description, whether or not it is your faith tradition; and it is more important to me that you be here on Saturday morning to go to synagogue than it is to help me go through yet another diagnostic and assessment process), and support. (Maybe it does not have to be a paid job to support my decision, but my paid staff can help me develop connections and friendships at the local (you fill in the blank), which is my major spiritual community.) A paper at the 1998 AAMR National Conference (Gleason, 1998, 2002) pointed to the importance placed on spiritual supports by one agency, which became convinced this was a major way to actively enhance quality of life. The importance of honoring and supporting choices as well as freedom in religious expression has been recognized in a policy statement adopted by both the AAMR and The Arc in 2001.

An intriguing component of spirituality in these theoretical underpinnings of self-determination is that it is connected to the fourth value of "responsibility," i.e.:

> the acceptance of a valued role in a person's community through competitive employment, organizational affiliations, spiritual development and general caring for others in the community, as well as accountability of spending public dollars in ways that are life-enhancing for persons with disabilities. . . . The intense over-regulation of programs and the setting of goals and objectives to meet the needs of the human service system more than the aspirations of people with disabilities, have conspired to prevent people with disabilities from truly contributing to the associational life of their communities, the spiritual life of our churches and synagogues, and the cultural and artistic life of our cities and towns. (Nerney & Shumway, 1996, p. 6)

These four theoretical foundations for expanding "spirituality" to a dimension of assessment and practice point to two other reasons that focus more on professional identity and practice than on assessment of another individual or plan for a system of supports. These are beyond the scope of this chapter, but let us outline them briefly.

The first is ethics. There are ethical issues and questions in almost every area of assessment, practice, and supports. The assumptions one makes about human life and growth, the ways we all discern and manufacture meaning and values, the influence of our cultural traditions on fundamental perceptions of what is right and wrong, and our political affirmations about what it means to be citizen as well as consumer of services, all shape the way we approach ethical questions in our work, issues with specific individuals in specific situations, and systemic issues of policy and resource allocation. The spiritual assumptions, foundations, and imperatives for ethical decision making and practice cannot be ignored.

The second is professional honesty, identity, and development. It may be hard to talk about, but if we are honest, it is the spiritual gifts, struggles, and pains of people with disabilities and their families that have "called" many of us into vocations that have provided meaning and purpose for professional caregivers. The questions that "they" face about independence, productivity, and integration are also our own journeys into meaning, values, and motivation. One could make a strong case for seeing people with disabilities as "our" spiritual guides. Seeing the diversity of spiritual gifts in different cultural contexts enriches our own. And being "professional," whether diagnostician, provider, planner, or policymaker, is a position of incredible power that we are struggling to share with those who say they are now community member and citizen, not consumer. In many ways, we are being pushed toward a much older definition of "profess-ional," one that is at least clear and open about values, loyalties, and willingness to share what one has to help fulfill a vision of community (Gaventa, 1993, 1998). The challenge of learning to reframe professional roles is an issue not just in developmental disabilities but in many areas of community development (Chambers, 1997).

SOME FURTHER MEDITATIONS (I.E., REFLECTIONS) ON THE DEFINITION

In a number of ways, the addition of spirituality as a fifth or sixth dimension could impact other areas of the 1992 or 2002 definitions. They include the tasks of assessing and defining gifts and strengths more carefully, exploring understandings of vocation, calling, and responsibility to the wider community, and providing clearer guidelines and models for assessing spirituality, supporting choice, and changing practice.

The parallels between discussions of the difficulty of assessing spirituality (substantive experiences or beliefs vs. functional interpretations of meaning and experience) and the difficulty of assessing mental retardation may or may not be obvious. Is mental retardation a substantial characteristic of some people's experience, i.e., real unto itself, or is it interpretation? Is it substance, experience, or interpretation, and what is the function of the definition at all levels? To whom is a definition real, by whom is it experienced, and how is it interpreted?

In the Judeo-Christian tradition, the power of "naming" is a gift given to Adam and Eve as a way of continuing the process of creation through ordering and naming that which God had created. (Note that in almost every one of the first six days, God paused to decide whether or not the new part of a named creation was "good.") There is also the fascinating account in the "second" story of creation in Genesis 2 that the naming of all the animals, birds, and fish was part of the process of bringing order but also of finding a helper as his partner, for "it is not good that man should be alone." But there are boundaries—some things shall not be touched or named. The tree of life was one. And later, it was the name of God—a refusal to give in to Moses' question for a clear classification: "I am That I Am."

That is one way of saying that a spiritual perspective on the process of defining and classification may need to recognize there are some parts of life which defy naming and dominion, and, instead, beg for respect and honor. Matters of the spiritual have been difficult to "classify." That may be a function of their "observable, measurable, material" elusiveness, and/or it may be a function of our innate awareness of their power. Wherever one stands, there remains the question of the purpose of naming, and whether or not we can respect depths of experience that call for wonder and mystery. How does it function? Whom does it help? And how?

But the second question for the definition and classification system comes from the Latin root of the word "assessment," which meant to "sit next to" (Hilsman, 1997). If we do indeed need to "sit next to" in order to see and understand what is real in and for another, to be with them in their context, to listen to self-report, observe behavior and skills, and then assess and plan, then that raises even further the question of the power of definition and the power of the definer. The question of "Who owns the definition?" is much more fundamental than whether it belongs to AAMR, APA (American Psychiatric Association), or CEC (Council for Exceptional Children). If, through defining, you own or have power over the person, then whose is the responsibility? If we sit next to, to observe and assess, are we honest about the impact of the event on the observer as well as the observed? As we evolve toward another paradigm that affirms the crucial importance of community embeddedness (which professional practice can support or hinder but not provide), and a paradigm of "empowerment," then the question of who owns the definition is even more important. Is the definition one that is functional and useful for the individual, his or her particular community, and his or her potential community?

A VIEW TOWARD THE FUTURE

My temptation was to call this section a "prophetic" look at the future. However, a self-named prophet is, by definition, not one. The argument in this chapter for more comprehensive recognition and use of the spiritual dimension on human life in a system of diagnosis, classification, and supports is based on the personal experience of many I know, on sound theory from a wide variety of theoretical perspectives, and, increasingly, on a significant body of research. Whether one recognizes and affirms the spiritual dimension as a substantial (i.e., real?) dimension of human experience, a functional process of discerning meaning and purpose in human experience (which is also real), a recognition of the role of spirituality in culture and community, or as a consumer right and choice that needs to be respected and honored, the theoretical foundation is there.

That recognition raises some interesting questions. How might we talk about "adaptive spirituality"? What does or might it mean to be "spiritually competent"? Or, even more provocatively, what does it mean to be "spiritually retarded" or "spiritually disabled"? Those questions raise the specter of the spiritual abuse very quickly, but if one goes back to the Tartaglia model, we all know in personal experience or professional practice what it means to be "disabled spiritually." To be caught in despair, to have lost hope, to have little experience of love or affirmation, to lack trust in anyone—we have seen that or been there, and the potential "client population" is much broader than that defined by "mental retardation." And many I know will give witness to the incredible spiritual strengths of people we label "retarded" in other dimensions of their life.

The real prophets in our time are the self-advocates who raise the real question outlined in the previous section: Who owns the definition and defining process? What is the function? How is it helpful, and to whom? Most self-advocates say it is time to change the definition and the name. To most, it feels hurtful. If "naming" is about the development of understanding and mastery over chaos, but also about the creation of a helpful partnership, it is time to hear and recognize the call for a new kind of partnership between "consumer" and "clinician" that is based on citizenship, collaboration, and self-determination.

That partnership would be not just between "consumer" and "clinician," but also between American perspectives and those of the rest of the world, where the emerging paradigm is either "mental disability" or "intellectual disability." It would put limitations in intellectual functioning, paired with other life-skill limitations, more firmly within the paradigm of "intellectual, physical, emotional," and, perhaps, spiritual disabilities.

Whatever the decisions about the construct and the diagnostic process, the future will see more and more research and practice focused on the integration of the spiritual dimension in human services and caregiving. Congregations continue to grow as a major source of community inclusion and natural supports. Individuals and families continue to say "This is an important part of our lives. Why is no one paying attention?" Anecdotes and stories are emerging about the power of having clergy or congregational members included in person-centered planning processes, but this is an area that begs for effective practice and research, such as recent examples exploring the participation in religious services by people with developmental disabilities (Minton & Dodder, 2003) and self reported perspectives (Shogren & Rye, 2005).

The challenge to clinical and professional practice is then multidimensional as well. There is first the question of developing effective models and processes for assessing the spiritual dimension as part of any diagnostic and support planning process. The models are there, and other areas of human service are, in many instances, much farther ahead. Given the current focus of research in a number of health-care disciplines and areas of need on the role of spirituality and faith, one hope is that same kind of research could develop in the area of developmental disabilities in relation to what the AAMR classification system calls primary, secondary, and tertiary prevention, and, more proactively, on the quality of lives of individuals and families.

Second, there is the question of how professional caregivers then help provide appropriate spiritual supports. Is it just a job for the "religious professional"? The nursing profession long ago decided that paying attention to spiritual care was one of the components of their responsibility (Schoenbeck, 1994). Research, training, and writing is being done in many disciplines about the responsibilities of professionals to pay attention to the spiritual dimension in the lives of the people they serve: social work (Dudley and Helfgott, 1990), occupational therapy (Farrar, 1995), psychology (Heifitz, 1987), psychiatry and medicine (Larson, 1994), and many more. The barriers cited to more effective practice include concern about "church/state" separation, understandings of "professional" identity, lack of knowledge, lack of funding, and personal history (Dudley, 1990; Hoeksema, 1995; Heifitz, 1987). All of those have and can be addressed if we believe this to be a crucial dimension of care (Gaventa, 1993, 2005). But more work needs to be done on what it means to be a "spiritual clinician" (Hilsman, 1997) or, borrowing a term from supported employment, a "church coach" (Gaventa, 1996).

The final challenge then comes back to professional identity as well as practice. Does "profess-ional" mean the one in control of a body of knowledge, the fixer, and the expert, or does it mean one who possesses some knowledge but also "professes" a commitment to walk alongside others as well as "sit next to them" in an assessment process, and a belief in the capacity of the partnership to support and sustain others in the challenges faced together? Professionals from many fields, both "scientific" and "religious," have been much better at naming, diagnosing, and classifying than at fixing or healing on the one hand and/or sustaining or supporting on the other.

To come back to where this chapter began, my hope is that the systems of definition, classification, and supports will proactively and intentionally expand to include the assessment of the spiritual dimensions of people with what we now call mental retardation, with both the belief and knowledge that this can contribute to more holistic understandings of individuals, families, and communities and more effective, and collaborative, systems of support and care. Spirituality is a dimension of life to be more intentionally addressed, explored, and tapped at the beginning of an assessment and supports process. Or, stated in faith language, it is an area to be "invoked" for understanding and assistance as well as one that can give a blessing, or "benediction," to a service and support plan that assumes it is already complete.

REFERENCES

Carder, M. (1984). Spiritual and religious needs of mentally retarded persons. *The Journal of Pastoral Care, 38*(2), 143–155.

Chambers, R. (1997). *Whose reality counts? Putting the first last.* London: Intermediate Technology.

Coles, R. (1990). *The spiritual life of children.* Boston: Houghton Mifflin.

Coulter, D. (1994). Spiritual supports in the 1992 AAMR system. *National Apostolate for Persons with Mental Retardation Quarterly, 25*(2), 10–12.

Downe, M. E. (1986). *A blessed weakness: The spirit of Jean Vanier and L'Arche.* San Francisco: Harper and Row.

Dudley, J., & Helfgott, C. (1990). Exploring a place for spirituality in the social work curriculum. *Journal of Social Work Education, 26*, 287–294.

Dudley, J., & Millison, M. (1992). Providing spiritual support: A job for all hospice professionals. *The Hospice Journal, 8*(4), 49–66.

Dudley, J., Smith, C., & Millison, M. (1995, March/April). Unfinished business: Assessing the spiritual needs of hospice clients. *The American Journal of Hospice and Palliative Care*, pp. 30–37.

Erikson, E. (1944). *Identity and the life cycle.* New York: Norton Press.

Farrar, J. (1995). *Client's spirituality and religious life: Challenging the scope of occupational therapy practice.* Unpublished master's thesis, Tufts University, Boston.

Fitchett, G. (1993a). *Assessing spiritual needs: A guide for caregivers.* Minneapolis: Augsburg/Fortress Press.

Fitchett, G. (1993b). *Spiritual assessment in pastoral care: A guide to selected resources.* Atlanta: Journal of Pastoral Care Publications.

Fitchett, G. (1996, March). The 7x7 model for spiritual assessment. *Vision, 6*(3), 10–11.

Fowler, J. (1981). *Stages of faith: The psychology of human development and the quest for meaning.* San Francisco: Harper and Row.

Gallimore, R., Weisner, T., Kaufman, S., & Bernheimer, L. (1989).The social construction of eco-cultural niches: Family accommodation of developmentally disabled children. *American Journal on Mental Retardation, 94*(3), 216–230.

Gaventa, W. (1986). Religious ministries and services with adults with developmental disabilities. In Summers, J. (Ed.), *The right to grow up: An introduction to adults with developmental disabilities* (pp. 191–224). Baltimore: Paul H. Brookes.

Gaventa, W. (1993). Gift and call: Recovering the spiritual foundations of friendships. In A. Amado (Ed.), *Friendships and community connections between people with and without developmental disabilities* (pp. 41–66). Baltimore: Paul H. Brookes.

Gaventa, W. (1993, September/October). From belief to belonging to belief: Trends in religious ministries and services with people with mental retardation. *Disability Rag/Resource*, pp. 27–29.

Gaventa, W. (1996). Honoring diversity through spirit and faith. *Impact, 9*(3), 10–11.

Gaventa, W. (1997). Pastoral care with people with disabilities and their families: An adaptable module for introductory courses. In M. Bishop (Ed.), *Thematic conversations regarding disability within the framework of courses of worship, scripture, and pastoral care* [Monograph]. Dayton, OH: National Council of Churches Committee on Disabilities.

Gaventa, W. (1998). Recovering the meaning of professional. *Frontline Initiative, 2*(4), 1–2.

Gaventa, W. (2005). A place for all of me and all of us: Rekindling the spirit in services and supports. *Mental Retardation, 43*(1), 48–54.

Gleason, T. (1998). *Spirituality and quality of life.* Paper presented at 1998 AAMR National Conference, San Diego, CA. Published as, Integrating spiritual supports into residential services: The PSCH model. *Impact, 14*(3), 30–31.

Haworth, A., Hill, A., & Glidden, L. (1996). Measuring the religiousness of parents of children with developmental disabilities. *Mental Retardation, 34*(5), 271–279.

Heifitz, L. (1987). Integrating religious and secular perspectives in the design and delivery of disability services. *American Journal on Mental Retardation, 25*, 127–131.

Hilsman, G. (1997, June). Spiritual pathways: One response to the current standards challenge. *Vision, 7*(7), 8–9.

Hoeksema, T. (1995). Supporting the free exercise of religion in the group home context. *Mental Retardation, 33*(5), 289–294.

Hornstein, B. (1997). How the religious community can support the transition to adulthood: A parent's perspective. *Mental Retardation, 35*(6), 485–487.

Kretzmann, J., & McKnight, J. (1993). *Building communities from the inside out: A path toward finding and mobilizing a community's assets.* Evanston, IL: Northwestern University.

Larson, D., & Larson, S. (1991). Religious commitment and health: Valuing the relationship. *Second Opinion, 17,* 27–40.

Larson, D., & Larson, S. (1994). *The forgotten factor in physical and mental health: What does the research show?* Rockville, MD: National Institute of Healthcare Research.

Laundau-Stanton, J., Clements, C., Tartaglia, A., Nudd, J., & Espaillat-Pina, E. (1993). Spiritual, cultural, and community systems. In J. Landau-Stanton & C. Clements (Eds.), *AIDS: Health and mental health. A primary sourcebook* (pp. 267–298). New York. Bruner/Mazel.

Luckasson, R., Borthwick-Duffy, S., Buntinx, W. H. E., Coulter, D. L., Craig, E. M., Reeve, A., et al. (2002). *Mental retardation: Definition, classification, and systems of supports* (10th ed.). Washington, DC: American Association on Mental Retardation.

Luckasson, R., Coulter, D. L., Polloway, E. A., Reiss, S., Schalock, R. L., Snell, M. E., et al. (1992). *Mental retardation: Definition, classification, and systems of supports* (9th ed.). Washington, DC: American Association on Mental Retardation.

Matthews, D., Larson, D., & Barry, C. (1993). *The faith factor: An annotated bibliography of clinical research on spiritual subjects.* Rockville, MD: National Institute for Healthcare Research.

Minton, C., & Dodder, R. (2003). Participation in religious services by people with developmental disabilities. *Mental Retardation, 41*(6), 430–439.

Moran, M., & Weiner, K. (1991). *Spiritual and faith community integration needs of Catholic developmentally disabled adults.* Holyoke, MA: Bureau for Exceptional Children.

Nerney, T., & Shumway, D. (1996). *Beyond managed care: Self determination for people with disabilities.* Concord: University of New Hampshire.

Poston, D., and Turnbull, A. (2004). Role of spirituality and religion in family quality of life for families of children with disabilities. *Education and Training in Developmental Disabilities, 39*(2), 95–108.

Prins, G. (1994, May). *Spiritual life plan.* Paper presented at the American Association on Mental Retardation National Conference, Boston.

Rice, D., & Dudley, J. (1997). Preparing students for the spiritual issues of their clients through a self-awareness exercise. *The Journal of Baccalaureate Social Work, 3*(1), 85–95.

Rogers-Dulan, J. (1998). Religious connectedness among urban African American families who have a child with disabilities. *Mental Retardation, 36*(2), 91–103.

Sacks, O. (1987). *The man who mistook his wife for a hat and other clinical tales.* New York: Harper and Row.

Schoenbeck, S. (1994). Called to care: Addressing the spiritual needs of patients. *The Journal of Practical Nursing, (44)*3, 19–23.

Schurter, D. (1994). Guidance for the journey: Fowler's stages of faith as a guide for ministry with people with mental retardation. In *A mutual ministry: Theological reflections and resources on ministry with people with mental retardation and other disabilities* (pp. 35-43). Denton, TX: Denton State School.

Schurter, D. (1998, May). *A developmental model for grief in people with mental retardation.* Paper presented at the American Association on Mental Retardation National Conference, San Diego, CA.

Shogren, K., & Rye, M. (2005). Religion and individuals with intellectual disabilities: An exploratory study of self reported perspectives. *Journal of Religion, Disability, and Health, 9*(1), 29–55.

Smith, J. *Parents' perceptions of the spiritual needs of their adult child with mental retardation.* Forthcoming doctoral dissertation, Lewis University, Chicago.

Sommer, D. (1994). Exploring the spirituality of children in the midst of illness and suffering. *The ACCH Advocate, 1*(2), 7–12.

Swinton, J. (2002). A space to listen: Spirituality and people with learning disabilities. *Learning Disability Practice, 5*(2), 6–7.

Vanier, J. (1975, May). L'Arche: A System of Service to the Handicapped. Unpublished keynote address at the American Association on Mental Retardation National Conference. Portland, OR.

Vanier, J. (1989). *Community and growth.* Mahwah, NJ: Paulist Press.

Wallis, C. (1996, June 24). Faith and healing. *Time Magazine, 147*(26), 58–64.

Webb-Mitchell, B. (1993). *God plays the piano too: The spiritual lives of disabled children.* New York: Crossroad.

Westerhoff, J. (1976). *Will our children have faith?* New York: Seabury Press.

Wolfensberger, W. (1979). An attempt toward a theology of social integration of devalued/handicapped people. *Information Service, 8*(1), 12–26. Republished in Gaventa, W., & Coulter, D. (2001). *The theological voice of Wolf Wolfensberger* (pp.49–70). Binghamton, NY: Haworth Press.

Wolfensberger, W. (1982). An attempt to gain a better understanding from a Christian perspective of what "mental retardation" is. *National Apostolate with Mentally Retarded Persons Quarterly, 13*(3), 2–7. Republished in Gaventa, W., & Coulter, D. (2001). *The theological voice of Wolf Wolfensberger* (pp.71–84). Binghamton, NY: Haworth Press.

Chapter Eleven

Mental Retardation in the Real World: Why the AAMR Definition Is Not There Yet

Stephen Greenspan

Introduction

The subtitle of this chapter was inspired by William E. Kiernan's AAMR presidential address in 1996. He asked a question about the mental retardation field, quoting the children's car-riding refrain: "Are we there yet?" With respect to the last two AAMR classification manuals, my reluctant reply is: "Unfortunately, in spite of some progress, we are still not there yet." My response may surprise some readers, when my ideas (especially about a tripartite model) were heavily cited in the theoretical section of the 2002 manual and, to a lesser extent, in the 1992 manual. This citing of my work has caused some to think, wrongly, that I played a major part in developing the definitions in both manuals. I am honored to have my work so recognized, but feel obligated to point out that the definitions of MR, in both the 2002 and 1992 manuals, do not fully reflect what I had been proposing, more or less consistently, in all of the works that were cited in support of those definitions.

My passion on this subject is driven less by abstract theoretical argument, or personal pique, than by practical considerations. While I have tried to ground my ideas on solid empirical work (mostly by others), and believe that my proposed definition has a fair amount of theoretical coherence, the main influence on my formulation and refinement of a definition of MR has always been my personal experience with people with MR—as a family member, as an advocate, and as a clinical consultant. I sincerely believe that my view best describes the real-world phenomenon of MR as I and others have experienced it. My recent experience in carrying out *Atkins* death-penalty exemption assessments (see Greenspan & Switzky, "Lessons from the Atkins Decision," elsewhere in this book), has greatly strengthened my belief that the 2002 AAMR definition, by moving in an even more formulaic direction, by suggesting the need for numerical adaptive-behavior scores; and by continuing to support the use of adaptive instruments, such as the Vineland-II and the ABAS, that emphasize tooth brushing far more than social vulnerability, still does not provide an adequate basis for determining whether a "marginally competent" person does or does not have MR.

The balance of this paper is divided into four sections. In the first section I discuss the question, "Is it better to use a cookbook formula or a natural intuitive 'taxon' to diagnose MR?" In the second section I describe the "tripartite model," both as it was proposed by me, and as it actually was used in the 1992 and 2002 AAMR manuals, as a search for a better and more adequate artificial cookbook formula. In the third section I discuss some reasons, particularly the hang-up with numbers, why the AAMR cannot come up with a better artificial cookbook. Finally, in the fourth section, I discuss why maybe it is time to abandon the artificial cookbook approach altogether and to get real.

A NATURAL TAXON VERSUS AN ARTIFICIAL FORMULA

According to the online version of the OED, a "taxon" is a unique species or classificatory group. Derived from biology, particularly botany, a taxon refers to what the psycho-diagnostician Paul Meehl (1973) referred to as "nature carved at the joints." While one taxonomic category may overlap somewhat with another, one or more essential qualities enable a knowledgeable observer, often intuitively, to rule a particular plant, animal, or disease in or out as belonging to a particular taxon. The notion that MR is a natural taxon—that is, that there are one or more essential qualities that a person with MR either has or does not have—seems to differ in fundamental ways from the formulaic approach reflected in the past few manuals, and especially the 1992 and 2002 AAMR manuals. That is not to say that we do not carry around inside our heads an intuitive sense of what the MR taxon is, such as the one that might cause you to think that the man depicted in the following example does not have MR, but the recent AAMR manuals, in spite of some loosening on the subject of clinical judgment, say basically, "Trust the formula, not your own gut."

Here is an example of what I am talking about. Let's say you are a new board member at a DD agency and you have a conversation at the annual holiday party with a well-groomed man whose name tag reads "Eric Jones." He is very articulate and talks with insight about current events and his own life. Mr. Jones strikes you as a little odd but is "normal" enough that you assume that he is a staff member. Later on, however, you find out that he is actually a client of the agency and has a diagnosis of mild MR. Your first reaction is to say, "No way. That is a misdiagnosis."

When you have a chance to find out more about Eric, you learn that he has several IQ scores below 70, his problems developed at an early age, and his adaptive behavior profile has sufficient deficit areas to qualify him as having MR under both the 1992 and 2002 manuals. Which is correct in this situation: your gut impression that Mr. Jones does not have MR, or the psychological evaluations that suggest that he does? If Eric's adaptive behavior scores were higher, then one could say, "This is a case where a low IQ score results in a 'false positive.'" However, in the current situation, the only basis for dismissing the test scores would be your clinical judgment, and that judgment is based only on a brief meeting and conversation in a party setting.

What if I told you, however, that Eric has a long history of being tricked and manipulated sexually, financially, and in every other way, and that his seeming social skills reflect a kind of superficial cocktail party patter that he can call upon with the same words when meeting people for the first time? In less conventional interpersonal situations, where there may be a hidden manipulative agenda or where a complex social narrative is unfolding, Eric either runs out of things to say or else gives clear evidence of being totally out of his depth. Then you might decide that Eric might have MR after all and that your first impression was mistaken.

You might think this is a totally hypothetical situation, although we all have wondered at one time or another about some of our colleagues, but I have seen some clinical reports recently in *Atkins* death-penalty exemption cases, in which an expert witness will conduct a one- two- or four-hour clinical interview with an individual and conclude, even in the face of significant test scores to the contrary, with words along the lines of "X's verbal skills and insights are really good, and on that basis I cannot concur with Dr. Y's judgment that he has MR." Is that good enough, or is it an inappropriate thing for a clinician to do in diagnosing a disorder that is officially to be defined according to a precise set of numerical specifications, and in which information about adaptive functioning is supposed to come mainly from others who know the individual well? I think most of us would say that a clinician's sense regarding whether a person fits the natural taxon should play a role when considering the differential diagnosis "MR" or "not-MR." The relevant question is: "What exactly is the natural taxon of MR?" One will look through the AAMR manual in vain, however, for an answer to that question.

The 1992 and 2002 AAMR manuals emphasize repeatedly that MR is a condition defined by weaknesses, and not ruled out by strengths. In fact, the manuals indicate that a person can have strengths in many areas (eight out of ten adaptive skill areas in 1992, two out of three adaptive skill domains in 2002) and still qualify as having MR. Other than an IQ score below a certain level, there are no behavioral (i.e., adaptive skill) domains in which normal or near-normal functioning would rule out a diagnosis of MR. In other words, it doesn't matter how brilliant a speaker Eric Jones is at a cocktail party or on a lecture stage, for that matter; neither verbal ability, nor any other isolated ability, justifies deciding that someone cannot have MR. This position may seem an exaggeration of what the 1992 and 2002 manuals say, but if it so, it is not much of one. By being tied to an artificial formula based on theory rather than reality, and since nothing is less natural than a standard deviation unit, there is the danger that one can classify a person as having MR or not having MR, without even having to look at the person in a holistic manner as a living, breathing entity.

An example from Blink, Malcolm Gladwell's best-seller about automatic cognitive processing (2005), involves a nearly too-perfect ancient Greek statue that a museum was considering buying for $10 million. To determine if it was a fake, the museum brought in chemists and x-ray specialists, who conducted a half-dozen sophisticated tests. They concluded it was for real, and the museum shelled out the cash. Then they asked an expert on Greek statues to look at it, and after a 10-second evaluation based solely on aesthetic impressions, he pronounced it fake. This expert, relying solely on his knowledge of hundreds of such statues, decided it did not fit the taxon for statues of this type. It turns out he was right.

To understand why the AAMR has moved toward the use of artificial formulas, and away from the use of intuitive judgments, one has to know something about the sad and sordid history of the MR field in the United States and other western countries. Seymour Sarason once told me a story about a woman working for the state of Connecticut whose job was to drive around to various towns and make snap judgments, based solely on eye-balling, about whether a child or adolescent should immediately be placed in one of the state's large residential institutions. As part of a research project (Dunaway, Granfield, Norton Greenspan, 1992), my colleagues and I once interviewed a few of these people finally deinstitutionalized after decades, some after being sterilized, and we found several cases where the person, based on today's cookbook formula, would not even come close to a diagnosis of MR. In fact, in the Connecticut Department of Mental Retardation database, a sizeable percentage of these now deinstitutionalized, but still-served, individuals have the diagnostic code "Non-MR." Similarly, in a quasi-scientific but highly cited study that contributed to the policy decision around 1920 to shut down the flow of immigration into the United States from eastern and southern Europe, allegedly because a large percentage of these immigrants had MR, psychologist Henry Goddard hired poorly trained "moron detectors" whose job was to scan the tired and disoriented and non-English-speaking immigrants debarking at Ellis island and decide, based on how they looked and acted, which of them had MR (Smith, 1985).

Ironically, although the use of today's artificial diagnostic formulas is an effort in part to avoid the misguided at best, evil at worst, past misuses of clinical judgment, it also owes it origins in part to the efforts of Henry Goddard and other eugenics-oriented psychologists to devise a more reliable method for rooting out hidden "morons" who were lurking unidentified in the general population (Trent, 1994). Goddard enthusiastically seized on the newly invented Stanford-Binet Intelligence Scales, because he had doubts about the ability of "eyeball methods" to reliably identify sufficient numbers of people who have what today would be called mild MR, in that such individuals may look or act in ways that on the surface are relatively normal. Thus, the use of intelligence test scores was promoted by early 20th-century psychologists such as Binet as a more scientific and valid basis for diagnosing MR. Guess what, folks? That same attitude still prevails today.

According to the late Stephen Jay Gould (1983), Henry Goddard began to suspect, toward the end of his life, that he may have grossly overestimated the prevalence of mild MR in the population. Specifically, he acknowledged that he produced many false positives when interpreting the results of intelligence test performance. A major reason was that in the early days of intelligence testing, psychologists relied on mental age (MA), and it was not yet understood that MA scores, a composite of knowledge and raw computing power, seems to reach an asymptotic value in early adolescence and does not continue to rise with chronological age. Thus, a 30-year-old man with a MA of 15 might look mentally deficient but in fact is probably functioning in the normal intellectual range. The same criticism, of course, can be made of the early-devised ratio IQ method, which is why today we use the deviation method, which employs percentile ranks derived from norms for persons of the same age when calculating IQ scores.

The raising or lowering of the IQ ceiling, along with the invention of the adaptive behavior criterion and its more "scientific" grounding in adaptive behavior standard scores, is an attempt to eliminate some of the mistakes that flow both from unfettered reliance on

clinical judgment and also from sole reliance on an IQ ceiling to define the MR populations. However, it still involves implicit acceptance of the following twin notions:

1. Mild MR is a hidden condition that cannot be reliably diagnosed from a judgment that a person's observed behaviors conform to the natural taxon.
2. The best way to discover if a person actually has mild MR is through the use of
   a scientific numeric formula that supposedly measures capacities residing inside
   the person.

A major reason why MR is defined in terms of an artificial numeric formula rather than
an intuitively-based natural taxon is something that is not generally understood, namely
that MR, particularly mild MR, is a socially constructed disability category rather than a
naturally constructed quasi-medical category. Although MR, like any disability, often is
caused by a medical disease, evidence of such a disease is not necessary to be diagnosed as
having MR, and in most cases of especially mild MR a cause may be suspected but is not
known. The taxon for most medical diseases is found not in observed symptoms/ behaviors, which can vary widely across and within diseases, but in the presence or absence of
critical etiological agents. Thus, tuberculosis (TB) is defined by the presence of the TB
bacillus, and before the identification of that microorganism, TB was as difficult to diagnose as is mild MR today.

The term "disability" originated in the vocational rehabilitation field and is used to
indicate that a person needs significant short- or long-term supports in order to be able
to hold down a job, if he can at all. It is, thus, a bureaucratic category, usually defined by
a committee, which may be influenced by political and economic considerations as much
as by "science," and the decision as to where to draw the line between disability and
nondisability, based on an estimate of the amount of supports needed to function normally, is relatively arbitrary. Given that MR is a socially constructed disability/bureau-
cratic category, is it any wonder that efforts to define it have mainly been based on
theoretically elegant formulas, rather than on complex and messy reality?

So here is the $64,000 question: "Does the fact that MR is a socially constructed
bureaucratic category mean that there is no point even talking about trying to find its natural taxon?" A related big question flowing from the above discussion is: "Since MR is a
socially rather than naturally defined category, should we just drop use of the category
altogether?" As an eternal optimist, I answer both of these questions with a qualified
"No." To take the last question first, I believe that some people are much less competent
than others in coping with the demands of life, and a point exists beyond which such
incompetence places these individuals at dire and potentially dangerous risk of catastrophic social or physical failure. I also believe that in some individuals, those whose primary impairment is not mental illness, a high potential vulnerability to catastrophic
failure can be traced to serious abnormalities in brain development which limits their ability to think and to learn.

The fact that there have always been some individuals who have developmental limitations in their ability to master and effectively apply cognitive schemas to challenges of
everyday life is reflected in the use in every society of descriptors and epithets such as "stupid" or "retarded." So it is useful to maintain some category, whether or not one calls it

"MR," to identify and bring needed supports and protections to those people who are viewed in such a light. Whether it will be possible to construct a definition of that class of people which is close to the category's natural taxon will hinge on the extent to which the definition/formula taps into the behavioral profile which laypeople use in deciding that some people have such a disorder. A practical implication for individual diagnosis, rather than defining the taxon, is that the best and maybe only way to establish whether a person qualifies as having MR is not how the person is viewed by a psychologist or other mental health professional in an artificial mental health setting, but in how he has been seen by peers and adults in his ecological world.

THE TRIPARTITE MODEL OF ADAPTIVE INTELLIGENCE

Something that I termed the "tripartite model" (Greenspan, 1979, 1981; Greenspan & Driscoll, 1997; Greenspan & Love, 1997; Greenspan, Switzky & Granfield, 1996), and which I borrowed and modified from an earlier formulation by E. L. Thorndike (1920), has been cited as a theoretical justification by both the 1992 and 2002 AAMR manuals. In fact, it was incorporated into the 2002 manual as the basis for its model of adaptive behavior. The tripartite model has been used by the T&C Committee as a foundation for devising a better, more valid, and thus more widely used formula for adaptive behavior and, thus, for devising a better cookbook recipe for defining and diagnosing MR. However, without using the term "natural taxon" (because this term has only recently entered into my vocabulary), I have argued that the model is useful mainly as a way of bringing awareness of the central importance of a critical aspect of "MR-ness" that has been overlooked, namely "social intelligence." Thus, the tripartite model has served both to tinker with the artificial formula and to bring that formula closer to the natural taxon.

To the extent that there has been tension between myself and the authors of the 2002 AAMR manual, it is that they have not gone nearly as far as I would have liked, although they have taken some welcome baby steps, toward stating that low social intelligence and its most dramatic expression, gullibility, is the universal and most important aspect of MR's natural taxon.

A point that I have been making over the past 25 years, hopefully with increasing clarity as my own understanding has deepened, is that MR is a condition characterized by deficits in three types of intelligence. The problem with the way that MR has typically been approached, however, is that one of those types of intelligence, conceptual (or academic) intelligence, measured by IQ tests, has received all of the emphasis. The construct of "adaptive behavior" was an attempt to loosen the overreliance on a single IQ score as the sole basis for definition and diagnosis. The adaptive behavior construct has muddied the waters, however, because of the failure to ground it solely in the other two types of intelligence.

Using Thorndike's tripartite model of multiple intelligences, I have suggested (Greenspan, 1979, 1997, 1999a, 1999b) that the best way to think of adaptive behavior, given that the term that was invented and used before it was defined or understood, is in terms of the two nonacademic domains in Thorndike's tripartite model. These are "social intelligence" (e.g., understanding of people and social processes) and "practical intelligence" (e.g., understanding of mechanical objects and processes). These two nonacademic domains of intelligence have been described (Greenspan, Switzky, & Granfield, 1996;

Sternberg, 1984) as comprising "everyday intelligence," which has to do with the application of intelligence to real-world settings and problems.

Given that the purpose of inventing the adaptive behavior construct was to reduce the likelihood that someone might be diagnosed as having MR solely on the basis on a single measure of academic intelligence (IQ), there is a major advantage in broadening the definition of MR to include the two aspects (social and practical) of everyday intelligence. The advantage is that, historically and logically, when we think of someone who has MR we think of someone who has low intelligence, and redefining adaptive behavior to encompass everyday intelligence keeps that historical and logical connection while weakening the tendency to think of low intelligence solely in IQ terms. Defining adaptive behavior, as has been done in all of the AAMR manuals since 1961, in ways that are not specifically tied to the notion of low but broadened intelligence, threatens to further confuse the definition of MR by bringing into the equation aspects of human competence/incompetence such as mental illness or antisocial behaviors other than those specifically reflecting low intelligence.

It is probably because adaptive behavior measures have not been clearly enough connected to intelligence, broadly defined, and thus to the historical construct of MR, that they have been ignored more than they have been used. In the field of adaptive behavior measurement, as with other constructs (including intelligence), current instruments have largely been modeled on the first widely used measure, which in this case was the AAMD (later AAMR) Adaptive Behavior Scale, widely known as the "ABS." In addition to providing a summary or overall index, the ABS, and its successors such as the Vineland-I and Vineland-II, have provided two subordinate scores, in addition to an overall adaptive behavior score. The two subordinate domains tapped by these instruments have both of the following:

1. Competence in dealing with practical aspects of life, what have been termed "self-help" and "community use" skills such as dressing and feeding oneself and using public transportation.
2. Competence in dealing with social-emotional aspects of life.

On the surface, these seem to have some logical connection with the everyday practical and social domains in Thorndike's tripartite model. A major problem, however, is that the social-emotional domain of adaptive behavior was termed "maladaptive behavior" and consisted of such things as the presence or absence of incompetent behaviors directed against oneself (e.g., anxiety, self-abuse) or others (e.g., aggression, noncompliance).

Anyone with deep experience in the MR field knows individuals whom they consider to clearly have MR but who have few if any maladaptive behaviors (i.e., they lack substantial psychopathology). Such individuals, however, if they are correctly diagnosed, almost always demonstrate deficits in social intelligence (i.e., they lack the ability to pick up social cues or anticipate reactions of others). A case that I have previously used to illustrate this point concerns "Bob," an adult man with Down syndrome who lived and worked in Omaha, Nebraska (Greenspan & Shoultz, 1981). The late Frank Menolascino, a mentor of mine who was one of the leading psychiatrists specializing in MR, actually used a videotape of an interview he did with Bob to show new psychiatry residents that one could have MR and yet be mentally healthy (i.e., lack maladaptive behaviors). Bob indeed was a very well-adjusted person, who possessed many positive qualities. However, he did have serious social intelligence deficits and, thus, was appropriately given the diagnosis of MR.

One example involved a time when Bob was at a going-away party for a female social worker and started telling the woman's mother that he had long wanted to have sex with her daughter and then elaborated on this story, even after the mother showed obvious signs of discomfort. Another example involved a meeting in which several self-advocates were complaining about a state legislator who opposed funding a program which they supported. Bob made the serious suggestion that the group send a letter to this politician threatening to shoot him if did not change his position, and had a hard time understanding why sending such a letter was not a good idea.

The use in adaptive behavior measures of maladaptive behavior (i.e., acting-out or self-abuse), rather than social intelligence items, to tap the "social" aspect of adaptive behavior, had the effect of muddying the distinction between two disorders, MR and mental illness, that historically and conceptually have been seen as distinct. Furthermore, it missed an aspect of incompetence that, much more than maladaptive behavior (which may or may not be present in persons with MR), goes to the heart (as in the case of Bob) of what it means to be viewed as having MR.

This failure to frame adaptive behavior mainly in terms of low everyday intelligence was also seen in the fact that many of the items on the ABS and other instruments tapped whether a person habitually did a certain activity, such as being nice, rather than on whether he or she possessed an adequate understanding of why such an activity is desirable. This problem of confusing understanding with outcome behavior (which could reflect personality and motivation as much or more than understanding) is one that still afflicts adaptive behavior measures.

Adaptive Skills in the 1992 Manual

The T&C Committee that wrote the 1992 AAMR manual was somewhat taken with my early writings about the connection between adaptive behavior and nonacademic aspects of intelligence, as reflected in the fact that the manual's second and theoretical chapter cited me quite a lot, and used the tripartite model as the theoretical justification for the way they approached that aspect of the definition. Given the emphasis on the notion of competence and incompetence in the 1992 manual, the T&C Committee apparently liked my suggestion that adaptive behavior should be conceptualized in ability rather than adjustment terms. However, in a foreshadowing of 2002, the model of adaptive behavior adopted in the final 1992 manual diverged significantly from what I had been suggesting.

What happened is that the next-to-last draft of the manual did base the definition of MR and of adaptive behavior on the tripartite model, but at a brief meeting when the final draft of the manual was being planned, the committee backed away from the tripartite model and took a very different tack. However, because of time constraints or the fact that the approach they finally took lacked an adequate theoretical justification, the tripartite model was kept in as the theoretical framework for a definition that now bore no resemblance to it. The reason why the tripartite model was dropped at the last minute, according to personal communications to me from committee members, was concern about the lack of empirical support and the lack of valid measures for the domain of social intelligence. So, with relatively little discussion, the committee took an adult community skills curriculum which possessed far less empirical support off the shelf and used it as the basis for a model of "adaptive skills" with nine dimensions. Later, after pressure from AAMR's recreation division, this was expanded to ten dimensions with the addition of leisure skills, as if more advertising were needed that science had little to do with the selection of this model.

In another arbitrary decision, the T&C Committee adopted a polythetic, so-called Chinese menu, approach to meeting the adaptive skills criterion, noting that in order to be eligible for a diagnosis of MR, a person had to show deficits in at least two out of the ten adaptive skills. Why two and not three, four, or five? The only answer given in the manual is that the committee wanted to make the criterion a fairly easy one to meet.

My biggest concern about the 1992 manual was its failure to recognize the importance and centrality of social intelligence deficit—which I have consistently argued is the most important, and most overlooked, domain—as the key to capturing the essence of the MR taxon. As already noted, skepticism about the importance of social intelligence framed mainly in terms of measures, but also reflecting doubts about the construct itself, was responsible for the decision to reject the tripartite model—except in the unchanged theoretical chapter—in the first place. Lack of appreciation for the importance of social intelligence was also reflected in the ten-domain model itself, in two ways:

1. Only one out of ten as opposed to my proposed one out of three domains dealt with social aspects of competence.
2. The construct of "social skills" is different, in very profound ways, from "social intelligence."

The term *social skills* is widely used by behaviorists and refers to the extent to which an individual engages in behaviors that are socially valued (Matson & Fee, 1991). In seeking to make people with MR more socially accepted, behaviorists have emphasized such isolated skills as eye contact, greeting verbalizations, and a range of other positive behaviors. There has been a consistent lack of emphasis in the behaviorist social skills literature on the cognitive underpinnings of socially competent behavior, which may explain why there is so much bemoaning of the lack of "generalizability" of acquired social skills from one situation to another. (I shall never forget a young woman with moderate MR who was trained to emit greetings, and then said "hello" so frequently and indiscriminately that her greeting verbalizations had to be extinguished, as they were driving the staff crazy.)

The Adaptive Behavior Assessment System (ABAS; Harrison & Oakland, 2000) was the first major adaptive behavior measure to base itself on the 1992 manual. In line with the 1992 manual, it had one subscale, termed "social," that mainly listed positive behaviors as "says 'thank you' when receiving a gift," "offers assistance to others," and "congratulates others." Such behaviors are more a function of what I have previously termed "character" (e.g., niceness toward others) than of social intelligence (e.g., understanding of others). The only other of the 10 adaptive skills in the 1992 manual that touched indirectly on the socio-emotional realm was "self-direction." On the ABAS, this domain was captured by a few other character items (i.e., "routinely arrives at places on time" and "stops a fun activity . . . when time is up"), but mainly contained items such as "controls anger," "controls disappointment," and "controls frustration" that reflect mostly what I have termed "temperament," which is the ability to control emotions and attention.

In the 2003 revision, now termed the ABAS-II, the authors recombined the original subscales, such that "self-direction" is now part of the "conceptual" domain, a combination that to me makes no sense. To have more than one subscale in the new "social" domain, the authors combined the "social" subscale with the "leisure" subscale, which contains mostly nonsocial items such as "plays alone with toys, games or other fun activities." In other words, in the ABAS-II—and, I can assure you, in other adaptive behavior scales such as the Vineland-II—we have a quantitative index that is conceptually and methodologically a mess. (See also Greenspan & Switzky, "Lessons from the Atkins Decision," this book.)

Thus, the construct of social skills, as defined by the 1992 manual and as operationalized on measures such as the ABAS, is not that different from what pre-1992 AB measures termed "maladaptive behavior" (i.e., the presence or absence of psychopathology), as good character is the absence of beating up on others, while good temperament is the absence of beating up on oneself. All of such information likely is useful in devising a service plan but is irrelevant to the main function of adaptive behavior assessment, namely the diagnosis of MR.

As Herman Spitz (1988) has pointed out, and I have also said repeatedly, MR is in essence a "thinking disorder." In contrast, behaviorists—and the 1992 adaptive skills model was essentially a behaviorist checklist—have tended to think of MR as a "learning disorder." To paraphrase Spitz, a learning disorder is characterized by a paucity of behavioral schemas, while a thinking disorder is characterized by an inability to apply those schemas flexibly and appropriately in novel and complex situations. People with MR likely have a greater ability than previously appreciated to learn new schemas (skills), but there are still real structural limitations, likely reflecting brain abnormalities, in the ability to apply those schemas/skills effectively, especially in complex and challenging situations. The term "intelligence" implies thinking, while "skill" implies learning. The essence of MR, from the standpoint of definition and diagnosis, is thus found not in the relative absence of especially routine skills but in the relative inability, especially under conditions of ambiguity or stress, to figure out when and how to apply those skills.

ADAPTIVE SKILLS IN THE 2002 MANUAL

On the surface, the 2002 manual appears to have incorporated the tripartite model into the definition of MR, but in fact it is not the tripartite model of "adaptive intelligence" that I had proposed but rather a transformed version of "adaptive skills" proposed by Robert Schalock (1997). He was a member of both the 1992 and 2002 T&C Committees and played a very influential role in coming up with the adaptive behavior component in the 2002 manual. I know that firsthand, as I served briefly during the early stages of that committee. The 2002 committee recognized early on that the ten-domain model of adaptive skills in the 1992 manual had been a mistake, as reflected in the widespread reluctance of clinicians and agencies to use the 1992 definition. The committee's solution was to restore into the definition of MR the term "adaptive behavior," thus defining MR as a disorder marked by deficits in both intelligence and adaptive behavior, but to now further define adaptive behavior as comprising three adaptive skill areas: "conceptual adaptive skills," "practical adaptive skills," and "social adaptive skills."

One can see that this differs fundamentally from my repeated insistence that MR is a disorder marked by deficits in three areas of intelligence. Specifically, the 2002 definition continued the practice, established in 1961, of viewing adaptive behavior as something different from intelligence and thus of less centrality to the diagnosis, given that persons with MR have historically been described mainly in terms of their low intelligence. If the committee had instead used, as I recommended, the tripartite model of intelligence, there would no longer be any need for this artificial invented construct of adaptive behavior. Or, if one wanted to continue using the term, perhaps because of some unwillingness to put other aspects of intelligence on quite the same level as IQ, then one could say that "MR is a disorder marked by deficits in academic intelligence (i.e., IQ) and adaptive behavior, with adaptive behavior operationally defined as everyday (i.e., practical and social) intelligence."

This last formulation would have been a slightly less direct and therefore less desirable way of saying "MR is a disorder marked by deficits in academic, practical and social intelligence," but it would have at least acknowledged an obvious and very simple truth, namely that MR is a disorder characterized by low intelligence, broadly defined. Instead, the solution adopted by the 2002 T&C Committee allowed continuation of the convoluted, artificial and, in my opinion, mistaken argument that intelligence equals IQ scores plus some set of behaviors other than intelligence.

The idea of morphing the tripartite model of adaptive intelligence into a tripartite model of adaptive skills was proposed in the chapter that Schalock (2003) wrote for the first e-book version of this volume. (A draft of the book was substantially completed well before the manual was completed, even if the e-book was published a year later in 2003.) That chapter built on an even earlier formulation of the same ideas, contained in a chapter written by Schalock (1999) for a book on adaptive behavior that he edited and in which I (Greenspan, 1999b) was also a contributor. In my chapter I argued that adaptive behavior should be viewed in terms of one's ability to negotiate challenging microsituations, such as a deceitful and manipulative interpersonal interaction. Schalock characterized his proposed solution as a way of "integrating" intelligence and adaptive behavior, by transforming the tripartite model of intelligence into a tripartite model of adaptive behavior/skills. On the contrary, I saw it as a way, whether intended or not, to continue to support the primacy of IQ scores in the diagnosis and definition of MR, by maintaining the shaky notion that "conceptual skills" is something other than conceptual or academic intelligence.

Schalock (2004) has acknowledged to me that the tripartite model has not been fully implemented, and he sees both the 1992 and 2002 as transitional documents that may, eventually, evolve into a fuller implementation of the model. I have no reason to doubt his sincerity and optimism, but 100 years of the field's infatuation with the twin notions that IQ scores = intelligence and MR = low intelligence leads me to question his estimate of that endpoint's being reached in the foreseeable future. Maintaining the idea that "adaptive skills" are anything other than "intelligence applied in various settings" is likely to perpetuate the idea that intelligence (i.e., IQ test scores) is central to what MR is all about, while adaptive behavior is still peripheral.

The compromise by which a tripartite model of adaptive intelligence morphed into a tripartite model of adaptive behavior may seem elegant in a Hegelian sense, and may make its adoption more politically attainable, given how resistant most psychologists are to any effort to suggest that IQ test scores no longer rule, but it does not, in my opinion, solve the problem of establishing a more valid basis for deciding if someone does or does not have MR. One reason it does not is that it contributes to the development and acceptance of measures such as the ABAS-II, on which an item such as "has pleasant breath" is taken seriously as a basis for diagnosing MR.

In the 2002 manual, a diagnosis of MR is now based on deficits in intelligence still defined as below minus two standard deviations on a measure of full-scale IQ, taking into account standard error of approximately five points and significant deficits in one out of the three adaptive skill domains of "conceptual skills," "practical skills," or "social skills." As was the case in 1992, the 2002 criterion was made fairly easy, in order that adaptive behavior not be too great an impediment to allowing someone with low-enough IQ to qualify as having MR.

A new step in making the definition more "scientific" is the strong indication for the first time in the various AAMR manuals that the adaptive behavior criterion should be derived from use of a formal instrument with population norms, and that a diagnostic decision be based on the same minus-two-standard-deviations equation that has been applied to IQ. The notion that use of a numerical index makes a definition more scientific is discussed later on, but one obvious problem with this notion is that if the number is based on a conceptual and methodological muddle (e.g., measures such as the ABAS-II and the Vineland-II), then what we have is a clear case not of science but of pseudoscience. That is not surprising, since the entire history of MR, starting with Goddard's bogus claim to have uncovered the menace of hidden mental defectives, is the history of a pseudoscience trying to pass as or turn itself into a real one, by using methods (MA or IQ cutting scores) whose main claim to scientific respectability is the fact that they produce a number.

Ranting aside, and aside also from the metatheoretical issues raised earlier, here is the main problem I have with the new formula. As indicated, a consequence of having the tripartite model become a model of "adaptive skills" rather than of "adaptive intelligence" is that it became necessary that the "conceptual skills" component of adaptive behavior be portrayed as something other than "conceptual intelligence" (i.e., IQ scores). Otherwise, using the formula MR = low IQ + low (one-out-of-three) adaptive skills, one would have a situation where an individual could be diagnosed as having MR on the basis of having deficits in IQ and academic incompetence only. In such a scenario, the idea that a diagnosis of MR must be based on more than academic incompetence somehow gets lost.

In order to avoid that problem, and to placate publishers who had invested heavily in the 1992 model, the approach taken by authors of the 2002 manual was to plug scales from the 1992 list into the three skill areas, including conceptual skill, in a relatively arbitrary manner. Thus, as depicted in Table 5.2 on page 82 of the 2002 manual, "Social Skills" was constituted by combining "social" and "leisure" from AAMR 1992, "Practical Skills" was constituted by combining "Self-Care," "Home Living," "Community Use," "Health and

Safety," and "Work" from AAMR 1992, and "Conceptual Skills" was constituted by combining "Communication," "Functional Academics," "Self-Direction," and "Health and Safety" from AAMR 1992.

This may have nicely solved a practical problem for the 2002 T&C Committee, but does it make sense, either theoretically or practically? I don't think so. Conceptual Intelligence has now morphed into a "Conceptual Skills" domain having only two subscales ("communication" and "functional academics") that have any connection to the conceptual intelligence piece of the original tripartite model, and it adds one subscale ("self-direction") that is really a measure of temperament which has nothing to do with the taxon of MR and another subscale ("health and safety") that really belongs in the practical skills domain.

If we are to remain saddled, as I am afraid we are, with the notion that adaptive behavior involves "skills" rather than "intelligences", then here is my own proposed Hegelian synthesis, which I believe is more acceptable both theoretically and practically than the one that the authors of the 2002 manual came up with (under, I suspect, very hasty circumstances). Simply drop "conceptual skills" from the right side of the plus sign, thus integrating it more into the notion of "intellectual processes" on the left side of the plus sign. Adaptive behavior would be redefined as significant deficits in "practical" and "social" skills in meeting everyday challenges, and these skills would, hopefully, be defined operationally more in terms of cognitive processing than in terms of personality styles. Thus, one would still have the tripartite model, but the conceptual piece would be moved over to the left side of the plus sign, as in the revised formula: MR = deficits in intellectual functioning (e.g., IQ, language, academics) + deficits in everyday functioning (e.g., practical and social skills).

This notion that adaptive behavior should be grounded in the idea of "everyday competence" (e.g., social plus practical deficits) was actually something that Robert Sternberg (1985) proposed in one of his few forays into the MR field, and that I proposed (Greenspan & Driscoll, 1997) in a revision of my model of personal competence a few years ago. One could still use a polythetic (one-out-of-two) decision criterion, if one wanted to stay with an artificial cookbook formula. Personally, I prefer an approach more grounded in the notion of requisite aspects of the MR taxon (e.g., all people with MR are practically and socially incompetent, defined in terms of "stupidity" rather than preference), as I discuss in the last section of this chapter.

Why the AAMR Seems Unable to Devise a Better Cookbook

I have already vented enough spleen, and there is no need to beat a dead—or, in this case, sick—horse. So I shall keep this section brief. There are lots of reasons why the AAMR keeps coming up with a flawed manual, two of them being the inevitable difficulty of getting a committee to agree on anything, and another being my own and others' failure to present a clear enough rationale or to come up with acceptable alternative measures, particularly for the "social" piece of the equation. Also, the "truth" is not always easy to figure out, especially in a situation where there are conflicting pressures from numerous constituencies.

In an obituary for the 1992 manual (Greenspan, 1997), I pointed out, without any pejorative intention, that the process of producing an AAMR manual is inherently "political."

Among the many conflicting political pressures faced by the T&C Committee were: the AAMR wanting the manual out fast (it is a major money maker for a financially strapped organization), psychologists threatening to bolt if their beloved IQ test was disrespected, researchers screaming "science," advocates wanting something respectful (i.e., the notion that one can have MR and still have normal talents), the international faction wanting the WHO to be honored, the DSM-IV threatening to go off in its own direction, internal factions on the T&C Committee, and various AAMR divisions wanting their own interests accommodated. In light of these pressures, it is a wonder that the 1992 and 2002 manuals turned out as well as they did.

In the most insightful analysis ever written about the political nature of any diagnostic manual, sociologists Stuart Kirk and Herb Kutchins (1992) described the writing of the path-breaking DSM-3, which has remained fundamentally unchanged in subsequent revisions, as the result of a tremendous internal battle within the psychiatric community between old-guard psychoanalysts and new-guard biological and descriptive psychiatrists. The new guard won this battle, not on the basis of their superior rhetoric—it is hard to beat psychoanalysts at that game—but on the basis of their superior claim to being "scientific," a notable weakness of psychoanalysts. They did this by demonstrating—debatably, it turns out—that the new diagnostic scheme was more reliable, using a newly invented statistic: Cohen's kappa. Thus, a diagnostic manual that was really grounded on a different kind of theory, was successfully sold on the basis that it was more reliable, and therefore more scientific (i.e., based on a number). Whether or not it did a better job of making true discriminations among people was another matter than was never really resolved.

A basic belief of most psychologists, perhaps reflecting a neurotic need to be seen as "real" scientists, is that high reliability leads inevitably to high validity. That is not always the case. J.P. Guilford (1965), using intelligence as an example, argued that while many constructs are multifaceted, the most internally reliable measures are reliable because they are narrow, which means that they hardly have adequate content validity. Thus, the best way to attain validity is to base it on the construct of interest, even if it may be a little hard, perhaps because of its fuzziness, to measure it reliably.

Assuming, as I argue, that "gullibility" is a hundredfold more important as an index of the MR taxon than brushing one's teeth daily, then a valid adaptive behavior scale is one which contains many gullibility items, even if one has to word these items in a way that can't be rated as reliably as "wipes up spills at home" (an item on the ABAS-II). This has important implications for the diagnosis of MR, as probably the most valid index that one has MR is also not completely reliable (which is why one should always use many raters), namely whether or not others in a person's community view him or her as having MR.

I have already indicated that probably the biggest obstacle to the full adoption of the tripartite model for defining MR is the idea that IQ is somehow more "scientific" than adaptive behavior, especially given that IQ measures are highly reliable (i.e., they produce roughly the same score from one time to another and regardless of who is administering the test, and the scales are fairly internally consistent). The need to be seen as more scientific is reflected in the debatable decision of the 2002 committee (debatable given the inadequate measures currently in use) to apply a statistical formula to the adaptive behavior criterion as well.

My main argument against sole reliance on the IQ score as a basis for diagnosing MR is that an IQ score does not provide a sufficiently valid basis for diagnosing a disorder that historically (i.e., before invention of the IQ test, and even before universal schooling) has been viewed mainly in terms of inability to function independently and safely in the social and practical world. The biggest myth in the intelligence field is that IQ scores equal intelligence. In fact, the first and all subsequent IQ measures assess academic potential, precisely because they were compiled by taking tasks from different grades within the school curriculum. If intelligence refers to the ability to apply "thinking" to challenges in the world, then it should be obvious that there are challenges in the world that people, whether children or, especially, adults, face that have nothing to do with what they learn at school. This brings me back to the point that falls at the heart of this chapter, and which I shall expand on in the final section: An artificial cookbook formula (i.e., minus two standard deviations in X and Y psychological tests) may look more scientific, and may be more reliable (which remains to be proven), but does not necessarily lead to a diagnosis that is true.

Can We Devise a Definition of MR Based on Its True Natural Taxon?

No one is more aware than I that people with mild MR can have a mixed profile of abilities and deficits, and that there may even be areas of near or actual normal functioning. The question is: Are there behavioral competencies which, if present, should rule out automatically any eligibility for a diagnosis of MR? The fact that Mr. Jones, in the example at the beginning of this chapter, can talk adequately in a conventional social setting does not, in my opinion, rule out such a diagnosis, even if some laypeople or clinicians—some of who are essentially laypeople when it comes to MR—might disagree. On the other hand, if Mr. Jones never gave any sign of being easily fooled or tricked in complex and deceitful social settings, then I would think it likely that the diagnosis of MR was a mistaken one, regardless of what score he may have received on one of the adaptive behavior scales in use. However Eric did, as described, have a history of frequent and dramatic gullibility, so that requirement of the universal natural taxon was met.

In the 2002 AAMR manual, there is only one absolute requirement, namely that an IQ be below 70 (75 if one takes into account standard error). In terms of the adaptive behavior criterion, one can be substantially average or even above average in two of the three areas in the tripartite model of adaptive skills and still have MR. To me that seems somehow wrong, based both upon theory and, more importantly, upon how people whom we believe to have MR actually function in the world. If the cookbook says that one can be normal in one's ability to see through deceptive manipulation, forgetting for a minute that no gullibility items are on the ABAS-II (and only one on the Vineland-II), then I say "Better ditch the cookbook." Fortunately, mention of the word "gullibility" finally made it into the 2002 manual, but hardly in a major way.

In the earlier (Greenspan, 2003) but now totally rewritten version of this chapter that was in the electronic edition of this book, I argued that essence of the MR taxon, which I then termed "prototype" or "behavioral phenotype," had three components:

1. It is grounded in the implicit, even if not always established, notion that a person has developmentally based abnormal brain structure or functioning.
2. It is grounded in the notion that a person has limitations in "thinking"—that is, he will be seen as "dumb" in coming up with solutions to real-world problems, particularly when these are novel, complex, or anxiety producing.
3. It is grounded in concern that, because of these brain-based limitations in thinking ability, a person will be vulnerable to catastrophic failure, academically, practically, socially, unless formal or informal supports and protections are put in place.

An obvious implication of this formulation of MR's natural taxon is that any definition of MR should emphasize clearly the idea of organicity, the idea that incompetence is solely based on thinking limitations, and the idea of vulnerability and need for supports. In fact, none of these three core components of the natural taxon are emphasized clearly in the 2002 model. With respect to organicity, the 2002 definition makes no real mention of etiology, and it is only very indirectly tied in with the idea of origination in the developmental period (because that is interpreted temporally and not etiologically). With respect to vulnerability and supports, there is no mention of vulnerability in the definition and only very indirectly is there mention of supports, in that the term "disability" implies need for supports. However, the notion of thinking limitations is partly satisfied in discussion of intellectual processes, but is undercut by the failure to specify that limitations in adaptive behavior must be considered only in regard to the application of thinking skills and not in terms of a grab-bag of behaviors reflecting inclination more than thinking applied to the everyday world.

Another major problem with the wording of the 2002 definition and previous ones is that by putting intelligence first (i.e., MR is "a disability characterized by significant limitations both in intellectual functioning and in adaptive behavior"), the definition encourages the tendency (documented in the Greenspan & Switzky chapter, "Lessons from the Atkins Decision," in this book), where adaptive behavior is considered only if a low-enough IQ score is attained, and not if IQ score is not low enough. In other words, an implication of the current cookbook formula is that adaptive behavior can be used only to rule out a false positive where low IQ gives a wrong diagnosis that a person has MR, but cannot be used to rule out a false negative where too-high IQ gives a wrong diagnosis that a person does not have MR. That seems to me to be fundamentally wrong, and if the cookbook formula is to be valid (i.e., to result in diagnoses that are in line with the natural taxon), then adaptive behavior needs to be able to rule out false negatives as well as false positives.

One way of doing this is to reverse the order of the wording and place adaptive behavior first in the equation. Here is one formulation of a definition in which this is done (this is also formulated in slightly different form in our *Atkins* chapter): MR (preferably called something else, perhaps Intellectual Disability) is "a form of disability, first suspected in childhood or adolescence, that is characterized by significant deficits in adaptive (social, academic, and practical) functioning that are attributable to significant brain-based limitations in the ability to think and process information adequately. These limitations in thinking make a person very vulnerable to catastrophic failure in various aspects of everyday life, and require the use of formal and informal supports and protections in order to minimize the occurrence and consequences of this vulnerability." This definition should also be expanded to indicate that MR is a condition inferred from how a person is viewed in his or her natural ecology, such that opinions by knowledgeable laypeople should be given infinitely more weight than opinions by a clinician based on a brief and limited interaction. Thus, in a very real sense, the best evidence that a person actually has MR is the fact that almost everyone who knows him thinks he has MR, and has given evidence in the past of using that or some similar term to describe him.

By placing the notion of adaptive functioning in front of "the ability to think," it is established both that the condition is defined first and foremost by actual behaviors, rather than by IQ scores, and that measures of adaptive functioning will always be needed in making a diagnosis of MR or not-MR. Furthermore, by indicating that these limitations are attributable to limitations in thinking, it is hoped that measures of adaptive behavior will contain many items such as "is vulnerable to trickery and deceit" or "cannot cook without producing an inedible mess or burning down the house" and very few items such as "has clean hair" or "has pleasant breath."

To get back to the example of Eric Jones with which I started this chapter, I want to delve a little bit into the fundamental question which needs to be answered if an adequate manual is to be devised, and that is: "Are there certain abilities or inabilities, derived from MR's natural taxon, which will universally need to be present or absent in deciding whether a person actually has or does not have MR?" The relativistic cookbook formula contained in the 2002 manual does not, as I have indicated, do this. It is my belief, however, that there are some universal aspects of the MR phenotype that must be in the definition if it is to be considered adequate.

At the risk of seeming somewhat crazed on the subject—it is hard to keep quiet when one feels one has made a major discovery—I think that a key to the universal natural prototype of MR is unusual gullibility (Greenspan, Loughlin, & Black, 2001). This is an aspect of the MR taxon that was mentioned in early textbooks (Ireland, 1877; Morrison, 1824), but has been almost absent from the recent research or clinical literatures. However, it is central to the MR taxon as it manifests in the real world, as seen in a story that appeared in my local newspaper.

It involved a woman, Sherri Bramer, who became lost at sprawling Denver International Airport when her plane was diverted to a gate other than the one posted. The main concern her frantic waiting family members felt, as they searched for the 52-year-old woman (described as having mild MR), was over a topic that is rarely even addressed in the scholarly literature: the possibility that her extreme gullibility made her vulnerable to being exploited if she fell into the wrong hands. As described by journalist Lynn Bartels (2004), Sherri's 57-year-old brother Keith said that the first thing that occurred to him and his 81-year-old mother, when they realized that Sherri was lost, was that "Sherri is very vulnerable. She'll do whatever you say, go wherever you want her to." In other words, their concern was fueled by a type of incompetence that is addressed in only a single item on one the leading adaptive behavior measure, namely Sherri's extreme gullibility and her tendency to believe anyone and trustingly do whatever was asked of her, even by strangers.

Similar evidence that gullibility is a major issue for cognitively impaired individuals can be found in fiction, as in the story of the gullible puppet Pinocchio (Greenspan, 2004), and more importantly in many other real-life examples. One such example can be found in the recent award-winning documentary *The Collector of Bedford Street*, by film maker Alice Eliot (2001). This film has won wide acclaim as the story of how neighbors in New York's Greenwich Village banded together to set up a trust fund to enable an unrelated man with mild MR, Larry Selman, to continue to live in their midst. The media emphasized that this act of caring was a form of thank-you to Mr. Selman for being such a kind person himself (he gets his nickname of "collector" from his having raised hundreds of thousands of dollars for charity in the neighborhood over the years). In fact, the main impetus for setting up the fund was that Larry's extreme gullibility had placed him and the other tenants in danger from repeated acts of exploitation by homeless people (e.g., taking his keys and ripping off his possessions, damaging the building, and terrorizing the residents). Yes, the neighbors are to be commended for caring about Mr. Selman, but they cared about him (and their own interests) not just because he was good but because he was extraordinarily socially vulnerable. This social vulnerability is not a collateral aspect to Mr. Selman's MR, similar to having pleasant breath. Larry's *extreme gullibility* was the central thing, far more than his IQ score (which most of the neighbors didn't even know), that caused all of the people who loved him to see him as having MR. Unless the next AAMR manual comes up with a definition that taps into such a universal aspect of the MR natural taxon, then the process of diagnosis and of fiddling around with the cookbook formula will be an artificial game with little relevance to the real world and the real people living in it.

REFERENCES

Bartels, L. (2004, January 3). Disabled woman lost at DIA for hours: Flight info changed, family grew frantic. *Rocky Mountain News, 146, 5–6.*

Dunaway, J., Granfield, J., Norton, K., & Greenspan, S. (1992). *Costs and benefits of privately-operated residential services for persons with mental retardation in Connecticut.* Storrs, CT: Pappanikou Center of the University of Connecticut.

Elliot, A. (Director). (2001). *The collector of Bedford street [Motion picture].* (Available from Welcome Change Productions, 107 Bedford Street, Upper One, New York, NY 10014)

Gladwell, M. (2005). *Blink: The power of thinking without thinking.* Boston: Little, Brown, & Co.

Gould, S. J. (1983). *The mismeasure of man.* New York: W. W. Norton.

Greenspan, S. (1979). Social intelligence in the retarded. In N. R. Ellis (Ed.), *Handbook of mental deficiency, psychological theory and research* (2nd ed., pp. 483–531). Hillsdale, NJ: Erlbaum.

Greenspan, S. (1997). Dead manual walking? Why the 1992 AAMR definition needs redoing. *Education and Training in Mental Retardation and Developmental Disabilities, 32,* 179–190.

Greenspan, S. (1999a). A contextualist perspective on adaptive behavior. In R. Schalock (Ed.), *Adaptive behavior and its measurement:Implications for the field of mental retardation.* (pp. 61–80). Washington, DC: American Association on Mental Retardation.

Greenspan, S. (1999b). What is meant by mental retardation? *International Review of Psychiatry, 11,* 6–18.

Greenspan, S. (2003). Perceived risk status as a key to defining mental retardation. In H. N. Switzky & S. Greenspan (Eds.), *What Is Mental Retardation? Ideas for an evolving disability.* Washington, DC: American Association on Mental Retardation [E-Book]. Available at http://www.disabilitybooksonline.com

Greenspan, S. (2004). Why Pinocchio was victimized: Factors contributing to social failure in people with mental retardation. In H. N. Switzky (Ed.), *International review of research in mental retardation* (Vol. 28, 121–144). San Diego, CA: Elsevier/Academic Press.

Greenspan, S., & Driscoll, J. (1997). The role of intelligence in a broad model of personal competence. In D. P. Flanagan, J. L. Genshaft, & P. L. Harrison (Eds.), *Contemporary intellectual assessment: Theories, tests and issues* (pp. 131–150). New York: Guilford.

Greenspan, S., Loughlin, G., & Black, R. S. (2001). Credulity and gullibility in people with developmental disorders: A framework for future research. In L. M. Glidden (Ed.), *International review of research in mental retardation* (Vol. 24, pp. 101–135). New York: Academic Press.

Greenspan, S., & Love, P. F. (1997). Social intelligence and developmental disorder: Mental retardation, learning disabilities and autism. In W. E. MacLean, Jr. (Ed.), *Ellis' handbook of mental deficiency, psychological theory, and research* (3rd ed., pp. 311–342). Mahwah, NJ: Erlbaum.

Greenspan, S., & Shoultz, B. (1981). Why mentally retarded adults lose their jobs: Social competence and work success of mentally retarded adults. *Applied Research in Mental Retardation, 2,* 23–38.

Greenspan, S., Switzky, H. N., & Granfield, J. M. (1996). Everyday intelligence and adaptive behavior: A theoretical framework. In J. W. Jacobson & J. A. Mulick (Eds.), *Manual of diagnosis and professional practice in mental retardation* (pp. 127–135). Washington, DC: American Psychological Association.

Guilford, J. P. (1965). *Fundamental statistics in psychology and education.* New York: McGraw-Hill.

Harrison, P. L., & Oakland, T. (2000). *Adaptive behavior assessment system (ABAS).* San Antonio: PsychCorp/Harcourt Assessment.

Ireland, W. W. (1877). *On idiocy and imbecility.* London: Churchill.

Kiernan, W. E. (1996). Presidential address 1996: Are we there yet? *Mental Retardation, 34,* 387–394.

Kirk, S. A. A., & Kutchins, H. (1992). *Selling of DSM: The rhetoric of science in psychiatry.* White Plains, NY: Aldine de Gruyter.

Matson, J. L., & Fee, V. E. (1991). Social skills difficulties among persons with mental retardation. In J. L. Matson & J. A. Mulick (Eds.), *Handbook of mental retardation* (2nd ed., pp. 468–478). New York: Pergamon.

Meehl, P. (1973). *Psychodiagnosis: Selected papers.* Minneapolis: University of Minnesota Press.

Morrison, A. (1824). *Outlines of mental diseases.* Edinburgh: MacLachlan & Stewart.

Schalock, R. L. (1999). The merging of adaptive behavior and intelligence: Implications for the field of mental retardation. In R.L. Schalock (Ed.), *Adaptive behavior and its measurement: Implications for the field of mental retardation* (pp. 43–60). Washington, DC: American Association on Mental Retardation.

Schalock, R. L. (2003). Mental retardation: A condition characterized by significant limitations in practical, conceptual and social skills. In H. N. Switzky & S. Greenspan (Eds.), *What Is Mental Retardation? Ideas for an evolving disability* (pp. 271–283). Washington, DC: American Association on Mental Retardation [E-Book]. Available at http://www.disabilitybooksonline.com

Smith, J. D. (1985). *Minds made feeble: The myth and legacy of the Kalikaks.* Rockville, MD: Aspen.

Spitz, H. H. (1988). Mental retardation as a thinking disorder: The rationalist alternative to empiricism. In N. Bray (Ed.), *International review of research in mental retardation* (Vol. 15, pp. 1–31). New York: Academic Press.

Sternberg, R. J. (1984). Macrocomponents and microcomponents of intelligence: Some proposed loci of mental retardation. In P. H. Brooks, R. Sperber, & C. McCauley (Eds.), *Learning and cognition in the mentally retarded* (pp. 89–115). Hillsdale, NJ: Erlbaum.

Thorndike, E. L. (1920, January). Intelligence and its uses. *Harper's Magazine, 140,* 227–235.

Trent, J. W. (1994). *Inventing the feeble mind: A history of mental retardation in the United States.* Berkeley: University of California Press

Chapter Twelve

Ten Years Later:
Two AAMR Tales of a Condition

———————

John W. Jacobson (Deceased) and James A. Mulick

Abstract

In 1992 and 2002 the American Association on Mental Retardation issued manuals, both of which altered the definition of mental retardation in potentially meaningful ways. Few states or practitioners adopted the 1992 definition. Potentially more states could adopt the definition issued in 2002, but many of the aspects that aroused concern about the 1992 definition persist in muted or altered form within the 2002 manual. This article discusses factors affecting adoption of these definitions, contrasts the two manuals, and focuses on issues related to the 2002 definition and clinical practice in the field of mental retardation and developmental disabilities.

Ten Years Later: Two AAMR Tales of a Condition

A decade has passed since publication of the 1992 AAMR manual on mental retardation (Luckasson et al., 1992), and AAMR has issued a new manual (Luckasson et al., 2002). In this essay we will compare, contrast, and critique the more recent manual in light of the earlier one, and also update some considerations in the use of the International Classification of Functioning, Disability and Health (ICF–World Health Organization [WHO], 2001) in mental retardation services.

Elsewhere we have critiqued the 1992 manual at length, and we will not repeat all of the concerns expressed at those times (Jacobson, 1994; Jacobson & Mulick, 1992, 1993, 1994, 2003), although most of them remain manifest in some form in the more recent manual. Thematically, these concerns center on issues involving ideology, pragmatics of application, clinical practice, and science. Here we focus on the concerns about clinical practice, and also, issues raised by Luckasson et al. (2002) regarding past adoption of the AAMR manual and prospects for adoption of the new manual.

Adoption of the AAMR Definition

As noted in Luckasson et al. (2002, p. 30) and Denning, Chamberlain, and Polloway (2000), few states adopted the 1992 definition set forth by AAMR. Luckasson et al. (2002) note professional commentaries presenting the 1992 definition in a positive or negative light, and discuss these in the context of considerations associated with adoption of the definition (p. 29). They note that adoption is explained by, among other things: "whether it is consistent with the values, past experiences, and needs of potential adopters; whether it is perceived as overly complex; whether the results of the innovation can be observed" (p. 29). Although many criticisms of the 1992 definition are mentioned and addressed in this segment of the book, they are not complete in terms of specific characteristics of the 1992 manual or definition that adversely affected its adoption and that persist to be problems in the new manual.

Are the Two Manuals Consistent with Values of Potential Adopters?

This has been a problem; for policymakers the benefits or costs of adopting the AAMR 1992 or 2002 definition are unclear. Although both manuals link the definition of MR to person-centered planning (PCP) as a planning format and thereby to the determination of needed supports, PCP, in principle if not in substance, has been more widely adopted than has the 1992 definition, by state and local services. However, at this time, whether PCP typically leads to its avowed outcomes of substantially superior tailoring of services and fuller community participation remains largely unverified [although there are indications of general trends toward achievement of these aims (Holburn et al., in preparation; Holburn & Vietze, 2002)]. Implementation of PCP remains fraught with logistical, organizational, and perhaps financial complexities (Holburn & Vietze, 1999). By linking the definition in numerous ways to PCP throughout the 1992 and 2002 manuals, the reforms represented by the definition may be perceived as substantially more complex to implement than state systems may be able to bear, stressed by fierce competition for human service resources, narrowed by the deteriorating economic climate and decreasing tax revenues, and reorientation of federal and state policy focus to address issues of national security.

As well, although firmly ideologically grounded advocates may perceive inherent socially constructed and sensitive issues embodied in the process of defining MR, administrators in states are usually more pragmatic. They may be more concerned with the impact of definitions on demand for services and eligibility, and view diagnosis and classification as a clinical matter, rather than one that should be legislated. Neither the 1992 nor the 2002 manual makes compelling arguments for adoption of the definition in terms of how it might positively impact on public policy issues with which states are grappling. Rather, adoption is stressed as, essentially, the right thing to do.

Is the 1992 or 2002 Definition Consistent with Past Experience of Administrators and Clinicians?

The 1992 definition and to a lesser extent, because of altered emphases on intelligence (i.e., IQ) and adaptive-behavior criteria, the 2002 definition, constituted significant breaks with past practice, which has tended to base diagnosis, as the manuals mention, on intellectual measures and age of onset, whereas the 1992 and 2002 manuals place equal weight on IQ and adaptive behavior. Although the 2002 manual continues arguments for increased emphasis on adaptive behavior, there remain gaps in the foundation of these arguments—for example, articulating fully the relevance of various adaptive measures to identification of needs for service and supportive provisions, or utilizing profiles from adaptive-behavior measures for purposes beyond those of identification of affected individuals.

To the degree that clinicians or administrators can minimize system or practice costs for identification of such individuals by reliance primarily on IQ and age of onset in diagnosis, as well as in-office assessment not augmented by in-situ observation, procedures not supported by sound clinical practice, compelling arguments countering such practices are not provided in either manual. Again, the manual does not address the attendant logistical demands for more adequate training in adaptive-behavior assessment, the need for more practitioners to be aware of standards for appraisal of the suitability of various adaptive-behavior scales and their performance in "grey" cases, and the concerns that many practitioners have about the quality and accuracy of informant information and the power of existing adaptive-behavior scales (i.e., Reschly, Myers, & Hartel, 2002).

Are the 1992 and 2002 Manuals Consistent with Needs of Potential Adopters?

The 2002 manual presents the same eclectic focus as the 1992 manual, and the evocative fervor of the 1992 manual is now more muted. But, in not focusing more narrowly on diagnosis and classification, instead of on the ideological backdrop and events following diagnosis, the manual fails to reach a suitable level of utility for most administrative or clinical purposes. Possibly, in aligning the new definition of MR with every conceivable progressive practice in the disability community (e.g., Luckasson et al., 2002, p. 189), the possible core sensibility of changes in the definition of MR per se is obscured. While it is true that administrators have continued to set policies (especially under the Home and Community Based Services waivers) that emphasize individual support and community membership, and clinicians have continued to set goals and establish interventions and supports that are consistent with this intent, insistence that this be achieved in the most idealized contexts, where all progressive practices are realized, may limit the degree to which administrators and clinicians perceive changes in the definition as useful in and of themselves. Simply put, evidence and substantial discussion is focused in neither manual on how the definition itself will benefit policymakers or clinicians in meeting their responsibilities. Instead, the manual concentrates on weaving a tapestry of definition with policy and some superficial aspects of practice.

Are the 1992 and 2002 Manuals Perceived as Overly Complex?

The 2002 definition for MR appears superficially more straightforward than the 1992 definition, because of stress on three adaptive-behavior factors, domains, or dimensions, rather than ten domains, but in fact diagnostic issues are not in any way simplified. Further, a team process for diagnosis is no longer emphasized as a cornerstone, and much greater emphasis has been placed on assessment of adaptive behavior "under changing circumstances" and observation of interaction with others in perhaps several different settings. The implications of observing children, for example, in settings typical of nondisabled peers, seems to allow for examination in a physician's office, but not in a psychologist's office or in offices or clinic rooms used by therapists (e.g., occupational therapists, speech and language therapists) if guidance is to be taken literally. Perhaps what is meant in the 2002 manual is the importance of not looking at adaptive behavior as solely a result of person-characteristics, but rather as a joint function of characteristics, past learning, and current (i.e., environmentally determined) opportunities to learn, practice, or perform adaptive skills. Unfortunately, the lack of clarity and full explanation of the wide range of recommendations and implicit guidelines offered in the 2002 manual heightens the complexity of translating numerous admonitions into clinical practice.

There is a fine line between clear and straightforward exposition on the one hand, and vague allusion or illustration on the other. Because the breadth of the book is so great and the substance with which many topics are addressed so limited, much of the 2002 manual is too vague to be applied without a great deal of ad hoc interpretation; this is surely not what was intended in developing a new manual. However, because the 2002 manual does refer to a widened array of research work (albeit still substantively limited), interested technical personnel and clinicians can investigate the particulars of related research findings more readily than was possible based on the 1992 manual.

Can the Results of Adopting the 2002 Definition as an Innovation Be Observed?

One problem with the adoption of a definition of a condition is that discernible effects of adoption may be not be easily detected. Regardless of the definition used, some people who are assessed will be diagnosed with MR and others will not. Regardless of the definition used, for example, the Grossman (1983) or 2002 definition, it remains likely that many school children who can be appropriately classified with milder MR will instead be misdiagnosed with learning disabilities (MacMillan, Gresham, & Bocian, 1998). Many children will continue not to be diagnosed with MR by criteria that meet general community standards, due to educational overclassification and misclassification of conditions other than mental retardation, thus obscuring developmental onset of the condition, and diminishing use of the classification when appropriate with young adults.

The frequency with which states adopt the 1992 or 2002 definition is one measure of whether innovation can be observed (Denning et al., 2000), and while not entirely inconsequential, the key issue is whether clinicians charged with responsibility for diagnosis, largely physicians, clinical psychologists, and school psychologists, adopted the definition from 1992 or will adopt the 2002 definition. It is problematic that the rate at which clinicians adopted the 1992 definition is unknown; although the continued policy emphasis, as opposed to analysis of clinical utility, in much of the 2002 manual suggests that many clinicians will not perceive the newly recommended definition as being relevant to their clinical practice, or have grounds to determine whether adoption of the definition as a set of clinical criteria has beneficial effects on diagnostic resolution. Adoption will remain limited by the extent to which alternate definitions are available and are considered to be clearer (e.g., DSM, ICD, APA).

CLINICAL PRACTICE AND THE 1992 AND 2002 DEFINITIONS

Superficially, there is more focus on clinical guidance within the 2002 manual when contrasted with the 1992 manual, although this guidance ranges from useful characterization of recent findings in assessment of adaptive behavior, discussion of bio-behavioral and behavioral phenotypic findings, and improved linkages to current adaptive-behavior measures to vague generalizations and mischaracterizations or understatements of the state of knowledge related to clinical research. Mischaracterizations range from a somewhat incompletely articulated and overinterpreted comparison of inclusion rates for two IQ tests having different standard deviations (Luckasson et al., 2002, p. 58) to superficially and factually inaccurate interpretations of research on rates of mental disorder among people with MR. In the first instance the implications of the comparison are inadequately framed, and in the second instance findings are distorted. Ridiculous ranges are noted for the prevalence of mental disorders among people with MR, sustainable only by inclusion of references to studies that *cannot* be used, due to limitations of their methodology, to project prevalence (Jacobson, 1990).

Moreover, it is purported that post traumatic stress disorders and anxiety disorders are more common mental disorders among people with MR than in the general population (pp. 172–173), yet the sole reference for this conclusion is a study not even listed in the references section of Luckasson et al. (2002), which could not be located through a search of PsycINFO as a book, chapter, article, or report, or through Medline (PubMed), or through a general internet search, and is presumably not a peer-reviewed epidemiologic study.

Ethnic and Linguistic Minority Concerns

One of the most difficult aspects of applying the 2002 manual clinically is the inadequacy with which it deals with central or critical concerns in clinical practice. One of these critical concerns involves the intellectual assessment, primarily, and adaptive-behavior assessment, secondarily, of children and adults who are members of racial, ethnic, or linguistic minorities. Overclassification of such individuals is a longstanding concern of practicing psychologists (e.g., Donovan & Cross, 2002). Remarkably, the 2002 manual, which stresses assessment and intervention issues related to ethnic status in at least seven places (pp. 43, 51, 181, 87, 94, 130, 163), never provides clear guidance on practices to possibly mitigate overclassification or refers to research findings (except for one well-known chapter in an AAMR publication) relevant to test performance by minority individuals, especially in intelligence testing. Yet, such sources do exist and do present findings pertinent to clinical practice (e.g., DeShon, Smith, Chan, & Schmitt, 1998; Finch et al., 2002; Frisby, 1999a, 1999b; Glutting, Oh, Ward, & Ward, 2000; Montie & Fagan, 1988; Oakland & Glutting, 1990; Paolo, Ryan, Ward, & Hilmer, 1996a, 1996b; Terrell et al., 2001; Uttal, Lummis, & Stevenson, 1988). That such sources could be identified in a matter of several hours and obtained within a week if not immediately, indicates that they were in no way inaccessible to the editors of the 2002 manual. Additionally, it may be noteworthy that guidelines on assessment and minority, ethnic, or linguistic concerns exist for psychologists but are not cited (APA Office of Minority Affairs, 1991/1993).

The Tough Issues in Diagnosis

Like the 1992 manual, the 2002 manual fails to grapple with the truly difficult issues that surround clinical decisions regarding diagnosis of MR at the border or borderline IQ-score criterion range associated with MR (e.g., Jacobson, 2001). Although the 2002 manual deals more explicitly with the issue of the standard error of measurement (SEM) of IQ tests than did the 1992 manual, this consideration appears not to apply to the interpretation of adaptive-behavior measures, as no mention is made of the existence of SEMs for these scores. They do exist, of course. Moreover, at one point in the manual, on page 79, Luckasson et al. (2002) recommend that if an adaptive-behavior score for a scale falls at within one standard deviation (SD) of the -2 SD criterion (which most would understand to mean, at -1 SD or lower), then this aspect of adaptive behavior should be further probed for indications of more severe limitations. While it is possible the editors meant an SEM in this instance rather than an SD, statistically, the likelihood of a -1 SD score is 15.9% and of a -2 SD score is 2.3%, indicating that, disregarding any basic notion that a measure has been developed to efficiently assess a construct, there is only a 14.5% chance that, when a score is observed at -1 SD with a suitable measure and an appropriately knowledgeable informant, the true score will be at -2 SD or less. In brief, the odds are greatly against any clinical utility of probes under these circumstances.

Of greater concern is that there is little substantive discussion of factors that are not specifically related to concurrent sensory or motor disorders, or that may be related to specific neurological conditions and that might depress IQ scores. Undiagnosed sensory deficits can distort both IQ test scores and everyday performance of adaptive skills. There is no discussion of the relative likelihood that, in clinical assessment situations, those factors that may be associated with depression of IQ scores in testing appear both logically and with respect to past research, to outnumber those that permit individuals to obtain a higher-than-true score. For example, factors that can depress observed scores can include concurrent mental disorder (e.g., motor slowing associated with depressed affect that diminishes performance on timed tasks; cognitive distortions that impair the quality of responses; specific acquired neurological conditions); ambient environmental conditions; motivational history of interactions in assessment situations; lack of rapport with the examiner; concurrent fatigue, illness, or discomfort; anxious responding; automatic responding; educational deprivation; socioeconomically linked language experience (e.g., Hart & Risley, 1995); differences in dialect in non-English testing between tester and testee; nonexistence of current dialect-relevant norms on many measures for people of various national origins; and possible subcultural biases pertinent to scoring by some minority-group members in American society.

On the other hand, reasons why people might obtain higher–than-true scores are limited to anomalies in the structural features of norming samples, possible gaps in the developmental spacing of item difficulties on some or most subtests of a comprehensive measure, and "pure" error variance. Since all tests with contemporary norms meeting prevailing professional standards either have known item biases or have been structured, during development, to remove item biases by linguistic- or ethnic-group membership, the influence of this factor on test scores has been systematically diminished over time.

On a somewhat different note, the 2002 manual mentions adverse effects of psychoactive medications on test performance due to side effects, including drowsiness or diminished alertness, but fails to note that, if effective or at least beneficial clinically, medications might also enhance test scores. Increases in IQ after drug treatment were responsible for the brief enthusiasm for administering fenfluramine to children with autism (Geller, Ritvo, Freeman, & Yuwiler, 1982), although subsequent double-blind studies failed to confirm this drug as an effective treatment for autism (Stern et al., 1990).

There remains an emphasis in the 2002 manual, as there was in the 1992 manual, on inclusiveness. Where scores are used as a formal criterion for mental retardation classification, in fact the issues most relevant to clinical assessment are those that are associated with achieving a lower-than-true IQ score, resulting in overclassification. The 2002 manual repeatedly stresses non-English primary language and possible ethnic influences, but essentially ignores the greater range of factors that may lead to overclassification, hence limiting the clinical relevance of the manual for professional practice. Indeed, although focusing on psychometric issues, and emphasizing the importance of psychometric criteria, accurately derived, to diagnosis of mental retardation, the manual also presents puzzlingly contradictory guidance through statements such as: "Given that the diagnostic process involves drawing a line of inclusion/exclusion, there can be little rationale for anything other a relativistic standard for significantly subaverage intellectual functioning" (Luckasson et al., 2002, p. 58).

THE INTERNATIONAL CLASSIFICATION AND THE AAMR MANUAL

Although the ICF is a far more complex and comprehensive typology of human functioning than we can appropriately portray here, the most recent edition of this typology was in development concurrently with the 2002 AAMR manual.

The 2002 manual discusses the ICF framework primarily in Chapter 7, on classification systems (pp. 106–113). Although several parallels are drawn between ICF and the AAMR structures for adaptive behavior and supports, the 2002 manual suggests that there is no inherent indication that either is superior to the other (Luckasson et al., 2002, p. 109), that the AAMR model is more desirable because it is specific to MR (pp. 112–113), and that "because of the elaborateness of the full ICF, a straightforward application of the detailed classification items might result in an impractical inventory and multitude of problems" (p. 112), especially for people with severe limitations. There is also the consideration that in the very last stages of development, the primary focus of application of several aspects of the ICF framework moved away from participation and attention to environmental and personal factors, resulting, in principle, in greater consideration of these domains or factors with the 2002 AAMR approach, a change not noted in the 2002 manual (but see pp. 106–108).

Clinical applications and drawbacks of overly comprehensive uses of the most recent ICF framework have been discussed by Lux et al. (2005), and we will not take on those issues here—it may be sufficient to note that, indeed, application of ICF as an entire system is extremely complex and requires augmentation with clarification of item content to promote validity. Nonetheless, its framework has evident clinical utility (see Jacobson, 2003), including utility for people with MR.

Certainly, interpretations of ICF in contrast to those of Luckasson et al. (2002) can be proffered. It can reasonably be suggested that as a framework that encompasses the full range of human function, illness, and activity, ICF represents a superior nomenclature for assessment, classification, description, and related purposes than does the AAMR framework—indeed, the AAMR framework could be considered, in principle, a simplification, or a coarse summary of aspects of ICF functional items. The purpose of ICF is not to identify problems but rather to fully consider "strengths and weaknesses" within a framework that encompasses all human activities, not only those sampled in typical adaptive-behavior measures, and then to further organize these characterizations in relation to activities that an individual performs. Thus, unlike adaptive-behavior measures, and other available measures that have been used in MR services, ICF can readily encompass aspects of such social performance factors as gullibility and credulousness, both in terms of people's characteristic personal behaviors and their skills in performing activities associated with independence or community membership.

Moreover, the ICF framework was developed to be universal, and applicable both across cultures and subcultures, and was revised in several waves to be unbiased in wording and to focus in the course of development; a claim that AAMR cannot make, lest one be led to disregard repeated statements cautioning administrators and clinicians about biases in measures that form the operational basis for application of AAMR's model. On a clinical basis, failure to consider the wider range of functioning contained in the ICF framework might, contrary to concerns that it might specify "too many" functional limitations for an individual, lead clinicians to overestimate the abilities and participation of an individual, or to miss critical aspects of functioning that would contribute to appropriate classification of a person with MR. Arguably, in contrast to AAMR, we would suggest that the ICF nomenclature and structure is distinctively superior and more suitable for considering the functioning of a person with MR because it is based on human functioning, regardless of disability: This is a strength of the nomenclature in description of disablement, not a weakness.

The most pronounced weakness of ICF rests on the question of the extent to which the World Health Organization will promote clinician awareness of its framework in North America, and federal and state or provincial governments will adopt aspects of the system as integral components of information, needs assessment, or decision support systems.

Conclusions

As a successor to the 1992 manual, the 2002 manual offers the preferred and superior depiction of issues surrounding diagnosis and classification in MR. But the 2002 manual retains, in more than residual form, weaknesses of the 1992 manual that likely limited adoption of that manual administratively or clinically, except as clinical practice devolves from administrative rule making in occasional circumstances. The manual continues to address system issues in a manner that is either hostile or indifferent to the conflicting and competing public policy priorities that are inherent in developmental and other human services settings today (e.g., Jacobson, 1991) because of its strong idealistic base.

The manual also fails to provide pragmatic guidance for clinicians that reflects the subtleties and complexity of issues and questions with which they grapple daily. Perhaps these characteristics are inherent in a manual that appears still to seek to appeal to all possible readers, but certainly the manual's intent is to engender adoption as opposed to constituting a grand gesture. As a guide to clinicians, or to students of assessment and developmental disability, it is woefully inadequate, a primer at best. In short, if AAMR, as the manuals demonstrate, has a stated objective of encouraging the adoption of a new definition of mental retardation by government and clinicians, then a new or additional vehicle is needed for this purpose, in the form of a clinician's manual that addresses the concerns of potential adopters, developed by scientist-practitioners, perhaps to augment rather than replace the Luckasson et al. (2002) manual.

REFERENCES

American Psychological Association Office of Minority Affairs. (1993). Guidelines for providers of psychological services to ethnic, linguistic and culturally diverse populations. *American Psychologist, 48*, 45–48.

Denning, C. B., Chamberlain, J. A., & Polloway, E. A. (2000). An evaluation of state guidelines for mental retardation: Focus on definition and classification practices. *Education and Training in Mental Retardation and Developmental Disabilities, 35*, 226–232.

DeShon, R. P., Smith, M. R., Chan, D., & Schmitt, N. (1998). Can racial differences in cognitive test performance be reduced by presenting problems in a social context? *Journal of Applied Psychology, 83*, 438–451.

Donovan, M. S., & Cross, C. T. (Eds.). (2002). *Minority students in special and gifted education.* Washington, DC: Committee on Minority Representation in Special Education, National Research Council.

Finch, S. J., Farberman, H. A., Neus, J., Adams, R. E., & Price-Baker, D. (2002). Differential test performance in the American educational system: The impact of race and gender. *Journal of Sociology & Social Welfare, 29*(3), 89–108.

Frisby, C. L. (1999a). Culture and test session behavior: Part I. *School Psychology Quarterly, 14*, 263–280.

Frisby, C. L. (1999b). Culture and test session behavior: Part II. *School Psychology Quarterly, 14*, 281–303.

Geller, E., Ritvo, E. R., Freeman, B. J., & Yuwiler, A. (1982). Preliminary observations on the effect of fenfluramine on blood serotonin and symptoms in three autistic boys. *New England Journal of Medicine, 307*, 165–169.

Glutting, J. J., Oh, H.-J., Ward, T., & Ward, S. (2000). Possible criterion-related bias of the WISC-III with a referral sample. *Journal of Psychoeducational Assessment, 18*, 17–26.

Grossman, H. J. (Ed.). (1983). *Manual on terminology and classification in mental retardation* (1983 revision). Washington, DC: American Association on Mental Deficiency.

Hart, B., & Risley, T. (1995). *Meaningful differences in the everyday experience of young American children.* Baltimore: Paul H. Brooks.

Holburn, S. C., Jacobson, J. W., Schwartz, A. A., Flory, M. J., & Vietze, P. M. *The Willowbrook futures project: A longitudinal analysis of person centered planning.* Manuscript in preparation.

Holburn, S. C., & Vietze, P. M. (1999). Acknowledging barriers in adopting person-centered planning. *Mental Retardation, 37*, 117–124.

Holburn, S. C., & Vietze, P. M. (Eds.). (2002). *Person-centered planning: Research, practice, and future directions.* Baltimore: Paul H. Brookes.

Jacobson, J. W. (1990). Assessing the prevalence of psychiatric disorders in a developmentally disabled population. In E. Dibble & D. B. Gray (Eds.), *Assessment of behavior problems in persons with mental retardation living in the community* (pp. 19–70). Rockville, MD: National Institute of Mental Health.

Jacobson, J. W. (1991). Administrative and policy dimensions of developmental services. In J. L. Matson & J. A. Mulick (Eds.), *Handbook of mental retardation* (2nd ed., pp. 1–27). Elmsford, NY: Pergamon Press.

Jacobson, J. W. (1994). Review of *Mental retardation: Definition, classification, and systems of supports. American Journal on Mental Retardation, 98*, 539–541.

Jacobson, J. W. (2001). Environmental postmodernism and rehabilitation of the borderline of mental retardation. *Behavioral Interventions, 16*, 209–234.

Jacobson, J. W. (2003). Focusing comprehensive functional assessment: A case formulation of dual diagnosis treatment priorities using ICIDH-2. In H. N. Switzky & S. Greenspan (Eds.), *What Is Mental Retardation? Ideas for an evolving disability.* Washington, DC: American Association on Mental Retardation [E-Book]. Available at http://www.disabilitybooksonline.com

Jacobson, J. W., & Mulick, J. A. (1992). A new definition of mental retardation or a new definition of practice? *Psychology in Mental Retardation and Developmental Disabilities, 18*(2), 9–14.

Jacobson, J. W., & Mulick, J. A. (1993). Pieces of the professional puzzle: Contents of a guide. *Psychology in Mental Retardation and Developmental Disabilities, 19*(2), 6–9.

Jacobson, J. W., & Mulick, J. A. (1994). The power of positive stereotyping, or Have you changed the way you think yet? *Psychology in Mental Retardation and Developmental Disabilities, 19*(3), 8–16.

Jacobson, J. W., & Mulick, J. A. (2003). Defining mental retardation, or the incurability of ideological imbecility. In H. N. Switzky & S. Greenspan (Eds.), *What Is Mental Retardation? Ideas for an evolving disability* (pp. 230–241). Washington, DC: American Association on Mental Retardation [E-Book]. Available at http://www.disabilitybooksonline.com

Luckasson, R., Borthwick-Duffy, S., Buntinx, W. H. E., Coulter, D. L., Craig, E. M., Reeve, A., et al. (2002). *Mental retardation: Definition, classification, and systems of supports* (10th ed.). Washington, DC: American Association on Mental Retardation.

Luckasson, R., Coulter, D. L., Polloway, E. A., Reiss, S., Schalock, R. L., Snell, M. E., et al. (1992). *Mental retardation: Definition, classification, and systems of supports* (9th ed.). Washington, DC: American Association on Mental Retardation.

Lux, J. B., Reed, G. M., Jacobson, J. W., Stark, S., Threats, T. T., Peterson, D. B., et al. (2005). Operationalizing the International Classification of Functioning, Disability, and Health (ICF) in clinical settings. *Social Science and Medicine, 50,* 122–131.

MacMillan, D. L., Gresham, F. M., & Bocian, K. M. (1998). Discrepancy between definitions of learning disabilities and school practices: An empirical investigation. *Journal of Learning Disabilities, 31,* 314–326.

Montie, J. E., & Fagan, J. F. (1988). Racial differences in IQ: Item analysis of the Stanford-Binet at 3 years. *Intelligence, 12,* 315–332.

Oakland, T., & Glutting, J. J. (1990). Examiner observations of children's WISC-R test-related behaviors: Possible socioeconomic status, race, and gender effects. *Psychological Assessment, 2,* 86–90.

Paolo, A. M., Ryan, J. J., Ward, L. C., & Hilmer, C. D. (1996a). Different WAIS-R short forms and their relation to ethnicity. *Personality & Individual Differences, 21,* 851–856.

Paolo, A. M., Ryan, J. J., Ward, L. C., & Hilmer, C. D. (1996b). White examiners generally do not impede the intelligence test performance of black children: To debunk a myth. *Journal of Consulting & Clinical Psychology, 50,* 196–208.

Reschly, D. J., Myers, T. G., & Hartel, C. R. (Eds.). (2002). *Mental retardation: Determining eligibility for SSI benefits.* Washington, DC: National Academy Press.

Stern, L. M., Walker, M. K., Sawyer, M. G., Oades, R. D., Badcock, N. R., & Spence, J. G. (1990) A controlled crossover trial of fendluramine in autism. *Journal of Child Psychology and Psychiatry, 31,* 569–585.

Terrell, S. L., Daniloff, R., Garden, M., Flint-Shaw, L., & Flowers, T. (2001). The effect of speech clinician race and Afro-American students' cultural mistrust on clinician-child conversation. *Clinical Linguistics & Phonetics, 15,* 169–175.

Uttal, D. H., Lummis, M., & Stevenson, H. W. (1988). Low and high mathematics achievement in Japanese, Chinese, and American elementary-school children. *Developmental Psychology, 24,* 335–342.

World Health Organization. (2001). *International classification of functioning, disability and health (ICF).* Geneva: Author.

CHAPTER THIRTEEN

Children with Mild Mental Retardation: A Challenge for Classification Practices–Revised

DONALD L. MACMILLAN, GARY N. SIPERSTEIN, AND JAMES S. LEFFERT

The disability category "mental retardation" has had a long and active life in science, education, habilitation and treatment, and law and public policy for at least two centuries. Throughout this period, the concept of mental retardation has endured in popular usage without expert intervention. However, this concept's utility for the specialized purposes listed above has depended upon the technical definitions that scientists, educators, advocates, and public officials have periodically promulgated for classifying individuals as having this disability. We believe that a critical test of any definition and classification scheme for mental retardation is whether it provides an adequate basis for eligibility determination, identification of subjects for research purposes, and service-delivery planning purposes for individuals who have mild forms of this disability.

This is a critical test for two reasons. First, individuals with mild mental retardation (MMR) represent the vast majority of individuals with mental retardation. [Note: At least 75–80% of all cases of mental retardation are diagnosed as mild cases (Grossman & Tarjan, 1987)]. Second, individuals with MMR represent 100% of the cases in which the answer to the question "Does this individual have mental retardation?" is actually in doubt and professionals must depend upon on a definition and classification system for help in resolving uncertainty.

In previous publications, we have argued that the 1992 American Association on Mental Retardation definition and classification scheme (Luckasson et al., 1992) failed the test of addressing the needs of children with MMR (MacMillan, Gresham, & Siperstein, 1993; 1995; 1996; MacMillan, Siperstein, & Leffert, 2002). In the present chapter we will review our objections to the 1992 AAMR definition, and as we do so, consider the qualities that any new definition and classification scheme must have if it will serve the needs of children with mild mental retardation. We will then examine the most recent revision of the AAMR definition and classification scheme (Luckasson et al., 1992)

and, in so doing, consider whether this revised scheme is more successful than its predecessor in addressing the needs of these children.

In order for a definition of mental retardation to address the needs of individuals with
MMR, its framers need to recognize that individuals with MMR have distinctive characteristics that differentiate them from individuals with moderate and severe forms of mental
retardation. The differences between the two groups, which are qualitative rather than
merely a matter of degree, were described most clearly by Zigler in a 1967 article entitled
"Familial Mental Retardation: A Continuing Dilemma." According to Zigler, the more
severe form of mental retardation (i.e., lower IQ, more obvious behavioral limitations)
includes a large percentage of cases with central nervous system damage linked to biomedical causes. The milder form, which in most cases lacks clear biomedical etiology, came to
attention with the advent of compulsory school attendance and the introduction of intelligence testing early in the century. This was the "feebleminded" group described by Goddard
and the source of alarm during the Eugenics Scare. Since that time, the mild group has continually been differentiated by the use of special terms, both formal and informal—cultural-
familial, familial, educable mentally retarded (EMR), and intergenerational.

The milder and more severe groups differ significantly, not only in etiology, but also in
the presentation of their disability. The more severe group demonstrates difficulties in
basic areas of daily functioning such as self-care and communication. Combined with
physical anomalies that are often present, these individuals clearly appear to the casual
observer to have a significant cognitive impairment. The milder group presents subtler
limitations—e.g., in academic skills, planning, problem solving and decision making, and
social understanding and judgment—that are often not evident to the casual observer.
The difference between the two groups is also evident in the formal process of classification. The more severe form is readily recognized by clinicians prior to school age and does
not rely on sophisticated diagnostic instruments to be identified. Milder forms, to the
contrary, have proven far more elusive to classify, particularly because the behavioral
deficits resulting from subaverage general intelligence are more subtle and emerge in
behavioral domains within the school context that are different from those of primary
concern for individuals with more severe forms of mental retardation.

Thus, a major challenge that any classification system must meet is that it be useful for
identifying individuals with the milder form of mental retardation, which is harder to
detect, as well as those who have more severe forms of mental retardation, which are easier to detect. This is a challenge that we believe was not met by the 1992 AAMR definition of mental retardation.

BACKGROUND: THE 1992 AAMR DEFINITION AND THE CONTROVERSY REGARDING MMR

The specific problems with the 1992 AAMR definition are worth reviewing because they
are representative of broader issues that surround the classification of individuals with
MMR. These issues continue to be relevant more than a decade later.

The past three decades have been marked by controversy over the use of the mental
retardation designation (including, at times, litigation), and by a remarkable decline in the
frequency of its use to identify schoolchildren who are in need of special education services.

The 1992 AAMR definition reflected and, we believe, contributed to the continuation of this trend of using terms other than "mental retardation" to describe individuals with MMR.

In the controversy regarding the application of the category of mental retardation to individuals with mild intellectual limitations, criticism has focused on three points: 1) the absence, in many cases, of a demonstrable biomedical basis for the diagnosis of mental retardation; 2) the high percentage of children from racial and ethnic minority groups who were so classified; and 3) the lack of clear-cut evidence that many children classified as having mental retardation were experiencing problems in daily adaptation outside of school settings (the phenomenon of "the six-hour retarded child").

Many educators and advocates have voiced concern that as a result of prevailing classification practices in school settings, children have often been mislabeled as having mental retardation. These criticisms have contributed to an ongoing tension within the community of professionals in the field of mental retardation between the desire to include and address the needs of children with intellectual impairment who are having adjustment difficulties on one hand, and the desire to avoid "false positive" decisions that misclassify children as having mental retardation on the other.

AAMR (in its previous incarnation as AAMD) adopted two major strategies to avoid overuse of the mental retardation classification. First, in revising the AAMD definition of mental retardation, the IQ cutoff point was lowered from 85 (Heber, 1961; 1959) to 70 (Grossman, 1973), and later to approximately 70 (Grossman, 1983). Second, by including limitations in adaptive behavior in the definition of mental retardation, AAMD continually emphasized that identification of an individual as having mental retardation should not occur on the basis of IQ scores alone, but should be reserved for cases with documented deficits in adaptive behavior.

Perhaps not coincidentally, as application of the term mental retardation to individuals with mild impairments drew criticism and the IQ criterion was tightened, there commenced a remarkable decline in the number of school-age children who were classified by school systems as having mental retardation, accompanied by an even greater rise in the use of the category of learning disabilities (LD). As the Annual Reports to Congress on the Implementation of the Individuals with Disabilities Education Act indicate, between 1976–77 and 1993–94 there was a 38% decline (a reduction of more than 335,000 children) in the number of students between 6 and 21 years of age served in the public schools who were classified as having mental retardation (U.S. Department of Education, 1995). During this same period, there was an increase of more than 1.5 million children classified as having learning disabilities.

Meanwhile, the use of the LD designation to include children closely resembling the MMR students of the 1960s has resulted in a drop in the mean IQ for school-identified LD students, particularly in urban schools (Gottlieb, Alter, Gottlieb, & Wishener, 1994; Macmillan & Siperstein, 2001). If the Centers for Disease Control were to monitor the changing incidence of disability conditions, we suspect that they would probably issue a statement proclaiming that MMR was well on its way to being cured while calling for a quarantine of public schools to contain an epidemic of LD.

Does this striking decline in the number of identified school-age cases of mental retardation reflect the tightening of eligibility standards (i.e., assuring the elimination of "false positives"), or are children who should properly be identified as having mental retardation being excluded from this category (i.e., a significant problem of "false negatives")? To address this question, we (MacMillan, Gresham, Siperstein, & Bocian, 1996; MacMillan, Siperstein, & Gresham, 1996) revisited the issue of how children with subaverage intelligence who exhibit severe and persistent academic failure in the schools are being categorized and served. We concluded that the term "mental retardation" is being reserved currently for cases exhibiting general dysfunction and lower IQs and that most children meeting the criteria for MMR are currently either being served as learning disabled (LD) or not being identified for any special education services. We also found that students were being classified as LD even though they met criteria for mental retardation, rather than legal criteria for learning disability.

Why the flight from mental retardation to learning disabilities as a diagnosis for children who meet the classification criteria for MMR? In the past, educators had to carefully follow established classification criteria, because the label they attached to the child was used to determine the particular educational services, i.e., type of classroom placement, that a child would receive. However, now that the classification process has been separated from the process of developing an individualized educational plan (IEP) that specifies the child's educational program, educators have greater latitude to choose whatever label they feel most comfortable applying to a given child. Educators often don't like to use the term "mental retardation" because it has pejorative connotations and suggests an "incurable" disability, with a limited prognosis for future independence. Interestingly, people with MMR who are active in the self-advocacy movement object to the term as well. Consequently, educators, parents, and individuals with MMR themselves are "voting with their feet" away from mental retardation and toward LD as the term that describes this disability.

Any new definition of mental retardation needs to respond constructively to this continuing shrinkage in the number of individuals classified as having mental retardation and corresponding increase in the use of the LD classification. Instead, the 1992 AAMR definition *implicitly* endorsed this trend toward redefining MMR as LD. Rather than working toward a creative resolution of the tension between inclusiveness and avoiding false positives, the 1992 AAMR definition resolved the tension by tilting heavily in the direction of narrowing the concept of mental retardation to refer primarily to individuals with more moderate or severe impairment. The major way it did this, as we shall see below, is by positing an operational definition of adaptive behavior that is of limited relevance for people with MMR, particularly for the key purposes of service delivery and research for which classification decisions are made.

1992 AAMR: A DEFINITION FOR ADVOCACY

Overall, our concern was that instead of serving the critical goals of determining eligibility for services, planning individualized services or treatment, and classifying and identifying individuals for research purposes, the 1992 definition appeared to be designed for the goal of advocacy for a particular ideology regarding the place in society of individuals with mental retardation—i.e., to advance inclusion and eliminate barriers to the full participation of individuals with mental retardation in school, community, and employment settings. The authors' focus on an advocacy agenda at the expense of the other "bread and butter" uses for a classification system resulted in a definition that blurred the distinctions between mild and more severe forms of mental retardation, and in doing so, neglected the MMR group. This neglect of individuals with MR was evident in two major problems with the 1992 definition:

Lack of Levels of Severity or a Defined MMR Group

The 1992 AAMR definition eliminated the differentiation of individuals with mental retardation based on levels of severity. For the first time, there was no specific MMR group. Instead, AAMR differentiated individuals with mental retardation on the basis of levels of support that they need for improved functioning. The motivation for this change appears to have been a concern to prevent the pigeonholing of individuals with mental retardation into categories, based on intellectual functioning, that might suggest limits on their potential for learning and skill development. Moreover, the drafters of the definition clearly wanted to emphasize the role of the environment in potentiating, mitigating, and even in some cases, eliminating the presence of mental retardation. This emphasis on the interaction between the person and the environment in the definition of mental retardation was evident in the substitution of levels of needed support for levels of severity. (*Note*: The authors' intention to substitute levels of support for levels of severity is explicitly stated in the Preface on p. x and in the text on p. 34.)

Unfortunately, 1) the four levels of needed supports specified in the 1992 definition are vague and unreliable for the purpose of measurement; 2) the nature and degree of "improvement" that might be expected to occur as a result of the provision of needed supports is undefined, so that the expected levels of improved functioning that might differentiate individuals are left unclear by this component of the definition; and 3) although the environment certainly plays an important role in the manifestation of a disability, the elimination of levels draws attention away from the fundamental role of cognitive limitations as the underlying feature of the disability.

Although the blurring of the boundaries between MMR and moderate and severe forms of mental retardation causes problems when the purpose of classification is service delivery or research, the 1992 AAMR definition may have also had a negative impact on advocacy for recognizing and addressing the needs of individuals with MMR. Research regarding the general public's perceptions and attitudes concerning mental retardation suggests that society's concept of mental retardation focuses on the moderate to severe exemplar whose physical stigmata and behavioral characteristics are most visible, rather than on individuals with MMR, who, although less visible, are in fact numerically more representative of the disability (Bak & Siperstein, 1986; Siperstein & Bak, 1985). A recent survey of 700 American adults' views of the capabilities of people with mental retardation documents this public perception of lower capabilities. The survey found that 83% of this sample group thought that people with mental retardation are able to wash and dress themselves, but only 53% thought that they are able to prepare food and only 44% thought that they can handle money (Siperstein, Norins, & Corbin, 2003).

By eliminating a separate category of MMR, AAMR-92 contributed to the invisibility of those with MMR by collapsing them into a general category of mental retardation that is already identified with moderate to severe cases in the public's mind. The risk is that the result, in popular usage, will resemble an "exemplar" classification system (Blashfield, 1993) in which only those who fit a certain "prototype" image that corresponds to the popular image of what the category "looks like" will be identified as belonging to that category, while others with milder forms will be viewed as being outside that category. We believe that this problem of classification by exemplar, which has in the past plagued the identification of mental health conditions (e.g., alcoholism, dissociative disorders) is already evident in the declining numbers of identified cases of mental retardation.

Problems with AAMR-92's Conceptualization of Intellectual Limitations and Adaptive Behavior

Regarding the intellectual-limitations criterion, the authors of the 1992 AAMR definition suggested that the IQ cutoff that they specified (between 70 and 75) represented continuity with previous definitions (i.e., "approximately 70" in the 1983 AAMR definition). However, by permitting cases up to 75, AAMR-92 opened the door to increasing the number of children who fit into the MMR category. The scope of the possible increase that resulted from this change is evident when we consider that shifting the IQ cutoff upward from IQ 70 to IQ 75 results in *twice as many* individuals being eligible. It is unclear whether this expansion of the pool of individuals who potentially have mental retardation was intentional or inadvertent. However, this upward adjustment of the IQ criterion brought to the forefront the problem of classifying individuals with MMR precisely at a time when a) AAMR ceased recognizing MMR as distinct level of mental retardation and b) most of the children who fit within the MMR range were being classified by schools as having LD rather than mental retardation (MacMillan, Gresham, Siperstein, & Bocian, 1996).

Since AAMR's 1992 definition was enlarging the pool of people who could be identified as having mental retardation on the basis of IQ at the very time that educators, parents, and individuals themselves were abandoning use of the term, it was essential that AAMR offer a conceptualization of MR that was relevant to the problems in daily functioning that individuals with MMR experience and to the purposes for which classification for this population is being carried out. This brings us to the second criterion for defining mental retardation, and therefore, a key component of any technical definition—limitations in adaptive behavior. In our view, this was the most problematic component of the 1992 AAMR definition.

As long as the concept of mental retardation has existed, it has been recognized that difficulties in everyday functioning, which are related to intellectual impairment, are an essential feature of this disability. Although the term "social competence" was often used during the first half of the twentieth century to describe the domain of daily life functioning; during the second half of the century "adaptive behavior" emerged as the preferred term and was incorporated into AAMD-sponsored definitions of mental retardation (Greenspan & Granfield, 1992; Luckasson et al., 1992). The 1992 AAMR definition took a radical turn by abandoning the conceptualization of adaptive behavior as a global construct, which was a feature of previous AAMR definitions. Instead, AAMR-92 required that an individual exhibit deficits in two or more of ten specified adaptive skill areas.

This multi-category definition of adaptive behavior raised numerous problems. First and foremost, the ten categories lacked adequate empirical justification, e.g., validation of their existence or independence from factor-analytic studies or data on the internal consistency of the skill areas. In this regard, the 1992 AAMR definition perpetuated a problem that has been the "Achilles' heel" of all previous definitions and classification systems for determining whether an individual has mental retardation for research purposes. Specifically, the definition specified that twin criteria of intellectual and adaptive-behavior limitations must *both* be met to identify an individual as having mental retardation. However, the operationalization of the adaptive behavior criterion was so imprecise and lacking in empirical foundation that it introduced variability (i.e., unreliability) into classification decisions—an untenable situation when the purpose of classification is research. Perhaps this is why individuals with mental retardation have often been selected for research studies on the basis of etiology of their disability and/or precisely measured IQ data, while the documentation of their limitations in adaptive behavior is, at best, imprecise and impressionistic.

A second serious problem with AAMR-92's conceptualization of adaptation is that it lacked any developmental perspective. This becomes evident when we consider the relevance of the various skill areas for the following two examples:

1. A child with Down syndrome being evaluated at 6 months.
2. A child with an IQ of 67 being evaluated for eligibility in the third grade.

The skill areas are: communication, self-care, home living, social skills, community use, self-direction, health and safety, functional academics, leisure, and work. It is unreasonable to expect any six-month-old, or any third-grader, for that matter, to be working or to be competent in home living or community use. What percentage of all initial diagnoses of cases of mental retardation occur after fourth or fifth grade? Many of the skill areas are not "age appropriate" for children at the time the evaluation is taking place and only really become salient as an individual approaches adulthood.

A third problem with the 1992 AAMR definition's conception of adaptive behavior, and perhaps the problem of greatest concern for MMR, is the lack of relevance of many of the domains to the difficulties in daily functioning experienced by individuals with MMR. The ten domains may be helpful in identifying adaptive-behavior limitations that are typical of individuals with moderate and severe forms of mental retardation. However, people with MMR do not typically show significant limitations in many of these domains. For this reason, existing scales of adaptive behavior (e.g., AAMR-ABS, Vineland Scales of Independent Behavior-I) have been largely unsuccessful at capturing the problems in adaptation encountered by students with MMR. When such scales are administered to children with MMR, one typically encounters ceiling effects, as these children do not exhibit problems in such fundamental areas as toileting, dressing, grooming, and other domains tapped by such scales. This is not meant as a criticism of the scales when used with individuals with mental retardation of a more severe form. It must be pointed out, however, that the domains tapped and the skills tapped within domains are inappropriate for the typical child with MMR.

Given the nature of the problems in adaptation that individuals with MMR exhibit, we would expect children with MMR, at most, to show difficulties in three of the ten domains: social, functional academics (a domain that only partially overlaps with the academic expectations that children are expected to meet in school), and self-direction. Even though adults with MMR might also show difficulties in other domains that become more relevant later in the life span, the problems that adults with MMR exhibit are often not in the mastery of concrete skills that are emphasized within these domains (e.g., knowing one's phone number, riding a bus, having a hobby), but rather in areas of planning, decision making, and social judgment, which receive only limited mention in the definition of these domains. Thus, the ten domains failed to conceptualize the particular adaptation problems of MMR and, moreover, the criterion of two or more out of the ten domains placed an undue burden on the detection of mild forms of mental retardation, particularly during childhood.

Any definition of adaptive behavior must be relevant to the environment in which the individual functions and in which classification takes place. Therefore, if a definition of adaptive behavior is to capture the subtle problems in daily functioning that children with MMR experience, it must be relevant to the environmental context of the public schools, which is the setting in which most classification decisions occur. The lack of relevance of the ten domains specified in the 1992 AAMR definition to the environmental context of the public school was one of that definition's most glaring defects. We have long known that the public schools are the primary labelers of cases of mental retardation, and almost exclusively the agency labeling cases of MMR. Mercer's research (1973), conducted in the 1960s, dramatically demonstrated the primacy of the public schools as labelers of mental retardation, as noted in the following passage:

> The public schools were the most significant formal organization in the social system epidemiology of mental retardation in the community. The schools not only labeled more persons as mentally retarded than did any other formal organization but also held the most central position in the network of formal organizations in the community dealing with mental retardation. Many other organizations used the results of the labeling process in the public schools as the basis for assigning persons to the status of mental retardate, that is, they borrowed the school labels. (p. 96)

What Mercer found in the 1960s persisted at least into the 1990s, as evidenced by findings in the Metropolitan Atlanta Developmental Disabilities Study (Murphy, Yeargin-Allsopp, Decouflé, & Drews, 1995), which reported that "Almost all (98%) of the children were initially identified through the public schools" (p. 320). Given the primary role of the public schools in the identification process, an appreciation of how schools operate and what prompts referrals by general education teachers is essential (MacMillan, Gresham, Siperstein, & Bocian, 1996). Only children referred by general education teachers are at risk for labeling as mentally retarded; stated differently, avoiding referral, regardless of one's IQ and adaptive skills, virtually guarantees that a child will not be labeled mentally retarded. Behaviors that precipitate referral are those relevant to the concept of *adaptation* in the context of public schools, and these behaviors differ significantly from what is tapped by scales of adaptive behavior, as will be discussed subsequently.

Those familiar with how schools operate have long noted the failure of existing adaptive behavior scales, which reflect the domains specified in the 1992 AAMR definition, to tap those failures in adaptation that prompt referral. Clearly, adaptation does not occur in a vacuum; rather, in the public schools, it is understood in terms of fulfilling social role expectations that are heavily weighted in favor of academic success and deportment. In describing the condition of MMR, Reschly (1988) emphasized the contextual nature of the problems that prompt referral of MMR:

> The critical question in the litigation, prominent also in theory and research, was whether mild mental retardation is an appropriate classification for persons whose handicapping condition is largely restricted to a particular context, the public school, and a particular age, roughly ages 6 or 7 to about age 17, and to a particular social role, performing as a student with demands to demonstrate literacy skills and abstract thinking. (p 27)

Reschly subsequently advanced the case for emphasizing academic competence in a conceptualization of adaptation in cases of MMR: "I have argued that school performance should be a major component of our conception of adaptive behavior for school-age children" (p. 36). This position was previously supported in an earlier piece by Ashurst and Meyers (1973), who also stressed the primacy of academics when they wrote: "The teacher is postulated here as serving the social system; it is he or she who has expectations based on age, sex, and status of the child, and observes the degree to which the child meets expectancies, especially the academic ones" (p. 154). When used in this context, the term "academic expectancies" should be interpreted broadly to include social behaviors that are "critically contiguous to academic performance." Such social behaviors are not well represented in adaptive-behavior scales (Gresham and Elliott, 1987).

In our view, therefore, the 1992 AAMR definition and published scales of adaptive behavior fall short in the authors' failure to capture dimensions of behavior relevant to the individual's environment. Specifically, this failure is apparent in the definition's relevance to the expectations that prevail in the public school environment, where most classification decisions occur. This is a major weakness of this classification system, and one that needs to be corrected in future definitions.

ASSESSMENT OF THE 2002 AAMR DEFINITION

The committee that produced the 2002 AAMR definition and classification system (Luckasson et al., 2002) acknowledged the concerns that we and other commentators raised regarding the 1992 AAMR definition. In the commentary that accompanied the new definition, they summarized the criticisms and in several instances offered clarifications and modifications to the 1992 classification system. In doing so, the committee demonstrated that they were listening to their critics. For example, they reduced the number of adaptive behavior domains from ten to three in order to place this component of the definition on a firmer conceptual and empirical footing. In addition, taking care to distinguish among the different uses to which classification systems are put, they cautioned that the specification of levels of needed support was reserved exclusively for use in planning for the delivery of services. Overall, the 2002 definition toned down the emphasis on advocacy that was a disturbing feature of the 1992 definition. The central question, however, is whether the 2002 definition and classification system is more useful than the previous one for classifying cases of MMR and stopping the "flight" away from the use of the mental retardation as a disability category. In our view, although the new definition is an improvement in some respects, it falls critically short in others. The flawed results are evident when we revisit the problems that we cited with the 1992 definition.

Lack of Levels of Severity or a Defined MMR Group

Similar to the 1992 AAMR definition, the 2002 classification system does not differentiate individuals with mental retardation based on levels of severity. Therefore, at a time when large numbers of children who meet eligibility criteria for MMR are instead being labeled as having LD, AAMR is again not offering consumers of the classification system a conceptual framework that they could use to differentiate mild from moderate to severe cases. Interestingly, although the commentary that accompanies the 2002 definition cites our criticism of the lack of levels in the 1992 definition, it does not explain why the authors of the 2002 definition continued to omit severity levels. We believe that the omission of levels of severity will contribute to the continuing "flight" of individuals who meet the criteria for MR to the LD designation.

The 1992 AAMR classification book clearly stated (in the Preface on p. x and in the text on p. 34) that its authors intended the introduction of levels of needed support into the operational definition of mental retardation to serve as a replacement for levels of severity. The authors of the 2002 definition responded positively to our strong objection to this substitution by stressing that levels of needed support cannot replace levels of severity. Distinguishing among the various purposes for which a definition and classification scheme can be used, the authors cautioned users of the classification system not to use the levels of needed support when establishing an individual's eligibility for services, benefits, or legal protections, in classifying groups for research purposes, or in assigning individuals to disability or service categories. Rather, they restricted the use of the support levels to the planning of individualized interventions. Having rightly imposed this restriction, they nonetheless offered nothing to fill the continuing absence in the AAMR system of a way to differentiate mild from moderate to severe cases for the remaining critical purposes. They allow this void to persist even though the distinction of levels of severity continues to have importance in research investigations of individuals' skill capabilities (e.g., McAlpine, Singh, Kendall, & Ellis, 1992; Moffat, Hanley-Maxwell, & Donellan, 1995).

AAMR-2002's Conceptualization of Intellectual Limitations and Adaptive Behavior

The intellectual limitations criterion.

The 2002 definition establishes a criterion for intellectual limitations that, similar to the 1992 definition, has the potential to include mild cases. In fact, despite differences in wording, the 2002 intellectual limitations criterion was designed to include the same number of individuals as the 1992 definition. Instead of AAMR-92's IQ cutoff boundary of "approximately 70 to 75," the 2002 IQ cutoff boundary is described as "approximately two standard deviations below the mean considering the standard error of measurement for the specific assessment instruments used and the instruments' strengths and limitations" (Luckasson et al., 2002, p. 58). In practice, this translates into the "approximately

70 to 75" range specified in the 1992 definition. As we mentioned earlier, it should be noted that both the 1992 and 2002 definitions are too imprecise, since the instruction to consider the standard error of measurement gives considerable latitude to clinicians and to governmental and educational authorities in applying these guidelines to cases between 70 and 75. The line should have been drawn more clearly, since the amount of imprecision may lead decision makers either to arbitrarily choose a particular number or to make subjective decisions in individual cases that will undermine the fairness of the classification process.

The adaptive-behavior criterion.

The 2002 AAMR definition departs most dramatically from its predecessor in its operational definition of adaptive behavior. We criticized AAMR-92's definition of adaptive behavior for specifying ten domains that lacked adequate empirical justification and that did not apply equally well to different developmental periods and levels of intellectual impairment. By contrast, the 2002 definition delineates three broad domains of adaptive behavior: conceptual, social, and practical skills. As the cutoff boundary for limitations in adaptive behavior, AAMR set a score of two standard deviations below the mean, either in one's overall score or in one's score for at least one domain, on an instrument for measuring adaptive behavior that has been normed on the general population.

The division of adaptive behavior into three domains represents a considerable improvement over the previous division into ten domains, because the three domains in the 2002 definition are empirically supported by factor analyses conducted with children and adults (see Luckasson et al., 2002, for a summary of research findings). In addition, at least two of the three domains, the conceptual and social domains, are relevant for measuring everyday functioning at the upper limits of mental retardation for both children and adults. Although the third domain, practical adaptive behavior, is perhaps less relevant to the problems in adaptation of school-age children with MMR, this is, perhaps, less of a problem, since a finding of limitations in either of the two remaining domains is sufficient for classifying a child as having mental retardation. An additional benefit of the three domains is that they have the potential to provide a conceptual foundation for investigating the linkages between adaptive behavior and intellectual limitations. This is because the three adaptive-behavior domains correspond to the domains specified in Thorndike's tripartite model of intelligence (Thorndike, 1920; see also Greenspan, 2003; Greenspan & Love, 1997; Greenspan, Switzky, & Granfield, 1996; Switzky, Greenspan, & Granfield, 1996).

Earlier, we mentioned the 2002 AAMR definition's lack of precision in establishing an upper cutoff score for intellectual limitations. This lack of precision is also true of the adaptive behavior criterion. In the text of the classification book (but, for some reason, not in the highlighted operational definition of adaptive behavior), professionals are urged to take the standard error of measurement of the instrument into consideration in deciding whether an individual has adaptive-behavior limitations. Furthermore, the text states that "scales with high reliability and low standard errors of measurement (SEMs) are recommended for use in diagnosis" (p. 79). However, the standard error of measurement cannot be easily minimized as a factor to consider when classification decisions are based on a single domain of adaptive behavior. The reason is that for any adaptive-behavior instrument, the SEM for a single domain score will be substantially higher than that for a global score. Thus, the intellectual limitations and adaptive behavior criteria in the 2002 definition combine to leave substantial leeway for clinicians and for governmental and educational authorities to differ in their classification decisions, thus introducing unreliability and, along with it, the potential perception of unfairness, into the classification process.

The balance between intelligence and adaptive behavior in making classification decisions.

In addition to the problems we have cited with the intelligence and adaptive behavior criteria, we have serious reservations about a seismic shift that the 2002 AAMR definition seeks to initiate regarding the relative importance that users of the classification system should ascribe to these two components. The authors point out that, for many decades, professional decision making and diagnosis has emphasized intellectual limitations (i.e., IQ scores), as the primary indicator for identifying cases of mental retardation. If the adaptive behavior criterion was used at all, it served, as we indicated earlier, merely as a corrective designed to eliminate false positive decisions. Taking issue with this "imbalance between intelligence and adaptive behavior," the authors of the 2002 AAMR definition contend that "diagnosis should include a balanced consideration of assessments of IQ and adaptive behavior" (p. 80). As evidence in support of this contention, the authors offer the assertion, which they attribute to Greenspan and Granfield (1992), that in the original concept of mental retardation, adaptive behavior was the central and distinguishing feature of this disability.

We question this premise. Of course, before standardized tests existed, professionals could only infer intellectual limitations from observations of everyday performance; nonetheless, the central and defining characteristic of mental retardation has always been impairment in adaptive functioning that clearly resulted from intellectual impairment as opposed to some other cause. The point that Greenspan and Granfield made was that other forms of adaptation besides school-based academic skills were central in the original conception of mental retardation as manifestations of the underlying intellectual limitation at the heart of the disability. Therefore, because prevailing conceptions of intellectual functioning focus on a limited subset of cognitive processes, i.e., those that are most closely associated with academic functioning, they have argued for an expanded model of intelligence that includes the cognitive substrate of nonacademic adaptive behavior.

We have consistently supported the inclusion of an adaptive behavior criterion in the definition of mental retardation as a corrective to identifying false positives, but we question the more radical position of giving "a balanced consideration" to assessments of IQ and adaptive behavior for the following three reasons:

First, unlike intelligence testing, which is designed to elicit a child's "maximal" performance of the processes assessed, adaptive behavior assessment instruments assess a child's "typical" performance of adaptive behavior over time, as described by informants familiar with the child's typical level of functioning over a period of time. Because many factors other than intellectual impairment (e.g., mental illness, motivational deficiencies, and environmental influences) can depress a child's typical behavior, we believe that on conceptual grounds, adaptive behavior should not serve as the starting point for defining and identifying cases of mental retardation. Second, even if we recognize the shortcoming of IQ tests cited by Greenspan and Granfield (1992) (that they too narrowly focus on school-related cognitive competencies to adequately assess the cognitive substrate of everyday adaptive functioning) we still hesitate to give balanced consideration, alongside data regarding intellectual functioning, to data from existing adaptive behavior assessment instruments. Our concern is that we cannot be confident that existing adaptive behavior assessment instruments operationally define adaptive functioning in a way that is sensitive to detecting mild impairments. This point requires us to consider the state of adaptive behavior assessment, particularly as it applies to cases of MMR.

The history of adaptive behavior assessment instruments is briefer than the history of intelligence testing, and these instruments are still evolving. Adaptive behavior instruments are clearly useful for identifying individuals with moderate to severe impairment, but we still cannot be confident that they do a satisfactory job of measuring subtle limitations in everyday functioning and that in doing so, that they sample behaviors that are relevant during different ages and in different environmental contexts. One recent development that we applaud is the inclusion in the new revision of the Vineland Adaptive Behavior Scale-II of items designed to measure subtle forms of adaptation. Examples include "refrains from entering group when nonverbal cues indicate that he or she is not welcome" and "responds to hints or indirect cues in conversation" (Sara Sparrow, personal communication, 3/26/2004). We note, however, that this addition of subtle behavioral items to the revised Vineland applies to only one of several widely used instruments. Moreover, even for the revised Vineland, can we be confident that this instrument, in its full, abridged, and classroom editions, has now been calibrated for measuring subtle limitations at all ages? In other words, do we actually understand what the difference between a standard score of 70 and 78 on a particular adaptive behavior instrument represents for a child in fourth grade or an adolescent at age 19 as an index of adaptation in relation to the subtle behavioral expectations of a typical age-appropriate environment? With regard to school-age children, for example, as far as we can determine, the lack of convergence between the behaviors that current adaptive behavior scales measure and the skill deficiencies that prompt teachers to refer children for special education services has not changed significantly since Gresham, Elliott, and Reschly (Gresham & Elliot, 1987; Gresham & Reschly, 1987) called attention to this problem during the 1980s. Third, as we mentioned above, both the 1992 and 2002 definitions are imprecise in their cutoff score for identifying intellectual limitations, because of the requirement that clinicians "take into consideration" the standard error of measurement that is an inevitable by-product of standardized testing. Moreover, the adaptive-behavior cutoff criterion specified in the 2002 AAMR definition is even more imprecise than the intellectual-limitations cutoff, because judgments regarding adaptive behavior can be based upon a single domain score. When these two sources of data are applied simultaneously, the lack of precision is compounded, thus introducing a substantial degree of unreliability into classification decisions.

For all three of these reasons, we reject the notion that mental retardation should represent, either conceptually or operationally, a balanced combination of intelligence and adaptive behavior. Rather, the field must strive to promote the idea that mental retardation is a *unitary* construct—it represents limitations in intellectual functioning that are *mani-*

fest in limitations in everyday adaptation. Our ultimate goal is to expand the assessment of intellectual limitations to include the cognitive processes that are most closely related to the different domains of adaptive functioning, not just in school-related academic tasks but in other areas of adaptive functioning. At the same time, we need to continue to refine our understanding of adaptive behavior to include subtle adaptive behaviors. Often, these subtle behaviors are the behavioral manifestation of mild cognitive impairment. The sample items added to the revised Vineland that we mentioned above provide an example of the refinement of adaptive behavior assessment to include subtle behaviors that are highly "saturated" with cognition. These new items, focusing on the awareness of nonverbal cues and indirect hints in conversation, reflect the underlying cognitive process of social perception (Leffert & Siperstein, 2002; Leffert, Siperstein, & Millikan, 2000) that contributes to subtle problems in adaptive behavior that disrupt social and academic functioning.

Suggestions for a Future Definition

The central theme of this chapter has been the inadequacies of the 1992 AAMR definition and the limited improvement of the 2002 AAMR definition for classifying cases of MMR and stopping the "flight" away from the use of the mental retardation as a disability category. Clearly, if the characteristics and needs of MMR are to be recognized and addressed, a different definition and classification system is needed. We will now present our recommendations for a revised definition of mental retardation.

Recognize Individuals with Mild Mental Retardation as a Distinct Subgroup

Because individuals with MMR have characteristics that set them apart from those with other types of disabilities, we believe that individuals with mental retardation should be recognized as a distinct subgroup. The MMR group and individuals with moderate and severe forms of mental retardation have some commonalities, but they also have distinct differences. Individuals with MMR and with moderate and severe forms of mental retardation are alike in that they have problems in adaptation that result from general limitations in their cognitive processing abilities. However, mild cases clearly differ from moderate and severe cases in the nature of their problems in adaptation, which are the outward manifestation of their intellectual impairment. For this reason, the concept of a large number of discrete areas of adaptive behavior that characterized the 1992 AAMR definition was appropriate only for conceptualizing the difficulties in adaptation that individuals with moderate to severe forms of mental retardation experience. This concept was not appropriate for individuals with MMR, who function successfully in many of these concrete areas of behavior, but have problems in adaptation that are subtler and that center on areas such as academic performance and social competence.

Individuals with MMR also have notable similarities to, as well as distinct differences from, individuals with LD. Children with MMR resemble children with LD in that the major problems in adaptation that they present in school settings are in the same areas where children with LD have difficulty, i.e., academic performance and social competence. Problems in academic performance are a defining characteristic of LD, and problems in social competence are sufficiently common among children with LD so that professionals have called for including a social component in the definition of LD (Conte & Andrews, 1993; Kavanaugh & Truss, 1988). Indeed, research studies involving teacher and parent ratings of children's social behavior have consistently found that children with MMR and LD have greater social behavior problems than nonclassified children; however, children with MMR and LD are so similar in their social behavior patterns that the two groups cannot be differentiated on social behavior assessment measures (Bramlett, Smith, & Edmonds, 1994; Cullinan & Epstein, 1985; Gresham, Elliot, & Black, 1987; Merrill, Sanders, & Popinga, 1993).

Despite these similarities, LD and MMR also differ in an important respect. LD is defined on the basis of a discrepancy, whether between aptitude (as measured by IQ tests) and academic achievement, or, as some have advocated, a discrepancy between achievement in one academic area and another (Louisiana Department of Education, 1983). By contrast, MMR is defined in terms of *consistency* between subaverage IQ and achievement, as indicated by consistently low performance across academic areas. In addition, for LD, the problems in academic achievement are *unexpected* given the child's average to above-average cognitive functioning, while for MMR, problems in academic achievement are *expected* given the child's below-average cognitive functioning.

This brief review of similarities and differences indicates that MMR is a distinct group that has characteristics in common with other forms of mental retardation and with LD, but also features striking dissimilarities with each of these classifications. The needs of individuals with MMR can only be met if MMR is recognized as a distinct category within mental retardation, with a distinct definition and set of classification criteria. Because of the commonality that exists between MMR and other types of mental retardation, we believe that the distinct needs of the MMR group can potentially be addressed within the overall construct of mental retardation, provided that the classification system recognizes MMR as a distinct category within this construct. The key feature would be a reconceptualization of adaptive skills to focus on the areas of academic competence, particularly in school settings, and social competence in all settings that are the primary areas of adaptive skill problems for individuals with MMR.

RECONCEPTUALIZE ADAPTATION TO FIT INDIVIDUALS WITH MMR

We believe that mild mental retardation is fundamentally a disability of intellectual limitations that are manifest not only on standardized IQ tests but also in daily adaptation. Thus, we agree that MMR needs to be identified on the basis of an adaptive skills criterion as well as an IQ criterion. The three domains of adaptive behavior in the 2002 AAMR represent a step in the right direction, because each of these broad domains includes behaviors that are heavily "saturated" with cognitive skills, and at least two of these domains are equally relevant for children and adults with MMR. How can we be sure that the specific behaviors that are most relevant to adaptation for MMR are well represented in the operational definition of adaptive behavior?

First, in establishing adaptive skill criteria for identifying MMR, we must be sensitive to the particular environment and stage in the life span in which classification is taking place. Leland (1973) described the construct of adaptive behavior as the level of coping a person has attained within an environment. The conceptualization of adaptive behavior, therefore, needs to focus on the skills that are required to meet the social role expectations of the particular environment(s) in which an individual is expected to function. Furthermore, the salience of a given environment is influenced, in turn, by the person's life stage, so that a person with MMR faces different social role expectations in different environments and at different points in the life span. Therefore, he or she must display different behaviors for successful functioning in adulthood than in childhood, and for successful functioning in the public school classroom than in the neighborhood. Because the public school is the environment in which the vast majority of cases of MMR are identified, we will focus on the school environment as a relevant example by specifying behaviors that indicate successful adaptation in school settings.

In the environment of the school, the ability to perform academically and not disrupt the ecology of the classroom and playground defines the level of adaptation. In the behavioral disorders literature, Walker and his colleagues (Hersh & Walker, 1983; Walker, Irwin, Noell, & Singer, 1992; Walker, McConnell, & Clark, 1985) described two behavior adjustments upon entering school, which capture school-related adaptation for children with MMR. The following two adjustments are required of children in order to be deemed competent within an academic setting:

1. Teacher-related, or the extent to which the child meets teacher demands.
2. Peer-related, or the extent to which a child meets the social expectations of peers.

The child's adaptation is acceptable if his or her behavioral repertoire does both of the following:

1. Facilitates academic performance
2. Is nondisruptive to the classroom ecology (Walker et al., 1992).

Impairments in adaptive behavior would then be defined by the extent to which a child's behavior deviates from this "Model Behavior Profile" (Hersh & Walker, 1983).

Teacher-related expectations include the following behaviors:

1. Prompt compliance to teacher directions and commands.
2. Following rules.
3. Making assistance needs known.
4. Producing work of acceptable quality.
5. Working independently.
6. Adjusting to different instructional situations.
7. Responding to teacher corrections.
8. Listening carefully to the teacher.

Nonperformance of these kinds of behaviors is associated with teacher rejection, school failure and/or dropout, low performance expectations, and referral by the teacher for specialized intervention (Walker et al., 1992). Peer-related expectations include the following behaviors:

1. Cooperates with peers.

2. Supports peers.
3. Remains calm.
4. Achieves well.
5. Leads peers.
6. Acts independently.
7. Compliments peers.
8. Affiliates with peers.

Nonperformance of these behaviors is associated with peer rejection or neglect and weak social involvement or engagement (Parker & Asher, 1987; Walker et al., 1992).

Typically, a child with MMR exhibits difficulties in these subtle behaviors constituting teacher-related and peer-related expectations rather than in the behavioral domains tapped by extant scales of adaptive behavior. If we conceptualize adaptation in terms of expectations in the environment (i.e., school-based in this example), this will lead to the development of instruments that are relevant to the concerns that prompt referral, and therefore, that will have treatment validity. It will pinpoint specific classes of behavior in which a child is deficient and permit designing treatments specifically targeting the academic and social behaviors in which a child is weak. For example, for a child who has difficulty adjusting to different instructional situations, adjustments can be made to accommodate the child's transitioning skills, or the child can be taught ways to cope with change using behaviors that are acceptable in that environment (e.g., anger management). A child who fails to master math instruction for multiplication tables, despite repeated and varied efforts, might be taught to use a calculator as a prosthetic that permits adapting to future challenges in math. By conceptualizing adaptation in this manner, we will provide a classification for *service delivery* that has treatment validity that would be lacking if IQ scores alone served as the basis for classification, owing to the omnibus nature of IQ tests and their lack of treatment validity.

We also believe that the conceptualization of adaptive behavior in MMR can be greatly advanced if the link between the cognitive processing limitations of individuals with MMR and their problems in academic and social functioning is made more explicit. For this reason, we preferred the term "adaptive skills," used in the 1992 AAMR definition in place of "adaptive behavior," to emphasize that observable behaviors reflect underlying cognitive processes. In standard definitions of mental retardation, intellectual limitations and adaptive behavior are measured separately and refer to different aspects of a person's functioning. Nonetheless, we presume that individuals with mental retardation have problems with tasks of daily functioning (i.e., adaptive behavior) in large part because of the cognitive processing demands that these tasks impose. Unfortunately, the two criteria of intellectual limitations and problems in adaptation are often considered separately without exploring the links between them (Greenspan, 1979; Greenspan & Granfield, 1992; Leffert & Siperstein, 1996). This leaves educators or other professionals who are carrying out the classification process open to the criticism that they are identifying as having MMR individuals whose problems in adaptive functioning have sources other than intellectual impairment.

The problems in adaptation of MMR, which are most manifest in the areas of social and academic competence, reflect subtle but meaningful limitations in their cognitive processes. However, since adaptive skills are often conceptualized exclusively in terms of observable behaviors, the nature of these cognitive limitations is often left unspecified. Fortunately, there is a growing research base that highlights the problems in cognition that underlie the difficulties individuals with MMR have in meeting the social role expectations in environments such as the school and the workplace. (See Glinou, 2004; Hickson & Khemka, 1999, 2001, 2004; Hickson & Khemka, in press; Murphy, 2004; Murphy & Clare, 2004.)

In the area of academic competence, research concerning the cognitive capacities that are involved in the performance of tasks that are primarily non-interpersonal in nature has highlighted components of intellectual functioning that impede the accomplishment of these tasks by individuals with MMR. In addition to the limitations in abstract reasoning that standard forms of intellectual assessment have documented, the research literature has focused on limitations in meta-components, knowledge acquisition components, and performance components (Sternberg, 1987; 1984) and difficulties in coordinating multiple dimensions when solving academic problems (Short & Evans, 1990). (See also Bebko & Luhaorg, 1998; Borkowski, Chan, & Muthukrisna, 2000; Borkowski, Smith, Weaver, & Akai, 2004; Van Haneghan & Turner, 2001).

Meanwhile, research in the field of social cognition has highlighted problems in processes such as social perception, the capacity to generate and select appropriate social strategies in response to social problems, and in individuals' knowledge of social scripts and schemes (Crick & Dodge, 1994) that help to explain why children and adults with MMR have difficulty demonstrating socially competent behavior in response to a complex and fast-changing social environment. (See Leffert & Siperstein, 2002, for a review of findings, as well as recent research studies by Hickson & Khemka, in press, and van Niewenhuizjen, 2004, among others.) Thus, it is possible, for example, when an adolescent with MMR initiates inappropriate conversational topics with customers while he is at a pre-vocational training site, to link this problem behavior to social cognitive skills such as:

1. Differentiating conversational topics by category, and choosing the conversation topic in relation to appropriate categories of social situations;
2. Social perception skills that involve recognizing and accurately interpreting the social cues that come from customers and fellow employees; and
3. Evaluation of social strategies in relation to a particular social context, including consequential reasoning.

In a related area of research, the social-cognitive components of the decision-making and self-direction skills that individuals with mental retardation need to apply in demonstrating self-determination in daily life have been explored and assessed by Wehmeyer and colleagues (Wehmeyer, 2001, 2004; Wehmeyer, Kelchner, & Richards, 1996).

Although, at this point, the measurement of social-cognitive processes is largely confined to research investigations, could social-cognitive assessment instruments become a useful clinical tool for the identification of individuals who have mental retardation? A report prepared by the National Research Council (National Research Council, 2002) to advise the Social Security Administration on disability determination practices has raised this as a possibility. Already, two norm-referenced instruments that test social-cognitive skills are commercially available:

1. The Test of Interpersonal Competence for Employment (Foss, Cheney, & Bullis, 1986), which assesses an adult's ability to select socially appropriate strategies in an employment setting.
2. The Arc's Self-Determination Scale (Wehmeyer, 1995; Wehmeyer & Kelchner, 1995) for adolescents and adults, which includes tests of means-end reasoning and the ability to generate strategies for meeting a goal.

Although these two items are far from a complete battery and tests for children are still in the development phase (Leffert, Siperstein, Freeman, & Sideridis, 2005), social-cognitive assessment is emerging as a means for direct assessment of the cognitive substrate of social adaptation. Greenspan (1999) has even suggested that if the social and practical components of intelligence can be directly measured, it will no longer be necessary to assess adaptive behavior in order to identify cases of mental retardation (see also Greenspan, 2003).

In summary, we are suggesting that adaptive behavior be reconceptualized to focus on the distinctive characteristics and needs of individuals with MMR. By focusing attention on those adaptive skills that pose the primary difficulties for individuals with MMR in relation to the social role expectations of particular environments, such as the public school, in which classification most often takes place, and by clarifying the links between the intellectual limitations of MMR and their problems in adaptation, AAMR can produce a definition and classification system that will be relevant and useful for the purposes of establishing eligibility for services and planning service delivery.

Adopt a New Name for the Disability

We have stated that MMR has characteristics in common with moderate and severe forms of mental retardation that would justify continuing to include individuals with MMR within the overall concept of mental retardation. However, we also recognize that the precipitous decline in the application of the term "mental retardation" in school settings is, to a significant extent, attributable to its pejorative connotation. In addition to the perhaps inevitable devolution of a long-established term into a pejorative term through popular usage, the label "mental retardation" has two specific disadvantages:

1. The concept of "mental" has the weakness of having broader connotations (e.g., mental illness; "mental case") that are not limited to intellectual processes.
2. The term "retardation" stigmatizes individuals because it is not used by nonprofessionals in any other context besides the description of this population.

If mental retardation is to serve as a unifying concept that includes MMR, a new term needs to be adopted that is less stigmatizing and more palatable to educators, parents, and the individuals with MMR themselves. In our view, a term such as "intellectual disability," which is increasingly becoming the standard term outside the United States, "cognitive impairment," or "general learning disability" would be more acceptable. Here in the United States, the use of other terms besides mental retardation is becoming more widespread. For example the President's Commission is now titled "For Persons with Intellectual Disability." Meanwhile, a number of states have changed the name of the statewide agency that serves individuals with mental retardation to the "Department of Developmental Disabilities Services."

In early 2005, AAMR announced that its membership voted down a proposal to change the name of the disability. This decision leaves "the oldest and largest interdisciplinary organization of professionals and others concerned about mental retardation and related disabilities" (according to AAMR's Web site) wedded to terminology that is almost never used in today's public schools to describe children who meet the criteria for MMR.

A FINAL NOTE

Following the promulgation of the 1992 AAMR definition, we argued that the historic inclusion of MMR under the general rubric of mental retardation might continue to be justified, provided that the framers of the next official definition recognized the distinct characteristics of MMR, e.g., by restoring levels of severity, adopted classification criteria that were more relevant and useful for the critical purposes of eligibility determination, research, and intervention planning for this population, and provided that the name of the disability was changed. What should happen at this point, now that AAMR has issued a revised definition of mental retardation that is still flawed for classifying individuals with MMR and, critically, continues to blur the distinct identity of MMR among a broad disability category simply called "mental retardation?" Furthermore, what should happen if AAMR continues to use a term that has pejorative connotations to describe this disability? In light of these circumstances, we continue to advocate for "secession" of MMR from the boundaries of mental retardation, so that it may take its place as a separate and distinct disability category. If this were to occur, of course, mental retardation would be recognized as a disability with a much lower incidence than is presently the case. The difficulties that self advocates and others who advocate for individuals with MMR would encounter in gaining recognition of a separate and distinct category of disability would be more than offset by the value that would accrue to individuals with MMR of having their problems and needs clearly recognized and addressed.

REFERENCES

Ashurst, D. I., & Meyers, C. E. (1973). Social system and clinical model in school identification of the educable mentally retarded. In R. K. Eyman, C. E. Meyers, & G. Tarjan (Eds.), *Monographs of the american association on mental deficiency* (Vol. 1, pp. 150–163). Washington, DC: American Association on Mental Deficiency.

Bak, J. J., & Siperstein, G. N. (1986). Protective effects of the label "mentally retarded" on children's attitudes toward their mentally retarded peers. *American Journal of Mental Deficiency, 91(1)*, 95–97.

Bebko, J. M., & Luhaorg, H. (1998). The development of strategy use and metacognitive processing in mental retardation: Some sources of difficulty. In J. A. Burack, R. M. Hodapp, & E. Zigler (Eds.), *Handbook of mental retardation and development* (pp. 382–407). New York: Cambridge University Press.

Belmont, J. M., & Borkowski, J. G. (1994). Prudence, indeed, will dictate. Review of Mental retardation: Definition, classification, and systems of supports (9th ed.). *American Journal on Mental Retardation, 98*, 541–544.

Blashfield, R. K. (1993). Models of classification as related to a taxonomy of learning disabilities. In G. R. Lyon, D. B. Gray, J. F. Kavanagh, & N. A. Krasnegor (Eds.), *Better understanding learning disabilities* (pp. 17–25). Baltimore: Brookes.

Borkowski, J. G., Chan, L. K. S., & Muthukrishna, N. (2000). A process oriented model of metacognition: Links between motivation and executive functioning. In G. Shaw (Ed.), *Issues in the measurement of metacognition* (pp. 1–41). Lincoln: University of Nebraska Press.

Borkowski, J. G., Smith, L., Weaver, C., & Akai, C. (2004). Metacognitive theory and classroom practices. In Ee, J., Chang, A., & Tan, O. (Eds.), *Thinking about thinking: What educators need to know.Singapore: McGraw-Hill.*

Bramlett, R. K., Smith, B. L., & Edmonds, J. (1994). A comparison of nonreferred, learning disabled, and mildly mentally retarded students utilizing the Social Skills Rating System. *Psychology in the Schools, 31,* 13–19.

Conte, R., & Andrews, J. (1993). Social skills in the context of learning disability definitions: A reply to Gresham and Elliott and directions for the future. *Journal of Learning Disabilities, 26*(3), 146–153.

Crick, N. R., & Dodge, K. A. (1994). A review and reformulation of social information processing mechanisms in children's social adjustment. *Psychological Bulletin, 115,* 74–101.

Cullinan, D., & Epstein, M. H. (1985). Adjustment problems of mildly handicapped and non-handicapped students. *RASE: Remedial and Special Education, 6*(2), 5–11.

Foss, G., Cheney, D., & Bullis, M. (1986). *TICE: Test of interpersonal competence for employment manual.* Santa Barbara, CA: James Stanfield.

Glinou, N. M. (2004). Impact of cognitive-motivational training on interpersonal negotiation strategies [Abstract]. *Journal of Intellectual Disabilities Research, 48,* 453.

Greenspan, S. (1979). Social intelligence in the retarded. In N. R. Ellis (Ed.), *Handbook of mental deficiency, psychological theory and research* (2nd ed., pp. 483–531). Hillsdale, NJ: Erlbaum.

Greenspan, S. (2003). Perceived risk status as a key to defining mental retardation. In H. N. Switzky & S. Greenspan (Eds.), *What Is Mental Retardation? Ideas for an evolving disability.* Washington, DC: American Association on Mental Retardation [E-Book]. Available at http://www.disabilitybooksonline.com

Greenspan, S. (2004). Why Pinocchio was victimized: Factors contributing to social failure in people with mental retardation. In H. N. Switzky (Ed.), *International review of research in mental retardation* (Vol. 28, pp. 121–144). San Diego, CA: Elsevier/Academic Press.

Greenspan, S., & Granfield, J. M. (1992). Reconsidering the construct of mental retardation: Implications of a model of social competence. *American Journal on Mental Retardation, 96*(4), 442–453.

Greenspan, S., & Love, P. F. (1997). Social intelligence and developmental disorder: Mental retardation, learning disabilities, and autism. In W. E. MacLean, Jr. (Ed.), *Ellis' handbook of mental deficiency, psychological theory, and research* (3rd ed., pp. 311–342). Mahwah, NJ: Erlbaum.

Greenspan, S., Switzky, H. N., & Granfield, J. M. (1996). Everyday intelligence and adaptive behavior: A theoretical framework. In J. W. Jacobson & J. A. Mulick (Eds.), *Manual of diagnosis and professional practice in mental retardation* (pp.127–135). Washington, DC: American Psychological Association.

Gresham, F. M., & Elliot, S. N. (1987). The relationship between adaptive behavior and social skills: Issues in definition and assessment. *Journal of Special Education, 21,* 168–181.

Gresham, F. M., Elliott, S. N., & Black, F. L. (1987). Teacher-rated social skills of mainstreamed mildly handicapped and non-handicapped children. *School Psychology Review, 16*(1), 78–88.

Gresham, F. M., & Reschly, D. J. (1987). Dimensions of social competence: Method factors in the assessment of adaptive behavior, social skills, and peer acceptance. *Journal of School Psychology, 25,* 367–381.

Grossman, H. J. (Ed.). (1973). *Manual on terminology and classification in mental retardation (1973 revision).* Washington, DC: American Association on Mental Deficiency.

Grossman, H. J. (Ed.). (1977). *Manual on terminology and classification in mental retardation* (1977 revision). Washington, DC: American Association on Mental Deficiency.

Grossman, H. J. (Ed.). (1983). *Manual on terminology and classification in mental retardation* (1983 revision). Washington, DC: American Association on Mental Deficiency.

Grossman, H. J., & Tarjan, G. (Eds.). (1987). *American Medical Association handbook on mental retardation.* Chicago: American Medical Association.

Heber, R. (1959). A manual on terminology and classification in mental retardation (Rev. ed.) [Monograph Supplement]. *American Journal of Mental Deficiency, 64*(2).

Heber, R. (1961). Modifications in the manual on terminology and classification in mental retardation. *American Journal of Mental Deficiency, 65(4),* 499–500.

Hersh, R. H., & Walker, H. M. (1983). Great expectations: Making schools effective for all students. *Policy Studies Review, 2,* 147–188.

Hickson, L., & Khemka, I. (1999). Decision making and mental retardation. In L. M. Glidden (Ed.), *International review of research in mental retardation* (Vol. 22, pp. 227–265). San Diego, CA: Academic Press.

Hickson, L., & Khemka, I. (2001). The role of motivation in the decision making of people with mental retardation. In H. N. Switzky (Ed.), *Personality and motivational differences in persons with mental retardation* (pp.199–255). Mahwah, NJ: Erlbaum.

Hickson, L., & Khemka, I. (2004). Impact of ESCAPE on the cognitive and motivational aspects of self–protective decision making [Abstract]. *Journal of Intellectual Disability Research, 48,* 453.

Hickson, L., & Khemka, I. (in press). The psychology of decision making. In G. H. Murphy & I. C. H. Clare (Eds.), *Decision making in people with intellectual disabilities.* Chichester, England: Wiley.

Jacobson, J. W., & Mulick, J. A. (1992). A new definition of mentally retarded or a new definition of practice? *Psychology in Mental Retardation and Developmental Disabilities, 18*(2), 9–14.

Kavanaugh, J. F., & Truss, T. J., Jr. (Eds.). (1988). *Learning Disabilities: Proceedings of the National Conference.* Parkton, MD: York Press.

Keogh, B. K. (1993). Linking purpose and practice: Social, political and developmental perspectives on classification. In G. R. Lyon, D. B. Gray, J. F. Kavanagh, & N. A. Krasnegor (Eds.), *Better understanding learning disabilities* (pp. 311–324). Baltimore: Paul H. Brookes.

Khemka, I., & Hickson, L.(2004). The role of motivation in the decision making of adolescents with mental retardation. In L. M. Glidden & H. N. Switzky (Ed.), *International review of research in mental retardation (Vol. 30).* San Diego, CA: Elsevier/Academic Press.

Leffert, J. S., & Siperstein, G. N. (1996). Assessment of social cognitive processes in children with mental retardation. *American Journal on Mental Retardation, 100,* 441–445.

Leffert, J. S., & Siperstein, G. N. (2002). Social cognition: A key to understanding adaptive behavior in individuals with mental retardation. In L. M. Glidden (Ed.), *International review of research in mental retardation* (Vol. 25, pp. 135–181). San Diego, CA: Academic Press.

Leffert, J. S., Siperstein, G. N., Freeman, B., & Sideridis, G. (2005). Assessment of social perception in children with mental retardation. Paper presented as part of a symposium titled, "Social-Cognitive Processes in Children and Adults with Mental Retardation" at the SRCD Biennial Meeting, Atlanta, GA.

Leffert, J. S., Siperstein, G. N., & Millikan, E. (2000). Understanding social adaptation in children with mental retardation: A social cognitive perspective. *Exceptional Children, 66*(4), 530–545.

Leland, H. (1973). Adaptive behavior and mentally retarded behavior. In G. Tarjan, R. K. Eyman, & C. E. Meyers (Eds.), *Sociobehavioral studies in mental retardation* (pp. 91–100). Washington, DC: American Association on Mental Deficiency.

Luckasson, R. Borthwick-Duffy, S., Buntinx, W. H. E., Coulter, D. L., Craig, E. M., Reeve. A., et al. (2002). *Mental retardation: Definition, classification, and systems of supports* (10th ed.). Washington, DC: American Association on Mental Retardation.

Luckasson, R., Coulter, D. L., Polloway, E. A., Reiss, S., Schalock, R. L., Snell, M. E., et al. (1992). *Mental retardation: Definition, classification, and systems of supports* (9th ed.). Washington, DC: American Association on Mental Retardation.

MacMillan, D. L., Gresham, F. M., & Siperstein, G. N. (1993). Conceptual and psychometric concerns about the 1992 AAMR definition of mental retardation. *American Journal on Mental Retardation, 98,* 325–335.

MacMillan, D. L., Gresham, F. M., & Siperstein, G. N. (1995). Heightened concerns over the 1992 AAMR definition: Advocacy versus precision. *American Journal on Mental Retardation, 100,* 87–97.

MacMillan, D. L., Gresham, F. M., Siperstein, G. N., & Bocian, K. M. (1996). The labyrinth of IDEA: School decisions on referred students with subaverage general intelligence. *American Journal on Mental Retardation, 101,* 161–174.

MacMillan, D. L., Siperstein, G. N., & Gresham, F. M. (1996). A challenge to the viability of mild mental retardation as a diagnostic category. *Exceptional Children, 62,* 356–371.

MacMillan, D. L., Siperstein, G. N., & Leffert, J. S. (2003). Children with mild mental retardation: A challenge for classification practices. In H. N. Switzky & S. Greenspan (Eds.), *What Is Mental Retardation? Ideas for an evolving disability* (pp. 242–261). Washington, DC: American Association on Mental Retardation [E-Book]. Available at http://www.disabilitybooksonline.com

McAlpine, C., Singh, N. N., Kendall, K. A., & Ellis, C. R. (1992). Recognition of facial expressions of emotion by persons with mental retardation. *Behavior Modification 16(4),* 543–558.

Mercer, J. R. (1973). *Labeling the mentally retarded.* Berkeley: University of California Press.

Merrell, K. W., Sanders, D. E., & Popinga, M. R. (1993). Teacher ratings of student social behavior as a predictor of special education status: Discriminant validity of the School Social Behavior Scale. *Journal of Psychoeducational Assessment, 11,* 220–231.

Moffatt, C. W., Hanley-Maxwell, C., & Donnellan, A. M. (1995). Recognition of facial expressions of emotion by persons with mental retardation. *Education and Training in Mental Retardation and Developmental Disabilities, 30(1),* 76–85.

Murphy, C. C., Yeargin-Allsopp, M., Decouflé, P., & Drews, C. D. (1995). The administrative prevalence of mental retardation in 10-year-old children in metropolitan Atlanta, 1985 through 1987. *American Journal of Public Health, 85,* 319–323.

Murphy, G. H. (2004). Making decisions [Abstract]. *Journal of Intellectual Disability Research, 48,* 285.

Murphy, G. H., & Clare, I. C. H. (in press). *Decision making in people with intellectual disabilities.* Chichester: Wiley.

National Research Council. (2002). *Mental retardation: Determining eligibility for social security benefits.* Committee on Disability Determination for Mental Retardation. D. J. Reschly, T. G. Myers, & C. R. Hartel (Eds). Division of Behavioral and Social Sciences and Education. Washington, DC: National Academy Press.

Ollendick, T. H., West, M. D., Borden, M. C., & Greene, R. W. (1992). Sociometric status and academic, behavioral and psychological adjustment: A five year longitudinal study. *Journal of Consulting and Clinical Psychology, 60(1),* 80–87.

Parker, J. G., & Asher, S. R. (1987). Peer relations and later personal adjustment: Are low-accepted children at risk? *Psychological Bulletin, 102(3),* 357–389.

Reiss, S. (1994). Issues in defining mental retardation. *American Journal on Mental Retardation, 99,* 1–7.

Reschly, D. J. (1992). Mental retardation: Conceptual foundation, definitional criteria, and diagnostic operations. In S. R. Hynd & R. E. Mattison (Eds.), *Assessment and diagnosis of child and adolescent psychiatric disorders: Volume II. Developmental disorders* (pp. 23–67). Hillsdale, NJ: Erlbaum.

Short, E. J., & Evans, S. W. (1990). Individual differences in cognitive and social problem solving skills as a function of intelligence. *International Review of Research in Mental Retardation, 16,* 89–123.

Siperstein, G. N., & Bak, J. J. (1985). Understanding factors that affect children's attitudes toward mentally retarded peers. In C. J. Meisel (Ed.), *Mainstreaming handicapped children: Outcomes, controversies, and new discoveries.* (pp. 55–75). Hillsdale, NJ: Erlbaum.

Siperstein, G. N., Norins, J., & Corbin, S. B. (2003, June). *Multinational study of attitudes toward individuals with intellectual disabilities* (Special Report). Washington, DC: Special Olympics.

Sternberg, R. J. (1984). Macrocomponents and microcomponents of intelligence: Some proposed loci of mental retardation. In P. H. Brooks, R. Sperber, & C. McCauley (Eds.), *Learning and cognition in the mentally retarded* (pp. 89–115). Hillsdale, NJ: Erlbaum.

Sternberg, R. J. (1987). A unified theory of cognitive exceptionality. In J. D. Day, & J. G. Borkowski (Eds.), *Intelligence and exceptionality: New directions for theory, assessment, and instructional practices* (pp. 135–173). Norwood, NJ: Ablex.

Switzky, H. N., Greenspan, S., & Granfield, J. (1996). Adaptive behavior, everyday intelligence and the constitutive definition of mental retardation. In A. F. Rotatori, J. O. Schwenn, & S. Burkhardt (Eds.), *Advances in special education* (Vol. 10, pp. 1–24). Greenwich, CT: JAI Press.

Thorndike, E. L. (1920, January). Intelligence and its uses. *Harper's Magazine, 140,* 227–235.

Van Haneghan, J. P., & Turner, L. (2001). Information processing and motivation in people with mental retardation. In H. N. Switzky (Ed.), *Personality and motivational differences in persons with mental retardation* (pp. 319–371). Mahwah, NJ: Erlbaum.

Von Nieuwenhuijzen, M. (2004). *Social information processing in children with mild intellectual disabilities.* Unpublished doctoral dissertation, University of Utrecht, The Netherlands.

Walker, H. M., Irwin, L., Noell, J., & Singer, G. (1992). A construct score approach to the assessment of social competence: Rationale, technological considerations, and anticipated outcomes. *Behavior Modification, 16,* 448–474.

Walker, H. M., McConnell, S., & Clark, J. (1985). Social skills training in school settings: A model of the social integration of handicapped children into less restrictive settings. In R. McMahon & R. Peters (Eds.), *Childhood disorders: Behavioral developmental approaches* (pp.140–168). New York: Brunner-Mazel.

Wehmeyer, M. L. (1995). *The Arc's Self-Determination Scale: Procedural guidelines.* Silver Spring, MD: The Arc of the United States.

Wehmeyer, M. L. (2001). Self determination and mental retardation: Assembling the puzzle pieces. In H. Switzky (Ed.), *Motivational and personality differences in mental retardation.* (pp. 147–198). Hillsdale, NJ: Erlbaum.

Wehmeyer, M. L. (2004). Self-determination, casual agency, and mental retardation. In L. M. Glidden & H. N. Switzky (Eds.), *International review of research in mental retardation (Vol. 28).* San Diego, CA: Elsevier/Academic Press.

Wehmeyer, M. L., & Kelchner, K. (1995). *The Arc's Self-Determination Scale.* Arlington, TX: The Arc of the United States.

Wehmeyer, M. L., Kelchner, K., & Richards, S. (1996). Essential characteristics of self-determined behavior of individuals with mental retardation. *American Journal on Mental Health, 100*(6), 632–642.

Zigler, E. (1967). Familial mental retardation: A continuing dilemma. *Science, 155,* 292–298.

CHAPTER FOURTEEN

Adaptation, Remission, and Growth: Conceptual Challenges to the Definition of Mental Retardation—Medical Implications and Applications

ALYA REEVE

In this brief chapter I will try to outline elements of the definition of mental retardation that are of particular relevance to the field of medicine with respect to medical understanding of brain function. For this reason, I have chosen terms describing neuronal and behavioral function to discuss the evolution of this field of clinical service and this term.

Mental retardation (MR) should be neither a sociologically dismissive label, nor an empty catch-all phrase. "A major hurdle in any attempt to bridge disciplines is terminology. Creative variation in language usage may produce lexically rich poetry but often fails to allow precise reporting. Ever present, the language problem becomes exacerbated when investigators must deal with terms that have acquired multiple meanings" (Benson, 1994). We must define mental retardation clearly for our time in order that we may apply it in educational, social, medical, developmental, and legal contexts in creative, meaningful and appropriate ways.

ADAPTATION TO NEW INFORMATION

The 1992 AAMR definition of mental retardation (Luckasson et al., 1992) bore reconsideration for a number of reasons, mostly because it was an initial paradigm shift, but an incompletely articulated one. The only partial adoption of its definition by DSM-IV and ICD-10 reflected the difficulty in changing our patterns of clinical thinking. Luckasson et al. (1992) reflected general experience that low IQ did not predict social talents, survival skills, or work habits of many individuals. As people who had been labeled as mentally retarded moved into living in community settings, the need for appropriate supports for functioning became more evident. Also, their ability to function in unexpected and creative ways became more visible. Hence, the rubric for anticipating the functional needs of individuals with mental retardation needed to shift to greater emphasis on other aspects of functioning and useful sources of support. The changes in use and labeling are summarized in the 2002 AAMR definition of mental retardation (Luckasson et al., 2002).

There are many purposes for which a diagnosis of mental retardation, or its predecessor diagnostic labels, is used. For example, the term "idiocy" has been used to describe limitations in cognitive reasoning and thereby to anticipate inability in social function. This line of thinking is evident in prior AAMR definitions, the 1959 definition and onward, with the delineations of borderline, mild, moderate, severe, and profound classes of mental retardation. Often behavioral and neuropsychiatric capacities have been mixed into the term mental retardation. Cognitive limitations and narrowness of behavioral repertoires have been assumed to be tightly and linearly related to each other. Yet our experiences show us that this is not the case. A universal definition for mental retardation is difficult to find, because people with mental retardation are not so different from those with normal intelligence. In some ways this diagnostic labeling dilemma reflects the deficiency of any unidimensional attempt to categorize and characterize human experience.

Greenspan (1997) has proposed that three types of intelligence be measured: social, practical and conceptual. He proposed that clinical impressions (implying qualitative measures to document strengths and deficits) are the source of evaluation of these types or aspects of intelligence. These three "naturalistic" types of intelligence are proposed to replace "artificial constructs" such as adaptive behavior or skills or functioning. From my perspective this is semantic nit-picking over which words are most intuitive of how humans successfully interact with each other. Social intelligence contributes directly and indirectly to a person's behavior. By replacing one IQ-based definition with a tripartite intelligence-based definition, we are not substantively changing the definition of mental retardation. The cognitive limitations and medical/neurological limitations must be tied to the behavioral expressions of the individual. Both Greenspan and the current AAMR definitions focus on the need to define requirements for external support to achieve maximal functional development.

Development of the brain involves internal nutritive support, appropriate rates of challenging experiences, and at the end of its "natural course" progressive decline in function and numbers of live cells. Mental retardation is distinguished from other disorders of brain function by the observation that onset of disordered function is during the developmental period, from gestation through late adolescence for humans. It is characterized by alteration in cognitive ability, by cognitive skills developing slower than normative rates of acquisition. There must also be lack of development of adaptive behaviors commensurate to the chronological age and culture of the individual. It is a chronic condition that may improve with support, opportunity to learn adaptive skills, and lack of catastrophic life experiences. Medical teaching has implied that neurological disorders resulting in mental retardation were static lesions that would not be expected to worsen over a lifetime.

More recent understanding of the development and function of the nervous system does not support such an opinion. Virtually no brain is static in its development or function. However, there is increasing awareness that the limitations of individual brains vary enormously and that these limitations are seen in the relative capacity for functioning across differing tasks that our brains perform. There is wide variety in the type of neuronal insult that is labeled mental retardation. Anoxia at birth can affect gross neuronal development, including motor and behavioral manifestations. Yet persistent physical, intellectual, and emotional therapeutic interactions throughout childhood can help a person develop a strong sense of self, independent mobility, and effective communication skills. Anoxic damage in late teen years may produce a much more dramatic limitation in functional and independent skills; in adulthood it is almost certainly likely to result in permanent disablement.

The emphasis placed on mental retardation as an expression of the interaction between individuals and their environment moved the definition from describing a specific trait toward a functional, dynamic understanding of an individual's abilities. It is assumed that the adaptive functioning of the person with mental retardation will generally improve with appropriate supports. In my view, mental retardation is an incomplete term to describe a type of chronic condition. Unlike acute discrete medical illnesses, chronic conditions may wax and wane in the severity of their symptoms, but individuals carry the susceptibility of exacerbation within themselves for their lifetime. This perpetual potential susceptibility to loss of functional adaptation underscores both the need for ongoing supportive services and the need for a realistic safety net of support services, should existing sources of support fail. I should immediately clarify that a chronic condition does not imply that the person is sick, or in the sick role. As with many neurologic and psychiatric illnesses, individuals may not require medical attention or special consideration during periods when they are functioning in their compensated "healthy" state.

The reason that the underlying condition is important is that it may put individuals at risk for other associated illness, or may complicate their response to medications, stress, and infection. For example, major depression is now understood to be a neurotransmitter-based experience-influenced disorder of the brain which may go into remission. For the person who has had depression, there are considerations to managing and minimizing the risk of becoming "ill" again, including awareness of other medications causing an exacerbation of symptoms. We do not treat persons who have recovered from an episode of depression differently when we evaluate their work or their ideas or their friendship. (However, during periods of exacerbation, dysfunction in cognition, attention, memory and mood all impair the person.) It is similar for people with mental retardation, whose condition may remit to allow them to function within normal expectations, with the inherent vulnerability to particular stressors.

New experiences and continual learning occur for all people at the neuronal level, even in the face of degeneration. In as extreme a case as Alzheimer's disease (a progressive dementing illness), at the same time that cells die, elevations in nerve growth factor occur and attempts are made to form new dendritic processes. The underlying etiology for any individual's condition will have an effect upon the nervous system's capabilities and capacities for growth. Development will be influenced by environmental stressors and repeated experiences (Schore, 1994). This variation in developed capacity is observed commonly in the length of time it may take a person with mental retardation to learn activities or habits: For some people it takes a long time and for others it can be very fast. The capacity for learning changes over the lifespan. Often new motor skills, such as a new sport or language, are more difficult to learn the older we become. Movements that build upon familiar actions are more easily incorporated into our repertoire. It is not surprising that each person has differing abilities and responses to similar opportunities. When there is a deficit in the normal redundancy in neuronal representation/function, these differences in capacity will be accentuated. Those pathways that are the most used become the most habitual and most easily relied upon. With any reduction in the numbers of neurons, in the numbers of pathways, in the connections of neurons to each other, there is a reduction in the flexibility of options for the entire system. Sometimes this reduction of flexibility is invisible to usual interactions; sometimes it can leave individuals with a much narrowed range of interests or behaviors, or a severely decreased tolerance of changes in their surrounding environment. As outsiders, we need a way to recognize that such an individual needs levels of support that are not immediately apparent to us, that we may not intuit without their help. For some people, the term mental retardation is a shorthand way to describe this kind of need for supports, without boxing it into the same supports for every person with MR. For other people, MR amounts to a method of dismissing interest in them, to avoid seeing their personhood.

Adaptation is a necessary physiologic and intellectual skill for survival. This is especially true if you have MR, because there are a lot of situations in which you need to follow other people's leads, or you are labeled as "trouble." It is instructive to notice that the U.S. Department of Health and Human Services left out such negative labels when constructing their model of "understanding and improving health." In Healthy People 2010, an individual has a dynamic interplay between his/her own biology and behavior while interacting with the physical and social environment (2001). This model represents the individual in dynamic interaction with the environment throughout his/her lifespan, just as early childhood development reflects the interaction of genetic and environmental influences (Zuckerman, Frank et al., 1999).

REMISSION FROM WHAT?

Remission and exacerbation are terms used to describe the patterns of worsening and alleviating clinical symptoms in many chronic illnesses, especially psychiatric illnesses. The underlying predilection for a chronic psychiatric condition renders the individual susceptible to becoming symptomatic, under certain environmental or psychological conditions. This quality of empirical visibility of symptoms can tempt some observers to consider MR to remit, when it is not providing barriers to an individual's functioning. I would interpret these observations to mean that the person's adaptive functioning has improved, or remitted, since we can all regress under stressful conditions, but that we are not measuring or directly assessing MR. The comprehensive assessment of MR requires careful attention to the psychological functioning of the individual. Not all changes in mood and behavior are attributable to having MR (Reiss & Szyszko, 1983).

The possibility of having mental illness(es) or disorders in addition to mental retardation has been discussed widely, often on the basis of strongly held opinion rather than clinical observation (Berrios, 1994). Some clinicians believe that the term means deformity in intellect and brain and is explanation enough for all subsequent disorders of behavior. The term "organic personality disorder" reflected this understanding. No such diagnosis is included among the definitions of psychiatric disorders (DSM-IV-TR, APA 2000), because it was too vague a term and was not tied to etiology. The prevailing custom is to include mental retardation with other chronic character pathology diagnoses on

Axis II in the DSM-IV-TR system. The misleading implication of this association is that mental retardation is a learned behavioral deficit. However, it correctly implies that proper supports can assist the individual to become less pathologic and less symptomatic.

Mental retardation is not a psychiatric illness. A person with mental retardation, or intellectual disabilities, behaves rationally at his or her operational level. "O.K. This is my definition of what retarded means. O.K. It doesn't necessarily have to do with what you look like on the outside. It's just that your brain doesn't think as fast as someone else. And you can't learn as fast as other people. That's all" (Castles, 1996). Emotional stability and maturity are learned experiences for all people, but may develop at different rates. Perceptual and emotional difficulties that are not flexibly handled can become permanent deficits in a person's ability to function. That is the moment of time when pathological processes in the brain are establishing themselves (Schore, 1994). Symptoms may wax and wane, but psychiatric function has become impaired. This is a relative definition for development of a psychiatric disorder as compared to an adjustment disorder, which is shorter lived and often of less severe pathology (DSM-IV-TR, definition and background for Adjustment Disorder).

Certain etiopathologies of mental retardation are associated with known psychiatric illnesses, such as Prader-Willi Syndrome with bipolar mood disorder. The cumulative interaction of epilepsy and mental retardation increases the risk of developing recurrent major depression or psychosis. Additionally, having mental retardation from any cause alters the response of the individual toward other more commonly seen psychiatric diagnoses. Anxiety disorders and sleep disorders are two of the most common problems in the general population (APA, 2000). Having anxiety to alert oneself to potential or real danger, to increase the intensity of effort and concentration, is a useful characteristic in normal humans. Too much anxiety is painfully arresting of a functional life. The need to modulate overwhelming anxiety is greater, in general, for individuals with mental retardation, than in the normal population. The reported prevalence of past experience of either physical or sexual abuse, or both, is threefold greater in persons with mental retardation than in persons with a personality disorder (Ryan, 1994). Sensitivity to sensory information may be heightened for people who are not verbal. This raises the level of discomfort, especially when the situation doesn't make sense.

"[T]he available studies agree on two essential points: that mental retardation is a risk factor for developing a mental disorder and that all categories of 'usual' mental disorders are seen in this population" (Szymanski, 1994). As more information about brain organization, development, and function becomes available, understanding will grow about how psychiatric illness develops in people with other manifestations of neuronal developmental disorders. Diagnosis of mental retardation/intellectual disability is needed as a means to communicate and to research etiologies and the course of development (as contrasted with the purposes of social isolation and segregation diagnosis), because we do not fully understand the interplay between the organ-based dysfunction and changes in mental state of the brain. The diagnosis currently is a descriptive term to communicate our presumption that developmental processes and dysfunction are different from subsequent behavioral/functioning dysfunction later in life. In the future we may look back at these concepts as academic exercises that were way off base!

Another important consideration in comprehensive appraisal of intellectual functioning is the effect of medications and drugs of abuse on brain and behavior. Greater incidence of psychiatric disorders is described in people with IQs between 45 and 70 and greater incidence of neurologic disorders in people with IQs less than 45. In part, these differences are due to increase in seizure disorder rates and the decrease in verbal communication abilities for people with IQs less than 45 as a group. These characterizations miss the point that conceptual/intellectual deficits by number do not predict social aptitude or physiologic and psychological responses to mind-altering substances from nicotine, to alcohol, to marijuana, and to ecstasy. Substance abuse is reported for 2–20% of people with known intellectual disability. Again, supports for any individual with addictions plays an enormous role in quitting the addiction and in learning new behavior. MR neither predicts nor prevents substance abuse or dependence.

The concepts of adaptation and remission, taken from the context of neuronal biology and applied to the topic of mental retardation, run straight into the societal and political meanings of the terminology. In this context, there is little advantage to seek what is "growing out of" mental retardation or "being normal." All individuals, including those with intellectual disabilities, are reacting and participating with their social and physical environments as their biological processes interpret them, and expressing it through their behavior. External attitudes and expectations mold both the behaviors and the environments, which is why the quality and types of supports must be tailored to individual needs in order to be effective. The accompanying schematic diagram shows these interactions:

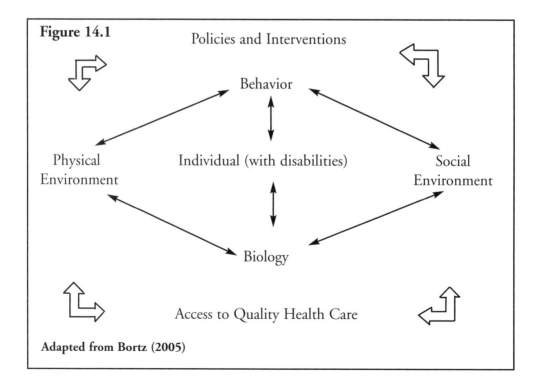

Figure 14.1

Policies and Interventions

Behavior

Physical Environment

Individual (with disabilities)

Social Environment

Biology

Access to Quality Health Care

Adapted from Bortz (2005)

How Do We Grow?

"The unique biological properties of man, as of all creatures, provide both abilities and limitations" (Baroff, 1986, p. 152) . . . "about people who have difficulty in coping with some of life adjustive tasks because of impaired general intelligence. The extent of their coping or adaptive difficulty is primarily related to the degree of intellectual impairment, though it is also much affected by both society's general attitude toward persons with limited intelligence and the services provided to them" (Baroff, 1986, p. 1).

The presence of a developmental disorder causes changes in responsivity of the neuronal substrate to sensory stimulation, including medications. There are alterations in threshold, raised and lowered, amplification of incoming stimuli, ability to modulate responses, outputs, and sensitivity to side effects, especially for drugs. Medical and metabolic illness or perturbations seem to more readily cause disturbances of associative pathways, even to the point of encephalopathy. The fundamental observation in clinical example after clinical example is that learning happens. Learning happens in multiple ways, and not all of them by intent of the learner. For this reason, clinicians and people who support individuals with disabilities must be willing to suspend prejudicial conceptions and expectations and truly assess the experiences they are sharing with the individual with disability.

Behavioral manifestations of distress in the person with mental retardation and/or head injury cannot be assumed to reflect neurotransmitter disruptions that have been ascribed to similar symptom constellations in the "normal population." Each therapeutic intervention must be tried in a systematic way to assess its effect on the overall functioning of the individual (Harris, 1995). This is true for behavioral and sensory therapies as well as for pharmacologic therapies.

One criticism levied against psychopharmacologic research efforts in mental retardation is that the high degree of individual variability in the cause of mental retardation obscures significant effects of specific treatment interventions. In other words, a known chemical compound will have very different effects in the brains of people with no pathology, from those with pathology, and the differences between the pathological processes, whether or not we know what they are, will cause differences in therapeutic response to the same compound.

The segregation of mental retardation into four categories by IQ cluster has not assisted in predicting response to psychopharmacologic agents. There is no data that assists us to anticipate on the basis of a diagnosis of mild MR how a person will respond to an antidepressant, or whether a person with profound MR will require either half or twice the dosage. Neither is there data that antipsychotics will have greater efficacy in one category than in another, depending upon MR severity. It is known that the more neurological and psychiatric illness individuals have, the more likely they are to have untoward side effects of the medications. This does not predict that there will be unwanted side effects, just that they are more likely to be encountered.

As a person grows older, over about 55–60 years, the likelihood of unwanted side effects increases. Unwanted side effects include problematic dry mouth and constipation, instability of gait, tendency to low blood pressure, fuzzy thinking, sleep disruption, and interference with sexual function. They do not include allergic reactions or nonresponsiveness to the intended pharmacologic effect. People with mental retardation will be affected by the aging process of all the organs of their body, including the brain. This becomes another factor to consider in anticipating responsiveness to the environment and exogenous agents, such as medicines.

PURPOSES OF DIAGNOSIS: WHERE ARE WE HEADING?

In medicine we seek common definitions for syndromes and symptoms. To that end we use diagnoses to communicate with other professionals. A *diagnosis* is defined as: "1. Process of identifying specific mental or physical disorders. 2. Comprehensive evaluation not limited to identification of specific disorders." *Diagnostic criteria* are defined as: "clearly articulated, exclusionary criteria for arriving at a diagnosis" (Ayd, 1995, p. 210). Diagnostic groups are organized into classes, or a classification system that may help us look at response to treatment interventions. *Classification of mental disorders* refers to a system of scientifically organizing mental disorders according to different criteria (e.g., behavioral symptoms) to yield uniform diagnoses (Ayd, 1995, p. 139). The diagnosis of mental retardation alone does not allow us to understand the degree of disability a person experiences. Disempowerment of individuals within society should not be the purpose of medical diagnoses. We, as physicians and other health professionals, strive to reduce human suffering and promote well-being. Medical practice and knowledge are changing as we learn more about the human body and the diseases that affect it. Our understanding of that which can be treated and prevented changes with new knowledge.

The importance of having a good definition of mental retardation/intellectual disability is that the application of those diagnostic criteria can assist our continued learning about the diagnosis, evaluating outcomes of different intervention, and developing reasonable prevention strategies (Bray, 1997). MR or intellectual disability is a biological condition of the brain, but not necessarily a disease. Chronic medical conditions do not require that people assume the "sick role." The incorporation of support and intensity of support needed by a person is an attempt to quantify the functional limitations that these disorders are placing on the person, rather than pigeon-holing them into marginal roles in society.

Review of supports required by a person will need to be incorporated into an ongoing assessment. Presumably the intensity of need for support will allow tracking of functional abilities (e.g., adaptive behavior). This would provide useful measures of the outcome of various strategies for intervention and opportunity in the lives of individuals with mental retardation. Performed perfunctorily and at artificial intervals, reevaluation is a meaningless exercise. It results in inaccurate assessments and misleading interpretation. Applied as an objective and thorough review of the changes a person has made over the period of one to several years, it documents the individual's changing adaptive capabilities, highlighting his or her strengths and interests. Whether named adaptive function or practical intelligence, these are aspects of the brain's capacity for effective expression to, and interaction with, the environment.

One limitation in allopathic medical practice is the tendency to present disease as an aberration from the normal state of the human experience. We are taught to seek cures to diseases. The medical curriculum teaches, with increasing emphasis, following people over the lifespan and cultivating awareness for the aging process. However, the practical application and delivery of services remains focused upon acute, intermittent delivery of care. Chronic illnesses, as a rule, are not served well by this model. Effective strategies for prevention are not assisted by this model. The recognition of mental retardation or intellectual or developmental disability as a chronic condition is important for communication and learning within the medical community. It is critical for increasing the awareness and realization that developmental disorders of the brain remain dynamic over the lifespan. This is an area of medical science that is in need of much multidisciplinary study.

REFERENCES

American Psychiatric Association. (2000). *Diagnostic and statistical manual of mental disorders-IV-TR.* Washington, DC: Author.

Ayd, F. J., Jr. (1995). *Lexicon of psychiatry, neurology, and the neurosciences.* Baltimore: Williams & Wilkins.

Baroff, G. S. (1986). *Mental retardation: Nature, cause, and management.* New York: Hemisphere.

Berrios, G. E. (1994). Mental illness and mental retardation: History and concepts. In N. Bouras (Ed.), *Mental health in mental retardation, recent advances and practices (pp. 5–18).* Cambridge, England: Cambridge University Press.

Bortz, W. M. (2005). Biological basis of determinants of health. *American Journal of Public Health, 95*(3), 389–392.

Bray, N. (Ed.). (1997). *International review of research in mental retardation.* New York: Academic Press.

Castles, E. E. (1996). *"We're people first": The social and emotional lives of individuals with mental retardation.* Westport, CT: Praeger.

Greenspan, S. (1997). Dead manual walking? Why the 1992 AAMR definition needs redoing. *Education and Training in Mental Retardation and Developmental Disabilities, 32,* 179–190.

Harris, J. C. (1995). *Developmental neuropsychiatry.* New York: Oxford University Press.

Luckasson, R., Borthwick-Duffy, S., Buntinx, W. H. E., Coulter, D. L., Craig, E. M., Reeve, A., et al. (2002). *Mental retardation: Definition, classification, and systems of supports* (10th ed.). Washington, DC: American Association on Mental Retardation.

Luckasson, R., Coulter, D. L., Polloway, E. A., Reiss, S., Schalock, R. L., Snell, M. E., et al. (1992). *Mental retardation: Definition, classification, and systems of supports* (9th ed.). Washington, DC: American Association on Mental Retardation.

Reiss, S., & Szyszko, J. (1983). Diagnostic overshadowing and professional experience with mentally retarded persons. *American Journal of Mental Deficiency, 87,* 396–402.

Ryan, R. (1994). Post traumatic stress disorder in persons with developmental disability. *Community Mental Health Journal, 30,* 45–54.

Schore, A. N. (1994). *Affect regulation and the origin of the self: The neurobiology of emotional development.* Hillsdale, NJ: Erlbaum.

Szymanski, L. (1994). Mental retardation and mental health: Concepts, aetiology and incidence. In N. Bouras (Ed.), *Mental health in mental retardation: Recent advances and practices (pp. 19–33).* Cambridge, England: Cambridge University Press.

United States Department of Health and Human Services. (2001). *Healthy people 2010: Understanding and improving health.* Washington, DC: Author.

Zuckerman, B. S., Frank, D. A., and Augustyn, M.A. (1999). Infancy and toddler years. In M. D. Levine, W. B. Carey, and A. C. Crocker *(Eds.), Developmental behavioral pediatrics* (pp. 24–37). Philadelphia: Saunders.

CHAPTER FIFTEEN

Scientific and Judgmental Issues Involved in Defining Mental Retardation

ROBERT L. SCHALOCK

OVERVIEW

In my chapter in the e-book *What Is Mental Retardation? Ideas for an Evolving Disability* (Switzky & Greenspan, 2003) I argued that mental retardation is a condition characterized by significant limitations in practical, conceptual, and social skills. The major rationale and context for the argument was based on recent conceptual and empirical formulations regarding the factor structure of adaptive behavior and intelligence. As discussed in the chapter, these recent formulations suggested to me two important points regarding defining the condition referred to as mental retardation (MR) in the United States:

1. The relevance of the multidimensionality of both adaptive behavior and intelligence to the definition of mental retardation.
2. The potential merging of the constructs of intelligence and adaptive behavior into a tripartite model of personal competence based on conceptual, social, and practical skills.

The concluding section of the chapter outlined a suggested approach to assessing personal (that is, overall) competence through the identification of typical and maximum performance indicators and measures of each skill area/performance domain (Schalock, 2003).

Since writing that chapter I have thought a lot about the condition of mental retardation, read widely in the area, and discussed with many valued colleagues the essential question, "What Is Mental Retardation?" (MR). Based on those efforts, I am not sure that we are yet ready to answer that question definitively. Although I do think that we can answer the question, I would like to suggest in the present chapter that in order to do so, we need to resolve four relevant and critical scientific and judgmental issues related to the following:

1. The construct of disability.
2. The essential characteristics of MR.
3. The relationship between intelligence and adaptive behavior.
4. Defining the MR class.

The discusssion of each of these four issues on subsequent pages includes an overview of the issue and a description of the two most important impacts (summarized in Table 15.1) that the issue has on answering the question, "What Is Mental Retardation?"

Table 15.1

Four Issues and Their Impacts on Answering the Question, "What Is Mental Retardation?"

Issue	Impacts
What is a disability	1. Conceptual model of disablement
	2. Focus of intervention
Essential characteristics of MR	1. Terminology
	2. Unifying concept of MR
Relation of intelligence adaptive behavior	1. Definition of MR
	2. Definitional criteria
Defining the class	1. Diagnosis
	2. Classification systems

ISSUE # 1: WHAT IS A DISABILITY?

Overview

Mental retardation is both a biomedical defect and a social construct. Therefore, it is important to begin the process of answering the question, "What Is Mental Retardation?" with a discussion of the basic question, "What is a disability?" Answers have varied significantly over time, ranging from a strong emphasis on human defectology to the current ecological, social-system perspective (Berkson, 2004; Schalock, 2004; Switzky & Greenspan, 2003).

Both the World Health Organization in their international classification of functioning, disability, and health (ICF; WHO, 2001) and the American Association on Mental Retardation in their 1992 and 2002 diagnostic, classification, and systems of supports manuals (Luckasson et al., 1992, 2002) have adopted a dual-approach to answering the question, "What is a disability?" Although both systems are functional and ecological in their conceptual models, both also recognize the biomedical aspects of disablement. In addition, both systems stress the multidimensionality of disablement. In the ICF model, for example, functioning and disability are conceived of as a complex, dynamic interaction among three components:

1. Health condition (e.g., disease/disorder).
2. Human functioning (with associated potential activity limitations, body function and structure impairments, and participation restrictions).
3. Contextual personal and environmental factors (i.e., barriers and hindrances).

In the AAMR multidimensional models, individual functioning is influenced by intellectual abilities; adaptive behavior; participation, interactions, and social roles; health; and context. As discussed by Buntinx (2003) and Switzky and Greenspan (2003), both systems are highly compatible in their focus on: human functioning within an ecological, social-system perspective; the need to incorporate the ecological perspective into one's assessment system, including contextual factors that can act as barriers or facilitators; the need to link intervention strategies to assessment results; and the integration of the interpretive and functionalist-objectivist paradigms.

Impacts

The current focus on defining disablement in terms of human functioning within an eco-logical, social-system perspective is consistent with other aspects of the emerging disability paradigm that is challenging cultural conceptions of normality (Fujiura, 2004; Vehmas, 2004). Schalock (2004) suggests, for example, that this emerging paradigm's four major characteristics are its focus on functional skills, personal well-being, the provision of individualized supports, and the concept of personal competence that is enhanced through skill acquisition, environmental modification, and/or the use of prosthetics. How a disability is defined will have a significant impact on both the conceptual model one has of disablement, which would include the differences between mental retardation and other disabling conditions, and the focus of one's intervention.

Conceptual model of disablement.

If one stresses a biomedical or organic model, then one might conceive of MR as Haywood (2003) does, "to reserve the diagnosis of MR for those individuals who are, by virtue of extreme genetic variation or severe alteration of the nervous system, functioning in a qual-itatively different manner than those whose variation in terms of intelligence is within the normal range of genetic variation" (p. 26). If, however, one stresses an ecological, social-sys-tem model, MR might be viewed "not as an illness, a disease, or a disorder but a term describing a human condition characterized primarily by functional limitations of learning and adaptation in meeting environmental demands" (Simeonsson et al., 2003, p. 318).

The focus of intervention.

Although neither Switzky (2003) nor Coulter (2003) subscribes to a single approach to intervention, their proposed definitions of mental retardation reflect how one's conception of disablement leads to different intervention foci. Switzky (2003, p. 285), for example, refers to "substantial limitations in present functioning due to very inefficient problem-solving behaviors in various domains of life experiences as the result of significantly sub-average intellectual cognitive functioning . . . interacting with personality and motivational variables as compared to others of the same age and cultural group." On the other hand, Coulter (2003, p. 149) suggests that intellectual disabilities "describe individuals who require meaningful supports in order to achieve optimal functioning within the commu-nity because of the presence of substantial limitations in social adaptation and intellectual abilities." Within either of these two conceptions, the focus of intervention would shift from the individual solely to environmentally based opportunities and supports:

1. It would enhance the person's motivational state and positive self-concept due to increased internal locus of control.

2. It would enhance the individual's personal well-being due to increased personal competence and support network.

ISSUE # 2: THE ESSENTIAL CHARACTERISTICS OF THE CONDITION

Overview

Intellectual and social impairments are the two essential characteristics that have historically been the basis for the construction of the concept of mental retardation. They, along with an early age of onset and organicity, appear repeatedly in the literature (e.g., Doll, 1941; Greenspan, 2003; Smith, 2003; Spitz, 2003; Trent, 1995). As discussed by Devlieger (2003), both dimensions have taken on different degrees of importance at various times and both have influenced language and practice. For example, early pioneers such as Itard, Seguin, and Howe focused on the educational remediation of the condition, with the label "idiot" (defined by Webster, 1986, as "ignorant or unschooled person") used commonly throughout the 19th century. However, around the end of the 19th century, the educational focus changed to a "feebleminded" emphasis, underscoring the condition's hereditary basis. This change in emphasis and importance from an educational to a biological/medical perception was reflected in a parallel change in institutions from education and habilitation facilities to places for custodial care (Braddock & Parish, 2002; DeKraai, 2002).

Changes in terminology and the ongoing shift from an educational to a biological/medical emphasis continued into the 20th century. New terminology was introduced, including the term mental deficiency (Begab, 1975; Scheerenberger, 1983). Each of these terms—feebleminded, mental defective, and mental deficiency—was associated with different conceptions of one's learning and moral capabilities. The term mental retardation was first used in the late 1940s (Mercer, 1994), was introduced in the 1959 AAMR Terminology and Classification Manual (Heber, 1959), and was added to the *New York Times Index* in 1981 (Devlieger, 2003). Two movements significantly affected the shifting emphasis between the intellectual and social components of the [then current] conception of mental retardation: intelligence testing and the parents' movement (Devlieger, 2003; Goode, 2003). With the widespread intelligence-testing movement, the intellectual component of the condition was strengthened, owing to the application of a quantitative method for its determination that was not available for the social component. By the 1950s, however, the social component was strengthened by the parents' movement and its emphasis on education, deinstitutionalization, and professional training.

Contributors to the e-book *What Is Mental Retardation?* (Switzky & Greenspan, 2003) continue to stress that intellectual and social limitations are the two essential characteristics of the condition. However, the operationalization of this dual criterion reflects ongoing and better understanding of disability, intelligence, and adaptive behavior. Specifically, one finds throughout the volume:

- An emphasis on cognitive functioning and cognitive-related limitations (Greenspan, 2003; Switzky, 2003).
- A focus on functional and performance limitations associated with learning (Baroff, 2003; MacMillan & Siperstein, 2003) and adapting to environmental demands (Simeonsson et al., 2003).

- A multidimensional conception of intelligence (Greenspan, 2003; Switzky, 2003) and adaptive skills (Schalock, 2003; Simeonsson et al., 2003).

Impact

Clarifying the essential characteristics of MR will have two significant impacts on defining mental retardation: the first relates to the terminology we use, and the second to the unifying concept of MR on which we base our diagnostic and classification systems.

Terminology.

Language (i.e., terminology) is critical in both scientific and public discourses about MR. The term used to define the condition should reflect its essential characteristics. For example, if mental retardation is characterized by significant limitations in intellectual and social/adaptive behavior domains, terminology should reflect these characteristics. Thus, the field needs to meet the challenges of aligning terminology with practice and the class to the taxon (Glidden, 2003; Greenspan, 2003). As asked by Glidden (2003) in the title of her chapter, "Where Are Mental and Retardation in MR?" both challenges are overcome by using terminology that describes the essential characteristics of the condition. Even though etiology is an essential part of terminology, it is a separate issue. As discussed later under the fourth issue, etiology impacts how one defines the class and, more specifically, serves as the basis for one or more classification systems.

Unifying concept of MR.

Mental retardation is not a single entity but rather, as Glidden (2003) suggests, has primary, secondary, and tertiary meanings. The current literature suggests strongly that its essential characteristics include four components that need to be integrated into a unifying concept: significant limitations in intelligence and adaptive behavior; onset during the developmental period; multiple causes; and the need for intervention and individualized supports related to the significant limitations and respective cause(s). Our challenge is to align these four characteristics so that terminology reflects the essential characteristics of mental retardation, diagnosis and classification relate to defining the class, and intervention and the provision of individualized supports follow the assessment process. The age-of-onset criterion will be established via the operational definition of the developmental period. Similarly, the operational definition of limitations in intelligence and adaptive behavior will be clearly defined, depending on how the next issue regarding the relationship between intelligence and adaptive behavior is resolved.

ISSUE # 3: THE RELATIONSHIP BETWEEN INTELLIGENCE AND ADAPTIVE BEHAVIOR

Overview

Today we know that psychometric intelligence is highly correlated with measures of adaptive behavior (Detterman & Gabriel, 2003). Historically, however, these two components have varied greatly in their understanding and relative use in defining, diagnosing, and classifying persons with mental retardation. Research and conceptual efforts are underway to understand better the multidimensionality of intelligence and adaptive behavior and how these two key components of mental retardation may be merging into an integrative construct. This work can be summarized in reference to the following:

1. Understanding the multidimensional aspect of intelligence and adaptive behavior.
2. Identifying their hierarchical structure.
3. Suggesting how one might merge the two constructs into a personal-competence model of functioning.

Multidimensional aspects.

Today, there is a strong trend to consider both intelligence and adaptive behavior as multidimensional. A tripartite model of both intelligence and adaptive behavior has been proposed. For intelligence, the three factors are generally described as conceptual, social, and practical (Greenspan, 2003; Sternberg, Wagner, Williams, & Horvath, 1995). For adaptive behavior, the primary factors are conceptual (such as cognitive, communication, academic skills), practical (such as independent living skills), and social (such as social competency) (Luckasson et al., 2002; Thompson, McGrew, & Bruininks, 1999; Widaman & McGrew, 1996).

Hierarchical structure.

Just as currently there is a strong trend to consider both intelligence and adaptive behavior as multidimensional, there is also evidence that they are hierarchically arranged. Carroll (1993), for example, identified three levels of cognitive factors varying in breadth and generality: many narrow, first-level stratum factors that represent greater specialization of abilities; a smaller number of broad second-stratum factors that represent general abilities; and a single broad third-stratum factor that represents general ability. Similarly, Widaman and McGrew (1996) suggest a parallel hierarchy based on specific adaptive-behavior items, item parcels, and subscales.

Merging of intelligence and adaptive behavior.

Historically, a distinction has been made between maximum and potential performance (i.e., intelligence) and typical performance (i.e., adaptive behavior). Currently, this distinction is being questioned. Simeonsson et al. (2003) argue, for example, that

> the extensive research literature that exists on the multidimensional and interrelated nature of human functioning in physical, cognitive, social, and affective domains suggests that a distinction between intelligence and adaptive functioning is artificial (p. 313) . . . and that intellectual and adaptive elements should not be seen as dichotomous but rather as varying expressions of underlying functions of a person's adaptation to the demands of the environment. (p. 315)

Greenspan (2003) agrees with this notion, suggesting the following:

1. That the tripartite model of intelligence would allow adaptive behavior to be reconceptualized as "everyday intelligence" composed of those practical and social aspects of intelligence not tapped well by IQ (p. 205).
2. That the solution to the problem of validly defining adaptive skills is to base it more fully on the tripartite model of intelligence, which would ground it in the natural MR prototype (p. 206).

What has still not emerged completely is the construct that might be used to integrate the multiple intelligences with the multiple adaptive-behavior factors. Personal or overall competence has been proposed by Schalock (1999; 2003) and Thompson, McGrew, and Bruininks (2002). This terminology is compatible with MacMillan and Siperstein's (2003, p. 256) suggestion that the key feature of individuals with mild mental retardation is adaptive skills that focus on the areas of academic competence (particularly in school settings) and social competence (in all settings).

Impact

The change in the relationship between intelligence and adaptive behavior that appeared in the 1961 and 1973 AAMR manuals was very significant. In 1961, the definition of mental retardation referred to "subaverage general intellectual functioning *associated with* impairment in adaptive behavior" (Heber, 1961); in 1973 and 1992 mental retardation was defined as significantly subaverage intellectual functioning existing *concurrently with* deficits in adaptive behavior (Grossman, 1973; Luckasson et al., 1992). The 2002 AAMR definition referred to significant limitations in *both* intelligence and adaptive behavior. As discussed by Greenspan and Switzky (2003, p. 45), the 1973 and subsequent AAMR definitions changed the belief that adaptive behavior was a necessary outgrowth of low intelligence to adaptive behavior as separate and orthogonal from intelligence. This change reflects how the concepts of intelligence and adaptive behavior have evolved over time, including the relationship between the two. This relationship effects significantly both the definition of the condition and the criteria used to operationalize the definition.

Definition of MR.

If IQ and adaptive behavior are considered separate phenomena, then a dual approach will continue to be used. If, however, they are combined into a multidimensional construct of intelligence (or some other construct such as personal competence), then the definition might be nearer to that proposed by Greenspan (2003, p. 203), "deficiencies in social, practical, and academic intelligence," or by Switzky (2003, p. 285), "significantly sub-average intellectual cognitive functioning—e.g., social, practical, and academic intelligences." If combined into a multiple conception of adaptive behavior (with maximum and typical performance indicators), the definition might be nearer to that proposed by Schalock (2003, p. 275), "a condition characterized by significant limitations in conceptual, social, and practical skills." As we continue to discuss the definition of mental retardation, the criteria for any definition need to be kept closely in mind (Glidden, 2003, p. 78):

1. Does it conform with current usage patterns?
2. Is it unambiguous?
3. Is it functional?
4. Does it define what the label suggests that it defines?

Definitional criteria.

How three terms are operationalized reflects the second impact of this issue regarding the relation of intelligence and adaptive behavior. The first term, as just discussed, relates to the verbs "associated with vs. concurrent." This distinction denotes whether limitations in adaptive behavior are an outgrowth of low intelligence or separate and orthogonal to it. The second term is "adaptive skills vs. adaptive behavior." As discussed by MacMillan and Siperstein (2003), adaptive skills—rather than adaptive behavior—reflect observable behavior underlying cognitive processes. The third term, "significant limitations," will require revisiting where the line should be drawn. The reader is familiar with the historical controversy regarding how many standard deviation units below the mean are necessary in order for one to be considered "mentally retarded." The role of the standard error of the mean will also be a part of this discussion. How these three terms are defined will have a significant impact on the fourth issue: defining the class.

ISSUE # 4: DEFINING THE CLASS

Overview

How the class is defined will logically establish the basis for future diagnostic and classification systems. Historically, individuals with mental retardation have been diagnosed on the basis of deficits in limited intelligence and some combination of social and adaptive behavior, and classified according to different criteria such as educational (e.g., idiot, moron), IQ level (e.g., mild, moderate, severe, profound), etiology (e.g., familial vs. social-cultural), or needed levels of support (e.g., mild, moderate, severe, profound). Currently, there is a considerable focus on multiple classification systems with an increasing trend to diagnose on the basis of significant functional limitations in multidimensional components of intelligence and adaptive behavior.

Historically, four approaches have been used to identify the "class" of persons with mental retardation: social, clinical, intellectual, and dual-criterion. Although these four approaches were not mutually exclusive during the late 19th and 20th centuries, their impact is still evident in current discussions regarding who is (or should be) diagnosed as an individual with mental retardation.

Social criterion.

Initially, persons (with mental retardation) were defined or identified because they failed to adapt socially to their environment. Since an emphasis on intelligence and the role of "intelligent people" in society was to come later, the oldest historical approach was to focus on social behavior, and as Greenspan (2003, p. 203) states, " natural behavioral prototype."

Clinical criterion.

With the rise of the medical model, the focus for defining the class shifted to one's symptom complex and clinical syndrome. This approach did not negate the social criterion, but gradually there was a shift toward the role of organicity, heredity, pathology, and need for segregation (Devlieger, Rusch, & Pfeiffer, 2003).

Intellectual criterion.

With the emergence of intelligence as a viable construct to explain the class and the rise of the mental testing movement, the criterion for defining the class shifted to intellectual functioning as measured by an IQ test. This emphasis led to the emergence of IQ-based statistical norms as a way to both define the class and classify individuals within it (Devlierger, 2003).

Dual criterion.

The first attempt to use both intellectual and social criteria to define the class was found in the 1959 AAMD manual (Heber, 1959), which defined mental retardation as referring to subaverage general intellectual functioning which originates during the developmental period and is associated with impairments in maturation, learning, and social adjustments. In the 1961 AAMD manual (Heber, 1961), maturation, learning, and social adjustments were folded into a single, largely undefined new term, "adaptive behavior."

The four historical approaches just described can still be seen in current discourses about defining the class. However, three trends in the literature affect these discourses and suggest to Simeonsson et al. (2003, p. 316) the need for a comprehensive framework.

1. Diagnosing on the basis of cognitively related impairments that originate during the developmental period.
2. Classifying on the basis of known etiology.
3. Recognizing the role of clinical judgment.

Diagnosing on the basis of cognitively-related impairments.

For some (e.g., Greenspan & Switzky, 2003), these impairments are in conceptual, social, and practical skills. For others it is learning that is impaired. Baroff (2003), for example suggests that MR should be defined as "a general learning disorder that affects all intellectual domains" (p. 73). Similarly, MacMillan and Siperstein (2003) discuss the need to recognize as a distinct group those individuals who have traditionally been diagnosed as mild mentally retarded. According to these authors, the key feature for this group is the need to emphasize adaptive skills that focus on the areas of academic and social competence.

Classifying on the basis of known etiology.

Numerous contributors to *What Is Mental Retardation?* support this trend. Baumeister (2003, p. 141), for example, argues that "mental retardation is a biological condition whose etiology is increasingly being understood." As definitive causes of MR become known, the utility of a classification system based on etiology is appealing. For example, the 2002 AAMR manual (Luckasson et al., 2002, p. 129) outlines a multifactorial and intergenerational model of mental retardation etiology and prevention including risk factors related to biomedical, social, environmental, and educational categories.

There are a number of advantages to an etiological-based classification system (Hodapp & Dykens, 2003). One is that it would align the "class" with the "taxon" and thereby implement a true taxonomy dealing with scientific classification as found in biological and medical sciences (Switzky, 2003, p. 252). Such a system would also meet the criterion discussed by Simeonsson et al. (2003, p. 317) that a classification system should organize information in mutually exclusive categories that are hierarchically arranged with subordinate items listed under superordinate goals. Although such a system could align classification with intervention strategies, much remains to be understood about the extent of genetically linked disabilities (Henderson, 2004).

Recognizing the role of clinical judgment.

Clinical judgment and clinical criteria have historically been part of defining the MR class and implementing a diagnostic and classification process. The concept of clinical judgment has emerged as one way to resolve many of the challenges surrounding the issue of defining the class (Luckasson et al., 2002). These challenges relate to the following:

1. Standardized testing that is less than optimal but for some reason cannot be improved.
2. Complex medical or behavioral conditions that require multiple perspectives and analysis.
3. Legal restrictions that impact assessment opportunities.
4. Cultural and/or linguistic diversity that affects the information needed for decisions.

Recognizing the role of clinical judgment in defining the class requires that one understands clinical judgment and how to increase its credibility by developing essential clinical competencies and implementing best practices.

Best practices in the field of mental retardation are grounded in research-based knowledge combined with professional ethics, professional standards, and clinical judgment. Clinical judgment is a special type of judgment rooted in a high level of clinical expertise and experience and emerging directly from extensive data. It is based on the clinician's explicit training, direct experiences with persons with whom the clinician is working, and familiarity with the person and the person's environment. Clinical judgment includes competencies that involve the knowledge and ability to: apply broad-based assessment strategies; conduct a through social history; implement and evaluate intervention best practices; plan, implement, and evaluate individualized supports; reflect cultural competence; and align data and its collection to the critical questions asked (Schalock & Luckasson, in preparation).

Impact

How one defines the class will provide the basis for any proposed diagnostic and classification systems. Building on the three trends just discussed regarding diagnosis, classification, and clinical judgment, a number of points need to be considered in reference to diagnosis and classification.

Diagnosis.

Generally, the primary purposes for diagnosis are to clarify etiology, to suggest treatment, and to certify eligibility. However, these purposes and the label associated with the diagnosis may differ depending on whose perspective is examined: individuals labeled as having mental retardation, parents and family members, or professionals (Snell & Voorhees, 2003). A related point is that these purposes may reflect two different types of thinking (Gelb, 1997): typological vs. population. Typological thinking focuses on sorting people into groups that differ from other groups and emphasizing measurement. In contrast, population thinking focuses on individual characteristics and current functioning, emphasizing the provision of individualized services and supports. These multiple purposes and types of thinking underlie the current debate about the term MR and the desire among many to find a term that is less stigmatizing (Nelis, 2003; Goode, 2003; Snell & Voorhees, 2003), more precise, and more humane (Smith, 2003). It may also account for the significant increase in the diagnosis of "learning disabled" as opposed to "mentally retarded" in public education (MacMillan & Siperstein, 2003).

Classification.

A classification system has many purposes including those related to description, intervention, and research. Although multiple classification systems are possible (Luckasson et al., 2002), their use involves both concerns and criteria. Hodapp and Dykens (2003), for example, discuss internal and external concerns. Internal concerns relate to how conceptually and practically straightforward the system is to implement; external concerns relate to what one gains from using a particular classification system. Other concerns are expressed by Greenspan (2003) and Verdugo (2003). Greenspan distinguishes between false negatives (i.e., some deserving cases declared ineligible) and false positives (i.e., wrongly given unnecessary and inappropriate services). Verdugo discusses concerns related to focusing on limitations rather than strengths, establishing a self-fulfilling prophecy, increasing one's negative self concept, creating a social hierarchy, and/or limiting an ecological approach to rehabilitation.

A number of criteria have been proposed for the development and use of a classification system. Seltzer (1983), for example, suggests the following five: clarity, coverage, reliability, clinical utility, and acceptability. To those, Jacobson and Mulick (2003) add consensual utility, and Simeonsson et al. (2003) add a hierarchical format with subordinate entities being subsumed under superordinate headings.

Summary and Conclusions

My sense is that there will always be outstanding issues and debates in the field of mental retardation due to the social construction of disability and disablement. If history is any guide, the concept of mental retardation and its amelioration will continue to evolve. In this chapter, I have discussed four issues that should establish our near-term agenda and that lie at the heart of defining mental retardation. The process needs to begin with asking and answering the question, "What is a disability?" Once the conceptual model of disablement and the focus of intervention are clear, then by combining the best of scientific and judgmental processes, we can collaboratively and successfully address key scientific and judgmental issues related to the essential characteristics of the condition, the relationship between intelligence and adaptive behavior, and how to define the class.

Some time ago, Sarason (1985) observed that "mental retardation is never a thing or characteristic of an individual, but rather a social invention stemming from time-bound societal values and ideology that makes diagnosis and management seem both necessary and socially desirable" (p. 233). It was good advice then, and it is good advice now, as we think about the scientific and judgmental issues that will impact how we answer the question, "What Is Mental Retardation?"

References

Baroff, G. S. (2003). Mental retardation: Some issues of concern. In H. N. Switzky & S. Greenspan (Eds.), *What Is Mental Retardation? Ideas for an evolving disability* (pp. 67–74). Washington, DC: American Association on Mental Retardation [E-Book]. Available at http://www.disabilitybooksonline.com

Baumeister, A. A. (2003). The meaning of mental retardation: Sentiment versus science. In H. N. Switzky & S. Greenspan (Eds.), *What Is Mental Retardation? Ideas for an evolving disability* (pp. 127–146). Washington, DC: American Association on Mental Retardation [E-Book]. Available at http://www.disabilitybooksonline.com

Begab, M. J. (1975). The mentally retarded and society: Trends and issues. In M. J. Begab & S. A. Richardson (Eds.), *The Mentally retarded and society: A social science perspective* (pp. 3–32). Baltimore: University Park Press.

Berkson, G. (2004). Intellectual and physical disabilities in prehistory and early civilization. *Mental Retardation, 42*(3), 195–208.

Braddock, D., & Parish, S. L. (2002). An institutional history of disability. In D. Braddock (Ed.), *Disability at the dawn of the 21st century and the state of the states* (pp. 3–76). Washington, DC: American Association on Mental Retardation.

Buntinx, W. (2003). Mental retardation: The relation between the AAMR definition and the International Classification of Functioning, Disability, and Health. In H. N. Switzky & S. Greenspan (Eds.), *What Is Mental Retardation? Ideas for an evolving disability* (pp. 352–370). Washington, DC: American Association on Mental Retardation [E-Book]. Available at http://www.disabilitybooksonline.com

Carroll, J. B. (1993). *Human cognitive abilities: A summary of factor analytic studies.* New York: Cambridge University Press.

Coulter, D. A. (2003). Neighbors and friends: Social implications of intellectual disabilities. In H. N. Switzky & S. Greenspan (Eds.), *What Is Mental Retardation? Ideas for an evolving disability* (pp. 147–154). Washington, DC: American Association on Mental Retardation [E-Book]. Available at http://www.disabilitybooksonline.com

DeKraai, M. (2002). In the beginning: The first hundred years (1850 to 1950). In R. L. Schalock (Ed.), *Out of the darkness and into the light: Nebraska's experience with mental retardation* (pp. 103–122). Washington, DC: American Association on Mental Retardation.

Detterman, D. K., & Gabriel, L. T. (2003). Look before you leap: Implications of the 1992 definition of mental retardation. In H. N. Switzky & S. Greenspan (Eds.), *What Is Mental Retardation? Ideas for an evolving disability* (pp. 155–166). Washington, DC: American Association on Mental Retardation [E-Book]. Available at http://www.disabilitybooksonline.com

Devlieger, J. P. (2003). From "idiot" to "person with mental retardation": Defining differences in an effort to dissolve it. In J. P. Devlieger, F. Rusch, & D. Pfeiffer (Eds.), *Rethinking disability: The emergence of new definitions, concepts, and communities* (pp. 169–188). Antwerp, Belgium: Garant.

Devlieger, J. P., Rusch, F., & Pfeiffer, D. (2003). Rethinking disability as same and different: Towards a cultural model of disability. In J. P. Devlieger, F. Rusch, & D. Pfeiffer (Eds.), *Rethinking disability: The emergence of new definitions, concepts, and communities* (pp. 9–16). Antwerp, Belgium: Garant.

Doll, E. A. (1941). The essentials of an inclusive concept of mental deficiency. *American Journal of Mental Deficiency, 46,* 214–219.

Fujiura, G. T. (2004, June). *Disability epidemiology in the developing world.* Paper presented at the 12th World Congress, International Association for the Scientific Study of Intellectual Disabilities, Montpellier, France.

Gelb, S. A. (1997). The problem of typological thinking in mental retardation. *Mental Retardation, 35,* 448–457.

Glidden, L. M. (2003). Where are the *mental* and *retardation* in mental retardation? In H. N. Switzky & S. Greenspan (Eds.), *What Is Mental Retardation? Ideas for an evolving disability* (pp. 75–86). Washington, DC: American Association on Mental Retardation [E-Book]. Available at http://www.disabilitybooksonline.com

Goode, D. A. (2003). What was "mental retardation"? In H. N. Switzky & S. Greenspan (Eds.), *What Is Mental Retardation? Ideas for an evolving disability* (pp. 167–181). Washington, DC: American Association on Mental Retardation [E-Book]. Available at http://www.disability-booksonline.com

Greenspan, S. (2003). Mental retardation: Some issues of concern. In H. N. Switzky & S. Greenspan (Eds.), *What Is Mental Retardation? Ideas for an evolving disability* (pp. 64–74). Washington, DC: American Association on Mental Retardation [E-Book]. Available at http://www.disabilitybooksonline.com

Grossman, H. J. (Ed.). (1973). *Manual on terminology and classification in mental retardation (1973 revision)*. Washington, DC: American Association on Mental Deficiency.

Haywood, H. C. (2003). Foreword: Global perspectives on mental retardation. In H. N. Switzky & S. Greenspan (Eds.), *What Is Mental Retardation? Ideas for an evolving disability* (pp. 20–26). Washington, DC: American Association on Mental Retardation [E-Book]. Available at http://www.disabilitybooksonline.com

Heber, R. (1959). A manual on terminology and classification in mental retardation [Monograph Supplement]. *American Journal of Mental Deficiency, 64*(2).

Heber, R. (1961). A manual on terminology and classification on mental retardation (2nd ed.) [Monograph Supplement]. *American Association of Mental Deficiency.*

Henderson, C. M. (2004). Genetically-linked syndromes in intellectual disabilities. *Journal of Policy and Practice in Intellectual Disabilities, 1*(1), 31–41.

Hodapp, R. M., & Dykens, E. M. (2003). Looking to the 21st century: Toward an etiology-based classification system. In H. N. Switzky & S. Greenspan (Eds.), *What Is Mental Retardation? Ideas for an evolving disability* (p. 219). Washington, DC: American Association on Mental Retardation [E-Book]. Available at http://www.disabilitybooksonline.com

Jacobson, J. W., & Mulick, J. A. (2003). Defining mental retardation or the incurability of ideological imbecility. In H. N. Switzky & S. Greenspan (Eds.), *What Is Mental Retardation? Ideas for an evolving disability* (pp. 230–241). Washington, DC: American Association on Mental Retardation [E-Book]. Available at http://www.disabilitybooksonline.com

Luckasson, R., Borthwick-Duffy, S., Buntinx, W. H. E., Coulter. D. L., Craig, E. M., Reeve, A., et al. (2002). *Mental retardation: Definition, classification, and systems of supports* (10th ed.). Washington, DC: American Association on Mental Retardation.

Luckasson, R., Coulter, D. L., Polloway, E. A., Reiss, S., Schalock, R. L., Snell, M. E., et al. (1992). *Mental retardation: Definition, classification, and systems of supports (9th ed.)*. Washington, DC: American Association on Mental Retardation.

MacMillan, D. L., Siperstein, G. N., & Leffert, J. S. (2003). Children with mild mental retardation: A challenge for classification practices. In H. N. Switzky & S. Greenspan (Eds.), *What Is Mental Retardation? Ideas for an evolving disability* (pp. 242–261). Washington, DC: American Association on Mental Retardation [E-Book]. Available at http://www.disabilitybooksonline.com

Mercer, J. R. (1994). Historical and current perspectives on the definition of mental retardation. *American Association on Mental Retardation Psychology Division Newsletter, 26–27.*

Nelis, T. (2003). Labels, labels, labels: Who needs them anyway? [Foreword]. In H. N. Switzky & S. Greenspan (Eds.), *What Is Mental Retardation? Ideas for an evolving disability* (pp. 33–35). Washington, DC: American Association on Mental Retardation [E-Book]. Available at http://www.disabilitybooksonline.com

Sarason, S. (1985). *Psychology and mental retardation: Perspectives in change*. Austin, TX: Pro-Ed.

Schalock, R. L. (2003). Mental retardation: A condition characterized by significant limitations in practical, conceptual and social skills. In H. N. Switzky & S. Greenspan (Eds.), *What Is Mental Retardation? Ideas for an evolving disability* (pp. 271–283). Washington, DC: American Association on Mental Retardation [E-Book]. Available at http://www.disabilitybooksonline.com

Schalock, R. L. (2004). The emerging disability paradigm and its implications for policy and practices. *Journal of Disability Policy Studies, 14*(4), 204–215.

Schalock, R. L. (Ed.). (1999). *Adaptive behavior and its measurement: Implications for the field of mental retardation.* Washington, DC: American Association on Mental Retardation.

Schalock, R. L., & Luckasson, R. (Manuscript in preparation.). *Clinical judgment in mental retardation: Framework and competence.*

Scheerenberger, R. (1983). *A history of mental retardation.* Baltimore: Paul H. Brookes.

Seltzer, G. B. (1983). Systems of classification. In J. L. Matson and J. A. Mulick (Eds.), *Handbook of Mental Retardation* (pp. 143–156). New York: Pergamon.

Simeonsson, R. J., Granlund, M., & Bjorck-Akesson, E. (2002). Classifying mental retardation: Impairment, disability, handicap, limitations, or restrictions? In H. N. Switzky & S. Greenspan (Eds.), *What Is Mental Retardation? Ideas for an evolving disability* (pp. 309–329). Washington, DC: American Association on Mental Retardation [E-Book]. Available at http://www.disabilitybooksonline.com

Smith, J. D. (2003). Constructing and deconstructing mental retardation: A history of aggregation and the hope for individual futures. In H. N. Switzky & S. Greenspan (Eds.), *What Is Mental Retardation? Ideas for an evolving disability* (pp. 87–96). Washington, DC: American Association on Mental Retardation [E-Book]. Available at http://www.disabilitybooksonline.com

Snell, M. E., & Voorhees, M. D. (2003). Mental retardation: Does the label bring support or stigma? In H. N. Switzky & S. Greenspan (Eds.), *What Is Mental Retardation? Ideas for an evolving disability* (pp. 97–116). Washington, DC: American Association on Mental Retardation [E-Book]. Available at http://www.disabilitybooksonline.com

Spitz, H. H. (2003). How we eradicated familial (hereditary) mental retardation. In H. N. Switzky & S. Greenspan (Eds.), *What Is Mental Retardation? Ideas for an evolving disability* (pp. 117–124). Washington, DC: American Association on Mental Retardation [E-Book]. Available at http://www.disabilitybooksonline.com

Sternberg, R. J., Wagner, R. K., Williams, W. M., & Horvath, J. A. (1995). Testing common sense. *American Psychologist, 50*(11), 912–927.

Switzky, H. N. (2003). A cognitive-motivational perspective on mental retardation. In H. N. Switzky & S. Greenspan (Eds.), *What Is Mental Retardation? Ideas for an evolving disability* (pp. 284–295). Washington, DC: American Association on Mental Retardation [E-Book]. Available at http://www.disabilitybooksonline.com

Switzky, H. N., & Greenspan, S. (2003a). Can so many diverse ideas be integrated? Multiparadigmatic models of understanding mental retardation. In *What Is Mental Retardation? Ideas for an evolving disability* (pp. 387–405). Washington, DC: American Association on Mental Retardation [E-Book]. Available at http://www.disabilitybooksonline.com

Switzky, H. N., & Greenspan, S. (Eds.). (2003b). *What Is Mental Retardation? Ideas for an evolving disability.* Washington, DC: American Association on Mental Retardation [E-Book]. Available at http://www.disabilitybooksonline.com

Thompson, J. R., McGrew, K. S., & Bruininks, R. H. (1999). Adaptive behavior and maladaptive behavior: Functional and structural characteristics. In R. L. Schalock (Ed.), *Adaptive behavior and its measurement: Implications for the field of mental retardation* (pp. 15–42). Washington, DC: American Association on Mental Retardation.

Thompson, J. R., McGrew, K. S., & Bruininks, R. H. (2002). Pieces of the puzzle: Measuring the personal competence and support needs of persons with mental retardation and related developmental disabilities. *Peabody Journal of Education, 77*(2), 21–37.

Trent, J. W., Jr. (1995). *Suffering fools.* New York: New York Academy of Sciences.

Vehmas, S. (2004). Ethical analysis of the concept of disability. *Mental Retardation, 42*(3), 209–222.

Verdugo, M. A. (2003). A step ahead of the paradigm shift. In H. N. Switzky & S. Greenspan (Eds.), *What Is Mental Retardation? Ideas for an evolving disability* (pp. 296–308). Washington, DC: American Association on Mental Retardation [E-Book]. Available at http://www.disabilitybooksonline.com

Webster. (1986). *Webster's 10th new collegiate dictionary.* Springfield, MA: Merriam-Webster.

Widaman, K. F., & McGrew, K. S. (1996). The structure of adaptive behavior: In J. W. Jacobson & J. A. Mulick (Eds.), *Manual of diagnosis and professional practice in mental retardation* (pp. 97–110). Washington, DC: American Psychological Association.

World Health Organization. (2001). *International classification of functioning, disability, and health (ICF)*. Geneva: Author.

Chapter Sixteen

The Concept and Classification of Mental Retardation

Rune J. Simeonsson, Mats Granlund, and Eva Bjorck-Akesson

While limited cognitive functioning has long been recognized as part of the human condition, how it has been defined has evolved over time. In the context of the middle 19th century, Howe (1848) defined idiocy as "that condition of a human being that in which, from some morbid cause in the bodily organization remain dormant or underdeveloped, so that the person is incapable of self-guidance, and of approaching that degree of knowledge usual with other of his age" (Howe, 1848, p. 20, in Trent, 2003, p. 18). Now in the 21st century, a dictionary defines *mental retardation* as "a disorder characterized by subaverage general intellectual function with deficits or impairments in the ability to learn and to adapt socially. The cause may be genetic, biologic, psychosocial or socio-cultural" (Mosby, 2002, p. 1080). A search in the same dictionary for the related term *mental deficiency* was only cross-referenced to mental retardation. On the other hand, the term *mental handicap* was defined as "any mental defect or characteristic resulting from a congenital abnormality, traumatic injury or disease that impairs normal intellectual functioning and prevents a person from participating normally in activities appropriate for a particular age group" (Mosby, 2002, p. 1080).

In another dictionary, no definitions were found for the terms mental deficiency or *mental handicap* but *mental retardation* was defined as "sub-average general intellectual functioning that originates during the developmental period and is associated with impairment in adaptive behavior. Mental retardation classification requires assignment of an index for performance relative to a person's peers on two interrelated criteria: measured intelligence (IQ scores) and overall socio-adaptive behavior. In general, an IQ of 70 or lower indicates mental retardation" (Stedman's, 2005, p. 906). This last definition is similar to the criteria provided in DSM-IV Technical Review (APA, 2000) for the diagnostic code for mental retardation. Specifically, there are three elements to the code:

(A) Significantly subaverage intellectual functioning: an IQ of approximately 70 or below on an individually administered IQ test (for infants, a clinical judgment of significantly subaverage intellectual functioning). (B) Concurrent deficit or impairments in present adaptive functioning (i.e., the person's effectiveness in meeting the standards expected for his or her age by his or her cultural group), in at least two of the following areas: communication, self-care, home living, social/interpersonal skills, use of community resources, self direction, functional academic skills, work, leisure, health, and safety. (C) The onset is before age 18 years.

In DSM-IV TR-2000, the severity of intellectual impairment is reflected by codes for the following IQ levels:(317) mild 50–55 to approx. 70; (318.0) moderate 35–40 to 50–55; (318.1) severe 20–25 to 35–40; (318.2) profound < 20–25; (319) severity unspecified.

The above definitions and diagnostic criteria reflect the variability currently surrounding the definition of mental retardation. The American Association on Mental Retardation, the U.S. professional organization in the field, has published 10 editions of its classification to provide a standard for the profession. The ninth and tenth editions, one published in 1992, and the other in 2002, Definition, Classification and Systems of Support (hereafter referred to as the AAMR 2002 system), however, differed significantly from earlier editions. A consequence of those differences was that the ninth edition was not widely accepted in the field and the place of the tenth edition as a standard has not been established. In the broader context of the changing paradigm of disability, there is clearly a need for a standard definition and classification of mental retardation with implications for policy, practice, and research on behalf of persons with mental retardation.

The purpose of this chapter is to address the following:

1. Examine the concept of mental retardation.
2. Review the AAMR 2002 system.
3. Propose steps to advance the definition and classification of mental retardation, building on a dimensional view of human functioning.

In the context of this chapter, the term *mental retardation* is used in light of its current acceptance to designate this human condition. However, as Devlieger (1998) has noted, acceptance of this term is specific to the United States, as different terms are used in other English speaking countries. In the United Kingdom for example, "learning disability" refers to mental retardation (O'Brien, 2001), and the International Association for the Scientific Study of Intellectual Disability uses the term "intellectual disability." Although the term mental retardation is used in this chapter, examination of it as a concept and review of the AAMR 2002 system are not tied to the term itself, but rather to the condition it represents.

THE CONCEPT AND CLASSIFICATION OF MENTAL RETARDATION

What Is Mental Retardation?

A review of books and journals pertaining to mental retardation reveals a wide variety of terms used to describe the condition. The title of a recent medical article, for example, used the term mental retardation as a frame for its content (Toutain et al., 1997). The body of the article included the terms intellectual handicap, mental handicap, and mental deficiency. Do these and other terms such as cognitive impairment, developmental disability, and intellectual disability all define the same phenomenon? Are the terms interchangeable? Alternatively, do the different terms convey different meanings? Is there a distinction between intellectual and mental functioning? In any case what constitutes the condition of limited cognitive functioning, and what should it be named?

In general, mental retardation and other terms such as those listed above appear to be used interchangeably to define a human condition of reduced cognitive ability. From scientific and policy perspectives, however, variability of definitions and terminology contributes to a number of fundamental problems related to measurement and to diagnostic and epidemiological studies of mental retardation. An example of these problems is the varying role of IQ in different approaches to defining the condition (O'Brien, 2001). As Greenspan (1999) has noted, defining the phenomenon of mental retardation has been a persistent challenge reflected by changing historical contexts as well as shifting criteria. Transcending terminological variability is the more basic issue of defining the concept of mental retardation.

Given the variability of nomenclature in the field, an examination of mental retardation as a concept would be useful as the context for a systematic review of the AAMR 2002 system. This examination will be couched within an analytic approach to the concept of mental retardation. Other approaches have been advanced for defining and framing mental retardation, including social construction and metaphor (Gustavsson, 2000; Smith, 1999), western epistemology (Stainton, 2001), and a contextual, narrative framework (Biklen & Schein, 2001). These approaches are acknowledged but not reviewed here, given the nature and analytic focus of this review.

The terminology for mental retardation should be based on the identification of the phenomenon it represents. In the English language, the current term mental retardation and earlier terms such as mental defect, mental deficiency, and mental handicap all involve the combination of the word "mental" with other words conveying a non-normal condition. Given that the word "mental" refers to the entity of mind, combining the words "mental" and "retardation" does not parallel the combination of other terms such as mental illness and mental disorders. Illness of the mind and disorders of the mind are logical combinations of words conveying a non-normal or atypical state of functioning of the mind. Retardation of the mind does not convey the similar logic. If it is essential that the word "mental" has to define the condition of mental retardation, logical combinations would take such forms as mental impairment or mental disability. The word "retardation" conveys delay or a decrease in rate. Logical uses of the word "retardation" would thus be to combine it with process words resulting in terms such as learning, cognitive or developmental retardation. While the above terminological problems may be specific to the English language, the issue of matching appropriate terminology to the concept of limited cognitive ability is likely to cut across languages.

One of the cardinal criteria defining mental retardation is that it originates during the developmental period, typically defined as the first two decades of life. While mental retardation has its origin in the developmental period, the functional status or outcome of the person in later life is not fixed but reflects the product of developmental processes. The focus on variations in developmental processes as defining features of the condition of mental retardation is consistent with research and theory that has emphasized level of functioning as continually modified by the person's interaction with the environment.

This premise has been defined in the developmental literature as the transactional model (Sameroff & Chandler, 1975), describing a continuum of developmental outcomes as a function of the nature of person-environment interactions over time. This model accounts for different developmental outcomes for individuals with disabilities in spite of the fact that they may share a common etiology.

The premise of ongoing transactions between the individual and the environment has also been acknowledged as the significant variable accounting for different manifestations of disability. In this context, there has been a rejection of the "medical model" in which disability was attributed to characteristics within a person. A broader "social model" has emerged in which disability is attributed to a person's interactions with environments which are inaccessible, inadequate, and unsupportive of the development of the individual. Disablement defines the process in which person-environment interactions contribute to, and exacerbate, disability over time.

The significance of the role of the environment in mediating the nature and extent of disability was recognized by Begab and Laveck (1972) more than three decades ago. Within their perspective of mental retardation, "the individual's functional performance is the product of the interaction of his biological makeup and environmental events" (1972, p. 1437). A similar position has been articulated by Soder's (1987) relative definition of handicap, which emphasized the interaction of individual and environmental factors in mental retardation.

At a phenomenological level, the central features of the interaction of the person with the environment are a reduced rate of learning and delayed acquisition of skills during development, resulting in a failure to achieve ultimate, mature levels of cognitive functioning. Variations in developmental processes reflecting reduced or delayed rates of learning served as a significant framework for mental retardation research in the middle of the 20th century. This approach was the basis for extensive contributions on the processes of memory, perception, habituation, discrimination, and learning in the experimental psychology of mental retardation (Ellis, 1966).

Variation in rates of learning and cognitive processes as the key features of mental retardation is also consistent with a qualitative perspective of development. Building on Piaget's cognitive theory, Inhelder (1966) defined mental retardation as the failure to achieve the stage of formal operations, reflected by hypothetical and deductive thinking at maturity. Increasing severity of mental retardation was seen to correspond with arrested functioning at lower stages of cognitive development. In a related application, Kylen (1985) drew on the nature of cognitive functioning in Piaget's theory in proposing a classification framework for mental retardation in Sweden. Three aspects of cognition were identified: organization-reorganization, operations within cognitive structures, and symbolization. The three aspects of cognitive functions and five content dimensions were incorporated within the four levels of abstraction in Piaget's theory. The first three levels describe cognitive functioning in persons with mental retardation. The classification framework has been used for the construction and provision of assistive technology for persons with mental retardation (Granlund et al., 1995). It has also been used as the basis for adaptation of information—for example, in the translation of daily news to a lower level of abstraction (Goransson, 1985).

As noted above, current terms include mental retardation in the United States, learning disability in the United Kingdom, and intellectual disabilities in international society. This variability is undoubtedly multiplied across different languages. A contributing factor to the variability is the use of imprecise words such as "mental" or "intellectual" in combination with terms denoting non-normal states. This chapter advances the position that variations in cognitive and learning processes are the essential features of the condition currently defined as mental retardation. Terminology should appropriately reflect these features. To that end, the contemporary use of the term "learning disability" in the United Kingdom most closely reflects the nature of the condition. It is unfortunate that this term has been pre-empted for another condition in the United States. A further irony is that the term explicitly excludes the condition of mental retardation. it is essential that the search for improved terms continue, with the goal of selecting words that most accurately reflect the nature of the condition and is respectful of persons.

REVIEW OF AAMR 2002 SYSTEM

Description

The AAMR's *Definition, Classification, and Systems of Support* (Luckasson et al., 2002) consist of a manual and a workbook. As the tenth edition of the Association's classification, it retains the essential features of the ninth edition published in 1992 while expanding selected elements. The AAMR 2002 system can be summarized as consisting of a definition with three elements, five supportive assumptions, a graphic framework encompassing five dimensions, and three functions of assessment. With reference to the definition, the term mental retardation continues to be defined as limitations of intellectual functioning and adaptive behavior with onset occurring before age 18. Specifically the manual states: "Mental retardation is a disability characterized by significant limitations both in intellectual functioning and in adaptive behavior as expressed in conceptual, social, and practical adaptive skills. The disability originates before age 18" (Luckasson et al., 2002, p. 8). The manual specifies that the application of the definition requires consideration of the following five assumptions, which were also specified for the 1992 definition:

1. Limitations in present functioning must be considered within the context of community environments typical of the individual's age, peers, and culture.
2. Valid assessment considers cultural and linguistic diversity as well as differences in communication, sensory, motor, and behavioral factors.
3. Within an individual, limitations often coexist with strengths.
4. An important purpose of describing limitations is to develop a profile of needed supports.
5. With appropriate personalized supports over a sustained period, the life functioning of the person with mental retardation will generally improve.

The theoretical model advanced for the 2002 definition emphasizes a multidimensional approach to mental retardation with five elements. The four dimensions of the ninth edition were expanded to five in the tenth edition for greater focus on participation, interaction and social roles, and context. This focus was designed to reflect the contribution of the

International Classification of Functioning, Disability and Health (ICF) (WHO, 2001). The dimensions of the AAMR 2002 system are as follows:

Dimension I: Intellectual abilities
Dimension II: Adaptive behavior (conceptual, social, practical skills)
Dimension III: Participation, interactions, and social roles
Dimension IV: Health (physical health, mental health, etiology)
Dimension V: Context (environments, culture)

A three-function process is presented as an approach to integrate the use of the AAMR 2002 system. In this framework, the first function is that of diagnosis of mental retardation. Classification is described as the second function, involving documentation of strengths and deficits within the five dimensions. The purpose of the third function is to identify the supports that an individual might need within nine support areas. Each function has a number of specific purposes together with associated measurement instruments and tools for assessment.

It is recognized at the outset that a primary purpose of the AAMR 2002 system is to provide a framework for advocacy to enhance the identification, planning, and implementation of resources and supports for persons with mental retardation. This review does not question the merit of the manual in this regard, although there may well be issues that need to be examined in that context. The purpose of this review is to analyze the AAMR 2002 system in terms of its structure and content as a scientific document. To that end, the review will draw on a set of guiding questions in the manual, initially written by Luckasson and Reeve (2001) to frame activities of naming, defining, and classifying in the development of the AAMR 2002 system. Selected questions are used to provide a systematic and ordered approach to the review process.

Review of Structure

Naming.

The questions that guide the review of naming are summarized as follows: Is the name exclusive to the phenomenon? Does it advance a consistent nomenclature for communication? Does it reflect the current state of knowledge and can it accommodate changes in that knowledge? Naming is the prerequisite for defining and ultimately for classifying the phenomenon of mental retardation. Although the authors maintain that naming was not within the scope of the AAMR 2002 manual's development, their use of the term "mental retardation" makes naming an implicit part of the process. Accordingly, it will be included in the focus of the review.

As noted earlier, mental retardation is a term that is neither logical nor precise and does not provide a parsimonious description of the phenomenon It fails to accurately convey the essence of what characterizes persons with this condition, namely a reduced ability to learn. Use of the term mental retardation in the 2002 system is a naming problem and does in fact influence what is defined and classified.

A related problem is confounding the classification of the condition with classification of persons with the condition. Any term describing reduced cognitive ability may become stigmatizing over time. The search should always be for one that is most parsimonious and respectful of persons. The term "learning disability" has a functional emphasis and is parsimonious, reflecting learning difficulties a person may have in meeting environmental demands. Framing it in this manner reflects the condition as a variation of a universal characteristic and makes it less likely to become pejorative.

Defining.

The questions that guide the review of defining the phenomenon of mental retardation are summarized as follows: Is the definition bounded by inclusion and exclusion criteria? Does the definition specify the class of things to which it belongs and does it differentiate the term from other members of the class? Are the words used in the definition no more complicated than the term itself? Is the definition based on a theoretical framework?

The phenomenon of mental retardation has been particularly challenging to define, as evidenced by changing terms over time and variability among current terms. Earlier terms such as feebleminded and moron often drew on nonscientific labels and were pejorative in nature. With the evolution of a more scientific approach, there was a shift in the terminology. The problem was defined as mental in nature and qualified by terms such as deficiency, defect, handicap, or more recently retardation.

While genetic and biological factors are etiologies for mental retardation, mental retardation is not an illness, disease, or disorder. It describes a human condition characterized by limitations in cognitive processes such as learning, memory, comprehension, reasoning, and problem solving, and it should be defined accordingly. Although a comprehensive classification of mental retardation should include associated etiological factors as well as physical manifestations, a primary component should be documentation of the nature and extent of limitations of cognitive functions.

An important consideration here is to use medical classifications or include etiological and medical information that is complementary to that of existing classifications. The need to distinguish between biological aspects and functional manifestations is not a problem unique to mental retardation; it applies to most conditions currently associated with the word "disability" (e.g., physical disability, learning disability, developmental disability).

The current definition (Luckasson et al., 1992) is not exclusive to MR in that it encompasses more than the condition of MR; it includes both intelligence and behavior. To be logically consistent with this definition, the term should be "mental and behavioral retardation." In the AAMR 2002 system, adaptive behavior is presented as a distinct element of mental retardation, separate from intelligence. Adaptive behavior, however, is not a separate and independent component of MR but an expression of underlying cognitive ability in meeting environmental demands. The fact that a variety of tools exist for measuring adaptive behavior does not mean that it is a separate element from measured cognitive ability. This is supported by the fact that the correlation between measures of intelligence and adaptive behavior is generally high. The definition of mental retardation should be restricted solely to the intellectual or cognitive dimension, a position that Zigler (1987) has maintained for some time.

Classifying.

Three questions can be considered with regard to the review of "classifying" a phenomenon: Does the classification contribute to a systematic, hierarchical way of organizing knowledge? Is the classification based on a coherent theoretical framework? Does the classification system contribute a base for efficient organization of knowledge for application to practice?

Classification requires that the objects or phenomena of interest be defined and assigned into a logical structure—a hierarchical one in which higher-order entries are followed by lower order entries defining subordinate elements. The central feature is that the classification should be inclusive of the phenomena defined. All of the phenomena should logically belong in the class. Inherent in any classification is a clear delineation of content and a structure for the systematic classification of that content. In the International Classification of Disease (ICD-10) and the Diagnostic and Statistical Manual (DSM-IV-TR), the content that is classified is defined by diseases and mental disorders, respectively. Diagnosis of a disease entity or disorder according to specified criteria serves as the basis for hierarchical and mutually exclusive classification in a dimensional or multi-axial structure. Based on the biological and mental characteristics associated with mental retardation, diagnostic entries have been included in the ICD-10 and DSM-IV-TR, respectively. In this context, aspects of mental retardation are included in the respective classifications as entities within broader arrays of physical and mental conditions found in the population.

In the AAMR 2002 system, by contrast, mental retardation is approached as a restricted segment of human cognitive functioning. As such, the system encompasses a particular characteristic of human functioning that applies to a limited group, approximately the lowest 3% of the population. . In the AAMR 2002 system, the name and the definition refer to a condition, however, the classification is of characteristics and things associated with the person. A question that derives from this contrast is, should the unit of classification be the phenomenon of mental retardation or the person identified with the condition of mental retardation? The phenomenon rather than the person with the condition should be the unit for classification and would serve as a logical basis for ordering dimensions of mental retardation.

In keeping with the title, the AAMR 2002 system consists of a definition, a classification for describing strengths and limitations, and a list of areas of supports. Ironically, there appears to be no clear stated purpose for the manual, although a practical application can be inferred from the statement that it "includes a framework for assessment that involves three functions: diagnosis, classification, and planning supports" (Luckasson et al., 2002, p. 10). The Workbook (Luckasson et al., 2002) states that it was designed to "put the 2002 diagnosis, classification and system of supports to work" (p. 3) and provides forms that can be completed to that end.

In its current form, the AAMR 2002 system can be seen as a composite document designed to organize the assessment functions related to the determination of eligibility and the planning of individualized interventions for persons with mental retardation. These functions are diagnosis, classification of limitations and strengths and identification of systems of support. Drawing on the description in the manual, the relationships of the three functions to the definition, dimensions, and lists of supports are summarized in Table 16.1. A review of the entries in Table 16.1 can serve as the basis for addressing the questions framed at the beginning of this section regarding the extent to which the AAMR 2002 system meets the criteria for a classification.

1. A hierarchical organization of knowledge.
2. Based on a coherent framework.
3. Contributes to efficient application.

Table 16.1
A summary of the tenth edition of the AAMR Definition,
Classification, and System of Supports

Function of assessment	Diagnosis	Classification and description of strengths and limitations	Identification of systems of supports
Element	Definition	Five dimensions	Systems of support
Documentation	1. Limitation in intellectual functioning 2. Limitations in adaptive behavior 3. Onset < 18 years	1. Intellectual ability 2. Adaptive behavior 3. Participation, interaction, and social roles 4. Health 5. Context	1. Human development 2. Teaching and education 3. Home living 4. Community living 5. Employment 6. Health and safety 7. Behavioral 8. Social 9. Protection and advocacy
Measurement	Standard scores	Description	Intensity ratings

As presented, the manual is a mixture of the three elements of the definition, five dimensions, and a list of areas of supports. As such the manual does not constitute a hierarchical organization of knowledge. Further, the five dimensions under classification and description are not ordered in a logical structure, nor are the individual domains characterized by a hierarchical structure with higher and subordinate categories. The dimension of intellectual ability is a single category, whereas that of adaptive behavior is divided into three separate categories of conceptual, social, and practical adaptive behaviors with seven, nine, and twelve specific skills under the respective categories. The three categories of adaptive skills are not operationalized, and the rationale for listing specific skills under one category rather than another is not provided. In the absence of operational criteria, questions can be raised about the validity of skills assigned under each of the three adaptive-behavior areas. For example, the justification for listing self-direction under conceptual rather than social skills, gullibility, and naïveté, and for listing following rules and obeying laws under social, rather than conceptual, skills, is not obvious. Similarly, the basis for separating money concepts and money management under conceptual and practical skills, respectively, is also not justified. In each of these cases, there is a need to differentiate the underlying cognitive functions from application of practical skills.

The third dimension of participation, interactions, and social roles, and the fifth dimension of context, each provide three broad categories for descriptive information without categorical detail. The fourth dimension defines health in two broad categories of physical and mental health together with a framework for the listing of etiological risk factors. With reference to health, the tenth chapter in the manual describes the importance of identifying physical and mental health conditions in terms of their impact on assessment, classification, and provision of support. While the manual states that "the ICD and DSM will be used to classify specific physical and mental health conditions, including the etiologies for mental retardation" (Luckasson et al., p.171), it is not clear in what way or at what level that will be done. Similarly, the form in the workbook refers only in general terms to the inclusion of diagnostic information.

With reference to etiological risk factors, the eighth chapter presents a classification approach in which etiology is framed in terms of their timing and nature. Prenatal, perinatal, and postnatal phases define the timing, whereas the nature of risk is grouped by biomedical, social, behavioral, and educational factors. The rationale stated for this multifactorial approach to etiology is "to identify strategies for supporting the individual and the family so that these risk factors might be prevented or ameliorated" (Luckasson et al., 2002, p. 135). There is a lack of information on how this approach is to be translated into practice, how ICD information and codes are to be used, and what level of expertise is needed to generate the information. The section pertaining to health in the Workbook is generic at best.

The final step in the assessment is to identify needed supports from a list of nine support areas. Listed under each of these areas are from three to twelve support activities with no apparent order or hierarchical structure. In fact, as presented in Table 5.2 of the Workbook (Luckasson et al., 2002), the activities resemble goals for achievement by the individual or goals for service provision.

In summary, the five dimensions of classification and description and the support needs profile are not presented in a hierarchical structure and lack the detail and coding conventions to constitute a classification. As such, the content of the manual does not meet the requirements of a classification. Instead, the description of the components in the manual and the accompanying forms in the Workbook seem consistent with their use as a framework to organize assessment activities and the planning of support for persons with mental retardation. A schematic model is presented in the manual and Workbook to represent an organizing framework for the AAMR 2002 system. In this schematic model the five dimensions are filtered through a prism of nine forms of support that determine an individual's functioning. What constitutes individual functioning, however, is not operationally defined. Specifically, it is not clear how individual functioning as presented in the schematic model differs from the characteristics of the person as documented under the first four dimensions of intellectual abilities, adaptive behavior, participation, and health. Further, a bidirectional relationship is posited between support and individual functioning, but the nature of the influence of one on the other is not described.

Table 16.2
A summary of key concerns about the AAMR 2002 system
1. Inadequate taxonomic structure
2. Dichotomy between limitations of intelligence and adaptive skills
3. Reliance on a single IQ score
4. Lack of conception of multiple intelligences
5. Lack of indicators of learning
6. Inadequate description of the three adaptive-behavior skill areas
7. Overlap of content across adaptive-behavior skill areas
8. Overlap of adaptive-behavior and participation
9. Inadequate sensitivity to characteristics of children

The model is posited to be a theoretical in nature, but *no theory* is specified in support of the elements of the model and their relationship to individual functioning. The manual draws a comparison of the AAMR 2002 system and the International Classification of Functioning Disabilities and Health (ICF) (WHO, 2001). In that comparison there is passing reference to a common base of ecological theory and a biopsychosocial paradigm, but no elaboration is provided for the model. Bronfenbrenner's (1979) framework is described in support of the dimension of context, but it also is not elaborated for the broader model.

In summary, while the model provides a schematic for the five dimensions and the systems of support, it cannot be seen to meet the criteria for the coherent theoretical framework needed for a classification. There are theories and models of person-environment interaction which could have been included to provide a substantive base for the framework of the manual.

Review of Content

This review of content examines the extent to which AAMR 2002 system contributes to organized knowledge that can be efficiently applied. Beyond the problem of an inadequate taxonomic structure, there are additional fundamental concerns as summarized in Table 16.2. Building on the earlier critique of the definition in this chapter, a second concern is the continuation of the dichotomy between limitations of intellectual functioning and adaptive skills. The criterion of requiring dual limitations of both intelligence and adaptive behavior to define mental retardation was instituted originally in recognition of the problem of false-positives associated with the sole use of IQ scores. It can be argued that the criterion of dual limitations reflected problems in measurement and the need to separate the confounding role of poverty and disadvantage rather than the conceptualization of mental retardation. This is consistent with Zigler's (1987) recommendation for defining mental retardation solely on the basis of intelligence in term of an IQ score that is two standard deviations below the mean. A single IQ score however, is not an adequate basis for defining mental retardation and the challenge is to draw on theory and research for indicators of cognitive function. In this context it should be pointed out that the

AAMR 2002 manual argues for three forms of adaptive behavior skills based on the work of Greenspan and his colleagues (Greenspan, 1996; Greenspan & Love, 1997). That work, however is framed in terms of dimensions of social intelligence, not adaptive behavior. Recognition of the complex and interrelated nature of intellectual functioning in a formal system of classification of mental retardation would be consistent with current research and theory on cognition and conceptions of disablement (Verbrugge & Jette, 1994).

A third concern is the exclusive reliance on the IQ score as an index of intellectual functioning for defining mental retardation. This is problematic in several ways. First, it focuses on one construct, intelligence, to define a second construct, mental retardation. As the default index of intellectual functioning, the IQ score is reductionistic and does not capture the range and diversity of cognitive functions.

A fourth concern is the lack of content related to current conceptions of multiple intelligences. The triarchic theory of intelligence (Torff & Sternberg, 1998) is such a conception, challenging the single "g" factor view of intelligence. Greenspan and his colleagues have advanced a similar conception (Greenspan, 2003; Greenspan & Granfield, 1992; Greenspan & Driscoll, 1997; Greenspan, Switzky, & Granfield, 1996), in which separate dimensions of intelligence have been spelled out. A comprehensive classification system of mental retardation should include the knowledge base of multiple intelligences (Gardner, 1993).

A fifth concern is that the term intellectual is restrictive and does not adequately reflect other essential aspects of mental functioning. Among these aspects are functional limitations associated with learning, arguably the most essential characteristic defining the condition of mental retardation. Findings from theory and extensive research on various learning functions support a focus on variations in the nature and rate of learning as a meaningful and nonstigmatizing approach to define the phenomenon of mental retardation.

The ability of persons with mental retardation to learn depends as much on the learning context available and the kind of teaching as on a specific level of cognitive ability. New experiences or information are easily mapped if they fit into the person's existing understanding of how knowledge transfer takes place. Different theories of intelligence are associated with different views of knowledge (Case, 1996). Intelligence defined by IQ scores is strongly related to formal schooling with its focus on instructions that deal with abstract principles separately from the context of their real-world applications (Watson, 1996). Other theories of intelligence, such as Piaget's epistemological theory (Piaget & Inhelder, 1969), emphasizes the internal mental activity in which a person engages as a result of a universal tendency to explore the environment. A primary difference between these two kinds of theories is the degree of intentionality involved. Informal learning is acquired without formal instruction and is consistent with the key role of incidental learning in social learning theory (Bandura, 1977). The primacy of functional limitations of learning as the indicator of mental retardation is supported by the fact that "learning disabilities" is the term used in the United Kingdom for mental retardation (Hart, 1999). Limitations in the nature, rate, and style of learning should be conceptual and terminological basis for classifying mental retardation.

The 6th, 7th, and 8th concerns pertain to the nature and significance of adaptive-skill areas as criteria for defining mental retardation. These concerns relating to inadequate description of adaptive behavior and overlap of ccontent of identified skills as elaborated below. One problem area of the 2002 system pertains to the nature and use of adaptive-skill areas to define mental retardation. As noted previously, intellectual and adaptive elements should not be seen as dichotomous but rather as varying expressions of underlying functions of a person's adaptation to demands of the environment. That said, there are three key issues concerning the ten adaptive skill areas specified in the 2002 system. First, the list is a mixture of two kinds of entries; one set defined by basic functional skills, and the other defined by contexts in which skills are applied. Functions involved in communication, social interaction, and self-direction transcend particular tasks or settings and can thus be seen as similar in nature to intellectual or cognitive functions. The remaining seven are defined by application of skills particular to a task (e.g., self-care, health/safety, academic) or a setting (e.g., home, community, leisure, work). Collapsing these two types of skill areas into a common set does not make sense on a conceptual or taxonomic basis. Functions that transcend particular tasks or settings are the most appropriate for defining mental retardation. In this regard the Swedish psychologist Kylen (1974) has suggested five dimensions of functions that transcend several tasks. These functions, based on Piaget's theory of cognitive development, include concepts of time, space, quality, quantity and causality.

The relevance of these functions for defining mental retardation is supported by the fact that task analysis of adaptive skills can be based on the five dimensions suggested by Kylen (1974). For example, choosing a leisure activity, catching a bus, and being on time all involve problems in understanding time and cause and effect. Analysis of adaptive skills indicates that usually only a limited number of actions within the task are intellectually challenging for persons with mental retardation (Granlund, Bond, Lindstrom, & Wenneberg, 1995). Granlund et al. (1995) report that such challenges can be overcome when assistive technology is provided based on the five dimensions.

A second problem of the 2002 system related to the adaptive-skill areas pertains to the requirement specifying limitations in two or more areas as criteria for diagnosing mental retardation. In addition to differences in skill areas by type as noted above, skills also vary in terms of their relative importance in documenting mental retardation. Using any two to meet the criteria for diagnosis of mental retardation is arbitrary and fails to account for the fact that some skill areas are more significant indicators than others. Limitations of communication and social-interaction skills, for example, would clearly have greater significance as indicators of mental retardation than limitations of leisure and community skills. If the number of areas is used as the criterion for the definition, a prerequisite weighting procedure should be developed to reflect the relative importance of the skill areas for defining mental retardation.

A related issue pertains to the fact that some skill areas are highly correlated with measured intelligence, such that they constitute a proxy measure for the diagnosis of mental retardation. The high correlations between IQ and language, and IQ and academic achievement, suggest two obvious skill areas in this regard: communication and functional academics. Speaking to this issue, Baroff and Olley (1999) have proposed that the criteria for diagnosis of limitations in any two or more adaptive-skill areas be modified in the 2002 system to specify functional academics as one of the two skill areas.

The 8th concern pertains to the overlap of the 2nd Dimension of Adaptive Behavior with the 3rd Dimension of Participation, Interactions and Social Roles. In this context, the manual seeks to make the distinction between the two dimensions building on a comparison with the dimensions of Activities/Participation in the International Classification of Functioning, Disability and Health (ICF) (WHO, 2001). This comparison in the narrative and in a table in the manual is generic and fails to clarify the distinction. In this regard, adaptive behavior items including interpersonal, occupational and instrumental activities of daily living skills more closely fit the ICF definition of participation. In the absence of clear operational definitions and inclusion and exclusion criteria for content in these two dimensions what differentiates the skills or functions to be assessed under respective dimensions is difficult to ascertain. This contributes to blurring of areas for assessment and redundancy of content which is likely to complicate implementation of the manual in practice.

A 9th and final concern is inadequate coverage related to documenting mental retardation in children (see MacMillan, Siperstein, & Leffert, this book). The insensitivity of the 2002 system to documenting developmental delay or retardation of the young child is similar to concerns raised previously in reference to the 1992 system by Vig and Jedrysek (1996) and responded to by Luckasson et al. (1996). Our concern with the 2002 system is more basic, focusing on its use with children with reference to a required IQ score and the nature of skill areas and measures of the environment. The continued reliance on the IQ score and selected adaptive-skill areas is problematic in terms of their applicability to define mental retardation in children. Specifically, variability of tests used with infants and young children and the derivation of indices such as Developmental Quotients (DQ) raise issues about validity, reliability and/or comparability to IQ scores. The administration of standardized tests is particularly problematic with young children with severe motor impairments.

A review of the adaptive-skill areas and the systems of support reveals that most of the content pertains to adult functioning and is not applicable to children, particularly infants and preschool children. In regard to adaptive-skill areas, it is crucial that adaptive skills of high frequency among children, for example symbolic and peer play, are identified in detail. Finally, it is important that the environments of children be fully represented in the system, including the family context, peers, and the built environment of home, school, and neighborhood.

The above concerns represent key problems with regard to the inadequacy of the 2002 system in terms of taxonomic structure and content. From the standpoint of application, the content listed for classification and description and the identification of supports is not exclusive to the phenomenon of mental retardation. The profile of identified needs and supports is not specific to mental retardation and, in fact, the information would be relevant and encompasses needs and support intensities applicable to a person with any disability.

Ongoing Issues in Defining and Classifying Mental Retardation

The above review has identified a number of problems in the definition of mental retardation in the 2002 system. Central to these problems has been the lack of a conceptually based, comprehensive framework for defining mental retardation with particular reference to dimensions of human functioning. For mental retardation to be a useful construct warranting a separate classification system, a comprehensive framework is needed encompassing the defining characteristics that make it unique as a human condition. While the 2002 system of diagnostic criteria does not provide an adequate conceptual and taxonomic standard, it may well constitute a comprehensive approach to planning for the individual with mental retardation. The existing classifications of ICD-10, DSM-IV, and ICD-10-MR have a medical focus and do not reflect the new paradigm of disability. As the leading professional organization advocating for persons with mental retardation, the AAMR should provide the definitional standards for the field not only for guiding practice but also to advance policy and research. To this end, several alternative approaches could be considered to meet the need for a comprehensive system for classification to support diagnostic and intervention efforts for persons with mental retardation. These alternatives are summarized in Table 16.3.

Table 16.3
Summary of Options for Classification of Mental Retardation

Options	Actions
Keep AAMR 2002 System—not open for revision	Remove the word "classification" from title of manual and advance as a comprehensive assessment and planning guide
Revise AAMR 2002 System with specific changes	Modify and incorporate specific content from ICF and Quebec classifications
Revise AAMR 2002 System with dimensional focus	Substitute selected sections, including codes, of ICD and ICF for relevant dimensions
Do not develop eleventh edition of AAMR 2002 System	Adopt ICF as the standard for AAMR

Essential to any alternative effort is the derivation of an organizing framework to define elements of the classification and their relationships. The articulation of such an integrated paradigm should be a guiding principle for defining and classifying mental retardation. Contributions could be drawn from a wealth of concepts, theories, and empirical findings as well as existing classification systems. As a starting point, key contributions are recommended here:

1. A transactional perspective on development and disablement.
2. A dimensional view of disability.
3. The primacy of cognitive functions in conceptualizing mental retardation.

If the AAMR 2002 system is not open to modification, it is recommended that the title be revised to reflect the use of the manual as a comprehensive guide to assessment and intervention planning. This would remove the premise that the manual has taxonomic properties and advance its use as a tool for systematic assessment and intervention planning. In keeping with the concerns raised above, steps should be taken to clarify the coverage of dimensions, reduce redundancy, add content relevant to children, and make the forms efficient for use.

If modification of the AAMR 2002 system as a classification is a possibility, a second option would be rethink the model desired to convey the classification scheme. Two choices that can be considered are either a model with conceptually defined dimensions or a multi-axial model that does not require a conceptual framework. An example of a limited application of a multi-axial approach to classification of mental retardation is that of Farmer and his associates (1994). If a dimensional approach is of interest, the content summarized in Table 16.1 can be reorganized in a systematic manner, drawing on the Quebec classification (Fugeyrollas et al., 1996) and the ICF. Without going into detail here, the health /etiology content of Dimension IV generally corresponds to the underlying risk factor dimension of the Quebec classification and selected content from the body functions/structures of the ICF model. The content of Dimension V of the 2002 system relates to the environment dimension of the respective classifications. The content of Dimensions II and III of the 2002 system covers several dimensions of disability, encompassing functions, activities, and participation. Reviewing the content of the 2002 system in this fashion, a revised classification manual could be developed that is unique to mental retardation while sharing a common organizing framework with two existing classifications of disability.

A third option would be to review the ICF with particular reference to identifying content appropriate for classifying mental retardation within a dimensional approach. As the content of the ICF provides coverage of universal functioning, selected content could be incorporated into the AAMR 2002 system on the basis of a joint agreement with the World Health Organization. Selected content from ICD-10 and DSM-IV-TR would also be relevant for inclusion. Precedents of this type include the use of the ICD-10 and International Classification of Primary Care (ICPC) (Hofmans-Okkes & Lamberts, 1996), in the classification of illness and disease. An interesting application of the ICPC has been its use to document the prevalence of persons with mental retardation and their health problems in a general-practice database (van Schrojenstein et al., 1997). Of specific relevance to the revision of the 1992 AAMR system is the ICD-10 *Guide for Mental Retardation* (WHO, 1996). Einfeld and Tonge (1999) found a number of problems with the guide but felt that it was a good first step to derive a multi-axial diagnosis of mental disorder in children and young adults with mental retardation.

A fourth option would be for AAMR to adopt the ICF as the classification tool for use in the field of mental retardation. With the availability of the ICF, opportunities exist to evaluate its utility for classifying manifestations of mental retardation and to examine its potential use in the field of mental retardation. The universal scope of the ICF provides a classification of disability across dimensions regardless of underlying etiology.

The ICF reflects the concept of disablement, defining a process in which aspects of disability are manifested over time (Hutchison, 1994). The adoption of a dimensional approach for the AAMR system can emphasize the multidimensional nature of mental retardation with manifestations of functional limitations by the individual at different planes of experience.

Given the extensive coverage the ICF provides of human functioning and disability, the four domains of the ICF should encompass the different manifestations of mental retardation and environmental factors. The domain of body functions would allow for classification of general mental functions as well as specific functions such as attention and memory. The activity domain covers aspects of learning, activities of daily living (ADLs), and instrumental activities of living (IADLs). The participation domain can provide coverage of the extent to which persons with mental retardation experience opportunities for full involvement in societal life. The environment domain could be used to identify the facilitators or barriers to such involvement. Classifying different manifestations of mental retardation across these dimensions will yield a profile of individual differences that can be used to identify needed supports or resources. This can document person-environment interaction to provide a basis for intervention planning to promote skill performance and participation.

Recent contributions and emerging trends in research and theory would suggest several themes that may need to be considered in future efforts on behalf of persons with mental retardation. The definition and classification of mental retardation has changed over time and will continue to evolve. Future efforts are likely to reflect increased precision in the definition and assessment of biological and functional manifestations of disability. It is also likely that mental retardation and other disabilities will be viewed as variations of human functioning, not as deficits or disorders. From the biological side, contributions from research on the human genome will generate more precise identification of etiology and markers of specific syndromes. Thus identification of individuals may well will be on the basis of specific syndromes rather than by a general term such as mental retardation. The result will be more frequent references to persons with "Williams Syndrome" or "Rett Syndrome" instead of "persons with mental retardation." From a perspective of functions, this will call for improved measurement involving direct observation as well as technological advances through imaging techniques and neuropsychological tests.

The focus on function is also likely to expand opportunities for personal independence and social participation.through ergonometric approaches coupled with assistive technology. The performance of activities, ranging from body movements to complex problem solving can be enhanced through more effective assessment and intervention practices. Current research on disability verifies that limitations and restrictions of activities and participation experienced by the person are more a function of opportunities and contexts than of the underlying etiology. Perhaps the most important and exciting challenges will come in identifying the mediating role of environments on human functioning. A particular focus in this regard would be to identify the characteristics of effective environments. Finally, in keeping with the holistic view of disability in social and cultural contexts, the concept of quality of life is increasingly likely to frame the nature and goals of interventions and supports.

REFERENCES

Akhutina, T. V. (1997). The remediation of executive functions in children with cognitive disorders: the Vygotsky-Luria neuropsychological approach. *Journal of Intellectual Disability Research, 41*, 144–151.

American Psychiatric Association. (2000). *Diagnostic and statistical manual of mental disorders-IV-TR*. Washington, DC: Author.

Baroff, G. S. (1999). General learning disorder: A new designation for mental retardation. *Mental Retardation, 37*(1), 68–70.

Begab, M. J., & LaVeck, G. D. (1972). Mental retardation: Development of an international classification scheme. *American Journal of Psychiatry, 128*(11), 121–122.

Bickenbach, J. E., Chatterji, S., Badley, E. M., & Ustun, T. B. (1999). Models of disablement, universalism and the international classification of impairments, disabilities and handicaps. *Social Science & Medicine, 48*, 1173–1187.

Biklen, D., & Schein, P. L. (2001). Public and professional constructions of mental retardation: Glen Ridge and the missing narrative of disability rights. *Mental Retardation, 39*(6), 436–451.

Burton, M., & Sanderson, H. (1998). Paradigms in intellectual disability: Compare, contrast, combine. *Journal of Applied Research in Intellectual Disabilities, 11*(1), 44–59.

Case, R. (1996). Changing views of knowledge and their impact on educational research and practice. In D. R. Olson & N. Torrance (Eds.), *The handbook of education and human development (pp. 75–96)*. London: Brookline Books.

Dawson, W. R. (1909, September 11). Considerations upon the report of the Royal Commission on the care and control of the feeble-minded. *British Medical Journal*, 665–667.

Devlieger, J. P. (1999). From handicap to disability: Language use and cultural meaning in the United States. *Disability and Rehabilitation, 21*(7), 346–354.

Einfeld, S. L., & Tonge, B. J. (1999). Observations on the use of the ICD-10 Guide for mental retardation. *Journal of Intellectual Disability Research, 43*(5), 408–412.

Farmer, R., Rohde, J., Bonsall, C., & Emami, J. (1994). Towards the development of a multi-axial classification of people with learning difficulties. *Journal of Intellectual Disability Research, 38*, 587–597.

Fryers, T. (1987). Epidemiological issues in mental retardation. *Journal of Mental Deficiency Research, 31*, 365–384.

Fugeyrollas, P., Cloutier, R., Bergeron, H., Cote, J., Cote, M., & St. Michel, G. (1996). *Revision of the Quebec Classification: Handicap creation process*. Lac St. Charles, QC: Canadian Society for the International Classification of Impairments, Disabilities, and Handicaps.

Gîransson, K. (1985). *Att skriva lÑttlÑst [To write texts for persons with intellectual disability]*. Stockholm: Ala Stiftelsen.

Granlund, M., Bond, A., Lindstrom, E., & Wennberg, B. (1995). Assistive technology for cognitive disability. *Technology and Disability, 4*, 205–214.

Greenspan, S. (1999). What is meant by mental retardation? *International Review of Psychiatry, 11*, 6–18.

Greenspan. S. (2003). Why Pinocchio was victimized: Factors contributing to social failure in people with mental retardation. In H. N. Switzky (Ed.), *International review of research in mental retardation (Vol. 28, pp. 121–144)*. San Diego, CA: Elsevier/Academic Press.

Greenspan, S., & Driscoll, J. (1997). The role of intelligence in a broad model of personal competence. In D. P. Flanagan, J. L. Genshaft, & P. L. Harrison (Eds.), *Contemporary intellectual assessment: Theories, tests and issues (pp. 131–150)*. New York: Guilford.

Greenspan, S., & Granfield, J. M. (1992). Reconsidering the construct of mental retardation: Implications of a model of social competence. *American Journal on Mental Retardation, 96*(4), 442–453.

Greenspan, S., Switzky, H. N., & Granfield, J. M. (1996). Everyday intelligence and adaptive behavior: A theoretical framework. In J. W. Jacobson & J. A. Mulick (Eds.), *Manual of diagnostic and professional practices in mental retardation* (pp. 127–135). Washington, DC: American Psychological Association.

Gustavsson, A. (2000). Utvecklingstorningens sociala inneborder och forstaelserformer. [Social aspects and comprehension associated with developmental disabilities]. In I. M. Tideman (Ed.), *Handikapp: Synsatt, Principer, Perspektiv* [Handicap: Views, principles, perspectives] (p. 47–65). Stockholm: Johansson & Skyttmo, Forlag.

Hutchison, T. (1994). The classification of disability. *Archives of Disease in Childhood, 73*, 91–99.

Inhelder, B. (1966). Cognitive development and its contribution to the diagnosis of some phenomena of mental deficiency. *Merrill-Palmer Quarterly, 12*, 299–321.

Institute of Medicine. (1991). *Disability in America: Toward a national agenda for prevention.* Washington, DC: National Academy Press.

Kirby, R. L. (1998). Impairment, disability and handicap. In J. A. DeLisa & B. M. Gans (Eds.), *Rehabilitation medicine: Principles and practice (3rd* ed., pp. 55–60). Philadephia: Lippincott-Raven.

KylÇn, G. (1974). *Psykiskt utvecklingshÑmmades first*Ünd* [The intellect of persons with mental retardation]. Stockholm: Ala Stiftelsen.

KylÇn, G. (1985). *En begÜvningsteori* [A theory of cognition]. Stockholm: Ala Stiftelsen.

Lower, T. A. (1999). Intellectual disabilities: Have we lost our senses? *Mental Retardation, 37*(6), 498–503.

Luckasson, R., Coulter, D. L., Polloway, E. A., Reiss, S., Schalock, R. L., Snell, M. E., et al. (1992). *Mental retardation: Definition, classification, and systems of supports* (9th ed.). Washington, DC: American Association on Mental Retardation.

MacMillan, D. L., Gresham, F. M., & Siperstein, G. N. (1995). Heightened concerns over the 1992 AAMR definition: Advocacy versus precision. *American Journal on Mental Retardation, 100*, 87–97.

McAllister, E. W. (1972). Thoughts on the use of the term mental retardation. *Mental Retardation, 10*, 40–41.

Mosby's medical, nursing & allied health dictionary (6th ed.). (2002). St. Louis: Mosby.

O'Brien, G. (2001). Defining learning disability: What place does intelligence testing have now? *Developmental Medicine and Child Neurology, 43*, 570–573.

Schalock, R. L., Stark, J. A., Snell, M. E., Coulter, D. L., Polloway, E. A., Luckasson, R., et al. (1994). The changing conception of mental retardation: Implications for the field. *Mental Retardation, 32*, 181–193.

Simeonsson, R. J., Bailey, D. B., Scandlin, D., Huntington, G. S., & Roth, M. (1999). Disability, secondary conditions and quality of life: Emerging issues in public health. In R. J. Simeonsson & L. McDevitt (Eds.), *Issues in disability and health: The role of secondary conditions and quality of life (pp. 239–255).* Chapel Hill: University of North Carolina.

Simeonsson, R. J., Chen, J., & Hu, Y. (1995). Functional assessment of Chinese children's disabilities with the ABILITIES Index. *Disability & Rehabilitation, 17, 400–410.*

Smith, P. (1999). Drawing new maps: A radical cartography of developmental disabilities. *Review of Educational Research, 2*, 117–144.

Soder, M. (1987). Relative definition of handicap: Implications for research. *Uppsala Journal of Medical Sciences—Supplement, 44*, 24–29.

Stainton, T. (2001). Reason and value: The thought of Plato and Aristotle and the construction of intellectual disability. *Mental Retardation, 39*(6), 452–460.

Stedman's medical dictionary for the health professions & nursing. (5th ed.). (2005). Philadelphia: Lippincott, Williams, & Wilkins.

Taylor, R. L., & Kaufmann, S. (1994). Trends in classification usage in the mental retardation literature. *American Journal on Mental Retardation, 29*(6), 367–371.

Torff, B., & Sternberg, R. J. (1998). Changing minds, changing world: Practical intelligence and tacit knowledge in adult learning. In M. C. Smith & T. Pourchat (Eds.), *Adult learning and development: Perspectives from educational psychology (pp. 109–126).* Hillsdale, NJ: Erlbaum.

Toutain, A., Ayrault, A. D., & Moraine, C. (1997). Mental retardation in Nance-Horan syndrome: Clinical and neuropsychological assessment in four families. *American Journal of Medical Genetics, 71,* 305–314.

Van Schrojenstein Lantman-de Valk, H. M., Metsemakers, J. F., Soomers-Turlings, M. J., Haveman, M. J., & Crebolder, H. F. (1997). People with intellectual disability in general practice: Case definition and case finding. *Journal of Intellectual Disability Research, 41*(5), 373–379.

Verbrugge, L. M., & Jette, A. M. (1994). The disablement process. *Social Science & Medicine, 38,* 1–14.

Vygotsky, L. S. (1965). Psychology and localization of function. *Neuropsychologia, 3,* 381–386.

Watson, R. (1996). Rethinking readiness for learning. In D. R. Olson & N. Torrance (Eds.), *The handbook of education and human development (pp. 148–170).* London: Brookline Books.

Wilson, P. T., & Spitzer, R. L. (1969). A comparison of three current classification systems for mental retardation. *American Journal of Mental Deficiency, 74*(3), 428–435.

World Health Organization. (1980). *International classification of impairments, disabilities, and handicaps. A manual of classification relating to the consequences of disease.* Geneva: Author.

World Health Organization. (1996). *ICD-10: Guide to classification in mental retardation.* Geneva: Author.

World Health Organization. (2001). *International classification of functioning, disability, and health (ICF).* Geneva: Author.

Wyatt, B. S., & Conners, F. A. (1998). Implicit and explicit memory in individuals with mental retardation. *American Journal on Mental Retardation, 102,* 511–526.

Zigler, E. (1987). The definition and classification of mental retardation. *Uppsala Journal of Medical Sciences—Supplement, 44,* 9–18.

CHAPTER SEVENTEEN

The Importance of Cognitive-Motivational Variables in Understanding Mental Retardation in the 21st Century

HARVEY N. SWITZKY

ASSESSMENT OF THE 2002 AAMR DEFINITION

Currently the field of mental retardation (MR) is undergoing a change in its constitutive theoretical model regarding its fundamental definition as a diagnostic category, its classifications systems, and its systems of supports and interventions analogous to a classical scientific paradigm shift, hence the need for this book (Devlieger, 1999; Devlieger, Rusch, & Pfeiffer, 2003; Greenspan & Switzky, Chapter 1 this book; Greenspan, Switzky, & Granfield, 1996; Jacobson & Mulick, 1996; Kuhn, 1970; Mercer, 1992; Rioux, 1997; Rioux & Bach, 1994; Switzky, Greenspan, & Granfield, 1996). The constitutive definition of MR is constantly changing in reflection of the sociopolitical zeitgeist of time, place, and societal values (Clarke & Clarke, 1985; Switzky, 1995a; Switzky & Haywood, 1984; Switzky, Dudzinski, Van Acker, & Gambro, 1988; Zigler, 2001). Each generation creates a constitutive definition of MR, which mirrors the values, emotions, and philosophies of the society at large. (See Boorstein, 1983, for numerous vignettes from the history of the clock, compass, telescope, and microscope documenting the tortuous road to true discovery deriving from contradictory and rival "world views.")

In viewing the 2002 AAMR definition, one needs to be able to adopt such a broad historical and world-view perspective. My own growing awareness of this context was discussed in an autobiographical chapter (Switzky, 1995a), in which I traced the changing roles of psychologists within the field of MR. Because some readers found such a personal emphasis useful, I have adopted a similar first-person approach in some sections of this paper.

The tradition of the American Association on Mental Retardation has been to lead the profession and society in promoting increased understanding of mental retardation, protection of their rights as citizens, and supports to establish personal life satisfaction. This tradition is represented in the 2002 AAMR Definition, Classification, and Systems of Supports. Such a volume, to be successful (i.e., accepted and used) needs to strike a balance among the various constituencies and the world views of the diverse stakeholders making up the field of mental retardation. The 1992 manual was strongly tilted toward the world views of stakeholders involved in treatment, service provision, and social advocacy within the context of the "community supports revolution" (Karan & Greenspan, 1995) and only minimally reflected the world views of researchers and scientists. The latter group found the 1992 AAMR definition too vague and ambiguous, as well as arbitrary and misleading, to be useful to them in carrying out the business of replicable research. The 2002 manual tries to remedy this by distinguishing among the various purposes that a manual may serve: naming, defining, and classifying (Luckasson & Reeve, 2001; Schalock & Luckasson, 2004).

Naming refers to assigning a specific term to something or someone. (See also Glidden, this book.) *Defining* refers to precisely explaining a name or term (e.g., definitions of diseases, International Statistical Classification of Diseases, 10th edition, WHO, 1993; and definitions of mental disorders, Diagnostic and Statistical Manual-IV, APA, 2000). *Classifying* refers to dividing into groups what has been included within the boundaries of a name or term (e.g., etiologies of diseases, or progress of a disease states). Much of the criticism of the 1992 manual (Switzky & Greenspan, 2003) had to do with the model's "defining" function (e.g., the Interpretive Postmodern world view of the 1992 manual, which was antithetical to the Functional-Objective Modern Positivistic world view of most researchers) and its "classifying" function (e.g., the elimination of the classification of groups of people with mental retardation into mild, moderate, severe, and profound categories and its replacement with a classification system based on the intensities of needed supports). The 2002 manual makes a move in the right direction in considering the various needs of the stakeholders within the mental retardation community of service providers, clinicians, parents, and researchers. However, the manual remains distinctively Interpretive Postmodern in its world view, though it does recognize the multiparadigmatic needs of the various users of the manual, who may prefer classification systems based on the intensities of needed supports, or on etiology, or on levels of measured intelligence, or on levels of adaptive behavior, and thereby it may be more useful to researchers (pp. 39–48, p. 200).

One specific lack in the 2002 definition, though to a lesser degree than in the 1992 manual, is sufficient emphasis on the role of motivational and related personality processes in both the constitutive and operational definitions of mental retardation. This problem is not of recent origin but has existed throughout the "Forty-Four Years of AAMR Manuals" described in Chapter 1.

A PROPOSED ALTERNATIVE TO THE 2002 AAMR DEFINITION

I offer here, somewhat crudely, my own definition of MR:

> Mental retardation refers to substantial limitations in present functioning due to very inefficient problem-solving behaviors in various domains of life experience as the result of significantly subaverage intellectual cognitive functioning (e.g., social, practical, and academic intelligences), interacting with personality and motivational variables (e.g., intrinsic motivation, mastery motivation, self-determination, and self-efficacy) as compared to others of the same age and cultural group.

Care must be taken when the details are worked out in the future to maintain discriminant validity from related intellectual disabilities such as learning disabilities.

We have to recognize that motivational variables are the key process, determining what kind of knowledge, gets into the cognitive information system, how it is organized in memory, and how it is used to solve problems. Motivation along with cognition rightfully belongs in the taxon of MR. Newer, more valid measures need to be invented to measure both motivational and cognitive processes in a variety of environmental settings, so that our model has practical utility in the real world. By the use of structural equation modeling we can discover precisely how much of the outcome performances in terms of percent variance explained are related to our measures of motivation and cognition in mentally retarded persons (Switzky & Greenspan, 2000).

We need to combine the levels-of-support–need matrix model (The Support Planning Matrix) of the 2002 manual with the deviation score from the mean IQ model of severity subcategories of the 1983 manual as a communication, diagnostic, and programming tool, as done in the 2002 manual. We also need to develop a more sophisticated model of person-environment interactions. (See Switzky, 2001, 2004, in press; Zigler, 2001). Also I hope that we can reduce our reliance on "clinical judgment," using more objective neuropsychological, neurodiagnostic, and diagnostic genetic measures, which relate to the processes underpinning the behavioral phenotypes of MR (Dilalla, 2004; Dykens, 2001; Holland, Whittington, & Hinton, 2003; Holland, Whittington, Butler, Webb, Boer, & Clarke, 2003; Plomin, Defries, Craig, & McGuffin, 2003). I am aware that these emerging technologies rooted in the biological sciences will have to be validated by clinical judgment, so we must make sure that we train people with superb clinical judgment. [I strongly agree with the position of Schalock and Luckasson (2004, 2005) supporting the importance of strong clinical judgment.] I would also like a model that aligns itself with the ICF WHO model of 2001 to increase cross-cultural communication. That will be very hard to do, I know, but not impossible.

More explicit attention needs to be paid to the construct of "mild" mental retardation and its operational definition, especially in its forensic applications, as in the *Atkins* decision (Switzky et al., 2003), since the AAMR 2002 manual is almost silent on this topic. The manual claims to "address the needs of the *forgotten generation*, defined as people with identified mental retardation at the higher IQ levels, those who currently reject or avoid the label but would be eligible for services or those who are not eligible for the label but experience significant problems due to cognitive limitations" (p. 200). The "forgotten generation" (Tymchuk et al., 2001) is mentioned in a sentence on page 208. [See Switzky (2003) for a more detailed examination of this topic.] However, I do not see how the needs of the *forgotten* generation are met in the AAMR 2002 manual. (See Greenspan & Switzky, "Lessons from the Atkins Decision for the Next AAMR Manual," this book.) Schalock & Luckasson (2004) speak of the importance of clinical judgment in legal matters but provide few details how this is to be done—no solace to the courts, the defendants, the attorneys, or the psychologists and psychiatrists who have to provide information to the forensic system on life-and-death matters such as *Atkins* cases.

It still is not clear in the 2002 AAMR manual whether mental retardation is a functional state, in the sense that one's status as being or not being a person with mental retardation can *change*, depending on one's satisfying the operational definition of mental retardation over time. The AAMR 2002 defines mental retardation as a *disability* on page 8 and on page 16, where a disability is conceptualized as a significant problem in functioning and is characterized in the ICF (WHO, 2001) model by marked and severe problems in performing ("impairment"), in the ability to perform ("activity limitations"), and in the opportunity to function ("participation restrictions"). What does having a *disability* mean operationally? It implies a condition that is serious and difficult to change. In using the descriptor *disability* was AAMR just trying to make its model more compatible with the ICF WHO model? Can a person have a diagnosis of mental retardation at age 6, or age 16, and not at age 25 even though the "*disability*" *of mental retardation* originated before age 18? In many *Atkins* cases the person may have had, or may have functioned to satisfy, a diagnosis of mental retardation in adolescence but not later in life at age 25. What does one do in such cases? I believe that having the functional state of mental retardation at the time of the murder is the deciding factor, not one's functional states at other times in life.

RATIONALE FOR THE PROPOSED DEFINITION: PERFORMANCE OUTCOMES AS A MEDIATED FUNCTION OF THE INTERACTION OF MOTIVATIONAL AND COGNITIVE INTELLECTUAL VARIABLES AND THE TAXON OF MENTAL RETARDATION

In the 2002 definition of MR, which stresses substantial limitations both in present intellectual functioning and in adaptive behavior as expressed in conceptual, practical, and social adaptive skills, the distinction between learning and performance, characteristic of modern cognitive-motivational learning theories, is forgotten. Since cognitive-motivational mediators intervene between the stimuli (setting events) and the response (performance outcomes), and since motivational limitations are commonly present in people with MR (Switzky, 1997a, 1999, 2001, 2004, in press), it is difficult to justify a definition of MR that makes little mention of intervening motivational processes (which was characteristic of all the AAMR manuals, as described in Chapter 1). Also the 2002 definition, as well as all the 44 years of definitions described in Chapter 1, stresses that MR at its core is a fundamental difficulty in intelligence.

Greenspan (2004), agreeing with Spitz (1988), argues that MR is not solely a problem of learning and acquiring knowledge but rather a problem of thinking and problem solving. Modern cognitive motivational learning theories (Bandura, 1997; Baumeister & Vohs, 2004; Boekaerts, Pintrich, & Zeidner, 2000; Deci, 2004; Elliot & Dweck, 2005; Gollwitzer & Bargh, 1996; McCombs, 2004; Pintrich & Blazevski, 2004; Sansone & Harackiewicz, 2000) are mindful of the interaction of a set of motivational operators with a set of cognitive operators which determines what kind of knowledge gets into the cognitive information-processing system, how that knowledge is organized in memory, and how it is used to solve problems—the performance outcome. My concern here is the neglect of motivational processes as not being part of the fundamental core of a definition of MR. This concern has been going on for a long time (Bialer, 1977; Hodapp & Zigler, 1997; Sloan & Birch, 1955; Switzky, 1997a, 1997b, 1998, 1999; Zigler, 1966, 1969, 1971, 1999, 2001; Zigler & Burack, 1989).

Zigler (1999) reflects on this controversy:

I must assert again that any cognitive theory cannot be a complete theory of the behavior of people with MR, because their behavior, like that of any other group of human beings, reflects factors other than cognitive ones. This leads one to reject the often implicitly held view that the cognitive deficiencies of individuals with MR are so ubiquitous and massive in their effects that we may safely ignore personality variables that also distinguish our subjects with MR from a comparison group without MR. (pp. 5–6)

I believe that motivational variables, because they interact with cognitive (intellectual) ones (Borkowski, Day, Saenz, Dietmeyer, Estrada, & Groteluschen, 1992; Switzky, 1999, 2001; 2004, in press), need to be part of the fundamental diagnostic "taxon" of MR and not dealt with indirectly, as the 2002 manual does in Dimension II: Adaptive Behavior (Conceptual, Social, and Practical Skills (pp. 41–43). It is of interest that Dimension II does include self-esteem, gullibility (likelihood of being tricked or manipulated), and naïveté as examples of social adaptive skills (p. 42) but largely ignores those aspects of personality and motivation—e.g., effectance motivation, intrinsic motivation, perceived self-efficacy, self-determination—which can substantially increase the competence of persons with MR to solve the important problems of living in the real world and to lead free, less dependent lives.

These issues, so important in raising quality of life, should be of utmost importance to service providers and parents as well as the person with MR. Though the 2002 manual excludes personality, temperament, and other personal-social and motivational factors as not essential to the definition of mental retardation, Self-Determination is mentioned under health-care support on page 180. Self-Determination appears similar to modern conceptions of self-regulation and self-determination. In the 1959 and 1961 manuals, personal-social factors (e.g., impairments in interpersonal relations, in cultural conformity, and in responsiveness) were included in a highly visible supplementary classification section as clearly outcome performances. The 1973 manual substantially downplayed the importance of these personal-social factors and viewed them also as outcome variables. The 1983 manual folded personal-social and motivational factors as outcome performances into adaptive behavior and included them in its multiaxial coding of social-environmental factors. In the 1992 manual, Dimension II—Psychosocial/Emotional Considerations mentioned only measures of psychopathology. The point is that 44 years of AAMR manuals virtually ignored mediating personality and motivational variables in favor of purely cognitive variables in the "taxon" of MR.

Considering that instruments are currently available to assess personality and motivational processes with fair construct validity for persons with MR—for instance, The Picture Choice Motivation Scale (Kunca & Haywood, 1969), EZ-Yale Personality Questionnaire (Zigler, Bennett-Gates, & Hodapp, 1999), Arc's Self-Determination Scale (Wehmeyer & Kelchner, 1995), The Reiss Profiles (Reiss & Havercamp, 1997)—one assumes they are underutilized only because of lack of awareness of their existence. Also, it is impossible to ignore the work on behavioral phenotypes concerning the interaction of different motivational and cognitive patterns of behavior, i.e., behavioral profiles, in familial, organic, dually diagnosed psychiatric disordered, and genetic (i.e., etiology-specific) populations of developmentally disabled learners (Dykens, 1995, 1998, 2001;

Dykens, Hodapp, & Finucane, 2000; Fidler, in press; Hodapp & Dykens, 2003), which stresses the importance of motivational as well as cognitive variables in understanding, defining, and classifying types of MR.

Finally, Greenspan and his colleagues, too (Greenspan, 2004, this book; Greenspan, Loughlin & Black, 2001), argue that credulity as well as gullibility have been neglected components of the taxon of MR, though historically (Ireland, 1877; Morrison, 1824), both were viewed as central to the taxon. In Greenspan's (2004) action-outcome model of personal competence, gullibility is viewed as an outcome performance of the interaction of credulity viewed as a limitation in social cognitive intelligence, a cognitive mediating variable (e.g., naive beliefs in deceptive claims, promises, or threats), and some motivational mediational operator (e.g., extrinsic motivational orientation).

I am sure that many in the field of MR would rather not include motivational operators in the taxon of MR (because of concern about further muddling an already muddled construct), thus maintaining the traditional (even if broadened) preoccupation with cognitive/intellectual limitations. The point is missed that it is a purely an operational definition that distinguishes cognitive from conative motivational variables. Do intellective variables also contain within them the operation of motivational variables? Can motivational variables operate only in the presence of cognitive variables? It is pointless to argue which set of variables are primary or secondary in understanding the taxon of MR, because outcome performance is an interactive function of both sets (see the following discussion of adaptive behavior).

Only by systematic research within a bounded miniature theory using structural equation modeling and the related techniques of hierarchical linear and nonhierarchical linear modeling (Kline, 1998) will it be possible to determine how much of the outcome performance can be attributed to cognitive variables, conative motivational variables, or their interaction. I hope we can agree that the taxon of MR is built upon cognitive and conative motivational variables and their interaction. This point of view leads to an assessment of both cognitive and motivational variables in order to invent the most useful diagnostic and classification system which has relevance to the descriptions of supports that the 2002 AAMR definition proposes as well as other educational interventions (Switzky, 1997b, 1998; Switzky & Greenspan, 2000).

Other Aspects of the AAMR Manual or Process

Adaptive Behavior

The AAMR manual of 2002 defines adaptive behavior as "the collection of conceptual, social, and practical skills that have been learned by people in order to function in their everyday lives" (p. 73). There is cognizance of the importance of the multidimensionality of adaptive behavior (Simeonsson & Short, 1996; Widaman & McGrew, 1996) and the importance of the developmental model in understanding MR and adaptive behavior (Hodapp, Burack, & Zigler, 1999; Switzky, 1999). There still is some confusion in the operational definition of adaptive behavior in the 2002 AAMR model. "For the diagnosis of mental retardation, significant limitations in adaptive behavior should be established through the use of standardized measures normed on the general population, including people with disabilities and people without disabilities. On these standardized measures, significant limitations in adaptive behavior are operationally defined as performance that is at least two standard deviations below the mean of either of the following:

1. One of the following three types of adaptive behavior: conceptual, social, or practical.
2. An overall score on a standardized measure of conceptual, social, and practical skills" (p. 76).

Unfortunately, no such valid measures of conceptual, social, and practical skills presently exist, so the clinician has to rely on what inadequate adaptive behavior measures exist and on clinical judgment with all its problems. Within the 2002 AAMR model significant limitations in adaptive behavior are operationalized as performance that is -2SD units below the mean of *one of the following three types* of adaptive behavior: conceptual, social, or practical, or an *overall score* on a standardized measure of conceptual, social, and practical skills, because of Widaman's concerns (p. 78) regarding the inadequate nature of current measures of adaptive behavior. This operational definition of adaptive behavior may not be useful, because no general consensus has emerged regarding which skills fall in the category of conceptual, social, or practical skills or what final factor structure of adaptive behavior will emerge within this model.

It is interesting to me that in both the definition of MR proposed in the Jacobson & Mulick manual (1996) where adaptive behavior is defined, and in the Widaman & McGrew's discussion (1996), adaptive behavior as an outcome performance is viewed as a function of the interaction of cognitive and motivational variables.

As Widaman and McGrew (1996) reflect:

> Measures of adaptive behavior are usually measures of *typical* performance, assessing the level of skill a person typically displays when responding to challenges in his or her environment. As a result, items measuring adaptive behavior often implicitly assess motivational components of behavior. Thus to exhibit a form of behavior typically, the person must be motivated to perform the behavior in most situations that she or he confronts. This motivation may be a stable trait-like attribute of the person or may result from contingencies in the environment. Nevertheless, the behavioral capacities assessed as adaptive behaviors implicitly include motivation to perform the behavior in typical life situation. (p. 98)

The American Psychological Association Editorial Board (Jacobson & Mulick, 1996), referring to the position of Zigler and Seitz (1982)—which stresses the central motivational determinants of adaptive behavior and social competence and the role of motivational processes in energizing these outcome performances and Scarr's (1981) suggestion that intellectual competence is the result of a "motivationally determined history of learning and that social competence is composed of physical health, formal cognitive ability, achievement in school, and motivational-emotional factors" (p. 20)—comes very close in placing motivational variables within the taxon of MR. The Editorial Board states (1996): "Clearly, poor generalization skills and motivational deficits are elements of the construct of MR, but the construct also refers to a condition of marked learning failure manifested by deficits in basic problem-solving process and in practical knowledge and skills" (p. 20).

The 2002 AAMR manual moves closer to these positions, since the model emphasizes the *expression* of relevant skills (p.73), *acknowledges that motivational factors can affect the expression of skills (performance deficit)* (p. 74), and even acknowledges the 1996 position of Widaman & McGrew, p. 74). Then why isn't the importance of motivational variables acknowledged more explicitly in the measurement of intelligence or within the total "taxon" of mental retardation?

Formal Assessment versus Clinical Judgment

Diagnosis, classification, and operationalization of levels of support always involve subjective clinical judgments related to the weakest kind of validity, content and judgment validity (Switzky & Heal, 1990). As a practicing clinical psychologist, who is a Diplomate in Clinical Psychology of the American Board of Professional Psychology, I am extremely nervous in making any decisions related to diagnosing, classifying, or operationalizing levels of support—for a variety of reasons:

1. Using traditional IQ test data does not tell much about the real-world everyday intelligence of individuals in the culture that they live in or give enough information concerning their personality and motivational self-regulatory systems. Can one really have confidence in the clinical expertise of the author of the report? When teaching a course in assessment of intelligence, I would always warn my students that it is easy to make an individual appear to be mentally retarded: just do a lousy job of assessing them. In my experience, most psychometrists are overworked and undertrained. If I am the one doing the evaluation, I go into the social-ecological world of the individual to examine his real-world problem-solving strategies of the individual as well as to meet the important persons in his world. When I was a consulting psychologist to a respected child development clinic in Chicago, the staff could not understand why it might be useful to visit the child in the context of home and school and view him/her beyond our office setting. It was not a question of time or money, since our clients were generally well-off financially. It was because the staff had never done this before. When undertaking formal psychometric assessment of intelligence, I would always use a variant of "testing the limits" and a "test-teach-test" approach based on the zone of proximal development and learning-potential assessment ideas of Vygotsky and Feuerstein, respectively (Switzky, 1999), to see if these procedural factors have any influence on test outcomes. Sometimes they really do, and the individual reveals more complex and sophisticated responses. I am aware that most clinicians are considerably busier than I am and cannot do even the basic psychometric assessment in a timely manner, let alone anything as individualized as this.

2. Adaptive-behavior assessment, even using the best instruments available, has only mediocre reliability as well as weak content or judgment validity (Switzky, 1995b), so how can one accurately assess the complex components of adaptive behavior? Direct observation of the individual in the real-world environment is extremely time consuming, and using informants because of the danger of unreliability is no real solution.

3. The use of interdisciplinary teams may or may not increase the validity of the diagnosis, classification, and levels of support process. It all depends on the quality of the reports presented to the team and on their clinical competence. Use of interdisciplinary teams will certainly increase the content and judgment validity of the clinical plan and process, assuming that the information presented to the team is valid and that the team members are competent clinicians themselves. The upshot is that clinicians need to be better trained.

Hopefully more objective and sophisticated procedures based on neuropsychological, neurodiagnostic technologies, and diagnostic genetics (Dykens, 1995, 2001; McClead, Menke, & Coury, 1996; Pennington & Bennetto, 1998; Schacter & Demerath, 1996; Simonoff, Bolton, & Rutter, 1998) in complement with our existing procedures will result in increasingly more valid clinical decision making.

THE FUTURE OF THE MR FIELD

The Sociopolitical Nature of the MR Construct

It took me some time to realize the sociopolitical nature of the definition of MR. When I first read the AAMR definition formulated by Grossman (1983), I thought that it was meant to be scientifically useful to researchers, service providers, physicians, educators, parents, and social advocates. At that time I was involved with educating severely and profoundly mentally retarded individuals as well as the teachers who would educate them (Switzky, 1973; Switzky & Haywood, 1985; Switzky & Rotatori, 1981; Switzky, Haywood & Rotatori, 1982; Switzky, Rotatori, & Cohen, 1978; Switzky, Woolsey-Hill, & Quoss, 1979; Switzky, Rotatori, Miller, & Freagon, 1979). I struggled to distinguish between severe, and profound mental retardation as the 1983 manual defined these categories. I really believed that the distinctions were based on scientific data. I was troubled because the research that I was doing at that phase of my career blatantly contradicted the manual. After discussions with the members of the AAMR Terminology and Classification Committee, I inferred that the constitutive definition of MR and the operational definitions of the committee were influenced by values, social/consensual validations, personal experience, personal philosophies, and best hunches rather than by hard scientific data. I really believed that the diagnostic categories of mild, moderate, severe ,and profound mental retardation were like diagnostic categories of diseases, e.g., mumps, measles, all with a set of diagnostic criteria based on signs and symptoms and measurements deriving from basic research and hard medical sciences. In this, I was naïve.

I have come to understand that MR is a social-politically constructed set of "classes" and not a real science of "taxons," i.e., a true taxonomy dealing with scientific classification as are biological and medical sciences. Invented "classes" in the area of MR are artificial constructions using somewhat arbitrary functional and indirect criteria, representing myriad "world views" among the stakeholders (e.g., researchers, service providers, physicians, educators, parents, social advocates) leading to often very emotional debates. (See Switzky & Greenspan, 2003.) Obviously one of our goals as stakeholders is to come up with a cohesive integrated constitutive theoretical model of MR, operationalized so that we can more closely align the "class" with the "taxon" (Greenspan, Switzky, & Granfield,

1996; Switzky, Greenspan, & Granfield, 1996). Rather than argue whether a constitutive definition of MR is true or false using "pilpul-like" (i.e., Talmudic-like nitpicking) casuistry, the more appropriate point of contention is whether one definition is more useful than another in respect to organizing our thinking, bringing clarity to areas of confusion, and giving direction to our empirical efforts and treatment practices regarding MR (Zigler, 1999, 2001).

In my own experiences as a service provider, a researcher, and a teacher educator, it appears to me that most teachers of persons with MR, and even parents of persons with MR, are not concerned with formal approaches leading to a definition of MR. These groups are much more concerned with improving the quality of life of persons with MR and increasing their competence. The only stakeholders who are seriously concerned with the constitutive definition of MR are researchers, physicians, administrators, and social advocates, stakeholders holding very diverse world views that are in conflict.

I believe that the field of MR is presently undergoing a set of processes analogous to a classical paradigm shift (Kuhn, 1970). Mercer (1992), discussing how changing "scientific" paradigm shifts have influenced our constitutive models of MR and other developmental disabilities, sheds much light and "food for thought" on our implicit conceptions of MR and our attempt to make our implicit world views explicit. Mercer (1992), drawing from Kuhn (1970), argues that "science" is a social collaboration among scientists who share a fundamental world view (i.e., scientific paradigm). This world view includes the scientists' beliefs, values, the nature of society, philosophies of "truth and reality," and the best methods to arrive at "truth and reality." (See also Guba, 1990; Rioux, 1997; Rioux & Bach, 1994.)

When scientific research conflicts with and cannot be assimilated within the current scientific paradigm, i.e., world view, a process of accommodation is forced by these anomalous phenomena, and the current scientific paradigm is modified to deal with these new "facts" in order to provide a framework which can account for them. Inevitably the new paradigm competes with the older paradigm for adoption as a world view. In the case of the "classes" of MR, this model needs to be expanded somewhat to take into consideration the paradigmatic views of the various stakeholders, who may not be only "scientists." Obviously a shared world view among the stakeholders in the area of MR needs to be constructed and operationalized to more closely align the "class" with the "taxon," leading to optimally useful outcomes for service and research. In the summary chapter (Switzky & Greenspan, this book) we explore more fully the paradigmatic assumptions of our authors in order to organize their various world views regarding the theoretical and operational models of MR and how these constitutive and operational models can be used to obtain the most useful shared viewpoint regarding the nature of MR.

IS THERE A NEW PARADIGM FOR MR?

I believe that since the 1950s MR has been understood in terms of the interaction of persons with MR and their environments (just like any other persons), especially as expressed in the research literature (Kuenzel, 1939; Rautman, 1949; Edgerton & Bercovici, 1976; Switzky & Haywood, 1984; Zigler, 2001). Learning is impossible without considering contextualized person-environmental interactions, so it is hard for me to understand why the AAMR 1992/2002 manuals claim the facts of person-environmental interactions as a major paradigm shift.

One must give credit to the AAMR 2002 model for recognizing the pragmatic value of multiple classification systems to meet the various needs of clinicians, service providers, and researchers using a model based on the intensities of need supports, etiology, measured levels of intelligence, or levels of assessed adaptive behavior. Taking such a pragmatic approach is a small tilt to rapprochement to the world views of stakeholders based on versions of "Psychomedical or Cognitive Models of Disability" (Mercer, 1992), such as scientists and researchers, which was recommended in Switzky & Greenspan (2003).

It is also a positive value in the 2002 AAMR manual to make explicit that assessment may have many functions, such as diagnosis, classification, or planning supports. In my view the 2002 AAMR manual is a substantial improvement over the 1992 manual but still presents some confusions that need to be resolved. See also Schalock and Luckasson (2004).

Conclusion

Our primary goal as stakeholders is to develop a cohesive, integrative, constitutive theoretical developmental model of MR operationalized so that we can closely align the "class" with the "taxon" of MR, which reflects the sometimes divergent world views of service providers, social advocates, and researchers. We need to develop a set of models that are useful in organizing our thinking, bring clarity to areas of confusion, and provide direction to our empirical efforts and treatment practices. As suggested by the range of ideas expressed in this book, a period of extended discussion among various stakeholders will likely be needed. The Summary chapter (Switzky & Greenspan, this book) summarizes and describes the points of agreement and disagreement among our authors in terms of their various paradigmatic world views and seeks to determine whether some consensual models emerge.

References

American Psychiatric Association. (2000). *Diagnostic and statistical manual of mental disorders* (Rev. ed.). Washington, DC: Author.

American Psychological Association Editorial Board. (1996). Definition of mental retardation. In J. W. Jacobson & J. A Mulick (Eds.), *Manual of diagnosis and professional practice in mental retardation* (pp. 13–53). Washington, DC: Author.

Bandura, A. (1997). *Self-efficacy: The exercise of control.* New York: W. H. Freeman.

Baumeister, R. F., & Vohs, K. D. (Eds.). (2004). *Handbook of self-regulation.* New York: Guilford.

Bialer, I. (1977). Mental retardation as a diagnostic construct. In I. Bialer & M. Sternlicht (Eds.), *The psychology of mental retardation: Issues and approaches* (pp. 67–123). New York: Psychological Dimensions.

Boekaerts, M., Pintrich, P. R., & Zeidner, M. (Eds.). (2000). *Handbook of self-regulation.* San Diego, CA: Academic Press.

Boorstein, D. J. (1983). *The discoverers.* New York: Random House.

Borkowski, J. G., Day, J. D., Saenz, D., Dietmeyer, J., Estrada, T. M., & Groteluschen, A. (1992). Expanding the boundaries of cognitive intervention. In B. Y. L. Wong (Ed.), *Contemporary intervention research in learning disabilities* (pp. 1–21). New York: Springer-Verlag.

Clarke, A. M., & Clarke, A. D. B. (1985). Criteria and classification. In A. M. Clarke, A. D. B. Clarke, & J. M. Berg (Eds.), *Mental deficiency: The changing outlook* (4th ed., pp. 27–52). New York: Free Press.

Deci, E. L. (2004) Promoting intrinsic motivation and self-determination in people with mental retardation. In H. N. Switzky (Ed.), *International review of research in mental retardation* (Vol. 28, pp. 1–29). San Diego, CA: Elsevier/Academic Press.

Devlieger, J. P. (1999). From handicap to disability: Language use and cultural meaning in the United States. *Disability and Rehabilitation, 21,* 346–354.

Devlieger, J. P., Rusch, F., & Pfeiffer, D. (2003). Rethinking disability as same and different: Towards a cultural model of disability. In J. P. Devlieger, F. Rusch, & D. Pfeiffer (Eds.), *Rethinking disability: The emergence of new definitions, concepts, and communities* (pp. 9–16). Antwerp, Belgium: Garant.

Dilalla, L. F. (Ed.). (2004). *Behavior genetics principles.* Washington, DC: American Psychological Association.

Dykens, E. M. (1995). Measuring behavioral phenotypes: Provocations from the "new genetics." *American Journal on Mental Retardation, 99,* 522–532.

Dykens, E. M. (1998). Maladaptive behavior and dual diagnosis in persons with genetic syndromes. In Burack, J. A., Hodapp, R. M., & Zigler, E. (Eds.), *Handbook of mental retardation* (pp. 542–562). New York: Cambridge University Press.

Dykens, E. M. (2001). Special issue on behavioral phenotypes. *American Journal on Mental Retardation, 106.*

Dykens, E. M., Hodapp, R. M., & Finucane, B. (2000). *Genetics and mental retardation. A new look at behavior and intervention.* Baltimore: Paul H. Brookes.

Edgerton, R. B., & Bercovici, S. (1976). The cloak of competence: Years later. *American Journal of Mental Deficiency, 80,* 485–497.

Elliot, A. J., & Dweck, C. S. (Eds.). (2005). *Handbook of competence and motivation.* New York: Guilford.

Fidler, D. J. (Ed.), Mental retardation and personality and motivational systems. In *International review of research in mental retardation.* (Vol. 31) San Diego.

Gollwitzer, P. M., & Bargh, J. A. (Eds.). (1996). *The psychology of action: Linking cognition and motivation to behavior.* New York: Guilford.

Greenspan, S. (2004). Why Pinocchio was victimized: Factors contributing to social failure in people with mental retardation In H. N. Switzky (Ed.), *International review of research in mental retardation and developmental disabilities* (Vol. 28, pp. 121–144). San Diego, CA: Elsevier/Academic Press.

Greenspan, S., Loughlin, G., & Black, R. S. (2001). Credulity and gullibility in people with developmental disorders: A framework for future research. In L. M. Glidden (Ed.), *International review of research in mental retardation and developmental disabilities* (Vol. 24, pp. 101–135). New York: Academic Press.

Greenspan, S., Switzky, H. N., & Granfield, J. M. (1996). Everyday intelligence and adaptive behavior: A theoretical framework: In J. W. Jacobson & J. A. Mulick (Eds.), *Manual of diagnosis and professional practice in mental retardation* (pp. 127–135). Washington, DC: American Psychological Association.

Grossman, H. J. (Ed.). (1983). *Manual on terminology and classification in mental retardation* (1983 revision). Washington, DC: American Association on Mental Deficiency.

Guba, E. G. (1990). The alternative paradigm dialog. In E. G. Guba (Ed.), *The paradigm dialog* (pp. 17–30). Newbury Park, CA: Sage.

Hodapp, R. M., Burack, J. A., & Zigler, E. (1998). Developmental approaches to mental retardation: A short introduction. In J. A. Burack, R. M. Hodapp, & E. Zigler (Eds.), *Handbook of mental retardation* (pp. 3–19). New York: Cambridge University Press.

Hodapp, R. M., & Dykens, E. M. (2003). Looking to the 21st century: Toward an etiology-based classification system. In H. N. Switzky & S. Greenspan (Eds.), *What Is Mental Retardation? Ideas for an evolving disability* (p. 219). Washington, DC: American Association on Mental Retardation [E-Book]. Available at http://www.disabilitybooksonline.com

Hodapp, R. M., & Zigler, E. (1997). New issues in the developmental approach to mental retardation. In W. E. MacLean, Jr. (Ed.), *Ellis' handbook of mental deficiency* (3rd ed., pp. 115–136).
Mahwah, NJ: Erlbaum.

Holland, A. J., Whittington, J. E., Butler, J., Webb, T., Boer, H., & Clarke, D. (2003). Behavioural
phenotypes associated with specific genetic disorders: Evidence from a population-based sample of people with Prader-Willi syndrome. *Psychological Medicine, 33,* 141–153.

Holland, A. J., Whittington, J. E., & Hinton, E. (2003). The paradox of Prader-Willi syndrome:
A genetic model of starvation. *The Lancet, 362,* 989–991.

Ireland, W. W. (1877). *On idiocy and imbecility.* London: Churchill.

Jacobson, J. W., & Mulick, J. A. (Eds.). (1996). *Manual of diagnosis and professional practice in
mental retardation.* Washington, DC: American Psychological Association.

Karan, O., & Greenspan, S. (Eds.). (1995). *Community rehabilitation services for people with disabilities.* Newton, MA: Butterworth & Heineman.

Kline, R. B. (1998). *Principles and practice of structural equation modeling.* New York: Guilford.

Kuenzel, M. W. (1939). Social status of foster families engaged in community care and training of
mentally deficient children. *American Journal of Mental Deficiency, 44,* 244–253.

Kuhn, T. S. (1970). *The structure of scientific revolutions* (2nd ed.). Chicago: University of Chicago
Press.

Kunca, D. F., & Haywood, N. P. (1969). The measurement of motivational orientation in low
mental age subjects. *Peabody Papers in Human Development, 7*(2).

Luckasson, R., & Reeve, A. (2001). Naming, defining, and classifying in mental retardation.
Mental Retardation, 39(1), 47–52.

McClead, R. E., Menke, J. A., & Coury, D. L. (1996). Major technological breakthroughs in the
diagnosis of mental retardation. In J. W. Jacobson & J. A. Mulick (Eds.), *Manual of diagnosis
and professional practice in mental retardation* (pp.179–190). Washington, DC: American
Psychological Association.

McCombs, B. L. (2004). Learner-centered principles and practices: Enhancing motivation and
achievement for children with learning challenges and disabilities. In H. N. Switzky (Ed.),
International review of research in mental retardation (Vol. 28, pp. 85–120). San Diego, CA:
Elsevier/Academic Press.

Mercer, J. R. (1992). The impact of changing paradigms of disability on mental retardation in the
year 2000. In L. Rowitz (Ed.), *Mental retardation in the year 2000* (pp. 15–38). New York:
Springer-Verlag.

Morrison, A. (1824). *Outlines of mental diseases.* Edinburgh: MacLachlan & Stewart.

Pennington, B. F., & Bennetto, L. (1998). Toward a neuropsychology of mental retardation. In J.
A. Burack, R. M. Hodapp, & E. Zigler (Eds.), *Handbook of mental retardation* (pp. 80–114).
New York: Cambridge University Press.

Pintrich, P. R., & Blazevski, J. L. (2004). Applications of a model of goal orientation and self-reg-
ulated learning to individuals with learning problems. In H. N. Switzky (Ed.), *International
review of research in mental retardation* (Vol. 28, pp. 31–830). San Diego, CA:
Elsevier/Academic Press.

Plomin, R., Defries, J. C., Craig, I. W., & Mcguffin, P. (Eds.). (2003). *Behavior genetics in the
postgenomic era.* Washington, DC: American Psychological Association.

Rautman, A. (1949). Society's first responsibility to the mentally retarded. *American Journal of
Mental Deficiency, 54,* 155–162.

Reiss, S., & Havercamp, S. H. (1997). Sensitivity theory and mental retardation: Why functional
analysis is not enough. *American Journal on Mental Retardation, 101,* 553–566.

Rioux, M. H. (1997). Disability: The place of judgement in a world of fact. *Journal of Intellectual
Disability Research, 41*(2), 102–111.

Rioux, M. H., & Bach, M. (Eds.). (1994). *Disability is not measles: New research paradigms in disability.* North York, ON: Roeher Institute.

Sansone, C., & Harackiewicz, J. M. (Eds.). (2000). *Intrinsic and extrinsic motivation.* San Diego, CA: Academic Press.

Scarr, S. (1981). Testing for children: Assessment and the many determinants of intellectual competence. *American Psychologist, 36,* 1159–1166.

Schacter, M., & Demerath, R. (1996). Neuropsychology and mental retardation. In J. W. Jacobson & J. A. Mulick (Eds.), *Manual of diagnosis and professional practice in mental retardation* (pp. 165–177). Washington, DC: American Psychological Association.

Schalock, R. L., & Luckasson, R. (2004). American Association on Mental Retardation's *Definition, Classification, and System of Supports* and its relation to international trends and issues in the field of intellectual disabilities. *Journal of Policy and Practice in Intellectual Disabilities, 3/4,* 136–146.

Schalock, R. L., & Luckasson, R. (2005). *Clinical judgement.* Washington, DC: American Association on Mental Retardation.

Sloan, W., & Birch, J. W. (1955). A rationale for degrees of retardation. *American Journal of Mental Deficiency, 60,* 258–264.

Simeonsson, R. J., & Short, R. J. (1996). Adaptive development, survival roles, and quality of life. In J. W. Jacobson & J. A. Mulick (Eds.), *Manual of diagnosis and professional practice in mental retardation* (pp. 137–146). Washington, DC: American Psychological Association.

Simonoff, E., Bolton, P., & Ruter, M. (1998). Genetic perspectives on mental retardation. In J. A. Burack, R. M. Hodapp, & E. Zigler (Eds.), *Handbook of mental retardation* (pp. 41–79). New York: Cambridge University Press.

Spitz, H. H. (1988). Mental retardation as a thinking disorder: The rationalist alternative to empiricism. In N. Bray (Ed.), *International review of research in mental retardation (Vol. 15, pp. 1–31).* New York: Academic Press.

Switzky, H. N. (1973). Short-term intake functions for sucrose in developmentally retarded children. *Perceptual and Motor Skills, 36,* 331–337.

Switzky, H. N. (1995a). The changing roles of psychologists: The influence of paradigm shifts and their implications for clinical practice, service, and research in the area of mental retardation and developmental disabilities. In O. Karen & S. Greenspan (Eds.), *Community rehabilitation services for people with disabilities* (pp. 399–419). Newton, MA: Butterworth & Heineman.

Switzky, H. N. (1995b). [Review of the article *The Adaptive Behavioral Evaluation Scale].* In J. C. Close & J. Impala (Eds.), *Buros: The twelve mental measurements yearbook* (pp. 1025–1026). Lincoln: University of Nebraska Press, Buros Institute of Mental Measurement.

Switzky, H. N. (1997a). Individual differences in personality and motivational systems in persons with mental retardation. In W. E. MacLean, Jr. (Ed.), *Ellis' handbook of mental deficiency* (3rd ed., pp. 343–373). Mahwah, NJ: Erlbaum.

Switzky, H. N. (1997b). Mental retardation and the neglected construct of motivation. *Education and Training in Mental Retardation and Developmental Disabilities, 32,* 194–197.

Switzky, H. N. (1998). The educational meaning of mental retardation: Toward a more helpful construct. Mental retardation and the neglected construct of motivation. *Resources in Education (RIE) & Educational Resource Information Center (ERIC).* (Document Reproduction Service No. EO 408767).

Switzky, H. N. (1999). Intrinsic motivation and motivational self-system processes in persons with mental retardation: A theory of motivational orientation. In E. Zigler & D. Bennett-Gates (Eds.), *Personality development in individuals with mental retardation* (pp. 70–106). New York: Cambridge University Press.

Switzky, H. N. (2001). Personality and motivational self-system processes in persons with mental retardation: Old memories and new perspectives. In *Personality and motivational self-system processes in persons with mental retardation* (pp. 57–143). Mahwah, NJ: Erlbaum.

Switzky, H. N. (2003). The plight of adults with mild cognitive limitations: Still forgotten? In A. J. Tymchuk, K. C. Lakin, & R. Luckasson (Eds.), *The forgotten generation: The status and challenges of adults with mild cognitive limitations. Contemporary Psychology, APA Review of Books, 48(3),* 363–365.

Switzky, H. N. (Ed.). (2004). Personality and motivational systems in mental retardation. In *International review of research in mental retardation (Vol. 28).* San Diego, CA: Elsevier/Academic Press.

Switzky, H. N. (Ed.) (in press). Mental retardation and personality and motivational systems. In *International review of research in mental retardation.* (Vol. 31) San Diego.

Switzky, H. N., Dudzinski, M., Van Acker, R., & Gambro, J. (1988). Historical foundations of out-of-home-residential alternatives for mentally retarded persons. In L. W. Heal, J. I. Haney, & A. R. N. Amado (Eds.), *Integration of developmentally disabled individuals into the community* (2nd ed., pp. 19–35). Baltimore: Paul H. Brookes.

Switzky, H. N., Everington, C., Keyes, D., Baroff, G., Greenspan, S., & Fulero, S. (2003, August). *Symposium. Mental Retardation and the Law: Atkins v. Virginia.* Paper presented at the Annual Meeting of the American Psychological Association, Divisions 33, 41, Toronto, ON.

Switzky, H. N., & Greenspan, S. (2000). New directions in motivation and personality research in persons with mental retardation. [Abstract No. 1129, New Millennium Research to Practice Congress Abstracts, 11th World Congress of the International Association for the Scientific Study of Intellectual Disabilities (IASSID), August 1–6, 2000, Seattle, WA]. *Journal of Intellectual Disability Research, 44*(Pt. 3 & 4)

Switzky, H. N., & Greenspan, S. (Eds.). (2003). *What Is Mental Retardation? Ideas for an evolving disability.* Washington, DC: American Association on Mental Retardation [E-Book]. Available at http://www.disabilitybooksonline.com

Switzky, H. N., Greenspan, S., & Granfield, J. (1996). Adaptive behavior, everyday intelligence and the constitutive definition of mental retardation. In A. F. Rotatori, J. O. Schwenn, & S. Burkhardt (Eds.), *Advances in special education* (Vol. 10, pp. 1–24). Greenwich, CT: JAI Press.

Switzky, H. N., & Haywood, H. C. (1984). Bio-social ecological perspectives on mental retardation. In N. S. Endler & J. M. Hunt (Eds.), *Personality and the behavior disorders* (2nd ed., Vol. 2, pp. 851–896). New York: Wiley.

Switzky, H. N., & Haywood, H. C. (1985). Perspectives on methodological and research issues concerning severely retarded persons. In D. Bricker & J. Filler (Eds.), *Severe mental retardation.* Reston, VA: Council for Exceptional Children.

Switzky, H. N., Haywood, H. C., & Rotatori, A. (1982). Who are the severely and profoundly mentally retarded? *Education and Training of the Mentally Retarded, 17*(4), 268–272.

Switzky, H. N., & Heal, L. (1990). Research issues and methods in special education. In R. Gaylord-Ross (Ed.), *Issues and research in special education* (pp. 1–81). New York: Teachers College Press.

Switzky, H. N., & Rotatori, A. (1981). Assessment of perceptual-cognitive functioning in non-verbal severely/profoundly handicapped children. *Early Child Development and Care, 7,* 29–44.

Switzky, H. N., Rotatori, A., & Cohen, H. (1978). The Community Living Skills Inventory: An instrument to facilitate the deinstitutionalization of the severely developmentally disabled. *Psychological Reports, 43,* 1335–1342.

Switzky, H. N., Rotatori, A., Miller, T., & Freagon, S. (1979). The developmental model and its implications for assessment and instruction for the severely/profoundly handicapped. *Mental Retardation, 17,* 167–170.

Switzky, H. N., Woolsey-Hill, J., & Quoss, T. (1979). Habituation of visual fixation responses: An assessment tool to measure visual sensory-perceptual processing in non-verbal profoundly handicapped children in the classroom. *AAWSPH Review, 4(2),* 136–147.

Tymchuk, A. J., Lakin, K. C., & Luckasson, R. (Eds.). (2001). *The forgotten generation: The status and challenges of adults with mild cognitive limitations.* Baltimore: Paul H. Brookes.

Wehmeyer, M. L., & Kelchner, K. (1995). *The Arc's Self-Determination Scale*. Arlington, TX: The Arc of the United States.

Widaman, K. F., & McGrew, K. S. (1996). The structure of adaptive behavior. In J. W. Jacobson & J. A. Mulick (Eds.), *Manual of diagnosis and professional practice in mental retardation*. (pp. 97–110). Washington, DC: American Psychological Association.

World Health Organization. (2001). *International classification of functioning, disability, and health (ICF)*. Geneva: Author.

Zigler, E. (1966). Research on personality structure in the retardate. In N. R. Ellis (Ed.), *International review of research in mental retardation* (Vol. 12, pp. 77–108). New York: Academic Press.

Zigler, E. (1969). Developmental versus difference theories of mental retardation and the problem of motivation. *American Journal of Mental Deficiency, 73,* 536–556.

Zigler, E. (1971). The retarded child as a whole person. In H. E. Adams & W. K. Boardman (Eds.), *Advances in experimental clinical psychology* (pp. 47–121). Oxford, England: Pergamon.

Zigler, E. (1999). The individual with mental retardation as a whole person. In E. Zigler & D. Bennett-Gates (Eds.), *Personality development in individuals with mental retardation* (pp. 1–16). New York: Cambridge University Press.

Zigler, E. (2001). Looking back 40 years and still seeing the person with mental retardation as a whole person. In H. N. Switzky (Ed.), *Personality and motivational self-system processes in persons with mental retardation* (pp. 3–55). Mahwah, NJ: Erlbaum.

Zigler, E., Bennett-Gates, D., & Hodapp, R. M. (1999). Assessing personality traits of individuals with mental retardation. In E. Zigler & D. Bennett-Gates (Eds.), *Personality development in individuals with mental retardation* (pp. 206–225). New York: Cambridge University Press.

Zigler, E., & Burack, J. (1989). Personality development and the dual diagnosed person. *Research in Developmental Disabilities, 10,* 225–240.

Zigler, E., & Seitz, V. (1982). Social policy and intelligence. In R. J. Sternberg (Ed.), *Handbook of human intelligence* (pp. 586–641). Cambridge, England: Cambridge University Press.

CHAPTER EIGHTEEN

Lessons from the Atkins Decision for the Next AAMR Manual

STEPHEN GREENSPAN AND HARVEY N. SWITZKY

INTRODUCTION

In the past, the main use of AAMR manuals was in determining whether a client would get access to agency-based services or benefits. In light of the U.S. Supreme Court's ruling in *Atkins* v. *Virginia* (2002), the manual is now being used to determine whether a criminal defendant should or should not be exempted from the death penalty on the grounds of having mental retardation (MR). Obviously, this makes the manual's adequacy or inadequacy a much more serious matter than it was before the *Atkins* ruling.

We have recently begun to serve as consultants in what are termed "Atkins hearings," which can occur either at the pretrial or habeus (postappeal) stage, and which are used to determine whether a death penalty can be considered or carried out. Thus far, our experience has been as defense consultants, but we have seen our share of reports by experts on both sides, and the same issues affect diagnostic evaluations conducted by both defense and prosecution experts. The responsibility of any expert witness is not to be an advocate, but to report the *truth*, regardless of whom it helps or hurts. It behooves an expert, therefore, to do some initial screening before getting too far into a case, so that he or she can feel free to tell the contacting attorney, "I don't think I can honestly take the position you want me to take." Unfortunately, this may not always be done, as the adversarial, not to mention lucrative, nature of the judicial process places pressures on experts to become what Hagen (1997) termed "whores of the court."

The likelihood that an *Atkins* hearing will be adversarial rather than a neutral search for the truth is increased by the stakes involved (a person's life) and also by the ambiguous nature of mild MR itself. Most *Atkins* applicants fall at the upper end of the MR severity continuum, and present a mixed competence profile. People on death row typically have a history of academic failure, marginal social and vocational competence, and even overt brain damage (Lewis & Balla, 1976). So what differentiates a worthy Atkins applicant from one who is unworthy? We hope to answer this question in the last part of this chapter. Does the 2002 AAMR diagnostic manual provide an adequate basis for resolving these disputes in a manner which one can consider just? If the answer to this last question is

"Not really," then that should shed some light on what needs to be done, and in a hurry, to improve the situation.

Although each state legislature has established its own criteria and procedures to be used by courts in deciding such litigation (in many cases, these predate the Supreme Court's ruling), the 2002 AAMR manual (Luckasson et al., 2002) has become the gold standard that is most typically reflected in the legislation and used by clinicians on both sides. Based on our experience with *Atkins* cases over the past couple of years, there are some problems that we think need to be addressed by the AAMR in its next round at producing a diagnostic manual.

As some of these cases are still moving through the litigation process, we are obliged to keep our comments very general and cannot discuss details of specific defendants. Because virtually all condemned prisoners in the United States are male (and we are unaware of any *Atkins* claims involving females), we have opted to refer to defendants as "he" rather than the more usual and cumbersome "he and she." The points made in the pages that follow have less to do with the definition of MR than with the procedures that are used in applying that definition in making a diagnosis. That is a critical feature of any diagnostic manual, and we hope that the next T&C Committee will give some thought to lessons that can be learned from the use of the 2002 manual in *Atkins* hearings. Because these lessons are very practical in nature, this chapter will be less abstract and more concrete than most of the other chapters in this volume. Hopefully, this will be seen to have some advantages in helping to ground future discussions of the manual in messy reality rather than, as in the past, mainly on less (but still) messy theory.

PROBLEMS with the ADAPTIVE BEHAVIOR CRITERION

Given that a court is unlikely to even take on an *Atkins* case unless the defendant's IQ scores are at least fluctuating around the 70–75 ceiling, the crux of most *Atkins* decisions will often hinge on the individual's adaptive behavior. This is not to deny that considerable disputation often occurs over whether a defendant meets the IQ criterion. But in our experience, there is usually less ambiguity over the IQ criterion (and an admirable reluctance, typically, to base an execution decision on one or two IQ points) than whether the individual meets the requirement of significant deficits in adaptive behavior. Thus, ironically, the *Atkins* decision has solved two major problems for the MR field.

The first problem solved is that the 2002 manual is now actually being followed, as the 1992 manual was not, which had as much to do with the problems inherent in the 1992 manual as with the fact that the Atkins ruling had not yet occurred. The second is that the adaptive behavior criterion is now, finally, being taken seriously by users of the AAMR manual. We both have had many experiences, in the very recent past, where adult service or educational agencies gave or withheld the MR label without even looking at an individual's adaptive behavior. The negative side of the courts' taking the adaptive behavior criterion seriously is that the inadequacies of the definition and measurement of adaptive behavior are now being brought into much greater relief. Hopefully, the lessons to be learned from *Atkins* cases about adaptive behavior will enable the next T&C Committee to come up with an approach to adaptive behavior that makes more *sense,* not just in terms of formal theory but in terms of guiding courts or other agencies to make just decisions.

To make our points about problems in the conceptualization and assessment of adaptive behavior as concrete as possible, we shall be using examples from a specific adaptive behavior instrument: the "Adaptive Behavior Assessment System, Second Edition," known as the "ABAS-II" (Harrison & Oakland, 2003), not because it is better or worse than other adaptive behavior instruments but because we have had the most experience with it. The problems we identify in the ABAS-II are likely found in all other existing instruments.

Inappropriateness of Relying on Self-Ratings

Some adaptive behavior instruments (e.g., the ABAS-II) have self-report forms. Sometimes an expert will ask the defendant to rate himself on such a form. In one such case, "John Doe's" adaptive behavior self-rating placed him in the "below-average" (but not MR) range, while another informant rated the individual as having adaptive behavior in the MR range. The expert chose to reject the third-party informant (for reasons addressed in the next section) and chose to give great weight (in deciding he did not have MR) to Mr. Doe's own self-rating.

There are two reasons why we believe it is inappropriate to use an individual's self-rating as a basis for deciding whether or not he has MR: (a) the near-universality of the tendency of people with mild MR to deny the extent of their limitations, and (b) the fact that MR is a status attributed by others, and that being viewed by others as "retarded" or "not retarded" is, thus, far more relevant for diagnostic purposes than how a subject views himself.

Typically, when a forensic psychologist evaluates a person's claim for criminal mitigation or civil monetary award, concern is expressed over possible "malingering." This term refers to a conscious effort on the part of the subject to make himself look crazy, incompetent, or disabled. Given that many defendants in Atkins cases have not previously been diagnosed as having MR, it is understandable that lawyers and experts would be on the lookout for possible malingering, when a defendant produces low IQ or adaptive behavior scores. When the person receives a high score, particularly when it falls squarely in the normal range, the tendency on the other hand is to assume, often wrongly, that there was no conscious effort at fakery, especially given the likely negative consequences for the defendant's claim. In fact, it is our contention that defendants with mild MR are much more likely to fake higher rather than lower competence when given an opportunity to rate or describe their adaptive behaviors.

"Reverse malingering" (for lack of a better word) is not really a problem when a subject obtains a high IQ score, given that one wants the subject to make his best effort anyway, and it is not really possible to make oneself brighter on such a test than one actually is. In the field of adaptive behavior measurement, in which rating instruments are used, reverse malingering is a real problem, in that what is required of the subject is not to make his best effort but to honestly admit whether or not he can perform certain tasks. In our experience, people with mild MR, whether or not they have adopted a criminal lifestyle, typically will go to great lengths to look more competent and "normal" than they actually are.

This problem was first written about by anthropologist Robert Edgerton (1993/1971) in his classic book *The Cloak of Competence*. In that book, and in later longitudinal follow-ups, Edgerton and his colleagues studied a number of people with mild MR as they went about their lives in community settings. A striking feature of all of these people was the great lengths to which they went to hide from others the extent of their limitations. A key strategy in "passing" (Edgerton's term) as normal was the use of nondisabled benefactors to help them do things (such as filling out forms) that they were unable to do on their own.

An example of how this strong need to look normal can contribute to reverse malingering can be found in the poignant documentary *The Collector of Bedford Street*, by the film maker Alice Elliot (2001). The film depicts the efforts on the part of residents in New York's Greenwich Village to set up a trust fund to provide case management, home visiting, and supplemental cash for a neighbor, 59-year-old Larry Selman, a man who has mild MR. The film gets its title from the fact that the impoverished Mr. Selman donates over $10,000 per year to charities from money he collects in the neighborhood on behalf of various causes. Before this fund can be set up, Larry (whose closest living relative, an elderly uncle, is no longer able to come around) is required to take an IQ test, in order that the agency that will be administering the fund is satisfied that Larry actually qualifies as having MR. Even though it is clearly in his interest to receive the diagnosis (and, therefore, to do poorly on the test), Larry agonizes that he will not do well and that his neighbors will no longer have a good opinion of him as a result. (Interestingly, from our standpoint, adaptive behavior does not seem to have been a focus of the evaluation process, and no mention was made of the main reason, aside from his extreme goodness, why the community banded together to help Larry: which was his extreme gullibility in the face of a repeated pattern of exploitation by street people.)

When Mr. Selman in fact received the needed diagnosis of MR, his first reaction was embarrassment, even though it was clearly in his interest to receive that label. This story, and the research of Edgerton and colleagues, illustrates that people with mild MR have a strong motivation to appear more competent than they are, and that this motivation can persist even in the face of very strong incentives to look incompetent. In fact, one can argue that the tendency to exaggerate one's competence, even in a situation as an *Atkins* evaluation where it is clearly in one's interest to be seen as incompetent, is itself a pretty good indication that an individual probably does have MR.

The other reason why it is inappropriate to give significant weight to self-ratings of adaptive behavior in diagnosing MR is that MR is a social status that is intricately tied in with how a person is perceived by peers, family members, and others in his community and social ecology. In a very real sense, the best definition of MR is "a label given to someone who behaves in his everyday life in a manner which causes others to refer to him as having MR." An individual's self-perception may be worth knowing for therapeutic purposes but has no relevance to diagnosing him as having or not having MR, except to the extent that an unrealistically positive self-image may support, rather than detract from, a diagnosis of MR. Experts in *Atkins* cases should always keep in mind that individuals with mild MR rarely are willing to see themselves as having MR, and many of the things they claim to be able to do are conscious or unconscious fictions of competent behavior. In that regard, we are reminded of one defendant who would fake reading the newspaper when in fact he was only looking at the pictures, another defendant who claimed to be making large sums per day for odd jobs when in fact he was paid a small fraction of that amount, and another defendant who claimed an ability to cook when in fact nothing he concocted was edible and letting him near a stove was considered a serious fire hazard.

Need to Use Multiple Raters

It is an interesting and little-known fact that publishers of clinical rating instruments often do not publish any data on inter-rater reliability. This is the case with two of the most widely used clinical rating instruments: the Child Behavior Checklist (Achenbach & Edelbrock, 1983) and the Conners Rating Scales (Conners, 1997). The closest authors of those two scales come is to present data comparing different categories of raters (e.g., parents vs. teachers), and they justify the extremely low correlations (around .4) between raters by attributing the differences to situational factors (e.g., children behaving differently at home versus in school) rather than to inherent problems in the rating process.

To their credit, the authors of the ABAS-II do present data on inter-rater reliability—for example, by having a sample of individuals rated by two raters on the same rating form, and then looking at correlations across these rater pairs. The inter-rater reliability coefficients reported for the ABAS-II are, in fact, quite high: around .9 on the composite standard score, around .8 on individual scale scores. The authors of the ABAS-II (or any other rating instrument) do not address one important issue, however, which is that no matter how reliable an instrument may be, there is always the possibility that any particular use of the scale may result in invalid scores.

As indicated by Suen and Ary (1989), the purpose of establishing an instrument's reliability (usually under relatively optimal conditions) is to be able to assure a user that any test error from a future application of the instrument is within acceptable limits. Thus, we talk about the reliability of the instrument and do not apply that term to any particular administration of it. For an instrument such as an IQ test, this is a safe thing to do, as we can be relatively assured that any two qualified testers will attain fairly similar results. For a rating instrument, however, the fact that the instrument has been found to have good inter-rater reliability does not enable one to say with assurance that any two raters will provide congruent scores, as there is always the possibility that one set of ratings will be "off the wall," for any number of reasons ranging from ignorance or dislike of the ratee, to having very deviant perceptions in general about the ratee.

There are two solutions to this problem (Driscoll & Greenspan, 1994), although neither has been discussed in manuals for adaptive behavior or other rating instruments. The first solution is to calculate the standard error of the difference between pairs of raters (which could be done easily from existing inter-rater reliability data) and then publish a table giving confidence intervals for difference scores between raters. The other solution, flowing from the existence of such a table, would be always to have an individual rated by at least two raters. Then if the scores fell within the confidence interval, one would be justified in averaging across the raters. If, on the other hand, the score differences between a pair of raters exceeded the confidence interval, one would know to seek one or more other raters, and then one would be in a position to know which rater's scores could be discarded as invalid. Thus, in the example given earlier, where John Doe's self-rating scores differed significantly from those of a third-party rater, the decision to disregard the self-rating (made for other stated reasons discussed in the previous section) could have been further justified had the two third-party ratings been found to agree within the confidence interval. Even in the present absence of such an inter-rater confidence-interval table, it seems much more desirable to obtain multiple adaptive behavior ratings, in order to attain some degree of "consensual validation" support for the adaptive behavior picture that emerges.

PROBLEMS WITH ADAPTIVE BEHAVIOR NORMS AND METRICS

In the evaluation of John Doe discussed earlier, the main reason the expert gave for rejecting the third party's scores (on the ABAS-II) was that her resulting scale scores were so uniformly low as to suggest that she was biased. An examination of her ratings showed considerable variation, however, as seen in the fact that on some of the ten subscales, she gave a fair number of "3"s (the highest score), a great many "2"s, and only a few "1"s and "0"s. The problem appeared to stem less from any (automatic "0" or "1") negative response bias on the part of the rater than from the likely skewed nature of the ABAS norms. The ABAS-II (adult version) has items such as "dresses himself/ herself" (from the "Self-Care" domain), "listens to music for fun or relaxation" (from the "Leisure" domain), "finds and uses a pay phone" (from the "Community Use" domain), and "goes out alone in daytime" (from the "Self-Direction" domain). For the vast majority of (nondisabled) adults, the score received on the above items will be a "2" ("sometimes when needed") or, more likely, a "3" ("always when needed"). All it takes is a few "1"s or "0"s on any of the ABAS-II subscales to produce a scale score well below the first percentile.

Contributing to this problem on the ABAS-II is the confusing nature of the rating metric. For each of the rating items (an example from "Functional Academics" would be "writes own name, including zip code"), a rater is asked to circle one of the following numbers: a "3" indicating the subject can "always when needed" perform the activity, a "2 indicating the subject can "sometimes when needed" perform the activity, a "1" indicating the subject can "never when needed" perform the activity, and a "0" indicating the subject "is not able" to perform the activity. For the life of us, we cannot figure out the difference between a "1" and a "0" and we imagine that lay raters have a similar problem. In the case of John Doe mentioned in the previous section, the third-party rater gave the defendant adaptive behavior scores which placed him at the bottom end of moderate MR. Because the defendant was relatively high functioning, the expert who administered this assessment concluded that the rater was biased and that her scores should be thrown out. We determined that part of the problem may have been that she may have been confused about when to give a "1" versus a "0," as she gave quite a few of the latter scores. Just to test this hypothesis, we decided to rescore her protocol, changing all of her "0"s to "1"s. When we did this, the defendant now received a composite adaptive behavior standard score in the mild MR range, which is much closer to how he actually functions. Thus it may be that the third-party rater's very low (below .1 percentile) ratings reflected problems with the ABAS-II (the skewed nature of the norms and confusion over the rating metric) rather than response bias. As mentioned in the preceding section, the best basis for concluding whether or not the rater was off in her perceptions of Mr. Doe would have been to use one or more other third-party raters.

PROBLEMS WITH ADAPTIVE BEHAVIOR CONTENT

The biggest problem with measures of adaptive behavior is that they don't measure all of the things which, in our opinion, they should be measuring (e.g., construct validity; see Switzky & Heal, 1990). This is a reflection of both of the following:

1   Confusion over the constitutive definition of adaptive behavior.
2.   Problems in the way in which adaptive behavior instruments have been constructed.

Problems in the content of adaptive behavior instruments are particularly evident in the domain of Social Skill, which numerous clinicians and theorists (Doll, 1941; Ireland, 1877; Greenspan & Love, 1997; Schalock, 1999; Tredgold, 1908) have indicated are universally problematic for people with MR.

Given that adaptive behavior is often the most critical criterion for diagnosing MR in Atkins hearings, it is vital that measures of adaptive behavior tap behavioral domains that are closely indicative of what might be termed the MR taxon, e.g., a true scientific taxonomy (See Switzky, Greenspan, & Granfield, 1996). After all, what good is the use of adaptive behavior standard scores in diagnosing MR, if the scores don't measure competencies that are central to the construct of MR? With the first (2000) edition of the ABAS, constructed in line with the 1992 AAMR operational definition of adaptive behavior (as comprising ten skills), there were ten subscales, but only one was described as measuring "social" functioning. When the 2002 AAMR manual shifted to a model of adaptive behavior comprised of the tripartite model of conceptual, practical, and social adaptive skills, the authors of the ABAS-II (Harrison & Oakland, 2003) were able to quickly respond to this change. They did this not by devising new subscales and items, but merely by combining the ten subscales of the earlier measure into the three major domains of the new AAMR manual. Thus, the "social" domain in the ABAS-II was constituted by combining two subscales—"Leisure" and "Social"—from the original ABAS instrument.

The Leisure subscale contains items such as "has a hobby or creative activity," "listens to music for fun or recreation," "looks at pictures or reads books," "plays alone with toys, games, or other fun activities," "selects television programs or videotapes," "tries a new activity to learn something new," "participates in an organized program for a sport or hobby." Our question is: What is there about these items that are particularly "social"? It is true that some of the other items on the Leisure subscale (for example, "organizes a game or other fun activity for a group of friends" or ""follows the rules in games and other fun activities") have an interpersonal component, but no more so than items in other subscales, such as "Helps other workers with their work" (from the "Work" subscale, which is part of the "Practical" adaptive skills domain).

On the one other subscale, termed "social" from the old ABAS, that is now folded into the new "social" adaptive-skills domain, all the items, obviously, have something to do with functioning in a social context. The problem is that they have more to do with the absence of maladaptive behavior than with the presence of what we (Switzky, Greenspan, & Granfield, 1996) and others have termed "social intelligence." This subscale is a mix of the following:

1.   Conventional politeness behaviors (e.g., "says 'thank you' when given a gift," "offers guests food or beverages," and "laughs in response to funny comments or jokes").
2.   Niceness versus nastiness behaviors (e.g., "offers assistance to others," "tries to please others," "apologizes if he/she hurts the feelings of others," and "offers to lend belongings to others").

3. Emotional intelligence items (e.g., "listens to friends or family members who need to talk about problems," "says when he/ she feels happy, sad, scared or angry," and "places reasonable demands on friends, for example, does not become upset when a friend goes out with another friend").

4. What might be termed social-outcome items (e.g., "keeps a stable group of friends," "has good relationships with family members," and "has one or more friends").

There are no items having to do with gullibility or its opposite (ability to see through and resist deceit or coercion), or other behaviors that speak to the social essence of the MR taxon, which is found more in things such as naïveté, innocence, and falling for practical jokes than in how nice or polite one is.

Another problem with the content of most adaptive behavior instruments is that they are a mix of items reflecting ability/competence with items reflecting motivational or personality dimensions. For example, under the subscale of "self-direction" are items such as "puts work or school over leisure activities," "controls temper when disagreeing with friends," "works on one home activity for at least 15 minutes," and "cancels fun activity when something important comes up." Similar examples of temperament (emotional and attentional self-regulation) and character (conformity to social norms) can be found in items scattered throughout the ABAS-II. Some examples are "puts things in their proper place" (from the "Home Living" subscale), "bathes daily" (from the "Self-Care" subscale), and "takes out trash when can is full" (from the "Home Living" subscale). Competence is confounded with motivation throughout the ABAS scales, as in items such as "keeps hair neat" or "gets hair cut" (both from "Self-Care").

The problem is that many of these items have nothing to do with MR. It may be desirable if a person "has pleasant breath" (an item in "Self-Care"), but can anyone inform us how having pleasant or unpleasant breath is related to the MR taxon? The same is true of all behaviors that reflect temperament or character. If social intelligence is, as we believe, the aspect of social competence that is most relevant to a diagnosis of MR, then the ABAS-II, as well as the Vineland-II and all other existing adaptive behavior instruments, has very little construct validity in the critical area of Social Skill.

Fortunately, we understand that the AAMR is devising its own adaptive behavior instrument that will have much more in the way of gullibility and related social intelligence items in the Social Skill area. That is certainly a welcome trend in the direction of bringing adaptive behavior assessment more in line with current thinking about the nature of MR and adaptive behavior. In particular, it is vital that adaptive behavior instruments maintain a clear focus on ability/competence as opposed to style/ personality, and that the abilities tapped are those, such as vulnerability to exploitation, that are particularly central to the MR taxon.

Can One Infer Adaptive Behavior Level from the Crime?

In an *Atkins* hearing, the two sides present their experts and supporting evidence for or against a diagnosis of MR, and the court then decides which side is right. Typically, these cases are decided solely by a judge, but we know of at least one state, and there likely are others, where the *Atkins* hearing is decided by the vote of a jury, even when the hearing takes place years after the original guilt trial and sentencing. In a sense, when the judge or jury decides the outcome of an *Atkins* hearing, he/she/they are functioning as their own expert, in that they are deciding whether to assign the defendant the diagnosis of "MR" or "Not-MR." To us, this is inherently problematic, in that judges, and even more so juries, are much more likely than a qualified expert to base their diagnostic judgment mainly on their own intuitive notions, and prejudices, concerning how people with MR are supposed to behave in the world.

If it were merely a matter of a judge or jury deciding which set of experts to believe, that would be bad enough. However, what typically happens is that the judge allows the presentation of evidence, for example, about the crime or crimes allegedly committed by the defendant, about which an expert is typically not allowed to comment. The reason is that judges believe such information can shed light on the defendant's level of adaptive functioning. This is problematic, not only because such information (e.g., about the heinousness of the crime) can be very prejudicial, but also because, even more than when choosing among experts, it is asking the judge or jury to make a diagnostic judgment based on whether they believe a person with MR is capable of carrying out certain behaviors.

Any type of defendant behavior could be subject to such a "hearing within a hearing." An example involved a defendant who allegedly carried out a string of armed robberies, one of which resulted in a death. In this case (which never came to trial, as the defendant died in jail just before the hearing was to start), the judge would have been asked by the prosecutor whether someone who could drive himself to and from the site, show some degree of planning (i.e., by doing some prior casing), and show some practical competence (i.e., operating a gun) and social competence (i.e., locking up witnesses) could be eligible for a diagnosis of MR. The correct answer to this should be "Who knows?" Unfortunately, some experts and judges/juries often act as if they do know, as they make inferences about whether the defendant could or could not have MR based on the criminal conduct that is depicted.

There are two reasons why one should avoid basing diagnostic inferences about a defendant's level of adaptive functioning, and about having MR, on information about his or her past criminal acts. The first reason has to do with the fact that not enough information is typically available (on a precise microlevel) regarding the exact situational demands and the level of cognitive skills required to navigate those demands. Among the situational factors we do not typically know about is the extent to which the defendant may have been coached and trained by a less impaired "robbery coach," as opposed to figuring out these things for himself. The second reason is that we simply do not possess normative information, adaptive behavior scales notwithstanding, about whether someone with MR can fire a gun, drive a car, case out a crime scene, or assert his will on victims. One of the lessons of the "support revolution" is that people with MR can do many things, including aspects of work and independent living, that previously one would not have thought they could do. Without meaning to be flip, one can think of a crime as a form of work. Just as people with mild MR have been found able to do jobs that previously might have been viewed as beyond their capabilities, it is possible that people with mild MR have a greater potential for a successful criminal career than might previously have been believed possible.

Herman Spitz (1988) has argued that MR is a "thinking disorder" and not a "learning disorder." By this, he meant that a person with MR can, through skillful instruction, be helped to learn many routine work and other schemas. But a person with MR has great difficulty when these learned schemas run up against novel challenges. In fact, that is precisely what seems to have happened with the defendant under discussion, as it is reported that on the two occasions when he fired his weapon (once with tragic consequences), something happened in the situation (e.g., a victim saying or doing something unexpected) that departed from his routine script. One lesson from our experience with Atkins cases is that there should perhaps be an attempt by the next T&C Committee to more fully delineate, based on research done or needing to be done, the kinds of behaviors that people with MR can and cannot perform. Such a delineation would, hopefully, limit the ability of experts in *Atkins* cases to make overgeneralizations about the meaning of isolated criminal or other behaviors for a diagnosis of MR.

Can One Infer Adaptive Behavior from Verbal Behavior?

The forensic evaluation process typically involves a clinical interview, in which the subject is asked to talk about himself, his history, ailments, interests, the circumstances of his current existence, and other matters that might shed light on his affective and mental state. Typically, experts are told not to delve into aspects of the current case, although information about other past criminal acts committed by the defendant will sometimes be discussed. Although not intended to be a primary basis for diagnosing MR, information from clinical interviews is often used to argue for, or more commonly against, a diagnosis of MR.

Most typically, the reason given for basing a "non-MR" diagnosis on clinical interview transcripts is that the defendant demonstrates average or above-average oral language, including occasional use of big words, along with a fair degree of insight into his past conduct and the dire situation in which he finds himself. As part of the insight into his current situation, a defendant may show a fair amount of understanding regarding which side the expert is working for, and may even show some degree of wariness and resistance to the interview that may be more in line with the suspicious style one associates more with hardened criminals than with the guileless/innocent stereotype that one often associates with the MR taxon. A problem with inferring non-MR status from normal language is that it is contradicted by research showing that adults with mild MR have relatively normal syntax, grammar and vocabulary (Kernan & Sabsay, 1988, 1992).Their deficits are more in the area of sociolinguistics (adjusting communication to take into account informational needs of others) rather than psycho-linguistics.

The same argument that we made in the previous section, involving problems in inferring MR status from someone's criminal history, can be made with respect to using material (e.g., vocabulary, verbal fluency, or seeming degree of verbal insight) from a clinical interview. This is nonstandardized data which is purely qualitative in nature and does not really provide a basis for making a diagnostic judgment. People with MR typically have normal language syntax and can be very facile verbally. In fact, some syndromes associated with MR, such as Williams syndrome, are associated with above-average verbal fluency that does not prevent the majority of individuals with these syndromes from being given a diagnosis of MR (Bellugi, Mills, & Jernigan, 1999). Forensic experts who do not have a great deal of experience with persons who have MR may apply their own stereotypic notions, applicable perhaps more to people with moderate or severe MR, about the limited verbal abilities of people with MR, and these stereotypes may be quite misleading when applied to people with mild MR.

One interesting fact that we have learned about life on death row is that condemned prisoners often spend a great deal of time watching "The History Channel," "The Discovery Channel," and other TV shows which contain relatively sophisticated information about the world. As a result, Atkins defendants may occasionally use words or make comments which one might assume are beyond the repertoire of people with MR. Such exposure might also be expected to elevate an individual's "General Information" and other "crystallized" subscale scores on IQ tests, although it would likely not affect the quality of one's "fluid" problem-solving or information-processing based scores. Because isolated bits of data taken from conversations or interviews can be misleading, the standard practice is to use formal IQ assessment, rather than clinical description, in determining the precise level of an individual's cognitive deficits.

With respect to the great deal of verbal insight that a defendant sometimes shows about the lessons to be learned from his criminal past, one can assume that some of that is a result of the group sessions used in the rehabilitation process in prison settings. Given the amount of time that a condemned prisoner has to think about his life, and to discuss his case with attorneys and others, it is not surprising that an *Atkins* applicant, even one who clearly has MR, might be able to show some surface sophistication in discussing what he would and should have done differently to have avoided his current predicament. People with MR often can be quite eloquent in talking about their lives, as can be seen in the stories told by "self-advocates" (Williams, Bratt, & Shoultz, 1995) and in the use by agencies of client spokespeople in fund-raising or public awareness campaigns. Such behavior may shed light on the need to revise stereotyped beliefs about the limitations of people with MR but provides a shaky basis for making diagnostic judgments.

The misuse of clinically obtained verbal and other kinds of information from forensic interviews has caused us to rethink our earlier call for an increased use of clinical judgment in the process used to diagnose MR. To be sardonic, our revised position is that "clinical judgment is all right when it is used correctly, by us, but is not all right when it is used incorrectly, by experts other than us." As we are not able to participate in every *Atkins* case in America, it would probably be better if constraints were placed on the use of clinical judgment. In particular, we feel that it is important to use clinical judgment to interpret test scores and be aware of the limitations of particular measures, but that it is not appropriate—given the tremendous variability in the qualifications of evaluators and the extent to which qualitative information can be misused—to base a diagnosis of "MR" or "Not-MR" solely or even largely on a clinician's judgment. To the extent that global perceptions are relevant in establishing a diagnosis of MR, they should be the perceptions of people who have known the individual well over a period of months or years and not those of a clinician who knows the individual superficially from one or two meetings, especially when that clinician has limited experience and training in the MR field.

Can One Assess Adaptive Behavior (and Diagnose MR) Retroactively?

One issue that has not been fully resolved in *Atkins* case law has to do with the time frame during which MR has to have been manifest. Is it all right, from a legal standpoint, to establish that a defendant is eligible for a diagnosis of MR today (when he may have already been on death row for a dozen or more years), even if one cannot establish that he would have been eligible during the period when the alleged crime was committed? The opposite case may be even more common—namely there might be evidence that the person had MR during his childhood years, or in the period, typically in his late teens or early 20s, when the crime was allegedly committed, but based on his current functioning he might no longer be eligible for the diagnosis. We are not qualified to comment on the legal questions (although we are told that competence at the time of the crime is probably the most relevant), but we can comment on how one might go about addressing this matter clinically.

The 1992 AAMR manual emphasized repeatedly, starting on the first page, that MR is a dynamic status that one can grow into, out of, and back into across the lifespan, depending on a number of factors, including developmental processes, situational challenges, and personal choice. The 2002 manual did not state this point as clearly, although we have been informed by David Coulter, President of AAMR (2004), a member of both the 1992 and 2002 committees, that no change in this emphasis was intended. The possibility that one can have MR at time one but not at time two might seem puzzling to those who think of it as an intrinsic aspect of a person. The 1992 manual (Luckasson et al., 1992) attempted to clarify this point, as follows: "Mental retardation is not something you have, like blue eyes or a bad heart. Nor is it something you are, like being short or thin. It is not a medical disorder. . . . Nor is it a mental disorder. Mental retardation refers to a particular state of functioning" (p. 9). This statement indicates that MR is a current social status which inheres not in the person but in how the person deals with the world and is perceived by others in that world at a particular point in time. It implies that one's status as a person with MR can change over time.

Certainly, for persons with moderate or severe MR, it is likely that one's status as having MR is permanent, but for persons with mild MR, it is possible that one could fluctuate above and below the boundary between the state of mental retardation and "normality." Furthermore, for many Atkins applicants it is possible, indeed likely, that a diagnosis of MR was never made at an earlier time, even though evidence such as IQ test scores below 70 might have justified such a diagnosis. The fact that someone was not diagnosed as having MR at an earlier time does not mean that such a diagnosis could not have been made; nor does it rule out the possibility that a diagnosis of MR could legitimately be made today.

Just as mental health professionals are often asked in murder cases, when the "insanity" defense is raised, to make a retroactive judgment as to whether a defendant could distinguish right from wrong at the time he committed a crime, it is also possible, and sometimes necessary, to make retroactive judgments regarding whether a defendant had MR at some point in the past. In terms of the intelligence and developmental criteria, it is typically the case with *Atkins* applicants that they came to the attention of school and mental health authorities early on, and a voluminous amount of testing and other data is available, Assuming it was not thrown out, such information could establish that during the developmental period an individual had significant cognitive problems, including, often,

IQ scores below or around the ceiling for a diagnosis of mild MR. Intellectual assessment is also typically available for the period before or after the trial, even if the defendant has been in prison for a decade or more.

The challenge for establishing the diagnosis retroactively is, thus, to identify two or more adaptive behavior informants who knew the individual well during various time frames (e.g., high school years, at the time of time of the crime, currently) and ask them to fill out a rating instrument such as the ABAS-II, and to be interviewed by the evaluator. In filling out the adaptive behavior instrument, the informant is asked to keep in mind a certain time frame and rate the defendant as he is remembered during that time period. Rating a condemned defendant on his current adaptive functioning can be a more difficult challenge, however, both in terms of locating appropriate raters and also because death row is a restricted environment in which there few if any opportunities to do most of the activities—cooking, working, or using public transportation—that are covered by the items. However, with some ingenuity, it is typically possible to find informants, such as inmates in neighboring cells, prison counselors or guards, or outside psychiatrists, who could fill out a rating instrument knowledgeably and with some guesswork and extrapolation on some items, assuming that they are willing and able to cooperate in such an endeavor. It should be noted that the use of retroactive assessment in Atkins cases has been endorsed as a legitimate practice in the recently-published "A User's Guide for AAMR's 2002 Definition, Classification and Systems of Supports" (Schalock et al, 2006).

OTHER LESSONS LEARNED FROM *ATKINS* CASES

In the preceding pages, we have focused mainly on practical issues in establishing the presence or absence of adaptive deficits in defendants subject to *Atkins* hearings. In the remainder of this paper, we shall address a range of other issues, including ones that speak more to the overriding conceptual question: "How can we be certain that an adult truly has mental retardation?"

Clarifying the Developmental Criterion

There is some confusion in the legal community about the meaning of the "developmental criterion," regarding the need to be able to trace the onset of one's MR to the period before the age of 18. Courts, in *Atkins* hearings, have increasingly interpreted this requirement to mean that one must demonstrate that one actually had MR before the age of 18. A more reasonable interpretation is that one must demonstrate that problems in development were apparent during the childhood or adolescent period, and that a diagnosis of MR made during the adult period should not be attributable solely to causes such as a car accident that occurred after the age of 18. Even if, as is usually the case with mild MR, one cannot identify a specific cause, it is essential that an individual have manifested problems in academic and other areas of functioning during the developmental period, and that, whether or not a formal diagnosis of MR was ever made, serious concerns about the individual were expressed by family members, educators, or medical professionals at a relatively early age.

Ironically, the success of the various AAMR manuals in reducing unfair application of the MR label to minority individuals has contributed to a situation in which deserving minority individuals have sometimes been unfairly denied the protections of the MR label. For example, we know of one Atkins case involving an African-American male, "James Smith," who was born over three months premature, had very low birth weight, and had other neurological insults, including severe head injuries, and symptoms in childhood. James was one of eight children in a profoundly disadvantaged family living in an impoverished rural area. In school, he was not given special education services until high school, and even then he was labeled as "Learning Disabled" rather than "Educable Mentally Retarded," in spite of the absence of the required (for LD) discrepancy between his below-70 IQ and his low educational achievement.

From indications in the school reports, it seems to have been assumed that Mr. Smith's intellectual deficits reflected his family's impoverished circumstances, and that it would be unfair, therefore, to give him a label of MR. In fact, except for a severely mentally retarded sister, Mr. Smith's other six siblings functioned in a normal manner, and he was seen by his adult relatives and by his brothers and sisters as very impaired and in need of special protections—for example, from exploitation by pranksters and con artists—from an early age. In line with the continuing emphasis in the AAMR manuals on the importance of sensitivity to cultural factors, the severity of Mr. Smith's cognitive limitations has been consistently discounted as due solely to growing up "Black and Poor."

This tendency to overlook the possibility that one can be a member of a minority group and also have biologically based problems might be termed "racial overshadowing." We have seen it reflected in other *Atkins* cases in which the most serious of organically caused developmental histories, even involving diagnosed genetic syndromes, is given little or no mention in the face of cultural and racial explanations. It seems important for the next AAMR manual to emphasize that culture and organicity are not mutually exclusive and that poor people have as much right as do middle class people to have the extent of their biologically based disabilities acknowledged and dealt with.

Need to Reverse the Weight Given to IQ and Adaptive Behavior

A special issue on the *Atkins* decision in the psychology journal *Ethics and Behavior*, edited by Gerald P. Koocher (2003), included six papers by various psychologists addressing a range of matters. In only one of these, the paper by the two of us (Greenspan & Switzky, 2003), was the term "adaptive behavior" even uttered. This demonstrates dramatically that for most psychologists, MR continues to equal "low IQ," in spite of the fact that the dual-criteria formula of low IQ plus significant deficits in adaptive behavior has been in existence for the past 44 years.

In a case discussed earlier, involving "John Smith," a referral to a developmental disabilities diagnostic center was made after his conviction and a decade or more before his Atkins petition was filed. As part of a sentencing mitigation effort, his appellate attorneys wanted to know if he qualified for a diagnosis of MR. The report that was submitted—this was before the recent AAMR effort to emphasize more strongly the need to take into account the standard error of IQ tests—concluded that James did not have MR because his most recent full-scale IQ score was a couple of points above 70. Interestingly, no effort whatsoever was made at that time to assess Mr. Smith's adaptive behavior. The reason, most likely, was that adaptive behavior has been viewed mainly as something that can rule a diagnosis of MR out if IQ is below 70, but not as something that can rule MR in if IQ is above

70. This tendency to view the IQ criterion as the "necessary but not sufficient" condition for diagnosing MR can be seen also in the declaration filed by a prosecution expert in preparation for Mr. Smith's Atkins hearing. Although one of us had interviewed and obtained ABAS-II data from a large number of informants indicating very significant adaptive behavior deficits at various stages in Mr. Smith's life, the prosecution psychologist's declaration focused entirely on raising questions about whether the IQ criterion for diagnosing MR had been met. In other words, he assumed that if he could raise sufficient doubts about the IQ test results, his diagnosis of "Not-MR" would clearly be justified without even needing to comment on the substantial adaptive behavior piece of the defendant's claim.

This tendency to see adaptive behavior as running a distant second in importance to intelligence, if it is even acknowledged at all, is at the heart of what is wrong with the current approach to diagnosing MR. Much as we commend the efforts of the last two T&C Committees to focus more attention on the importance of adaptive behavior, we feel that there continues to be a fundamental flaw in the basic definition of MR which, unless corrected, will likely contribute to a continued slighting of adaptive behavior, if it is even assessed at all. This flaw is that adaptive behavior is always the second part of the definition, as in the 2002 statement that MR "is a disability characterized by significant limitations both in intellectual functioning and . . ." (p. 1). This, in addition to the fact that adaptive behavior is described as something separate from intelligence, contributes in our opinion to the notion that intellectual deficit must first be established before adaptive behavior even comes into play.

The solution seems fairly simple, and that is to reverse the order of the wording. Doing so, the definition might read as follows: "MR is a form of disability, first suspected in childhood or adolescence, that is characterized by significant deficits in adaptive social, academic, and practical functioning that are attributable to significant limitations in the ability to think and process information adequately." This proposed definition does several things that could, if taken seriously, serve to finally put "King IQ" in its place and raise adaptive behavior to an equal if not greater level of importance. The first is that adaptive behavior—termed "adaptive functioning" to free ourselves from all of the baggage associated with that poorly defined term—is now put toward the beginning of the definition, such that the starting point for the diagnosis is now establishing limitations in adaptive functioning rather than first establishing limitations in intelligence. By describing the intellectual criterion with the nonjargon words "ability to think and process information," we are indicating that what is important is not a score on an IQ test but an exploration of an individual's intellectual processes. However, by inserting the words "that are attributable," we hope to indicate that adaptive behavior deficit is not separable from intellectual deficit, but rather flows from it. This would, hopefully, cause a refocusing of adaptive behavior measures away from personality or stylistic aspects of incompetence, such as not having pleasant breath, and toward aspects of incompetence, such as vulnerability to exploitation, that are more clearly an outgrowth of difficulty in cognitively processing social or other challenges.

Need to Revisit the Borderline Category, but with a New Twist

There has been significant discussion that a concern underlying both the 1992 and 2002 AAMR manuals was to shift attention away from addressing the problem of "false positives," which was a major concern of the authors of the 1961 and 1973 manuals, and toward addressing the problem of "false negatives." In the next-to-last page of the 2002 manual, for example, mention is made of what Tymchuk, Lakin, and Luckasson (2001) termed "the lost generation"—a term which refers mainly to individuals who do not quite qualify for the MR label, in part because there no longer is a "Borderline" subcategory, but who still have significant needs for supports and protections. In raising the IQ ceiling to take into account standard error, and in adopting an easy-to-satisfy (e.g., deficits in only one out of three domains) adaptive behavior criterion, the 2002 T&C Committee obviously wished to swing the pendulum back in order that more of this disenfranchised population could be accommodated under the MR rubric.

In spite of the fairly overt desire on the part of the authors of the 2002 AAMR manual to accommodate a broader sample of the universe of cognitively impaired people, it seems unlikely the manual will have much success in attaining this objective, unless a more direct assault on the problem of false negatives is undertaken. A solution that has occurred to us, and to others such as MacMillan, Siperstein, and Gresham (1996), is to bring back something like the Borderline subcategory. It would have to be done in a very different way, however, in order to avoid the problems (i.e., gross overidentification of poor minority children), that caused the Borderline subcategory to be abandoned in 1973.

Two mistakes sank the Borderline subcategory in the first place. The first was that it was defined solely on where one fell in an IQ range, given that adaptive behavior was not really used or acknowledged in the 1960s or 1970s. The second was that it was identified as a new and separate subcategory, rather than being grounded in the broader pre-existing subcategory, unfortunately known as "moronity." While the previous subcategory had been believed to cover a fairly large chunk, at least up to 3%, of the general population, the new subcategory of mild MR defined on the basis of the minus-two-standard-deviations statistic reduced that population to a maximum of 2%, which arbitrarily threw out about one-third of the deserving population of people considered to have MR. The way to recapture the spirit of the Borderline subcategory (i.e., to allow deserving members of the "forgotten generation" to receive needed protections flowing from the diagnosis of MR) is to do three things:

1. Raise the IQ ceiling, if one has to have one at all, dramatically (say, to 80 or 85).
2. Base the diagnosis of MR, once one has gotten into that very broad IQ range, solely on adaptive deficits and, of course, the developmental criterion.
3. Place qualifying individuals not in a separate "Borderline" subcategory but rather in a somewhat expanded subcategory of "mild MR."

Thus, mild MR would now be a subcategory defined primarily by deficits in adaptive functioning attributable to problems in cognitive ability, but not necessary defined by an IQ level that fell below an arbitrarily, and statistically, defined score.

This proposed solution would go far toward addressing another problem that concerns lawyers and others who have written about the Atkins decision, and that is the need to expand that decision to cover other deserving individuals who do not quite qualify under the existing narrowly defined rubric of MR. The arbitrary diving line of IQ = 70 does not, unfortunately, correspond with the natural division between people who are vulnerable and deserve protection and people who are not vulnerable and are not deserving of protection. Especially, as the mean IQ of people with various brain-based disorders (e.g., Prader-Willi syndrome) has risen, thanks to various medical and educational interventions, there are now many vulnerable people who at one time, even after the abolition of the Borderline category, would have qualified by use of an IQ score as having MR but no longer do. The proposed solution of bringing the Borderline subcategory back but in a different guise would solve this problem and would put attention where it belongs, namely on how an individual functions in the world rather than on whether his IQ score falls above or below some less-than-meaningful dividing line.

CONCLUSION: NEED TO CLARIFY THE MR TAXON

A basic problem with the various AAMR definitions of MR is that they rely on artificial rather than natural criteria, and use jargon terms needing further definition rather than everyday words which need no further definition. In virtually every category in DSM-IV, the definition uses everyday words which describe behaviors that everyone can understand. Some examples would be pica ("the persistent eating of nonnutritive substances for a period of at least 1 month"); autism ("the presence of markedly abnormal or impaired development in social interaction and communication and a markedly restricted repertory of activity and interests"); and separation anxiety ("excessive anxiety concerning separation from the home or from those to whom the person is attached"). Here is the 2002 definition of MR: "a disability characterized by significant limitations both in intellectual functioning and in adaptive behavior as expressed in conceptual, social, and practical adaptive skills" (p. 1). The meanings of "disability," "adaptive behavior," and "adaptive skills" are not evident and need further definition. "Intellectual functioning" is probably somewhat more of a natural/everyday term, but the way it is later operationally defined as minus two standard deviations below the population mean on a measure of IQ is nothing if not artificial. The application of the same statistical criterion to the assessment of adaptive behavior is also a step in the direction of greater artificiality, even if one assumes that measures of adaptive behavior tap into the natural taxon of MR, which we have argued that they do not do sufficiently.

The artificiality and arbitrariness of the 2002, and previous, AAMR definitions of MR contribute to the bickering and nit-picking over interpretation of IQ scores that can be found in the typical Akins hearings and shakes one's confidence that a just and correct decision will always be reached. It would be useful if the definition of the category of MR could be grounded in something more natural, such that the dividing line between "MR" and "Not-MR" would correspond to what Paul Meehl (1973), in describing medical categories such as TB, called "nature carved at the joints." Such a naturally based definition (taxon) hopefully would increase the likelihood that diagnostic decisions in *Atkins* cases were *true* in a real and not just a bureaucratic sense.

Given that MR is really a bureaucratic/disability category, rather than a medical one, although many medical conditions contribute to MR, it may be difficult to come up with a more natural, taxonically-based, definition. However, until a more natural definition is devised, there will always be problems in making the diagnosis, especially at the upper boundary where virtually all Atkins defendants can be found. We have discussed repeatedly in this paper the need to devise a definition of adaptive behavior and, by extension, of MR, that taps into the "natural taxon " of MR. Because MR is a condition grounded in the perception of others, this natural taxon has to be based on the factors that other people use in deciding that someone has MR and needs the protections associated with that status. Greenspan (1997, 2003) has contended that the behavioral phenotype for MR is most likely to be found in the notion of social vulnerability in general, and gullibility in particular. This notion, explored more fully in another chapter by Greenspan in this book, might be expressed in an elaboration on the definition expressed earlier. To repeat, that definition went as follows: "MR is a form of disability, first suspected in childhood or adolescence, that is characterized by significant deficits in adaptive social, academic, and practical functioning that are attributable to significant limitations in the ability to think and process information adequately." The elaboration, bringing it closer to the pre-20th-century taxon, might add the following: "People with MR are seen by others as extremely naïve, trusting, and vulnerable in their dealings with others, and need protections against exploitation by others who would take advantage of their gullibility."

In every *Atkins* case where we feel that a legitimate claim for execution exemption can be made, we have found that the individual is described by everyone who has known him with words such as: "_____ is one of the most gullible people on the planet." Interestingly, although Justice John Paul Stephens, in his majority opinion in *Atkins v. Virginia*, justified the opinion on the basis of emerging national consensus about the inhumanity of executing people with MR, he did devote some attention to discussing adaptive deficits that justify such an exemption. His explanation focused on the inability of people with MR to see through manipulation by a less-disabled confederate, inability of people with MR to see through manipulation by police officers seeking a confession, inability of people with MR to understand how to cut a deal that might save their life, and inability of people with MR to understand the court proceedings well enough to be of assistance to their counsel. In other words, the taxon of MR, as expressed by a member of the U.S. Supreme Court, was grounded in social vulnerability in general, and gullibility in particular. Maybe the *Atkins* decision itself, and not just the experience of expert witnesses in *Atkins* proceedings, has something important to tell the authors of the next AAMR diagnostic manual about how to devise a definition of MR that will finally be found adequate.

REFERENCES

Achenbach, T. M., & Edelbrock, C. S. (1983). *Manual for the child behavior checklist and revised child behavior profile*. Burlington: University of Vermont.

Atkins v. Virginia. U. S. Case No. 8452. (2002).

Bellugi, U., Mills, D., & Jernigan, T. (1999). Linking cognition, brain structure, and brain function in Williams Syndrome. In H. Tager-Flusberg (Ed.), *Neurodevelopmental disorders* (pp. 111–136). Cambridge: Massachusetts Institute of Technology Press.

Conners, C. K. (1997). *Conners Rating Scales (Rev. ed.)*. Minneapolis: Pearson Assessments.

Doll, E. A. (1941). The essentials of an inclusive concept of mental deficiency. *American Journal of Mental Deficiency, 46*, 214–219.

Driscoll, J. H., & Greenspan, S. (1994, April). *How do we know when a rating of child behavior is off the wall?* Paper presented at the annual conference of the New England Educational Research Organization, Camden, ME.

Edgerton, R. B. (1993). *The cloak of competence: Revised and updated*. Berkeley: University of California Press.

Elliot, A. (Director). (2001). *The collector of Bedford street [Motion picture].* (Available from Welcome Change Productions, 107 Bedford Street, Upper One, New York, NY 10014)

Greenspan, S. (1997). A contextualist perspective on adaptive behavior. In R. L. Schalock (Ed.), *Adaptive behavior and its measurement: Implications for the field of mental retardation* (pp. 61–80). Washington, DC: American Association on Mental Retardation.

Greenspan, S. (2004). Why Pinocchio was victimized: Factors contributing to social failure in people with mental retardation. In H. N. Switzky (Ed.), *International review of research in mental retardation (Vol. 28*, pp. 122–147). San Diego, CA: Elsevier/Academic Press.

Greenspan, S., & Love, P. F. (1997). Social intelligence and developmental disorder: Mental retardation, learning disabilities and autism. In W. E. MacLean, Jr. (Ed.), *Ellis' handbook of mental deficiency, psychological theory, and research* (3rd ed., pp. 311–342). Mahwah, NJ: Erlbaum.

Greenspan, S., & Switzky, H. N. (2003). Execution exemption should be based on actual vulnerability, not disability label. *Ethics & Behavior, 13,* 19–26.

Hagen, M. A. (1997). *Whores of the court: The fraud of psychiatric testimony and the rape of American justice.* New York: HarperCollins.

Harrison, P. L., & Oakland, T. (2003). *Adaptive behavior assessment system (ABAS-II)* (2nd ed.). San Antonio: PsychCorp/Harcourt Assessment.

Ireland, W. W. (1877). *On idiocy and imbecility.* London: Churchill.

Kernan, K. T., & Sabsay, S. (1988). Communication in social interaction: Aspects of an ethnography of mildly mentally handicapped adults. In M. Beveridge, G. Conti-Ramsden, & I. Leudar (Eds.), *Language and communication in mentally handicapped people* (pp. 239–353). London: Chapman and Hall.

Kernan, K. T. & Sabsay, S. (1992). Discourse and conversational skills of mentally retarded adults. In A. M. Bauer (Ed.), *Students who challenge the system* (pp. 145–185). Norwood, NJ: Ablex.

Lewis, D. O., & Balla, D. A. (1976). *Delinquency and psychopathology.* Philadelphia: Saunders.

Luckasson, R., Borthwick-Duffy, S., Buntinx, W. H. E., Coulter, D. L., Craig, E. M., Reeve, A., et al. (2002). *Mental retardation: Definition, classification, and systems of supports* (10th ed.). Washington, DC: American Association on Mental Retardation.

Luckasson, R., Coulter, D. L., Polloway, E. A., Reiss, S., Schalock, R. L., Snell, M. E., et al. (1992). *Mental retardation: Definition, classification and systems of supports* (9th ed.). Washington, DC: American Association on Mental Retardation.

MacMillan, D. L., Siperstein, G. N., & Gresham, F. M. (1996). A challenge to the viability of mild mental retardation as a diagnostic category. *Exceptional Children, 62,* 356–371.

Meehl, P. (1973). *Psychodiagnosis: Selected papers.* Minneapolis: University of Minnesota Press.

Schalock, R. L. (1999). The merging of adaptive behavior and intelligence: Implications for the field of mental retardation. In R. L. Schalock (Ed.), *Adaptive behavior and its measurement: Implications for the field of mental retardation* (pp. 43–60). Washington, DC: American Association on Mental Retardation

Schalock, R. L., Buntinx, W., Borthwick-Duffy, S., Luckasson, R., Snell, M., Tasse, M., et al. (2006). *A user's guide for AAMR's 2002 definition, classification and systems of supports: Applications for clinicians, educators, disability program managers, and policy makers.* Washington, DC: American Association on Mental Retardation.

Spitz, H. H. (1988). Mental retardation as a thinking disorder: The rationalist alternative to empiricism. In N. Bray (Ed.), *International review of research in mental retardation* (Vol. 15, pp. 1–31). New York: Academic Press.

Suen, H. K., & Ary, D. (1989). *Analyzing quantitative behavioral observation data.* Hillsdale, NJ: Erlbaum.

Switzky, H. N., Greenspan, S., & Granfield, J. (1996). Adaptive behavior, everyday intelligence and the constitutive definition of mental retardation. In A. F. Rotatori, J. O. Schwenn, & S. Burkhardt (Eds.), *Advances in special education* (Vol. 10, pp.1–24). Greenwich, CT: JAI Press.

Switzky, H. N., & Heal, L. (1990). Research issues and methods in special education. In R. Gaylord-Ross (Ed.), *Issues and research in special education* (pp. 1–81). New York: Teachers College Press.

Tredgold, A. F. (1908). *Mental deficiency.* London: Baillere, Tindall, & Fox.

Tymchuk, A. J., Lakin, K. C., & Luckasson, R. (Eds.). (2001). *The forgotten generation: The status and challenges of adults with mild cognitive limitations.* Baltimore: Paul H. Brookes.

Williams, P., Bratt, B., & Shoultz, B. (1995). *We can speak for ourselves: Self-advocacy by mentally handicapped people* (Rev. ed.). Bloomington: University of Indiana Press.

Chapter Nineteen

The Relationship Between the WHO-ICF (International Classification of Functioning, Disability, and Health) and the AAMR 2002 System

Wil H. E. Buntinx

This chapter discusses the relationship between the International Classification of Functioning, Disability, and Health (ICF) of the World Health Organization (WHO, 2001), and the Definition, Classification and Systems of Supports of the American Association on Mental Retardation (AAMR) (Luckasson et al., 2002). This comparison is inspired by two questions:

1. Are the two systems compatible?
2. What can be learned from the ICF for the application and further development of the AAMR 2002 system?

There are at least three reasons for a comparative examination. First, there is a growing international need for unification of conceptualizations of disability across a wide range of collaborating clinical disciplines, including medicine, rehabilitation, education, psychology, social work, and nursing. A common frame of reference is also increasingly being asked for by advocates, self-advocates, researchers, policymakers, managers, and administrators in the areas of public health policy, social security, and health care organization at large (Drotar & Sturm, 1996; Greenspan, 1999; Halbertsma, 1995; WHO, 2001). Therefore, it is important to examine whether the AAMR model of intellectual disability (ID) is congruent with international developments in the conceptualization of disability.

Second, the ICF's claim to offering a unifying language needs to be tested: If "intellectual disability" represents a particular class of disability, the general characteristics of disability as described by the ICF should be recognized in the AAMR 2002 system. To examine compatibility between the two systems, we ask how well the conceptualization of ID in the AAMR 2002 system can be expressed in the ICF model and vice versa.

Third, a closer look at the ICF system may generate ideas for effective inter-disciplinary application and for further development of the AAMR 2002 system in the future.

In this chapter, the name "intellectual disability" (ID) is equivalent to the name "mental retardation" as used in Luckasson et al., 2002 (see also Luckasson & Reeve, 2000). First, in preparation for the comparison, an overview of the ICF will be presented. Second, the compatibility between the ICF and the AAMR 2002 system will be examined. Third, some implications of the outcome of that comparison will be discussed in the context of application and development of the AAMR 2002 system. Fourth, a conclusion will be formulated.

OVERVIEW OF THE ICF

The overview of the ICF will be organized around four themes:

1. The historical background of the system.
2. The presentation of the dimensions of "human functioning."
3. The presentation of the dimensions of "health" and "contextual factors."
4. A brief discussion of the dynamics of the ICF model.

Historical Roots

A good understanding of the ICF system should start with a brief explanation of its predecessor, the International Classification of Impairments, Disabilities, and Handicaps (ICIDH) (WHO, 1980). This ICIDH was designed for the evaluation of the effectiveness of health care processes. The primary goal was to provide a tool for epidemiological research and outcome-related evaluations of care systems on a national and international level. It was based on the extension of the classification system of "diseases" and "causes of death" already available in the International Classification of Diseases (ICD) and on a sequence of "etiology → pathology → manifestation" (WHO, 1999a). This sequence, however, does not reflect the whole range of problems felt by people who face a disability or the consequences of a chronic health condition. Neither does it reflect their needs for supports. The ICIDH offered an important extension by introducing different perspectives or planes of experience for looking at disability. The health condition as an "interiorized state" or "intrinsic situation" is the first perspective; a corresponding classification system was and still is available in the ICD system. The ICIDH goes beyond this and adds three other perspectives:

1. Exteriorization of pathology in body functions and anatomy.
2. Objectified pathology as expressed in the person's activities.
3. Social consequences of pathology (WHO, 1980, p. 30; see also Figure 19.1.)

These three perspectives coincide with the functional levels of the body, the individual, and society. The ICIDH was a breakthrough in integrating the medical model with the social model of disability and combining the individual perspective with the social perspective. The ICIDH provided clear definitions of concepts and an extensive system of classification and codes for characteristics of its three dimensions (not discussed here). It became both a conceptual model and a classification tool.

Core Components of disability process	**Disease** ➡	**Impairment** ➡ **Disability** ➡ **Handicap**		
Perspective	Intrinsic situation	Exteriorized	Objectified	Socialized
Functional level	Pathology or Health Condition	Body	Individual activities	Social context
WHO Classification System	ICD	ICIDH		

Figure 19.1. The ICIDH model: Core Components (bold face) with their relationship and distinctive Perspective, Functional level and corresponding Classification System

However, the ICIDH was criticized for conceptual as well as technical reasons (Fougeyrollas, 1998; Kraijer, 1993; Tarlov, 1993; WHO Collaborating Center, 1994; WHO, 1999b, p. 195). We will not discuss the technical (coding and classification) problems. We briefly mention the conceptual criticism, which referred to the following:

1. The unidirectional and alleged causal nature of the disabling process (not intended but strongly suggested by the unidirectional arrows).
2. The absence of the impact of the environment on the disabling process.
3. Weaknesses of application in problems of children and the elderly (the system is not sensitive to development).
4. The use of negative language ("impairment," "disability," "handicap").
5. A paradigmatic issue: The ICIDH conceives "disability" as a separate phenomenon without reference to the functioning of people "without a disability." This would enhance categorization and conceptually separate persons-with from persons-without disabilities. Disability is seen as a class in its own and not on a continuum of human functioning.

This criticism, as well as feedback from the worldwide use of the ICIDH in research, gave input to a fundamental revision that started in 1993 and ended in November 2001 with the official release of the International Classification of Functioning, Disability, and Health under the new acronym ICF. The new conceptual model of human functioning comprises six components. Usually, the three components of "human functioning" are distinguished from the "health" component and the two "contextual components" that are seen as influencing factors. The next two sections will explain the conceptual model along this dual approach. Although the focus will be on the model itself, references will also be made to the more technical classification systems without going into detail.

ICF: A Multidimensional Description of Human Functioning

The ICF provides a framework for the description of human functioning and its restrictions along three dimensions representing the body, the individual, and the societal perspective. Each dimension can be seen as a particular aspect of human functioning and is further organized into domains. *Functioning* is used as an umbrella term for neutral or nonproblematic functional states, whereas *disability* is used as an umbrella term for problems of functioning. On the model level, the three dimensions of human functioning (now formulated in positive language) are defined as shown in the center of Figure 19.2 (see WHO, 2001, pp. 10–18). This figure shows the "neutral" terminology with the corresponding problematic state in italics.

The body functions and structures dimension comprises two major domains, defined as:

- Body Functions: the physiological and psychological functions of the body systems, and
- Body Structures: anatomical parts of the body such as organs, limbs, and their components.

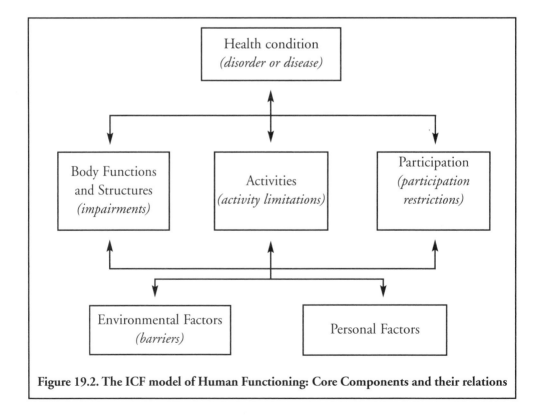

Figure 19.2. The ICF model of Human Functioning: Core Components and their relations

Impairments are problems in body functions or structures such as a significant deviation or loss. In the context of ID, intellectual functions and cognitive functions are subdomains of "body functions" (code: b117). The activity dimension refers to a person's execution of a task or action. Difficulties a person may have in the capacity and/or performance of activities are referred to as "*activity limitations.*"

The participation dimension refers to a person's involvement in life situations in relation to health conditions, body functions and structures, activities, and contextual factors. It denotes the degree of the person's involvement in the community, including the society's response to the person's functioning. Problems that an individual may have in the manner or extent of involvement in life situations are called "participation restrictions." Unlike the activity dimension, which is about individual performance and the presence of skills that are relevant to various aspects of life, the participation dimension is about the actual involvement of the person in real social life settings. Restrictions must be understood as problems resulting from the availability or accessibility of resources, accommodations and/or services, relative to impairments and limitations. Participation restrictions are about disadvantages that limit the fulfillment of social roles that are normal (considering age, sex, culture) for the individual. The term participation restrictions is congruent with the term *handicap* in the original ICIDH (WHO, 1980). Although the concepts of activity and participation are conceptually different from each other (as recognized in the ICF general model), the classification system eventually combines them into one single component. At this point, the ICF classification system is less consistent with the ICF model then was the case in the older ICIDH and also in the draft ICIDH Beta-2 version of the revision process. Further discussion of this feature is beyond the scope of the present article.

ICF: Health Conditions and Contextual Factors

Human functioning and disability are both conceived as processes and outcomes of interactions between health conditions on one hand and contextual factors on the other hand. These two concepts complete the model.

Health conditions.

It is important to realize that the ICF is a frame of reference for the description of human functioning in relation to health conditions. Functional states of the individual that are not related to health conditions are not within the scope of the ICF. The ICF system is not meant for describing and classifying restrictions of human functioning because of gender, religion, race, socioeconomic problems, or any other circumstances that are not health related. Health, however, should be seen according to the WHO definition comprising physical, psychological, and social well-being and not just the absence of disease. As an international classification system of health conditions, the most recent 10th edition of the WHO's International Statistical Classification of Diseases and Related Health Problems (ICD-10) is complementary to the ICF (WHO, 1999a). Actually, the ICD-10 represents an etiological framework in which health conditions can be identified that affect the individual on the three dimensions of functioning. However, the use of the ICF does not presuppose a clearly identified disease or etiology. In other words, the ICF can be used without reference to the ICD-10. Another remark should be made about the complex interrelatedness in the model. Even in the event of the absence of a health condition at the onset of, for example, a participation restriction or activity limitation, the continuation of such a situation eventually may result in a health condition that did not exist before but was induced as a consequence of prolonged stress.

Contextual factors.

Recent paradigms of disability conceive human functioning (whether or not "disabled") as multidimensional *person-environment* interactions that can be approached at different levels (Bronfenbrenner, 1979; Landesman-Ramey, Dossett, & Echols, 1996; Luckasson et al., 2002; Mercer, 1992; Rioux, 1997; Schalock & Kiernan, 1990; Schalock & Verdugo, 2002). In the ICF, contextual factors represent the complete background of living conditions that may affect the state of functioning of a particular individual.

Contextual factors comprise two components: environmental factors and personal factors. Environmental factors make up the physical, social, and attitudinal background and environment in which people live and conduct their lives. They refer to the environment that the individual shares with others in his or her family, community, culture, and nation. The environmental factors are external to the individual and can have a positive or a negative effect on the individual's body structure or function, on his or her performance of activities, or on his participation as a member of society. Environmental factors can act as barriers or facilitators of functioning on two levels:

- *Individual level:* The immediate personal environment including settings such as home, school, and workplace; it includes material features as well as people, relationships, supports, values and attitudes.
- *Societal level:* The formal and informal social structures, organizations, and services in the community including housing services, communication services, transportation, health, and educational services, social security services, and governmental agencies that are relevant to service providing. The societal level also includes the overarching systems established in the cultural and national service patterns including values, ideology, laws, and regulations.

The importance of the societal environment in both the disabling process and the provision of supports has now been widely recognized. Several declarations and conventions of the United Nations are aimed at improving social conditions and particularly at enhancing equal rights and opportunities for people with disabilities (Maes, 1998). Among these, the *Standard Rules on the Equalization of Opportunities for Persons with Disabilities* (United Nations, 1994) are of particular importance (Table 19.1).

Personal factors are the individual background of a person's life and living, composed of features that are not part of the person's health condition or functional state. Personal factors include: age, race, gender, educational background, fitness, lifestyle, habits, coping styles, social background, profession, past and current experiences. Personal factors are not further classified in the ICF. However, they may influence the functioning of the individual with a health condition as well as the outcome of interventions.

Health conditions and contextual factors are the two dynamic factors that influence human functioning on its three dimensions. These two factors, together with the three

---

Table 19.1
Target Areas of the United Nations Standard Rules on Equalization of Opportunities for Persons with Disabilities (summarized)

1. Accessibility by removing obstacles to participation in the physical environment; access of people with disabilities and their families and advocates to full information on diagnosis, rights, services, and programs; facilitating communication and accessibility of media, television, radio, and newspapers.
2. Educational opportunities for children, youth, and adults in integrated settings and education of people with disabilities as an integral part of national educational planning.
3. The active support of integration of people with disabilities in employment and the implementation of nondiscriminatory laws and regulations in the employment field.
4. Provision of adequate income support and social security schemes that do not exclude or discriminate against people with disabilities.
5. Full participation in family life, personal integrity, opportunity to experience sexuality, and protection against abuse.
6. Opportunities to utilize their creative, artistic, and intellectual potential, not only for their own benefit, but also for the enrichment of their community.
7. Equal opportunities for recreation and sports.
8. Participation in the religious life of their communities.

---

dimensions of functioning and disability, are the building blocks of the ICF *classification system*. The ICF *model of disability* refers also to *health conditions*. For reasons of simplification and for comparison with the AAMR 2002 model, these "building blocks" or "components" are all referred to as "dimensions" of the model.

ICF Dynamics

The ICF represents a multidimensional and dynamic frame of reference that allows multiple interactions on different levels of functioning. The model offers five conceptual dimensions and their interrelations as an aid to understanding the complex reality of human functioning and disability:

1. Health/etiology.
2. Body functions and structures.
3. Activities.
4. Participation.
5. Context, comprising both environmental and personal factors.

In the ICF, functioning and disability are conceived as resulting from a complex dynamic interaction between health conditions and contextual factors. Interactions work in two directions. A health condition can lead to a disability. The presence of a disability, though, may also modify a person's health condition and lead to a disorder. A person can have impairments without having activity limitations (e.g., a disfigurement as an impairment of body structure) or may experience activity limitations without evident impairments or may have participation problems without impairments or activity limitations (e.g., as a result of stigma). A person with mental retardation, for example, could experience participation restrictions in work or informal relationships, not primarily as a result of mental, motor, speech impairments, or limitations in communication, but as a result of stigma (e.g., living in an institution and/or having a reputation of behavior problems). In this case, attitudes and beliefs of the (work or living) environment affect the person's involvement in work and social relationships.

It is obvious that the complex interactions of disorders, impairments, limitations, restrictions, and environmental barriers in different degrees of magnitude and relevance to the situation may affect the a person's functioning considerably and in different ways. The same participation restrictions can be the outcome of quite different antecedents in terms of ICF dimensions. The scheme in Figure 19.2 illustrates the potential roles of health conditions and contextual factors as well as the potential interactions between the three dimensions of functioning itself. The ICF offers a frame of reference to help us understand a person's actual functioning and identify areas for intervention or support to improve that functioning.

Note that the ICF is not a diagnostic manual. It is a way of conceiving human functioning and disability, and therefore it may contribute to the conceptualization of disability in general. As a general frame of reference, it helps explain the disabling process to individuals who experience disability, to the general public, to clinicians involved in assessment or rehabilitation, and to policymakers who have a responsibility in providing support systems or creating more equal opportunities for people with disabilities in society. In specific situations, the more detailed classifications of the ICF can support the assessment process by enabling the construction of more specific instruments (e.g., Maeda et al., 2005; Simeonsson et al., 2003). The ICF therefore is both a common language for understanding disability and a reference tool that can be used in clinical assessment and data collection in research.

LINKING THE AAMR 2002 SYSTEM TO THE ICF: ARE THEY COMPATIBLE?

The AAMR 2002 system includes a theoretical model of intellectual disability as well as a three-step multidimensional assessment system:

1. Diagnosis.
2. Description of strengths and weaknesses of the person's functioning.
3. Establishing a profile of supports needs.

Therefore an examination of compatibility with the ICF should be conducted on different levels. We will consider the following:

1. The theoretical model.
2. The definition (diagnosis).
3. The assessment of strengths and weaknesses in functioning.
4. The supports profile.
5. An analysis of similarities and differences.

Theoretical Model

The AAMR 2002 system describes ID as a state of functioning that requires an understanding of the person's capabilities as well as the structure and expectations of the person's environment (Luckasson et al., 2002). ID therefore is approached from an ecological paradigm of disability and is not conceived as a state or defect "within" the person. The outcome of this person-environment interaction can be influenced by factors within as well as outside the person. This influence can be actively directed to enhance the person's capabilities, e.g., by providing education, training, and appropriate health care, by making changes in the demands of settings of the person, or by facilitating access to resources of the social environment and community. Both the AAMR 2002 concept of ID and the ICF focus on "human functioning" as a multidimensional person-environment interaction (Figure 19.3).

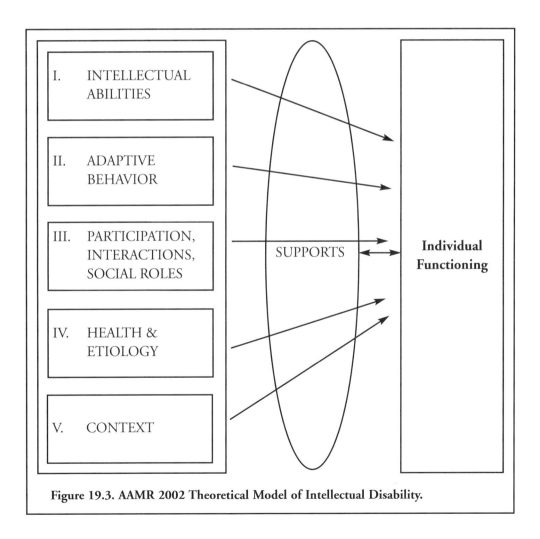

Figure 19.3. AAMR 2002 Theoretical Model of Intellectual Disability.

The AAMR 2002 model's five dimensions clearly encompass a multidimensional approach to ID. This multidimensionality is also reflected in the Supports function of the system.

Both the AAMR and the ICF systems are similar in their ecological conceptualization of functioning and disability. Both systems also present a dynamic concept of functioning and disability that does not imply a permanent state of being and recognizes positive and negative aspects of functioning: limitations as well as strengths; environmental barriers as well as facilitators. Moreover, both explicitly refer to interactions between the dimensions. Both systems bear a positive orientation toward improving the lives of people with disabilities. Both systems have a multi-paradigmatic background. That means that they do not rely on a one-sided objective or subjective worldview and attempt to integrate medical, psychological, and social models of disability (Mercer, 1992). The ICF states this explicitly (WHO, 2001, p. 20); the AAMR system demonstrates it in the multidimensional model of functioning and the multiple assessment dimensions (Luckasson et al., 2002).Without going into more detail on the complex issues involved in paradigm comparison, there is ample evidence for compatibility on the theoretical level of both systems.

Definition Level
The AAMR 2002 definition of ID comprises the following (Luckasson et al., 2002, p. 110; Luckasson & Reeve, 2000):

a statement:	mental retardation is a disability (expression of limitations in individual functioning within a social context and representing a substantial disadvantage to the individual);
a first requirement:	significantly limitations in intellectual functioning;
a second requirement:	significant limitations in adaptive behavior as expressed in conceptual, social, and practical adaptive skills;
a third requirement:	originates before age 18.

The statement places ID clearly in the realm of (problematic) human functioning. The first inclusion criterion for ID is the significant subaverage intellectual functioning, which clearly is an element of the ICF domain of body functions (mental/intellectual functions). The second AAMR inclusion criterion is the presence of limitations in adaptive-skills areas, which clearly are within the scope of the ICF activities dimension. The third requirement may be seen as a "personal factor" in terms of ICF.

It may be concluded that the core concepts and criteria of the AAMR definition fit the frame of reference of the ICF (see Figure 19.4). It should be clear that with respect to the theoretical construct of "disability," the theoretical models of the AAMR 2002 system and the ICF are compatible.

ICF AAMR 2002	Health Condition	Body Functions & Structures	Activities	Participation	Context (environment & personal)
Statement		*	*	*	
Requirement 1		*			
Requirement 2			*		
Requirement 3					*

Figure 19.4. Relation between the central concepts of the AAMR 2002 definition of ID and corresponding ICF components

A diagnosis of ID depends on the application of the definition criteria. The first requirement can be expressed in the ICF code b117, eventually with the qualifier extension b117.4 for "complete problem." The second requirement can also be expressed in terms of ICF activities codes, as shown in Table 19.2. This table shows the adaptive-skills areas of both the AAMR 2002 and AAMR 1992 system with examples of corresponding ICF activities codes.

Assessment of Strengths and Weaknesses in Functioning

The AAMR 2002 manual describes a three-step assessment process for (a) diagnosis, (b) description of strengths and weaknesses, and (c) development of a profile of needed supports. After establishing a diagnosis, a multidimensional analysis of strengths and weaknesses, facilitators and barriers, is performed along the five dimensions of the theoretical model. The similarities between the AAMR 2002 dimensions and those of the ICF are already obvious in a comparison of Figures 19.2 and 19.3. The relationship between the two models can be further demonstrated by showing the conceptual similarities in the dimensions, as in Figures 19.5a–f. These figures show the simplified models of the ICF (top) and the AAMR 2002 system (bottom) with arrows linking the corresponding dimensions (a: intellectual functioning; b: adaptive behavior; c: participation; d: health and etiology; e: health; f: supports).

Figure 19.6 summarizes the relationship between the two systems and shows that the AAMR 2002 assessment dimensions can be projected on the corresponding components of the ICF and vice versa.

Supports

At the heart of the AAMR 2002 system is the function of Supports. One of the assumptions underlying this model is that the descriptions of strengths and weaknesses, and facilitators and barriers, serve the purpose of developing a profile of supports needs. Therefore,

Table 19.2

AAMR Adaptive-Skills Areas (2002 and 1992) and Related Classification of ICF Activities and Participation Domains

AAMR 2002 Adaptive skills	AAMR 1992 Adaptive skills (corresponding)	Related ICF Activities and Participation Classifications (ICF codes and examples for AAMR 1992 skill)
Conceptual adaptive skills: Language Reading and writing Money concepts Self-direction	Communication	Communication (d310–d399) (understanding and producing messages; using communication devices and techniques)
	Self-direction	General tasks and demands (d210–d299) (undertaking single tasks; multiple tasks; handling stress, and other psychological demands)
	Health and safety	Self-care (d570) (looking after one's health)
	Functional academics	Learning and applying knowledge (d130–d150) (school education; copying, rehearsing, learning to read, write, calculate)
Social adaptive skills: Interpersonal responsibility Self-esteem Gullibility Naïveté Follows rules Obeys laws Avoids victimization	Social skills	Interpersonal interactions and relationships (d710–d799) (relating with strangers; family relationships; informal social relationships; intimate relationships)
	Leisure	Performing in recreation (d920) (recreation and leisure)
Practical adaptive skills: Daily living activities Occupational skills Maintaining safe environments	Self-care	Self-care (d510–d599) (washing oneself; toileting; eating; drinking; dressing)
	Home-living	Domestic life (d61–d699) (acquiring necessities, household, caring for possessions)
	Community use	Mobility (d450–d499) Community, social and civic life (d910–d999) (walking; using transportation; moving around in different locations; community life)
	Health and safety	Self-care (d570) (looking after one's health)
	Work	Performing in work and employment (d840–d859) (apprenticeship; acquiring, keeping, and terminating a job)

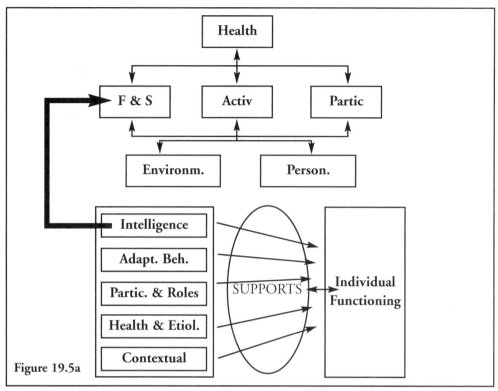

Figure 19.5a

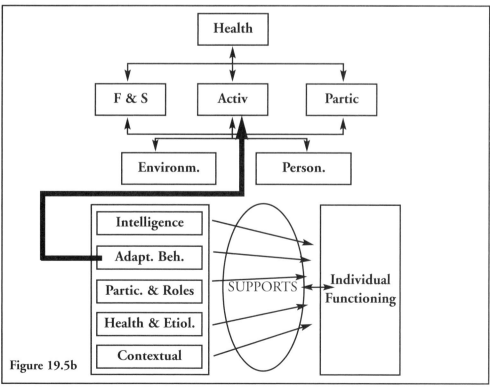

Figure 19.5b

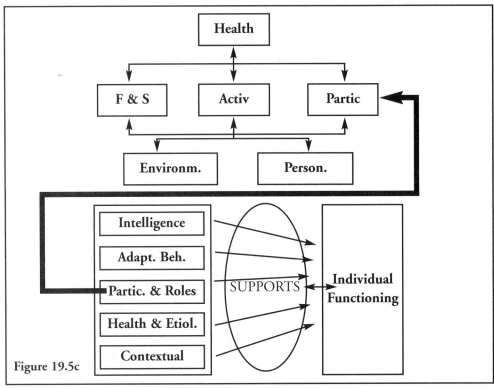

Figure 19.5c

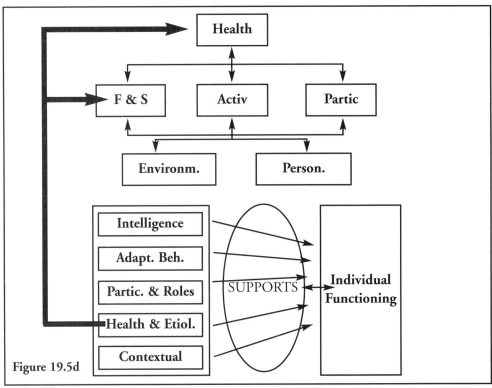

Figure 19.5d

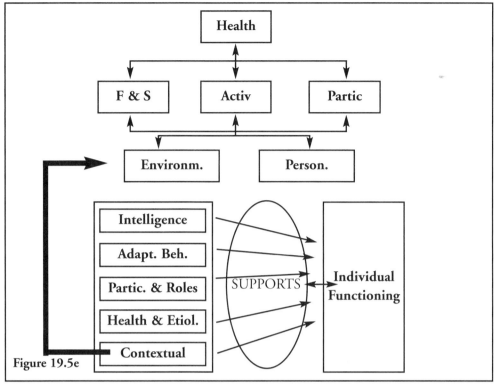

Figure 19.5e

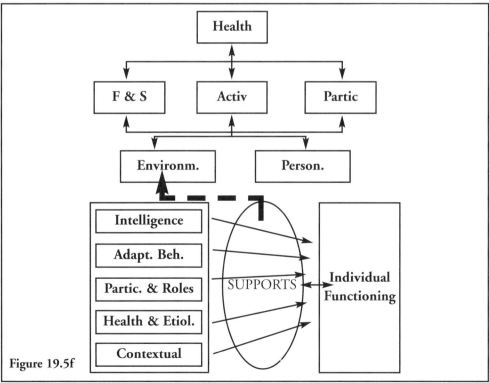

Figure 19.5f

ICF AAMR 2002	Health Condition	Body Functions & Structures	Activities	Participation	Context (environment & personal)
Dimension I (intellectual functioning)		*			
Dimension II (adaptive behavior skills)			*		
Dimension III (participation, interactions, and social roles)			*		
Dimension IV (health & etiology)	*	*			
Dimension V (context)					*
Figure 19.6. Relation between the assessment dimensions of the AAMR 2002 system and the analogous ICF dimensions (* show corresponding analogous dimensions)					

the AAMR 2002 is firmly rooted in a supports paradigm of disability. From the previous discussions, it will be clear that supports also could be described in terms of the dimensions of the AAMR 2002 model of individual functioning. In theory, this can be done. On the basis of their analysis of the person's functioning, professionals should, of course, discuss supports needs, goals, activities, and other measures with the person, his family, and/or specialized service providers in order to enhance and improve that person's functioning. However, the world of day-to-day practical situations is not best reflected in the specialized and analytic language of professionals. Therefore, the AAMR 2002 system offers a more suitable supports model that is discussed in depth in Chapter 9 of Luckasson et al. (2002). This model provides support areas, functions, systems, and outcomes. Recently AAMR published the Supports Intensity Scale that offers an instrument for mapping supports profiles and for the measurement of intensity of supports needs (Thompson et al., 2004). The ICF model does not separately reflect the supports function in its diagram, but nevertheless incorporates it within the "environmental factors" dimensions. Chapter 3 of the ICF "environmental factors dimension" is devoted to the function of personal supports and supportive relationships. Chapter 5 of the same ICF dimension comprises structured services, organizations, and policies that provide (special) supports to persons with disabilities. However, the ICF model is not focused on the provision of supports, but again, it is not impossible to relate the AAMR 2002 support function to the ICF model (Figure 19.5f).

Similarities and Differences

The similarities and differences between the AAMR 2002 system and the ICE model of functioning and disability can be summarized as follows.

Similarities:

1. Both focus on human functioning as a whole.
2. "Functioning" is defined as the person-environment interaction, placing both systems in the realm of ecological theory.
3. The systems share a multiparadigmatic background (bio-psycho-social model).
4. Congruent frames of reference (Figures 19.5a–f).
5. Congruence between adaptive skill areas and activities domains (Table 19.2).
6. Common approach to assessment of the functioning of the person as a whole within the context (expectations and resources) of the environment.
7. On a more philosophical level, both systems do not just clarify differences between disabled and nondisabled states of functioning but emphasize social equality and share a vision of a-society-for-all and full community participation for persons with disabilities.

Differences:

1. The ICF is a general model of disability, whereas the AAMR 2002 system is specific to mental retardation.
2. The ICF is not a diagnostic or an assessment system, whereas the AAMR 2002 system is.
3. The ICF reflects a professional and rather objective view on functioning and disability, whereas the AAMR 2002 system allows space for including subjective aspects of functioning (e.g., personal appraisal; quality-of-life issues) and has a strong orientation toward support.
4. The ICF has been developed as a result of consensus procedures involving international professional as well as consumer views on disability and functioning. In addition to including information from field consultation (professionals and consumers), the development of the AAMR 2002 system has also been guided by emerging evidence-based views, e.g., on the nature of intelligence and adaptive behavior.

IMPLICATIONS

Although the AAMR 2002 and ICF systems were conceived along independent lines, there is a high degree of compatibility between the two. Compatibility should be understood in terms of a high degree of similarity between concepts and theoretical models of disability and underlying paradigm. This places the AAMR 2002 approach in line with the present international orientation as adopted by the WHO to improve our understanding by studying disability in an ecological and multidimensional context and applying this understanding in a context of social egalitarianism. This compatibility may be seen as support for the validity of the AAMR 2002 conceptual model and assessment system.

A practical implication of this compatibility is the potential use of the ICF as a supplementary assessment resource in the context of the AAMR 2002 system. First, the classification domains of the various ICF dimensions can serve as (additional) checklists for clinicians in the assessment process. However, because of the elaborateness of the full ICF, a straightforward application or detailed inventory in individual cases might result in the registration of an impractical multitude of "problems," especially in people with severe intellectual disability (Kraijer, 1993). The use of the ICF as an assessment aid should therefore be made with professional discretion. Second, existing diagnostic tools can be used with the ICF framework and therefore with the AAMR 2002 system. Examples are the ICD-10 for classifying health conditions and etiology, and the Diagnostic and Statistical Manual of Mental Disorders (DSM-IV) (American Psychiatric Association, 1994) for classifying aspects of mental health or psychiatric disorders. Third, new instruments and assessment frameworks that are being designed for use in the ICF-environment can also be applied in the AAMR 2002 environment. For example, the studies of Simeonsson et al. (2003) and Maeda et al. (2005) describe assessment instruments that are based on the ICF but, because of the high degree of compatibility between the two systems, are also relevant to be studied and used with the AAMR 2002 system. Another effort to relating the ICF to the assessment of disability is currently being made by the American Psychological Association (Holloway, 2004) and eventually may provide useful information for the further development of the AAMR 2002 system.

Another consideration for the development of the AAMR 2002 system could be a more elaborated discussion of "personal factors" as formulated in the ICF model. Actually, personal factors such as gender, race, age, and lifestyle (e.g., maintaining nutritious and healthy food patterns) do have a significant impact on the health and functioning of persons with ID. It might be useful to address these factors more explicitly in the model and the assessment system in the future. Another rather simple supplement to the present AAMR 2002 system would be the mentioning of ICF codes whenever useful in the discussion of adaptive-behavior skills, participation problems, health conditions and etiology, and contextual factors.

The ICF model emphasizes the complex, variable, dynamic, and—most important of all—the continuous or gradual nature of disability. This system does not categorize persons or human functioning but offers a frame of reference for describing functioning and problems in functioning in a gradual way. However, *defining* a specific disability is always a process of categorization. Maybe this process would not in principle deny complexity and gradualism, but it certainly reduces the phenomenon to the most "economic" description possible and to the lowest common multiple of characteristics. Because boundaries and criteria need to be specified to distinguish the class of "ID" from "not-ID," categorization will inevitably lead to reduction of the complexity and dynamics of disability. Applying a definition to categorize (i.e., diagnose) a disability will inevitably tell little about the general functioning of a particular person and virtually nothing about his or her needs for supports. If in a bureaucratic context definitions are considered useful instruments—e.g., in the context of eligibility for services—they acquire this status on the basis more of their simplicity and practical usefulness than of their scientific validity and relevance for supports. One may wonder how useful it would be to put more energy into refining the boundaries of IQ and adaptive-behavior scale outcomes in defining ID. There will always be problems of boundaries and hence problems of accessibility of resources due to categorization of the concept of ID, whereas it is evident that ID as a disability represents a gradual phenomenon implying a wide and highly individual variety of supports needs. An alternative approach would be to focus on the assessment of needed supports as a function of problems in individual functioning. The relationship between disability and needed supports in individual situations would then become more relevant as a characteristic of "the problem," and it has already been advocated for (Greenspan, 1999). A combination of, on the one hand, the ICF multidimensional assessment of human functioning and, on the other hand, the strong focus of the AAMR 2002 on supports needs and the planning of supports might be an interesting option for future development and research.

Conclusion

The two questions raised at the beginning of this chapter can now be answered. First, there is ample evidence of compatibility between the AAMR 2002 system of ID and the ICF general model of functioning and disability of the WHO. Congruence between the systems can be demonstrated on the levels of theoretical constructs and models of individual functioning and disability. ID as defined in the AAMR 2002 system can be seen as a congruent subclass of the broader class of disability as defined and conceptualized in the ICF. Although the ICF does not include a definition of ID, it offers relevant concepts as well as a relevant framework for defining, assessing, classifying, explaining, and even coding the complex phenomenon of ID. On a general level, it may therefore be seen as an auxiliary instrument for interdisciplinary communication about ID and for teaching the AAMR system, not just to professionals, but also to family, policymakers, administrators, students, and other stakeholders in the field of ID.

In the context of individual assessment, the ICF may facilitate communication between professional disciplines in the field of ID with colleagues in other disability or rehabilitation sectors. Because there is an obvious and growing international collaboration between ID professionals and stakeholders in research and also in international disability policy (e.g., at the United Nations and in the European Union), it is also important to understand and resolve the tensions that come from the use of different language and models (Drotar & Sturm, 1996). The ICF can facilitate this process in the domain of ID.

Second, although the ICF constitutes a relevant framework for conceptualizing and understanding ID, it must be clear that the AAMR 2002 system is fine-tuned to the particular needs of the field of ID. However, the ICF system can act as a bridge for applying the AAMR definition, classification, and supports system to relevant domains in society. Especially in situations where stakeholders are less familiar with the AAMR 2002 system, the ICF can help translate and promote its approach. Because of its general validity for developing conceptualizations, assessment instruments, and support policies of disability, the ICF may play a role in the development of the AAMR 2002 system in the future. By further focusing on the effective assessment of complex problems of functioning (through developing instruments on the basis of ICF), and by further developing instruments for assessing needs of supports (through developing the AAMR support system and the Supports Intensity Scale), the collaboration between these two systems is a most promising way to go.

REFERENCES

American Association on Mental Retardation. (1999). *Policy statements on legislative and social issues.* Washington, DC: Author.

American Psychiatric Association. (1994). *Diagnostic and statistical manual of mental disorders* (4th ed.). Washington, DC: Author.

Bronfenbrenner, U. (1979). *The ecology of human development: Experiments by nature and design.* Cambridge, MA: Harvard University Press.

Drotar, D. D., & Sturm, L. (1996). Interdisciplinary collaboration in the practice of mental retardation. In J. W. Jacobson & J. A. Mulick (Eds.), *Manual of diagnosis and professional practice in mental retardation* (pp. 393–401). Washington, DC: American Psychological Association.

Fougeyrollas, P. (Ed.). (1998). ICIDH and environmental factors [Special Issue]. *International Network, 9.* Monograph Supplement.

Greenspan, S. (1999). What is meant by mental retardation? *International Review of Psychiatry, 11,* 6–18.

Halbertsma, J. (1995). The ICIDH: Health problems in a medical and social perspective. *Disability and Rehabilitation, 17*(3/4), 128–134.

Halbertsma, J., Heerkens, Y. F., Hirs, W. M., de Kleijn-de Vrankrijker, M. W., Van Ravensberg, C. D., & Ten Napel, H. (1999). Towards a new ICIDH. *Disability and Rehabilitation, 22,* 144–156.

Halbertsma, J., Heerkens, Y. F., Hirs, W. M., de Kleijn-de Vrankrijker, M. W., Van Ravensberg, C. D., & Ten Napel, H. (2000). *Comments on the* ICIDH-*2 Beta-2 draft and results of field trials.* Bilthoven, Netherlands: National Institute of Public Health and the Environment—WHO Collaborating Center for the ICIDH in the Netherlands.

Holloway, J. D. (2004). A new way of looking to health status. *American Psychological Association Monitor on Psychology, 35*(1), 32.

Landesman-Ramey, S., Dossett, E., & Echols, K. (1996). The social ecology of mental retardation. In J. W. Jacobson & J. A. Mulick (Eds.), *Manual of diagnosis and professional practice in mental retardation* (pp. 55–65). Washington, DC: American Psychological Association.

Luckasson, R., Borthwick-Duffy, S., Buntinx, W. H. E., Coulter, D. L., Craig, E. M., Reeve, A., et al. (2002). *Mental retardation: Definition, classification, and systems of supports* (10th ed.). Washington, DC: American Association on Mental Retardation.

Luckasson, R., Coulter, D. L., Polloway, E. A., Reiss, S., Schalock, R. L., Snell, M. E., et al. (1992). *Mental retardation: Definition, classification, and systems of supports* (9th ed.). Washington, DC: American Association on Mental Retardation.

Luckasson, R., & Reeve, A. (2001). Naming, defining, and classifying in mental retardation. *Mental Retardation, 39*(1), 47–52.

Maeda, S., Kita, F., Miyawaki, T., Takeuchi, K., Ishida, R., Egusa, M., et al. (2005). Assessment of patients with intellectual disability using the International Classification of Functioning, Disability, and Health to evaluate dental treatment tolerability. *Journal of Intellectual Disability Research, 49*(4), 253–259.

Maes, B. (1998). Quality of care and the rights of children with disabilities. *European Journal on Mental Disability, 5,* 26–35.

Mercer, J. R. (1992). The impact of changing paradigms of disability on mental retardation in the year 2000. In L. Rowitz (Ed.), *Mental retardation in the year 2000* (p. 15–38). New York: Springer-Verlag.

Rioux, M. H. (1997). Disability: The place of judgment in a world of fact. *Journal of Intellectual Disability Research, 41*(2), 102–111.

Schalock, R. L., & Kiernan, W. E. (1990). *Habilitation planning for adults with disabilities.* New York: Springer-Verlag.

Schalock, R. L., & Verdugo-Alonso, M. A. (2002*). Handbook of quality of life for human service practitioners.* Washington, DC: American Association on Mental Retardation.

Simeonsson, R. J., Leonardi, M., Lollars, D., Bjork-Akesson, E., Hollenweger, J., & Martinuzzi, A. (2003). Applying the *International Classification of Functioning, Disability and Health (*ICF) to measure childhood disability. *Disability and Rehabilitation, 25,* 602–610.

Tarlov, A. R. (1993). Persons with disabilities: Definition and conceptual framework. *Dolentium Hominum: Journal of the Pontifical Council for Pastoral Assistance to Health Care Workers, 22,* 40–43.

Thompson, J. R., Bryant, B. R., Campbell, E. M., Craig, E. M., Hughes, C. M., Rotholz, D. A., et al. (2004). *Supports intensity scale users manual.* Washington, DC: American Association on Mental Retardation.

United Nations. (1994). *Standard rules on the equalization of opportunities for persons with disabilities.* United Nations General Assembly, 48th session, agenda item 109.

World Health Organization. (1980). *International classification of impairments, disabilities, and handicaps. A manual of classification relating to the consequences of disease.* Geneva: Author.

World Health Organization. (1999a). ICD-10*: International statistical classification of diseases and related health problems* (10th ed., Vols. 1–3). Geneva: Author.

World Health Organization. (1999b). *International classification of functioning and disability (*ICIDH*-2 Beta 2 version).* Geneva: Author.

World Health Organization. (2001). *International classification of functioning, disability, and health (*ICF*).* Geneva: Author.

World Health Organization Collaborating Center for the ICIDH. (1994). *A survey of criticism about the* ICIDH. Zoetermeer, Netherlands: WCC Dutch Classification and Terminology Committee for Health.

CHAPTER TWENTY

Focusing Comprehensive Functional Assessment: A Case Formulation of Dual Diagnosis Treatment Priorities Using ICF (ICIDH-2)

JOHN W. JACOBSON (DECEASED)

Functional assessment has a long and well-established history in the field of developmental disabilities. Adaptive-behavior measures, for example, are functional assessment instruments that tap aspects of performance of basic and instrumental activities of daily living (ADLs) and, to a lesser degree, aspects or components of social roles. Performance of ADLS has been blended into definitions of mental retardation (e.g., Grossman, 1983) as a means to cross-validate the clinical and pragmatic significance of measured intellectual performance and to enhance linkage between the assessment process and possible priorities for intervention.

Over the past decade, there have been continuing concerns regarding the adequacy of adaptive-behavior measures:

1. Deformation of assessment findings due to environmental constraints upon performance (e.g., underestimation of skills).
2. Insensitivity of these measures to social role performance generally and their social cognitive components specifically (Greenspan, Switzky, & Granfield, 1996).
3. A growing sense of relative orthogonally between adaptive behavior and quality of life or social role participation theoretically (e.g., Simeonsson, Granlund, & Bjork-Akesson, 2003; Simeonsson & Short, 1996).

There is also the issue that complex intervention frameworks, such as the interdisciplinary team or person-centered methods, have typified assessment and intervention or support services design, and that adaptive behavior and other functional assessment measures may lack the breadth, subtlety, or sensitivity required for effective design (e.g., see Holburn & Vietze, 1999, on related issues). Moreover, there may also be some confusion within professional literatures regarding general functional assessment at the molar level and functional behavior analytic assessment at the situational or molecular level, which may obscure a continuing role for general functional assessment.

The history of application of functional assessment in the field of developmental disabilities (Halpern, 1984) includes utilization both within clinical processes and as the source of both independent and dependent variables in research (Editorial Board, 1996). Functional assessment continues to have evident utility in the form of informant-completed measures relevant to job and other aspects of performance of social roles, but it does not, in itself, provide a comprehensive picture of the social or behavioral ecology of the individual. Functional assessment has been used in similar ways, and with similar limitations that are evident, in mental health or psychiatric disability services (Cohen & Anthony, 1984) and in rehabilitation services (Brown, Gordon, & Diller, 1984). Indeed, functional assessment data are probably used most commonly in clinical practice and in clinical and policy research in the field of rehabilitation (Rucker, Wehman, & Kregel, 1996; Schuntermann, 1996).

A Comprehensive Functional Assessment Framework

International Classification of Impairments, Disabilities, and Handicaps (ICIDH)

The 1980 ICIDH is a classification framework that was developed as a companion to earlier versions of the WHO (1993) International Statistical Classification of Diseases and Related Health Problems (ICD). The ICIDH was developed in order to provide a consistent and uniform means of documenting the functional consequences of health conditions (Kennedy, 1999). Briefly, it utilized a framework based on three components, with physical impairments (due to psychological or physical illness, disease, or injury) contributing to and causing disability, and with disability, in social context, treated as a precursor to handicap. Since its inception the ICIDH has been adopted or emulated internationally—in Canada, France, and the Netherlands, for example—but, despite research use, has not been implemented on a wide scale in health or long-term care systems in the United States (Furrie, 1995; Kennedy, 1999).

Since its publication, although ICIDH (1980) has addressed health problems in terms of daily living or social factors as well as medical terms (Halbertsma, 1995), it has been criticized for including psychological conditions in their own right as opposed to limiting their inclusion to conditions secondary to impairments (Dickson, 1996), and as requiring greater clarity with respect to the definitions of impairment, disability, and handicap (Brandsma, Lakerveld-Heyl, Van Ravensberg, & Heerkens, 1995). More compelling, however, have been recommendations that a greater stress in orientation was needed within ICIDH on social roles, social factors, and social environment (Marks, 1997; Peters, 1995; Wiersma, 1996) and to health-related quality of life (Wood-Dauphinee, 1998).

Furthermore, the need to base functional assessment on an interactive synergistic or potentiating model, rather than a linear model, of causality of handicap, such as the 1980 ICIDH model, has been acknowledged on the basis of subsequent research and sociopolitical analysis of the relationship among psychological and health conditions, functional impacts of conditions, social or environmental contexts, and quality of life (Post, de Witte, & Schrijvers, 1999).

Since the early 1980s, there have also been substantial changes in disability policy relating to the affirmation or guarantee of human and civil rights of people with disabilities in many nations, and evident in the United States in the Americans with Disabilities Act. While the enactment of such legislation has formalized policy that treats people with disabilities as a minority group subjected to discrimination, it also represents adoption of a more social model of disability nationally, and has provided further impetus to development of a more interactive model or framework for functional assessment.

The social model disavows or minimizes the causal significance of health or related conditions to disability, and attributes disability principally to the unresponsiveness of society to individual citizens' needs for reasonable adjustments or accommodations in working and living: "It explains disablement as the result of any behavior or barriers which prevent people with impairments choosing to take part in the life of society" (Valid, 2000, p. 1). However, just as earlier, more medical, models of handicap placed excessive emphasis on physical or medical conditions as causal factors, so may a strong social model place excessive emphasis on social or political factors. Thus, a comprehensive assessment model might most appropriately encompass measures or reporting of both types of factors, providing a basis for empirical analysis of disability at several levels and expanding the applicability and utility of functional assessment for both individuals and groups.

International Classification of Functioning and Disability (ICIDH-2 Beta 2 Version) and the Final ICF

The considerations noted above contributed to efforts to redevelop the ICIDH to be more comprehensive, and more useful, and to incorporate an interactive domain or factor model. Efforts to develop and field test the ICIDH-2, through focus groups, international task forces on issues such as mental health and assessment of children, and empirical studies of coherence, clarity, utility, validity, and reliability, have been underway for several years, and ICIDH-2 was published as the ICF in late 2001.

Rather than an exclusively social model, ICF is based on a universal model, in that its content is applicable, and comparable in its suitability, in assessment of functional aspects and personal and social consequences of the entire range of psychological, medical, and health conditions (Ustun, Bickenbach, Badley, & Chatterje, 1998). The components of the ICF model include body functions, body structure, activity, participation, and environmental factors, rated by qualifiers that are consistent across conditions and circumstances (see Table 20.1 for definitions of these components and related levels and forms of individual or group interventions; also see Simeonsson, Granlund, & Bjorck-Akesson, 2003; Simeonsson, Lollar, Hollowell, & Adams, 2000; and Simeonsson, & Short, 1996).

As reported by WHO (1999b) the objective of the ICF is to "develop an operational classification system on human functioning and disability that is applicable to people universally. It addresses multiple dimensions regarding the person and environment, and incorporates "international practices that are culture sensitive, based on user needs, and empirical field trials on applicability, reliability and utility" (see also Bickenbach, Chatterji, Badley, & Ustun, 1999). In developing this system, the focus has shifted from ICIDH to ICIDH-2, from

disabilities to functioning and disability, from impairments to body functions and structures, from disabilities to activities, handicaps to participation, from no environmental content to use of environmental factors, from a causal-linear to an interactive-integrative model, from undefined content to use of operational definitions, and from no linkages to assessment instruments to the development of linked instruments. (WHO, 1999b, closely paraphrased)

Presently, the linked instruments include a checklist for each component that allows reporting on each one systematically, and a brief functional assessment measure that reflects the ICF framework.

Although the intended use of ICF is to document and organize information about the functional ramifications of specific psychological and medical or health conditions occurring in individuals and groups, rather than to be used as a model of classifying effects of poverty, abuse prejudice, conflict, or social injustice, a range of applications has been proposed. These include: scientific applications to study the impact of illness, use in services to assess interventions and outcomes, use with individuals to specify needs, use in economic contexts for planning of services and supports, and use at the social level to identify issues in social policy formulation relating to the rights of the individual and duties of the society (WHO, 1999b).

ICF CLASSIFICATION, MENTAL HEALTH, AND DEVELOPMENTAL DISABILITIES

As noted above, the ICF is structured to be applicable to both psychological and physical health conditions and psychological conditions per se, including those that neither are directly associated with nor regularly follow the occurrence of particular health conditions (e.g., postpartum depression, or reactive depression or agitation following limb amputation or traumatic injury). There is no differentiation in the classification model based upon whether a condition is behavioral or physical in character (Kennedy, 1999; Ustun et al., 1995; Ustun, van Duuren-Kristen, Bertolote, Cooper, & Sartorius, 1996; Wiersma, 1996). Although the utility of ICF's framework for assessment of childhood disability has been of some concern, functional assessment of adolescents and adults with developmental disabilities can be achieved in a manner quite comparable with applications involving adults participating in or requiring rehabilitative interventions and services.

The suitability of the ICF framework in appraisal of the functional and social ramifications of developmental disabilities and psychiatric disabilities, and concurrent presence of these conditions, is evident in the structural features and content of several domains. Table 20.2 illustrates the type of content contained in the ICF that is likely to allow suitable documentation of body function, activity, and participation concerns associated with severe and persistent, or perhaps transient, mental disorders. As these items indicate, ICF addresses psychosocial factors in a comprehensive manner, identifying abilities and impairments that contribute to quality of performance, everyday and common activities that are difficult for a person to perform or are well performed, and environmental factors, both social and cultural, that inhibit or facilitate participation in culturally typical activities.

Each of the items listed in the second column of Table 20.2 represents either a group of items with greater specificity or a content area with exclusionary and inclusionary criteria relating to other items in the framework. For example "Emotional Functions" are "specific mental functions related to the feeling and affective component of the processes of the mind." They include "functions of appropriateness of emotion, regulation and range of emotion; affect; sadness, happiness, love, fear, anger, hate, tension, anxiety, joy, sorrow; lability of emotion; and flattening of affect" and exclude "temperament and personality functions; energy and drive functions" (WHO, 1999a). In turn, more specific items, such as "appropriateness of emotion," are defined and an example is provided; however, multiple indicators are not provided for each of these more specific terms.

As Tables 20.1 and 20.2 indicate, the IASSID model is complex and multifaceted. In order to further illustrate the model, a case report, focusing on assessment, is presented below.

A Sample Case Formulation: Gerald

Historical or Conventional Formulation

This case formulation is based on a young man whom I served as a behavioral consultant over twenty years ago. Noncritical aspects of this case summary have been fabricated in order to further obscure his identity and establish further information that can be recast through the ICIDH-2 system. The particular usage of activities and participation ratings in this chapter and case formulation reflects the format used in a late, but not final, version of the ICF as it went to publication in late 2001. Usage in the final form of ICF of ratings or scales related to activities and participation is largely at the discretion of the rater, clinician, or organization, and as noted in the final document, may take a variety of forms, adapted to the particular application of the ICF elements taken as a whole.

Demographics and Disability History

(1) A boy in his mid-teens.
(2) Developmental disability: Mild ID (IQ = 60–65) and
(3) Psychiatric disability: Schizoaffective disorder or Affective disorder hypothesized (his diagnostic workup was not definitive).
(4) Prior assessments, history, course of psychiatric disability condition were unilluminating and largely untargeted.
(5) History of institutionalization: (state school for people with mental retardation) since age seven years.
(6) Lived at a new institutional unit (new institution) with planned transition to community group home (and subsequently, at about age 17.5, moved to a specialized foster care home, and later, a group home).

Adaptive Skills

(1) Had marked academic delays.
(2) Did not read or perform pragmatic math.
(3) Attended an on-grounds school with several peers who also lived at the facility and others who lived in the local area, with small classes of about 10 students.
(4) Had adequate community resource use skills, in terms of recreational participation and everyday activities such as going to and using community shops and

stores, but required supervision due to elopement risk and lack of functional independence (e.g., self-protection or safety awareness).

Psychosocial Functioning

(1) Was frequently affable but conversational content was impoverished with respect to self-description and self-reference (i.e., "insight").

(2) Had difficulty discussing his feelings whether calm or agitated; had no confidants among staff or peers; sought interaction with staff in preference to peers.

(3) There was some evidence of affective cycling (periodic agitation); occasional lability.

(4) Presented with some emotional blunting; was occasionally wary and suspicious (based on demeanor and character of statements).

(5) As a comparatively capable institutional resident, had been acculturated primarily within the attendant culture as a "go'fer" or junior trustee, secondarily into status structure of youth within that facility (e.g., Edgerton, 1963).

(6) Probably was acculturated within the psychosexual culture of the institution (a factor not addressed at that time).

(7) Infrequent family contacts; although they had increased with his move (transfer) closer to his family's home, contacts remained infrequent at once every two months, and were limited to one parent (he had two siblings).

Psychosocial Treatment Concerns

(1) Periodically resisted supervision and attempts to engage him in conversation or in activities, but not in relation to particular topics or activities.

(2) Participated in a school program but regularly engaged in maladaptive behavior, primarily verbal teasing of peers or hostile statements to staff; when queried, did not or would not stipulate specific situational concerns.

(3) Participated in daily outings and weekly special activities, but occasionally displayed pseudoseizures in public settings.

(4) Periodically, and predictably, eloped and sought to return to his prior institutional setting, but lacked functional skills to achieve this (e.g., lacked hitch-hiking skills, knowledge of proper direction to travel in order to return to the setting).

(5) Set a fire in public restroom in mall while eloping; and later stated he did so in order to be arrested and sent back to his prior institutional setting.

(6) Principal personal preferences were not feasible (i.e., wanted to move back to prior, large institutional setting, but his former residential unit had closed, and the facility was due to close in its entirety).

(7) He was unable or unwilling to make specific statements regarding present feasible daily or short-term preferences despite interview and probing.

Treatment and Intervention: The Services Gerald Received

(1) Treatment at the time included psychiatric counseling, apparently without effect.

(2) He received pharmacological treatment with phenothiazine and antidepressant—achieving principally sedative and appetitive effects.

(3) Behavioral treatment was hindered by inconsistent staff implementation, and imperceptions or denial by staff of cyclic character of elopement and affective shifts.

(4) Unit staff periodically indulged him, did not recognize precipitating factors for elopement or pseudoseizures, and inadvertently encouraged him to make negative statements.

(5) Unit staffed considered various behavior problems to be isolated instances, reflecting "frustration" or occasional "unhappiness."

(6) Behavioral specialists were consultants to the unit, without supervisory authority; they were members of a geographic team that operated this unit; the team leader was a psychiatrist.

(7) Behavioral treatment incorporated a token system for prosocial and cooperative behavior in the school program; school and residential unit interventions were not closely coordinated.

ICIDH-Based Reformulation

An ICF reformulation of Gerald's functioning and situation should be structured in terms of the domains of the system, i.e., body functions, body structure, activities, participation, and environment. The ICF permits comprehensive assessment identifying normal range, or typical functioning and societal participation, within all elements of the system. However, in practice it is likely that purposeful clinical, as opposed to research, applications of the system will fail to fully report all aspects of functioning that can be assessed, but rather will focus on aspects of functioning and situational factors most salient to formulation of treatment. Generally, in the following formulation, it should be assumed that Gerald's functioning in areas not listed either approaches or approximates typical functioning for a person his age and having a comparable educational background in the general population.

Body Functions and Degree of Limitation

(1)	Global Mental Functions	
	Intellectual functions (b120)	Moderate (i.e., MR)
(2)	Temperament and Personality Functions	
	Emotional stability (b1253)	Moderate
(3)	Emotional Functions	
	Regulation of function (b1551)	Severe
(4)	Thought Functions	
	Content of thought (b1652)	Moderate
	Control of thought (b1653)	Moderate

   (5) Higher-Level Cognitive Functioning
      Abstraction (b1700)   Moderate
      Insight (b1704)   Severe
      Judgment (b1705)   Severe

Summary: Gerald was classified with mild mental retardation, which had a moderate impact on his general intellectual functioning (i.e., the use of a score range in classification or description of a condition is not necessarily synonymous with impact relative to peers). He also manifested moderate emotional instability, severe difficulty with regulation of emotional functions, moderate impairments with respect to content and control of thought, moderate impairment in abstraction, and severe impairments of insight and judgment.

Body Structure and Degree of Impairment

   (1) Nervous System
      Unspecified structure of the nervous system (s199)   Moderate

Summary: Medical history and examination had identified no notable physical or biochemical anomalies associated with diagnosed developmental or psychiatric disabilities. No pertinent neurological findings were apparent, and there was no evidence of a neurological basis for Gerald's seizure (i.e., pseudoseizure) episodes. There were no persisting medical concerns of note and there was no identified etiological diagnosis for mental retardation. Nonetheless, since ICF eschews a mind-body dualistic model (Ustun et al., 1995), unspecified involvement of the central nervous system would be coded.

Activities and Degree of Performance Difficulty

   Activities of learning and applying knowledge

   (1) Thinking Activities
      Problem-solving activities (a140)
      Evaluating potential effects of solution (a1453)   Severe
      Decision-making activities (a150)
      Evaluating effects of decisions (a1502)   Severe
   (2) General Interpersonal Activities
      Responding to criticism (a7103)   Severe
      Regulating emotions and impulses for interactions (a7201) Moderate
      Regulating verbal aggression (a7202)   Severe
      Regulating physical aggression (a 7203)   Moderate
   (3) Activities of Handling Stress and Other
      Psychological Demands
      Handling stress (a8301)   Severe
   (4) Activities of Performing in School
      Activities of being supervised at school (a8453)   Moderate

Summary: Gerald evaluated potential effects of solutions to problems, evaluated effects of decisions, responded to criticism, regulated verbal behavior, and handled stress with great difficulty. He regulated emotions and impulses for interaction, regulated physical aggression, and performed activities of being supervised at school with moderate difficulty. He required personal assistance with all of these activities.

Participation and Degree of Restriction

    (1) Participation in Mobility
        Participation in mobility outside the home and
        other buildings (p230)   Moderate
        Participation in mobility with transportation (p240)   Severe
    (2) Participation in Social Relationships
        Participation in family relationships (p410)   Severe
        Participation in informal social relationships (p430)   Severe
        Participation in relationships with friends (p4300)   Severe
    (3) Participation in Education
        Participation in education in school (p630)   Moderate
    (4) Participation in Community, Social, and Civic Life
        Participation in informal associations (p9100)   Moderate
        Participation in formal associations (p9200)   Mild

Summary: Gerald experienced severe restriction in participation in the use of vehicles to participate in desired activities due to requirements for individual safeguarding, and severe restrictions in family relationships, extended family relationships, and relationships with friends, due to infrequent or absent contact or lack of opportunity to meet a wider range of peers. He experienced moderate restriction in participation in mobility outside the home, especially in other buildings and in participation in informal associations due to safeguarding, participation in education in school due to consequences for other students of his verbal or physical aggression, and mild restriction in participation in informal associations, due to the considerations noted above.

Environmental Factors and Extent of Barriers or Facilitators

    (1) Support and Relationships
        Immediate family (e310)   Severe (–)
        Extended family (e320)   Severe (–)
        Friends (e330)   Severe (–)
        People in positions of authority (e335)   Moderate (+)
        Personal care providers and personal assistants (e340)   Mild (–)
    (2) Services
        Housing services (e525)   Severe (–)
        Rehabilitation services (e575)   Severe (–)
        School services (e580)   Severe (–)
        Secondary school services (e5802)   Severe (–)
    (3) Systems and Policies
        Housing system and policies (e620)   Severe (–)

Summary: There were numerous severe environmental barriers to Gerald's broadened participation in society and community, including severe barriers in terms of immediate family, extended family, and friend involvement in his life, and mild barriers associated with personal care providers (direct service staff) who did not initiate and maintain interventions to assist him (although they did so with other people they served). There were also severe barriers posed by the character of housing services available to him, the intensity of rehabilitation (i.e., focused clinical services) that could be brought to bear, and the character of the non-community-based educational services in which he was enrolled. Prevailing housing systems capacities and policies also hindered his participation by delaying his movement to a more typical community residential situation (e.g., a foster family care or group home setting). People in positions of authority, who sought to develop more effective services and supports for Gerald, and who persisted in locating a community living situation for him, constituted moderately important environmental resources for him.

ISSUES AND IMPLICATIONS

The example above indicates how an ICF-based formulation of clinical concerns can help to clarify potential intervention priorities at several levels of social ecology—and arguably this is the purpose of comprehensive functional assessment. ICF formulation focuses professional attention on multiple factors—activities, participation, and environmental factors as well as impairments—that affect the person, and identifies a range of points and purposes toward which interventions may be directed (e.g., Gardner & Whalen, 1996).

Not all strengths, impairments, limitations, or barriers are necessarily noted in a given formulation, and they may be limited to only those most pertinent to the salient condition. However, the framework does present the capacity for rating of performance, including personal and social assets, if practitioners, teams, researchers, and managers desire to do so. The framework is more extensive, and more broadly applicable to use with people with a wide range of disabilities, than existing alternatives.

At the individual level, use of the ICF can help to clarify interventions and perhaps to identify critical environmental contingencies or pivotal skills. At the local level of services it can encourage communication through a shared classification structure among practitioners of different disciplines, who may otherwise be serving a person in disparate and even inconsistent ways. With respect to policy analysis and formulation, ICF data could clarify impacts of an array of behavioral and physical health conditions on engagement of people with disabilities in society, to stimulate service sector reforms and perhaps cross-cutting initiatives as well. Finally, broad application of the ICF framework could enhance the coherence of clinical, pragmatic, economic, and policy research regarding disability, including physical, psychological or behavioral, and developmental disabilities and conditions.

Potential breadth of utility ranging from the level of individual clinical usage to policy development, however, comes at a cost. That cost is complexity. The ICF is a very complicated and exacting framework, which will require special training and considerable familiarization if clinicians are to use it in more than a very cursory way (although WHO has taken some steps to make the framework more user-friendly—see WHO, 2000). Considerations of behavioral and human economics will tend to emphasize use of ICF broadly, particularly in managed care and managed behavioral health care in the near future, but most likely in very limited and superficial ways. For econometrists and other researchers and evaluators in government and the health-care industry, even minor applications of ICF codes may represent a substantial step forward in the breadth of information available for monitoring trends, projecting utilization, engaging in oversight, and better understanding both the human and economic costs and benefits of health and rehabilitative care policies.

At the same time, however, for many purposes, the ICF, as complex as it is, may not be complex enough. Regardless of whether the people being served have relatively unique and diverse, or shared and common, needs, for the purposes of functional assessment leading to skilled, informed, well-founded and not merely well-intended interventions, substantially greater detail will be required in terms of indicator items. Item indicators or definitions are needed that both explain and quantify the assessment ratings and that enhance the precision of the system beyond global ratings of degree of impairment, level of difficulty in performing activities, and breadth and depth of barriers to participation.

Each of the global ratings represents a summative appraisal of complex behavior, activities, and contextual influences. Similar indices in mental health assessment have not consistently demonstrated adequate concurrent and predictive validity of these types of ratings (Moos, McCoy, & Moos, 2000), and clinical utility of functional assessment instruments is often associated with depth or incorporation of critical items, as well as breadth (Bracken, Keith, & Walker, 1998). Ironically, although broadened use of the ICF as a direct clinical assessment methodology would be strengthened, and on practical and ethical grounds, might require more stringent operationalization, the likely immediate future broad uses of the ICF will be in collection of population and health survey data and limited data sets by managed-care organizations and other health insurers. There is clear potential, however, in the use of the ICF framework in functional assessment of people with mental retardation at the level of the individual, and in particular, it is a methodology that may be particularly effective in interleaving information related to developmental and mental health status within a coherent assessment process.

Table 20.1:
ICF (ICIDH-2) Domains, Content of Domains, and Focus of Interventions
Stemming from Assessment

ICF Domains	Content of Domain or Focus of Intervention
BODY FUNCTIONS	are the physiological or psychological functions of body systems.
BODY STRUCTURES	are anatomic parts of the body, such as organs, limbs and their components.
–Impairments	are problems in body function or structure, such as a significant deviation or loss.

Table 20.1 (continued):
ICF (ICIDH-2) Domains, Content of Domains, and Focus of Interventions Stemming from Assessment

ICF Domains	Content of Domain or Focus of Intervention
ACTIVITY	is the performance of a task or action by an individual.
–Activity Limitations	are difficulties an individual may have in the performance of activities.
PARTICIPATION	is an individual's involvement in life situations in relation to Health Conditions, Body Functions and Structure, Activities, and Contextual Factors.
–Participation Restrictions	are problems an individual may have in the manner or extent of involvement in life situations.
ENVIRONMENTAL FACTORS	make up the physical, social, and attitudinal environment in which people live and conduct their lives.

Intervention Strategies Stemming from Assessment

IMPAIRMENT INTERVENTIONS	medical and psychosocial interventions to deal with the impairment, and preventive interventions to avoid activity limitation
ACTIVITY LIMITATION INTERVENTIONS	rehabilitative interventions and provision of assistive devices and personal assistance to mitigate the activity limitation, and preventive interventions to avoid participation restrictions
PARTICIPATION RESTRICTION INTERVENTIONS	entail public education, equalization of opportunities, social reform and legislation, architectural universal design applications, and other ways of accommodating activity limitations in major life areas

Source: ICIDH-2 Beta-2 Draft Manual (WHO, 1999a), and WHO (2000) at www.who.int/icidh.htm.

Table 20.2:

Examples of Content within the ICF (ICIDH-2) Framework Relevant to Assessment of Several Dimensions of Psychiatric Disability

General Component	Examples of Content Relevant to Psychiatric Disability
MENTAL FUNCTIONS: Global Mental Functions (Examples)	1) Consciousness functions / Orientation functions 2) Intellectual functions 3) Temperament and personality functions 4) Energy and drive functions 5) Sleep functions 6) Other specified and unspecified general mental functions
MENTAL FUNCTIONS: Specific Mental Functions (Examples)	1) Attention functions / Memory functions 2) Psychomotor functions 3) Emotional functions 4) Perceptual functions 5) Thought functions 6) Higher-level cognitive functions 7) Specific mental functions of language 8) Calculation functions 9) Mental function of sequencing complex movements 10) Other specified and unspecified attention functions
PERFORMING ACTIVITIES (Examples)	General Task and Performance Demand Activities 1) Activities of performing a task 2) Activities of performing multiple tasks 3) Activities of organizing daily routines 4) Activities of sustaining task performance 5) Activities of handling stress and other psychological demands 6) Other specified and unspecified general tasks and demands Activities of Performing in Major Life Situations 1) Activities of performing in work 2) Activities of performing in school 3) Activities of using money and finance 4) Activities for performance in recreation 5) Activities of religious or spiritual pursuits 6) Activities of responding to unusual situations 7) Other specified and unspecified activities of performing in major life situations

Table 20.2 (continued):
Examples of Content within the ICF (ICIDH-2) Framework Relevant to
Assessment of Several Dimensions of Psychiatric Disability

General Component	Examples of Content Relevant to Psychiatric Disability
PARTICIPATION (Examples)	Participation in Social Relationships 1) Participation in family relationships 2) Participation in intimate relationships 3) Participation in informal social relationships 4) Participation in formal relationships 5) Other specified participation in social relationships 6) Unspecified participation in social relationships Participation in Home Life and Assistance to Others 1) Participation in housing for self and others 2) Participation in management of the home and possessions 3) Participation in caring for others 4) Participation in nutrition for others 5) Participation in health maintenance for others 6) Participation in mobility and transportation for others
ENVIRONMENT (Example)	Attitudes, Values, and Beliefs (promoting or inhibiting participation) 1) Individual attitudes 2) Individual values 3) Individual beliefs 4) Societal attitudes 5) Societal values 6) Societal beliefs 7) Social norms, conventions and ideologies 8) Other specified attitudes, values and beliefs

Source: WHO (1999a)

REFERENCES

American Psychological Association Editorial Board. (1996). Definition of mental retardation. In J. W. Jacobson & J. A Mulick (Eds.), *Manual of diagnosis and professional practice in mental retardation* (pp. 13–53). Washington, DC: Author.

Bickenbach, J. E., Chatterji, S., Badley, E. M., & Ustun, T. B. (1999). Models of disablement, universalism and the international classification of impairments, disabilities and handicaps. *Social Science & Medicine, 48*, 1173–1187.

Bracken, B. A., Keith, L. K., & Walker, K. C. (1998). Assessment of preschool behavior and social-emotional functioning: A review of thirteen third-party instruments. *Journal of Psychoeducational Assessment, 16*, 153–169.

Brandsma, J. W., Lakerveld-Heyl, K., Van Ravensberg, C. D., & Heerkens, Y. F. (1995). Reflection on the definition of impairment and disability as defined by the World Health Organization. *Disability & Rehabilitation, 17*, 119–127.

Brown, M., Gordon, W. A., & Diller, L. (1984). Rehabilitation indicators. In A. S. Halpern & M. J. Fuhrer (Eds.), *Functional assessment in rehabilitation* (pp. 187–204). Baltimore: Paul H. Brookes.

Cohen, B. F., & Anthony, W. (1984). Functional assessment in psychiatric rehabilitation. In A. S. Halpern & M. J. Fuhrer (Eds.), *Functional assessment in rehabilitation* (pp. 79–100). Baltimore: Paul H. Brookes.

Department of Health and Human Services. (2000). Disability and secondary conditions. *Healthy people 2010* (Vol. 1, Pt. A, Focus Area 6). Washington, DC: Author. Retrieved from http://www.health.gov/healthypeople/Document/default.htm

Dickson, H. G. (1996). Problems with the ICIDH definition of impairment. *Disability & Rehabilitation, 18*, 52–54.

Edgerton, R. B. (1963). A patient elite: Ethnography in a hospital for the mentally retarded. *American Journal of Mental Deficiency, 68*, 372–385.

Furrie, A. D. (1995). The Canadian database on disability issues: A national application of the ICIDH. *Disability & Rehabilitation, 17*, 344–349.

Greenspan, S., Switzky, H. N., & Granfield, J. M. (1996). Everyday intelligence and adaptive behavior: A theoretical framework. In J. W. Jacobson & J. A. Mulick (Eds.), *Manual of diagnosis and professional practice in mental retardation* (pp. 127–135). Washington, DC: American Psychological Association.

Grossman, H. J. (Ed.). (1983). *Manual on terminology and classification in mental retardation* (1983 revision). Washington, DC: American Association on Mental Deficiency.

Halbertsma, J. (1995). The ICIDH: Health problems in a medical and social perspective. *Disability and Rehabilitation, 17*(3/4), 128–134.

Halpern, A. S. (1984). Functional assessment and mental retardation. In A. S. Halpern & M. J. Fuhrer (Eds.), *Functional assessment in rehabilitation* (pp. 61–78). Baltimore: Paul H. Brookes.

Holburn, S. C., & Vietze, P. M. (1999). Acknowledging barriers in adopting person-centered planning. *Mental Retardation, 37*, 117–124.

Kennedy, C. (1999). *Social Security Administration's disability determination of claims based on mental impairments and the World Health Organization's International Classification of Impairments, Activities, and Participation (ICIDH–2): Toward an agenda for research.* Washington, DC: Institute of Medicine, National Academy of Sciences.

Moos, R. H., McCoy, L., & Moos, B. S. (2000). Global Assessment of Functioning (GAF) ratings: Determinants and role as predictors of one-year treatment outcomes. *Journal of Clinical Psychology, 56*, 449–461.

Post, M. W. M., de Witte, L. P., & Schrijvers, A. J. P. (1999). Quality of life and the ICIDH: Towards an integrated conceptual model for rehabilitation outcomes research. *Clinical Rehabilitation, 13*, 5–15.

Rucker, K. S., Wehman, P., & Kregel, J. (1996, July*). Analysis of functional assessment instruments for disability/rehabilitation programs: Report on findings and recommendations for future directions.* Richmond: Medical College of Virginia, Virginia Commonwealth University. Retrieved from www.ssa.gov/DPRT/future.html

Schuntermann, M. F. (1996). The International Classification of Impairments, Disabilities and Handicaps (ICIDH): Results and problems. *International Journal of Rehabilitation Research, 19*, 1–11.

Simeonsson, R. J., Granlund, M., & Bjorck-Akesson, E. (2003). Classifying mental retardation: Impairment, disability, handicap, limitations, or restrictions? In H. N. Switzky & S.Greenspan (Eds.), *What Is Mental Retardation? Ideas for an evolving disability* (pp. 309–329). Washington, DC: American Association on Mental Retardation [E-Book]. Available at http://www.disabilitybooksonline.com

Simeonsson, R. J., Lollar, D., Hollowell, J., & Adams, M. (2000). Revision of the International Classification of Impairments, Disabilities, and Handicaps: Developmental issues. *Journal of Clinical Epidemiology, 53*, 113–124.

Simeonsson, R. J., & Short, R. J. (1996). Adaptive development, survival roles, and quality of life. In J. W. Jacobson & J. A. Mulick (Eds.), *Manual of diagnosis and professional practice in mental retardation* (pp. 137–146). Washington, DC: American Psychological Association.

Valid. (2000). *The social model of disability*. Internet document. Retreived on August 29, 2000, from http://www.ppweb.com/valid/smdis.htm

Wiersma, D. (1996). Measuring social disabilities in mental health. *Social Psychiatry & Psychiatric Epidemiology, 31*, 101–108.

Wood-Dauphinee, S. (1998). Competing conceptual frameworks for assessing rehabilitation outcomes. *Canadian Journal of Rehabilitation, 11*, 165–167.

World Health Organization. (1980). *International classification of impairments, disabilities, and handicaps. A manual of classification relating to the consequences of disease*. Geneva: Author.

World Health Organization. (1993). *International statistical classification of diseases and related health problems* (10th ed.). Geneva: Author.

World Health Organization. (1999a). *International classification of functioning and disability (ICIDH-2 Beta 2 version)*. Geneva: Author.

World Health Organization. (1999b). *ICIDHWeb.pps (Powerpoint instructional slideshow about the ICIDH–2)*. Geneva: Author. Available at http://www.who.int/icidh

World Health Organization. (2000). *ICIDH browser (Executable expert assistant program)*. Geneva: Author.

Chapter Twenty-One

Summary and Conclusions: Can So Many Diverse Ideas Be Integrated? Multiparadigmatic Models of Understanding Mental Retardation in the 21st Century

Harvey N. Switzky and Stephen Greenspan

This book has presented the often-divergent world views of our contributors, representing a broad cross section of philosophical and epistemological paradigms underpinning current conceptions of mental retardation. It is obvious to us that the field of MR is in the midst of a classic paradigm shift (Kuhn, 1970), and that is the cause of the very strong reactions for and against the 1992/2002 AAMR system and the search for new conceptions and new definitions of mental retardation suitable for the 21st century.

Science and Scientific Paradigms

Mercer in 1992 wrote a most prophetic chapter, "The impact of changing paradigms of disability on mental retardation in the year 2000," about how changing "scientific" paradigmatic shifts influence our conceptual models of MR as well as social policy decisions. Well, we are now in the 21st century, and we want to review some of Mercer's ideas to show what an excellent seer and oracle she was and to see if her thoughts can provide us with some organizing schemas to enable us to sort out the very diverse worldviews of our contributors. Additionally, we believe that the work of Rioux and her collaborators (Rioux, 1997; Rioux & Bach, 1994) in ways of viewing disability and justifying research methodologies may provide valuable insights in providing scaffolding to allow us to integrate the diverse views of our contributors. We will first discuss Mercer's ideas and then those of Rioux and her collaborators.

THE CONTRIBUTION OF MERCER

Mercer (1992), borrowing from Kuhn (1970), argues that "science" involves social collaboration among scientists who share a fundamental world view (i.e., a scientific and epistemological paradigm). This world view includes the scientists' values and beliefs, their concept of the nature of society, philosophies of "truth and reality," and ideas about the best methods for arriving at "truth and reality." When scientific research conflicts and cannot be contained within the current (dominant) scientific paradigm, i.e., world view, a crisis occurs, and the current (dominant) scientific paradigm is modified to deal with these new "facts" in order to provide a framework which can account for them. Inevitably the new paradigm competes with the older one for adoption and acceptance as a world view. This sequence of events is currently occurring in the field of mental retardation.

Drawing from Burrell and Morgan's (1979) typology of scientific paradigmatic assumptions, Mercer (1992) uses their two orthogonal dimensions, Nature of Reality and Nature of Society, to define the major paradigms, which in her opinion underpin current world views regarding the nature of mental retardation. (See Figure 21.1.)

The Nature of Reality dimension is a continuous bipolar dimension consisting of Extreme Subjectivity to Extreme Objectivity. The subjective world view regarding the Nature of Reality, we believe, derives from Phenomenology, *Geisteswissenschaft*, and the various qualitative research traditions (Denzin & Lincoln, 1994; Dilthey, [1900], 1976; Lancy, 1993; Lincoln & Guba, 1985; Husserl, [1913], 1962; Taylor & Bogdan, 1984). The subjective view of the Nature of Reality dimension emphasizes that reality is created by observers who through their experiences become the main measurement tools for understanding the phenomena they experience. Observers and phenomena interact to influence one another and are inseparably interconnected. The meaning of reality is created through dynamic social interactions among researchers and the observed individuals, and among fellow researchers, leading to a common consensus regarding phenomena and their value. The subjective world view is that there are *no* human characteristics or processes from which generalizations can emerge. Each individual or phenomenon is uniquely different and can only be studied holistically; thus it is impossible to break complex phenomena into parts and study the parts separately. Since the total setting of a phenomenon is never the same, prediction and control are not possible, but meaning, value, and understanding may be possible.

Models of mental retardation located on the subjective pole of the Nature of Reality axis consider the phenomena of disability, intelligence, and mental retardation as social constructs varying not only from society to society but also over time in the same society, as groups of researchers and groups of observed individuals reevaluate their joint dynamic interconnected realities (e.g., *verstehen*): ability and disability are subjective constructs which can only be understood by entering the subjective reality of the individuals observed, participating in their systems of meanings and values and their subjective world views.

The objective world view, we believe, derives from Empiricism, Logical Positivism (Logical Empiricism), and the current variants of these quantitative world views (Buchler, 1955; Compte, 1896; Durkheim, 1938; Mills, [1843], 1906; Poincare, 1952; Sarkar, 1996a, 1996b). The objective view of the Nature of Reality dimension emphasizes that reality exists outside of and independent of the observer. Through a combination of

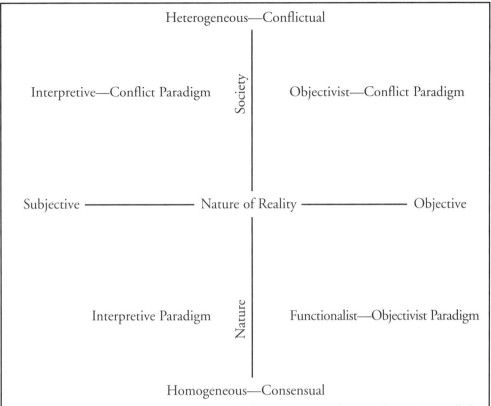

Figure 21.1. Mercer's typology of four fundamental scientific paradigms. From "The impact of changing paradigms of disability on mental retardation in the year 2000," by J. Mercer. In *Mental retardation in the year 2000* **(p. 17), ed. by L. Rowitz, 1992, New York: Springer-Verlag. Copyright 1992 by Springer-Verlag. Reprinted by permission. Originally adapted from** *Sociological paradigms and organizational analysis* **(p. 22), by G. Burrell and G. Morgan, 1979, Portsmouth, NJ: Heinemann. Adapted by Mercer with permission.**

inductive and deductive methodologies (i.e., the scientific method), observers can infer phenomena that are casual and lawful, and therefore measurable, controllable, predicable, and universal. The ultimate goal of the researcher is to develop a body of knowledge that can be generalized. Knowledge of reality is created by varieties of scientific empirical methodologies that are inquiry free and not value bound and that need to be valid and replicable, leading to a common consensus regarding the nature of empirical phenomena.

Models of mental retardation located on the objective pole of the Nature of Reality Axis assume the independent reality of disability, intelligence, mental retardation, and society: Ability and disability are objective entities that exist in individuals and can be measured and diagnosed.

The Nature of Society Dimension is bipolar, with one pole representing a Homogeneous-Consensual view (i.e., that society is primarily homogeneous, stable, integrative, coordinated, and in homeostasis), and the other pole representing a

Heterogeneous-Conflictual view (i.e., that society is primarily heterogeneous, conflict laden, unstable, and ever changing, where severe conflict exists among social classes and ethnic groups for power). Heterogeneous-Conflictual viewpoints are concerned with the cultural and linguistic backgrounds and the norms and values of the conflicting social classes and ethnic groups and the inevitable domination of one group over the others with the purpose of imposing their norms, languages, values, and culture upon the subordinated groups. Models of mental retardation and disability representing a Homogeneous-Consensual point of view define individuals with mental retardation and other disabilities as possessing behaviors that interfere with societal stability and therefore as being dysfunctional and deviant. Intervention is concerned with making persons with mental retardation more "functional" for society and thereby increasing social stability.

Models of mental retardation and disability representing a Heterogeneous-Conflictual point of view define individuals with mental retardation and other disabilities as belonging to the subordinate groups and by definition possessing unacceptable "disabling" behaviors which preclude any acceptable social role in the larger society. Such disabled populations, having no function in the larger society, are viewed as surplus and valueless.

The Nature of Society Dimension and the orthogonal Nature of Reality Dimension form the basis of four paradigms: The Functionalist-Objectivist Paradigm, whose world view is based on the presence of an objective reality and social stability, the Objectivist-Conflict Paradigm, whose world view is based on the presence of an objective reality and social conflict, the Interpretive Paradigm, whose world view is based on the presence of a subjective reality and social stability, and the Interpretive-Conflict Paradigm, whose world view is based on the presence of a subjective reality and social conflict (included for completeness but not used in the construction of any mental retardation paradigms).

Mental Retardation, Science, and Scientific Paradigms

Mercer defines seven models of MR/DD within the four fundamental scientific paradigms that have been used by individuals working in the 20th century and now in the 21st century: The Medical model, the Psychomedical model, the Cognitive model, the Social System model, the Humanistic model, the Cultural Pluralism model, and the Conflict model. (See Figure 21.2.)

The medical model.

Medicine provided the earliest model of mental retardation, based on purely biological anomalies. The Medical model occupies an extreme position on both axes in Figure 21.2 in the most extreme version of the Functionalist-Objectivist Paradigm, which assumes the objective reality of the observed symptoms and the facticity of a disabling condition that exists in the individual because of disease processes and genetic causes. The cultural setting is not relevant to the diagnosis of the disorder nor to its prevention or treatment, because diagnosis and treatment are the same across cultures and societies. Because many untreated disorders become worse when undetected and untreated, there is a strong tendency to commit type 2 errors (finding a disability where none exists) and avoid type 1 errors (finding health when in reality there is unrecognized disease).

Mercer believes that the Medical model had an all-inclusive impact on practice in the field of mental retardation. "Its emphasis on the centrality of diagnosis, its focus on

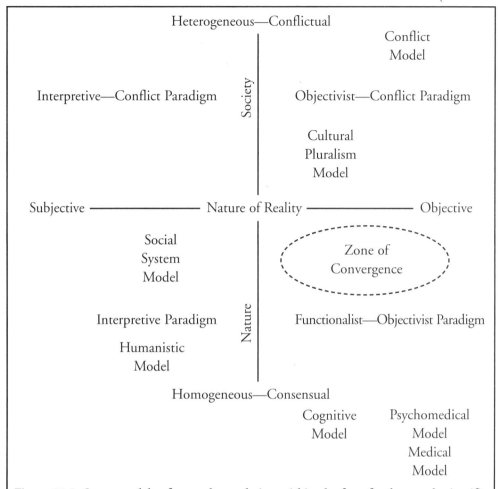

Figure 21.2. Seven models of mental retardation within the four fundamental scientific paradigms. From "The impact of changing paradigms of disability on mental retardation in the year 2000," by J. Mercer.

categorization before treatment, its preference for segregated settings [training schools, colonies, hospitals, developmental centers] where training can be administered by experts, and its insistence on certification of eligibility through diagnosis by experts before treatment is made available is tacit knowledge in the field of mental retardation. From it flows the focus on cause, the assumption that there is a biological basis to all disability, the rejection of social and cultural factors as relevant to diagnosis, the bias toward type 2 errors, and the belief that treatment is benign" (Mercer, 1992, p. 21).

The psychomedical model.

The Psychomedical model is an extension of the Medical model, where a statistical definition of "normal" derived from the invention of intelligence and the "IQ" testing movement is combined with the Medical model. The Psychomedical model assumes that "IQ" tests measure "intelligence" defined as a relatively stable genotype. The Medical model uses low scores on an "IQ" test as a hard scientific objective index of mental retardation. The model assumes that tests of academic achievement are valid measures of what individuals have learned vs. IQ tests which are valid measures of intelligence, i.e., what individuals are capable of learning, their learning potential. Thus "intelligence" and "achievement" can be treated as dimensions that can be separated both conceptually and operationally. The Psychomedical model argues that IQ tests are valid measures of "intelligence" because they accurately predict performance on "achievement" tests. Additionally, their construct validity is supported because of their intercorrelations with other IQ tests.

Tests of IQ are not culturally biased, because they have similar predictive validities for persons of different cultural groups, i.e., the regression lines predicting academic achievement test scores from IQ test scores have similar slopes for different ethnic and cultural groups. Additionally, IQ tests have similar internal validities for different ethnic and cultural groups, i.e., similar patterns of internal reliabilities and stabilities, similar patterns of item difficulty levels, and similar factor structures (Jensen, 1980). Also, because society is culturally homogeneous, a single set of test norms is appropriate for all cultural and ethnic groups (Jensen, 1980).

Mercer believes that "one major consequence of applying the psychomedical model in the public schools [during the 1950s and 1960s] was that disproportionately large numbers of children who had no biological stigmata but were from racial, ethnic, and linguistic minorities were diagnosed as 'educable mentally retarded' [which was accepted as objective fact by the psychometric community]" (Mercer, 1992, p. 23).

The cognitive model.

A variety of cognitive models of learning difficulties (which for Mercer consist of the work of Feuerstein and his group, 1979 and the cognitive-motivational–information-processing learning theories as described by Gelsheiser and Shepherd, 1986, though many other versions of this viewpoint exist) have come into prominence which fall within the Functionalist-Objectivist Paradigm, slightly left of the Psychomedical models along the Objective-Subjective axis. These models are similar enough to be treated as operating within the same conceptual framework, having an objectivist view of reality and a consensual view of society. They are not based on the Medical model nor are they concerned with the normal distribution of intelligence. Their major constructs (e.g., learning, learning problems, learning strategies, metacognitive processes, motivational self-systems, self-regulation, motivational attributions, perceived self-efficacy, executive processing) are conceived as objective realities.

Theorists view learning difficulties as the result of inefficient learning strategies due to insufficient mediated learning rather than to biologically based disabilities. Learning will improve if learners become more actively involved in their learning process, use more effective learning strategies, and energize their motivational and self-regulatory systems. The role of assessment is to directly understand the information processes underlying learning, using a variant of the test-teach-test or test-mediate-observe-retest learning potential assessment approach rather than some standardized IQ or achievement test, which is viewed as not very useful, since only the products of experience are assessed. The role of instruction is to teach more efficient learning strategies and to optimize the individual's motivation and expectation to learn effectively.

Mercer believes that the switch to a Cognitive model from a Psychomedical model has profound implications for policy. Those who use the various cognitive models would probably reserve the term "mental retardation" to refer to persons who have discernible biological anomalies and perform at the lowest levels of functioning. Normal-bodied children can learn if properly motivated to apply themselves and if they are taught effective and appropriate learning strategies. "The categories 'educable mentally retarded,' 'borderline mentally retarded,' and 'mildly mentally retarded' atrophy. They disappear from the thought and vocabularies of persons using a Cognitive model because they serve no purpose in that model. . . . [Because motivational systems are so important in the Cognitive model,] children must believe that they can learn before they will make the effort to use the cognitive strategies that make learning possible. This movement away from Medical model thinking is a major break with the past" (Mercer, 1992, p. 31).

The social system model of disability.

The Social System model is in the Interpretive Paradigm whose world view is based on the presence of subjective reality and social stability. Mental retardation is viewed as a subjective cognition,

> a social construction emerging from social interaction in which social actors evaluate each other's behavior in relation to socially agreed on norms as to what constitutes "intelligent" behavior. Persons in society develop a consensus on what they consider to be "normal" or "intelligent" behavior, and that consensus becomes part of their intersubjective reality. The nature of the intersubjective reality that they create is not predetermined. From the perspective of the interpretive paradigm, mental retardation is a socially constructed category [which does not have universal meaning]. Individuals and groups with the greatest social power have the greatest influence on the consensus formation, which creates the intersubjective reality that guides societal action. They are able to establish their view of "normal" behavior as the societal standard against which everyone will be judged. Inevitably, members of the dominant group will be advantaged because those standards will reflect their values, beliefs, language, and customs while nondominant groups will be disadvantaged. Because the scientists who devised the IQ tests were members of the dominant English-speaking group in American society, they created tests that covered the linguistic and cognitive skills valued by their own group and normed them on populations consisting primarily of members of their own group. Inevitably, outsiders, such as racial and linguistic minorities, do less well on such tests than members of the dominant group and earn lower average scores because they do not share the same intersubjective reality. Consequently, they are more likely to be labeled as "mentally retarded." (Mercer, 1992, pp. 24–25)

Obviously there are great differences among the paradigms based in the Functionalist-Objectivist Paradigm and those based in the Interpretive Paradigm. The Psychomedical model views mental retardation as an objective empirical fact that one "has," whereas the Social System model views mental retardation as a social construction and a social status that one "holds" due to social forces: Mental retardation depends on what group one is in. Mental retardation is a social proclamation.

In regard to social policy Mercer points out that the fundamental underpinnings of the Interpretive Paradigm—value neutral regarding tests, norms or assessment procedures, value neutral as regards one intersubjective reality over another—were perceived by those operating within the Functionalist-Objectivist Paradigm as an attack on their professional practices. The very act of applying an interpretive analysis to professional practices in the field of mental retardation was viewed as a frontal assault on fundamental belief systems. Additionally, civil rights advocates seized upon the premises of the Interpretive Paradigm to construct legal arguments concerning the placement of minority students in special education classes. "If the meaning of mental retardation has been socially negotiated and has changed over time, then that meaning can be renegotiated. If diagnoses are social constructions rather than 'facts' then they are open to dispute. Whose intersubjective reality shall prevail?" (Mercer, 1992, p. 25).

Those who use the Social System model embedded in the Interpretive Paradigm study the process of deviance formation, stigmatization, and the achievement of a devaluated achieved social status and directly challenge the fundamental assumptions of the Psychomedical model that type 2 errors (finding a disability where none exists) are preferable to type 1 errors (finding health when in reality there is unrecognized disease) in making the diagnose of mental retardation. "Overdiagnosis, formerly seen as benign because it provided special education services to children having educational difficulties, was redefined as malignant because it stigmatized persons who were not disabled by assigning them to a disesteemed social status and by triggering a deviant career" (Mercer, 1992, pp. 25–26). The Social System model was used to challenge current diagnostic practices in medicine, the psychological sciences, the legal system, and in education.

The humanistic model.

The Humanistic model is in the Interpretive Paradigm and is far more subjective than the Social System model. The Humanistic model stresses the uniqueness of each individual and the process of *verstehen*, that individuals can only be understood by entering their subjective realities and participating in their systems of meanings and values. The Humanistic model stresses individualized instruction based on sensitive interpersonal interaction between students and teachers in a warm and caring environment. Standardized testing that categorizes, compartmentalizes, and dehumanizes is anathema. Individuals can only be viewed in a holistic open-system mode (Heshusius, 1988, Poplin, 1984). Mercer views the power of the Humanistic model as "its affirmation of the worth and individuality of each student and teacher and its rejection of categorization, standardization, and mechanization."

The cultural pluralism model of mental retardation.

The Cultural Pluralism model is based in the Objectivist-Conflict Paradigm: It assumes the facticity of mental retardation but, unlike the Medical, Psychomedical, and Cognitive models, it assumes that society is heterogeneous and full of social, racial, and cultural conflicts and societal diversity. The Cultural Pluralism model builds from the Psychomedical model by being concerned with the individual's social adaptation to his or her own social group rather than with psychometric intelligence, and constructing multiple normative frameworks for interpreting measures of intelligence. Only in this way can persons with real mental retardation be identified in a culturally diverse set of subcultures and in a diverse set of environments including school and nonschool settings.

Mercer was a strong advocate for this model and developed the System of Multicultural Pluralistic Assessment (SOMPA) for Anglo, Hispanic, and African American children (Mercer, 1979), which both measured adaptive behavior and contained sociocultural norms for the Wechsler Intelligence Scale for Children-Revised (WISC-R) administered in English and in Spanish. "These norms are based on the educational and cultural characteristics of each child's family. Only the sociocultural norms are used to make inferences about the child's 'intelligence'" (Mercer, 1992, p. 27). In this model mental retardation is identified by measures of psychometric intelligence and adaptive behavior, taking into consideration pluralistic cultural diversity.

For Mercer, the policy implications for the Cultural Pluralistic model of mental retardation were important. By using sociocultural pluralistic norms for psychometric intelligence and adaptive behavior, type 2 error was reduced, shrinking the number of children diagnosed as mentally retarded who were not truly mentally retarded. "Although the SOMPA was adopted in some states and several thousand psychologists were trained to use the system, the Cultural Pluralism model of mental retardation has never been widely accepted. Although it is based on objectivist assumptions, it moves further into the conflict paradigm than the scientific community has been prepared to go" (Mercer, 1992, p. 28).

The conflict model.

The Conflict model is part of the Objectivist-Conflict paradigm and moves even further than the Pluralistic model upward toward the view of society as heterogeneous-conflictual, full of linguistic, racial, and social class struggles for dominance and power among groups.

> The groups who prevail are able to make their language, values, beliefs, and cultural systems the standard for the entire society and the yardstick by which all members of the society are judged. Dominant groups determine the language of instruction and content of the curriculum of the schools, which exist as an instrument to preserve their social and economic dominance. They determine the language and content of the tests used in public education and the categories to which students will be assigned. Consequently, persons from nondominant groups are disadvantaged in gaining access to the educational and economic resources of the society. Through the standardized testing and sorting that takes place in the schools, they are systematically devalued, oppressed, and discriminated against. [The categories of mental retardation] are defined entirely by low test scores . . . and used as mechanisms to control racial and cultural minorities and persons from the lower classes. If the tests are tools for discrimination and segregation, there is but one remedy—abolish the tests and the segregated classes. (Mercer, 1992, pp. 28–29)

In terms of policy, Mercer comments

> Needless to say, the Conflict model of mental retardation has never been accepted by the scientific community of measurement psychology because it sees them as the intelligentsia providing scientific legitimacy to the administration of culturally biased tests that discriminate against social and cultural minorities. However,

the Conflict model of mental retardation formed the philosophic basis of the class action suits against the state of California filed on behalf of Hispanic and African American students who had been placed in classes for the mentally retarded using their scores on IQ tests as the main criterion {*Diana* v. *California Board of Education*, 1969; *Larry P. et al.* v. *Wilson Riles*, 1979}. Consequently, the Conflict model has had a profound influence on public policy. (Mercer, 1992, p. 29)

THE CONTRIBUTION OF RIOUX

Rioux and her colleagues (Rioux, 1997, Rioux & Bach, 1994) argue that how disability is perceived is related to assumptions about social responsibility toward persons with disability, and therefore it is important to examine the social and scientific conceptions of disability that underpin the various research agendas and the ways of knowing disability. Rioux conceives of four social and scientific conceptions of disability: The Bio-Medical model and the Functional model based on ideas of Individual Pathology that resides in the individual, and the Environmental model and the Rights Outcome model based on ideas of Structural Social Pathology inherent to the social structure. (See Figure 21.3)

The Bio-Medical Model and the Functional Model

The Bio-Medical and Functional models are based on paradigms that focus on disability as a result of individual pathology that resides in the individual. These paradigms have a number of common characteristics (Rioux, 1997):

1. Disability is approached as a field of professional expertise.
2. A positivist paradigm is used.
3. Primary prevention, including biological and environmental conditions, is emphasized.
4. Disability is characterized as incapacity in relation to nondisabled people, i.e., a comparative incapacity.
5. Disability is viewed as an anomaly and social burden, including costs.
6. The inclusion of people with disabilities is seen as a private responsibility.
7. The unit of analysis is the individual.
8. The point of intervention is the individual condition (p. 103).

The Bio-Medical model conceives of disability as a result of a disease process in which the condition itself becomes the focus of attention. The goal of the professional or the researcher is to reduce the prevalence of the disorder through biological/genetic intervention or screening and also treat/cure the biological condition through medical and technological means. There is less emphasis on the role society has in limiting and enabling people with disability. Social responsibility is to eliminate or cure the biologically based disability.

The Functional model also conceives of disability as the result of an individual pathological state. The goal of the professional or researcher is to ameliorate the condition through a variety of rehabilitative services (e.g., behavior modification, developmental programming, skills for independent living, vocational and academic teaching) so that individuals with a disability can develop their potential to become as socially functional as possible (as "normal" as possible) to enable them to function more independently and

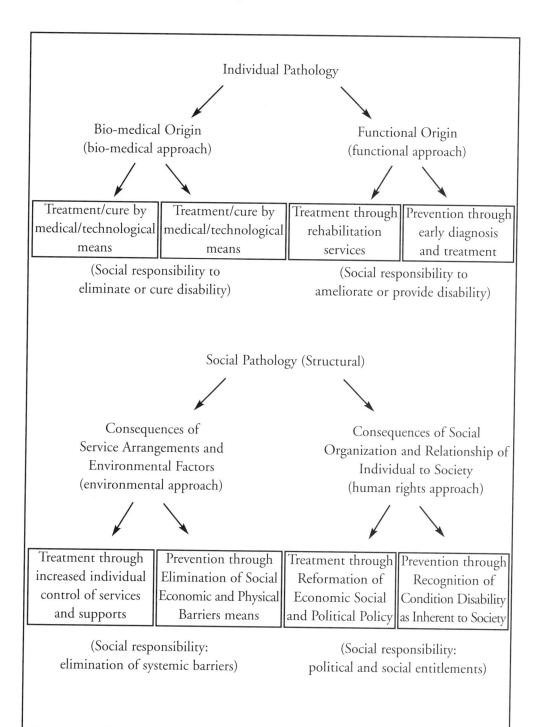

Figure 21.3. Rioux's social and scientific formulations of disability. From "Disability: The place of judgement in a world of Fact," by M. Rioux, 1997, *Journal of Intellectual Disability Research*, 40 (Pt. 2), p. 104. Copyright 1997 by *Journal of Intellectual Disability Research*. Reprinted with permission.

become more productive members of society. Social responsibility is to ameliorate and provide comfort. Rioux is concerned that in placing the focus on the individual, a functional [model] can lose sight of environmental and situational factors that may limit individuals from achieving their ambitions. In targeting the individual for change, professionals operating [in the functional model] run the risk of operating on assumptions about the person's "best interests" that may not always coincide with what the person wants for him or herself. The way services are organized can also produce a power imbalance that creates tensions between people with disabilities and the professional community. (Rioux, 1997, p. 105)

The Environmental Model and the Rights Outcome Model

The Environmental and Rights Outcome models are based on paradigms that focus on disability as a result of social pathology inherent to the social structure. Disability is not inherent to the individual: It is inherent to the social structure. The problem resides in a society that needs fixing rather than in the individual that we need to fix. These paradigms have a number of common characteristics (Rioux, 1997, p.105).

1. Disability is assumed not to be inherent in the individual independent of the social structure.
2. Priority is given to the political, social, and built environment.
3. Secondary rather than primary prevention is emphasized.
4. Disability is recognized as difference rather than as an anomaly.
5. Disability is viewed as the interaction of the individual with society.
6. Inclusion of people with disabilities is seen as a public responsibility.
7. The unit of analysis is the social structure.
8. The points of intervention are the social, environmental, and economic systems.

The Environmental model conceives that along with personal limitations residing in the individual, the interaction between the individual and the environment can exacerbate as well as improve the impact of the disability on the individual. Barrier-free environments can give persons who are wheelchair bound independence and mobility that in essence neutralizes their disability. Individuals with communication disorders can have their disability neutralized if a variety of alternative methods of communication are provided such as bliss symbols or sign-language instruction. Disability is the result of increased structural social pathology due to service arrangements and environmental factors. The individual control of services and supports can ameliorate the effects of the disability. The disability can be prevented through the elimination of social and economic physical barriers. Social responsibility is to eliminate systemic barriers. "[T]he impact of disability can be lessened as environments are adapted to enable participation. Building codes, principles of barrier-free design, adapted curricula, targeted policy and funding commitments are shown in policy research to be useful tools to this end. Research shows that these tools enable modifications and supports to be made in home, school, work and leisure environments which increase the participation of people with disabilities in society and limit the disadvantages they otherwise would face" (Rioux, 1997, p. 105).

The Rights Outcome model is based on the idea that disability is a function of the way society is organized and of the relationship of the disabled individual to the total society that may prevent persons with disabilities from participating in society with equal civil and social rights. Disability issues are human rights issues. Disability is the result of structural social pathology due to the organization of the total society and the relationship of the individual with a disability to the total society. The treatment of disability is through reformulation of economic social and political policy that can ameliorate the effects of disability. The disability can be prevented through the recognition of disability as inherent to society. Social responsibility is to provide political and social entitlements.

> [Disabilities] are inherent in the human condition and . . . people with disabilities do contribute to society. . . . [P]ublic policy and programmes should aim to reduce civic inequalities to address social and economic disadvantage . . . [V]arious supports (e.g., personal services, aids and devices) will be needed by some people in order to gain access to, participate in and exercise self-determination as equals in society. Research from a rights outcome approach constructs an analysis of how society marginalizes people with disabilities, and how it could be adjusted to respond more effectively to their presence and needs. This approach focuses on the disabling aspects of society, on supporting human diversity and on empowering disadvantaged individuals. (Rioux, 1997, p. 106)

In both the Environmental model and the Rights Outcome model the social obligation of research "is to reduce civic inequalities, i.e., social and economic disadvantages are addressed through providing supports, and aids and devices that enable social and economic integration, self-determination, and legal and social rights" (p. 106). The social obligation of research in the Bio-Medical model is to eliminate or cure biologically based disability. The social obligation of research in the Functional model is to ameliorate the condition and provide comfort.

THE CONTRIBUTIONS OF MERCER AND RIOUX

How exactly are the models of mental retardation and disability identified by Mercer and Rioux related? We believe that Rioux's Bio-Medical model and Functional model fall within Mercer's Functionalist-Objectivist Paradigm. Rioux's Bio-Medical model is identical to Mercer's Medical model. Rioux's Functional model is not quite like Mercer's Psychomedical model or Cognitive model but is similar to both of them. We believe that Rioux's Environmental Approach model and Rights Outcome model fall within Mercer's Interpretive Paradigm. Rioux's Environmental model is very similar to Mercer's Social Systems model. Rioux's Rights Outcome model, we believe, is a more extreme version of Mercer's Social System model. Mercer's and Rioux's formulations of the nature of mental retardation and disability are not identical and stress different facets of the phenomena of mental retardation and the construct of disability in general. However, Mercer and Rioux's ideas do provide us with some organizing schemas and scaffolding to allow us to sort out the very diverse world views of our contributors.

Can So Many Diverse Ideas Be Integrated?

If we superposed (i.e., mentally factor analyzed) the ideas, world views, and epistemological underpinnings of our contributors' conceptions of mental retardation on the organizing schemas and scaffolding of Mercer's and Rioux's typologies, we believe our contributors' conceptions of mental retardation would cluster roughly into the Functionalist-Objectivist Paradigm, whose world view is based on the presence of an objective reality and social stability, and into the Interpretative Paradigm, whose world view is based on the presence of a subjective reality and social stability. This is the source of the paradigm clash that is now occurring in the field of mental retardation. Every AAMR manual from 1959 to 1983 was firmly grounded in the Functionalist-Objectivistic Paradigm representing variants of Mercer's Medical and Psychomedical models and Rioux's Bio-Medical and Functional models. The AAMR 1992 and 2002 Manuals represent viewpoints firmly grounded in the Interpretive Paradigm representing variants of Mercer's Social System model and Rioux's Environmental model and perhaps Rioux's even more radical Rights Outcome model. Simply put, our contributors are lining up for and against a world view of mental retardation based in the Functionalist-Objective Paradigm characteristic of the AAMR Manuals of 1959–1983 vs. a world view of mental retardation based in the Interpretive Paradigm characteristic of the 1992 and 2002 AAMR manuals. This is the paradigm clash currently facing the field of mental retardation.

How do our contributors line up? We can only roughly sort those who favor a Functionalist-Objective Paradigm and those who favor an Interpretive Paradigm. The attempt to exactly place each contributor is fraught with danger. Only the individual contributor can really know which of Mercer's and Rioux's paradigms he/she really favors. We looked over the table of contents and guessed that contributors who favor the Functionalist-Objective Paradigm include: Baroff, Glidden, Spitz, Baumeister, Detterman and Gabriel, Greenspan (?), Jacobson and Mulick, MacMillan, Siperstein and Leffert, Switzky (?), Reeve (?), Simeonson, Granlund and Bjorck-Akesson (?), and Buntinx (?). We guessed that contributors who favor the Interpretive Paradigm include: Smith, Snell and Voorhees, Coulter, Gaventa, and Schalock (?).

As mentioned previously, there are almost irresolvable differences among the models based in the Functionalist-Objective Paradigm and those based in the Interpretive Paradigm. The Medical and Psychomedical models view mental retardation as an objective empirical fact that one "has" and uses a positivist (i.e., scientific method) system of inquiry to conduct research. The Social System model views mental retardation as a social construction, a social proclamation that one "holds" due to social forces. Disability is assumed not to be inherent to the individual independent of the social structure and is viewed as due to the interaction of the individual with society. "Mental retardation is not something you have, like blue eyes or a bad heart. Nor is it something you are, like being short or thin. It is not a medical disorder. . . . Nor is it a mental disorder. Mental retardation refers to a particular state of functioning that begins in child hood and in which limitations in intelligence coexist with related limitations in adaptive skill" (Luckasson et al., 1992, p. 9).

> In summary, mental retardation is not something you have, like blue eyes or a bad heart. Nor is it something you are, like being short or thin. It is not a medical

disorder, although it may be coded in a medical classification of diseases; nor is it a mental disorder, although it may be coded in a classification of psychiatric disorders. *Mental retardation* refers to a particular state of functioning that begins in childhood, is multidimensional, and is affected positively by individualized supports. . . . As a model of functioning, it includes the structure and expectations of the systems within which the person functions and interacts: micro-, meso-, and macrosystem. Thus a comprehensive and correct understanding of the condition of mental retardation requires a multidimensional and ecological approach that reflects the interaction of the individual and his or her environment, and the person-referenced outcomes of that interaction related to independence, relationships, contributions, school and community participation, and personal well-being. (Luckasson et al., 2002, p. 48)

"Disability is not measles" is the title of an edited book published by the Roeher Institute, Canada's national institute for the study of public policy affecting persons with an intellectual impairment and other disabilities (Rioux & Bach, 1994). The Social System model uses a postmodern (i.e., qualitative and inductive) system of inquiry to conduct research. The Interpretive Paradigm by its very nature is viewed as a fundamental attack on the professional practices of those following the Functionalist-Objective Paradigm, who in turn are suspicious of postmodern research methods.

Mental retardation in the 21st century has become multiparadigmatic. Rioux (1997) argues that all the conceptions of disability she discusses—The Bio-Medical model, The Functional model, The Environmental model, and the Rights Outcome model—are myopic. What has to be recognized is the potential harm that the advocates of these models can do by claiming the field of disability as their exclusive domain. Social, economic, ethical, and professional forces, she believes, have made the Bio-Medical and Functional models dominant in the field of mental retardation. "Research on policy, programmes and services that have an impact on individuals with intellectual disabilities have overly emphasized [the Bio-Medical and Functional] perspective to the detriment of the broader systemic conditions that disable people [as represented and recognized in the Environmental and Rights Outcome models]" (Rioux, 1997, p. 107).

Mercer also recognized the problem of the multiparadigmatic nature of mental retardation in the 21st century. "There is little agreement on the nature of the phenomenon being studied and, consequently, little agreement on treatments. People talk past each other because they are operating from different assumptions. The field is in the midst of a scientific revolution" (Mercer, 1992, p. 32). She predicted that by the year 2000, the field of mental retardation would "undoubtedly be multiparadigmatic and the center of intellectual gravity will have moved [closer to where the Nature of Society axis crosses with the Nature of Reality axis in Figure 21.2, the Zone of Convergence]" (Mercer, 1992, p. 33). She predicted that by the year 2000 only two dominant paradigmatic clusters for mental retardation would emerge: the Medical model and some amalgam of the Interpretive and Conflict Paradigms. The diagnostic construct of mental retardation would only be applied to the small number of individuals with clear biomedical anomalies. For the large number of individuals with learning problems without clear biomedical anomalies a new multiparadigmatic model would emerge combining elements of the

Cognitive, Humanistic, and Cultural Pluralism models. She hoped that the scientific community would become more comfortable using multiparadigmatic ideas and use the best model for understanding the needs of each individual. Mercer and Rioux's ideas concerning the multiparadigmatic nature of mental retardation in the 21st century substantially overlap.

We believe that mental retardation is a social-politically constructed set of "classes" and not a real science of "taxons," i.e., a true taxonomy dealing with scientific classification, as are biological and medical classes. Our goal as stakeholders is to come up with a cohesive, integrated constitutive theoretical model of mental retardation operationalized so that we can more closely align the "class" with the "taxon," which we believe is Mercer's goal and the goal of the contributors to this volume.

We can clearly see the emergence of a new paradigm that is some amalgam of the Interpretive and Functionalist-Objectivist approach as represented in WHO's International Classification of Impairments, Disabilities and Handicaps (ICIDH-2) (2000) and WHO's International Classification of Functioning, Disability, and Health (ICF) (2001); that is why, in our classification of which of our authors favored a Functionalist-Objectivistic Paradigm or an Interpretive Paradigm, we added a question mark to our contributor (Buntinx) who explicitly discussed this model, because ICIDH-2 and ICF are an amalgam of both paradigms.

Have Mercer's predictions come true? Yes and no. There has surely been a movement away from the Functionalistic-Objectivistic Paradigm as represented by the AAMR manuals of 1959–1983 and APA Division 33's *The Manual of Diagnosis and Professional Practices in Mental Retardation* and toward the Interpretive Paradigm as represented by the AAMR manuals of 1992 and 2002 and the emergence of a paradigm that is some amalgam of the Interpretive and Functionalist-Objective Paradigms as represented by WHO's ICIDH-2. and ICF. AAMR (2002) tried very hard to integrate its model into the ICF and in this sense there is movement toward Mercer's and Rioux's sense of the multiparadigmatic nature of mental retardation and into Mercer's Zone of Convergence. We know that Greenspan and Switzky, and we guess that Simeonson, Granlund and Bjorck-Akesson, Reeve, and Schalock, have moved more closely into Mercer's Zone of Convergence in their thinking, which indicates our initial ambiguity about their position. However, the scientific community is still not comfortable using a multiparadigmatic perspective.

We hope this book will contribute to a shared world view among all the stakeholders in the field of mental retardation to expand the various paradigms somewhat in order to take into consideration the paradigmatic views of both "modernists-positivists" and "postmodernists-qualitative inductive" researchers. Can we construct a shared world view that can more closely align the "class" of mental retardation with the "taxon" leading to optimally useful outcomes for service and research? Can we come up with a multiparadigmatic perspective that is useful in ordering our thinking, provides clarity rather than confusion, and provides a pathway to guide both our service and research efforts? We can imagine models of mental retardation that are driven by the heuristic meaningfulness of the context and the appropriateness of the problem-solving situation. Just as in modern physics, where light can be considered simultaneously as either a particle or a wave, whichever is appropriate to the context and problem-solving situation, mental retardation can also be considered simultaneously both within a Functionalistic-Objectivistic modernist positivistic Paradigm and within an Interpretive postmodernistic qualitative Social System Paradigm. Mental retardation can be considered as existing within the "levels of severity of intellectual impairments" models that are heuristic (useful) to scientists and researchers who follow some variant of the Functionalistic-Objectivistic Paradigm and at the same time as existing within the levels of intensity and patterns of supports-needs matrix models that are most heuristic to educators and service providers who follow some variant of the Interpretive Paradigm. Depending on one's purposes, mental retardation can be either "a particle or a wave" and perceived within a multiparadigmatic set of models and world views. As suggested by the range and scope of ideas in this book, a period of extensive discussion among the various stakeholders in the field of mental retardation is warranted. We believe this book will provide the genesis to these encounters and help resolve the paradigm clash and shift currently underway in the field of mental retardation.

REFERENCES

Buchler, J. (1955). *Philosophical writings of Peirce.* New York: Dover.

Burrell, G., & Morgan, G. (1979). *Sociological paradigms and organizational analysis.* Portsmouth, NH: Heineman.

Compte, A. (1896). *The positive philosophy* (H. Martineau, Trans.). London: George Bell & Sons.

Denzin, N. K., & Lincoln, Y. S. (Ed.). (1994). *Handbook of qualitative research.* Thousand Oaks, CA: Sage.

Diana v. California Board of Education, United States District Court, Northern District of California, C-70 37 RFP(1969).

Dilthey, W. L. (1976). *Selected writings.* Cambridge, England: Cambridge University Press.

Durkheim, E. (1982). *The rules of sociological method* (W. D. Halls, Trans.). New York: Free Press.

Heshusius, L. (1988). The arts, science, and study of exceptionality. *Exceptional Children, 55*(1), 60–65.

Husserl, E. (1962). *Ideas: General introduction to pure phenomenology.* New York: MacMillan.

Jenson, A. R. (1980). *Bias in mental testing.* New York: Free Press.

Kuhn, T. S. (1970). *The structure of scientific revolutions* (2nd ed.). Chicago: University of Chicago Press.

Lancy, D. F. (1993). *Qualitative research in education.* New York: Longman.

Larry, P., et al. v. Wilson Riles, Superintendent of Public Instruction for the State of California, et al., C71 2270 REP (U.S. District Court for the Northern District of California, 1979).

Lincoln, Y. S., & Guba, E. G. (1985). *Naturalistic inquiry.* Newbury Park, CA: Sage.

Luckasson, R., Borthwick-Duffy, S., Buntinx, W. H. E., Coulter, D. L., Craig, E. M., Reeve, A., et al. (2002). *Mental retardation: Definition, classification, and systems of supports (10th ed.).* Washington, DC: American Association on Mental Retardation.

Luckasson, R., Coulter, D. L., Polloway, E. A., Reiss, S., Schalock, R. L., Snell, M. E., et al. (1992). *Mental retardation: Definition, classification, and systems of supports (9th ed.).* Washington, DC: American Association on Mental Retardation.

Mercer, J. R. (1979). *SOMPA: Technical and conceptual manual.* New York: Psychological Corporation.

Mercer, J. R. (1992). The impact of changing paradigms of disability on mental retardation in the year 2000. In L. Rowitz (Ed.), *Mental retardation in the year 2000 (pp. 15–38).* New York: Springer-Verlag.

Mills, J. S. (1906). *A system of logic.* London: Longman.

Poincare, H. (1952). *Science and hypothesis.* New York: Dover.

Poplin, M. (1984). Toward an holistic view of persons with learning disabilities. *Learning Disabilities Quarterly, 7,* 290–294.

Rioux, M. H. (1997). Disability: The place of judgement in a world of fact. *Journal of Intellectual Disability Research, 41(2),* 102–111.

Rioux, M. H., & Bach, M. (Eds). (1994). *Disability is not measles: New research paradigms in disability.* North York, ON: Roeher Institute.

Sarkar, S. (Ed.). (1996a). *The legacy of the Vienna circle: Modern reppraisals.* New York: Garland Press.

Sarkar, S. (Ed.). (1996b). *Logical empiricism at its peak: Schlick, Carnap, and Neurath.* New York: Garland Press.

Taylor, S. J., & Bogdan, R. (1984). *Introduction to qualitative research methods (2nd ed.).* New York: John Wiley.

World Health Organization. (2000). *International classification of functioning, and disability (ICIDH-2 Beta 2 full version).* Geneva: Author.

World Health Organization. (2001). *International classification of functioning, disability, and health (ICF).* Geneva: Author.